The Vest-Pocket
CFO

JAE K. SHIM, Ph.D.
Chief Financial Officer
NBRF Incorporated
Professor of Accounting and Finance
California State University, Long Beach

JOEL G. SIEGEL, Ph.D., CPA
Financial Consultant
Professor of Accounting and Finance
Queens College

PRENTICE HALL
Englewood Cliffs, New Jersey 07632

Prentice-Hall International (UK) Limited, *London*
Prentice-Hall of Australia Pty. Limited, *Sydney*
Prentice-Hall Canada, Inc., *Toronto*
Prentice-Hall Hispanoamericana, S.A., *Mexico*
Prentice-Hall of India Private Limited, *New Delhi*
Prentice-Hall of Japan, Inc., *Tokyo*
Simon & Schuster Asia Pte. Ltd., *Singapore*
Editora Prentice-Hall do Brasil, Ltda., *Rio de Janeiro*

© 1992 *by*

Prentice Hall

Englewood Cliffs, New Jersey

10 9 8 7 6

Library of Congress Cataloging-in-Publication Data

Shim, Jae K.
   The vest-pocket CFO / by Jae K. Shim and Joel G. Siegel.
     p.   cm.
   Includes index.
   ISBN 0-13-952870-9   —ISBN 0-13-952862-8 (pbk.)
   1. Corporations—United States—Finance—Handbooks,
manuals, etc.   I. Siegel, Joel G.   II. Title.
HG4061.S48   1992
658.15—dc20
                                        92-6155
                                           CIP

ISBN 0-13-952870-9

PRENTICE HALL
Professional Publishing
Englewood Cliffs, NJ 07632
Simon & Schuster. A Paramount Communications Company

Printed in the United States of America

Acknowledgments

Our sincere thanks and appreciation to Gerald Galbo for his outstanding editorial advice and input on this book. We are very fortunate to have received the valuable assistance of this superb editor. His hard work, dedication, and suggestions helped to make this book possible.

Thanks also to Barbara O'Brien our production manager at Prentice Hall and Nancy Marcus Land at Publications Development Company for their help in the production of this book.

Thanks to Anthony Akel, Ph.D. (Northwestern University), a managerial consultant, for coauthoring the chapter on inventory management; Stan Chu, M.S., CPA, a consultant and professor at the City University of New York for coauthoring the chapter on mergers and acquisitions; Loc T. Nguyen, LL.M., CPA, a tax consultant, who coauthored the chapter on taxation; and Chung J. Liew, Ph.D., consultant and associate professor of decision sciences at the University of Oklahoma and the University of Central Oklahoma for coauthoring the chapter on working capital and cash management.

Thanks goes to Roberta M. Siegel for her excellent editorial assistance and professional comments.

About the Authors

JAE K. SHIM is chief financial officer of NBRF Incorporated and Professor of Accounting and Finance at California State University, Long Beach. Dr. Shim is president of the National Business Review Foundation (NBRF), a financial consulting firm. He received his Ph.D. degree from the University of California at Berkeley. Dr. Shim is a certified cost analyst.

He has served as a consultant in financial management to Ernst and Whinney, CPAs, and Deloitte Touche, CPAs.

Dr. Shim has 35 books to his credit and has published over 50 articles in accounting and financial journals including *Financial Management, Decision Sciences, Management Science, Long Range Planning, Cost and Management, Econometrica,* and *Advances in Accounting.*

Dr. Shim is a recipient of the 1982 Credit Research Foundation Award for his article on financial management. He also received a research grant from Arthur Andersen, CPAs.

JOEL G. SIEGEL, Ph.D., CPA is a financial consultant and Professor of Accounting and Finance at Queens College of the City University of New York.

He was previously employed by Coopers and Lybrand, CPAs, and Arthur Andersen, CPAs. Dr. Siegel has acted as a consultant to many organizations including Citicorp, International Telephone and Telegraph, United Technologies, American Institute of CPAs, and Person-Wolinsky Associates.

Dr. Siegel is the author of 35 books and about 200 articles on accounting and financial topics. His books have been published by Prentice Hall, McGraw-Hill, Harper and Collins, John Wiley, Macmillan, International Publishing, Barron's, and the American Institute of CPAs.

His articles have been published in many accounting and financial journals including *Financial Executive, The Financial Analysts Journal, The CPA Journal, Practical Accountant,* and the *National Public Accountant.*

In 1972, he was the recipient of the Outstanding Educator of America Award. Dr. Siegel is listed in *Who's Where Among Writers* and *Who's Who in the World.* His international reputation lead to his appointment in 1992 as chairperson of the National Oversight Board.

This book is dedicated to
Chung Shim, dedicated wife;
Roberta M. Siegel, loving wife and colleague;
and
Sylvia and Arnold Siegel
loving mother and brother

What This Book
Will Do for You

Here is a handy pocket problem-solver for today's busy chief financial officer (CFO). It's a working guide to help you quickly pinpoint

- What to look for
- What to watch out for
- What to do
- How to do it

in the complex world of business. You'll find checklists, ratios, formulas, measures, guidelines, procedures, rules of thumb, illustrations, step-by-step instructions, real life examples, tables, charts, and exhibits to help you analyze and evaluate any business-related problem. Throughout, you'll find this book practical, quick, comprehensive, and useful.

Uses for this book are as varied as the topics presented. It can be used by CFOs employed by large, medium, or small companies.

You'll be able to move quickly to take advantage of favorable situations and avoid unfavorable ones. Here is the guide that will help you make smart decisions. The book provides analysis of recurring problems as well as unusual ones that may occur. "Red flags" are posted of potential difficulties. It gives vital suggestions throughout on correcting financial sickness and inefficiency. The latest developments, such as new tax laws, are included.

The book covers the major areas and problems of corporate financial management and accounting. It is directed to the modern chief financial officer who must follow some traditional elements common to controllership and financial management but must be cognizant of the ever-changing financial markets and technology of today. These factors make some of the traditional techniques of financial management obsolete—new strategies and techniques are necessary in order to do an effective job that ensures financial survival.

Guidelines are presented for evaluating proposals, whether they be short- or long-term, for profit potential, and risk-return comparison. Ways to analyze and measure operations and activities are presented. Tips for preparing necessary reports are also provided.

The book is a practical reference that contains approaches and techniques for understanding and solving problems of:

- Financial accounting
- Managerial accounting
- Financial management and planning
- Management of assets and liabilities
- Investments
- Financing the business
- Quantitative analysis and modeling
- Taxation
- Mergers and acquisitions
- Divestitures
- Multinational finance
- Forecasting corporate bankruptcy
- Economics

Part I (Chapters 1–2) covers the financial reporting responsibilities of the chief financial officer including the types of reports that must be prepared. Securities and Exchange Commission filings are required by public companies.

Part II (Chapters 3–8) discusses the financial accounting requirements applicable to the income statement, balance sheet, and statement of cash flows. Generally accepted accounting principles are delved into including such important topics as leases, pensions, and accounting for income taxes.

Part III (Chapters 9–19) is on managerial accounting. It covers what the chief financial officer should know about cost management and analysis, break-even analysis, contribution margin analysis, budgeting and financial modeling, variance analysis, just-in-time costs, capital budgeting, managerial reports, segmental performance, and quantitative techniques.

Part IV (Chapters 20–23) addresses the management of working capital and assets including cash, accounts receivable, and inventory. The management of payables is also highlighted.

Part V (Chapters 24–29) deals with how to adequately obtain financing for the business to meet its goals and financial needs. Short-term, intermediate-term, and long-term financing requirements are discussed as well as indicating under what circumstances each would be appropriate. Cost of capital determination and capital structure decisions are presented. The factors in establishing a dividend policy are noted. The financial management of overseas operations is crucial to multinational companies.

Part VI (Chapters 30–33) is directed toward financial analysis areas including risk/reward relationships and financial statement analysis for internal evaluation. Ways to analyze and control revenue and expenses are addressed. The economic environment has to be studied to see its impact on the business and what can be done in recessionary times. Proper insurance is needed to assure the sustenance of the business. A knowledge of law is required to guard against legal exposure such as from product defects.

Part VII (Chapter 34) covers investment portfolio selection so as to earn a satisfactory return while controlling risk.

Part VIII (Chapter 35) discusses the tax consequences in making financial decisions. Tax planning is essential to minimizing the tax obligation of the business.

Part IX (Chapters 36–39) presents the planning and financial aspects for mergers and acquisitions. The reasons and ways of divesting of business segments are discussed. The signs of potential business failure must be noted so timely corrective action may be taken. The steps in a reorganization are discussed.

The content of the book is clear, concise, and to the point. It is a valuable reference tool with practical applications and "how-to's" for you, the up-to-date knowledgeable CFO. Keep this book handy for easy reference and daily use.

In the index, a specific area of interest may easily be found.

Contents

PART 1

REPORTS AND FILINGS

Chief Financial Officer's Reports

The chief financial officer must communicate important and accurate financial information to senior-level executives, the board of directors, divisional managers, employees, and various third parties. The reports must be prepared in a timely fashion and be comprehensible and relevant to readers.

The needs of management differ among organizations. Management reports should be sufficiently simplistic in order to enable the reader to concentrate on problems and difficulties that may arise. The reports should not be cumbersome to read through. The reports should be consistent and uniform in report format. The facts presented should be based on supportable financial and accounting data. The CFO should use less accounting jargon and more operating terminology when reporting to management. Also, the reports should generate questions for top management discussions.

What are prospective financial statements?

Prospective financial statements include financial forecasts and projections. This category excludes pro forma financial statements and partial presentations.

Financial forecasts are prospective financial statements that present the company's expected financial position, results of operations and cash flows, based on assumptions about conditions actually *anticipated* to occur and the management action expected to be taken.

A financial forecast may be presented in a single dollar amount based on the best estimate, or as a reasonable range. However, this range cannot be selected in a misleading way.

In contrast, financial projections are prospective statements that present the company's financial position, results of operations and cash flows,

based on assumptions about conditions anticipated to exist and the action management is expected to take, given the *hypothetical* (what-if)
assumptions.

Financial projections may be most useful to
limited users, who seek answers to questions involving hypothetical questions. These users may
want to change the scenarios based on expected
changing situations. A financial projection may
contain a range.

A financial projection may be prepared for
general users *only* if it supplements a financial
forecast. However, financial projections may not
be contained in general-use documents and tax
shelter prospectuses.

What should be contained in financial forecasts and financial projections?

Financial forecasts and financial projections
may be in the form of either complete basic financial statements or financial statements containing the following minimum items: sales or
gross revenues; net income; gross profit; primary
and fully diluted earnings per share; income
from continuing operations; income from discontinued operations; unusual income statement
items; tax provision; material changes in financial positions; and summary of significant accounting policies and assumptions.

Management's intent of preparing the prospective financial statements should be stated. However, there should be a mention that prospective
results may not materialize. Also, it should be
clearly stated that the assumptions used by management are based on information and circumstances in existence at the time when the financial
statements were prepared.

What are the various kinds of planning reports that may be prepared?

The CFO may prepare short-term company-
wide or division-wide planning reports. This
includes forecasted balance sheet, forecasted

income statement, forecasted statement of cash flows, and projections of capital expenditures.

Special short-term planning studies of specific business segments may also be prepared. These reports may relate to the following: product distribution by territory and market; product line mix analysis; warehouse handling; salesperson performance; and logistics. Long-range planning reports may include five to ten-year projections for the company and its major business segments.

Specialized planning and control reports may include the effects of cost-reduction programs, production issues in cost/quality terms, cash flow plans for line-of-credit agreements, evaluating pension/termination costs in plant closings, contingency and downsizing plans, and appraising risk factors in long-term contracts.

Why are informational reports useful?

The CFO may prepare information reports for other members of top management. The reports may show and discuss long-term financial and operating trends. For example, the reasons and analytical implications of trends in revenue, production, and costs may be presented over the last three years. While the format of such reports may vary depending upon the environmental considerations and user needs, graphic depiction is often enlightening.

How can reports be used to analyze and control operations?

Reports may be prepared dealing with controlling financial activities and related analytical implications. Analytical procedures include comparing financial and nonfinancial information over time. The reports may highlight the reasons for significant change between prior and current year performance. For example, a sharp increase in promotion and entertainment expense or telephone expense may require investigation. Analytical reports are also used to summarize and evaluate variances from forecasts and budgets. Appraisal of variances may be by revenue, expense, profit, assets, product, division, and territory.

Why are exceptions to the norm significant to note?

Exception reports present detailed enumeration of the problems and difficulties faced by the business over a given time period. Such reports might "zero in on" internal control structure inadequacies or improper employment of accounting or auditing procedures in violation of generally accepted accounting principles (GAAP) and generally accepted auditing standards (GAAS). Exception reports should be automatically outputed by the computer when a "red flag" is posted such as when a customer's balance exceeds the credit limit.

What should the Board of Directors know?

The Board of Directors is usually concerned with overall policy matters, general trends in revenue and earnings, and what the competition is doing. It is also interested in short-term and long-term issues. Relevant information in reports directed to the Board of Directors include company and divisional performance reports, historical and forecasted financial statements, status reports applicable to capital expenditures, and special studies.

What special occurrences should be reported upon?

Special situations and circumstances may occur requiring separate evaluation and study. For example, it may be necessary to identify the cause for a repeated decline in profitability of a given product, service, or territory. There may be a need for a feasibility analysis of whether to open a new store location or plant. Other reports may be in connection with union negotiations, commercial contract reviews, pension plan administration, bonus plans, and product warranty issues. It is essential that the reports contain narrative and statistical analyses of the decision with graphic presentations as needed.

What reports may segment managers find useful in decision making?

Reports prepared to assist divisional managers in evaluating performance and improving operating results include: dollar sales and volume; profitability by product line, service, project, program, and territory; return on investment and residual income; divisional contribution margin, segment margin, and short-term performance margin; actual and budgeted costs by cost center; cash flow; labor and plant utilization; backlog, and comparisons of each division's performance to other divisions within the company and to competing divisions in other companies.

The CFO should determine whether current reporting may be improved. In one case, the author consulted with a company in which a maintenance and repair department manager prepared reports solely focusing on machine downtime. The reports concentrated on expenditures for repairs due to equipment breakdowns. Instead, the author recommended that the focus of attention should be on improving the productivity of manufacturing facilities. Hence, it is more constructive to look at *uptime* (machine usage) rather than downtime, and allocate resources accordingly. A machine uptime index may be computed. The production cycle period may also be analyzed. This is the time between the receipt of an order and delivery to the customer which should be monitored on a regular basis.

How may reports be directed to improving quality?

Reports may be prepared with the view of improving the quality of goods and/or services while controlling costs. What is the cost-effectiveness of contemplated quality improvements? Of course, there is a trade-off between better quality and increased costs. Attention should be directed to curing defects causing project delays. Cost considerations include overtime, rework, scrap, and capital outlays. The reports should concentrate on the accumulated costs of actions that promote quality. The costs include material inspection, quality control, preventive maintenance, and sampling. The CFO should also consider the increased costs associated with "poor quality" products and/or services, such as warranties, promotional expenditures to improve the company's image, and legal liability settlements.

What types of information might employees be interested in?

Reports may be directed toward the interests and concerns of employees and contain the following information: revenue and/or profitability per employee; revenue relative to employee salaries; assets per employee; profit margin; sales volume or service hours; investments made to directly or indirectly benefit employees; explanation of changes in benefit programs (e.g., health insurance, pension plan); percentage increase in salaries, fringe benefits, and overtime; dividends relative to wages and number of employees; corporate annual growth rate; comparison of employee salaries to that of competing companies and industry averages; real earnings after adjusting for inflation; analytical profit and cost information by responsibility center; assets by business segment; future prospects and problems in the company, industry, and economy; break-even point; actual and expected production; employee safety; compliance with federal, state and local laws pertaining to employee working conditions; sources of financing; nature and type of assets held; and overall financial health of the company. (See Exhibit 1–1.)

GOVERNMENTAL REPORTING _____

The CFO may have to prepare reports to federal, state, and city governmental agencies. Antitrust laws, environmental protection laws, pension laws, product liability laws, pollution laws, laws

EXHIBIT 1-1 ABC COMPANY STATEMENT OF REVENUE AND EXPENSE FOR EMPLOYEES FOR THE YEAR ENDED DECEMBER 31, 19XX

	Total Amount	Amount per Employee	Costs per Dollar of Receipts
The Business Received:			
From customers for merchandise or services performed			
Interest			
Dividends			
Total amount received			
Business Expenses Incurred:			
For raw materials, supplies, and other expenses			
Depreciation			
Taxes			
Total expenses			
Residual for salaries, dividends, and reinvestment in the company			
This Was Divided as Follows:			
Paid to employees (excluding officers) as salaries			
Paid for employee fringe benefits			
Total			
Executive salaries			
Executive fringe benefits			
Dividends to stockholders			
Reinvested in the company for expansion			
Total division			

governing international trade and commerce, and tax laws are but a few of the myriad of reports with which the company must contend. Penalties may be assessed for the failure to file reports on time.

What does the New York Stock Exchange want to know?

The listing application to the New York Stock Exchange contains an agreement to provide annual and interim reports including financial statements and disclosures. The reports are filed on a timely basis since the information contained may have a material influence on market price of stock, bond ratings, and cost of financing.

OTHER REPORTING

Many groups compile statistics on business performance, such as trade associations, state commerce departments, federal bureaus and agencies, and credit agencies. Questionnaires and reports of a wide scope are received and completed.

The CFO's role in reporting information cannot be understated. Besides the ability to formulate relevant financial and nonfinancial data, the CFO must be able to effectively and efficiently communicate to management, employees, government, investors, creditors, and other interested parties. Financial reports should be timely submitted so up-to-date information is available for decision-making purposes.

2

Securities and Exchange Commission Filings

The Securities and Exchange Commission (SEC) requires full and fair disclosure in connection with the offering and issuance of securities to the public. The CFO should be familiar with the major provisions of the Securities Act of 1933 and the Securities Act of 1934.

What SEC rules apply to the issuance of securities for the first time?

The Securities Act of 1933 (as amended) pertains to the *initial* offering and sale of securities. It does *not* apply to the subsequent trading of securities. The Act requires the filing of a registration statement with the SEC so as to prevent misrepresentation.

What SEC rules apply to the subsequent trading of securities?

The Securities Act of 1934 regulates the *subsequent trading* of securities on the various national stock exchanges. A scaled-down version of the 1933 Act registration statement must be filed by the company if its securities are to be traded on a national exchange. The annual Form 10-K and the quarterly Form 10-Q are required to be filed.

What should the Basic Information Package contain?

The complexity of the reporting requirements under the 1933 and 1934 Acts were somewhat relieved when the SEC adopted the Integrated Disclosure System, which requires the Basic Information Package (BIP). The BIP includes:

- Audited balance sheets for the last two years and audited statements of income, retained earnings, and cash flows for the most recent three years.

- Management's discussion and analysis of the company's financial position and operating results.
- A five-year summary consisting of selected financial information.

What information is required in the S Forms?

Form S-1

Form S-1 is typically used by a company that wants to sell securities and that has been subject to the SEC reporting requirements for less than three years and typically includes:

- A description of the securities being registered.
- A summary of the business including pertinent industry and segment information.
- A listing of properties.
- Background and financial information concerning the company's directors and officers.
- Selected financial information over the last five years including sales, profit, divisions, and total assets.

Form S-2

Form S-2 is a short form that is used by issuers who have been reporting to the SEC for at least three years and have voting stock held by nonaffiliates of less than $150 million.

Form S-3

Form S-3 may generally be used by a company that has at least $150 million of voting stock owned by nonaffiliates. It may also be used if the company issues $100 million of securities and the annual trading volume is at least 3 million shares.

Form S-4

Form S-4 is filed for securities issuances arising from business combinations.

What should the CFO discuss when reporting to stockholders?

Management's discussion and analysis is an important element of the registration filing and provides an explanation of the significant changes in financial position and results of operations, including:

- Results of operations.
- Unusual or infrequent items.
- Liquidity.
- Capital resources.
- Significant uncertainties.

What disclosures are required under Regulation S-X?

In general, the accounting rules under Regulation S-X parallel generally accepted accounting principles (GAAP). However, some disclosure rules under Regulation S-X are more expansive. For example, financial statements filed with the SEC require the following disclosures which are not usually included in financial statements under GAAP:

- Lines of credit.
- Compensating balance arrangements.
- Current liabilities if they represent in excess of 5% of the entity's total liabilities.

What information must be filed annually with the SEC?

To comply with the Securities Act of 1934, most registrants must file each year a Form 10-K. It is due within 90 days after the reporting year-end. Some required disclosures are financial statements, management's discussion of operations, litigation, executive compensation, and related party transactions.

What if something important suddenly happens?

Form 8-K has to be filed immediately after a significant event occurs materially affecting the company's financial status and/or operating performance. Such events may include bankruptcy, acquisition or disposition of assets, change in control, change in outside auditor, and other important issues (e.g., litigation).

What information should be filed on an interim basis?

Form 10-Q is a quarterly filing updating for changes in financial position and operations since the filing of the last Form 10-K. Form 10-Q is due within 45 days after the end of each of the first three fiscal quarters.

PART II

FINANCIAL
ACCOUNTING

3

Financial Statement Reporting: The Income Statement

In preparing the income statement, revenue and expenses must be properly recognized. Many revenue recognition methods exist. Extraordinary and nonrecurring items must be separately shown. The income statement must be in the proper format with earnings per share disclosed.

How is the income statement presented?

The format of the income statement follows:

Income from continuing operations before tax
Less: Taxes
Income from continuing operations after tax
Discontinued operations:
    Income from discontinued operations (net of tax)
    Loss or gain on disposal of a division (net of tax)
Income before extraordinary items
Extraordinary items (net of tax)
Cumulative effect of a change in accounting principle
    (net of tax)
Net income

The earnings per share effect for each of the above items is presented.

What is comprehensive income?

Comprehensive income is the change in equity resulting from transactions and other activities with nonowners. The owners' investments and disinvestments are excluded. The items included in comprehensive income but excluded from net income are:

• Cumulative effect of a change in accounting principle.

- Unrealized losses and gains on long-term investments.
- Foreign currency translation gains and losses.

Comprehensive income is subdivided into revenues and gain, and expenses and losses. These are further classified as either recurring or extraordinary.

What are extraordinary items?

Extraordinary items are unusual *and* infrequent. Unusual means the occurrence is abnormal and unrelated to the usual activities of the business. Infrequent means the transaction is not expected to occur in the foreseeable future considering the company's environment. Materiality looks at items individually and not in the aggregate. However, if arising from a single event extraordinary items are aggregated. Extraordinary items are presented net of tax between income from discontinued operations and cumulative effect of a change in accounting principle. Examples of extraordinary items are:

- Casualty losses.
- Loss or gain on the early extinguishment of debt.
- Gain on troubled debt restructuring.
- Losses on expropriation of property by a foreign government.
- Gain on life insurance proceeds.
- Gain or loss on disposal of a major part of the assets of a previously separate company in a business combination when sale is made within two years after the combination date.
- Loss from prohibition under a newly enacted law or regulation.

Losses on receivables and inventory take place in the ordinary course of business and therefore are *not* extraordinary. However, losses on receivables and inventory are extraordinary if they relate to a casualty loss (e.g., earthquake) or governmental expropriation (e.g., withdrawal of a product deemed hazardous to health).

What is a nonrecurring item and how is it presented?

Nonrecurring items are unusual *or* infrequent. They are shown separately before tax in arriving at income from continuing operations. An example is the gain or loss on the sale of a fixed asset.

How are discontinued operations presented?

A business segment is a major line of business or customer class. A discontinued operation is one discontinued during the year or will be discontinued shortly after year-end. It may be a segment that has been sold, abandoned, or spun off. The footnote disclosure for a discontinued operation includes an identification of the segment, the manner of disposal, disposal date, and description of the remaining net assets of the segment.

The two components of discontinued operations are: (1) income or loss from operations and (2) loss or gain on disposal of division.

Income or Loss from Operations. In a year that includes the measurement date, it is the income from the beginning of the year to the measurement date. The measurement date is the one on which management obligates itself to a formal plan of action. Reasonable estimates may be required.

If comparative financial statements are presented including periods before the measurement date, discontinued operations should be separately shown from continuing operations.

Loss or Gain on Disposal of Division. Income or loss from activities after the measurement date and before the disposal date is an element of the gain or loss on disposal. The disposal date is the date of closing by sale or the date activities end because of abandonment. The gain or loss is shown in the disposal year. However, if losses are expected, they are recorded in the year of the measurement date even if disposal is not completed in that year. Loss or gain should include estimated net losses from operations between the measurement date and the disposal date. If the loss cannot be estimated, a footnote is required. Loss on disposal includes the costs directly applicable to the disposal decision. On the other hand, if a gain is anticipated, it should be recognized at the disposal date. The estimated gain or loss is computed at the measurement date and includes consideration of the net realizable value of the segment's assets. Also, loss or gain on disposal includes costs and expenses *directly* related to the disposal decision. These costs include employment relocation, severance pay, additional pension costs, and future rentals on long-term leases where subrentals are not possible. *Note:* Normal business adjustments (e.g., routinely writing down accounts receivable) are not included in the loss on disposal. These ordinary adjustments apply to the discontinued segment's operation instead of to the disposal of the segment. Typically, disposal is expected within one year of the measurement date.

EXAMPLE 1

On 6/16/19X8, ABC Company set up a plan to dispose of segment X. It is expected that the sale will occur on 3/1/19X9 for a selling price of $800,000. In 19X8, disposal costs were $100,000. Segment X's actual and estimated operating losses were:

1/1/19X8 to 6/14/19X8	$85,000
6/15/19X8 to 12/31/19X8	40,000
1/1/19X9 to 3/1/19X9	12,000

The carrying value of the segment on 3/1/19X9 is expected to be $900,000. The loss on disposal of segment X in the 19X8 income statement is:

Selling price		$800,000
Less: Disposal costs	$100,000	
Actual and expected operating losses after the measurement date	52,000	
Carrying value	900,000	1,052,000
Loss on disposal		$ 252,000

REVENUE RECOGNITION ——————

Revenue may be recognized under different methods depending on the circumstances. (Special revenue recognition guidelines exist for franchisors and in right of return situations. A product financing arrangement may also exist.) The basic methods of recognition are:

- Realization.
- Completion of production.
- During production.
- Cash basis.

When does realization occur?

Revenue is recognized when goods are sold or services are performed. This method is used most of the time. At realization, the earnings process is complete. Further, realization is in conformity with accrual meaning that revenue is recognized when earned rather than when received. Realization should be used when the selling price is determinable, future costs can be estimated, and an exchange has occurred that can be objectively measured. There are other cases in which another method of revenue recognition should be used as discussed below.

When can revenue be recorded when production is completed?

Revenue can be recognized before sale or exchange. There must be a stable selling price, absence of significant marketing costs, and interchangeability in units. This approach is used with agricultural products, byproducts, and precious metals when the aforementioned criteria are satisfied. It is also used in accounting for construction contracts under the completed contract method.

When can revenue be recognized in stages?

Revenue can be recognized gradually as work is performed on a long-term contract. There must be an assured selling price and reliable estimation of costs. An example is the percentage of completion method for long-term construction contracts.

Construction Contracts. Under the completed contract method, revenue is only recognized in the final year the project is completed. The method should only be used when the percentage of completion method is inappropriate.

Under the percentage of completion method, revenue is recognized with production activity. The gradual recognition of revenue levels out earnings over the years and is more realistic since revenue is recognized as performance occurs. This method is preferred over the completed contract method and should be used when reliable estimates of the degree of completion are possible. Percentage of completion results in a matching of revenue against expenses in the benefit period.

Using the cost-to-cost method, revenue recognized for the period equals:

$$\frac{\text{Actual costs to date}}{\text{Total estimated costs}} \times \frac{\text{Contract}}{\text{price}} = \frac{\text{Cumulative}}{\text{revenue}}$$

Revenue recognized in previous years is deducted from the cumulative revenue to determine the revenue in the current period, for example:

> Cumulative revenue (1–4 years)
> Revenue recognized (1–3 years)
> Revenue (Year 4 – Current year)
> Revenue less expenses equals profit.

EXAMPLE 2

In year 4 of a contract, the actual costs to date were $50,000. Total estimated costs are $200,000. The contract price is $1,000,000. Revenue recognized in the prior years (years 1–3) were $185,000.

$$\frac{\$50,000}{\$200,000} \times \$1,000,000 = \frac{\$250,000}{\text{Cumulative revenue}}$$

Cumulative revenue	$250,000
Prior year revenue	185,000
Current year revenue	$ 65,000

Regardless which method is used, conservatism requires that a loss on a contract be *immediately* recognized.

Journal entries under the construction method using assumed figures include:

	Percentage of Completion		Completed Contract	
Construction-in-Progress (CIP)	100,000		100,000	
Cash		100,000		100,000
Construction costs				
Progress Billings Receivable	80,000		80,000	
Progress Billings on CIP		80,000		80,000
Periodic billings				
Construction-in-Progress	25,000		No Entry	
Profit		25,000		
Yearly profit recognition				

In the last year when the construction project is completed, the following additional entry is made to record the profit in the final year:

	Percentage-of-Completion	Completed Contract
Progress Billings on Construction-in-Progress	Total Billings	Total Billings
Construction-in-Progress	Cost + Profit	Cost
Profit	Incremental Profit for Last Year	Profit for All the Years

Construction-in-Progress less Progress Billings is shown net. Typically, a debit figure results that is shown as a current asset. Construction-in-progress is an inventory account for a construction company. If a credit balance occurs, the net amount is shown as a current liability.

When must revenue recognition await cash receipt?

If a company sells inventory, the accrual basis is used. However, when certain circumstances exist, the cash basis of revenue recognition is used. Namely, revenue is recognized when cash is received. The cash basis rather than the accrual basis must be used when one or more of the following exist:

- Selling price not objectively determinable at the time of sale.
- Inability to estimate expenses at the time of sale.
- Collection risk exists.
- Uncertain collection period.

Revenue recognition under the *installment method* equals the cash collected times the gross profit percent. Any gross profit not collected is deferred on the balance sheet until collection occurs. When collections are received, realized gross profit is recognized by debiting the deferred gross profit account. The balance sheet presentation is:

> Accounts receivable (Cost + Profit)
> Less: Deferred gross profit (Profit)
> Net accounts receivable (Cost)

Under the *cost recovery method,* profit is only recognized after all costs have been recovered.

Note: Since a service business does not have inventory, it has the option of either using the accrual basis or cash basis.

What if the buyer has the privilege to return the merchandise?

If a buyer has the right to return merchandise, the seller can only recognize revenue at the time of sale according to FASB 48 if *all* of the following criteria are met:

- Selling price is known.
- Buyer has to pay for the product even if the buyer is unable to resell it.
- If the buyer loses or damages the item, the buyer still has to pay for it.
- Purchase by the buyer makes economic sense.
- Seller does not have to perform future services so that the buyer will be able to resell the item.
- Returns may be reasonably estimated.

If any one of the above criteria are not satisfied, revenue must be deferred along with deferral of related expenses until the criteria have been met or the right of return provision has expired. An alternative to deferring the revenue would be to record a memo entry.

The ability of a company to predict future returns involves consideration of the following:

- Predictability is detracted from when there is technological obsolescence risk of the product, uncertain product demand changes, or other significant external factors.
- Predictability is lessened when there is a long-time period for returns.
- Predictability is enhanced when there are many similar transactions.
- Seller's prior experience in estimating returns for similar products.
- Nature of customer relationship and types of products sold.

What is a product financing arrangement?

According to FASB 49, the sale and repurchase of inventory is in substance a financing arrangement. The product financing arrangement must be accounted for as a borrowing not a sale. In many instances, the product is stored on the company's (sponsor's) premises. Further, the sponsor often guarantees the debt of the other entity.

The types of product financing arrangements include:

- Sponsor sells a product to another business and contracts to reacquire it or an identical one. The price paid by the sponsor usually includes financing and storage costs.
- Sponsor controls the distribution of the product that has been bought by another company based on the aforementioned terms.

In each case, the company (sponsor) either agrees to repurchase the product at specified prices over given time periods, or guarantees resale prices to third parties.

When the sponsor sells the product to the other business and in a related transaction agrees to repurchase it, the sponsor records a liability when the proceeds are received. A sale should *not* be recorded and the product should be retained as inventory on the sponsor's balance sheet.

If another entity buys the product for the sponsor, inventory is debited and liability credited at the time of purchase.

Costs of the product, excluding processing costs, exceeding the sponsor's original cost represents finance and holding costs. The sponsor accounts for these costs based on its customary accounting policies. Interest expense will also be recognized.

EXAMPLE 3

On 1/1/19X1, a sponsor borrows $100,000 from another company and gives the inventory as collateral. The entry is:

| Cash | 100,000 | |
| Liability | | 100,000 |

A sale is *not* recorded and the inventory continues on the books of the sponsor.

On 12/31/19X1, the sponsor remits payment to the other company. The collateralized inventory item is returned. If the interest rate on the loan is 8% and storage costs are $2,000, the journal entry is:

Liability	100,000	
Interest expense (or Deferred interest)	8,000	
Storage expense	2,000	
Cash		110,000

In most cases, the product in the financing agreement is ultimately used or sold by the sponsor. However, in some instances, small amounts of the product may be sold by the financing entity to other parties.

The entity providing financing to the sponsor is typically an existing creditor, nonbusiness entity, or trust. It is also possible that the finansor may have been established for the *sole* purpose of providing financing to the sponsor.

Footnote disclosure should be made of the product financing terms.

How should franchisors recognize revenue?

According to FASB 45, the franchisor can only record revenue from the initial sale of the franchise when all significant services and obligations applicable to the sale have been substantially performed. Substantial performance is indicated by:

- Absence of intent to give cash refunds or relieve the accounts receivable due from the franchisee.
- Nothing material remains to be done by the franchisor.
- Initial services have been rendered.

The earliest date that substantial performance can take place is the franchisee's commencement of operations unless there are special circumstances. When it is probable that the franchisor will eventually repurchase the franchise, the initial fee may be deferred and treated as a reduction of the repurchase price.

If revenue is deferred, the related expenses must be deferred for later matching in the year in which the revenue is recognized. This is illustrated below.

> Year of initial fee:
> Cash
> > Deferred revenue
> Deferred expenses
> > Cash
> Year when substantial performance occurs:
> Deferred revenue
> > Revenue
> Expenses
> > Deferred expenses

If the initial fee includes both services and property (real or personal), there should be an allocation based on fair market values.

When part of the initial fee applies to *tangible property* (e.g., equipment, signs, inventory), revenue recognition is based on the fair value of the assets. Revenue recognition may occur before or after recognizing the portion of the fee related to initial services. For example, part of the fee for equipment may be recognized at the time title passes with the balance of the fee being recorded as revenue when future services are performed.

Recurring franchise fees are recognized as earned with related costs being expensed. There is one exception. If the price charged for the continuing services or goods to the franchisee is less than the price charged to third parties, it infers that the initial franchise fee was in essence a partial *prepayment* for the recurring franchise fee. In this case, part of the initial fee has to be deferred and recognized as an adjustment of the revenue from the sale of goods and services at bargain prices.

When there is a probability that continuing franchise fees will not cover the cost of the continuing services and provide for a reasonable profit to the franchisor, part of the initial franchise fee should be deferred to satisfy the deficiency and amortized over the life of the franchise. The deferred amount should be adequate to meet future costs and generate a profit on the recurring services. This situation may arise if the continuing fees are minimal considering the services rendered or the franchisee has the option to make bargain purchases over a stated time period.

Unearned franchise fees are recorded at present value. Where a part of the initial fee represents a nonrefundable amount for services already performed, revenue should be accordingly recognized.

The initial franchise fee is *not* usually allocated to specific franchisor services before all services are performed. This practice can only be done if actual transaction prices are available for individual services.

If the franchisor sells equipment and inventory to the franchisee at no profit, a receivable and payable is recorded. There is *no* revenue or expense recognition.

When there is a repossessed franchise, refunded amounts to the franchisee reduce current revenue. In the absence of a refund, the franchisor records additional revenue for the consideration retained which was not previously recorded. In either case, *prospective* accounting treatment is given for the repossession. Warning: Do *not* adjust previously recorded revenue for the repossession.

Indirect costs of an operating and recurring nature are immediately expensed. Future costs are accrued no later than the period in which related revenue is recognized. A bad debt provision for uncollectible franchise fees should be recorded in the year of revenue recognition.

Installment or cost recovery accounting may be used to account for franchise fee revenue *only* if there is a long collection period and future uncollectibility of receivables cannot be reliably estimated.

Footnote disclosure should be made of outstanding obligations and segregation of franchise fee revenue between initial and continuing.

What are research and development costs and how are they accounted for?

Research is the testing in search for a new product, process, service, or technique. Research can be directed at substantially improving an existing product or process. Development is translating the research into a design for the new product or process. Development may also result in a significant improvement to an existing product or process. According to FASB 2, research and development costs are expensed as incurred. However, R&D costs incurred under contract for others that is reimburseable are charged to a receivable account. Further, materials, equipment and intangibles bought from others that have alternative future benefit in R&D activities are capitalized. The depreciation or amortization on such assets are classified as R&D expense. If there is no alternative future use, the costs should be expensed.

R&D cost includes the salaries of personnel involved in R&D efforts. R&D cost also includes a rational allocation of indirect (general and administrative) costs. If a group of assets are acquired, allocation should be made to those that relate to R&D activities. When a business combination is accounted for as a purchase, R&D costs are assigned their fair market value.

Expenditures paid to others to conduct R&D activities are expensed.

Examples of R&D activities include:

- Formulation and design of product alternatives and testing thereof.
- Pre-production models and prototypes.
- Design of models, tools, and dies involving latest technology.
- Laboratory research.
- Pilot plant costs.
- Engineering functions until the product meets operational guidelines for manufacture.

Examples of activities that are not for R&D include:

- Legal costs to obtain a patent.
- Quality control.
- Seasonal design modifications.
- Market research.
- Commercial use of the product.
- Rearrangement and start-up operations including design and construction engineering.
- Recurring efforts to improve the product.
- Identifying breakdowns during commercial production.

FASB 2 does not apply to either regulated or extractive (e.g., mining) industries.

According to FASB 86, costs incurred for computer software to be sold, leased, or otherwise marketed are expensed as R&D costs until technological feasibility has been established as evidenced by the development of a detailed program or working model. After technological feasibility, software production costs should be deferred and recorded at the lower of unamortized cost or net realizable value. Examples of such costs include debugging the software, improvements to subroutines, and adaptions for other uses. Amortization starts when the product is available for customer release. The amortization expense should be based on the higher of the straight line amortization amount or the percent of current revenue to total revenue from the product.

As per FASB 68, if a company enters into an agreement with other parties to fund the R&D efforts, the nature of the obligation must be determined. If the company has an obligation to repay the funds regardless of the R&D results, a liability must be recognized with the related R&D expense. The journal entries are:

```
Cash
    Liability
Research and development expense
    Cash
```

A liability does not arise when the transfer of financial risk to the other party is substantive. If the financial risk is transferred because repayment depends only on the R&D possessing future benefit, the company accounts for its obligation as a contract to conduct R&D for others. In this case, R&D costs are capitalized and revenue is recognized as earned and becomes billable under the contract. Footnote disclosure is made of the terms of the R&D agreement, the amount of compensation earned, and the costs incurred under the contract.

When repayment of loans or advances to the company depends only on R&D results, such amounts are considered R&D costs incurred by the company and charged to expense.

If warrants or other financial instruments are issued in an R&D arrangement, the company records part of the proceeds to be provided by the other parties as paid-in-capital based on their fair market value on the arrangement date.

How are EPS computed?

APB 15 requires the computation of earnings per share. In a simple capital structure, there are no potentially dilutive securities. (Potentially dilutive means the security will be converted into common stock at a later date reducing EPS). Thus, only one EPS figure is needed. In a complex capital structure, dilutive securities exist requiring dual presentation as follows:

$$\frac{\text{Primary}}{\text{EPS}} = \frac{\text{Net income} - \text{Preferred dividend}}{\substack{\text{Weighted-average common stock} \\ \text{outstanding} + \text{Common stock equivalents}}}$$

$$\frac{\text{Fully}}{\substack{\text{diluted} \\ \text{EPS}}} = \frac{\text{Net income} - \text{Preferred dividend}}{\substack{\text{Weighted-average common stock} \\ \text{outstanding} + \text{Common stock equivalents} \\ + \text{Other fully diluted decurities}}}$$

Fully diluted EPS reflects the *maximum* potential dilution per share on a prospective basis. Weighted-average common stock shares outstanding considers the number of months in which those shares were outstanding.

EXAMPLE 4

On 1/19X1 10,000 shares were issued. On 4/1/19X1 2,000 of those shares were reacquired. The weighted-average common stock outstanding is:

$$(10,000 \times 3/12) + (8,000 \times 9/12) = 8,500 \text{ shares}$$

Common stock equivalents are securities that can become common stock at a later date and are shown in both primary EPS and fully diluted EPS, including:

- Stock options and warrants.
- Subscribed stock.
- Two-class common stock.
- Contingent shares only related to the passage of time.
- Convertible securities (convertible bonds, convertible preferred stock) when the yield at the time of issuance is less than 2/3 of the average Aa corporate bond yield at the time of issuance. Once a convertible security qualifies as a common stock equivalent, it continues as such. Aa bonds are defined by Standard and Poor's and Moody's as of the highest quality. For zero-coupon bonds, the effective yield is the interest rate that discounts the maturity value of the bond to its present value. This rate is then used to determine common stock equivalency by comparing the rate to 2/3 of the average yield. If convertible securities are issued in a foreign country, we use the most comparable long-term yield in that country in performing the cash yield test.

Note: Although stock options are *always* considered common stock equivalents, they are only included in computing EPS if the market price of common stock is greater than the option price for substantially all of the last *three* months of the year. In this case, we assume the stock options were exercised at the *beginning* of the year (or at time of issuance, if later). While convertible securities are classified as common stock equivalents based on the circumstances at time of issue, warrants are classified according to the conditions at each period.

In computing EPS, common stock equivalents are included if they have a dilutive effect. Dilutive effect means that inclusion of a common stock equivalent reduces EPS by at least 3% in the aggregate and is applied by type of security. The 3% dilution also relates to presenting fully diluted EPS. Fully diluted EPS is also shown if it reduces primary EPS by 3% or more. Antidilutive securities that increase EPS are not shown in the EPS computation because they will increase EPS which violates conservatism.

When shares are issued because of a stock dividend or stock split, the computation of weighted-average common stock shares outstanding requires retroactive adjustment as if the shares were outstanding at the beginning of the year.

The common stock equivalency of options and warrants is determined using the *treasury stock method.* Options and warrants are assumed exercised at the beginning of the year (or at time of issuance, if later). The proceeds received are assumed used to: (1) reacquire common stock at the average market price for the year provided it does not exceed 20% of the shares outstanding at year-end; (2) with the balance remaining reduce long or short-term debt; and (3) with any balance left over invest in U.S. government securities and commercial paper.

We assume the exercise of options only when the market price of stock exceeds the exercise price for three consecutive months ending with the year-end month.

In computing fully diluted EPS, the treasury stock method is modified in that the market price at the end of the accounting period is used if it is higher than the average market price for the period.

EXAMPLE 5

100 shares are under option at an option price of $10. The average market price of stock is $25. The common stock equivalent is 60 shares as calculated below:

Issued shares from option	100 shares × $10 = $1,000
Less: Treasury shares	40 shares × $25 = $1,000
Common stock equivalent	60 shares

Convertible securities are accounted for using the "if converted method." The convertible securities are assumed converted at the beginning of the earliest year presented or date of security issuance. Interest or dividends on them are added back to net income since the securities are considered part of equity in the denominator of the EPS calculation.

Other fully diluted securities are defined as convertible securities that did not meet the $2/3$ test. They are included only in the calculation of fully diluted EPS. Thus, fully diluted EPS will be a lower figure than primary EPS because of the greater shares in the denominator. Contingent issuance of shares in computing fully diluted EPS is assumed to have occurred at the beginning of the year, or at the time of issuance, if later. Fully diluted EPS is a pro forma presentation showing what EPS would be if *all* potential contingencies of common stock issuances having a dilutive effect occurred.

To achieve the fullest dilution in obtaining fully diluted EPS, we assume that all common stock issuances on exercise of options or warrants during the period were made at the start of the year. The *higher* of the closing price or the average price of common stock is used in determining the number of shares of treasury stock to be purchased from the proceeds received upon issuance of the options. If the ending market price exceeds the average market price, the assumed treasury shares acquired will be lessened resulting in higher assumed outstanding shares with the resulting decrease in EPS.

Net income less preferred dividends is in the numerator of the EPS fraction representing earnings available to common stockholders. On cumulative preferred stock, preferred dividends for the current year are subtracted whether or not paid. Further, preferred dividends are only subtracted for the current year. Thus, if preferred dividends in arrears were for five years, all of which were paid plus the sixth-year dividend, only the sixth-year dividend (current year) is deducted. Note that preferred dividends for each of the prior years would have been deducted in those years.

In computing EPS, preferred dividends are only subtracted on preferred stock that was not included as a common stock equivalent. If the preferred stock is a common stock equivalent, the preferred dividend would *not* be deducted because the equivalency of preferred shares into common shares are included in the denominator.

If convertible bonds are included in the denominator of EPS, they are considered as equivalent to common shares. Thus, interest expense (net of tax) has to be added back in the numerator.

Disclosure of EPS should include information on the capital structure, explanation of the computation of EPS, identification of common stock equivalents, number of shares converted, and assumptions made. Rights and privileges of the securities should also be disclosed. Such disclosure includes dividend and participation rights, conversion ratios, call prices, and sinking fund requirements.

A stock conversion occurring during the year, or between year-end and the audit report date may have significantly impacted EPS if it had occurred at the beginning of the year. Thus, supplementary footnote disclosure should be made reflecting on an "as if" basis what the effects of these conversions would have had on EPS if they were made at the start of the accounting period.

If a subsidiary has been acquired under the *purchase accounting method* during the year, the weighted-average shares outstanding for the year is used from the purchase date. But if a *pooling of interests* occurred, the weighted-average shares outstanding for all the years are presented.

If common stock or a common stock equivalent is issued during the year and the cash received was used to buy back debt or retire preferred stock, supplemental EPS figures should be presented.

When comparative financial statements are presented, there is a retroactive adjustment for stock splits and stock dividends. Assume in 19X5 a 10% stock dividend occurs. The weighted-average shares used for previous years' computations has to be increased by 10% to make EPS data comparable.

When a prior period adjustment occurs that results in a restatement of previous years' earnings, EPS should be restated.

EXAMPLE 6

The stockholders' equity section of ABC Company's balance sheet as of 12/31/19X3 appears below:

$1.20 cumulative preferred stock (par value of $10 per share, issued 1,200,000 shares, of which 500,000 were converted to common stock and 700,000 shares are outstanding)	$7,000,000
Common stock (par value of $2.50, issued and outstanding 6,000,000 shares)	15,000,000
Paid-in-capital	20,000,000
Retained earnings	32,000,000
Total stockholders' equity	$74,000,000

On 5/1/19X3, ABC Company acquired XYZ Company in a pooling-of-interest. For each of XYZ Company's 800,000 shares, ABC issued one of its own shares in the exchange.

On 4/1/19X3, ABC Company issued 500,000 shares of convertible preferred stock at $38 per share. The preferred stock is convertible to common stock at the rate of 2 shares of common for each share of preferred. On 9/1/19X3, 300,000 shares and on 11/1/19X3 200,000 shares of preferred stock were converted into common stock. The market price of the convertible preferred stock is $38 per share.

During August, ABC Company granted stock options to executives to buy 100,000 shares of common stock at an option price of $15 per share. The market price of stock at year-end was $20.

ABC Company has 8%, $10,000,000 convertible bonds payable issued at fair value in 19X1. The conversion rate is 4 shares of common stock for each $100 bond. No conversions have occurred.

The Aa corporate bond yield is 10%. The tax rate is 34%. Net income for the year is $12,000,000.

The convertible bonds are not common stock equivalents because the interest rate of 8% is more than $2/3$ of the Aa bond yield of 10%.

The convertible preferred stock is a common stock equivalent because its yield of 3.16% ($1.20/$38.00) is less than $2/3$ of the Aa bond yield of 10%.

Note: Stock options are always considered common stock equivalents.

Shares outstanding from 1/1/19X3 (including 800,000 shares issued upon acquisition of XYZ company):		
6,000,000 − 1,000,000		5,000,000
Shares issued upon conversion of 500,000 shares of preferred stock to common stock:		
Issued 9/1/19X3 600,000 × 4/12	200,000	
Issued 11/1/19X3 400,000 × 2/12	66,667	266,667
Total shares of common stock		5,266,667
Common stock equivalents:		
Convertible preferred stock:		
500,000 shares of convertible preferred issued on 4/1/19X3 500,000 × 2 × 9/12	750,000	
Less: Common shares applicable to 500,000 preferred shares converted during the year	266,667	
Common stock equivalents of convertible preferred stock		483,333
Common stock equivalents of stock options:		

Option	$100,000 \times \$15 = \$1,500,000$	
Less:		
Treasury stock	$\underline{75,000} \times \$20 = \$1,500,000$	
Common stock equivalent of stock options	25,000	25,000

Weighted-average common stock outstanding plus common stock equivalents for primary EPS	5,775,000
Convertible bonds payable assumed converted at 1/1/19X3 ($10,000,000/$100) = 100,000 bonds 100,000 bonds × 4 shares per bond	400,000
Weighted-average common stock outstanding plus common stock equivalents plus other fully diluted securities for fully diluted EPS	6,175,000

Primary EPS equals:

$$\frac{\$12,000,000}{5,775,000 \text{ shares}} = \$2.08$$

Fully diluted EPS equals:

$$\frac{\$12,000,000 + \$528,000*}{6,175,000 \text{ shares}} = \$2.03$$

*$10,000,000 × 8% = $800,000 × 66% = $528,000

4

Financial Statement Reporting: The Balance Sheet

On the balance sheet, the CFO is concerned with the accounting for and reporting of assets, liabilities, and stockholders' equity.

How are assets recorded?

An asset is recorded at the price paid plus the cost of putting the asset in service (e.g., freight, insurance, installation). If an asset is acquired in exchange for a liability, the asset is recorded at the discounted values of the future payments.

EXAMPLE 1

A machine was bought by taking out a loan requiring ten $10,000 payments. Each payment includes principal and interest. The interest rate is 10%. While the total payments (principal and interest) are $100,000, the present value will be less since the machine is recorded at the present value of the payments. The asset would be recorded at $61,450 ($10,000 × 6.145). The factor is obtained from the present value of annuity table for n = 10, i = 10%.

Note: The asset is recorded at the principal amount excluding the interest payments. If an asset is acquired for stock, the asset is recorded at the fair value of the stock issued. If it is impossible to ascertain the fair market value of the stock (e.g., closely held company), the asset will be recorded at its appraised value.

Unearned discounts (except for quantity or cost), finance charges, and interest included in the face of receivables should be deducted to arrive at the net receivable.

Some of the major current and noncurrent assets are accounts receivable, inventory, fixed assets, and intangibles.

What is an assignment of accounts receivable?

When accounts receivable are *assigned*, the owner of the receivables borrows cash from a lender in the form of a note payable. The accounts receivable serves as security. New receivables substitute for receivables collected. The *assignment* of accounts receivable usually involves a financing charge and interest on the note.

The transferor's equity in the assigned receivables equals the difference between the accounts receivable assigned and the balance of the line (e.g., $50,000). When payments on the receivables are received, they are remitted by the company to the lending institution to reduce the liability. Customers are *not* notified of the assignment. Assignment is with recourse meaning the company has to make good for uncollectible accounts.

EXAMPLE 2

On 4/1/19X1, X Company assigns accounts receivable totalling $600,000 to A Bank as collateral for a $400,000 note. X Company will continue to receive customer remissions since the customers are not notified of the assignment. There is a 2% finance charge of the accounts receivable assigned. Interest on the note is 13%. Monthly settlement of the cash received from assigned receivables is made. During April there were collections of $360,000 of assigned receivables less cash discounts of $5,000. Sales returns were $10,000. On 5/1/19X1, April remissions were made plus accrued interest. In May, the balance of the assigned accounts receivable was collected less $4,000 that were uncollectible. On 6/1/19X1, the balance due was remitted to the bank plus interest for May. The journal entries follow:

4/1/19X1

Cash	388,000	
Finance charge (2% × $600,000)	12,000	

Accounts receivable assigned	600,000	
Notes payable		400,000
Accounts receivable		600,000
During April:		
Cash	355,000	
Sales discount	5,000	
Sales returns	10,000	
Accounts receivable assigned		370,000
5/1/19X1		
Interest expense	4,333[a]	
Notes payable	355,000	
Cash		359,333
During May:		
Cash	226,000	
Allowance for bad debts	4,000	
Accounts receivable assigned ($600,000 – $370,000)		230,000
6/1/19X1		
Interest expense	488[b]	
Notes payable ($400,000 – $355,000)	45,000	
Cash		45,488

[a] $\$400,000 \times .13 \times 1/12 = \$4,333$
[b] $\$45,000 \times .13 \times 1/12 = \$488$

How does factoring of accounts receivable work?

When *factoring* accounts receivable, the receivables are sold to a finance company. The factor buys the accounts receivable at a discount from face value, typically at a discount of 6%. Customers are usually notified. The factoring arrangement is usually without recourse, where the risk of uncollectibility of the customer's account rests with the financing institution. Billing and collection is typically done by the factor. The factor charges a commission ranging from 3/4% to 1 1/2% of the net receivables acquired. The entry is:

Cash (proceeds)
Loss on sale of receivables

Due from factor (proceeds kept by factor to cover
  possible adjustments such as sales discounts,
  sales returns and allowances)
Accounts receivable (face amount of
  receivables)

Factoring is usually a continual process. The seller of merchandise receives orders and transmits them to the factor for acceptance; if approved, the goods are shipped; the factor advances the money to the seller; the buyers pay the factor when payment is due, and the factor periodically remits any excess reserve to the seller of the goods. There is a continual circular flow of goods and money among the seller, the buyers, and the factor. Once the agreement is in effect, funds from this source are spontaneous.

EXAMPLE 3

T Company factors $200,000 of accounts receivable. There is a 4% finance charge. The factor retains 6% of the accounts receivable. Appropriate journal entries are:

Cash	180,000	
Loss on sale of receivables (4% × $200,000)	8,000	
Due from factor (6% × $200,000)	12,000	
Accounts receivable		200,000

Factors provide a dependable source of income for small manufacturers and service businesses.

EXAMPLE 4

You need $100,000 and are considering a factoring arrangement. The factor is willing to buy the accounts receivable and advance the invoice amount less a 4% factoring commission on the receivables purchased. Sales are on 30-day terms. A 14% interest rate will be charged on the total invoice price and deducted in advance. With the factoring arrangement, the credit department will be eliminated, reducing monthly credit expenses by $1,500. Also, bad debt losses of 8% on the factored amount will be avoided.

To net $100,000, the amount of accounts receivable to be factored is:

$$\frac{\$100,000}{1-(0.04+0.14)} = \frac{\$100,000}{0.82} = \$121,951$$

The effective interest rate on the factoring arrangement is:

$$\frac{0.14}{0.82} = 17.07\%$$

The annual total dollar cost is:

Interest ($0.14 \times \$121,951$)	$17,073
Factoring ($0.04 \times \$121,951$)	4,878
Total cost	$21,951

What if receivables are transferred with recourse?

As per FASB 77, a sale is recorded for the transfer of receivables with *recourse* if *all* of the following conditions are met:

1. The transferor gives up control of the future economic benefits applicable to the receivables (e.g., repurchase right).

2. The liability of the transferor under the recourse provisions can be estimated.

3. The transferee cannot require the transferor to repurchase the receivables unless there is a recourse stipulation in the contract.

When the transfer is treated as a sale, gain or loss is recognized for the difference between the selling price and the net receivables. The selling price includes normal servicing fees of the transferor and probable adjustments (e.g., debtor's failure to pay on time, effects of prepayment, and defects in the transferred receivable). Net receivables equals gross receivables plus finance and service charges minus unearned finance and service charges.

If the selling price varies during the term of the receivables because of a variable interest rate provision, the selling price is estimated with the use of an appropriate "going market interest rate" at the transfer date. Subsequent changes in the rate results in a change in estimated selling price, not in interest income or interest expense.

If one of the aforementioned criteria is not met, a liability is recognized for the amount received.

Footnote disclosure includes: amount received by transferor and balance of the receivables at the balance sheet date.

Inventory

Inventory may be valued at the lower of cost or market value. Specialized inventory methods may be used such as retail, retail lower of cost or market, retail LIFO, and dollar value LIFO. Losses on purchase commitments should be recognized in the accounts.

If ending inventory is understated, cost of sales is overstated, and net income is understated. If beginning inventory is understated, cost of sales is understated, and net income is overstated.

How does the lower of cost or market value method work?

Inventories are recorded at the lower of cost or market value for conservatism purposes applied on a total basis, category basis, or individual basis. The basis selected must be consistently used.

If cost is less than market value (replacement cost), cost is selected. If market value is below cost, we start with market value. However, market value cannot exceed the ceiling which is net realizable value (selling price less costs to complete and dispose). If it does, the cost is used. Further, market value cannot be less than the floor which is net realizable value less a normal profit margin. If market value is less than the floor, the floor value is chosen. Of course, market value is

FIGURE 4–1

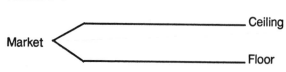

used when it lies between the ceiling and floor.
(See Figure 4–1.)

EXAMPLE 5

The lower of cost or market value method is
applied on an item-by-item basis. The circled
figure is the appropriate valuation.

Product	Cost	Market	Ceiling	Floor
A	$ ⑤	$ 7	$ 9	$ 6
B	14	12	⑪	7
C	18	⑮	16	12
D	20	12	18	⑯
E	⑥	5	12	7

Note that in case E, market value of $5 was
originally selected. The market value of $5 ex-
ceeded the floor of $7, so the floor value would
be used. However, if after applying the lower of
cost or market value rule, the valuation derived
($7) exceeds the cost ($6), the cost figure is more
conservative and thus is used.

If market (replacement cost) is below the original cost but the selling price has not likewise
declined, no loss should be recognized. To do so,
would result in an abnormal profit margin in the
future period.

The lower of cost or market value method is
not used with LIFO since under LIFO current
revenue is matched against current costs.

How does the retail method work?

The retail method is used by some large retail
concerns. These businesses may carry inventory
items at retail selling price. The retail method is

used to estimate the ending inventory at cost by employing a cost to retail (selling price) ratio. The ending inventory is first determined at selling price and then converted to cost. Markups and markdowns are both considered in arriving at the cost to retail ratio resulting in a higher ending inventory than the retail lower of cost or market value method.

Retail Lower of Cost or Market Value Method (Conventional Retail). This is a modification of the retail method and is preferable to it. In computing the cost to retail ratio, markups but not markdowns are considered resulting in a lower inventory figure.

The following example illustrates the accounting difference between the retail method and the retail lower of cost or market value method.

EXAMPLE 6

RETAIL METHOD VS. RETAIL LOWER OF COST OR MARKET VALUE METHOD

		Cost	Retail
Inventory—1/1		16,000	30,000
Purchases		30,000	60,000
Purchase returns		(5,000)	(10,000)
Purchase discount		(2,000)	
Freight in		1,000	
Markups	25,000		
Markup cancellations	5,000		20,000
Total (40%)		40,000	100,000
Markdowns	22,000		
Markdown cancellations	2,000		20,000
Cost of goods available (50%)		40,000	80,000
Deduct:			
Sales	55,000		
Less: sales returns	5,000		50,000
Inventory-Retail			30,000

	Cost	Retail
Retail method:		
At cost 50% × 30,000		15,000
Retail lower of cost		
or market method:		
40% × 30,000		12,000

Retail LIFO. In computing ending inventory, the mechanics of the retail method are basically used. Beginning inventory is *excluded* and both markups and markdowns are *included* in computing the cost to retail ratio. A decrease in inventory during the period is deducted from the most recently layer and then subtracted from layers in the inverse order of addition. A retail price index is used in restating inventory.

EXAMPLE 7

Retail price indices follow:

19X7	100
19X8	104
19X9	110

	Cost	Retail
19X8		
Inventory—Jan. 1 (base inv.)	80,000	130,000
Purchases	240,000	410,000
Markups		10,000
Markdowns		(20,000)
Total (exclude beg. inv.) 60%	240,000	400,000
Total (include beg. inv.)	320,000	530,000
Sales		389,600
19X8 Inv.—end-retail		140,400[a]
Cost Basis		
19X8 Inventory in terms of 19X7 prices 140,400 ÷ 1.04		135,000
19X7 base	80,000	130,000
19X8 layer in 19X7 prices		5,000
19X8 layer in 19X8 prices		5,200

	Cost	Retail
19X8 LIFO cost 60% × 5,200	3,120	
	83,120	140,400[a]
19X9		
Inventory—Jan. 1	83,120	140,400
Purchases	260,400	430,000
Markups		20,000
Markdowns		(30,000)
Total (exclude beg. inv.) 62%	260,400	420,000
Total (include beg. inv.)	343,520	560,400
Sales		408,600
19X9 Inventory—end at retail		151,800
Cost Basis		
19X9 Inventory in 19X7 prices		
151,800 ÷ 1.10		138,000
19X7 base	80,000	130,000
Excess over base year		8,000
19X8 layer in 19X8 prices	3,120	5,000
19X9 layer in 19X7 prices		3,000
19X9 layer in 19X9 prices		3,300
19X9 increase in 19X9 prices		
LIFO cost 62% × 3,300	2,046	
	85,166	151,800[b]

[a] $130,000 \times 1.04 = 135,200$
    $5,000 \times 1.04 = \underline{5,200}$
              $140,400$

[b] $130,000 \times 1,10 = 143,000$
    $5,000 \times 1.10 = 5,500$
    $3,000 \times 1.10 = \underline{3,300}$
              $151,800$

What are the mechanics of the dollar value LIFO method?

Dollar value LIFO is an extension of the historical cost principle. The method aggregates dollars rather than units into homogeneous groupings. The method assumes that an inventory decrease came from the last year.

The procedures under dollar value LIFO are:

• Restate ending inventory in the current year into base dollars by applying a price index.

• Subtract the year 0 inventory in base dollars from the current year's inventory in base dollars.

• Multiply the incremental inventory in the current year in base dollars by the price index to obtain the incremental inventory in current dollars.

• Obtain the reportable inventory for the current year by adding to the year 0 inventory in base dollars the incremental inventory for the current year in current dollars.

EXAMPLE 8

At 12/31/19X1, the ending inventory is $130,000 and the price index is 1.30. The base inventory on 1/1/19X1 was $80,000. The 12/31/19X1 inventory is computed below:

12/31/19X1 inventory in base dollars	
$130,000/1.30	$100,000
1/1/19X1 beginning base inventory	80,000
19X1 Increment in base dollars	$ 20,000
19X1 Increment in current year dollars	× 1.3
	$ 26,000
Inventory in base dollars	$ 80,000
Increment in current year dollars	26,000
Reportable inventory	$106,000

Losses on Purchase Commitments. Significant net losses on purchase commitments should be recognized at the end of the reporting period.

EXAMPLE 9

In 19X8, ABC Company committed itself to buy raw materials at $1.20 per pound. At the end of the year, before fulfilling the purchase commitment, the price of the materials dropped to $1.00 per pound. Conservatism requires that a loss on purchase commitment of $.20 per pound be recognized in 19X8. Loss on purchase commitment is debited and allowance for purchase commitment loss is credited.

Inventory Valuation Problems. While the basics of inventory cost measurement is easily stated, difficulties exist in cost allocation. For example, idle capacity costs and abnormal spoilage costs may have to be written off immediately in the current year rather than being allocated as a component of inventory valuation. Further, general and administrative expenses are inventoriable when they are directly related to production.

Inventory Stated at Market Value in Excess of Cost. In unusual cases, inventories may be stated in excess of cost. This may arise when there is no basis for cost apportionment (e.g., meat packing industry). Market value may also be used when there is immediate marketability at quoted prices (e.g., certain precious metals or agricultural products). Disclosure is necessary when inventory is stated above cost.

How do we account for fixed assets?

A fixed asset is recorded at its fair market value or the fair market value of the consideration given, whichever is more clearly evident.

The cost of *buying an asset* includes all costs required to place that asset into existing use and location, including freight, installation, insurance, taxes, and breaking-in costs (e.g., instruction).

The additions to an existing building (such as constructing a new garage) are capitalized and depreciated over the shorter of the life of the addition or the life of the building. Rearrangement and reinstallation costs are deferred when future benefit exists. If not, they should be expensed. Obsolete fixed assets should be reclassified from property, plant and equipment to other assets and shown at salvage value recognizing a loss.

When *two or more assets are purchased for one price,* cost is allocated to the assets based on their relative fair market values. If an old building is demolished to make way for the construction of a new building, the costs of demolishing the old building are capitalized to land.

Self-constructed assets are recorded at the incremental costs to build assuming idle capacity. However, they should not be recorded at more than the outside price.

EXAMPLE 10

Incremental costs to self-construct equipment is $12,000. The equipment could have been bought outside for $9,000. The journal entry is:

Equipment	$9,000	
Loss	3,000	
Cash		$12,000

A donated fixed asset should be recorded at fair market value. The entry is to charge fixed assets and credit paid-in-capital (donation).

Note: Fixed assets cannot be written-up except in the case of a discovery on a natural resource or in a purchase combination. In a discovery of a natural resource (e.g., oil), the land account is debited at appraised value and then depleted by the units of production method.

Land improvements (e.g., driveways, sidewalks, fencing) are capitalized and depreciated over useful life. Land held for investment purposes or for a future plant site should be classified under investments and not fixed assets.

Ordinary repairs (e.g., tune-up for a car) are expensed because they have a benefit period of less than one year.

Extraordinary repairs are deferred since they benefit a period of more than one year. An example is a new motor for a car. Extraordinary repairs increase the life of an asset or make the asset more useful. Capital expenditures improve the quality or quantity of services to be derived from the asset.

What is depreciation and how is it accounted for?

Depreciation is the allocation of the historical cost of a fixed asset into expense over the period benefited to result in matching expense against revenue.

Fractional year depreciation is computing depreciation when the asset is bought during the year. A proration is needed.

EXAMPLE 11

On 10/1/19X7, a fixed asset costing $10,000 with a salvage value of $1,000 and a life of 5 years is acquired.

Depreciation expense for 19X8 using the sum-of-the-years' digits method is:

1/1/19X8 – 9/30/19X8 5/15/ × $9,000 × 9/12	$2,250
10/1/19X8 – 12/31/19X8 4/15 × $9,000 × 3/12	600
	$2,850

Depreciation expense for 19X8 using double declining balance is:

Year	Computation	Depreciation	Book Value
0			$10,000
10/1/19X7– 12/31/19X7	3/12 × $10,000 × 40%	$1,000	9,000
1/1/19X8– 12/31/19X8	$9,000 × 40%	3,600	5,400

What are the group and composite depreciation methods?

Group and composite depreciation methods involve similar accounting. The group method is used for similar assets while the composite method is used for dissimilar assets. Both methods are generally accepted. There is one accumulated depreciation account for the entire group. The depreciation rate equals:

$$\frac{\text{Depreciation}}{\text{Gross cost}}$$

Depreciation expense for a period equals:

Depreciation rate × Gross cost

The depreciable life equals: $\dfrac{\text{Depreciable cost}}{\text{Depreciation}}$

When an asset is sold in the group, the entry is:

Cash (proceeds received)
Accumulated depreciation (plug figure)
  Fixed asset (cost)

Upon sale of a fixed asset in the group, the difference between the cash received and the cost of the fixed asset is plugged to accumulated depreciation. No gain or loss is recognized upon the sale. The only time a gain or loss is recognized is if all the assets were sold.

EXAMPLE 12

Calculations for composite depreciation follow:

Asset	Cost	Salvage	Depreciable Cost	Life	Depreciation
A	$25,000	$5,000	$20,000	10	$2,000
B	40,000	2,000	38,000	5	7,600
C	52,000	4,000	48,000	6	8,000
	$117,000	$11,000	$106,000		$17,600

Composite rate: $\dfrac{\$17,600}{\$117,000} = 15.04\%$

Composite life: $\dfrac{\$106,000}{\$17,600} = 6.02$ years

The entry to record depreciation is:

| Depreciation | 17,600 | |
| Accumulated depreciation | | 17,600 |

The entry to sell asset B for $36,000 is:

Cash	36,000	
Accumulated depreciation	4,000	
Fixed asset		40,000

When is interest deferred?

Disclosure should be made of the interest capitalized and expensed. Interest incurred on borrowed funds is expensed. However, interest on borrowed funds is deferred to the asset and then amortized in the following instances:

- Self-constructed assets for the company's own use. To justify interest capitalization, a time period must exist for assets to be prepared for use.
- Assets for sale or lease constructed as discrete, individual projects (e.g., real estate development).
- Assets purchased for the entity's own use by arrangements requiring a down payment and/ or progress payments.

Interest is *not* capitalized for:

- Assets in use or ready for use.
- Assets not in use and not being prepared for use.
- Assets produced in large volume or on a recurring basis.

Interest capitalized is based on the average accumulated expenditures for that asset. The interest rate used is either:

- Interest rate on the specific borrowing.
- Weighted-average interest rate on corporate debt.

EXAMPLE 13

In the purchase of a qualifying asset, a company expends $100,000 on January 1, 19X1 and

$150,000 on March 1, 19X1. The average accumulated expenditures for 19X1 are computed as follows:

Expenditure	Number of Months	Average Expenditure
$100,000	12	$100,000
150,000	10	125,000
$250,000		$225,000

The interest capitalization period begins when the following exist:

- Interest is being incurred.
- Expenditures have been incurred.
- Work is taking place to make the asset ready for intended use. These activities are not limited to actual construction but may also include administrative and technical activities before construction. This includes costs of unforeseen events occurring during construction such as labor instability and litigation.

The capitalization period ends when the asset is substantially complete and usable. When an asset consists of individual elements (e.g., condominium units), the capitalization period of interest costs applicable to one of the separate units ends when the particular unit is substantially finished. Capitalization of interest is not continued when construction ends, except for brief or unanticipated delays.

When the total asset must be completed to be useful, interest capitalization continues until the total asset is materially finished, for example, a manufacturing plant where sequential production activities must occur.

How are exchanges of assets accounted for?

Nonmonetary transactions covered under APB Opinion 29 primarily deal with exchanges or distributions of fixed assets.

In an exchange of *similar assets* (e.g., truck for truck), the new asset received is recorded at the book value of the old asset plus the cash paid. Since book value of the old asset is the basis to charge the new asset, no gain is possible. However, a loss is possible because the new asset can never be recorded in excess of the fair market value of the new asset.

In an exchange of *dissimilar* assets (e.g., truck for machine), the new asset is recorded at the fair market value of the old asset plus the cash paid. Thus, a gain or loss may take place because the fair market value of the old asset will be different than the book value of the old asset. However, the new asset cannot be shown at more than its fair market value. Fair market value in a nonmonetary exchange may be based upon:

- Quoted market price.
- Appraisal
- Cash transaction for similar items.

EXAMPLE 14

An old fixed asset that cost $10,000 with accumulated depreciation of $2,000 is traded in for a *similar,* new fixed asset having a fair market value of $22,000. Cash paid on the exchange is $4,000. The fair market value of the old asset is $5,000.

In a similar exchange the entry is:

Fixed asset (8,000 + 4,000)	12,000	
Accumulated depreciation	2,000	
Fixed asset		10,000
Cash		4,000

Assume instead that the fair market value of the new asset was $11,000, resulting in the exception where the new fixed asset must be recorded at $11,000. *Note:* The new fixed asset cannot be shown at more than its fair market value. In this case, the entry is:

Fixed asset	11,000	
Accumulated depreciation	2,000	
Loss	1,000	
Fixed asset		10,000
Cash		4,000

Assume the original facts except there is a *dissimilar* exchange. The entry is:

Fixed asset (5,000 + 4,000)	9,000	
Accumulated depreciation	2,000	
Loss	3,000	
Fixed asset		10,000
Cash		4,000

In a nonmonetary exchange, the entity receiving the monetary payment (boot) recognizes a gain to the degree the monetary receipt is greater than the proportionate share of the book value of the asset given up.

$$\text{Gain} = \frac{\text{Monetary}}{\text{receipt}} - \frac{\text{Monetary receipt}}{\substack{\text{Fair market value of total} \\ \text{consideration received}}}$$

$$\times \text{Book value of asset given up}$$

The company receiving the "boot" records the asset acquired at the carrying value of the asset surrendered minus the portion considered sold.

What happens in the case when a fixed asset is damaged?

There may be an involuntary conversion of nonmonetary assets into monetary assets, followed by replacement of the involuntarily converted assets (e.g., a building is destroyed by a fire, and the insurance recovery is used to buy a similar building).

According to Interpretation 30, gain or loss is recognized for the difference between the insurance recovery and the book value of the destroyed asset.

Caution: A contingency arises if the old fixed asset is damaged in one period, but the insurance recovery is received in a later period. A contingent gain or loss is reported in the period the old fixed asset was damaged. The gain or loss may be recognized for book and tax purposes in different years resulting in a temporary difference for income tax allocation purposes.

How do we account for intangible assets?

Intangible assets have a life of one year or more and lack physical substance (e.g., goodwill), or represent a right granted by the government (e.g., patent) or another company (e.g., franchise fee). APB 17 covers accounting for intangible assets whether purchased or internally developed. The costs of intangibles *acquired* from others should be reported as assets. The cost equals the cash or fair market value of the consideration given. The individual intangibles that can be separately identified must be costed separately. If not separately identified, the intangibles are assigned a cost equal to the difference between the total purchase price and the cost of identifiable tangible and intangible assets. Note "goodwill" does not include identifiable assets.

The cost of developing and maintaining intangibles should be charged against earnings if the assets are not specifically identifiable, have indeterminate lives, or are inherent in the continuing business (e.g., goodwill). An example of internally developed goodwill that is expensed are the costs incurred in developing a name (e.g., Cuisinart).

All intangible assets are amortized over the period benefited using the straight-line method not exceeding 40 years. The factors in estimating useful lives include:

- Legal, contractual, and regulatory provisions.
- Renewal or extension provisions. If a renewal occurs, the life of the intangible may be increased.
- Obsolescence and competitive factors.
- Product demand.
- Service lives of "key" employees within the company.

For example, an intangible may be enhanced due to a strong public relations staff.

Footnote disclosure should be made of the amortization period and method.

When the purchase of assets results in goodwill, the subsequent sale of a separable part of the entity acquired requires a proportionate reduction of the goodwill account. A portion of the unamortized goodwill is included in the cost of assets sold.

Goodwill is only recorded in a business combination accounted for under the purchase method when the cost to the acquirer exceeds the fair market value of the net assets acquired. Goodwill may be determined by an individual appraiser, a purchase audit done by the acquiring company's public accounting firm, etc. Goodwill is then amortized into expense. If the cost to the acquirer is less than the fair market value of the net assets acquired, a credit arises which reduces the noncurrent assets acquired on a proportionate basis (excluding long-term investments). If a credit still remains, it is treated as a deferred credit not to be amortized over more than 40 years under the straight line method.

Goodwill is theoretically equal to the discounted value of future excess earnings of a company over other companies in the industry. However, it is difficult to forecast the years in which superior earnings will occur.

In acquiring a new business, goodwill must be estimated. Two possible methods to value goodwill are (1) capitalization of earnings and (2) capitalization of excess earnings.

EXAMPLE 15

The following information applies to a business we are considering buying:

Expected average annual earnings	$10,000
Expected future value of net assets exclusive of goodwill	$45,000
Normal rate of return	20%

Using the capitalization of earnings approach, goodwill is estimated at:

Total asset value implied ($10,000/20%)	$50,000
Estimated fair value of assets	45,000
Estimated goodwill	$ 5,000

Assuming the same facts as above except a capitalization rate of excess earnings of 22% and using the capitalization of excess earnings method, goodwill is estimated at:

Expected average annual earnings	$10,000
Return on expected average assets ($45,000 × 20%)	9,000
Excess earnings	$ 1,000

Goodwill ($1,000/.22) = $4,545

EXAMPLE 16

The net worth of ABC Company excluding goodwill is $800,000 and earnings for the last four years were $750,000. The latter figure includes extraordinary gains of $50,000 and nonrecurring losses of $30,000. It is desired to determine a selling price of the business. A 12% return on net worth is typical for the industry. The capitalization of excess earnings is 45% in determining goodwill.

Net income for 4 years	$750,000
Less: Extraordinary gains	50,000
Add: Nonrecurring losses	30,000
Adjusted 4-year earnings	$730,000
Average earnings ($730,000/4)	$182,500
Normal earnings ($800,000 × .12)	96,000
Excess annual earnings	$ 86,500

Excess earnings capitalized at 45%:
$$\frac{\$86,500}{.45} = \$192,222$$

The determination of goodwill and its amortization can have a significant effect on the financial position of a company. An example is when Turner Broadcasting attempted to acquire CBS. Turner assigned the difference of what he would pay for CBS and its book value entirely to goodwill and amortized this amount over 40 years. CBS claimed a smaller amount should be assigned to goodwill and their assets revalued which would have lowered the net income of the combined Turner-CBS Company. The valuation of goodwill was very important in this takeover battle.

Internally generated costs to derive a patented product are expensed such as R&D incurred in developing a new product. The patent is recorded at the registration fees to secure and register it, legal fees in successfully defending it, and the cost of acquiring competing patents. The patent is amortized over its useful life not exceeding 17 years. If an intangible asset is worthless, it should be written-off immediately as an extraordinary loss.

Organization costs are the costs to incorporate a business (e.g., legal fees). They are deferred and amortized.

Leaseholds are rent paid in advance and are amortized over the life of the lease.

If the amortization expense of an intangible is not tax deductible (e.g., amortization of goodwill), a permanent difference arises that does not involve interperiod tax allocation.

How do we account and report liabilities?

In accounting for liabilities, the CFO must consider many reporting and disclosure responsibilities:

• Bonds payable may be issued between interest dates at a premium or discount.

• Bonds may be amortized using the straight-line method or effective interest method.

• Debt may be extinguished prior to the maturity date when the company can issue new debt at a lower interest rate.

• Estimated liabilities must be recognized when it is *probable* that an asset has been impaired or liability has been incurred by year-end, and the amount of loss can be reasonably estimated.

• An accrued liability may be recognized for future absences, for example, sick leave or vacation time.

- Special termination benefits such as early retirement may also be offered to and accepted by employees.
- Short-term debt may be rolled over to long-term debt, requiring special reporting.
- A callable obligation by the creditor may exist.
- Long-term purchase obligations have to be disclosed.

How are bonds payable handled?

The cost of a corporate bond is expressed in terms of yield. Two types of yield are:

1. *Simple Yield.*

$$\frac{\text{Nominal interest}}{\text{Present value of bond}}$$

It is not as accurate as yield to maturity.

2. *Yield to Maturity* (Effective Interest Rate).

$$\frac{\text{Nominal interest} + \dfrac{\text{Discount}}{\text{Years}} - \dfrac{\text{Premium}}{\text{Years}}}{\dfrac{\text{Present value} + \text{Maturity value}}{2}}$$

EXAMPLE 17

A $100,000, 10% 5-year bond is issued at 96. The simple yield is:

$$\frac{\text{Nominal interest}}{\text{Present value of bond}} = \frac{\$10,000}{\$96,000} = 10.42\%$$

The yield to maturity is:

$$\frac{\text{Nominal interest} + \dfrac{\text{Discount}}{\text{Years}}}{\dfrac{\text{Present value} + \text{Maturity value}}{2}}$$

$$= \frac{\$10,000 + \dfrac{\$4,000}{5}}{\dfrac{\$96,000 + \$100,000}{2}} = \frac{\$10,800}{\$98,000} = 11.02\%$$

When a bond is issued at a *discount,* the yield (effective interest rate) exceeds the nominal (face, coupon) interest rate.

When a bond is issued at a *premium,* the yield is below the nominal interest rate.

The two methods of amortizing bond discount or bond premium are:

1. *Straight Line Method.* It results in a constant dollar amount of amortization but a different effective rate each period.

2. *Effective Interest Method.* It results in a constant rate of interest but different dollar amounts each period. This method is preferred over the straight line method. The amortization entry is:

Interest expense (Yield × Carrying value of bond at the beginning of the year)
    Discount
    Cash (Nominal interest × Face value of bond)

In the early years, the amortization amount under the effective interest method is lower relative to the straight line method (either for discount or premium).

EXAMPLE 18

On 1/1/19X1, a $100,000 bond is issued at $95,624. The yield rate is 7% and the nominal interest rate is 6%. The schedule below is the basis for the journal entries.

Date	Debit Interest Expense	Credit Cash	Credit Discount	Carrying Value
1/1/19X1				$95,624
12/31/19X1	$6,694	$6,000	$694	96,318
12/31/19X2	6,742	6,000	742	97,060

The entry on 12/31/19X1 is:

Interest expense	6694	
Cash		6000
Discount		694

At maturity, the bond will be worth its face value of $100,000. When bonds are issued between interest dates, the entry is:

Cash	
Bonds payable	
Premium (or debit discount)	
Interest expense	

EXAMPLE 19

A $100,000, 5% bond having a life of 5 years is issued at 110 on 4/1/19X0. The bonds are dated 1/1/19X0. Interest is payable on 1/1 and 7/1. Straight line amortization is used. The journal entries are:

4/1/19X0 Cash		
(110,000 + 1,250)	111,250	
Bonds payable		100,000
Premium on bonds payable		10,000
Bond interest expense		
$(100,000 \times 5\% \times 3/12)$		1,250
7/1/19X0 Bond interest expense	2,500	
Cash		2,500
$100,000 \times 5\% \times 6/12$		
Premium on bonds payable	526.50	
Bond interest expense		526.50
4/1/19X0—1/1/19X5 4 years, 9 months = 57 months		
$\dfrac{\$10,000}{57} = \$175.50$ per month		
$\$175.50 \times 3$ months = $\$526.50$		
12/31/19X0 Bond interest expense	2,500	
Interest payable		2,500
Premium on bonds payable	1,053	
Bond interest expense		1,053
1/1/19X1 Interest payable	2,500	
Cash		2,500

Bonds payable is presented on the balance sheet at its present value in the following manner:

Bonds payable
Add: Premium
Less: Discount
Carrying value

Bond issue costs are the expenditures in issuing the bonds such as legal, registration, and printing fees. Bond issue costs are preferably deferred and amortized over the life of the bond. They are shown under Deferred charges.

In computing the price of a bond, the face amount is discounted using the present value of $1 table. The interest payments are discounted using the present value of an ordinary annuity of $1 table. The yield serves as the discount rate.

EXAMPLE 20

A $50,000, 10-year bond is issued with interest payable semiannually at an 8% nominal interest rate. The yield rate is 10%. The present value of $1 table factor for n = 20, i = 5% is .37689. The present value of annuity of $1 table factor for n = 20, i = 5% is 12.46221. The price of the bond equals:

Present value of principal	
$50,000 × .37689	$18,844.50
Present value of interest payments	
$20,000 × 12.46221	24,924.42
	$43,768.92

What if bonds are converted to stock?

In converting a bond into stock, there are three alternative methods as follows: book value of bond, market value of bond, and market value of stock. Under the book value of bond method, no gain or loss on bond conversion arises because the book value of the bond is the basis to credit equity. Under the market value methods, gain or loss will result because the book value of the bond will be different from the market value of bond or market value of stock which is the basis to credit the equity accounts.

EXAMPLE 21

A $100,000 bond with unamortized premium of $8420.50 is converted to common stock. There are 100 bonds ($100,000/$1,000). Each bond is converted into 50 shares of stock. Thus, there are 5,000 shares of common stock. Par value is $15 per share. The market value of the stock is $25 per share. The market value of the bond is 120. Using the book value method, the entry for the conversion is:

Bonds payable	100,000	
Premium on bonds payable	8,420.50	
Common stock (5,000 × 15)		75,000
Premium on common stock		33,420.50

Using the market value of stock method, the entry is:

Bonds payable	100,000	
Premium on bonds payable	8,420.50	
Loss on conversion	16,579.50	
Common stock		75,000
Premium on common stock		50,000
5,000 × $25 = $125,000		

Using the market value of the bond method, the entry is:

Bonds payable	100,000	
Premium on bonds payable	8,420.50	
Loss on conversion	11,579.50	
Common stock		75,000
Premium on common stock		45,000
$100,000 × 120% = $120,000		

How do we account for the early extinguishment of debt?

Long-term debt may be retired early when new debt can be issued at a lower interest rate. It can also occur when the company has excess cash and desires to avoid paying interest and having the debt on its balance sheet. The gain or loss on the early extinguishment of debt is an extraordinary item presented net of tax. Extraordinary classification occurs whether the extinguishment is early, at scheduled maturity, or later. There is an exception that the gain or loss on extinguishment is an ordinary item if it meets a sinking fund requirement due within one year of the date of extinguishment. However, serial bonds do not have characteristics of sinking fund requirements.

Debt may be considered extinguished if the debtor is relieved of the principal liability and it is probable the debtor will not have to make future payments.

EXAMPLE 22

A $100,000 bond payable with an unamortized premium of $10,000 is called at 85. The entry is:

Bonds payable	100,000	
Premium on bonds payable	10,000	
Cash (85% × 100,000)		85,000
Extraordinary gain		25,000

Footnote disclosures regarding extinguishment of debt include description of extinguishment transaction including the source of funds and per share gain or loss net of tax.

If convertible debt is converted to stock in connection with an "inducement offer" where the debtor alters conversion privileges, the debtor recognizes an expense rather than an extraordinary item. The amount is the fair value of the securities transferred in excess of the fair value of securities issuable according to the original conversion terms. This fair market value is measured at the earlier of the conversion date or date of the agreement. An inducement offer may be accomplished by giving debt holders a higher conversion ratio, payment of additional money, or other favorable changes in terms.

As per FASB 76, if the debtor puts cash or other assets in a trust to be only used for paying interest and principal on debt on an irrevocable basis, there should be disclosure of the particulars including a description of the transaction and the amount of debt extinguished.

How is recognition given to estimated liabilities?

A loss contingency should be accrued if *both* of the following criteria exist:

- At year-end, it is *probable* (likely to occur) that an asset was impaired or a liability was incurred.
- The amount of loss can be reasonably estimated.

The loss contingency is booked based on conservatism. The entry for a probable loss is:

Expense (Loss)
    Estimated liability

A probable loss that cannot be estimated should be footnoted.

EXAMPLE 23

On 12/31/19X6, warranty expenses are estimated at $20,000. On 3/15/19X7, actual warranty costs paid were $16,000. The journal entries are:

12/31/19X6 Warranty expense	20,000	
Estimated liability		20,000
3/15/19X7 Estimated liability	16,000	
Cash		16,000

If a loss contingency exists at year-end but no asset impairment or liability incurrence exists (e.g., uninsured equipment), footnote disclosure may be made.

A probable loss occurring after year-end but before the audit report date only requires subsequent event disclosure.

Examples of probable loss contingencies are warranties, lawsuits, claims and assessments, casualties and catastrophes (e.g., fire), and expropriation of property by a foreign government.

If the amount of loss is within a range, the accrual is based on the best estimate within that range. However, if no amount within the range is better than any other amount, the *minimum amount* (not maximum amount) of the range is booked. The exposure to additional losses should be disclosed.

There is *no* accrual for a reasonably possible loss (more than remote but less than likely). However, footnote disclosure is required of the nature of the contingency and the estimate of probable loss or range of loss. If an estimate of loss is not possible, that fact should be noted.

A remote contingency (slight chance of occurring) is usually ignored and no disclosure is made. There are exceptions when a remote contingency would be disclosed in the case of guarantees of indebtedness, standby letters of credit, and agreements to repurchase receivables or properties.

General (unspecified) contingencies are not accrued. Examples are self-insurance and catastrophe losses. Disclosure and/or an appropriation of retained earnings can be made for general contingencies. To be booked as an estimated liability, the future loss must be *specific* and *measurable* such as parcel post and freight losses.

Gain contingencies cannot be recognized because it violates conservatism. However, footnote disclosure can be made.

Accounting for Compensated Absences

Compensated absences include sick leave, holiday, and vacation time. FASB 43 is *not* applicable to severance or termination pay, post retirement benefits, deferred compensation, stock option plans, and other long-term fringe benefits (e.g., disability, insurance).

The employer accrues a liability for employees' compensation for future absences if *all* of the following conditions are satisfied:

- Employee services have already been performed.
- Employee rights have vested.
- Probable payment exists.
- Amount of estimated liability can reasonably be determined.

Note: If the criteria are met except that the amount is not determinable, only a footnote can be made because an accrual is not possible.

The accrual for sick leave is required when the employer allows employees to take accumulated sick leave days off regardless of actual illness. The accrual is not required if employees may only take accumulated days off for actual illness, since losses for these are usually insignificant.

EXAMPLE 24

Estimated compensation for future absences is $30,000. The entry is:

Expense	$30,000	
Estimated liability		$30,000

If at a later date a payment of $28,000 is made, the entry is:

Estimated liability	$28,000	
Cash		$28,000

What if there is a special termination benefit?

An expense is accrued when an employer offers special termination benefits to an employee, the employee accepts the offer, and the amount can be reasonably estimated. The amount equals the current payment plus the discounted value of future payments.

When it can be objectively measured, the effect of changes on the employer's previously accrued expenses applicable to other employee benefits directly associated with employee termination should be included in measuring termination expense.

EXAMPLE 25

On 1/1/19X1, as an incentive for early retirement, the employee receives a lump sum payment today of $50,000 plus payments of $10,000 for each of the next 10 years. The discount rate is 10%. The journal entry is:

Expense	111,450	
Estimated liability		111,450
Present value $10,000 × 6.145* =	61,450	
Current payment	50,000	
Total	$111,450	

*Present value factor for n = 10, i = 10% is 6.145

What if short-term debt is rolled over into long-term debt?

A short-term obligation shall be reclassified as a long-term liability in the following cases:

1. After the year end of the financial statements but before the audit report is issued, the short-term debt is rolled over into a long-term obligation or an equity security is issued in substitution.

or

2. Before the audit report date, the company contracts for refinancing of the current obligation on a long-term basis and *all* of the following are satisfied:

- Agreement does not expire within one year.
- No violation of the agreement exists.
- The parties are financially able to meet the requirements of the arrangement.

The proper classification of the refinanced item is under long-term debt and *not* stockholders' equity even if equity securities were issued in substitution of the debt. When short-term debt is excluded from current liabilities, a footnote should describe the financing agreement and the terms of any new obligation.

If the amounts under the agreement for refinancing vary, the amount of short-term debt excluded from current liabilities will be the *minimum* amount expected to be refinanced based on conservatism. The exclusion from current liabilities cannot be greater than the net proceeds of debt or security issuances, or amounts available under the refinancing agreement.

Once cash is paid for the short-term debt even though the next day long-term debt of a similar amount is issued, the short-term debt is presented under current liabilities since cash was paid.

What if the creditor has the right to call the bond?

Under current liabilities is a long-term debt callable by the creditor because of the debtor's violation of the agreement except if *one* of the following conditions exist:

- The creditor waives or lost the right to demand repayment for a period in excess of one year from the balance sheet date.
- There is a *grace period* in which the debtor may correct the violation which makes it callable, and it is probable that the violation will be so rectified.

What footnote information should be presented of long-term purchase commitments?

An unconditional purchase obligation provides *funds* for goods or services at a determinable future date. An example is a take-or-pay contract in which the buyer must pay specified periodic amounts for products or services. Even if the buyer does not take delivery of the goods, periodic payments must still be made.

When unconditional purchase obligations are recorded in the balance sheet, disclosure is made of payments for recorded unconditional purchase obligations and maturities and sinking fund requirements for long-term borrowings.

Unconditional purchase obligations not reflected in the balance sheet should be disclosed if they meet the following conditions:

- Noncancellable. However, it may be cancellable upon a remote contingency.
- Negotiated to arrange financing to provide contracted goods or services.
- A term exceeding one year.

The disclosure for unconditional purchase obligations when not recorded in the accounts are:

- Nature and term.
- Fixed and variable amounts.
- Total amount for the current year and for the next five years.
- Purchases made under the obligation for each year presented.

Optional disclosure exists of the amount of imputed interest required to reduce the unconditional purchase obligation to present value.

How must stockholders' equity be accounted for?

In accounting for stockholders' equity, consideration is given to preferred stock characteristics, conversion of preferred stock to common stock, stock retirement, appropriation of retained earnings, treasury stock, quasi-reorganization, dividends, fractional share warrants, stock options, stock warrants, and stock splits.

The stockholders' equity section of the balance sheet includes major categories for:

- Capital stock (stock issued and stock to be issued).
- Paid-in capital.
- Retained earnings.
- Unrealized loss on long-term investments.
- Gains or losses on foreign currency translation.
- Treasury stock.

Note: Disclosure should be made for provisions of capital stock redeemable at given prices on specific dates.

What are the types and provisions for preferred stock?

Participating preferred stock is rare. If it does exist, it may be partially or fully participating. In partially participating, preferred stockholders participate in excess dividends over the preferred dividend rate proportionately with common stockholders up to a maximum additional rate. For example, a 6% preferred stock may allow participation up to 11%, so that an extra 5% dividend may be added. In fully participating, a distribution for the current year is at the preference rate plus any cumulative preference. Further, the preferred stockholders share in dividend distributions in excess of the preferred stock rate on a proportionate basis using the total par value of the preferred stock and common stock. For example, a 12% fully participating preferred stock will get the 12% preference rate plus a proportionate share based on the total par value of the common and preferred stock of excess dividends once common stockholders have obtained their matching 12% of par of the common stock.

EXAMPLE 26

Assume 5% preferred stock, $20 par, 5,000 shares. The preferred stock is partially participating up to an additional 2%. Common stock is $10 par, 30,000 shares. A $40,000 dividend is declared. Dividends are distributed as follows:

	Preferred	Common
Preferred stock, current year ($100,000 × 5%)	$5,000	
Common stock, current year ($300,000 × 5%)		$15,000
Preferred stock, partial ($100,000 × 2%)	2,000	
Common stock, matching ($300,000 × 2%)		6,000
Balance to common stock		12,000
Total	$7,000	$33,000

Cumulative preferred stock means that if dividends are not paid, the dividends accumulate and must be paid before any dividends can be paid to noncumulative stock.

The *liquidation value* of preferred stock means that in corporate liquidation, preferred stockholders will receive the liquidation value (sometimes stated as par value) before any funds may be distributed to common stockholders.

Disclosure for preferred stock includes liquidation preferences, call prices, and cumulative dividends in arrears.

When preferred stock is converted to common stock, the preferred stock and paid-in-capital accounts are eliminated and the common stock and paid-in-capital accounts are credited. If a deficit results, retained earnings would be charged.

EXAMPLE 27

Preferred stock having a par value of $300,000 and paid-in-capital (preferred stock) of $20,000 are converted into common stock. There are 30,000 preferred shares having a $10 par value per share. Common stock issued are 10,000 shares having a par value of $25.

The journal entry is:

Preferred stock	300,000	
Paid-in-capital		
(Preferred stock)	20,000	
Common stock		
(10,000 × $25)		250,000
Paid-in-capital (Common stock)		70,000

What is done for retired shares?

A company may retire its stock. If common stock is retired *at par value,* the entry is:

Common stock ⎫
  Cash   ⎬   Par value
          ⎭

If common stock is retired for *less than par value,* the entry is:

Common stock
  Cash
  Paid-in-capital

If common stock is retired for *more than par value,* the entry is:

Common stock
Paid-in-capital (original premium per share)
Retained earnings (excess over original premium
     per share)
  Cash

Note: In retirement of stock, retained earnings can only be debited, not credited.

What is done if retained earnings must be restricted?

Appropriation of retained earnings means setting aside retained earnings and making them unavailable for dividends. Examples include appropriations for plant expansion, debt retirement, sinking fund, and general contingencies (e.g., self-insurance).

How is treasury stock accounted for and reported?

Treasury stock are issued shares bought back by the company. The two ways to account for treasury stock are:

1. Cost Method. Treasury stock is recorded at the cost to purchase it. If treasury stock is later sold above cost, the entry is:

Cash
  Treasury stock
  Paid-in-capital

If treasury stock was sold instead at below cost, the entry is:

Cash
Paid-in-capital—Treasury stock (up to amount
     available)
Retained earnings (if paid-in-capital is unavailable)
  Treasury stock

If treasury stock is donated, only a memo entry is made. When the treasury shares are later sold the entry based on the market price at that time is:

Cash
   Paid-in-capital—Donation

An appropriation of retained earnings equal to the cost of treasury stock on hand is required.

Treasury stock is shown as a reduction from total stockholders' equity.

2. Par Value Method. Treasury stock is recorded at its par value when bought. If treasury stock is purchased at more than par value, the entry is:

Treasury stock—Par value
Paid-in-capital—Original premium per share
Retained earnings—If necessary
   Cash

If treasury stock is purchased at less than par value, the entry is:

Treasury stock—Par value
   Cash
   Paid-in-capital

Upon sale of the treasury stock above par value, the entry is:

Cash
   Treasury stock
   Paid-in-capital

Upon sale of the treasury stock at less than par value, the entry is:

Cash
Paid-in-capital (Amount available)
Retained Earnings (If paid-in-capital is insufficient)
   Treasury stock

An appropriation of retained earnings equal to the cost of the treasury stock on hand is required. Treasury stock is presented as a contra account to the common stock it applies to under the capital stock section of stockholders' equity.

What is a quasi-reorganization?

A quasi-reorganization provides a financially troubled firm with a deficit in retained earnings a "fresh start." A quasi-reorganization occurs to avoid bankruptcy. A revaluation of assets is made.

• Stockholders and creditors must consent to the quasi-reorganization. Net assets are reduced to fair market value. If fair value is not readily determinable, then conservative estimates of such value may be made.

• Paid-in-capital is reduced to eliminate the deficit in retained earnings. If paid-in-capital is insufficient, then capital stock is charged.

• Retained earnings becomes a zero balance. Retained earnings will bear the quasi-reorganization date for 10 years after the reorganization.

The retained earnings account consists of the following components:

Retained earnings – Unappropriated

Dividends	Net income
Appropriations	
Prior period adjustments	
Quasi-reorganization	

The entry for the quasi-reorganization is:

Paid-in-capital
Capital stock (if necessary)
   Assets
   Retained earnings

Caution: If potential losses exist at the readjustment date but the amounts of losses cannot be determined, there should be a provision for the maximum probable loss. If estimates are later shown to be incorrect, the difference adjusts paid-in-capital.

Note: New or additional common stock or preferred stock may be issued in exchange for existing *indebtedness.* Thus, the current liability account would be charged for the indebtedness and the capital account credited.

EXAMPLE 28

A company having a $3,500,000 deficit undertakes a quasi-reorganization. There is an overstatement in assets of $800,000 relative to fair market value. The balances in capital stock and paid-in-capital are $5,000,000 and $1,500,000, respectively. The following entry is made to effect the quasi-reorganization:

Paid-in-capital	1,500,000	
Capital stock	2,800,000	
Assets		800,000
Retained earnings		3,500,000

Since the paid-in-capital account has been fully wiped out, the residual debit goes to capital stock.

How are dividends accounted for?

Dividends are distributions by the company to stockholders. After the declaration date is the record date. A person is qualified to receive a dividend only if he or she is the registered owner of the stock on the date of record. Several days before the date of record, the stock will be selling "ex-dividend." This is done to alert investors that those owning the stock before the record date are entitled to receive the dividend, and that those selling the stock prior to the record date will lose their rights to the dividend.

A dividend is typically in cash or stock. A dividend is based on the outstanding shares (issued shares less treasury shares).

EXAMPLE 29

Issued shares are 5,000, treasury shares are 1,000, and outstanding shares are therefore 4,000. The par value of the stock is $10 per share.

If a \$.30 dividend per share is declared, the dividend is:

$$4,000 \times \$.30 = \$1,200$$

If the dividend rate is 6%, the dividend is:

4,000 shares × \$10 par value = \$40,000
$$\begin{array}{r} \times .06 \\ \hline \$\ 2,400 \end{array}$$

Assuming a cash dividend of \$2,400 is declared, the entry is:

Retained earnings	2,400	
Cash dividend payable		2,400

No entry is made at the record date. The entry at the payment date is:

Cash dividend payable	2,400	
Cash		2,400

A property dividend is payable in assets other than cash. When the property dividend is declared, the company restates the distributed asset to fair market value, recognizing any gain or loss as the difference between the fair market value and carrying value of the property at the declaration date.

EXAMPLE 30

A company transfers investments in marketable securities costing \$10,000 to stockholders by declaring a property dividend on December 16, 19X8, to be distributed on 1/15/19X9. At the declaration date, the securities have a market value of \$14,000. The entries are:

Declaration:
12/16/19X8

Investment in securities	4,000	
Gain on appreciation of securities		4,000
Retained earnings	14,000	
Property dividend payable		14,000

The net reduction is still the $10,000 cost of the asset.

Distribution:
1/15/19X9

Property dividend payable	14,000	
Investment in securities		14,000

A stock dividend is issued in the form of stock. Stock dividend distributable is shown in the capital stock section of stockholders' equity. It is *not* a liability. If the stock dividend is less than 20% to 25% of outstanding shares at the declaration date, retained earnings is reduced at the market price of the shares. If the stock dividend is in excess of 20 to 25% of outstanding shares, retained earnings is charged at par value. Between 20 to 25% is a gray area.

EXAMPLE 31

A stock dividend of 10% is declared on 5,000 shares of $10 par value common stock having a market price of $12. The entry at the declaration and issuance dates follow:

Retained earnings		
(500 shares × $12)	6,000	
Stock dividend distributable		
(500 shares × $10)		5,000
Paid-in-capital		1,000
Stock dividend distributable	5,000	
Common stock		5,000

Assume instead that the stock dividend was 30%. The entries would be:

Retained earnings (1500 × $10)	15,000	
Stock dividend distributable		15,000
Stock dividend distributable	15,000	
Common stock		15,000

A liability dividend (scrip dividend) is payable in the form of a liability (e.g., notes payable). This type of dividend sometimes occurs when a company has financial difficulties.

EXAMPLE 32

On 1/1/19X2, a liability dividend of $20,000 is declared in the form of a one year, 8% note. The entry at the declaration date is:

Retained earnings	20,000	
Scrip dividend payable		20,000

When the scrip dividend is paid, the entry is:

Scrip dividend payable	20,000	
Interest expense	1,600	
Cash		21,600

A liquidating dividend can be deceptive as it is not actually a dividend. It is a return of capital and not a distribution of earnings. The entry is to debit paid-in-capital and credit dividends payable. The recipient of a liquidating dividend pays no tax on it.

How is a stock split handled?

In a *stock split,* the shares are *increased* and the par value per share is *decreased.* However, total par value is the same.

A memo entry is only made.

EXAMPLE 33

Before: 1,000 shares, $10 par value
         = $10,000 total par value
         2 for 1 stock split declared

After: 2,000 shares, $5 par value
         = $10,000 total par value

A reverse split has the opposite effect.

How are stock options accounted for and reported?

A stock option gives a company's officers and other employees the right to buy shares of the company's stock, at a stated price, within a specified time period. A stock option is typically in a form of compensation or incentive for employee services.

Noncompensatory plans are *not* primarily designed to give employees compensation for services. Compensation expense is *not* recognized. A noncompensatory plan has *all* of the following characteristics:

- All employees are offered stock on some basis (e.g., equally, percent of salary).
- Most full-time employees may participate.
- A reasonable time period exists to exercise the options.
- The price discount for employees on the stock is not better than that afforded to corporate stockholders if there was an additional issuance.

The objective of a noncompensatory plan is to obtain funds and to reduce widespread ownership in the company among employees.

Accounting for a noncompensatory stock plan is one of simple sale. The option price is the same as the issue price.

A compensatory plan exists if any one of the above four criteria are *not* met. Consideration received by the firm for the stock equals the cash, assets, or employee services.

In a compensatory stock option plan for executives, compensation expense should be recognized in the year in which the services are performed. The deferred compensation is determined at the measurement date as the difference between the market price of the stock at that date and the option price. When there exists more than one option plan, compensation cost should be computed separately for each. If treasury stock is used in the stock option plan, its market value and not cost is used in measuring the compensation.

The measurement date is the date upon which the number of shares to be issued and the option price are known. The measurement date cannot be changed by provisions that reduce the number of shares under option in the case of employee termination. A new measurement date occurs when there is an option renewal. The measurement date is not changed when stock is transferred to a trustee. If convertible stock is awarded to employees, the measurement date is the one upon which the conversion rate is known. Compensation is measured by the higher of the market price of the convertible stock or the market price of the securities to which the convertible stock is to be transferred.

There may be a postponement in the measurement date to the end of the reporting year if all of the following conditions exist:

- There is a formal plan for the award.
- The factors determining the total dollar award is designated.
- The award relates to employee services rendered in the current year.

EXAMPLE 34

On 1/1/19X1, 1,000 shares are granted under a stock option plan. At the measurement date, the market price of the stock is $10 and the option price is $6. The amount of the deferred compensation is:

Market price	$10
Option price	6
Deferred compensation	$ 4

Deferred compensation equals:
1,000 shares × $4 = $4,000

Assume the employees must perform services for four years before they can exercise the option.

On 1/1/19X1, the journal entry to record total deferred compensation cost is:

Deferred compensation cost	4,000	
Paid-in capital—Stock options		4,000

Deferred compensation is a contra account against stock options to derive the net amount under the capital stock section of the balance sheet.

On 12/31/19X1, the entry to record the expense is:

| Compensation expense | 1,000 | |
| Deferred compensation | | 1,000 |

$4,000/4 years = $1,000

The capital stock section on 12/31/19X1 would show stock options as follows:

Stock options	$4,000
Less: Deferred compensation	1,000
Balance	$3,000

Compensation expense of $1,000 would be reflected for each of the next three years as well.

At the time the options are exercised when the market price of the stock at the exercise date exceeds the option price, an entry must be made for stock issuance.

Assuming a par value of $5 and a market price of $22, the journal entry for the exercise is:

Cash ($6 × 1,000)	6,000	
Paid-in-capital—Stock options	4,000	
Common stock ($5 × 1,000)		5,000
Paid-in-capital		5,000

If the market price of the stock was below the option price, the options would lapse requiring the following entry:

| Paid-in-capital—Stock options | 4,000 | |
| Paid-in-capital | | 4,000 |

Note: If an employee leaves after completing the required service years, no effect is given to recorded compensation and the nonexercised options are transferred to paid-in-capital. If the employee leaves before the exercise period, previously recognized compensation is adjusted currently.

If the grant date is before the measurement date, deferred compensation costs must be estimated until the measurement date so that compensation expense is recognized when services are performed. The difference between the actual figures and estimates are considered a change in estimate during the year in which the actual cost is determined.

When the measurement date is after the grant date, compensation expense for each period from the date of award to the measurement date should be based on the market price of the stock at the close of the accounting period.

In a variable plan granted for previous services, compensation should be expensed in the period the award is granted.

If the employee performs services for several years before the stock is issued, there should be an accrual of compensation expense for the shares earned.

When employees receive cash in settlement of a previous option, the cash paid is used to measure the compensation. If the ultimate compensation differs from the amount initially recorded, an adjustment is made to the original compensation.

The accrual of compensation expense may require estimates which have to be modified at a later date. An example is an employee resignation that precludes him or her from exercising the stock option. Compensation expense should be reduced when employee termination occurs. The adjustment is accounted for as a change in estimate.

Footnote disclosure for a stock option plan includes the number of shares under option, status of the plan, option price, number of shares exercisable, and the number of shares issued under the option plan during the year.

Compensation expense is deductible for tax purposes when paid but deducted for book purposes when accrued. This results in interperiod income tax allocation involving a deferred income tax credit. If for some reason reversal of the temporary difference will not take place, a permanent difference exists which does not affect earnings. The difference should adjust paid-in capital in the year the accrual occurs.

What if a bond is issued along with warrants?

If bonds are issued along with *detachable* stock warrants, the portion of the proceeds applicable to the warrants is credited to paid-in-capital. The basis for allocation is the relative values of the securities at the time of issuance. If the warrants are *not detachable,* the bonds are accounted for only as convertible debt with *no* allocation of the proceeds to the conversion right.

EXAMPLE 35

A $20,000 convertible bond is issued at $21,000 with $1,000 applicable to stock warrants. If the warrants are not detachable, the entry is:

Cash	21,000	
Bonds payable		20,000
Premium on bonds payable		1,000

If the warrants are detachable, the entry is:

Cash	21,000	
Bonds payable		20,000
Paid-in-capital—Stock		
warrants		1,000

If the proceeds of the bond issue were only $20,000 rather than $21,000 and $1,000 is attributable to the warrants, the entry is:

Cash	20,000	
Discount	1,000	
Bonds payable		20,000
Paid-in-capital—Stock		
warrants		1,000

How are fractional shares accounted for?

Fractional share warrants may be issued.

EXAMPLE 36

There are 1,000 shares of $10 par value common stock. The common stock has a market price of $15. A 20% dividend is declared resulting in 200 shares (20% × 1,000). The 200 shares include fractional share warrants. Each warrant equals 1/5 of a share of stock. There are 100 warrants resulting in 20 shares of stock (100/5). Therefore, we have 180 regular shares and 20 fractional shares. The journal entries follow:

At the declaration date:

Retained earnings (200 shares × 15)	3,000	
Stock dividends distributable (180 shares × 10)		1,800
Fractional share warrants (20 shares × 10)		200
Paid-in-capital		1,000

At time of issuance:

Stock dividend distributable	1,800	
Common stock		1,800
Fractional share warrants	200	
Common stock		200

If only 80% of the fractional share warrants were turned in the entry is:

Fractional share warrants	200	
Common stock		160
Paid-in-capital		40

5

The Statement of Cash Flows

In accordance with FASB 95, a Statement of Cash Flows is included in the annual report. This chapter discusses how the Statement may be prepared as well as the analytical implications for the CFO. The purpose of the Statement is to provide useful information about the company's cash receipts and cash payments. A reconciliation between net income and net cash flow from operations is included. There is also disclosure of *noncash* investments and financing transactions.

What is the definition of cash flow?

The Statement of Cash Flows explains the change in *cash and cash equivalents* for the period. A cash equivalent is a short-term liquid investment having an original maturity of three months or less. Examples are Treasury bills and commercial paper.

The Statement of Cash Flows classifies cash receipts and cash payments as arising from operating, investing, and financing activities.

What is included in the Operating Section?

Operating activities relate to manufacturing and selling goods or the performance of services. They do not apply to investing or financing activities. Cash flow from operating activities usually applies to the cash effects of transactions entering into profit computations. Cash inflows from operating activities include: (1) cash sales or collections on receivables arising from the initial sale of merchandise or rendering of service; (2) cash receipts from returns on loans, debt securities (e.g., interest income), or equity securities (e.g., dividend income) of other entities; (3) cash received from licensees and lessees; (4) receipt of a litigation settlement;

(5) and reimbursement under an insurance policy. Cash outflows for operating activities include: (1) cash paid for raw material or merchandise for resale; (2) principal payments on accounts payable; (3) payments to suppliers for operating expenses (e.g., office supplies, advertising, insurance); (4) salaries; (5) payments to governmental agencies (e.g., taxes, penalties); (6) interest expense; (7) lawsuit payment; (8) charitable contributions; and (9) cash refund to customers for defective goods.

What is reported in the Investing Section?

Investing activities include buying debt and equity securities in other entities, purchasing and selling fixed assets, and making and collecting loans. Cash inflows from investing are: (1) receipts from sales of equity or debt securities of other companies; (2) amount received from selling fixed assets; and (3) collections or sales of loans made by the company. Cash outflows for investing activities include: (1) disbursements to buy equity or debt securities of other companies; (2) payments to buy fixed assets; (3) and disbursements for loans made by the company.

What is included in the Financing Section?

Financing activities include cash flows resulting from changes in long-term liabilities and stockholders' equity items. Financing activities relate to receiving equity funds and providing owners with a return on their investment. They also include debt financing and repayment or settlement of debt. Another element is obtaining and paying for other resources derived from noncurrent creditors. Cash inflows from financing activities are comprised of (1) funds received from the issuance of stock and (2) funds obtained from the incurrence of debt. Cash outflows for financing activities include (1) paying-off debt, (2) repurchase of stock, (3) dividend payments, and (4) other principal payments to long-term creditors.

Are cash inflows and cash outflows shown gross for each major item?

There should be separate presentation of cash inflows and cash outflows from investing and financing activities. For example, the purchase of fixed assets is a use of cash while the sale of a fixed asset is a source of cash. These are shown separately. The issuance of debt would be a source of cash while debt payment would be an application. Thus, cash received of $800,000 from debt incurrence would be shown as a source while the payment of debt of $250,000 would be presented as an application. The net effect is $550,000.

What disclosure is made for noncash activities?

There is separate disclosure for investing and financing activities impacting upon assets or liabilities that do *not* affect cash flow. Examples of noncash activities of an investing and financing nature are bond conversion, purchase of a fixed asset by the incurrence of a mortgage payable, capital lease, and nonmonetary exchange of assets. This disclosure may be footnoted or shown in a schedule.

EXAMPLE

Net increase in cash	$980,000
Noncash investing and financing activities:	
Purchase of land by the issuance of common stock	$400,000
Conversion of bonds payable to common stock	200,000
	$600,000

What if an item applies to more than one section within the statement?

If a cash receipt or cash payment applies to more than one classification (operating, investing, financing), classification is made as to the activity that is the primary source of that cash flow. For example, the purchase and sale of equipment to be used by the company is usually considered an investing activity.

How about foreign currency exposure?

In the case of foreign currency cash flows, use the exchange rate at the time of the cash flow in reporting the currency equivalent of foreign currency cash flows. The effect of changes in the exchange rate on cash balances held in foreign currencies should be reported as a separate element of the reconciliation of the change in cash and cash equivalents for the period.

How is the direct method different from the indirect method?

The *direct method* is *preferred* in that companies should report cash flows from operating activities by major classes of gross cash receipts and gross cash payments and the resulting net amount in the operating section. A reconciliation of net income to cash flow from operating activities should be shown in a separate schedule after the body of the statement. *Note:* This schedule has the same net result as gross cash receipts and cash payments from operating activities.

Although the direct method is preferred, a company has the option of using the indirect (reconciliation) method. In practice, most companies use the indirect method because of its easier preparation. Under the indirect method, the company reports net cash flow from operating activities indirectly by adjusting profit to reconcile it to net cash flow from operating activities. This is shown in the operating section within the body of the Statement of Cash Flows or in a separate schedule. If presented in a separate schedule, the net cash flow from operating activities is presented as a single line item. The adjustment to reported earnings for noncash revenues and expenses involves:

• Effects of deferrals of past operating cash receipts and cash payments (e.g., changes in inventory and deferred revenue), and accumulations of expected future operating cash receipts and cash payments (e.g., changes in receivables and payables).

• Effects of items whose cash effect apply to investing or financing cash flows (e.g., depreciation, amortization expense, and gain or loss on the sale of fixed assets).

From this discussion, we can see that there is basically one difference in presentation between the direct and indirect method. It only relates to the operating section. Under the direct method, the operating section presents gross cash receipts and gross cash payments from operating activities with a reconciliation of net income to cash flow from operations in a separate schedule. Under the indirect method, gross cash receipts and gross cash payments from operating activities are *not* shown. Instead, there is only presented the reconciliation of net income to cash flow from operations in the operating section *or* in a separate schedule with the final figure of cash flow from operations reported as a single line item in the operating section.

Since the indirect method is the one commonly used, we will concentrate on it.

Exhibit 5–1 shows the reconciliation process of net income to cash flow from operating activities and Exhibit 5–2 outlines the indirect method.

ANALYSIS OF THE STATEMENT OF CASH FLOWS

The Statement of Cash Flows provides CFOs with information about the company's cash receipts and cash payments for operating, investing, and financing activities.

What useful information is obtained from doing a comparative analysis?

Comparative Statements of Cash Flows hold clues to a company's earning potential, risk, and liquidity. Comparative Statements show the repeatability of the company's sources of funds,

EXHIBIT 5-1   INDIRECT METHOD OF COMPUTING CASH PROVIDED BY OPERATIONS

	Add (+) or deduct (−) to adjust net income
Net income	$XXX
Adjustments required to convert net income to cash basis:	
Depreciation, depletion, amortization expense, and loss on sale of noncurrent assets	+
Amortization of deferred revenue, amortization of bond premium, and gain on sale of noncurrent assets	−
Add (deduct) changes in current asset accounts affecting revenue or expenses[a]	
Increase in the account	−
Decrease in the account	+
Add (deduct) changes in current liability accounts affecting revenue or expense[b]	
Increase in the account	+
Decrease in the account	−
Add (deduct) changes in the Deferred Income Taxes account	
Increase in the account	+
Decrease in the account	−
Cash provided by operations	$XXX

[a]*Examples include accounts receivable, accrued receivables, inventory, and prepaid expenses.*
[b]*Examples include accounts payable, accrued liabilities, and deferred revenue.*

their costs, and whether such sources may be relied upon in the future. The uses of funds for growth and for maintaining competitive position are revealed. An analysis of Comparative Statements of Cash Flows helps in understanding the entity's current and prospective financial health.

**EXHIBIT 5-2   FORMAT OF THE STATEMENT OF CASH
FLOWS (INDIRECT METHOD)**

Net cash flow from operating activities:		
Net income	x	
Adjustments for noncash expenses, revenues, losses and gains included in income:	x	
	(x)	
Net cash flow from operating activities		x
Cash flows from investing activities:	x	
	(x)	
Net cash flows provided (used) by investing activities		x
Cash flows from financing activities:	x	
	(x)	
Net cash provided (used) by financing activities		x
Net increase (decrease) in cash		xx
Schedule of noncash investing and financing activities:	x	
	x	

It facilitates planning future ventures and financing needs. Comparative data help the CFO identify abnormal or cyclical factors, and changes in the relationship among each flow element.

The Statement is a basis to forecast earnings based on plant, property, and equipment posture. It assists in appraising growth potential and incorporates cash flow requirements, highlighting specific fund sources and future means of payment. Will the company be able to pay its obligations and dividends?

The Statement reveals the type and degree of financing required to expand long-term assets and to bolster operations.

The CFO should compute for analytical purposes cash flow per share equal to net cash flow divided by the number of shares. A high ratio indicates the company is liquid.

We now discuss the analysis of the operating, investing, and financing sections of the Statement of Cash Flows.

What should you look at in evaluating the Operating Section?

An analysis of the Operating Section enables the CFO to determine the adequacy of cash flow from operating activities to satisfy company requirements. Can the firm obtain positive future net cash flows? The reconciliation tracing net income to net cash flow from operating activities should be examined to see the effect of noncash revenue and noncash expense items.

A high ratio of cash from sales to total sales points to quality sales dollars.

The cash debt coverage ratio equals cash flow from operations less dividends divided by total debt. Cash flow from operations less dividends is referred to as retained operating cash flow. The ratio indicates the number of years current cash flows will be needed to pay debt. A high ratio reflects the company's ability to repay debt. Another related ratio is cash flow from operations less dividends divided by the current maturities of long-term debt. These ratios could include adding to the denominator current liabilities or other fixed commitments such as lease obligations.

The cash dividend coverage ratio equals cash flow from operations divided by total dividends. It reflects the company's ability to pay current dividends from operating cash flow.

The capital acquisitions ratio equals cash flow from operations less dividends divided by cash paid for acquisitions. The ratio reveals the entity's ability to finance capital expenditures from internal sources.

The cash return on assets equals cash flow from operations before interest and taxes divided by total assets. A higher ratio means a greater cash return earned on assets employed. However, this ratio contains no provision for the replacement of assets or for future commitments.

The ratio of cash flow from operations divided by total debt plus stockholders' equity indicates the internal generation of cash available to creditors and investors.

The ratio of cash flow from operations to stockholders' equity indicates the return to stockholders.

An award under a lawsuit is a cash inflow from operating activities that results in a nonrecurring source of revenue.

An operating cash outlay for refunds given to customers for deficient goods indicates a quality problem with merchandise.

Payments of penalties, fines, and lawsuit damages are operating cash outflows that show poor management in that a problem arose which required a nonbeneficial expenditure.

What investing activities should be examined?

An analysis of the Investing Section identifies an investment in another company that may point to an attempt for ultimate control for diversification purposes. It may also indicate a change in future direction or change in business philosophy.

An increase in fixed assets indicates capital expansion and growth. The CFO should determine which assets have been purchased. Are they assets for risky (specialized) ventures or are they stable (multipurpose) ones? This is a clue as to risk potential and expected return. The nature of the assets shows future direction and earning potential of product lines, business segments, and territories. Are these directions viable?

The CFO should ascertain whether there is a contraction in the business arising from the sale of fixed assets without adequate replacement. Is the problem corporate (e.g., product line is weakening) or industry wide (e.g., industry is on the downturn)?

What is the importance of financing activities?

An appraisal of the Financing Section will help the CFO form an opinion of the company's ability to obtain financing in the money and capital markets as well as its ability to satisfy its obligations. The financial mixture of equity, bonds, and long-term bank loans impact the cost of financing. A major advantage of debt is the tax deductibility of interest. However, dividends on stock are not tax deductible. In inflation, paying debt back in cheaper dollars will result in purchasing power gains. The risk of debt financing is the required repayment of principal and interest. Will the company have the funds at maturity? The CFO must analyze the stability of the fund source to ascertain whether it may be relied upon in the future even in a tight money market. Otherwise, there may be problems in maintaining corporate operations in a recession. The question is: Where can the company go for funds during times of "tight money."

By appraising the financing sources, the financing preferences of management are revealed. Is there an inclination toward risk or safety?

The ability of a company to finance with the issuance of common stock on attractive terms (high stock price) indicates that investors are positive about the financial health of the business.

The issuance of preferred stock may be a negative indicator because it may mean the company has a problem issuing common stock.

An appraisal should be made of the company's ability to meet debt. Excessive debt means greater corporate risk especially in an economic downturn. The problem is acute if earnings are unstable or declining. On the other hand, the reduction in long-term debt is favorable because it lessens corporate risk.

The CFO should appraise the company's dividend paying ability. Stockholders favor a company with a high dividend payout.

Why are noncash activities worth considering?

A bond conversion is positive because it indicates that bondholders are optimistic about the company's financial well-being and/or the market price of stock has increased. A conversion of preferred stock to common stock is favorable because it shows preferred stockholders are impressed with the company's future and are willing to have a lower priority in liquidation.

How is managerial planning facilitated by analyzing the Statement of Cash Flows?

Profitability is only one important ingredient for success. Current and future cash flows are also important.

Management is responsible for planning how and when cash will be used and obtained. When planned expenditures require more cash than planned activities are likely to produce, managers must decide what to do. They may decide to obtain debt or equity financing or to dispose of some fixed assets or a business segment. Alternatively, they may decide to reduce planned activities by modifying operational plans such as ending a special advertising campaign or delaying new acquisitions. Or, they may decide to revise planned payments to financing sources such as delaying bond repayment or reducing dividends. Whatever is decided, the managers' goal is to balance, over both the short and the long term, the cash available and the needs for cash.

Managerial planning is aided when evaluating the Statement of Cash Flows in terms of coordinating dividend policy with other corporate activities, financial planning for new products and types of assets needed, strengthening a weak cash posture and credit availability, and ascertaining the feasibility and implementation of existing top management plans.

The ratio of net cash flows for investing activities divided by net cash flows from financing activities compares the total funds needed for investment to funds generated from financing. Are fund sources adequate to meet investment needs? Similarly, the ratio of net cash flows for investing divided by net cash flows from operating and financing activities compares the funds needed for investment to the funds obtained from financing and operations.

The analysis and evaluation of cash flows is essential if the CFO is to appraise an entity's cash flows from operating, investing, and financing activities. The company's liquidity and solvency positions as well as future directions are revealed. Inadequacy in cash flow has possible serious implications because it may lead to declining profitability, greater financial risk, and even bankruptcy.

EXAMPLE 1

X Company provides the following financial statements:

X Company
Comparative Balance Sheets
December 31
(In Millions)

	19X9	19X8
ASSETS		
Cash	$ 40	$ 47
Accounts receivable	30	35
Prepaid expenses	4	2
Land	50	35
Building	100	80
Accumulated depreciation	(9)	(6)
Equipment	50	42
Accumulated depreciation	(11)	(7)
Total assets	$254	$228
LIABILITIES AND STOCKHOLDERS' EQUITY		
Accounts payable	$ 20	$ 16
Long-term notes payable	30	20
Common stock	100	100
Retained earnings	104	92
Total liabilities and stockholders' equity	$254	$228

X Company
Income Statement
For the Year-End December 31, 19X9
(In Millions)

Revenue		$300
Operating expenses (excluding depreciation)	$200	
Depreciation	7	207
Income from operations		$ 93
Income tax expense		32
Net income		$ 61

Additional information:

1. Cash dividends paid $49.

2. The company issued long-term notes payable for cash.

3. Land, building, and equipment were acquired for cash.

We can now prepare the Statement of Cash Flows under the *indirect method* as follows:

X Company
Statement of Cash Flows
For the Year-End December 31, 19X9
(In Millions)

Cash flow from operating activities		
Net income		$61
Add (deduct) items not affecting cash		
Depreciation expense	$ 7	
Decrease in accounts receivable	5	
Increase in prepaid expenses	(2)	
Increase in accounts payable	4	14
Net cash flow from operating activities		$75
Cash flow from investing activities		
Purchase of land	($15)	
Purchase of building	(20)	
Purchase of equipment	(8)	(43)

Cash flow from financing activities

Issuance of long-term notes payable	$10	
Payment of cash dividends	(49)	(39)
Net decrease in cash		$ 7

A financial analysis of the Statement of Cash Flows reveals that the profitability and operating cash flow of X Company improved. This indicates good earnings performance as well as earnings being backed-up by cash. The decrease in accounts receivable reveals better collection efforts. The increase in accounts payable is a sign that suppliers are confident in the company and willing to give interest-free financing. The acquisition of land, building, and equipment points to a growing business undertaking capital expansion. The issuance of long-term notes payable indicates that part of the financing of assets is through debt. Stockholders will be happy with the significant dividend payout of 80.3% (dividends divided by net income, or $49/$61). Overall, there was a decrease in cash of $7 but this should *not* cause alarm because of the company's profitability and the fact that cash was used for capital expansion and dividend payments. We recommend that the dividend payout be reduced from its high level and the funds be reinvested in the profitable business. Also, the curtailment of dividends by more than $7 would result in a positive net cash flow for the year. Cash flow is needed for immediate liquidity needs.

EXAMPLE 2

Y Company presents the following statement of cash flows:

Y Company
Statement of Cash Flows
For the Year-End December 31, 19X8

Cash flows from operating activities

Net income	$134,000
Add (deduct) items not affecting cash	

Depreciation expense	$ 21,000	
Decrease in accounts receivable	10,000	
Increase in prepaid expenses	(6,000)	
Increase in accounts payable	35,000	60,000
Net cash flow from operating activities		$194,000
Cash flows from investing activities		
Purchase of land	$(70,000)	
Purchase of building	(200,000)	
Purchase of equipment	(68,000)	
Cash used by investing activities		(338,000)
Cash flows from financing activities		
Issuance of bonds	150,000	
Payment of cash dividends	(18,000)	
Cash provided by financing activities		132,000
Net decrease in cash		$(12,000)

An analysis of the Statement of Cash Flows reveals that the company is profitable. Also, cash flow from operating activities exceeds net income, which indicates good internal cash generation. The ratio of cash flow from operating activities to net income is a solid 1.45 ($194,000/$134,000). A high ratio is desirable because it shows that earnings are backed up by cash. The decline in accounts receivable indicates better collection efforts. The increase in accounts payable shows the company can obtain interest-free financing. The company is in the process of expanding for future growth as evidenced by the purchase of land, building, and equipment. The debt position of the company has increased indicating greater risk. The dividend payout was 13.4% ($18,000/$134,000). Stockholders look positively on a firm that pays dividends. The decrease in cash flow for the year of $12,000 is a negative sign.

6

Accounting and Disclosures

This chapter discusses the accounting involved in changes in principle, estimate, and reporting entity. Corrections of errors are also presented. In a troubled debt situation, the debtor wants relief from the creditor. Noninterest bearing notes and futures contracts are presented. Disclosure about financial instruments with off-balance-sheet risk are discussed.

ACCOUNTING CHANGES

The types of accounting changes as per APB 20 are principle, estimate, and reporting entity.

What do we do if an accounting principle is changed?

A change in accounting principle or method is shown in the current year's income statement in an account called "cumulative effect of a change in accounting principle" (net of tax). The amount equals the difference between retained earnings at the beginning of the year with the old method compared to what retained earnings would have been at the beginning of the year if we had used the new method in previous years. The new principle is used in the current and future years. A change in depreciation method for a *new* fixed asset is *not* a change in principle. A footnote discloses the nature and justification of a change in principle including an explanation of why the new principle is preferred. Justification may be a new FASB pronouncement, new tax law, new AICPA statement of position or industry audit guide, a change in circumstances, and to more readily conform to industry practice.

If comparative financial statements are not presented, pro forma disclosures should be made between the body of the financial statements and the footnotes of what earnings would have been in prior years if the new principle was used in those years. If income statements are presented for comparative purposes, they should reflect the change on a pro forma basis as if the change had been in effect in each of such years. Financial statements of prior years, presented for comparative purposes, are presented *as previously reported.* However, income before extraordinary items, net income, and earnings per share for previous years presented are *recalculated* and disclosed on the face of the prior periods' income statements as if the new principle had been in use in those periods. If space does not permit, this information may be presented in separate schedules showing both the original and recalculated figures. If only the current period's income statement is presented, the actual and pro forma (recalculated) figures for the immediate preceding period should be disclosed.

In unusual cases, pro forma amounts are not determinable for previous years even though the cumulative effect on the opening retained earnings balance can be computed. The cumulative effect of a change in principle is presented in the usual fashion with reasons given for omitting pro forma figures. Similarly, when the cumulative effect of a change in principle is impossible to compute, disclosure is given for the effect of the change on income data of the current period and explaining the reason for omitting the cumulative effect and pro forma amounts for prior periods. An example of a situation where the cumulative effect is not determinable is a change from the FIFO to LIFO inventory method.

If an accounting change in principle is immaterial in the current year but it is expected to be material in the future, disclosure is needed.

Certain types of changes in accounting principle instead of being shown in a cumulative effect account require the restatement of prior years as if the new principle was used in those years. These changes are:

• Change from LIFO to another inventory method.

• Change in accounting for long-term construction contracts (e.g., changing from the completed contract method to the percentage of completion method).

• Change to or from the full cost method used in the extractive industry. The full cost method defers both successful and unsuccessful exploration costs to the asset account with subsequent amortization. An alternative method is successful efforts under which only successful costs are deferred while unsuccessful ones are expensed.

The following are *not* considered a change in accounting principle:

• A principle adopted for the first time on new or previously immaterial events or transactions.

• A principle adopted or changed because of events or transactions clearly different in substance.

According to Interpretation 1, a *change in composition* of the cost elements (e.g., material, labor, and overhead) of inventory qualifies as an accounting change.

EXAMPLE 1

X Company changed from double declining balance to straight-line depreciation in 19X7. It uses ACRS depreciation for tax purposes which results in depreciation higher than the double declining balance method for each of the three years. The tax rate is 34%. Relevant data follow:

Year	Double Declining Balance Depreciation	Straight-Line Depreciation	Difference
19X5	$250,000	$150,000	$100,000
19X6	200,000	150,000	50,000
19X7	185,000	150,000	35,000

The entries to reflect the change in depreciation in 19X7 follow:

Depreciation	150,000	
Accumulated depreciation		150,000

For current year depreciation under the straight line method:

Accumulated depreciation (100,000 + 50,000)	150,000	
Deferred income tax credit (150,000 × .34)		51,000
Cumulative effect of a change in accounting principle		99,000

What if an estimate is revised?

A change in accounting estimate results from new circumstances such as a change in salvage value or bad debt experience. A change in accounting estimate is recognized prospectively over current and future years. There is *no* restatement of past years. A footnote describes the nature of a *material* change.

If a change in estimate is coupled with a change in principle and the effects cannot be distinguished, it is accounted for as a change in estimate. For example, there may be a change from deferring and amortizing a cost to expensing it because future benefits are uncertain. This should be accounted for as a change in estimate.

EXAMPLE 2

Equipment was bought on 1/1/19X2 for $40,000 having an original estimated life of 10 years with a salvage value of $4,000. On 1/1/19X6, the estimated life was revised to 8 more years remaining with a new salvage value of $3,200. The journal entry on 12/31/19X6 for depreciation expense is:

Depreciation	2,800	
Accumulated depreciation		2,800

Computations follow:

Book value on 1/1/19X6:

Original cost	$40,000
Less: Accumulated depreciation	
$\dfrac{\$40,000 - \$4,000}{10} = \$3,600 \times 4$	14,400
Book value	$25,600

Depreciation for 19X6:

Book value	$25,600
Less: New salvage value	3,200
Depreciable cost	$22,400

$\dfrac{\text{Depreciable cost}}{\text{New life}}$

$\dfrac{\$22,400}{8} = \$2,800$

How do we account and report when the makeup of the entity is changed?

A change in reporting entity (e.g., two previously separate companies merge) is accounted for by restating previous years' financial statements as if both companies were always combined. The restatement helps to show trends in comparative financial statements and historical summaries. The effect of the change on income before extraordinary items, net income and per share amounts is reported for all periods presented. The restatement does not have to go back more than 5 years. Footnote disclosure should be made of the nature of and reason for the change in reporting entity only in the year of change. Examples of changes in reporting entity are:

- Presenting consolidated statements rather than statements of individual companies.
- Change in subsidiaries included in consolidated statements or combined statements.
- A business combination accounted for under the pooling-of-interests method.

How is a prior period adjustment handled?

The two types of prior period adjustments are:

- Correction of an error that was made in a previous year.
- Recognition of a tax loss carryforward benefit arising from a purchased subsidiary (curtailed by the 1986 Tax Reform Act).

When a single year is presented, prior period adjustments adjust the beginning balance of retained earnings. The presentation follows:

Retained earnings—1/1 Unadjusted
Prior period adjustments (net of tax)
Retained earnings—1/1 Adjusted
Add: Net income
Less: Dividends
Retained earnings—12/31

Errors may arise from mathematical mistakes, misapplication of accounting principles, or misuse of facts existing when the financial statements were prepared. Further, a change in principle from one that is not GAAP to one that is GAAP is an error correction. Disclosure should be made of the nature of the error and the effect of correction on profit.

When comparative statements are prepared, a retroactive adjustment for the error is made to prior years. The retroactive adjustment is disclosed by showing the effects of the adjustment on previous years' earnings and component items of net income.

EXAMPLE 3

In 19X1, a company incorrectly charged furniture for promotion expense amounting to $30,000. The error was discovered in 19X2. The correcting journal entry is:

Retained earnings	30,000	
Furniture		30,000

EXAMPLE 4

X Company acquired Y Company on 1/1/19X3 recording goodwill of $60,000. Goodwill was not amortized. The correcting entry on 12/31/19X5 follows:

Amortization expense		
(1500 × 1 for 19X5)	1,500	
Retained earnings (1500		
× 2 for 19X3 and 19X4)	3,000	
Goodwill		4,500

EXAMPLE 5

At the end of 19X2, a company failed to accrue telephone expense which was paid at the beginning of 19X3. The correcting entry on 12/31/19X3 is:

Retained earnings	16,000	
Telephone expense		16,000

EXAMPLE 6

On 1/1/19X2, an advance retainer fee of $50,000 was received covering a 5 year period. In error, revenue was credited for the full amount. The error was discovered on 12/31/19X4 before closing the books. The correcting entry is:

12/31/19X4		
Retained earnings	30,000	
Revenue		10,000
Deferred revenue		20,000

EXAMPLE 7

A company bought a machine on January 1, 19X4 for $32,000 with a $2,000 salvage value and a five-year life. By mistake, repairs expense was charged. The error was uncovered on December 31, 19X7 before closing the books. The correcting entry follows:

Depreciation expense	6,000	
Machine	32,000	
Accumulated depreciation		24,000
Retained earnings		14,000

Accumulated depreciation of $24,000 is calculated below:

$$\frac{\$32,000 - \$2,000}{5} = \$6,000 \text{ per year} \times 4 \text{ years}$$
$$= \$24,000$$

The credit to retained earnings reflects the difference between the erroneous repairs expense of $32,000 in 19X4 versus showing depreciation expense of $18,000 for three years (19X4–19X6).

EXAMPLE 8

At the beginning of 19X5, a company bought equipment for $300,000 with a salvage value of $20,000 and an expected life of 10 years. Straight line depreciation is used. In error, salvage value was not deducted in computing depreciation. The correcting journal entries on 12/31/19X7 follow:

		19X5 and 19X6
Depreciation taken		
$300,000/10 × 2 years		$60,000
Depreciation correctly stated		
$280,000/10 × 2 years		56,000
		$ 4,000
Depreciation	28,000	
Accumulated depreciation		28,000
Depreciation for current year		
Accumulated depreciation	4,000	
Retained earnings		4,000

Correct prior year depreciation misstatement

What policies should be disclosed?

Accounting policies are the specific accounting principles and methods of applying them that are selected by management. Accounting policies should be those that are most appropriate in the circumstances to fairly present financial position and operating results. Accounting policies can relate to reporting and measurement methods as well as disclosures. They include:

- A selection from GAAP or unusual applications thereof.
- Practices peculiar to the industry.

The first footnote or a section preceding the notes to the financial statements should describe the accounting policies used.

The application of GAAP requires the use of *judgement* when alternative acceptable principles exist and when there are varying methods of applying a principle to a given set of facts. Disclosure of these principles and methods is essential to the full presentation of financial position and operations.

Examples of accounting policy disclosures are inventory pricing method, depreciation method, consolidation bases, and amortization period for intangibles.

Some types of financial statements do not have to describe the accounting policies followed. Examples are quarterly unaudited statements when there has not been a policy change since the last year-end, and statements only for internal use.

What if the debtor has trouble paying?

In a troubled debt restructuring, the debtor has financial problems and is relieved of part or all of the obligation. The concession arises from the debtor-creditor agreement, law, or applies to foreclosure and repossession. The types of troubled debt restructurings are:

- Debtor transfers to creditor receivables from third parties or other assets.
- Debtor gives creditor equity securities to satisfy the debt.
- Modification of the debt terms including reducing the interest rate, extending the maturity date, or reducing the principal of the obligation.

The debtor records an extraordinary gain (net of tax) on the restructuring while the creditor recognizes a loss. The loss may be ordinary or extraordinary, depending on whether the arrangement is unusual and infrequent. Typically, the loss is ordinary.

Debtor

The gain to the debtor equals the difference between the fair value of assets exchanged and the book value of the debt including accrued interest. Further, there may arise a gain on disposal of assets exchanged equal to the difference between the fair market value and the book value of the transferred assets. The latter gain or loss is *not* a gain or loss on restructuring, but rather an ordinary gain or loss in connection with asset disposal.

EXAMPLE 9

A debtor transfers assets having a fair market value of $80 and a book value of $65 to settle a payable having a carrying value of $90. The gain on restructuring is $10 ($90 – $80). The ordinary gain is $15 ($80 – $65).

A debtor may give the creditor an equity interest. The debtor records the equity securities issued based on fair market value and not the recorded value of the debt extinguished. The excess of the recorded payable satisfied over the fair value of the issued securities constitutes an extraordinary item.

A modification in terms of an initial debt contract is accounted for prospectively. A new interest rate may be determined based on the new terms. This interest rate is then used to allocate future payments to lower principal and interest. When the new terms of the agreement results in the sum of all the future payments to be *less* than the carrying value of the payable, the payable is reduced and a restructuring gain recorded for the difference. The future payments only reduce principal. Interest expense is not recorded.

A troubled debt restructuring may result in a *combination* of concessions to the debtor. This may occur when assets or an equity interest are given in *partial* satisfaction of the obligation and the balance is subject to a modification of terms. There are two steps. First, the payable is reduced by the fair value of the assets or equity transferred. Second, the balance of the debt is accounted for as a "modification of terms" type restructuring.

Direct costs, such as legal fees, incurred by the debtor in an equity transfer reduce the fair value of the equity interest. All other costs reduce the gain on restructuring. If there is no gain, they are expensed.

EXAMPLE 10

The debtor owes the creditor $200,000 and because of financial problems may have difficulty making future payments. There should be footnote disclosure of the problem by both the debtor and creditor.

EXAMPLE 11

The debtor owes the creditor $80,000. The creditor relieves the debtor of $10,000. The balance of the debt will be paid at a later time.

The journal entry for the debtor is:

Accounts payable	10,000	
Extraordinary gain		10,000

The journal entry for the creditor is:

Ordinary loss	10,000	
Accounts receivable		10,000

EXAMPLE 12

The debtor owes the creditor $90,000. The creditor agrees to accept $70,000 in full satisfaction of the obligation.

The journal entry for the debtor is:

Accounts payable	90,000	
Extraordinary gain		20,000
Cash		70,000

The journal entry for the creditor is:

Cash	70,000	
Ordinary loss	20,000	
Accounts receivable		90,000

The debtor should disclose the following in the footnotes:

- Terms of the restructuring agreement.
- The aggregate and per share amounts of the gain on restructuring.
- Amounts that are contingently payable including the contingency terms.

Creditor

The creditor's loss is the difference between the fair value of assets received and the book value of the investment. When terms are modified, the creditor recognizes interest income to the degree that total future payments are greater than the carrying value of the investment. Interest income is recognized using the effective interest method. Assets received are reflected at fair market value. When the book value of the receivable is in excess of the aggregate payments, an ordinary loss is recognized for the difference. All cash received in the future is accounted for as a recovery of the investment. Direct costs of the creditor are expensed.

The creditor does not recognize contingent interest until the contingency is removed and interest has been earned. Further, future changes in the interest rate are accounted for as a change in estimate.

The creditor discloses the following in the footnotes:

- Loan commitments of additional funds to financially troubled companies.
- Loans and/or receivables by major type.
- Debt agreements in which the interest rate has been downwardly adjusted, including an explanation of the circumstances.
- Description of the restructuring provisions.

What if a note does not provide for interest?

If the face amount of a note does not represent the present value of the consideration given or received in the exchange, imputation of interest is needed to avoid the misstatement of profit. Interest is imputed on noninterest bearing notes, notes that provide for an unrealistically low interest rate, and when the face value of the note is substantially different from the "going" selling price of the property or market value of the note.

If a note is issued only for cash, the note should be recorded at the cash exchanged regardless of whether the interest rate is reasonable. The note has a present value at issuance equal to the cash transacted. When a note is exchanged for property, goods, or services there is a presumption that the interest rate is reasonable. Where the stipulated interest rate is unreasonable, the note is recorded at the fair value of the merchandise or services or at an amount that approximates fair value. If fair value is not ascertainable for the goods or services, the discounted present value of the note is used.

The imputed interest rate is the one that would have resulted if an independent borrower or lender had negotiated an "arms length" transaction. For example, it is the prevailing interest rate the borrower would have paid for financing. The interest rate is based on economic circumstances and events.

The factors to be taken into account in deriving an appropriate discount rate include:

- Prime interest rate.
- "Going" market rate for similar quality instruments.
- Collateral.
- Issuer's credit standing.
- Restrictive covenants and other terms in the note agreement.
- Tax effects of the arrangement.

APB 21 applies to *long-term* payables and receivables. Short-term payables and receivables are typically recorded at face value. The pronouncement is *not* applicable to:

- Receivables or payables occurring within the ordinary course of business.
- Security deposits.
- Amounts that do not require repayment.
- Transactions between parent and subsidiary.

The difference between the face value of the note and its present value represents discount or premium which has to be accounted for as an element of interest over the life of the note. Present value of the payments of the note is based on an imputed interest rate.

The interest method is used to amortize the discount or premium on the note. The interest method results in a constant rate of interest. Under the method, amortization equals:

Interest Rate × Present Value of the Liability/
Receivable at the Beginning of the Year

Interest expense is recorded for the borrower while interest revenue is recorded for the lender. Issuance costs are treated as a deferred charge.

The note payable and note receivable are presented in the balance sheet as follows:

Notes payable (principal plus interest)
Less: Discount (interest)
Present value (principal)

Notes receivable (principal plus interest)
Less: Premium (interest)
Present value (principal)

EXAMPLE 13

On 1/1/19X1 equipment is acquired in exchange for a one year note payable of $1,000 maturing on 12/31/19X1. The imputed interest rate is 10% resulting in the present value factor for n = 1, i = 10% of .91. Relevant journal entries follow:

1/1/19X1

Equipment	910	
Discount	90	
Notes payable		1,000

12/31/19X1

Interest expense	90	
Discount		90
Notes payable	1,000	
Cash		1,000

EXAMPLE 14

On 1/1/19X1, a machine is bought for cash of $10,000 and the incurrence of a $30,000, five-year, noninterest bearing note payable. The imputed interest rate is 10%. The present value factor for n = 5, i = 10% is .62. Appropriate journal entries follow:

1/1/19X1

Machine (10,000 + 18,600)	28,600	
Discount	11,400	
Notes payable		30,000
Cash		10,000

Present value of note equals
$30,000 × .62 = $18,600

On 1/1/19X1, the balance sheet shows:

Notes payable	$30,000
Less: Discount	11,400
Present value	$18,600

12/31/19X1

| Interest expense | 1,860 | |
| Discount | | 1,860 |

10% × $18,600 = $1,860

1/1/19X2

Notes payable	$30,000
Less: Discount	
(11,400 − 1,860)	9,540
Present value	$20,460

12/31/19X2
   Interest expense   2,046
      Discount   2,046
   $10\% \times \$20,460 = \$2,046$

Do you engage in futures contracts?

A futures contract is a legal arrangement between the purchaser or seller and a regulated futures exchange in the United States or overseas. However, FASB 80 does not apply to foreign currencies futures that are dealt with in FASB 82. Futures contracts involve:

• A buyer or seller receiving or making a delivery of a commodity or financial instrument (e.g., stocks, bonds, commercial paper, mortgages) at a specified date. Cash settlement rather than delivery typically exists (e.g., stock index future).

• A futures contract may be eliminated before the delivery date by engaging in an offsetting contract for the particular commodity or financial instrument. For example, a futures contract to buy 200,000 pounds of a commodity by December 31, 19X4, may be cancelled by entering into another contract to sell 200,000 pounds of that same commodity on December 31, 19X4.

• Changes in value of open contracts are settled regularly (e.g., daily). The usual contract provides that when a decrease in the contract value occurs, the contract holder has to make a cash deposit for such decline with the clearinghouse. If the contract increases in value, the holder may withdraw the increased value.

The change in the market value of a futures contract involves a gain or loss that should be recognized in earnings. An exception exists that for certain contracts the timing of income statement recognition relates to the accounting for the applicable asset, liability, commitment, or transaction. This accounting exception applies when the contract is designed as a hedge against price and interest rate fluctuation. When the criteria below are satisfied, the accounting for the contract relates to the accounting for the hedged item. Thus, a change in market value is recognized in the same accounting period that the effects of the related changes in price or interest rate of the hedged item is reflected in income.

What is a hedge?

A *hedge* exists when both of the following criteria are met:

• The hedged item places price and interest rate risk on the firm. Risk means the sensitivity of corporate earnings to market price changes or rates of return of existing assets, liabilities, commitments, and expected transactions. This criteria is *not* met in the case where other assets, liabilities, commitments, and anticipated transactions *already* offset the risk.

• The contract lowers risk exposure and is entered into as a hedge. High correlation exists between the change in market value of the contract and the fair value of the hedged item. In effect, the market price change of the contract offsets the price and interest rate changes on the exposed item. An example is a futures contract to sell silver that offsets the changes in the price of silver.

A change in market value of a futures contract that meets the hedging criteria of the related asset or liability adjusts the carrying value of the hedged item. For example, a company has an investment in a government bond that it expects to sell in the future. The company can reduce its susceptibility to changes in fair value of the bonds by entering into a futures contract. The changes in the market value of the futures contract adjusts the book value of the bonds.

A change in market value of a futures contract that is for the purpose of hedging a firm commitment is included in measuring the transaction satisfying the commitment. An example is when the company hedges a firm purchase commitment by using a futures contract. When the acquisition takes place satisfying the purchase commitment, the gain or loss on the futures contract is an element of the cost of the acquired item. Assume ABC Company has a purchase commitment for 30,000 pounds of a commodity at $2 per pound, totaling $60,000. At the time of the consummation of the transaction, the $60,000 cost is *decreased* by any gain (e.g., $5,000) arising from the "hedged" futures contract. The net cost is shown as the carrying value (e.g., $55,000).

A futures contract may apply to transactions the company *expects* to carry out in the ordinary course of business. It is not obligated to do so. These expected transactions do not involve existing assets or liabilities, or transactions applicable to *existing* firm commitments. For example, your company may *anticipate* buying a commodity in the future but has not made a formal purchase commitment. The company may minimize risk exposure to price changes by making a futures contract. The change in market value of this "anticipatory hedge contract" is included in measuring the subsequent transaction. The change in market value of the futures contract adjusts the cost of the acquired item. The following criteria must be satisfied for "anticipatory hedge accounting":

1. and 2. are the same as the criteria for regular hedge contracts related to *existing* assets, liabilities, or firm commitments.

3. Identification exists of the major terms of the contemplated transaction. This includes the type of commodity or financial instrument, quantity, and expected transaction date. If the financial instrument carries interest, the maturity date should be given.

4. It is probable that the expected transaction will occur.

Probability of occurrence depends on the following:

- Monetary commitment.
- Time period.
- Financial soundness to conduct the transaction.
- Frequency of previous transactions of a similar nature.
- Adverse operational effects of not engaging in the transaction.

- Possibility that other types of transactions may be undertaken to accomplish the desired objective.

How do we account for and disclose "hedge type" contracts?

The accounting for a "hedge type" futures contract related to an expected asset acquisition or liability incurrence should be consistent with the company's accounting method used for those assets and liabilities. For example, the company should recognize a loss for a futures contract that is a hedge of an expected inventory acquisition if the amount will not be removed from the sale of inventory.

If a "hedged" futures contract is closed before the expected transaction, the accumulated value change in the contract should be carried forward in measuring the related transaction. If it is probable that the quantity of an expected transaction will be less than the amount initially hedged, recognize a gain or loss for a pro rata portion of futures results that would have been included in the measurement of the subsequent transaction.

A "hedged" futures contract requires disclosure of:

- Nature of assets and liabilities.
- Accounting method used for the contract including a description of events resulting in recognizing changes in contract values.
- Expected transactions that are hedged with futures contracts.
- Firm commitments.

What footnote information should be presented for financial instruments?

FASB No. 105 requires disclosure of information about financial instruments with off-balance sheet risk and financial instruments with concentrations of credit risk. A financial instrument is defined as cash, evidence of an ownership interest in another entity, or a contract that *both:* (1) imposes on one entity a contractual obligation to deliver cash or another financial instrument to a second entity, or exchange financial instruments on unfavorable terms, and (2) conveys to the second entity a contractual right to receive cash, another financial instrument, or exchange financial instruments on favorable terms with the first entity. Examples of financial instruments include letters of credit or loan commitments written, foreign currency or interest rate swaps, financial guarantees written, forward or futures contracts, call and put options written, and interest rate caps or floors written.

The company must disclose information about financial instruments that may result in future loss but have *not* been recognized in the accounts as liabilities and are thus not reported in the income statement or balance sheet. A financial instrument has an off-balance sheet risk of accounting loss if the risk of loss exceeds the amount recognized as an asset (if any), or if the ultimate obligation may exceed the amount recognized as a liability.

The following must be footnoted:

- The face amounts of the financial instruments.
- The extent, nature, and terms of the financial instruments, including any cash requirements.
- The entity's policy for requiring security on financial instruments it accepts.
- Identification and description of collateral.
- A discussion of credit risks associated with financial instruments because of the failure of another party to perform.
- A discussion of market risk that will make a financial instrument less valuable including future changes in market prices caused by foreign exchange and interest rate fluctuations.
- Information about a region, activity, or economic factor that may result in a concentration of credit risk.
- The *potential* loss from the financial instrument if a party fails to perform under the contract.
- The entity's accounting policies for financial instruments.

7

Key Financial Accounting Areas

This chapter discusses the accounting requirements for major financial areas including consolidation, investing in stocks and bonds, leases, pensions, post retirement benefits excluding pensions, tax allocation, and foreign currency translation and transactions.

How are convertible bonds accounted for?

Consolidation occurs when the parent owns more than 50% of the voting common stock of the subsidiary. The prime purpose of consolidation is to present as one economic unit the financial position and operating results of a parent and subsidiaries. It shows the group as a single company (with one or more branches or divisions) rather than separate companies. It is an example of theoretical substance over legal form. The companies constituting the consolidated group keep their individual legal identity. Adjustments and eliminations are only for financial statement reporting. Disclosure should be made of the company's consolidation policy in footnotes or by explanatory headings.

A consolidation is negated, even if more than 50% of voting common stock is owned by the parent, in the following situations:

- Parent is not in actual control of subsidiary (e.g., subsidiary is in receivership, subsidiary is in a politically unstable foreign country).
- Parent has sold or contracted to sell subsidiary shortly after year-end. The subsidiary is a temporary investment.
- Minority interest is substantive relative to the parent's interest, thus individual financial statements are more useful.

Intercompany eliminations include those for intercompany receivables and payables, advances, and profits. However, in the case of certain regulated companies, intercompany profit does not have to be eliminated to the extent the profit represents a reasonable return on investment. Subsidiary investment in the parent's shares is not consolidated outstanding stock in the consolidated balance sheet. Consolidated statements do not reflect capitalized earnings in the form of stock dividends by subsidiaries subsequent to acquisition.

Minority interest in a subsidiary is the stockholders' equity of those outside to the parent's controlling interest in the partially owned subsidiaries. Minority interest should be shown as a separate component of stockholders' equity. When losses applicable to the minority interest in a subsidiary exceed the minority interest's equity capital, the excess and any subsequent losses related to the minority interest are charged to the parent. If profit subsequently occurs, the parent's interest is credited to the degree of prior losses absorbed.

If a parent acquires a subsidiary in more than one block of stock, each purchase is on a step-by-step basis and consolidation does not occur until control exists.

If the subsidiary is acquired within the year, the subsidiary should be included in consolidation as if it had been bought at the start of the year with a deduction for the preacquisition part of earnings applicable to each block of stock. An alternative, but less preferable approach, is to include in consolidation the subsidiary's profit after the acquisition date.

The retained earnings of a subsidiary at the acquisition date is not included in the consolidated financial statements.

When the subsidiary is disposed of during the year, the parent should present its equity in the subsidiary's earnings before the sale date as a separate line item in conformity with the equity method.

A subsidiary whose *major business activity* is leasing to a parent should always be consolidated.

Consolidation is allowed without adjustments when the fiscal year-ends of the parent and subsidiary are three months or less apart. However, disclosure is required of significant events in the intervening period.

The equity method of accounting is used for unconsolidated subsidiaries unless there is a foreign investment or a temporary investment. In a case where the equity method is not used, the cost method is followed. The cost method recognizes the difference between the cost of the subsidiary and the equity in net assets at the acquisition date. Depreciation is adjusted for the difference as if consolidation of the subsidiary was made. There is an elimination of intercompany gain or loss for unconsolidated subsidiaries to the extent the gain or loss exceeds the unrecorded equity in undistributed earnings. Unconsolidated subsidiaries accounted for with the cost method should have adequate disclosure of assets, liabilities, and earnings. Such disclosure may be in footnote or supplementary schedule form.

There may be cases when combined rather than consolidated financial statements are more meaningful, such as where a person owns a controlling interest in several related operating companies (brother-sister corporation).

There are instances where besides consolidated statements, parent company statements are required to properly provide information to creditors and preferred stockholders. In this case, *dual columns* are needed—one column for the parent and other columns for subsidiaries.

INVESTMENTS IN STOCKS AND BONDS

Investments in stock may be accounted for under the cost or equity method depending on the percentage of ownership in the voting common stock.

Note: Nonvoting stock (e.g., preferred stock) is always accounted for under the cost method.

A security is typically classified as current if it is liquid and used for temporary excess cash. A security is usually classified as long-term if the intent is to hold for one year or more, it is for capital appreciation, dividend income is desired, there is possible ultimate control, a lack of market price quotations exist, and there is restricted marketability. "Restricted" stock is noncurrent except if it qualifies for sale within one year of the balance sheet date and there are readily available price quotations.

When is the cost method used?

The cost method of accounting for investments is used when the holder owns less than 20% of the voting common stock of the company. However, the cost method could be used instead of the equity method when the holder owns between 20 to 50% of the voting common stock but *lacks* significant influence (effective control).

Significant influence may be indicated by one or more of the following:

- Investor owns a high percentage of investee's shares compared to other stockholders.
- Input into the decision making of the owned company.
- Managerial personnel are interchanged between the investor and investee.
- Significant intercompany transactions.
- Investor provides investee with technological knowledge.
- Representation on the Board of Directors of the investee company.

The signs of an absence of significant influence follow:

- Concentration of majority ownership of investee among a few stockholders, particularly when the group operates the investee disregarding the investor's viewpoints.
- Investee opposes the investment (e.g., a lawsuit or complaint is filed).
- Investor cannot obtain the financial information required from the investee to use the equity method.
- Investor and investee sign a contract (called "standstill") in which the investor surrenders

significant shareholder rights. The "stand-still" agreement is usually used to settle disputes between the parties.

The cost method is used for equity securities. While it is not required for debt securities, debt securities are typically reflected in the investment portfolio at the lower of cost or market value.

How do we account for the investment portfolio?

The investment portfolio is classified into current and noncurrent. Current securities are presented as marketable securities under current assets. Noncurrent securities are presented as noncurrent assets. The lower of cost or market value is applied to each portfolio separately.

If market value exceeds cost, the securities are presented at cost with market value either disclosed parenthetically or in a footnote. If market value is below cost, conservatism dictates that the securities portfolio be written down to market value recognizing an unrealized loss. Thus, a temporary decline in value of the portfolio is reflected. The portfolio is presented on the balance sheet at the lower of total cost or total market value. The entry at year-end is:

Unrealized loss
    Allowance to reduce securities
       from cost to market value

In the case of short-term securities, the unrealized loss is presented in the income statement. For long-term securities, the unrealized loss is shown as a separate item in the stockholders' equity section. The allowance account is a contra account to Investments to obtain the net amount. The allowance account is only adjusted at year-end.

In the following year, if there is a partial or full recovery from cost to market value, the entry is:

Allowance to reduce securities
    from cost to market value
       Unrealized gain

However, in recording the recovery from cost to market value, the portfolio can never be written-up above the original cost.

If securities are sold, a realized loss or realized gain is recognized. The realized loss or gain is presented in the income statement regardless of whether the portfolio is current or noncurrent. The same realized loss or gain on sale appears on the tax return.

The entry to record the sale of securities is:

Cash (proceeds received)
Loss
    Securities (at cost)
    Gain

A loss or gain will either be involved in the above entry.

A security cannot be recorded at more than cost since that will lack conservatism. The only time market value can be used for valuation is the case of a *permanent* increase in value. However, accountants are reluctant to state that a permanent increase has occurred because of legal liability exposure.

If a balance sheet is unclassified, the investment security portfolio is considered noncurrent.

A permanent decline in value of a particular security is immediately recognized with a realized loss being booked shown in the income statement even if it is a noncurrent portfolio. The investment account is credited directly. The new market value becomes the new cost basis which means it cannot later be written up.

A permanent decline in market price of stock may be indicated when the company has several years of losses, is in a very weak financial condition, and has issued a liquidating dividend. For example, if the company sells some of its major divisions and distributes the proceeds to stockholders, a write-down of the investment may be appropriate.

EXAMPLE 1

In a long-term investment portfolio, one stock in ABC Company has suffered a permanent decline in value from cost of $6,000 to market value of $5,000. The entry is:

Realized loss	1,000	
Long-term investment		1,000

The new cost now becomes $5,000 (the market value). If in a later period, the market value increased above $5,000, the stock would *not* be written up above $5,000.

If a particular stock is reclassified from noncurrent to current, or vice versa, it is transferred at the lower of cost or market value at the transfer date. If market value exceeds cost, it is transferred at cost with no unrealized gain being recorded. If market value is less than cost, a realized loss in the income statement is recognized and the investment account is credited. The new cost basis becomes the market value which means the portfolio cannot be written up above cost.

EXAMPLE 2

XYZ stock is reclassified from noncurrent to current. If cost is $3,000 and market value is $2,700, the entry for the reclassification is:

Short-term securities	2,700	
Realized loss	300	
Long-term investment		3,000

If there is a later recovery and market value becomes $2,900, there is no entry.

If market value of a portfolio significantly declines below cost between year-end and the audit report date, subsequent event disclosure is needed.

There is interperiod income tax allocation with investments because of temporary differences. A deferred tax arises because unrealized losses and gains on securities are not recognized on the tax return.

EXAMPLE 3

On 1/1/19X1, Company X buys long-term securities of $480,000 plus brokerage commissions of $20,000. On 5/12/19X1, a cash dividend of $15,000 is received. On 12/31/19X1, the market value of the portfolio is $490,000. On 2/6/19X2 securities costing $50,000 are sold for $54,000. On 12/31/19X2, the market value of the portfolio is $447,000. The journal entries follow:

1/1/19X1

Long-term investment	500,000	
Cash		500,000

5/12/19X1

Cash	15,000	
Dividend revenue		15,000

12/31/19X1

Unrealized loss	10,000	
Allowance		10,000

The balance sheet presentation of the long-term investments is:

Long-term investments	$500,000
Less: Allowance	10,000
Net balance	$490,000

If market value were $510,000 rather than $490,000, the securities portfolio would remain at $500,000 with the market value of $510,000 disclosed:

2/2/19X2

Cash	54,000	
Long-term investments		50,000
Gain		4,000

12/31/19X2

Allowance	7,000	
Unrealized loss		7,000

The balance sheet presentation of the long-term securities is:

Long-term investments	$450,000
Less: Allowance	3,000
Net balance	$447,000

If instead market value was $435,000, the entry would have been:

Unrealized loss	5,000	
Allowance		5,000

If instead market value was $452,000, the entry would have been:

Allowance	10,000	
Unrealized loss		10,000

If two or more securities are purchased at one price, the cost is allocated among the securities based on their relative fair market value. In the exchange of one security for another, the new security received in the exchange is valued at its fair market value.

EXAMPLE 4

Preferred stock costing $10,000 is exchanged for 1,000 shares of common stock having a market value of $15,000. The entry is:

Investment in common stock	15,000	
Investment in preferred stock		10,000
Gain		5,000

There is a memo entry for a stock dividend indicating that there are more shares at no additional cost. In consequence, the cost per share decreases.

EXAMPLE 5

The company owns 50 shares at $12 per share of stock for a total cost of $600. A 20% stock dividend is declared. A memo entry reflects the additional shares as follows:

Investment

50	$12	$600
10		0
60	$10	$600

If 10 shares are later sold at $15, the entry is:

Cash	150	
Long-term investment		100
Gain		50

A stock split increases the shares and reduces the cost basis proportionately. There is a memo entry. Assume 100 shares costing $20 per share were owned. A 2 for 1 split results in 200 shares at a cost per share of $10. Total par value is still $2,000.

When is the equity method used?

If an investor owns between 20 to 50% of the voting common stock of an investee, the equity method is used. The equity method also applies if the holder owned less than 20% of the voting common stock but had significant influence (effective control). The equity method is also employed if more than 50% of the voting common stock was owned but a negating factor for consolidation existed. Further, investments in joint ventures have to be accounted for under the equity method.

How do we account under the equity method?

The accounting under the equity method can be illustrated by examining the following "T-accounts":

Investment in Investee

Cost	Dividends
Ordinary profit	Amortization expense
Extraordinary gain	on goodwill
	Depreciation on excess of fair market value less book value of specific assets
	Permanent decline

Equity in Earnings of Investee

Amortization expense	Ordinary profit
Depreciation	

Loss	
Permanent decline	

Extraordinary Gain	
	Extraordinary gain

The cost of the investment includes brokerage fees. The investor recognizes his percentage ownership interest in the ordinary profit of the investee by debiting investment in investee and crediting equity in earnings of investee. The investor's share in investee's earnings is computed after deducting cumulative preferred dividends, whether or not declared. The investor's share of investee net income should be based on the investee's most current income statement applied on a consistent basis. Extraordinary gains or losses and prior period adjustments are also recognized on the investor's books. Dividends reduce the carrying value of the investment account.

The excess paid by the investor for the investee's net assets is first assigned to the specific assets and liabilities and depreciated. The unidentifiable portion of the excess is considered goodwill which is amortized over the period benefited not exceeding 40 years. The amortization expense on goodwill and depreciation on excess value of assets reduce the investment account and are charged to equity in earnings. Temporary decline in price of the investment in the investee is ignored. Permanent decline in value of the investment is reflected by debiting loss and crediting investment in investee.

When the investor's share of the investee's losses is greater than the balance in the investment account, the equity method should be discontinued at the zero amount unless the investor has guaranteed the investee's obligations or where immediate profitability is assured. A return to the equity method is made only after offsetting subsequent profits against the losses not recorded.

When the investee's stock is sold, a realized gain or loss arises for the difference between selling price and the cost of the investment.

The mechanics of consolidation basically apply with the equity method. For example, there is an elimination of intercompany profits and losses. Investee capital transactions affecting the investor's share of equity should be accounted for as in a consolidation. For example, when the investee issues common stock to third parties at a price exceeding book value, there will be an increase in the value of the investment and a related increase in the investor's paid-in-capital.

Interperiod income tax allocation occurs because the investor recognizes the investee's earnings for book reporting but dividends for tax purposes resulting in a deferred income tax liability.

If the ownership goes below 20% or the investor for some reason is unable to control the investee, the investor should cease recognizing the investee's earnings. The equity method is discontinued but the balance in the investment account is maintained. The cost method should then be applied.

If the investor increases his ownership in the investee to 20% or more, the equity method should be used for current and future years. Further, the effect of using the equity method rather than the cost method on prior years at the old percentage (e.g., 15%) should be recognized as an adjustment to retained earnings and other accounts so affected such as investment in investee. The retroactive adjustment on the investment, earnings, and retained earnings should be applied in the same manner as a step-by-step acquisition of a subsidiary.

Disclosures should be made by the investor in footnotes, separate schedules, or parenthetically of the following: name of investee, percent owned, investor's accounting policies, significant effects of possible conversions and exercises of investee common stock, and quoted market price (for investees not qualifying as subsidiaries). Further, summarized financial data as to assets, liabilities, and earnings should be given in footnotes or separate schedules for material investments in unconsolidated subsidiaries. Material realized and unrealized gains and losses relating to the subsidiary's portfolio occurring between the dates of the financial statements of the subsidiary and parent must also be disclosed.

EXAMPLE 6

On 1/1/19X5, X Company bought 30,000 shares for a 40% interest in the common stock of AB Company at $25 per share. Brokerage commissions were $10,000. During 19X5, AB's net income was $140,000 and dividends received were $30,000. On 1/1/19X6, X Company received 15,000 shares of common stock as a result of a stock split by AB Company. On 1/4/19X6, X Company sold 2,000 shares at $16 per share of AB stock. The journal entries follow:

1/1/19X5

Investment in investee	760,000	
Cash		760,000

12/31/19X5

Investment in investee	56,000	
Equity in earnings of investee		56,000

40% × $140,000 = $56,000

Cash	30,000	
Investment in investee		30,000

1/1/19X6 Memo entry for stock split

1/4/19X6

Cash (2,000 × $16)	32,000	
Loss on sale of investment	2,940	
Investment in investee (2,000 × $17.47)		34,940

$$\frac{\$786,000}{45,000} = \$17.47 \text{ per share}$$

Investment in Investee

1/1/19X5	760,000	12/31/19X5	30,000
12/31/19X5	56,000		
	816,000		
	786,000		

EXAMPLE 7

On 1/1/19X6, investor purchased 100,000 shares of investee's 400,000 shares outstanding for $3 million. The book value of net assets acquired was $2.5 million. Of the $500,000 excess paid over book value, $300,000 is attributable to undervalued tangible assets and the remainder is attributable to unidentifiable assets. The depreciation period is 20 years and the maximum period is used to amortize goodwill. In 19X6, investee's net income was $800,000 including an extraordinary loss of $200,000. Dividends of $75,000 were paid on June 1, 19X6. The following journal entries are necessary for the acquisition of investee by investor accounted for under the equity method.

1/1/19X6

Investment in investee	3,000,000	
Cash		3,000,000

6/1/19X6

Cash	18,750	
Investment in investee		18,750

$25\% \times \$75,000$

12/31/19X6

Investment in investee	250,000	
Equity in earnings of investee		250,000

$\$1,000,000 \times 25\% = \$250,000$

Extraordinary loss from investment	50,000	
Investment in investee		50,000

$\$200,000 \times 25\% = \$50,000$

Equity in earnings of investee	20,000	
Investment in investee		20,000

Computation follows:

Undervalued depreciable assets $300,000/20 years	$15,000
Unrecorded goodwill $200,000/40 years	5,000
	$20,000

How are bond investments handled?

The provisions of FASB 12 do *not* require the write-down of debt securities from cost to market value for a *temporary change*. A company has the option, which is usually exercised, of retaining investments in debt securities (e.g., bonds) at cost. However, a *permanent* decline in the price of bonds must be recognized.

The difference between the cost of a bond and its face value is discount or premium. Discount or premium is amortized over the life of the bond from the *acquisition date*.

The bond investment account is usually recorded *net* of the discount or premium. If bonds are acquired between interest dates, accrued interest should be recorded separately.

The market price of the bond takes into account the financial health of the company, "prevailing" interest rates in the market, and the maturity date.

The market price is computed by discounting the principal and interest using the yield rate.

EXAMPLE 8

On 3/1/19X5, an investor purchases $100,000, 6%, 20-year bonds. Interest is payable on 1/1 and 6/30. The bonds are bought at face value.

3/1/19X5

Investment in bonds	100,000	
Accrued bond interest receivable	1,000	
Cash		101,000

$100,000 \times 6\% = \$6,000$ per year
$\$6,000 \times 2/12 = \$1,000$

6/30/19X5

Cash	3,000	
Accrued bond interest receivable (2 months)		1,000
Interest income (4 months)		2,000

$\$6,000 \times 6/12 = \$3,000$

12/31/19X5

Accrued bond interest receivable	3,000	
Interest income		3,000

1/1/19X6

Cash	3,000	
Accrued bond interest receivable		3,000

6/30/19X6

Cash	3,000	
Interest income		3,000

EXAMPLE 9

On 1/1/19X5, $10,000 of ABC Company 6%, 10 year bonds are bought for $12,000. Interest is payable 1/1 and 6/30. On 4/1/19X6, the bonds are sold for $11,000. There is a commission charge on the bonds of $100. Applicable journal entries follow:

1/1/19X5

Investment in bonds	12,000	
Cash		12,000

6/30/19X5

Interest income	100	
Investment in bonds		100

Amortization of premium computed as follows:

$2,000/10 years = $200 per year × 6/12 = $100

Cash	300	
Interest income		300

6% × $10,000 × 6/12 = $300

12/31/19X5

Accrued bond interest receivable	300	
Interest income		300
Interest income	100	
Investment in bonds		100

4/1/19X6

Accrued bond interest receivable	150	
Interest income		150

6% × $10,000 × 3/12 = $150

Interest income	50	
Investment in bonds		50

Amortization of premium computed as follows:

$200 per year $\times$ 3/12 = $50

Cash (11,000 + 150 − 100)	11,050	
Loss on sale of investments	850	
Investment in bonds		
(12,000 − 100 − 100 − 50)		11,750
Accrued bond interest receivable		150

LEASES

Leases are usually long-term noncancellable commitments. The lessee acquires the right to use property owned by the lessor. Although there is no legal transfer of title, many leases transfer substantially all the risks and ownership rights. A capital lease is recorded as an asset and liability by the lessee because theoretical substance governs over legal form.

A lease may be between related parties such as when a company has significant control over the operating and financial policies of another business.

The *date of inception* of a lease is the date of the lease *agreement or commitment*, if earlier. A commitment has to be in writing, signed, and provide the major terms. If substantive provisions are to be negotiated in the future, a commitment does *not* exist.

Lessee

The two ways to account for a lease by the lessee are the operating method and capital method.

What does the operating method entail?

An operating lease is a regular rental of property. As rental payments become payable, rent expense is charged and cash and/or payables credited. The lessee does not report anything on the balance sheet. Rent expense is accrued on the straight-line basis unless another method is more suitable.

What criteria must be met for there to be a capital lease?

The lessee uses the capital lease method if any *one* of the following four conditions are satisfied:

1. The lessee obtains ownership to the property at the end of the lease term.
2. A bargain purchase option exists where either the lessee can buy the property at a nominal amount or renew the lease at minimal rental payments.
3. The life of the lease is 75% or more of the life of the property.
4. The discounted value of minimum lease payments at the inception of the lease equals or exceeds 90% of the fair market value of the property. Minimum lease payments exclude executory costs to be paid by the lessee to reimburse the lessor for its costs of maintenance, insurance, and property taxes.

If criteria 1 or 2 are met, the depreciation period is the life of the property. Otherwise, the depreciation period is the life of the lease.

The 3rd and 4th criteria do not apply when the beginning of the lease term falls within the last 25% of the total economic life of the property.

The asset and liability are recorded at the present value of the minimum lease payments plus the present value of the bargain purchase option. The lessee is expected to pay the nominal purchase price. If the present value of the minimum lease payments plus the bargain purchase option exceeds the fair value of the leased property at the time of lease inception, the asset should be capitalized at the fair market value of the property. The lessee's discount rate is the *lower* of the lessee's incremental borrowing rate (the rate the lessee would have to borrow at to be able to buy the asset) or the lessor's implicit interest rate. The lessor's implicit interest rate is the one implicit in the recovery of the fair value of the property at lease inception through the present value of minimum lease payments including the lessee's guarantee of salvage value. The liability is divided between current and noncurrent.

The lessee's minimum lease payments (MLP) usually includes MLP over the lease term plus any guaranteed salvage value. The guarantee is the determinable amount for which the lessor has the right to require the lessee to buy the property at the lease termination. It is the stated amount when the lessee agrees to satisfy any dollar deficiency below a stated amount in the lessor's realization of the residual value. MLP also includes any payment lessee must pay due to failure to extend or renew the lease at expiration. If there exists a bargain purchase option, MLP includes *only* MLP over the lease term and exercise option payment. MLP does *not* include contingent rentals, lessee's guarantee of lessor's debt, and lessee's obligation for executory costs.

Each minimum lease payment is allocated as a reduction of principal (debiting the liability) and as interest (debiting interest expense). The interest method is used to result in a constant periodic rate of interest. Interest expense equals the interest rate times the carrying value of the liability at the beginning of the year.

The balance sheet shows the "Asset Under Lease" less "Accumulated Depreciation." The income statement shows interest expense and depreciation expense. In the first year, the expenses under a capital lease (interest expense and depreciation) are greater than the expenses under an operating lease (rent expense).

According to Interpretation 26, when a lessee buys a leased asset during the lease term which has been originally capitalized, the transaction is considered an *extension* of a capital lease not a termination. Thus, the difference between the purchase price and the carrying value of the lease obligation is an *adjustment* of the book value of the asset. There is *no loss recognition* when a capital lease is extended.

EXAMPLE 10

On 1/1/19X1, the lessee enters into a capital lease for property. The minimum rental payment is $20,000 a year for 6 years to be made at the end of the year. The interest rate is 5%. The present value of an ordinary annuity factor for n = 6, i = 5% is 5.0757. The journal entries for the first two years follow:

1/1/19X1		
Asset	101,514	
Liability		101,514
12/31/19X1		
Interest expense	5,076	
Liability	14,924	
Cash		20,000

$5\% \times \$101,514 = \$5,076$

Depreciation	16,919	
Accumulated depreciation		16,919

$\dfrac{\$101,514}{6} = \$16,919$

The liability as of 12/31/19X1 appears below:

Liability

12/31/19X1	14,924	1/1/19X1	101,514
		12/31/19X1	86,590

12/31/19X2		
Interest expense	4,330	
Liability	15,670	
Cash		20,000

$5\% \times \$86,590 = \$4,330$

Depreciation	16,919	
Accumulated depreciation		16,919

The footnote disclosures under a capital lease are:

- Description of leasing arrangement including purchase options, escalation clause, renewal terms, and restrictions.
- Assets under lease by category.
- Future minimum lease payments in total and for each of the next five years.
- Total future sublease rentals.
- Contingent rentals (rentals based on other than time such as based on profit).

Lessor

The lessor may account for leases under the operating, direct-financing, and sales-type methods.

How does the lessor account under the operating method?

The operating method is a regular rental by the lessor. An example is Hertz renting cars. The income statement shows rental revenue less related expenses. The balance sheet presents the asset under lease less accumulated depreciation to obtain book value.

Rental income is recognized as earned using the *straight-line* basis over the lease term except if there is another preferable method. *Initial direct costs* are deferred and amortized over the lease term on a pro rata basis based on rental income recognized. However, if immaterial relative to the allocation amount, the initial direct costs may be expensed.

EXAMPLE 11

Hall Corporation produced machinery costing $5 million which it held for resale from January 1, 19X1 to June 30, 19X1, at a price to Travis Company under an operating lease. The lease is for four years with equal monthly payments of $85,000 due on the first of the month. The initial payment was made on July 1, 19X1. The depreciation period is 10 years with no salvage value.

Lessee's rental expense for 19X1:

$85,000 × 6	$510,000

Lessor's income before taxes for 19X1:

Rental income	$510,000
Less: Depreciation $\dfrac{\$5,000,000}{10} \times \dfrac{6}{12}$	250,000
Income before taxes	$260,000

What is the accounting and financial statement reporting under the direct financing method?

The direct financing method satisfies 1 of the 4 conditions for a capital lease by the lessee plus both of the following two requirements for the lessor:

- Collectibility of lease payments is assured.
- No important uncertainties surround future costs to be incurred.

The lessor is *not* a manufacturer or dealer. The lessor acquires the property for the sole purpose of leasing it out. An example is a bank leasing computers. The carrying value and fair value of the leased property are the same at the inception of the lease.

The lessor uses as the discount rate the interest rate implicit in the lease.

Interest income is only recognized in the financial statements over the life of the lease using the interest method. Unearned interest income is amortized as income over the lease term to result in a constant rate of interest. Interest revenue equals the interest rate times the carrying value of the receivable at the beginning of the year.

Contingent rentals are recognized in earnings as earned.

The lessor's MLP includes the (1) MLP made by the lessee (net of any executory costs together with any profit thereon) and (2) any guarantee of the salvage value of the leased property, or of rental payments after the lease term, made by a third party unrelated to either party in the lease provided the third party is financially able to satisfy the commitment. A guarantee by a third party related to the lessor makes the residual value unguaranteed. A guarantee by a third party related to the lessee infers a guaranteed residual value by the lessee.

A modification of lease provisions, that would have resulted in a different classification had they occurred at the beginning of the lease, require that the lease be treated as a new agreement and classified under the new terms. However, exercise of existing renewal options are not considered lease changes. A change in estimate does not result in a new lease.

A provision for escalation of the MLP during a construction or preacquisition period may exist. The resulting increase in MLP is considered in determining the fair value of the leased property at the lease inception. There may also exist a salvage value increase that takes place from an escalation clause.

Initial direct costs are incurred by the lessor to negotiate and consummate a *completed* lease transaction including commissions, legal fees, credit investigation, document preparation and processing, and the relevant percentage of salespersons' and other employees' compensation. It does *not* include costs for leases *not consummated* nor administrative, supervisory, or other indirect expenses. Initial direct costs of the lease are expensed as incurred. A portion of the unearned income equal to the initial direct costs should be recognized as income in the same accounting period.

If the contract includes a penalty for nonrenewal or becomes inoperative because of a time extension, the unearned interest income account must be adjusted for the difference between the present values of the old and revised agreements. The present value of the future minimum lease payments under the new arrangement should be computed using the original rate for the initial lease.

Lease termination is accounted for by the lessor through eliminating the net investment, recording the leased property at the lower of cost or fair value, and the net adjustment is charged against earnings.

The lessor reports on his balance sheet as the gross investment in the lease the total minimum lease payments plus salvage value of the property accruing to the lessor. This represents lease payments receivable. Deducted from lease payments receivable is unearned interest revenue. The balance sheet presentation follows:

Lease payments receivable (Principal + Interest)
Less: Unearned interest revenue (Interest)
Net receivable balance (Principal)
The income statement shows:
Interest revenue
Less: Initial direct costs
Less: Executory costs
Net income

Footnote disclosure includes assets leased by type, future lease payments in total and for each of the next five years, contingent rentals, and lease provisions.

How do we account for and present the sales-type method?

The sales-type method must satisfy the same criteria as the direct financing method. The only difference is that the sales-type method involves a lessor who is a manufacturer or dealer in the leased item. Thus, a manufacturer or dealer profit results. Although legally there is no sale of the item, theoretical substance governs over legal form and a sale is assumed to have taken place. *Note:* The distinction between a sales-type lease and a direct financing lease affects only the lessor; as to lessee, either type would be a capital lease.

If there is a renewal or extension of an existing sales-type or financing lease, it shall *not* be classified as a sales-type lease. There is an *exception* which may exist when the renewal occurs toward the end of the lease term.

In a sales-type lease, profit on the assumed sale of the item is recognized in the year of lease as well as interest income over the life of the lease. The cost and fair value of the leased property are different at the inception of the lease.

An annual appraisal should be made of the salvage value and where necessary reduce the net investment and recognize a loss but do not adjust the salvage value.

The cost of the leased property is matched against the selling price in determining the assumed profit in the year of lease. Initial direct costs of the lease are expensed.

Except for the initial entry to record the lease, the entries are the same for the direct financing and sales-type methods.

EXAMPLE 12

Assume the same facts as in the capital lease example. The accounting by the lessor assuming a direct financing lease and a sales-type lease follow:

Direct Financing

1/1/19X1

Receivable	120,000	
Asset		101,514
Unearned interest revenue		18,486

Sales-Type

Receivable	120,000	
Cost of sales	85,000	
Inventory		85,000
Sales		101,514
Unearned interest revenue		18,486

Direct Financing

12/31/19X1

Cash	20,000	
Receivable		20,000
Unearned interest revenue	5,076	
Interest revenue		5,076

12/31/19X2

Cash	20,000	
Receivable		20,000

| Unearned interest revenue | 4,330 | |
| Interest revenue | | 4,330 |

Sales-Type
Same entries as Direct Financing.

The income statement for 19X1 presents:

Direct Financing

Interest revenue	$5,076

Sales-Type

Sales	$101,514
Less: Cost of sales	85,000
Gross profit	$ 16,514
Interest revenue	5,076

EXAMPLE 13

On October 1, 19X1, Jones leased equipment to Tape Company. It is a capital lease to the lessee and a sales-type lease to the lessor. The lease is for eight years with equal annual payments of $500,000 due on October 1 each period. The first payment was made on October 1, 19X1. The cost of the equipment to Tape Company is $2,500,000. The equipment has a life of 10 years with no salvage value. The interest rate is 10%.

Tape reports the following in its income statement for 19X1:

Asset cost ($500,000 × 5.868 = $2,934,000)

Depreciation $\dfrac{\$2,934,000}{10} \times \dfrac{3}{12}$		$73,350
Interest expense:		
Present value of lease payments	$2,934,000	
Less: Initial payment	500,000	
Balance	$2,434,000	
Interest expense		
$2,434,000 × 10% × $\dfrac{3}{12}$		60,850
Total expenses		$134,200

Jones' income before tax is:

Interest revenue		$60,850
Gross profit on assumed sale of property:		
Selling price	$2,934,000	
Less: Cost	2,500,000	
Gross Profit		434,000
Income before tax		$494,850

How do we treat a sales-leaseback?

A sales-leaseback is when the lessor sells the property and then leases it back. The lessor may do this when he needs money.

The profit or loss on the sale is deferred and amortized as an adjustment on a proportionate basis to depreciation expense in the case of a capital lease or in proportion to rental expense in the case of an operating lease. However, if the fair value of the property at the time of the sales-leaseback is below its book value, a loss is immediately recognized for the difference between book value and fair value.

EXAMPLE 14

The deferred profit on a sales-leaseback is $50,000. An operating lease is involved where rental expense in the current year is $10,000 and total rental expense is $150,000. Rental expense is adjusted as follows:

Rental expense	$10,000
Less: Amortization of deferred gross profit	
$50,000 \times \dfrac{\$10,000}{\$150,000}$	3,333
	$ 6,667

What if there is a sublease?

There are three types of transactions. In a *sublease,* the original lessee leases the property to a third party. The lease agreement of the original parties remains intact. Another possibility is where a new lessee is substituted under the original agreement. The original lessee may still be secondarily liable. Finally, the new lessee is substituted in a new agreement. There is a cancellation of the original lease.

The original lessor continues his present accounting method if the original lessee subleases or sells to a third party. If the original lease is replaced by a new agreement with a new lessee, the lessor terminates the initial lease and accounts for the new one in a separate transaction.

In accounting by the original lessee, if the lessee is relieved of primary obligation by a transaction other than a sublease, terminate the original lease:

• If original lease was a capital lease remove the asset and liability, recognize a gain or loss for the difference including any additional consideration paid or received, and accrue a loss contingency where secondary liability exists.

• If the original lease was an operating one and the initial lessee is secondarily liable, recognize a loss contingency accrual.

If the original lessee is not relieved of *primary* obligation under a sublease, the original lessee (now sublessor) accounts in the following manner:

• If original lease met lessee criteria 1 or 2, classify the new lease per normal classification criteria by lessor. If sublease is sales-type or direct financing lease, the unamortized asset balance becomes the cost of the leased property. Otherwise, it is an operating lease. Continue to account for the original lease obligation as before.

• If original lease met only lessee criteria 3 or 4, classify the new lease using lessee criteria 3 and lessor criteria 1 and 2. Classify as a direct financing lease. The unamortized balance of the asset becomes the cost of the leased property. Otherwise, it is an operating lease. Continue to account for original lease obligation as before.

If the original lease was an *operating lease,* account for old and new leases as operating leases.

What is the accounting under a leveraged lease?

A leveraged lease occurs when the lessor (equity participant) finances a small part of the acquisition (retaining total equity ownership) while a third party (debt participant) finances the balance. The lessor maximizes his leveraged return by recognizing lease revenue and income tax shelter (e.g., interest deduction, rapid depreciation).

A leveraged lease meets *all* of the following:

• It satisfies the tests for a direct financing lease. Sales-type leases are not leveraged leases.

• It involves at least three parties: lessee, long-term creditor (debt participant) and lessor (equity participant).

• The long-term creditor provides nonrecourse financing as to the general credit of the lessor. The financing is adequate to give the lessor significant leverage.

• The lessor's net investment (see below) decreases during the initial lease years, then increases in the subsequent years just before its liquidation by sale. These increases and decreases in the net investment balance may take place more than once during the lease life.

The lessee classifies and accounts for leveraged leases in the same way as non-leveraged leases.

The lessor records *investment in the leveraged lease net* of the nonrecourse debt. The net of the following balances represent the initial and continuing investment: rentals receivable (net of the amount applicable to principal and interest on the nonrecourse debt), estimated residual value, and unearned and deferred income. The initial entry to record the leveraged lease is:

Lease receivable
Residual value of asset
   Cash investment in asset
   Unearned income

The lessor's *net investment in the leveraged lease* for computing net income is the *investment in the leveraged lease less* deferred income taxes. *Periodic net income* is determined in the following manner using the *net investment in the leveraged* lease:

• Determine annual cash flow equal to the following:

> Gross lease rental (plus residual value of asset in last year of lease term)
> Less: Loan interest payments
> Less: Income tax charges (or add income tax credits)
> *Less: Loan principal payments*
> Annual cash flow

• Determine the return rate on the *net investment in the leveraged lease.* The rate of return is the one when applied to the *net investment* in the years when it is positive will distribute the net income (cash flow) to those positive years. The *net investment* will be positive (but declining rapidly due to accelerated depreciation and interest expense) in early years; it will be negative during the middle years; and it will again be positive in the later years (because of the declining tax shelter).

PENSION PLANS

The company must conform to FASB and governmental rules on the accounting and reporting for its pension plan. FASB 87 requires the accrual of pension expense based on services rendered. The pension plan relationship between the employer, trustee, and employee is shown in Figure 7–1.

What are the two kinds of pension arrangements?

The two types of pension plans are:

Defined Contribution. The employer's annual contribution is specified rather than the benefits to be paid.

Defined Benefit. The determinable pension benefit to be received by participants upon

FIGURE 7-1 PENSION PLAN RELATIONSHIP

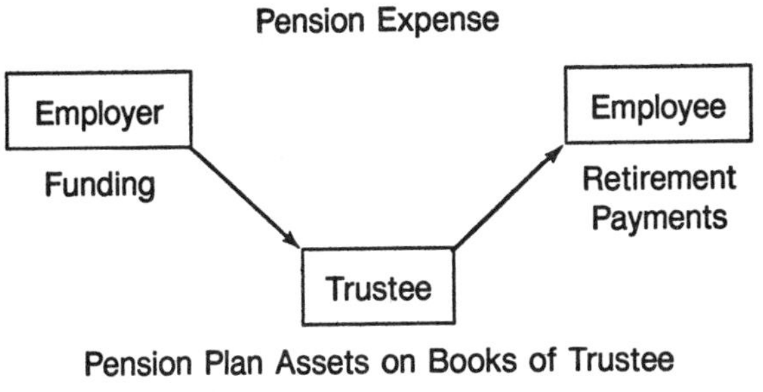

Pension Expense

Pension Plan Assets on Books of Trustee

retirement is specified. In determining amounts, consider such factors as salary, service years, and age. The employer makes contributions so that adequate funds are accumulated to pay benefits when due. Typically, there is an annuity of payments. Pension cost for administrative staff is expensed while pension cost for factory personnel is inventoriable.

What are some important pension plan terms?

The following pension plan terminology should be understood:

Actuarial Assumptions. Actuaries make assumptions as to variables in determining pension expense and related funding. Examples of estimates are employee turnover, mortality rate, return rates, and compensation.

Actuarial Cost (Funding) Method. The method actuaries use to compute the employer contribution to assure adequate funds will be available when employees retire. The method used determines the pension expense and related liability.

Actuarial Present Value of Accumulated Plan Benefits. The discounted amount of money required to meet retirement obligations for active and retired employees.

Benefit Information Date. The date the actuarial present value of accumulated benefits is presented.

Vested Benefits. The employee vests when he or she has accumulated pension rights to receive benefits upon retirement. The employee no longer has to be with the company to receive pension payments.

Projected Benefit Obligation. The projected benefit obligation is the year-end pension obligation based on *future* salaries. It is the actuarial present value of vested and nonvested benefits for services performed before a particular actuarial valuation date based on expected *future* salaries.

Accumulated Benefit Obligation. The accumulated benefit obligation is the year-end obligation based on *current* salaries. It is the actuarial present value of benefits (vested and nonvested) applicable to the pension plan based on services rendered prior to a given date based on *current* salaries.

The accumulated and projected benefit obligation figures will be the same in the case of plans having flat-benefit or nonpay-related pension benefit formulas.

Net Assets Available for Pension Benefits. Net assets represents plan assets less plan liabilities. The plan's liabilities exclude participants' accumulated benefits.

What are the accounting and disclosures for a defined contribution pension plan?

Pension expense equals the employer's cash contribution for the period. There is no deferred charge or deferred credit. If the defined contribution plan specifies contributions are to be made for years after an employee's performance of services (e.g., after retirement), there should be an accrual of costs during the employee's service period.

Footnote disclosure includes cost recognized for the period, basis of determining contributions, and description of plan including employee groups covered.

What are the elements of pension expense?

The components of pension expense in a defined benefit pension plan are:

- Service cost.
- Amortization expense of prior service cost.
- Return on plan assets.
- Interest on projected benefit obligation.
- Amortization of actuarial gain or loss.

Service cost is based on the present value of future payments under the benefit formula for employee services of the current period. It is recognized in full in the current year. The calculation involves actuarial assumptions.

Prior service cost is the pension expense for services performed before the adoption or amendment of a pension plan. The cost of the retroactive benefits is the increase in the projected benefit obligation at the date of amendment. It involves the allocation of amounts of cost to future service years. Prior service cost determination involves actuarial considerations. The total pension cost is *not* booked but rather there are periodic charges based on actuarial determinations. Amortization is achieved by assigning an equal amount to each service year of active employees at the amendment date who are anticipated to receive plan benefits. The amortization of prior service cost takes into consideration future service years, period employees will receive benefits, change in the projected benefit obligation, and decrement in employees receiving benefits each year.

EXAMPLE 15

X Company changes its pension formula from 2 to 5% of the last three years of pay multiplied by the service years on January 1, 19X1. This results in the projected benefit obligation being increased by $500,000. Employees are anticipated to receive benefits over the next 10 years.

$$\text{Total future service years} = \frac{n\,(n+1)}{2} \times P$$

Where n is the number of years services are to be made and P is the population decrement each year.

$$\frac{10\,(10+1)}{2} \times 9 = 495$$

Amortization
of prior service $= \$500,000 \times \dfrac{10 \times 9}{495} = \$90,909$
cost in 19X1

The return on plan assets (e.g., stocks, bonds) reduces pension expense. Plan assets are valued at the moving average of asset values for the accounting period.

Interest is on the projected benefit obligation at the beginning of the year. The settlement rate is employed representing the rate that pension benefits could be settled for.

$$\text{Interest} = \text{Interest rate} \times \begin{array}{c}\text{Projected benefit} \\ \text{obligation at} \\ \text{the beginning} \\ \text{of the year}\end{array}$$

Actuarial gains and losses are the difference between estimates and actual experience. For example, if the assumed interest rate is 11% and the actual interest rate is 14%, an actuarial gain results. There may also be a change in actuarial assumptions regarding the future. Actuarial gains and losses are deferred and amortized as an adjustment to pension expense over future years. Actuarial gains and losses related to a single event *not* related to the pension plan and not in the ordinary course of business are immediately recognized in the current year's income statement. Examples are plant closing and segment disposal.

How does a deferred pension asset or deferred pension liability arise?

Pension expense will not typically equal the employer's cash funding. Pension expense is usually based on the unit credit method. Under this approach, pension expense and related liability depends on estimating future salaries for total benefits to be paid.

> If Pension expense > Cash paid
> = Deferred pension liability (Credit)

> If Pension expense < Cash paid
> = Deferred pension asset (Charge)

Interest on the deferred pension liability reduces future pension expense. Conversely, interest on the deferred pension asset increases pension expense.

How does the minimum pension liability arise and how is it accounted for?

A minimum pension liability must be recognized when the accumulated benefit obligation exceeds the fair value of pension plan assets. However, no minimum pension asset is recognized because it violates conservatism. When there is an accrued pension liability, an additional liability is booked up to the minimum pension liability.

When an additional liability is recorded, the debit is to an intangible asset under the pension plan. However, the intangible asset cannot exceed the unamortized prior service cost. If it does, the excess is reported as a separate component of stockholders' equity shown net of tax. While these items may be adjusted periodically, they are not amortized.

EXAMPLE 16

Accumulated benefit obligation	$500,000
Less: Fair value of pension plan assets	200,000
Minimum pension liability	$300,000
Less: Accrued pension liability	120,000
Additional liability	$180,000

If instead of an accrued pension liability, there was an accrued pension asset of $120,000, the additional liability would be $420,000.

Assume unamortized prior service cost is $100,000. The entry is:

Intangible asset under pension plan	100,000	
Stockholders' equity	80,000	
Additional liability		180,000

EXAMPLE 17

Mr. A has 6 years before retirement. The estimated salary at retirement is $50,000. The pension benefit is 3% of final salary for each service year payable at retirement. The retirement benefit is computed below:

Final annual salary	$50,000
Formula rate	× 3%
	$ 1,500
Years of service	× 6
Retirement benefit	$ 9,000

EXAMPLE 18

On 1/1/19X1, a company adopts a defined benefit pension plan. The return and interest rate are both 10%. Service cost for 19X1 and 19X2 are $100,000 and $120,000, respectively. The funding amounts for 19X1 and 19X2 are $80,000 and $110,000, respectively.

The entry for 19X1 is:

Pension expense	100,000	
Cash		80,000
Pension liability		20,000

The entry in 19X2 is:

Pension expense	122,000	
Cash		110,000
Pension liability		12,000

Computation:

Service cost	$120,000
Interest on projected benefit obligation 10% × $100,000	10,000
Return on plan assets 10% × $80,000	(8,000)
	$122,000

At 12/31/19X2:

Projected benefit obligation = $230,000
($100,000 + $120,000 + $10,000).

Pension plan assets = $198,000
($80,000 + $110,000 + $8,000).

EXAMPLE 19

Company X has a defined benefit pension plan for its 100 employees. On 1/1/19X1, pension plan assets have a fair value of $230,000, accumulated benefit obligation is $285,000, and the projected benefit obligation is $420,000. Ten employees are expected to resign each year for the next 10 years. They will be eligible to receive benefits. Service cost for 19X1 is $40,000. On 12/31/19X1, the projected benefit obligation is $490,000, fair value of plan assets is $265,000, and accumulated benefit obligation is $340,000. The expected return on plan assets and the interest rate are both 8%. No actuarial gains or losses occurred during the year. Cash funded for the year is $75,000.

Pension expense equals:

Service cost	$40,000
Interest on projected benefit obligation 8% × $420,000	33,600
Expected return on plan assets 8% × $230,000	(18,400)
Amortization of actuarial gains and losses	—
Amortization of unrecognized transition amount	34,545*
Pension expense	$89,745

Projected benefit obligation	$420,000
Fair value of pension plan assets	230,000
Initial net obligation	$190,000

Amortization $\dfrac{\$190,000}{5.5 \text{ years}} = \$34,545$

$\dfrac{n\,(n+1)}{2} \times P = \dfrac{10\,(10+1)}{2} \times 10 = 550$

$\dfrac{550}{100} = 5.5$ years (average remaining service period)

The journal entries at 12/31/19X1 follow:

Pension expense	89,745	
Cash		75,000
Deferred pension liability		14,745
Intangible asset—Pension plan	60,255	
Additional pension liability		60,255
Computation follows:		
Accumulated benefit obligation—12/31/19X1		$340,000
Fair value of plan assets—12/31/19X1		265,000
Minimum liability		$75,000
Deferred pension liability		14,745
Additional pension liability		$60,255

What disclosures should be made?

Footnote disclosures for a pension plan follow:

- Description of the plan including employee groups covered, benefit formula, funding policy, and retirement age.
- Pension assumptions (e.g., employee turnover, interest rate, mortality rate).
- Components of pension expense.
- Reconciling funded status of plan with employer amounts recognized on the balance sheet including fair value of plan assets, projected benefit obligation, and unamortized prior service cost.
- Weighted-average discount rate used to measure the projected benefit obligation.
- Weighted-average return rate on pension plan assets.
- Present value of vested and nonvested benefits.
- Amounts and types of securities held in pension assets.
- Approximate annuity benefits to employees.

What if part of the employer's pension obligation is relieved?

According to FASB 88, a settlement is discharging some or all of the employer's pension benefit obligation. Excess plan assets revert back to the employer. A settlement must meet *all* of the following conditions:

- Relieves pension benefit responsibility.
- Substantially reduces risk of the pension obligation.
- Irrevocable.

The amount of gain or loss when a pension obligation is settled is limited to the unrecognized net gain or loss from realized or unrealized changes in either the pension benefit obligation or plan assets arising from the difference between actual experience and assumptions. All or a proportion of the unrecognized gain or loss is recognized when a plan is settled. If there is a full settlement, all unrecognized gains or losses are recognized. If only a part of the plan is settled, a pro rata share of the unrecognized net gain or loss is recognized.

An example of a settlement is when the employer pays employees a lump sum to waive their pension rights. The gain or loss is included in the current year's income statement.

What if employee services in the future are to be reduced?

According to FASB 88, there is a curtailment when an event materially reduces future service years of current employees or eliminates for most employees the accumulation of defined benefits for future services. An example is a plant closing terminating employee services before pension plan expectations. The gain or loss is recognized in the current year's income statement and includes the following elements:

- Unamortized prior service cost for employee services no longer required.
- Change in pension benefit obligation because of the curtailment.

What if there is early retirement?

When termination benefits are offered by the employer, accepted by employees, and the amount can reasonably be determined, an expense and liability are recorded. The amount of the accrual equals the down payment plus the discontinued value of future employer payments. The entry is to debit loss and credit cash (down payment) and liability (future payments). The terms of the arrangement should be disclosed.

POST RETIREMENT BENEFITS EXCLUDING PENSIONS _____

FASB No. 106 titled "Employers' Accounting For Postretirement Benefits Other Than Pensions" is effective for fiscal years beginning after December 15, 1992. Although the pronouncement deals with all types of postretirement benefits, it *concentrates* on postretirement health care benefits. However, brief references are made to long-term care, tuition assistance, legal advisory services, and housing subsidies.

How are postretirement benefits accounted for?

The pronouncement drastically changes the prevalent current practice of accounting for postretirement benefits on the pay-as-you-go (cash) basis by requiring *accrual* of the expected cost of postretirement benefits during the years in which active employee services are rendered. These expected postretirement benefits may be paid to employees, employees' beneficiaries, and covered dependents.

Companies must also charge-off the cost of benefits earned previously, either all at one time or in installments over a period of up to twenty years. For example, in 1990, the Aluminum Company of America deducted about $1 billion from its earnings because of this immediate charge-off. In 1990, International Business Machines charged off $2.3 billion against earnings to pay for retirement costs of current employees.

The employer's obligation for postretirement benefits expected to be provided must be *fully accrued* by the date that the employee attains full eligibility for all of the benefits expected to be received (the full eligibility date), even if the employee is expected to perform additional services beyond that date.

The beginning of the accrual (attribution) period is the *date of employment* unless the plan only grants credit for service from a later date, in which instance benefits are generally attributed from the beginning of that credited service period. An equal amount of the anticipated postretirement benefit is attributed to each year of service unless the plan provides a disproportionate share of the expected benefits to early years of service.

The pronouncement requires a single measurement approach to spread costs from the date of hire to the date the employee is *fully* eligible to receive benefits. If information on gross charges is not available, there is a measurement approach based on net claims cost (e.g., gross changes less deductibles, copayments, Medicare). There is a projection of future retiree health care costs based on a health care cost trend assumption to current costs.

The transition obligation is the unfunded and unrecognized accumulated postretirement benefit obligation for all plan participants. There are two acceptable methods of recognizing the transition obligation. An employer may *immediately recognize* the transition obligation as the effect of an accounting change, subject to certain limits. Alternatively, the employer may recognize the transition obligation on a delayed basis over future years of service, with disclosure of the unrecognized amount. However, this delayed recognition cannot result in less rapid recognition than using the cash basis for the transition obligation. The *amortization* of the transition obligation to expense would be over the *greater of the average remaining service period of active plan participants or 20 years*.

The *expected postretirement benefit obligation* is the *actuarial present value* as of a given date of the *postretirement benefits expected to be paid* to the employees, their beneficiaries, or covered dependents.

What are the elements of postretirement benefit expense?

Net periodic postretirement benefit cost is comprised of the following components:

• *Service cost.* Actuarial present value of benefits applicable to services performed during the *current year.*

• *Interest cost.* Interest on the accumulated postretirement benefit obligation at the beginning of the period.

• *Actual return on plan assets.* Return based on the fair value of plan assets at the beginning and end of the period, adjusted for contributions and benefit payments.

• *Amortization expense on prior service cost.* Expense provision for the current year due to amortization of the prior service cost arising from adoption or amendment to the plan. Prior service cost applies to credited services *before* adoption or amendment, and is accounted for over current and future years.

• *Amortization of the transition obligation or transition assets.* Applies to the effect of switching from the pay-as-you-go basis to the accrual basis of accounting for postretirement benefits.

• *Gain or loss component.* Gains and losses apply to changes in the amount of either the accumulated postretirement benefit obligation or plan assets resulting from actual experience being different from the actuarial assumptions. Gains and losses may be realized (i.e., sale of securities) or unrealized.

What disclosures are necessary?

Footnote disclosure includes:

• A description of the postretirement plan including employee groups covered, type of benefits provided, funding policy, types of assets held and liabilities assumed.

• The components of net periodic postretirement cost.

• The fair value of plan assets.

• Accumulated postretirement benefit obligation showing separately the amount applicable to retirees, other fully eligible participants, and other active plan participants.

• Unamortized prior service cost.

• Unrecognized net gain or loss.

• Unrecognized transition obligation or transition asset.

• The amount of net postretirement benefit asset or liability recognized in the balance sheet.

• The assumed health care cost trends used to measure the expected postretirement benefit cost for the next year.

• The discount rate used to determine the accumulated postretirement benefit obligation.

• The return rate used on the fair value of plan assets.

• The cost of providing termination benefits recognized during the period.

Individual deferred compensation contracts must be fully *accrued* by the date the employee is fully eligible to receive benefits. (For further information, see J. Siegel, *The Sourcebook on Postretirement Health Care Benefits,* 1990 Supplement, Panel Publishers, pp. 165–184.)

INCOME TAX ALLOCATION _____

How do you account for the differences between book income and taxable income?

FASB No. 96 requires that income taxes be accounted for using the *liability method.* Tax allocation applies to *temporary differences* not permanent ones.

The deferred tax liability or asset is measured at the tax rate under *current* law which will apply when the temporary difference reverses. Further, the deferred tax liability or asset must be adjusted for tax law changes.

Comprehensive deferred tax accounting is followed where tax expense equals taxes payable plus the tax effects of all temporary differences.

Income taxes is accounted for on the *accrual basis* providing for *matching* of tax expense to income before tax.

Interperiod tax allocation recognizes current (or deferred) tax liability or asset for the current (or deferred) tax effect of transactions that have occurred at year-end. Tax effects of *future* events should be recognized in the year they occur. It is incorrect to anticipate them for recognizing a deferred tax liability or asset in the current year.

What are the examples of temporary differences?

Temporary differences are the differences between the years in which transactions affect taxable income and book income. They originate in one year and reverse in another. Temporary differences arise from the following four types of transactions:

1. Income included in taxable income after being recognized in accounting income (e.g., installment sales).

2. Expenses deducted for taxable income after being recognized for accounting income (e.g., bad debts, warranties).

3. Income included in taxable income before being recognized in accounting income (e.g., revenue received in advance such as a retainer).

4. Expenses deducted for taxable income before being recognized for accounting income (e.g., accelerated depreciation).

If tax rates are graduated based on taxable income, aggregate calculations may be made using an estimated average rate.

What effect do permanent differences have?

Permanent differences do not reverse (turn around), and therefore do not require tax allocation. Examples of nontaxdeductible expenses are goodwill amortization, premiums on officers' life insurance, fines, and penalties. An example of income that is not taxable is interest on municipal bonds.

How are deferred taxes reported?

In the balance sheet, deferred tax charges and credits are offset and shown (a) net current and (b) net noncurrent. However, offset is not allowed for deferred tax liabilities or assets of different tax jurisdictions.

Deferred taxes are classified as current or noncurrent based on the expected reversal dates of the temporary differences. Temporary differences reversing within one year are current while those reversing in more than one year are noncurrent.

In the income statement, disclosure is made of (a) income tax expense currently payable (the liability) and (b) the *deferred portion* of the expense (this is the portion of the expense based on temporary differences). (The total expense provision is based on financial reporting income excluding permanent differences.)

The presentation of these two expense portions (with numbers and a 40% tax rate assumed) are as follows:

Income before income taxes		$200
Income tax expense:		
Amount currently payable	$400	
Deferred portion	(320)	80
Net income		$120

What is intraperiod tax allocation?

Intraperiod tax allocation is when tax expense is shown in different parts of the financial statements for the current year. The income statement shows the tax allocated to (a) income from continuing operations, (b) income from discontinued operations, (c) extraordinary items, and (d) cumulative effect of a change in accounting principle. In the retained earnings statement, prior period adjustments are shown net of tax.

What can be done for current year losses for tax purposes?

The tax effects of net operating *loss carry-backs* should be allocated to the loss year. The company may carryback a net operating loss three years and receive a refund for taxes paid in those years. The loss is first applied to the earliest year. Any remaining loss is carried forward up to fifteen years.

The presentation of a *loss carryback* with recognition of refund during the loss year is as follows:

Loss before refundable income taxes	$1,000
Refund of prior years' income taxes arising from carryback of operating loss	485
Net loss	$515

(*Note:* The refund should be computed at the amount actually refundable regardless of current tax rates.)

The tax effects of net operating *loss carryforwards* and tax credits (e.g., alternative minimum tax credit) generally cannot be recognized until the year realized (the year in which the tax liability is reduced). A journal entry usually *cannot* be made in the loss year for any possible tax benefits because of the uncertainty of future profitability. There is recognition only in the year realized.

When the tax benefit of a loss carryforward is recognized when realized in a later year, it is classified in the same way as the income enabling recognition (typically reducing tax expense).

Presentation of the loss carryforward with recognition of benefit in year realized (numbers and 50% rate assumed):

Income before income taxes		$1,000
Income tax expense:		
Without carryforward	$500	
Reduction of income taxes arising from carryforward of prior years' operating losses	(300)	200
Net income		$800

There is an exception to the general rule of not allowing the recognition of a net operating loss carryforward in the current year. The net operating loss carryforward may be recognized up to the deferred tax liability balance.

The amounts and expiration dates of operating loss carryforwards should be footnoted.

Deferred Tax Liability vs. Deferred Tax Asset

If book income exceeds taxable income, tax expense exceeds tax payable so a deferred tax liability results. If book income is less than taxable income, tax expense is less than tax payable so a deferred tax asset results.

How do we account for a deferred tax liability?

EXAMPLE 20

Assume book income and taxable income are $1,000. Depreciation for book purposes is $50 based on the straight line method and $100 for tax purposes based on the accelerated cost recovery system. Assuming a tax rate of 34%, the entry is:

Income tax expense (950 × 34%)	323	
Income tax payable (900 × 34%)		306
Deferred tax liability		17

At the end of the life of the asset, the deferred tax liability of $17 will be completely reversed.

EXAMPLE 21*

At the end of year 1, future recovery of the reported amount of an enterprise's installment receivables will result in taxable amounts totaling $240,000 in years 2 to 4. Also, a $20,000 liability for estimated expenses has been recognized in

---

*Source: Financial Accounting Standards Board, FASB No. 96, "Accounting for Income Taxes," Stamford, Connecticut, December 1987, p. 32.

the financial statements in year 1, and those expenses will be deductible for tax purposes in year 4 when the liability is expected to be paid. Those temporary differences are estimated to result in net taxable amounts in future years as presented below.

	Year 2	Year 3	Year 4
Taxable amounts	$70,000	$110,000	$60,000
Deductible amount	—	—	(20,000)
Net taxable amounts	$70,000	$110,000	$40,000

This example assumes that the enacted tax rates for years 2 to 4 are 20% for the first $50,000 of taxable income, 30% for the next $50,000, and 40% for taxable income over $100,000. The liability for deferred tax consequences is measured as follows:

	Year 2	Year 3	Year 4
20% tax on first $50,000	$10,000	$10,000	$8,000
30% tax on next $50,000	6,000	15,000	—
40% tax on over $100,000	—	4,000	—
	$16,000	$29,000	$8,000

A deferred tax liability is recognized for $53,000 (the total of the taxes payable for years 2 to 4) at the end of year 1.

How do we account for a deferred tax asset?

A deferred tax asset results in a future deductible amount (for tax purposes) which can only be recognized as an asset in the current year if the company is assured of having taxable income in the future. Thus, a deferred tax asset can only be recognized up to the deferred tax liability balance. In other words, there cannot be reported on the balance sheet a *net* deferred tax asset balance. This rule is based on *conservatism*.

EXAMPLE 22

In 19X8, a company sold a fixed asset reporting a gain of $70,000 for book purposes which was deferred for tax purposes (installment method) until 19X9. In addition, in 19X8, $40,000 of subscription income was received in advance. The income was recognized for tax purposes in 19X8 but was deferred for book purposes until 19X9.

The deferred tax asset may be recorded because the deductible amount in the future ($40,000) offsets the taxable amount ($70,000). Assuming a 34% tax rate and income taxes payable of $100,000, the entry in 19X8 is:

Income tax expense	110,200	
Deferred tax asset		
($40,000 × 34%)	13,600	
Deferred tax liability		
($70,000 × 34%)		23,800
Income taxes payable		100,000

Note: The deferred tax asset can only be recognized up to the later years' deferred tax liabilities caused from temporary differences. Thus, if the gain on the sale of fixed assets was $25,000, the maximum amount of deferred revenue that could be recognized as a deferred tax asset would be $25,000. In this case, the entry is:

Income tax expense	100,000	
Deferred tax asset (maximum		
up to deferred liability)	8,500	
Deferred tax liability		
(25,000 × 34%)		8,500
Income taxes payable		100,000

A deferred tax asset can also be recognized for the tax benefit of deductible amounts realizable by carrying back a loss from future years to reduce taxes paid in the current or a previous year.

Tax Rates

The tax rates over the years may be different. Further, there may be a change in tax law.

What happens when tax rates are different?

Deferred taxes are reflected at the amounts of settlement when the temporary differences reverse.

EXAMPLE 23

Assume in 19X3 a cumulative temporary difference of $200,000 which will reverse in the future generating the following taxable amounts and tax rate:

	19X4	19X5	19X6	Total
Reversals	$60,000	$90,000	$50,000	$200,000
Tax rate	×.34	×.30	×.25	
Deferred tax liability	$20,400	$27,000	$12,500	$ 59,900

On December 31, 19X3, the deferred tax liability is recorded at $59,900.

A future tax rate can *only* be used if it has been enacted by law.

While there may be graduated tax rates, the highest tax rate may be used when the difference is insignificant.

What happens if tax rates change?

A change in tax rate must be immediately recognized by adjusting tax expense and deferred taxes in the year of change.

EXAMPLE 24

Assume at the end of 19X2, a new tax law reduces the tax rate from 34 to 30% beginning in 19X4. In 19X2, there was deferred profit of $100,000 showing a deferred tax liability of

$34,000 as of 19X2. The gross profit is to be reflected equally in 19X3, 19X4, 19X5, and 19X6. Thus, the deferred tax liability at the end of 19X2 is $31,000 as shown below:

	19X3	19X4	19X5	19X6
Reversals	$25,000	$25,000	$25,000	$25,000
Tax rate	×.34	×.30	×.30	×.30
Deferred tax liability	$8,500	$7,500	$7,500	$7,500

Total = $31,000

The appropriate entry in 19X2 is:

Deferred tax liability	3,000	
Income tax expense		3,000

How is tax allocation treated in a business combination accounted for under the purchase method?

In a business combination accounted for as a purchase, the net assets acquired are recorded at their gross fair values with a separate deferred tax balance for the tax effects. Further, a temporary difference arises for the difference between the financial reporting and tax basis of assets and liabilities acquired. If the acquired company has an operating loss, it reduces the deferred tax liability of the acquired business.

What footnote disclosures should be made?

There should be disclosure of the types of temporary differences. An example is the disclosure that warranties are deducted for taxes when paid but are deducted for financial reporting in the year of sale.

If a deferred tax liability is *not* recognized, disclosure should be made of the following:

• Description of the types of temporary differences for which *no* recognition is made to a deferred tax liability and the kinds of occurrences that would result in tax recognition of the temporary differences.

- Cumulative amount of each type of temporary difference.

A reconciliation should exist between the reported amount of tax expense and the tax expense that would have occurred using federal statutory tax rates. The reconciliation should be in terms of percentages or dollar amounts. If statutory tax rates do not exist, use the regular tax rates for alternative tax systems. Disclosure should be made of the estimated amount and the nature of each material reconciling item.

There should be disclosure of the terms of intercorporate tax sharing arrangements and tax-related balances due to or from affiliates.

Extensions of Tax Allocation

APB Opinions No. 23 and 24 provide that undistributed earnings (parent/investor share of subsidiary/investee income less dividends received) are temporary differences.

The reasoning for this treatment is the assumption that such earnings will ultimately be transferred.

Temporary Difference. In the case of investee income arising from applying APB No. 18, if evidence indicates ultimate realization by disposition of investment, income taxes should be determined at capital gains or other appropriate rates.

What happens in the case of indefinite reversal?

There is no interperiod tax allocation in the case of indefinite reversal. Indefinite reversal is when undistributed earnings in a foreign subsidiary will indefinitely be postponed or when earnings will be remitted in a tax-free liquidation.

If there is a change in circumstances and the presumption of indefinite reversal no longer is valid, an adjustment to tax expense is required.

Disclosure should be made of the declaration to reinvest indefinitely or to remit tax free, and the cumulative amount of undistributed earnings.

Amount of Temporary Difference. Eighty percent of the dividends received from affiliated corporations are generally exempt from tax. Consequently, the temporary difference is equal to 20% of the undistributed earnings (parent/investor interest less dividends received).

FOREIGN CURRENCY ACCOUNTING ———

How do you account for and report foreign currency translation and transaction gains and losses?

FASB 52 applies to foreign currency transactions such as exports and imports denominated in other than a company's functional currency. It also relates to foreign currency financial statements of branches, divisions, and other investees incorporated in the financial statements of a U.S. company by combination, consolidation, or the equity method.

An objective of translation is to provide information of expected effects of rate changes on cash flow and equity. Translation also provides data in consolidated financial statements relative to the financial results of each individual foreign consolidated entity.

FASB 52 covers the translation of foreign currency statements and gains and losses on foreign currency transactions. The translation of foreign currency statements is usually required when the statements of a foreign subsidiary having a functional currency other than the U.S. dollar are to be included in the consolidated financial statements of a domestic enterprise. In general, the foreign currency balance sheet should be translated using the exchange rate at the end of the reporting year. The income statement should be translated using the average exchange rate for the year. The resulting translation gains and losses are shown as a separate component in the stockholders' equity section.

Any gains or losses arising from transactions denominated in a foreign currency are presented in the current year's income statement.

What are some important terms in foreign currency?

Some key terminology that the CFO should be familiar with are:

• *Conversion*—An exchange of one currency for another.

• *Currency Swap*—An exchange between two companies of the currencies of two different countries according to an agreement to re-exchange the two currencies at the same rate of exchange at a specified future date.

• *Denominate*—Pay or receive in that *same* foreign currency. It can only be denominated in one currency (e.g., lira). It is a real account (asset or liability) fixed in terms of a foreign currency regardless of exchange rate.

• *Exchange Rate*—The ratio between a unit of one currency and that of another at a specified date. If there is a *temporary lack of exchangeability* between two currencies at the transaction date or balance sheet date, the first rate available thereafter is used.

• *Foreign Currency*—A currency other than the functional currency of the business (for example, the dollar could be a foreign currency for a foreign entity).

• *Foreign Currency Statements*—The financial statements using as the unit of measure a functional currency.

• *Foreign Currency Transactions*—Transactions whose terms are denominated in a currency other than the entity's functional currency. Foreign currency transactions occur when a business (a) buys or sells on credit goods or services whose prices are denominated in foreign currency, (b) borrows or lends funds and the amounts payable or receivable are denominated in foreign currency, (c) is a party to an unperformed forward exchange contract, or (d) acquires or disposes of assets, or incurs or settles liabilities denominated in foreign currency.

• *Foreign Currency Translation*—The expression in the reporting currency of the company those amounts that are denominated or measured in a different currency.

• *Foreign Entity*—An operation (e.g., subsidiary, division, branch, joint venture) whose financial statements are prepared in a currency other than the reporting currency of the reporting entity.

• *Functional Currency*—*What is the functional currency?* An entity's functional currency is the currency of the *primary economic environment* in which the business operates. It is usually the currency of the foreign country that the company primarily obtains and uses cash.

Before translation, the foreign country figures are remeasured in the functional currency. For example, if a company in France is an independent entity and received cash and incurred expenses in France, the franc is the functional currency. However, if the French company was an extension of an Italian parent, the functional currency is the lira. The functional currency should be consistently used except if unusual material economic changes occur. However, previously issued financial statements are not restated for a change in the functional currency.

If a company's books are *not* kept in its functional currency, remeasurement into the functional currency is required. The remeasurement process occurs before translation into the reporting currency. When a foreign entity's functional currency is the reporting currency, remeasurement into the reporting currency obviates translation. The remeasurement process generates the same result as if the company's books had been kept in the functional currency.

How do you determine the functional currency?

There are guidelines to determine the functional currency of a foreign operation. The "benchmarks" apply to selling price, market, cash flow, financing, expense, and intercompany transactions. The following is a detailed discussion:

• *Selling Price*—The functional currency is the foreign currency when the foreign operation's selling price of products or services primarily arise from local factors such as government law. It is *not* caused by changes in exchange rate. The functional currency is the parent's currency when foreign operation's sales prices apply in the short-run to fluctuation in the exchange rate emanating from international factors (e.g., worldwide competition).

• *Market*—The functional currency is the foreign currency when the foreign activity has a strong local sales market for products or services even though a significant amount of exports may exist. The functional currency is the parent's currency when the foreign operation's sales market is mostly in the parent's country.

• *Cash Flow*—The functional currency is the foreign currency when the foreign operation's cash flows are predominately in foreign currency not directly impacting the parent's cash flow. The functional currency is the parent's currency when the foreign operation's cash flows affect the parent's cash flows. They are typically available for remittance via intercompany accounting settlement.

• *Financing*—The functional currency is the foreign currency if financing the foreign activity is in foreign currency and funds obtained by the foreign activity are adequate to satisfy debt payments. The functional currency is the parent's currency when financing foreign activity is provided by the parent or occurs in U.S. dollars. The funds obtained by the foreign activity are inadequate to meet debt requirements.

• *Expenses*—The functional currency is the foreign currency when foreign operation's production costs or services are usually incurred locally. However, there may be some foreign imports. The functional currency is the parent's currency when foreign operation's production and service costs are mostly component costs obtained from the parent's country.

• *Intercompany Transactions*—The functional currency is the foreign currency when minor interrelationships exist between the activities of the foreign entity and parent except for competitive advantages (e.g., patents). There are a few intercompany transactions. The functional currency is the parent's currency when significant interrelationships exist between the foreign entity and parent. There are many intercompany transactions.

There should be consistent use of the functional currency of the foreign entity over the years unless there is a significant change in circumstances. If a change in the functional currency occurs, it is treated as a change in estimate.

• *Local Currency*—The currency of the foreign country.

• *Measure*—A translation into a currency other than the original reporting currency. The foreign financial statements are measured in U.S. dollars by using the appropriate exchange rate.

• *Reporting Currency*—The currency the business prepares its financial statements in which is typically U.S. dollars.

• *Spot Rate*—The exchange rate for immediate delivery of currencies exchanged.

• *Transaction Gain or Loss*—Transaction gains or losses arise from a change in exchange rates between the functional currency and the currency in which a foreign currency transaction is denominated. They represent an increase or decrease in (a) the actual functional currency cash flows realized upon settlement of foreign currency transactions and (b) the expected functional currency cash flows on unsettled foreign currency transactions.

• *Translation Adjustments*—Translation adjustments arise from translating financial statements from the entity's functional currency into the reporting one.

How is translation accomplished and reported upon?

The foreign entity's financial statements in a highly *inflationary* economy is not sufficiently stable and should be remeasured as if the functional currency were the reporting currency. Thus, the financial statements of those entities should be remeasured into the reporting currency (the U.S. dollar becomes the functional currency). In effect, the reporting currency is used directly.

A *highly inflationary environment* is one that has cumulative inflation of about *100% or more over a three year period.* In other words, the inflation rate must be increasing at a rate of about 35% a year for three consecutive years. *Tip:* The International Monetary Fund of Washington, D.C. publishes monthly figures on international inflation rates.

Translation of Foreign Currency Statements When the Foreign Currency Is the Functional Currency

The balance sheet accounts are translated using the *current exchange rate.* Assets and liabilities are converted at the exchange rate at the balance sheet date. If a current exchange rate is not available at the balance sheet date, use the first exchange rate available after that date. The *current exchange rate* is also used to translate the statement of cash flows except for those items found in the income statement which are translated using the weighted-average rate. The income statement items are translated using the weighted-average exchange rate.

A significant change in the exchange rate between year-end and the audit report date should be disclosed as a subsequent event. Disclosure should also be made of the effects on unsettled balances applicable to foreign currency transactions.

What are the steps in the translation process?

There are several steps in translating the foreign country's financial statements into U.S. reporting requirements. They are:

1. Conform the foreign country's financial statements to U.S. GAAP.

2. Determine the functional currency of the foreign entity.

3. Remeasure the financial statements in the functional currency, if necessary. Gains or losses from remeasurement are includable in remeasured current net income.

4. Convert from the foreign currency into U.S. dollars (reporting currency).

If a company's functional currency is a foreign currency, *translation adjustments* arise from translating that company's financial statements into the reporting currency. Translation adjustments are unrealized and should not be included in the income statement but should be reported separately and accumulated in a *separate component of equity.* However, if remeasurement from the recording currency to the functional currency is required before translation, the gain or loss is reflected in the income statement.

Upon sale or liquidation of an investment in a foreign entity, the amount attributable to that entity and accumulated in the translation adjustment component of equity is removed from the stockholders' equity section and considered a part of the gain or loss on sale or liquidation of the investment in the income statement for the period during which the sale or liquidation occurs.

As per Interpretation 37, a sale of an investment in a foreign entity may include a partial sale of an ownership interest. In that case, a pro rata amount of the cumulative translation adjustment reflected as a stockholders' equity component is includable in arriving at the gain or loss on sale. For example, if a business sells a 40% ownership interest in a foreign investment, 40% of the translation adjustment applicable to it is included in calculating gain or loss on sale of that ownership interest.

How are foreign currency transactions handled?

Foreign currency transactions are denominated in a currency other than the company's functional currency. Foreign currency transactions may result in receivables or payables fixed in the amount of foreign currency to be received or paid.

A foreign currency transaction requires settlement in a currency other than the functional currency! A change in exchange rates between the functional currency and the currency in which a transaction is denominated increases or decreases the expected amount of functional currency cash flows upon settlement of the transaction. This change in expected functional currency cash flows is a *foreign currency transaction gain or loss* that typically is included in arriving at earnings in the *income statement* for the period in which the exchange rate is changed. An example of a transaction gain or loss is when an Italian subsidiary has a receivable denominated in lira from a British customer.

Similarly, a transaction gain or loss (measured from the *transaction date* or the most recent intervening balance sheet date, whichever is later) realized upon settlement of a foreign currency transaction usually should be included in determining net income for the period in which the transaction is settled.

EXAMPLE 25

An exchange gain or loss occurs when the exchange rate changes between the purchase date and sale date.

Merchandise is bought for 100,000 pounds. The exchange rate is 4 pounds to 1 dollar. The journal entry is:

Purchases	25,000	
Accounts payable		25,000
100,000/4 = $25,000		

When the merchandise is paid for, the exchange rate is 5 to 1. The journal entry is:

Accounts payable	25,000	
Cash		20,000
Foreign exchange gain		5,000
100,000/5 = $20,000		

The $20,000 using an exchange rate of 5 to 1 can buy 100,000 pounds. The transaction gain is the difference between the cash required of $20,000 and the initial liability of $25,000.

Note that a foreign transaction gain or loss has to be determined at each balance sheet date on all recorded foreign transactions that have not been settled.

EXAMPLE 26

A U.S. company sells goods to a customer in England on 11/15/X7 for 10,000 pounds. The exchange rate is 1 pound is $.75. Thus, the transaction is worth $7,500 (10,000 pounds × .75). Payment is due 2 months later. The entry on 11/15/X7 is:

Accounts receivable—England	7,500	
Sales		7,500

Accounts receivable and sales are measured in U.S. dollars at the transaction date employing the spot rate. Even though the accounts receivable is measured and reported in U.S. dollars, the receivable is fixed in pounds. Thus, there can occur a transaction gain or loss if the exchange rate changes between the transactions date (11/15/X7) and the settlement date (1/15/X8).

Since the financial statements are prepared between the transaction date and settlement date, receivables which are denominated in a currency other than the functional currency (U.S. dollar) have to be restated to reflect the spot rate on the balance sheet date. On December 31, 19X7 the exchange rate is 1 pound equals $.80. Hence, the 10,000 pounds are now valued at $8,000 (10,000 × $.80). Therefore, the accounts receivable denominated in pounds should be upwardly adjusted by $500. The required journal entry on 12/31/X7 is:

Accounts receivable—England	500	
Foreign exchange gain		500

The income statement for the year-ended 12/31/X7 shows an exchange gain of $500. Note that sales is not affected by the exchange gain since sales relates to operational activity.

On 1/15/X8, the spot rate is 1 pound = $.78. The journal entry is:

Cash	7,800	
Foreign exchange loss	200	
Accounts receivable—England		8,000

The 19X8 income statement shows an exchange loss of $200.

Which transaction gain or loss should not be reported in the income statement?

Gains and losses on the following foreign currency transactions are not included in earnings but rather reported as translation adjustments:

• Foreign currency transactions designated as *economic hedges* of a net investment in a foreign entity, beginning as of the designation date.

• Intercompany foreign currency transactions of a *long-term investment* nature (settlement is not planned or expected in the foreseeable future), when the entities to the transaction are consolidated, combined, or accounted for by the equity method in the reporting company's financial statements.

A gain or loss on a forward contract or other foreign currency transaction that is intended to *hedge* an identifiable foreign currency commitment (e.g., an agreement to buy or sell machinery) should be deferred and included in the measurement of the related foreign currency transaction. Losses should *not* be deferred if it is expected that deferral would result in recognizing losses in later periods. A foreign currency transaction is deemed a hedge of an identifiable foreign currency commitment if both of the following conditions are met:

• The foreign currency transaction is designated as a hedge of a foreign currency commitment.

• The foreign currency commitment is firm.

What is a forward exchange contract and how is it accounted for?

A forward exchange contract is an agreement to exchange different currencies at a specified future date and at a given rate (forward rate). A forward contract is a foreign currency transaction. A gain or loss on a forward contract that does not satisfy the conditions described below are included in earnings.

Note: Currency swaps are accounted for in a similar way.

A gain or loss (whether or not deferred) on a forward contract, except a speculative forward contract, should be computed by multiplying the foreign currency amount of the forward contract by the difference between the *spot rate* at the balance sheet date and the spot rate at the date of inception of the forward contract.

The *discount or premium on a forward contract* (that is, the foreign currency amount of the contract multiplied by the difference between the contracted forward rate and the spot rate at the date of inception of the contract) should be accounted for separately from the gain or loss on the contract and typically should be included in computing net income over the life of the forward contract.

A gain or loss on a *speculative forward contract* (a contract that does not hedge an exposure) should be computed by multiplying the foreign currency amount of the forward contract by the difference between the forward rate available from the remaining maturity of the contract and the contracted forward rate (or the forward rate last used to measure a gain or loss on that contract for an earlier period). *No* separate *accounting recognition* is given to the *discount or premium* on a *speculative forward contract.*

How may you hedge foreign currency exposure to reduce risk?

Foreign currency transactions gains and losses on assets and liabilities, denominated in a currency other than the functional currency, can be hedged if the U.S. company engages into a forward exchange contract.

There can be a hedge even if there is not a forward exchange contract. For example, a foreign currency transaction can serve as an economic hedge offsetting a parent's net investment in a foreign entity.

EXAMPLE 27

A U.S. parent owns 100% of a French subsidiary having net assets of $3 million in francs. The U.S. parent can borrow $3 million francs to hedge its net investment in the French subsidiary. Assume the French franc is the functional currency and the $3 million obligation is denominated in francs. The variability in the exchange rate for francs does *not* have a net effect on the parent's consolidated balance sheet because increases in the translation adjustments balance arising from translation of the net investment will be netted against decreases in this balance arising from the adjustment of the liability denominated in francs.

8

Interim and
Segmental Reporting

This chapter discusses the requirements for the preparation of interim financial statements and segmental disclosures included in the annual report.

What should be reported and disclosed in interim periods?

Interim reports may be issued periodically, such as quarterly or monthly. Complete financial statements or summarized data may be provided, but interim financial statements do not have to be certified by the outside auditors.

Interim balance sheets and cash flow information should be given. If these statements are not presented, material changes in liquid assets, cash, long-term debt, and stockholders' equity should be disclosed.

Interim reports typically include results of the current interim period and the cumulative year-to-date figures. There are usually comparisons to the results of comparable interim periods for the previous year.

Interim results should be based on the accounting principles used in the last year's annual report unless a change has been made in the current year.

A gain or loss cannot be deferred to a later interim period except if such deferral would have been allowable for annual reporting.

Revenue from merchandise sold and services performed should be accounted for as earned in the interim period in the same manner as in annual reporting. If an advance is received in the first quarter and benefits the whole year, it should be allocated ratably to the interim periods affected.

Expenses should be matched to revenue in the interim period. If a cost cannot be traced to revenue in a future interim period, it should be expensed in the current one. Yearly expenses such as administrative salaries, insurance, pension plan expense, and year-end bonuses should be allocated to the quarters. The allocation basis may be based on such factors as time spent, benefit obtained, and activity.

The gross profit method can be used to estimate interim inventory and cost of sales. Disclosure should be made of the method, assumptions, and material adjustments by reconciliations with the annual physical inventory.

A permanent inventory loss should be recognized in the interim period it occurs. A subsequent recovery is considered a gain in the later interim period. However, if the change in inventory value is temporary, no recognition is given in the accounts.

If a temporary liquidation of the LIFO base occurs with replacement expected by year-end, cost of sales should be based on replacement cost.

EXAMPLE 1

The historical cost of an inventory item is $10,000 with replacement cost expected to be $15,000. The entry is:

Cost of sales	15,000	
Inventory		10,000
Reserve for liquidation of LIFO base		5,000

The Reserve for liquidation of LIFO base is reported as a current liability.

When there is replenishment at year-end the entry is:

Reserve for liquidation of LIFO base	5,000	
Inventory	10,000	
Cash		15,000

Volume discounts to customers tied into annual purchases should be apportioned to the interim period based on the ratio of:

$$\frac{\text{Purchases for the interim period}}{\text{Total estimated purchases for the year}}$$

When a standard cost system is used, variances expected to be reversed by year-end may be deferred to an asset or liability account.

How are taxes provided for in interim periods?

The income tax provision includes current and deferred taxes. Taxes include federal and local. The tax provision for an interim period should be cumulative (e.g., total tax expense for a 9-month period is shown in the third quarter based on 9 months' income). The tax expense for the three month period based on 3 months revenue may also be presented (e.g., third quarter tax expense based on only the third quarter). In computing tax expense, use the estimated annual effective tax rate based on income from continuing operations. If a reliable estimate is not feasible, the actual year-to-date effective tax rate may be used.

At the end of each interim period, a revision to the effective tax rate may be needed using the best estimates of the annual effective tax rate. The projected tax rate includes adjustment for net deferred credits. Adjustments should be considered in deriving the maximum tax benefit for year-to-date figures.

The estimated effective tax rate should incorporate all available tax credits (e.g., foreign tax credit). A change in taxes arising from a new tax law is immediately reflected in the interim period it occurs.

Income statement items after income from continuing operations (e.g., income from discontinued operations, extraordinary items, cumulative effect of a change in accounting principle) should be presented net of taxes. The tax effect on these unusual line items should be reflected only in the interim period they actually occur. Prior period adjustments in the retained earnings statement are also shown net of tax.

The tax implication of an interim loss is recognized *only* when realization of the tax benefit is assured beyond reasonable doubt. If a loss is expected for the remainder of the year, and carryback is not possible, the tax benefits typically should not be recognized.

The tax benefit of a previous year operating loss carryforward is recognized as an extraordinary item in each interim period to the extent that income is available to offset the loss carryforward.

What if a change in principle occurs?

When a change in principle is made in the first interim period, the cumulative effect of a change in principle account should be shown net of tax in the first interim period. If a change in principle is made in a quarter other than the first (e.g., third quarter), we assume the change was made at the beginning of the first quarter showing the cumulative effect in the first quarter. The interim periods will have to be *restated* using the new principle (e.g., first, second, and third quarters).

When interim data for previous years is presented for comparative purposes, there should be a restatement to conform with newly adopted policies. Alternatively, disclosure can be made of the effect on prior data had the new practice been applied to that period.

If there is a change in principle, disclosure should be made of the nature and justification. The effect of the change on per share amounts should be given.

There should be disclosure of seasonality affecting interim results. Contingencies should be disclosed. When a change in the estimated effective tax rate occurs it should be disclosed. Further, if a fourth quarter is not presented, any material adjustments to that quarter must be commented upon in the footnotes to the annual report. If an event is immaterial on an annual basis but material in the interim period, it should be disclosed. Purchase or pooling transactions should be noted.

What about financial statement presentation?

The financial statement presentation for prior period adjustments follow:

- Include in net income for the current period, the portion of the effect related to current operations.
- Restate earnings of impacted prior interim periods of the current year to include the portion related thereto.
- If the prior period adjustment affects prior years, include it in the earnings of the first interim period of the current year.

The criteria for prior period adjustments in interim periods are materiality, subject to estimation, and identifiable to a prior interim period. Examples of prior period adjustments for interim reporting are error corrections, settlement of litigation or claims, renegotiation proceedings, and adjustment of income taxes.

Segmental disposal is separately shown in the interim period it occurs.

What is presented in segmental reports?

The financial reporting for business segments is useful in appraising segmental performance, earning prospects, and risk. Segmental reporting may be by industry, foreign geographic area, major customers, and government contracts. The financial statement presentation for segments may appear in the body, footnotes, or separate schedule to the financial statements. Segmental information is not required in interim reports. An industry segment sells products or renders services to outside customers.

Segmental data occurs when a company prepares a full set of financial statements (balance sheet, income statement, statement of cash flows, and related footnotes). Segmental information is shown for each year presented.

Accounting principles employed in preparing financial statements should be used for segment information, except that intercompany transactions eliminated in consolidation are included in segmental reporting.

What segments should be reported upon?

A segment must be reported if one or more of the following conditions are satisfied:

- Revenue is 10% or more of total revenue.
- Operating income is 10% or more of the combined operating profit.
- Identifiable assets are 10% or more of the total identifiable assets.

The factors to be taken into account when determining industry segments are:

- *Nature of the Market.* Similarity exists in geographic markets serviced or types of customers.
- *Nature of the Product.* Related products or services have similar purposes or end uses (e.g., similarity in profit margins, risk, and growth).
- *Nature of the Production Process.* Homogeneity exists when there is interchangeable production or sales facilities, labor force, equipment, or service groups.

Reportable segments are determined by:

- Identifying specific products and services.
- Grouping those products and services by industry line into segments.
- Selecting material segments to the company as a whole.

There should be a grouping of products and services by industry lines. A number of approaches exist. However, not one method is appropriate in determining industry segments in every case. In many instances, management judgment determines the industry segment. A starting point in deciding upon an industry segment is by *profit center.* A profit center is a component that sells mostly to outsiders for a profit.

When the profit center goes across industry lines, it should be broken down into smaller groups. A company in many industries not accumulating financial information on a segregated basis must disaggregate its operations by industry line.

Although worldwide industry segmentation is recommended, it may not be practical to gather. If foreign operations cannot be disaggregated, the firm should disaggregate domestic activities. Foreign operations should be disaggregated where possible and the remaining foreign operations should be treated as a single segment.

What should you know about the 10% and 75% rules?

According to FASB 14, a segment that was significant in previous years, even though not meeting the 10% test in the current year, should still be reported upon if it is expected that the segment will be significant in future years.

Segments should represent a substantial portion, meaning 75% or more, of the company's total revenue to outside customers. The 75% test is applied separately each year. However, in order to derive 75%, as a matter of practicality not more than 10 segments should be shown. If more than 10 are identified, it is possible to combine similar segments.

Even though intersegment transfers are eliminated in the preparation of consolidated financial statements, they are included for segmental disclosure in determining the 10% and 75% rules.

In applying the 10% criteria, the CFO should note the following:

• *Revenue.* A separation should exist between revenue to unaffiliated customers and revenue to other business segments. Transfer prices are used for intersegmental transfers. Accounting bases followed should be disclosed.

• *Operating Profit or Loss.* Operating earnings of a segment excludes general corporate revenue and expenses that are not allocable, interest expense (unless the segment is a financial type, such as one involved in banking), domestic and foreign income taxes, income from unconsolidated subsidiaries or investees, income from discontinued operations, extraordinary items, cumulative effect of a change in accounting principles, and minority interest. Traceable and allocable costs should be charged to segments.

• *Identifiable Assets.* Assets of a segment include those directly in it and general corporate assets that can rationally be allocated to it. Allocation methods should be consistently applied. Identifiable assets include those consisting of a part of the company's investment in the segment (e.g., goodwill). Identifiable assets do not include advances or loans to other segments except for income therefrom that is used to compute the results of operations (e.g., a segment of a financial nature).

EXAMPLE 2

A company provides the following data regarding its business segments and overall operations:

	Segment A	Segment B	Company*
Revenue	$2,000	$1,000	$12,000
Direct costs	500	300	5,000
Company-wide costs (allocable)			800
General company costs (not allocable)			1,700

*Excludes segment amounts

Company wide costs are allocable based on the ratios of direct costs. The tax rate is 34%.

The profits to be reported by segment and for the company as a whole are as follows:

	Segment A	Segment B	Company
Revenues	$2,000	$1,000	$15,000
Less:			
Direct costs	(500)	(300)	(5,800)
Indirect costs (allocated)			
$800 × $500/$5,800	(69)		
$800 × $300/$5,800		(41)	
			(800)
Segment margin	$1,431	$ 659	
General company costs			(1,700)
Income before tax			$6,700
Income tax (34%)			2,278
Net income			$4,422

What should be disclosed?

Disclosures are not required for 90% enterprises (e.g., a company that derives 90% or more of its revenue, operating profit, and total assets from one segment). In effect, that segment is the business. The dominant industry segment should be identified.

Segmental disclosure includes:

- Allocation method for costs.
- Capital expenditures.
- Aggregate depreciation, depletion and amortization expense.
- Transfer price used.
- Unusual items affecting segmental profit.
- Company's equity in vertically integrated unconsolidated subsidiaries and equity method investees. Note the geographic location of equity method investees.
- Effect of an accounting principle change on the operating profit of the reportable segment. Also include its effect on the company.

- Material segmental accounting policies not already disclosed in the regular financial statements.
- Type of products.

What if consolidation is involved?

If a segment includes a *purchase method* consolidated subsidiary, segmental information is based upon the consolidated value of the subsidiary (e.g., fair market value and goodwill recognized) and *not* on the book values recorded in the subsidiary's own financial statements.

Segmental information is *not* required for *unconsolidated subsidiaries* or other *unconsolidated investees.* Each subsidiary or investee is subject to the rules of FASB 14 that segment information be reported.

Some types of typical consolidation eliminations are *not* eliminated when reporting for segments. For example, revenue of a segment includes intersegmental sales and sales to unrelated customers.

A complete set of financial statements for a foreign investee that is *not* a subsidiary does not have to disclose segmental information when presented in the same financial report of a primary reporting entity except if the foreign investee's separately issued statements already disclose the required segmental data.

What other reporting requirements are there?

Segmental disclosure is also required when:

- 10% or more of revenue or assets is applicable to a foreign area. Presentation must be made of revenue, operating profit or loss, and assets for foreign operations in the aggregate or by geographic locality.
- 10% or more of sales is to one customer. A group of customers under common control is considered one customer.
- 10% or more of revenue is obtained from domestic government contracts or a foreign government.

In the above cases, the source of the segmental revenue should be disclosed along with the percent derived.

The *restatement* of prior period information may be required for *comparative* purposes. The nature and effect of restatement should be disclosed. Restatement is needed when financial statements of the company as a whole have been restated. Also, restatement occurs when there is a pooling-of-interests. Restatement is also needed when a change has occurred in grouping products or services for segment determination or change in grouping of foreign activities into geographic segments.

As per FASB 24, segmental data are not required in financial statements that are presented in another company's financial report if those statements are:

- Combined in a complete set of statements and both sets are presented in the same report; or
- Presented for a foreign investee (not a subsidiary of the primary enterprise) unless the financial statements disclose segment information (e.g., those foreign investees for which such information is already required by the SEC).

If an investee uses the cost or equity method and is not exempted by one of the above provisions, its full set of financial statements presented in another enterprise's report must present segment information if such data are significant to statements of the primary enterprise. Significance is determined by applying the percentage tests of FASB 14 (i.e., 10% tests) in relation to financial statements of the primary enterprise without adjustment for the investee's revenue, operating results, or identifiable assets.

PART III

MANAGEMENT ACCOUNTING

9

Cost Management and Analysis

How do American firms fare in the world market? Do American firms really measure the costs of products and services they offer *accurately?* Only recently has this question been seriously addressed. American managers are finding themselves operating in a highly competitive global economy. Manufacturing and service industries are seeing their profits squeezed by the pinch of foreign price and quality competition.

Firms who do know how to accurately measure product costs will find the going tough, while firms who fail to recognize and solve cost measurement problems and to analyze cost data are probably destined for extinction.

Today's CFOs have the tremendous responsibility for this task. They are the ones that ensure that their cost accounting systems produce accurate (not distorted) cost data for managerial uses for performance measurement and for strategic decisions on pricing, product mix, process technology, and product design. They must know how to analyze cost information for operational planning and control and make operational and tactical decisions.

What is cost management and analysis?

Cost management and analysis involves obtaining accurate product-costing data and managing it to assist managers in making critical decisions such as pricing, product mix, and process technology decisions and analyzing cost data, translating them into the information useful for managerial planning and control, and for making short-term and long-term decisions. This phase involves measurement of accurate and relevant cost data and analyzing them for decision making. *Activity-Based Costing (ABC)* and *Just-in-Time (JIT) costing* are two new developments that enhance product costing accuracy.

Cost management and analysis facilitates better decision making. Decision making, which can be described as problem solving, is largely a matter of choosing among alternative courses of action. The questions that arise from time to time are many and varied. Should the new product be introduced? Should one of the products or services in a line be dropped? Should a special order be accepted at below the normal selling price? Should parts now being manufactured be purchased? Should the present equipment be replaced? Should equipment be purchased or leased? Should production capacity be expended? A cost management system is used to support management's needs for better decisions about product design, pricing, marketing, and mix and to encourage continual operating improvements.

Quantitative methods may be used in various phases of cost analysis to determine costs and their financial effects, correlations, and the financial feasibility of adopting alternatives. They include learning curves, linear programming, inventory planning techniques, and program evaluation and review technique (PERT).

What is wrong with traditional cost systems?

Many companies use a traditional cost system such as job-order costing or process costing, or some hybrid of the two. This traditional system may provide distorted product cost information. In fact, companies selling multiple products are making critical decisions about product pricing, making bids, or product mix, based on inaccurate cost data. In all likelihood, the problem is not with assigning the costs of direct labor or direct materials. These prime costs are traceable to individual products, and most conventional cost systems are designed to ensure that this tracing takes place.

However, the assignment of overhead costs to individual products is another matter. Using the traditional methods of assigning overhead costs to products, using a single predetermined overhead rate based on any single activity measure, can produce distorted product costs.

Overhead Costing: A Single-Product Situation

The accuracy of overhead cost assignment becomes an issue only when multiple products are manufactured in a single facility. If only a single product is produced, all overhead costs are caused by it and traceable to it. The overhead cost per unit is simply the total overhead for the year divided by the number of hours or units produced.

The cost calculation for a single-product setting is illustrated in Table 9–1. There is no question that the cost of manufacturing the product illustrated in Table 9–1 is $28.00 per unit. All manufacturing costs were incurred specifically to make this product. Thus, one way to ensure product-costing accuracy is to focus on producing one product. For this reason, some multiple product firms choose to dedicate entire plants to the manufacture of a single product.

By focusing on only one or two products, small manufacturers are able to calculate the cost of manufacturing the high-volume products more accurately and price them more effectively.

Overhead Costing: A Multiple-Product Situation

In a multiple-product situation, manufacturing overhead costs are caused jointly by all products.

TABLE 9–1 UNIT COST COMPUTATION: SINGLE PRODUCT

	Manufacturing Costs	Units Produced	Unit Cost
Direct materials	$ 800,000	50,000	$16.00
Direct labor	200,000	50,000	4.00
Factory overhead	400,000	50,000	8.00
Total	$1,400,000	50,000	$28.00

The problem becomes one of trying to identify the amount of overhead caused or consumed by each. This is accomplished by searching for *cost drivers,* or activity measures that cause costs to be incurred.

In a traditional setting, it is normally assumed that overhead consumption is highly correlated with the volume of production activity, measured in terms of direct labor hours, machine hours, or direct labor dollars. These volume-related cost drivers are used to assign overhead to products. Volume-related cost drivers use either *plant-wide* or *departmental* rates.

EXAMPLE 1

To illustrate the limitation of this traditional approach, assume that Delta Manufacturing Company has a plant that produces two high-quality fertilizer products; Nitro-X and Nitro-Y. Product costing data are given in Table 9–2. Because the quantity of Nitro-Y produced is five times greater than that of Nitro-X, Nitro-X can be labelled a low-volume product and Nitro-Y a high-volume product.

For simplicity, only four types of factory overhead costs are assumed: setup, quality control, power, and maintenance. These overhead costs are allocated to the two production departments using the *direct* method.

Assume that the four service centers do not interact. Setup costs are allocated based on the number of production runs handled by each department. Quality control costs are allocated by the number of inspection hours used by each department. Power costs are allocated in proportion to the kilowatt hours used. Maintenance costs are allocated in proportion to the machine hours used.

Plant-Wide Overhead Rate

A common method of assigning overhead to products is to compute a plant-wide rate, using a volume-related cost driver. This approach assumes that all overhead cost variation can be

TABLE 9-2 PRODUCT COSTING DATA

	Nitro-X	Nitro-Y	Total
Units produced per year	10,000	50,000	60,000
Production runs	20	30	50
Inspection hours	800	1,200	2,000
Kilowatt hours	5,000	25,000	30,000
Prime costs (direct materials and direct labor)	$50,000	$250,000	$300,000

Departmental Data	Department 1	Department 2	Total
Direct labor hours:			
Nitro-X	4,000	16,000	20,000
Nitro-Y	76,000	24,000	100,000
Total	80,000	40,000	120,000
Machine hours:			
Nitro-X	4,000	6,000	10,000
Nitro-Y	16,000	34,000	50,000
Total	20,000	40,000	60,000
Overhead costs:			
Setup costs	$ 48,000	$ 48,000	$ 96,000
Quality control	37,000	37,000	74,000
Power	14,000	70,000	84,000
Maintenance	13,000	65,000	78,000
Total	$112,000	$220,000	$332,000

explained by one cost driver. Assume that machine hours is chosen.

Dividing the total overhead by the total machine hours yields the following overhead rate:

$$\text{Plant-wide rate} = \$332,000/60,000$$
$$= \$5.53/\text{machine hour}$$

Using this rate and other information from Table 9-2, the unit cost for each product can be calculated, as given in Table 9-3.

TABLE 9-3   UNIT COST COMPUTATION: PLANT-WIDE RATE

Nitro-X	
Prime costs	$ 50,000
Overhead costs $5.53 × 10,000	55,300
	$105,300
Unit cost $105,300/10,000 units	$10.53

Nitro-Y	
Prime costs	$250,000
Overhead costs $5.53 × 50,000	276,500
	$526,500
Unit cost $526,500/50,000 units	$10.53

Departmental Rates

Based on the distribution of labor hours and machine hours in Table 9-2, Department 1 is labor intensive and Department 2 machine oriented. Furthermore, the overhead costs of Department 1 are about one half those of Department 2. Based on these observations, it is obvious that departmental overhead rates would reflect the consumption of overhead better than a plant-wide rate. Product costs would be more accurate, using departmental rates rather than a plant-wide rate.

This approach would yield the following departmental rates, using direct labor hours for Department 1 and machine hours for Department 2:

$$\text{Department 1 rate} = \$112,000/80,000$$
$$= \$1.40/\text{labor hour}$$
$$\text{Department 2 rate} = \$220,000/40,000$$
$$= \$5.50/\text{machine hour}$$

Using these rates and the data from Table 9-2, the computation of the unit costs for each product is shown in Table 9-4.

TABLE 9-4 UNIT COST COMPUTATION: DEPARTMENT RATES

Nitro-X	
Prime costs	$ 50,000
Overhead costs	
Department 1: $1.40 × 4,000 = $ 5,600	
Department 2: $5.50 × 6,000 = 33,000	38,600
	$ 88,600
Unit cost $88,600/10,000 units	$ 8.86

Nitro-Y	
Prime costs	$250,000
Overhead costs	
Department 1: $1.40 × 76,000 = $106,400	
Department 2: $5.50 × 34,000 = 187,000	293,400
	$543,400
Unit cost $543,400/50,000 units	$10.87

Plant-Wide Rate Versus Departmental Rates

Using a single, plant-wide overhead rate based on machine hours gave the same overhead application and cost per unit for Nitro-X and Nitro-Y, or $10.53. But this would not be an accurate measurement of the underlying relationship, because Nitro-X made light use of overhead incurring factors while Nitro-Y made heavy use of such services.

To summarize, when products are heterogeneous, receiving uneven attention and effort as they move through various departments, departmental rates are necessary to achieve more accurate product costs.

Problems with Costing Accuracy

The accuracy of the overhead cost assignment can be challenged regardless of whether the plant-wide or departmental rates are used. The main problem with either procedure is the assumption that machine hours or direct labor hours drive or cause all overhead costs.

From Table 9–2, we know that Nitro-Y—with five times the volume of Nitro-X—uses five times the machine hours and direct labor hours. Thus, if a plant-wide rate is used, Nitro-Y will receive five times more overhead costs. But does it make sense? Is all overhead driven by volume? Use of a single driver—especially volume-related—is not proper.

Examination of the data in Table 9–2 suggests that a significant portion of overhead costs is not driven or caused by volume. For example, setup costs are probably related to the number of setups and quality control costs to the number of hours of inspection.

Notice that Nitro-Y only has 1.5 times as many setups as the Nitro-X (30/20) and only 1.5 times as many inspection hours (1,200/800). Use of a volume-related cost driver (machine hours or labor hours) and a plant-wide rate assigns five times more overhead to the Nitro-Y than to Nitro-X. For quality control and setup costs, then, Nitro-Y is overcosted, and Nitro-X is undercosted.

The problems worsened when departmental rates were used. Nitro-Y consumes 19 times as many direct labor hours (76,000/4,000) as Nitro-X and 5.7 times as many machine hours (34,000/6,000). Thus, Nitro-Y receives 19 times more overhead from Department 1 and 5.7 times more overhead from Department 2.

As Table 9–4 shows, with departmental rates the unit cost of Nitro-X decreases to $8.86, and the unit cost of Nitro-Y increases to $10.87. This change emphasizes the failure of volume-based cost drivers to reflect accurately each product's consumption of setup and quality control costs.

Why do volume-related cost drivers fail?

At least two major factors impair the ability of a volume-related cost driver to assign overhead costs accurately: (1) the proportion of nonvolume-related overhead costs to total overhead costs; and (2) the degree of product diversity.

Nonvolume-Related Overhead Costs. In our example, there are four overhead activities: quality control, setup, maintenance, and power. Two, maintenance and power, are volume-related. Quality control and setup are less dependent on volume. As a result, volume-based cost drivers cannot assign these costs accurately to products.

Using volume-based cost drivers to assign nonvolume-related overhead costs creates distorted product costs. The severity of this distortion depends on what proportion of total overhead costs these nonvolume-related costs represent. For our example, setup costs and quality control costs represent a substantial share—51 percent—of total overhead ($170,000/$332,000). This suggests that some care should be exercised in assigning these costs. If nonvolume-related overhead costs are only a small percentage of total overhead costs, the distortion of product costs would be quite small. In such a case, the use of volume-based cost drivers may be acceptable.

Product Diversity. When products consume overhead activities in different proportions, a firm has product diversity.

To illustrate, the proportion of all overhead activities consumed by both Nitro-X and Nitro-Y is computed and displayed in Table 9–5. The proportion of each activity consumed by a product is defined as the consumption ratio. As you can see from Table 9–5, the consumption ratios for these two products differ from the nonvolume-related categories to the volume-related costs.

Since the nonvolume-related overhead costs are a significant proportion of total overhead and their consumption ratio differs from that of the volume-based cost driver, product costs can be distorted if a volume-based cost driver is used. The solution to this costing problem is to use an *activity-based costing (ABC)* approach.

TABLE 9-5 PRODUCT DIVERSITY: PROPORTION OF CONSUMPTION

Overhead Activity	Mix[a]	Nitro-X	Nitro-Y	Consumption Measure
Setup	(1)	.40	.60	Production runs
Quality control	(2)	.40	.60	Inspection hours
Power	(3)	.17	.83	Kilowatt hours
Maintenance	(4)	.17	.83	Machine hours

[a] (1) 20/50 (Nitro-X) and 30/50 (Nitro-Y)
(2) 800/2,000 (Nitro-X) and 1,200/2,000 (Nitro-Y)
(3) 5,000/30,000 (Nitro-X) and 25,000/30,000 (Nitro-Y)
(4) 10,000/60,000 (Nitro-X) and 50,000/60,000 (Nitro-Y)

How ABC product costing corrects the situation?

An activity-based cost system is one which first traces costs to activities and then to products. Traditional product costing also involves two stages, but in the first stage costs are traced to departments, not to activities. In both traditional and activity-based costing, the second stage consists of tracing costs to the product. The principal difference between the two methods is the number of cost drivers used. Activity-based costing uses a much larger number of cost drivers than the one or two volume-based cost drivers typical in a conventional system. In fact, the approach separates overhead costs into overhead cost pools, where each cost pool is associated with a different cost driver. Then a predetermined overhead rate is computed for each cost pool and each cost driver. In consequence, this method has enhanced accuracy.

First-Stage Procedure

In the first stage of activity-based costing, overhead costs are divided into homogeneous cost pools. A *homogeneous* cost pool is a collection of overhead costs for which cost variations can be explained by a single cost driver. Overhead activities are homogeneous whenever they have the same consumption ratios for all products.

Once a cost pool is defined, the cost per unit of the cost driver is computed for that pool. This is referred to as the *pool rate*. Computation of the pool rate completes the first stage. Thus, the first stage produces two outcomes: (1) a set of homogeneous cost pools and (2) a pool rate.

For example, in Table 9–5, quality control costs and setup costs can be combined into one homogeneous cost pool and maintenance and power costs into a second. For the first cost pool, the number of production runs or inspection hours could be the cost driver. Since the two cost drivers are perfectly correlated, they will assign the same amount of overhead to both products. For the second pool, machine hours or kilowatt hours could be selected as the cost driver.

Assume for the purpose of illustration that the number of production runs and machine hours are the cost drivers chosen. Using data from Table 9–2, the first-stage outcomes are illustrated in Table 9–6.

Second-Stage Procedure

In the second stage, the costs of each overhead pool are traced to products. This is done using the pool rate computed in the first stage and the measure of the amount of resources consumed by each product. This measure is simply the quantity of the cost driver used by each product. In our example, that would be the number of production runs and machine hours used by each product. Thus, the overhead assigned from each cost pool to each product is computed as follows:

Applied overhead = Pool rate × Cost driver units used

To illustrate, consider the assignment of costs from the first overhead pool to Nitro-X. From Table 9–6, the rate for this pool is $3,400 per production run. From Table 9–2, Nitro-X uses 20 production runs. Thus, the overhead assigned

TABLE 9-6 ACTIVITY-BASED COSTING: FIRST-STAGE PROCEDURE

Pool 1:	
Setup costs	$ 96,000
Quality control costs	74,000
Total costs	$170,000
Production runs	50
Pool rate (cost per run) $170,000/50	$ 3,400
Pool 2:	
Power cost	$ 84,000
Maintenance	78,000
Total costs	$162,000
Machine hours	60,000
Pool rate (cost per machine hour) $162,000/60,000	$2.70

from the first cost pool is $68,000 ($3,400 × 20 runs). Similar assignments would be made for the other cost pool and for the other product (for both cost pools).

The total overhead cost per unit of product is obtained by first tracing the overhead costs from the pools to the individual products. This total is then divided by the number of units produced. The result is the unit overhead cost. Adding the per-unit overhead cost to the per-unit prime cost yields the manufacturing cost per unit. In Table 9-7, the manufacturing cost per unit is computed using activity-based costing.

Comparison of Product Costs

In Table 9-8, the unit cost from activity-based costing is compared with the unit costs produced by conventional costing using either a plant-wide or departmental rate. This comparison clearly illustrates the effects of using only volume-based cost drivers to assign overhead costs. The activity-based cost reflects the correct pattern of overhead consumption and is, therefore, the most accurate of the three costs shown in Table 9-8.

TABLE 9-7 ACTIVITY-BASED COSTING: SECOND-STAGE PROCEDURE UNIT COSTS

Nitro-X		
Overhead:		
Pool 1: $3,400 × 20	$ 68,000	
Pool 2: $2.70 × 10,000	27,000	
Total overhead costs		$ 95,000
Prime costs		50,000
Total manufacturing costs		$145,000
Units produced		10,000
Unit cost		$14.50

Nitro-Y		
Overhead:		
Pool 1: $3,400 × 30	$102,000	
Pool 2: $2.70 × 50,000	135,000	
Total overhead costs		$237,000
Prime costs		250,000
Total manufacturing costs		$487,000
Units produced		50,000
Unit cost		$ 9.74

Activity-based product costing reveals that the conventional method undercosts the Nitro-X significantly—by at least 37.7% = ($14.50 − 10.53)/$10.53) and overcosts the Nitro-Y by at least 8.1% = ($10.53 − $9.74)/$9.74.

Note: Using only volume-based cost drivers can lead to one product subsidizing another. This

TABLE 9-8 COMPARISON OF UNIT COSTS

	Nitro-X	Nitro-Y	Source
Conventional:			
Plant-wide rate	10.53	10.53	Table 3
Department rates	8.86	10.87	Table 4
Activity-based cost	$14.50	$9.74	Table 7

subsidy could create the appearance that one group of products is highly profitable and adversely impact the pricing and competitiveness of another group of products. In a highly competitive environment, accurate cost information is critical for sound planning and decision making.

Which cost drivers should be used?

At least two major factors should be considered in selecting cost drivers: (1) the cost of measurement and (2) the degree of correlation between the cost driver and the actual consumption of overhead.

The Cost of Measurement. In an activity-based cost system, a large number of cost drivers can be selected and used. However, it is preferable to select cost drivers that use information that is readily available. Information that is not available in the existing system must be produced, which will increase the cost of the firm's information system. A homogeneous cost pool could offer a number of possible cost drivers. For this situation, any cost driver that can be used with existing information should be chosen. This choice minimizes the costs of measurement.

In our example, for instance, quality control costs and setup costs were placed in the same cost pool, giving the choice of using either inspection hours or number of production runs as the cost driver. If the quantities of both cost drivers used by the two products are already being produced by the company's information system, then which is chosen is unimportant. Assume, however, that inspection hours by product are not tracked, but data for production runs are available. In this case, production runs should be chosen as the cost driver, avoiding the need to produce any additional information.

Indirect Measures and the Degree of Correlation. The existing information structure can be exploited in another way to minimize the costs of obtaining cost driver quantities. It is sometimes possible to replace a cost driver that directly measures the consumption of an activity with a cost driver that indirectly measures that consumption. For example, inspection hours could be replaced by the actual number of inspections associated with each product; this number is more likely to be known. This replacement only works, of course, if hours used per inspection are reasonably stable for each product. *Linear regressions,* can be utilized to determine the degree of correlation.

A list of potential cost drivers is given in Table 9–9. Cost drivers that indirectly measure the consumption of an activity usually measure the number of transactions associated with that activity. It is possible to replace a cost driver that directly measures consumption with one that only indirectly measures it without loss of accuracy provided that the quantities of activity consumed per transaction are stable for each product. In such a case, the indirect cost driver has a high correlation and can be used.

EXAMPLE 2

To further illustrate the limitation of this traditional approach, assume that OC Metals, Inc. has established the overhead cost pools and cost drivers for their product shown on the next page.

TABLE 9-9 COST DRIVERS

Manufacturing:

Number of setups	Direct labor hours
Weight of material	Number of vendors
Number of units reworked	Machine hours
Number of orders placed	Number of labor transactions
Number of orders received	Number of units scrapped
Number of inspections	Number of parts
Number of material handling operations	Square footage

Non-manufacturing:
Number of hospital beds occupied
Number of take-offs and landings for an airline
Number of rooms occupied in a hotel

TABLE 9-9 COST DRIVERS, (continued)

Overhead Cost Pool	Budgeted Overhead Cost	Cost Driver	Predicted Level for Cost Driver	Predetermined Overhead Rate
Machine setups	$100,000	Number of setups	100	$1,000 per set-up
Material handling	100,000	Weight of raw material	50,000 pounds	$2 per pound
Waste control	50,000	Weight of hazardous chemicals used	10,000 pounds	$5 per pound
Inspection	75,000	Number of inspections	1,000	$75 per inspection
Other overhead costs	$200,000	Machine hours	20,000	$10 per machine hour
	$525,000			

Job No. 3941 consists of 2,000 special purpose machine tools with the following requirements:

Machine set-ups	2 set-ups
Raw material required	10,000 pounds
Waste materials required	2,000 pounds
Inspections	10 inspections
Machine hours	500 machine hours

The overhead assigned to Job No. 3941 is computed in Table 9–10.

The total overhead cost assigned to Job No. 3941 is $37,750, or $18.88 ($37,750/2,000) per tool. Compare this with the overhead cost that is assigned to the job if the firm uses a single predetermined overhead rate based on machine hours:

$$\frac{\text{Total budgeted overhead cost}}{\text{Total predicted machine hours}} = \frac{\$525,000}{20,000}$$

$$= \$26.25 \text{ per machine hour}$$

Under this approach, the total overhead cost assigned to Job No. 3941 is $13,125 ($26.25 per machine hour × 500 machine hours). This is only $6.56 ($13,125/2,000) per tool, which is about 1/3 of the overhead cost per tool computed when multiple cost drivers are used.

The reason for this wide discrepancy is that these special purpose tools require a relatively large number of machine set-ups, a sizable amount of waste materials, and several inspections. Thus, they are relatively costly in terms of driving overhead costs. Use of a single predetermined overhead rate obscures that fact.

Inaccurately calculating the overhead cost per unit to the extent illustrated above can have serious adverse consequences for the firm. For example, it can lead to poor decisions about pricing, product mix, or contract bidding.

Note: The CFO needs to weigh carefully such considerations in designing a product costing system. A costing system using multiple cost drivers is more costly to implement and use, but it may save millions through improved decisions.

TABLE 9-10 OVERHEAD COMPUTATION

Overhead Cost Pool	Predetermined Overhead Rate	Level of Cost Driver	Assigned Overhead Cost
Machine setups	$1,000 per setup	2 setups	$ 2,000
Material handling	$2 per pound	10,000 pounds	20,000
Waste control	$5 per pound	2,000 pounds	10,000
Inspection	$75 per inspection	10 inspections	750
Other overhead costs	$10 per machine hour	500 machine hours	5,000
Total			$37,750

10

Cost-Volume-Profit Analysis and Leverage

What is cost-volume-profit analysis?

Cost-volume-profit (CVP) analysis, together with cost behavior information, helps CFOs perform many useful analyses. CVP analysis deals with how profit and costs change with a change in volume. More specifically, it looks at the effects on profits of changes in such factors as variable costs, fixed costs, selling prices, volume, and mix of products sold. By studying the relationships of costs, sales, and net income, the CFO is better able to cope with many planning decisions.

Break-even analysis, a branch of CVP analysis, determines the break-even sales. Break-even point —the financial crossover point when revenues exactly match costs—does not show up in corporate earnings reports, but CFOs find it an extremely useful measurement in a variety of ways.

How may you use CVP analysis in solving business problems?

CVP analysis tries to answer the following questions:

- What sales volume is required to break even?
- What sales volume is necessary to earn a desired profit?
- What profit can be expected on a given sales volume?
- How would changes in selling price, variable costs, fixed costs, and output affect profits?
- How would a change in the mix of products sold affect the break-even and target income volume and profit potential?

What does contribution margin mean?

For accurate CVP analysis, a distinction must be made between costs as being either variable or fixed. Mixed costs must be separated into their variable and fixed components.

In order to compute the break-even point and perform various CVP analyses, note the following important concepts.

• Contribution Margin (CM). The contribution margin is the excess of sales (S) over the variable costs (VC) of the product or service. It is the amount of money available to cover fixed costs (FC) and to generate profit. Symbolically, $CM = S - VC$.

• Unit CM. The unit CM is the excess of the unit selling price (p) over the unit variable cost (v). Symbolically, unit $CM = p - v$.

• CM Ratio. The CM ratio is the contribution margin as a percentage of sales, i.e.,

$$CM \text{ ratio} = \frac{CM}{S} = \frac{S - VC}{S} = 1 - \frac{VC}{S}$$

The CM ratio can also be computed using per-unit data as follows:

$$CM \text{ ratio} = \frac{Unit\ CM}{p} = \frac{p - v}{p} = 1 - \frac{v}{p}$$

Note that the CM ratio is 1 minus the variable cost ratio. For example, if variable costs account for 70% of the price, the CM ratio is 30%.

EXAMPLE 1

To illustrate the various concepts of CM, consider the following data for Delta Toy Store:

	Total	Per Unit	Percentage
Sales (1,500 units)	$37,500	$25	100%
Less: Variable costs	15,000	10	40
Contribution margin	$22,500	$15	60%
Less: Fixed costs	15,000		
Net income	$ 7,500		

From the data listed above, CM, unit CM, and the CM ratio are computed as:

$$CM = S - VC = \$37{,}500 - \$15{,}000 = \$22{,}500$$

$$\text{Unit CM} = p - v = \$25 - \$10 = \$15$$

$$\text{CM ratio} = \frac{CM}{S} = \frac{\$22{,}500}{\$37{,}500} = 60\% \text{ or}$$

$$\frac{\text{Unit CM}}{p} = \frac{\$15}{\$25} = 0.6 = 60\%$$

How can the break-even sales be computed?

The break-even point represents the level of sales revenue that equals the total of the variable and fixed costs for a given volume of output at a particular capacity use rate. For example, you might want to ask the break-even occupancy rate (or vacancy rate) for a hotel or the break-even load rate for an airliner.

Generally, the lower the break-even point, the higher the profit and the less the operating risk, other things being equal. The break-even point also provides CFOs with insights into profit planning. It can be computed using the following formulas:

$$\text{Break-even point in units} = \frac{\text{Fixed costs}}{\text{Unit CM}}$$

$$\text{Break-even point in dollars} = \frac{\text{Fixed costs}}{\text{CM ratio}}$$

EXAMPLE 2

Using the same data given in Example 1, where unit CM = $25 - $10 = $15 and CM ratio = 60%, we get:

Break-even point in units = $15,000/$15 = 1,000 units

Break-even point in dollars = $15,000/0.6 = $25,000

Or, alternatively,

$$1{,}000 \text{ units} \times \$25 = \$25{,}000$$

How do you determine target income volume?

Besides determining the break-even point, CVP analysis determines the sales required to attain a target net income. The formula is:

$$\frac{\text{Target income}}{\text{sales volume}} = \frac{\text{Fixed costs plus Target income}}{\text{Unit CM}}$$

EXAMPLE 3

Using the same data given in Example 1, assume that Delta Toy Store wishes to attain a target income of $15,000 before tax. Then, the target income volume would be:

$$\frac{\$15,000 + \$15,000}{\$25 - \$10} = \frac{\$30,000}{\$15} = 2,000 \text{ units}$$

What is the impact of income taxes on target income volume?

If target income is given on an after-tax basis, the target income volume formula becomes:

$$\frac{\text{Target income}}{\text{volume}} = \frac{\text{Fixed costs} + [\text{Target after-tax income}/(1 - \text{Tax rate})]}{\text{Unit CM}}$$

EXAMPLE 4

Assume in Example 1 that Delta Toy Store wants to achieve an after-tax income of $6,000. The tax rate is 40%. Then,

$$\frac{\text{Target income}}{\text{volume}} = \frac{\$15,000 + [\$6,000/(1 - 0.4)]}{\$15}$$

$$= \frac{\$15,000 + \$10,000}{\$15} = 1,667 \text{ units}$$

What is the cash break-even point?

If a company has a minimum of available cash or the opportunity cost of holding excess cash is too high, management may want to know the volume of sales that will cover all cash expenses during a period. This is known as the cash break-even point. Not all fixed operating costs involve cash payments. For example, depreciation expenses are non-cash fixed charges. To find the cash break-even point, the non-cash charges must be subtracted from fixed costs. Therefore, the cash break-even point is lower than the usual break-even point. The formula is:

$$\text{Cash break-even point} = \frac{\text{Fixed costs} - \text{Depreciation}}{\text{Unit CM}}$$

EXAMPLE 5

Assume from Example 1 that the total fixed costs of $15,000 include depreciation of $1,500. Then the cash break-even point is:

$$\frac{\$15,000 - \$1,500}{\$25 - \$10} = \frac{\$13,500}{\$15} = 900 \text{ units}$$

Delta Toy Store has to sell 900 units to cover only the fixed costs involving cash payments of $13,500 and to break even.

What is the use of Margin of Safety?

The margin of safety is a measure of difference between the actual sales and the break-even sales. It is the amount by which sales revenue may drop before losses begin, and is expressed as a percentage of expected sales:

$$\text{Margin of safety} = \frac{\text{Expected sales} - \text{Break-even sales}}{\text{Expected sales}}$$

The margin of safety is used as a measure of operating risk. The larger the ratio, the safer the situation since there is less risk of reaching the break-even point.

EXAMPLE 6

Assume Delta Toy Store projects sales of $35,000 with a break-even sales level of $25,000. The projected margin of safety is

$$\frac{\$35,000 - \$25,000}{\$35,000} = 28.57\%$$

How is CVP analysis used in solving "what-if" scenarios?

The concepts of contribution margin and the contribution income statement have many applications in profit planning and short-term decision making. Many "what-if" scenarios can be evaluated using them as planning tools, especially utilizing a spreadsheet program such as Lotus 1-2-3. Some applications are illustrated in Examples 7 to 11 using the same data as in Example 1.

EXAMPLE 7

Recall from Example 1 that Delta Toy Store has a CM of 60% and fixed costs of $15,000 per period. Assume that the company expects sales to go up by $10,000 for the next period. How much will income increase?

Using the CM concepts, we can quickly compute the impact of a change in sales on profits. The formula for computing the impact is:

$$\text{Change in net income} = \text{Dollar change in sales} \times \text{CM ratio}$$

Thus,

Increase in net income = $10,000 × 60% = $6,000

Therefore, the income will go up by $6,000, assuming there is no change in fixed costs.

If we are given a change in unit sales instead of dollars, then the formula becomes:

$$\text{Change in net income} = \text{Change in unit sales} \times \text{Unit CM}$$

EXAMPLE 8

Assume that the store expects sales to go up by 400 units. How much will income increase? From Example 1, the company's unit CM is $15. Again, assuming there is no change in fixed costs, the income will increase by $6,000.

400 units × $15 = $6,000

EXAMPLE 9

What net income is expected on sales of $47,500?

The answer is the difference between the CM and the fixed costs:

CM: $47,500 × 60%	$28,500
Less: Fixed costs	15,000
Net income	$13,500

EXAMPLE 10

Delta Toy Store is considering increasing the advertising budget by $5,000, which would increase sales revenue by $8,000. Should the advertising budget be increased?

The answer is no, since the increase in the CM is less than the increased cost:

Increase in CM: $8,000 × 60%	$4,800
Increase in advertising	5,000
Decrease in net income	$ (200)

EXAMPLE 11

Consider the original data. Assume again that Delta Toy Store is currently selling 1,500 units per period. In an effort to increase sales, management is considering cutting its unit price by $5 and increasing the advertising budget by $1,000.

If these two steps are taken, management feels that unit sales will go up by 60%. Should the two steps be taken?

A $5 reduction in the selling price will cause the unit CM to decrease from $15 to $10. Thus,

Proposed CM: 2,400 units × $10	$24,000
Present CM: 1,500 units × $15	22,500
Increase in CM	$ 1,500
Increase in advertising outlay	1,000
Increase in net income	$ 500

The answer, therefore, is yes.

What effect does the sales mix have?

Break-even and cost-volume-profit analysis requires some additional computations and assumptions when a company produces and sells more than one product. In multi-product firms, sales mix is an important factor in calculating an overall company break-even point.

Different selling prices and different variable costs result in different unit CM and CM ratios. As a result, the break-even points and cost-volume-profit relationships vary with the relative proportions of the products sold, called the *sales mix*.

In break-even and CVP analysis, it is necessary to predetermine the sales mix and then compute a weighted average unit CM. It is also necessary to assume that the sales mix does not change for a specified period. The break-even formula for the company as a whole is:

$$\text{Break-even sales in units (or in dollars)} = \frac{\text{Fixed costs}}{\text{Weighted average unit CM (or CM ratio)}}$$

EXAMPLE 12

Assume that Knibex, Inc. produces cutlery sets out of high-quality wood and steel. The company makes a deluxe cutlery set and a standard set that have the following unit CM data:

	Deluxe	Standard
Selling price	$15	$10
Variable cost per unit	12	5
Unit CM	$ 3	$ 5
Sales mix	60%	40%
Fixed costs	$76,000	

The weighted average unit CM = ($3)(0.6) + ($5)(0.4) = $3.80. Therefore the company's break-even point in units is:

$$\$76,000/\$3.80 = 20,000 \text{ units}$$

which is divided as follows:

A: 20,000 units × 60% = 12,000 units
B: 20,000 units × 40% =   8,000
                         20,000 units

EXAMPLE 13

Assume that Dante, Inc. is a producer of recreational equipment. It expects to produce and sell three types of sleeping bags—the Economy, the Regular, and the Backpacker. Information on the bags is given below:

BUDGETED

	Economy	Regular	Backpacker	Total
Sales	$30,000	$60,000	$10,000	$100,000
Sales mix	30%	60%	10%	100%
Less: VC	24,000	40,000	5,000	69,000
CM	$ 6,000	$20,000	$ 5,000	$ 31,000
CM ratio	20%	33⅓%	50%	31%
Fixed costs				$18,600
Net income				$12,400

The CM ratio for Dante, Inc. is $31,000/$100,000 = 31%. Therefore the break-even point in dollars is

$$\$18,600/0.31 = \$60,000$$

which will be split in the mix ratio of 3:6:1 to give us the following break-even points for the individual products:

Economy: $60,000 × 30% = $18,000
Regular: $60,000 × 60% = 36,000
Backpacker: $60,000 × 10% =   6,000
                             $60,000

One of the most important assumptions underlying CVP analysis in a multi-product firm is that the sales mix will not change during the planning period. But if the sales mix changes, the break-even point will also change.

EXAMPLE 14

Assume that total sales from Example 13 was achieved at $100,000 but that an actual mix came out differently from the budgeted mix (i.e., for Regular, 60 to 30% and for Backpacker, 10 to 40%).

ACTUAL

	Economy	Regular	Backpacker	Total
Sales	$30,000	$30,000	$40,000	$100,000
Sales mix	30%	30%	40%	100%
Less: VC	24,000	20,000*	20,000**	64,000
CM	$ 6,000	$10,000	$20,000	$ 36,000
CM ratio	20%	33¹/₃%	50%	36%
Fixed costs				$18,600
Net income				$17,400

*$20,000 = $30,000 × (100% − 33¹/₃%) = $30,000 × 66²/₃%
**$20,000 = $40,000 × (100% − 50%) = $40,000 × 50%

Note: The shift in sales mix toward the more profitable line C has caused the CM ratio for the company as a whole to go up from 31% to 36%.

The new break-even point will be:

$$\$51,667 = \$18,600/0.36$$

The break-even dollar volume has decreased from $60,000 to $51,667. The improvement in the mix caused net income to go up. It is important to note that generally, the shift of emphasis from low-margin products to high-margin ones will increase the overall profits of the company.

How can CVP analysis be applied to nonprofit organizations?

Cost-volume-profit (CVP) analysis and break-even analysis is not limited to profit firms. CVP is appropriately called *cost-volume-revenue (CVR) analysis,* as it pertains to nonprofit organizations. The CVR model not only calculates the break-even service level, but helps answer a variety of "what-if" decision questions.

EXAMPLE 15

LMC, Inc., a Los Angeles county agency, has a $1,200,000 lump-sum annual budget appropriation for an agency to help rehabilitate mentally ill patients. On top of this, the agency charges each patient $600 a month for board and care. All of the appropriation and revenue must be spent. The variable costs for rehabilitation activity average $700 per patient per month. The agency's annual fixed costs are $800,000. The agency manager wishes to know how many patients can be served. Let x = number of patients to be served.

$$\text{Revenue} = \text{Total expenses}$$

$$\frac{\text{Lump sum}}{\text{appropriation}} + \$600\,(12)\,x = \frac{\text{Variable}}{\text{expenses}} + \frac{\text{Fixed}}{\text{costs}}$$

$$\$1,200,000 + \$7,200\,x = \$8,400\,x + \$800,000$$
$$(\$7,200 - \$8,400)\,x = \$800,000 - \$1,200,000$$
$$-\$1,200\,x = \$400,000$$
$$x = \$400,000/\$1,200$$
$$x = 333 \text{ patients}$$

We will investigate the following two "what-if" scenarios:

1. Suppose the manager of the agency is concerned that the total budget for the coming year will be cut by 10% to a new amount of $1,080,000. All other things remain unchanged. The manager wants to know how this budget cut affects the next year's service level.

$$\$1,080,000 + \$7,200\,x = \$8,400\,x + \$800,000$$
$$(\$7,200 - \$8,400)\,x = \$800,000 - \$1,080,000$$
$$-\$1,200\,x = -\$280,000$$
$$x = \$280,000/\$1,200$$
$$x = 233 \text{ patients}$$

2. The manager does not reduce the number of patients served despite a budget cut of 10%.

All other things remain unchanged. How much more does he/she have to charge his/her patients for board and care? In this case, x = board and care charge per year

$$\$1,080,000 + 333\, x = \$8,400\,(333) + \$800,000$$
$$333x = \$2,797,200 + \$800,000$$
$$- \$1,080,000$$
$$333\, x = \$2,517,200$$
$$x = \$2,517,200/333 \text{ patients}$$
$$x = \$7,559$$

Thus, the monthly board and care charge must be increased to $630 ($7,559/12 months).

What are the assumptions underlying break-even and CVP analysis?

The basic break-even and CVP models are subject to a number of limiting assumptions. They are:

1. The selling price per unit is constant throughout the entire relevant range of activity.

2. All costs are classified as fixed or variable.

3. The variable cost per unit is constant.

4. There is only one product or a constant sales mix.

5. Inventories do not change significantly from period to period.

6. Volume is the only factor affecting variable costs.

What is leverage and what are the types?

Leverage is that portion of the fixed costs which represents a risk to the firm. Operating leverage, a measure of operating risk, refers to the fixed operating costs found in the firm's income statement. Financial leverage, a measure of financial risk, refers to financing a portion of the firm's assets, bearing fixed financing charges in hopes of increasing the return to the common stockholders. The higher the financial leverage, the higher the financial risk, and the higher the cost of capital. Cost of capital rises because it costs more to raise funds for a risky business. Total leverage is a measure of total risk.

How do you measure operating leverage?

Operating leverage is a measure of operating risk and arises from fixed operating costs. A simple indication of operating leverage is the effect that a change in sales has on earnings.

The formula is:

$$\text{Operating leverage at a given level of sales (x)} = \frac{\text{Percentage change in EBIT}}{\text{Percentage change in sales}}$$

$$= \frac{\Delta \text{EBIT}/\text{EBIT}}{\Delta x / x} = \frac{(p-v)\Delta x / (p-v)x - FC}{\Delta x / x}$$

$$= \frac{(p-v)x}{(p-v)x - FC}$$

where EBIT = earnings before interest and taxes = $(p-v)x - FC$.

EXAMPLE 16

The Peters Company manufactures and sells doors to home builders. The doors are sold for $25 each. Variable costs are $15 per door, and fixed operating costs total $50,000. Assume further that the Peters Company is currently selling 6,000 doors per year. Its operating leverage is:

$$\frac{(p-v)x}{(p-v)x - FC} = \frac{(\$25 - \$15)(6,000)}{(\$25 - \$15)(6,000) - \$50,000}$$

$$= \frac{\$60,000}{\$10,000} = 6$$

which means if sales increase (decrease) by 1 percent, the company can expect net income to increase (decrease) by six times that amount, or 6 percent.

How do you calculate financial leverage?

Financial leverage is a measure of financial risk and arises from fixed financial costs. One way to measure financial leverage is to determine how earnings per share are affected by a change in EBIT (or operating income).

$$\begin{aligned}\text{Financial leverage} \\ \text{at a given level} \\ \text{of sales (x)}\end{aligned} = \frac{\text{Percentage in change in EPS}}{\text{Percentage in change in EBIT}}$$

$$= \frac{(p-v)x - FC}{(p-v)x - FC - IC}$$

where EPS is earnings per share, and IC is fixed finance charges, that is, interest expense or preferred stock dividends. (Preferred stock dividend must be adjusted for taxes i.e., preferred stock dividend/$(1-t)$.)

EXAMPLE 17

Using the data in Example 16, the Peters Company has total financial charges of $2,000, half in interest expense and half in preferred stock dividend. Assume a corporate tax rate of 40%.

First, the fixed financial charges are:

$$IC = \$1,000 + \frac{\$1,000}{(1-0.4)} = \$1,000 + \$1,667 = \$2,667$$

Therefore, Peters's financial leverage is computed as follows:

$$\begin{aligned}&\frac{(p-v)x - FC}{(p-v)x - FC - IC}\\ \\ &= \frac{(\$25 - \$15)(6,000) - \$50,000}{(\$25 - \$15)(6,000) - \$50,000 - \$2,667}\\ \\ &= \frac{\$10,000}{\$7,333} = 1.36\end{aligned}$$

which means that if EBIT increases (decreases) by 1%, Peters can expect its EPS to increase (decrease) by 1.36 times, or by 1.36%.

How do you determine total leverage?

Total leverage is a measure of total risk. The way to measure total leverage is to determine how EPS is affected by a change in sales.

$$\begin{array}{c} \text{Total leverage} \\ \text{at a given level} \\ \text{of sales (x)} \end{array} = \frac{\text{Percentage in change in EPS}}{\text{Percentage in change in sales}}$$

$$= \frac{\text{operating}}{\text{leverage}} \times \frac{\text{financial}}{\text{leverage}}$$

$$= \frac{(p-v)x}{(p-v)x - FC} \times \frac{(p-v)x - FC}{(p-v)x - FC - IC}$$

$$= \frac{(p-v)x}{(p-v)x - FC - IC}$$

EXAMPLE 18

From Examples 16 and 17, the total leverage for Peters company is:

$$\frac{\text{Operating}}{\text{leverage}} \times \frac{\text{financial}}{\text{leverage}} = 6 \times 1.36 = 8.16$$

or

$$\frac{(p-v)x}{(p-v)x - FC - IC}$$

$$= \frac{(\$25 - \$15)(6,000)}{(\$25 - \$15)(6,000) - \$50,000 - \$2,667}$$

$$= \frac{\$60,000}{\$7,333} = 8.18 \text{ (due to rounding error)}$$

which means that if sales increase (decrease) by 1%, Peters can expect its EPS to increase (decrease) by 8.18%.

11

Short-Term Decisions

What are the typical short-term nonrecurring decisions that you face?

When performing the manufacturing and selling functions, management is constantly faced with the problem of choosing between alternative courses of action. Typical questions to be answered include: What to make? How to make it? Where to sell the product? What price should be charged? The CFO is faced with many short-term, nonroutine decisions. In a short-term situation, fixed costs are generally irrelevant to the decision at hand. CFOs must recognize two important concepts as major decision tools: *relevant costs* and *contribution margin*.

What are relevant costs?

In each short-term situation, the ultimate management decision rests on cost data analysis. Cost data are important in many decisions, since they are the basis for profit calculations. Cost data are classified by function, behavior patterns, and other criteria, as discussed previously.

However, not all costs are of equal importance in decision making, and CFOs must identify the costs that are relevant to a decision. Such costs are called relevant costs.

Which costs are relevant in a decision?

The relevant costs are the expected future costs (and also revenues) which differ between the decision alternatives. Therefore, the sunk costs (past and historical costs) are not considered relevant in the decision. What is relevant are the incremental or differential costs.

What is incremental analysis?

Under the concept of relevant costs, which may be appropriately titled the incremental, differential, or relevant cost approach, the decision involves the following steps:

1. Gather all costs associated with each alternative.

2. Drop the sunk costs.

3. Drop those costs that do not differ between alternatives.

4. Select the best alternative based on the remaining cost data.

When should a company accept special orders?

A company often receives a short-term, special order for its products at lower prices than usual. In normal times, the company may refuse such an order since it will not yield a satisfactory profit. If times are bad, however, such an order should be accepted if the incremental revenue obtained from it exceeds the incremental costs. The company is better off receiving some revenue, above its incremental costs, than to receive nothing at all.

Such a price, one lower than the regular price, is called a *contribution price.* This approach to pricing is often called the contribution approach to pricing or the variable pricing model.

This approach is most appropriate under the following conditions:

1. When operating in a distress situation,

2. When there is idle capacity, and

3. When faced with sharp competition or in a competitive bidding situation.

EXAMPLE 1

Assume that a company with 100,000-unit capacity is currently producing and selling only 90,000 units of product each year at a regular price of $2. If the variable cost per unit is $1 and the annual fixed cost is $45,000, the income statement looks as follows:

Sales (90,000 units)	$180,000	$2.00
Less: Variable cost (90,000 units)	90,000	1.00

Contribution margin	$ 90,000	$1.00
Less: Fixed cost	45,000	0.50
Net income	$ 45,000	$0.50

The company has just received an order that calls for 10,000 units at $1.20 per unit, for a total of $12,000. The buyer will pay the shipping expenses. The acceptance of this order will not affect regular sales. The company's president is reluctant to accept the order, however, because the $1.20 price is below the $1.50 factory unit cost ($1.50 = $1.00 + $0.50). Should the company accept the order?

The answer is yes. The company can add to total profits by accepting this special order even though the price offered is below the unit factory cost. At a price of $1.20, the order will contribute $0.20 per unit (CM per unit = $1.20 − $1.00 = $0.20) toward fixed cost, and profit will increase by $2,000 (10,000 units × $0.20).

Using the contribution approach to pricing, the variable cost of $1 will be a better guide than the full unit cost of $1.50. Note that the fixed costs do not change because of the presence of idle capacity.

The same result can be seen in more detail as follows:

	Per Unit	Without Special Order (90,000 Units)	With Special Order (100,000 Units)	Difference
Sales	$2.00	$180,000	$192,000	$12,000
Less: Variable costs	1.00	90,000	100,000	10,000
CM	$1.00	$ 90,000	$ 92,000	$ 2,000
Less: Fixed cost	0.50	45,000	45,000	—
Net income	$0.50	$ 45,000	$ 47,000	$ 2,000

EXAMPLE 2

The marketing manager had decided that for Product A he wants a markup of 30% over cost. Particulars concerning a unit of Product A are given as follows:

Direct material	$ 4,000
Direct labor	10,000
Overhead	2,500
Total cost	$16,500
Markup on cost (30%)	4,950
Selling price	$21,450

Total direct labor for the year equals $1,200,000. Total overhead for the year equals 25% of direct labor ($300,000), of which 40% is fixed and 60% is variable. The customer offers to buy a unit of Product A for $18,000. Idle capacity exists.

You should accept the extra order because it provides an increased contribution margin, as indicated below:

Selling price		$18,000
Less: Variable costs		
Direct material	$ 4,000	
Direct labor	10,000	
Variable overhead ($10,000 × 15%)*	1,500	(15,500)
Contribution margin		$ 2,500
Less: Fixed overhead		(0)
Net income		$ 2,500

*Variable overhead equals 15% of direct labor, calculated as follows:

$$\frac{\text{Variable overhead}}{\text{Direct labor}} = \frac{60\% \times \$300,000}{\$1,200,000} = \frac{\$180,000}{\$1,200,000} = 15\%$$

How do you determine a bid price?

The relevant cost approach can be used to determine the bid price on a contract.

EXAMPLE 3

Travis Company has received an order for 6,000 units. The CFO wants to know the minimum bid price that would produce a $14,000 increase in profit. The current income statement follows:

Income Statement

Sales (30,000 units × $20)		$600,000
Less cost of sales		
Direct material	$ 60,000	
Direct labor	150,000	
Variable overhead (150,000 × 40%)	60,000	
Fixed overhead	80,000	(350,000)
Gross margin		$250,000
Less selling and administrative expenses		
Variable (includes transportation costs of $0.20 per unit)	15,000	
Fixed	85,000	(100,000)
Net income		$150,000

If the contract is taken, the cost patterns for the extra order will remain the same, with these exceptions:

- Transportation costs will be paid by the customer.
- Special tools costing $6,000 will be required for just this order and will not be reusable.
- Direct labor time for each unit under the order will be 10% longer.

The bid price is derived in this manner:

	Current Cost Per Unit	
Selling price	$20	($600,000/30,000)
Direct material	2	($60,000/30,000)
Direct labor	5	($150,000/30,000)
Variable overhead	40% of direct labor cost	($60,000/$150,000)

Variable selling and adminis- trative expense	$0.50	($15,000/30,000)

As can be seen in the income statement that follows, the contract price for the 6,000 units should be $80,000 ($680,000 – $600,000), or $13.33 per unit ($80,000/6,000).

The contract price per unit of $13.33 is less than the $20 current selling price per unit. Note, by accepting the order, total fixed cost will remain the same except for the $6,000 cost of special tools. (See example on the next page.)

What is a make-or-buy decision?

The decision whether to produce a component part internally or to buy it externally from an outside supplier is called a "make-or-buy" decision. This decision involves both quantitative and qualitative factors. The qualitative factors include ensuring product quality and the necessity for long-run business relationships with the supplier. The quantitative factors deal with cost. The quantitative effects of the make-or-buy decision are best seen through the relevant cost approach.

EXAMPLE 4

Assume that a firm has prepared the following cost estimates for the manufacture of a subassembly component based on an annual production of 8,000 units:

	Per Unit	Total
Direct materials	$ 5	$ 40,000
Direct labor	4	32,000
Variable factory overhead applied	4	32,000
Fixed factory overhead applied (150% of direct labor cost)	6	48,000
Total cost	$19	$152,000

INCOME STATEMENT

	Current (30,000)	Projected (36,000)	
Sales	$600,000	$680,000[d]	(Computed last)
Cost of sales			
Direct material	$ 60,000	$ 72,000	($2 × 36,000)
Direct labor	150,000	183,000	($150,000 + [6,000 × $5.50[a]])
Variable overhead	$ 60,000	$ 73,200	($183,000 × 40%)
Fixed overhead	80,000	86,000	($80,000 + $6,000)
Total	$350,000	$414,200	
Variable selling and administration costs	$ 15,000	$ 16,800	($15,000 + [6,000 × $0.30])[b]
Fixed selling and administrative costs	85,000	85,000	
Total	$100,000	$101,800	
Net income	$150,000	$164,000[c]	

[a]$5 × 1.10 = $5.50
[b]$0.50 − $0.20 = $0.30
[c]$150,000 + $14,000 = $164,000
[d]Net income + Selling and administrative expensive + Cost of sales = sales
$164,000 + $101,800 + $414,200 = $680,000

242

The supplier has offered to provide the sub-assembly at a price of $16 each. Two-thirds of fixed factory overhead, which represents executive salaries, rent, depreciation, and taxes, continue regardless of the decision. Should the company buy or make the product?

The key to the decision lies in the investigation of those relevant costs that change between the make-or-buy alternatives. Assuming that the productive capacity will be idle if not used to produce the subassembly, the analysis takes the following form:

	Per Unit		Total of 8,000 Units	
	Make	Buy	Make	Buy
Purchase price		$16		$128,000
Direct materials	$ 5		$ 40,000	
Direct labor	4		32,000	
Variable overhead	4		32,000	
Fixed overhead that can be avoided by not making	2	—	16,000	
Total relevant costs	$15	$16	$120,000	$128,000
Difference in favor of making	$1		$8,000	

The make-or-buy decision must be investigated, along with the broader perspective of considering how best to utilize available facilities. The alternatives are:

1. Leaving facilities idle.

2. Buying the parts and renting out idle facilities.

3. Buying the parts and using idle facilities for other products.

What is a sell-or-process-further decision?

When two or more products are produced simultaneously from the same input by a joint process, these products are called *joint products*. The term *joint costs* is used to describe all the manufacturing costs incurred prior to the point where the joint products are identified as individual products, referred to as the split-off point. At the split-off point, some of the joint products are in final form and saleable to the consumer, whereas others require additional processing.

In many cases, however, the company might have an option: it can sell the goods at the split-off point or process them further in the hope of obtaining additional revenue. In connection with this type of decision, called the "sell-or-process-further" decision, joint costs are considered irrelevant, since the joint costs have already been incurred at the time of the decision, and therefore represent sunk costs. The decision will rely exclusively on additional revenue compared to the additional costs incurred due to further processing.

EXAMPLE 5

The Gin Company produces three products, A, B, and C from a joint process. Joint production costs for the year were $120,000. Product A may be sold at the split-off point or processed further. The additional processing requires no special facilities and all additional processing costs are variable. Sales values and cost needed to evaluate the company's production policy regarding product A follow:

Units Produced	Sales Value at Split-Off	Additional Cost & Sales Value After Further Processing	
		Sales	Costs
3,000	$60,000	$90,000	$25,000

Should product A be sold at the split-off point or processed further?

Incremental sales revenue	$30,000
Incremental costs, additional processing	25,000
Incremental gain	$ 5,000

In summary, product A should be processed as shown above. Keep in mind that the joint production cost of $120,000 is not included in the analysis, since it is a sunk cost and, therefore, irrelevant to the decision.

How do you decide whether to keep or drop a product line?

The decision whether to drop an old product line or add a new one must take into account both qualitative and quantitative factors. However, any final decision should be based primarily on the impact the decision will have on contribution margin or net income.

EXAMPLE 6

The Beta grocery store has three major product lines: produce, meats, and canned food. The store is considering the decision to drop the meat line because the income statement shows it is being sold at a loss. Note the income statement for these product lines below:

	Produce	Meats	Canned Food	Total
Sales	$10,000	$15,000	$25,000	$50,000
Less: Variable costs	6,000	8,000	12,000	26,000
CM	$ 4,000	$ 7,000	$13,000	$24,000
Less: Fixed costs				
Direct	$ 2,000	$ 6,500	$ 4,000	$12,500
Allocated	1,000	1,500	2,500	5,000
Total	$ 3,000	$ 8,000	$ 6,500	$17,500
Net income	$ 1,000	$(1,000)	$ 6,500	$ 6,500

In this example, direct fixed costs are those costs that are identified directly with each of the product lines, whereas allocated fixed costs are the amount of common fixed costs allocated to the product lines using some base such as space occupied. The amount of common fixed costs typically continues regardless of the decision and thus cannot be saved by dropping the product line to which it is distributed.

The following calculations show the effects on the company as a whole with and without the meat line:

	Keep Meats	Drop Meats	Difference
Sales	$50,000	$35,000	$(15,000)
Less: Variable cost	26,000	18,000	(8,000)
CM	$24,000	$17,000	$ (7,000)
Less: Fixed cost			
Direct	$12,500	$ 6,000	$ (6,500)
Allocated	5,000	5,000	—
Total	$17,500	$11,000	$ (6,500)
Net Income	$ 6,500	$ 6,000	$ (500)

Alternatively, the incremental approach would show the following:

If Meats Dropped

Sales revenue lost		$15,000)
Gains:		
Variable cost avoided	$8,000	
Direct fixed costs avoided	6,500	14,500
Increase (decrease) in net income		$ (500)

From either of the two methods, we see that by dropping meats the store will lose an additional $500. Therefore, the meat product line should be kept. One of the dangers in allocating common fixed costs is that such allocations can make a product line look less profitable than it really is. Because of such an allocation, the meat line showed a loss of $1,000, but it in effect contributes $500 ($7,000 – $6,500) to the recovery of the company's common fixed costs.

How do you make the best use of scarce resources?

In general, the emphasis on products with higher contribution margin maximizes a firm's total net income, even though total sales may decrease. This is not true, however, where there are constraining factors and scarce resources. The constraining factor may be machine hours, labor hours, or cubic feet of warehouse space.

In the presence of these constraining factors, maximizing total profits depends on getting the highest contribution margin per unit of the factor (rather than the highest contribution margin per unit of product output).

EXAMPLE 7

Assume that a company produces two products, A and B, with the following contribution margins per unit.

	A	B
Sales	$8	$24
Variable costs	6	20
CM	$2	$ 4
Annual fixed costs		$42,000

As is indicated by CM per unit, B is more profitable than A since it contributes more to the company's total profits than A ($4 vs. $2). But let us assume that the firm has a limited capacity of 10,000 labor hours. Further, assume that A requires two labor hours to produce and B requires five labor hours. One way to express this limited capacity is to determine the contribution margin per labor hour.

TABLE 11-1 DECISION GUIDELINES

Decision	Description	Decision Guidelines
Special order	Should a discount-priced order be accepted when there is idle capacity?	If regular orders are not affected, accept order when the revenue from the order exceeds the incremental cost. Fixed costs are usually irrelevant.
Make or buy	Should a part be made or bought from a vendor?	Choose lower-cost option. Fixed costs are usually irrelevant. Often opportunity costs are present.
Closing a segment	Should a segment be dropped?	Compare loss in contribution margin with savings in fixed costs.
Sell or process further	Should joint products be sold at split-off or processed further?	Ignore joint costs. Process further if incremental revenue exceeds incremental cost.
Scarce resources	Which products should be emphasized when capacity is limited?	Emphasize products with highest contribution margin per unit of scarce resource (e.g., CM per machine hour).

	A	B
CM/unit	$2.00	$4.00
Labor hours required per unit	2	5
CM per labor hour	$1.00	$0.80

Since A returns the higher CM per labor hour, it should be produced and B should be dropped.

Table 11–1 summarizes guidelines for typical short-term decisions.

12

Financial Forecasting, Planning, and Budgeting

What and why of financial forecasting?

Financial forecasting, an essential element of planning, is the basis for *budgeting* activities. It is also needed when estimating future financing requirements. The company may look either internally or externally for financing. Internal financing refers to cash flow generated from the company's normal operating activities. External financing refers to funds provided by parties external to the company. You need to analyze how to estimate *external* financing requirements. Basically, forecasts of future sales and related expenses provide the firm with the information to project future external financing needs.

The basic steps in projecting financing needs are:

1. Project the firm's sales. The sales forecast is the initial step. Most other forecasts (budgets) follow the sales forecast.

2. Project additional variables such as expenses.

3. Estimate the level of investment in current and fixed assets to support the projected sales.

4. Calculate the firm's financing needs.

How does the percent-of-sales method work?

The most widely used method for projecting the company's financing needs is *the percent-of-sales method.* This method involves estimating the various expenses, assets, and liabilities for a future period as a percent of the sales forecast and then using these percentages, together with the projected sales, to construct forecasted balance sheets. The following example illustrates how to develop a pro forma balance sheet and determine the amount of external financing needed.

EXAMPLE 1

Assume that sales for 19X1 = $20, projected sales for 19X2 = $24, net income = 5% of sales, and the dividend payout ratio = 40%. Table 12–1 illustrates the method, step by step. All dollar amounts are in millions.

The steps for the computations are outlined as follows:

1. Express those balance sheet items that vary directly with sales as a percentage of sales. Any item such as long-term debt that does not vary directly with sales is designated "na," or "not applicable."

2. Multiply these percentages by the 19X2 projected sales = $24 to obtain the projected amounts as shown in the last column.

3. Simply insert figures for long-term debt, common stock and paid-in-capital from the 19X1 balance sheet.

4. Compute 19X2 retained earnings as shown in (b).

5. Sum the asset accounts, obtaining a total projected assets of $7.2, and also add the projected liabilities and equity to obtain $7.12, the total financing provided. Since liabilities and equity must total $7.2, but only $7.12 is projected, we have a shortfall of $0.08 "external financing needed."

Although the forecast of additional funds required can be made by setting up pro forma balance sheets as described here, it is often easier to use the following formula:

$$\begin{aligned} \text{External funds} \atop \text{needed (EFN)} &= {\text{Required increase} \atop \text{in assets}} \\ &- {\text{Spontaneous increase} \atop \text{in liabilities}} \\ &- {\text{Increase in} \atop \text{retained earnings}} \end{aligned}$$

$$\text{EFN} = (A/S)\,\Delta S - (L/S)\,\Delta S - (PM)(PS)(1-d)$$

where A/S = Assets that increase spontaneously with sales as a percentage of sales;

TABLE 12-1 PRO FORMA BALANCE SHEET (IN MILLIONS OF DOLLARS)

	Present (19X1)	% of Sales (19X1 Sales = $20)	Projected (19X2 Sales = $24)	
Assets				
Current assets	2	10	2.4	
Fixed assets	4	20	4.8	
Total assets	6		7.2	
Liabilities and Stockholders' Equity				
Current liabilities	2	10	2.4	
Long-term debt	2.5	n.a.	2.5	
Total liabilities	4.5		4.9	
Common stock	0.1	n.a.	0.1	
Paid-in capital	0.2	n.a.	0.2	
Retained earnings	1.2		1.92[a]	
Total equity	1.5		2.22	
Total liabilities and stockholders' equity	6		7.2	
			7.12	Total financing provided
			0.08[b]	External financing needed
			7.2	Total

[a] *19X2 retained earnings = 19X1 retained earnings + projected net income − cash dividends paid*
$= \$1.2 + 5\%(\$24) - 40\%[5\%(\$24)] = \$1.2 + \$1.2 - \$0.48 = \$2.4 - \$0.48 = \$1.92$

[b] *External financing needed = projected total assets − (projected total liabilities + projected equity)*

252

L/S = Liabilities that increase spontaneously with sales as a percentage of sales;

ΔS = Change in sales;

PM = Profit margin on sales;

PS = Projected sales; and

d = Dividend payout ratio.

In Example 1,

A/S = \$6/\$20 = 30%

L/S = \$2/\$20 = 10%

ΔS = (\$24 – \$20) = \$4

PM = 5% on sales

PS = \$24

d = 40%

Plugging these figures into the formula yields:

$$EFN = 0.3(\$4) – 0.1(\$4) – (0.05)(\$24)(1 – 0.4)$$
$$= \$1.2 – \$0.4 – \$0.72 = \$0.08$$

Thus, the amount of external financing needed is \$800,000, which can be raised by issuing notes payable, bonds, stocks, or any combination of these financing sources.

The major advantage of the percent-of-sales method of financial forecasting is that it is simple and inexpensive to use. One important assumption behind the use of the method is that the firm is operating at full capacity. This means that the company has no sufficient productive capacity to absorb a projected increase in sales and thus requires additional investment in assets. Therefore, the method must be used with extreme caution if excess capacity exists in certain asset accounts.

To obtain a more precise projection of the firm's future financing needs, however, the preparation of a cash budget (to be presented later) is required.

What is a budget?

A comprehensive (master) budget is a formal statement of the CFO's expectation regarding sales, expenses, volume, and other financial

FIGURE 12-1 COMPREHENSIVE (MASTER) BUDGET

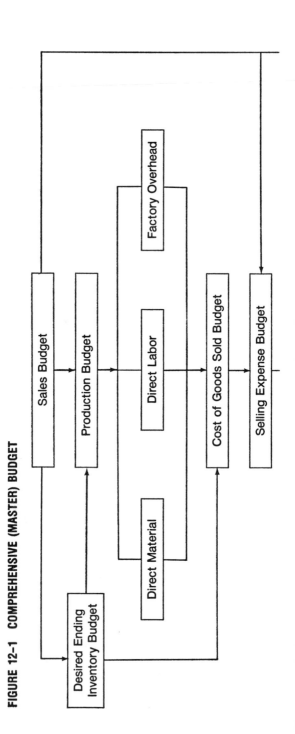

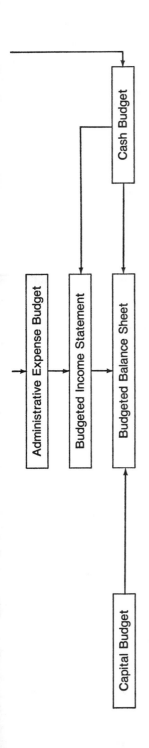

Administrative Expense Budget

Budgeted Income Statement

Budgeted Balance Sheet

Cash Budget

Capital Budget

transactions of an organization for the coming period. Simply put, a budget is a set of pro forma (projected or planned) financial statements. It consists basically of a pro forma income statement, pro forma balance sheet, and cash budget.

A budget is a tool for both planning and control. At the beginning of the period, the budget is a plan or standard; at the end of the period it serves as a control device to help the CFO measure its performance against the plan so that future performance may be improved.

With the aid of computer technology, budgeting can be used as an effective device for evaluation of "what-if" scenarios. Such scenarios allow management to move toward finding the best course of action among various alternatives through simulation.

If management does not like what they see on the budgeted financial statements in terms of various financial ratios such as liquidity, activity (turnover), leverage, profit margin, and market value ratios, they can always alter their contemplated decision and planning set.

What are the types of budgets?

The budget is classified broadly into two categories:

1. Operating budget, reflecting the results of operating decisions.

2. Financial budget, reflecting the financial decisions of the firm.

What is an operating budget?

The operating budget consists of:

- Sales budget.
- Production budget.
- Direct materials budget.
- Direct labor budget.
- Factory overhead budget.
- Selling and administrative expense budget.
- Pro forma income statement.

What does the financial budget contain?

The financial budget consists of:

- Cash budget.
- Pro forma balance sheet.

How do you prepare a budget?

The major steps in preparing the budget are:

1. Prepare a sales forecast.
2. Determine expected production volume.
3. Estimate manufacturing costs and operating expenses.
4. Determine cash flow and other financial effects.
5. Formulate projected financial statements.

Figure 12–1 shows a simplified diagram of the various parts of the comprehensive (master) budget, the master plan of the company.

EXAMPLE 2

To illustrate how all these budgets are developed, we will focus on a manufacturing company called the Delta Company, which produces and markets a single product. We will assume that the company develops the master budget in contribution format for 19XX on a quarterly basis. We will highlight the variable cost-fixed cost breakdown throughout the illustration.

The Sales Budget

The sales budget is the starting point in preparing the master budget, since estimated sales volume influences nearly all other items appearing throughout the master budget. The sales budget ordinarily indicates the quantity of each product expected to be sold. After sales volume has been estimated, the sales budget is constructed by multiplying the expected sales in units by the expected unit sales price. Generally, the sales budget includes a computation of expected cash collections from credit sales, which will be used later for cash budgeting. (See example on page 258.)

THE DELTA COMPANY
Sales Budget for the Year Ending December 31, 19XX

	Quarter				
	1	2	3	4	Total
Expected sales in units	800	700	900	800	3,200
Unit sales price	× $80	× $80	× $80	× $80	× $80
Total sales	$64,000	$56,000	$72,000	$64,000	$256,000
Schedule of Expected Cash Collections					
Accounts receivable, 12/31/19A	$ 9,500[a]				$9,500
1st quarter sales ($64,000)	44,800[b]	$17,920[c]			62,720
2d quarter sales ($56,000)		39,200	$15,680		54,880
3d quarter sales ($72,000)			50,400	$20,160	70,560
4th quarter sales ($64,000)				44,800	44,800
Total cash collections	$54,300	$57,120	$66,080	$64,960	$242,460

[a]All $9,500 accounts receivable balance is assumed to be collectible in the first quarter.
[b]70% of a quarter's sales are collected in the quarter of sale.
[c]28% of a quarter's sales are collected in the quarter following, and the remaining 2% are uncollectible.

258

The Production Budget

After sales are budgeted, the production budget can be determined. The number of units expected to be manufactured to meet budgeted sales and inventory requirements is set forth in the production budget. The expected volume of production is determined by subtracting the estimated inventory at the beginning of the period from the sum of the units expected to be sold and the desired inventory at the end of the period. The production budget is illustrated as follows:

THE DELTA COMPANY
Production Budget
For the Year Ending December 31, 19XX

	1	2	3	4	Total
			Quarter		
Planned sales	800	700	900	800	3,200
Desired ending inventory[a]	70	90	80	100[b]	100
Total needs	870	790	980	900	3,300
Less: Beginning inventory[c]	80	70	90	80	80
Units to be produced	790	720	890	820	3,220

[a]*10% percent of the next quarter's sales.*
[b]*Estimated.*
[c]*The same as the previous quarter's ending inventory.*

The Direct Material Budget

When the level of production has been computed, a direct material budget should be constructed to show how much material will be required for production and how much material must be purchased to meet this production requirement. (See example on pages 260–261.)

THE DELTA COMPANY

Direct Material Budget for the Year Ending December 31, 19XX

	Quarter				Total
	1	2	3	4	
Units to be produced	790	720	890	820	3,220
Material needs per unit (lbs)	× 3	× 3	× 3	× 3	× 3
Material needs for production	2,370	2,160	2,670	2,460	9,660
Desired ending inventory of materials[a]	216	267	246	250[b]	250
Total needs	2,586	2,427	2,916	2,710	9,910
Less: Beginning inventory of materials[c]	237	216	267	246	237
Materials to be purchased	2,349	2,211	2,649	2,464	9,673
Unit price	× $2	× $2	× $2	× $2	× $2
Purchase cost	$4,698	$4,422	$5,298	$4,928	$19,346

Schedule of Expected Cash Disbursements

Accounts payable, 12/31/19A	$2,200			$ 2,200
1st quarter purchases ($4,698)	2,349	$2,349[d]		4,698
2d quarter purchases ($4,422)		2,211	$2,211	4,422
3d quarter purchases ($5,298)			2,649	2,649	5,298
4th quarter purchases ($4,928)				2,464	2,464
Total disbursements	$4,549	$4,560	$4,860	$5,113	$19,082

[a] 10% of the next quarter's units needed for production.

[b] Estimated.

[c] The same as the prior quarter's ending inventory.

[d] 50% of a quarter's purchases are paid for in the quarter of purchase; the remainder are paid for in the following quarter.

The purchase will depend on both expected usage of materials and inventory levels. The formula for computation of the purchase is:

$$\underset{\text{in units}}{\text{Purchase}} = \text{Usage} + \underset{\text{inventory units}}{\text{Desired ending material}}$$

$$- \text{Beginning inventory units}$$

The direct material budget is usually accompanied by a computation of expected cash payments for materials.

The Direct Labor Budget

The production requirements as set forth in the production budget also provide the starting point for the preparation of the direct labor budget. To compute direct labor requirements, expected production volume for each period is multiplied by the number of direct labor hours required to produce a single unit. The direct labor hours to meet production requirements is then multiplied by the direct labor cost per hour to obtain budgeted total direct labor costs. (See page 263.)

The Factory Overhead Budget

The factory overhead budget should provide a schedule of all manufacturing costs other than direct materials and direct labor. Using the contribution approach to budgeting requires the development of a predetermined overhead rate for the variable portion of the factory overhead. In developing the cash budget, we must remember that depreciation does not entail a cash outlay and therefore must be deducted from the total factory overhead in computing cash disbursement for factory overhead. (See page 264.)

To illustrate the factory overhead budget, we will assume that

- Total factory overhead budgeted = $6,000 fixed (per quarter), plus $2 per hour of direct labor.
- Depreciation expenses are $3,250 each quarter.
- All overhead costs involving cash outlays are paid for in the quarter incurred.

THE DELTA COMPANY
Direct Labor Budget for the Year Ending December 31, 19XX

	Quarter				
	1	2	3	4	Total
Units to be produced	790	720	890	820	3,220
Direct labor hours per unit	× 5	× 5	× 5	× 5	× 5
Total hours	3,950	3,600	4,450	4,100	16,100
Direct labor cost per hour	× $5	× $5	× $5	× $5	× $5
Total direct labor cost	$19,750	$18,000	$22,250	$20,500	$80,500

THE DELTA COMPANY

Factory Overhead Budget for the Year Ending December 31, 19XX

| | Quarter | | | | |
	1	2	3	4	Total
Budgeted direct labor hours	3,950	3,600	4,450	4,100	16,100
Variable overhead rate	× $2	× $2	× $2	× $2	× $2
Variable overhead budgeted	$7,900	$ 7,200	$8,900	$8,200	$32,200
Fixed overhead budgeted	6,000	6,000	6,000	6,000	24,000
Total budgeted overhead	$13,900	$13,200	$14,900	$14,200	$56,200
Less: Depreciation	3,250	3,250	3,250	3,250	13,000
Cash disbursement for overhead	$10,650	$ 9,950	$11,650	$10,950	$43,200

The Ending Inventory Budget

The desired ending inventory budget provides us with the information required for the construction of budgeted financial statements. Specifically, it will help compute the cost of goods sold on the budgeted income statement. Secondly, it will give the dollar value of the ending materials and finished goods inventory to appear on the budgeted balance sheet.

THE DELTA COMPANY

Ending Inventory Budget
For the Year Ending December 31, 19XX

	Ending Inventory Units	Unit Cost	Total
Direct materials	250 pounds	$ 2	$ 500
Finished goods	100 units	$41*	$4,100

The unit variable cost of $41 is computed as follows:

	Unit Cost	Units	Total
Direct materials	*$2*	*3 pounds*	*$ 6*
Direct labor	*5*	*5 hours*	*25*
Variable overhead	*2*	*5 hours*	*10*
Total variable manufacturing cost			*$41*

The Selling and Administrative Expense Budget

The selling and administrative expense budget lists the operating expenses involved in selling the products and in managing the business. In order to complete the budgeted income statement in contribution format, variable selling and administrative expense per unit must be computed. (See example on page 266.)

THE DELTA COMPANY
Selling and Administrative Expense Budget for the Year Ending December 31, 19XX

	Quarter				
	1	2	3	4	Total
Expected sales in units	800	700	900	800	3,200
Variable selling and administrative expense per unit[a]	× $4	× $4	× $4	× $4	× $4
Budgeted variable expense	$ 3,200	$ 2,800	$ 3,600	$ 3,200	$12,800
Fixed selling and adminstrative expenses:					
Advertising	1,100	1,100	1,100	1,100	4,400
Insurance	2,800				2,800
Office salaries	8,500	8,500	8,500	8,500	34,000
Rent	350	350	350	350	1,400
Taxes			1,200		1,200
Total budgeted selling and administrative expenses[b]	$15,950	$12,750	$14,750	$13,150	$56,600

[a]Includes sales agents' commissions, shipping, and supplies.
[b]Paid for in the quarter incurred.

The Cash Budget

The cash budget is prepared for the purpose of cash planning and control. It presents the expected cash inflow and outflow for a designated time period. The cash budget helps management keep cash balances in reasonable relationship to its needs. It aids in avoiding unnecessary idle cash and possible cash shortages. The cash budget consists typically of four major sections:

1. The *receipts* section, which is the beginning cash balance, cash collections from customers, and other receipts

2. The *disbursements* section, which comprises all cash payments made by purpose

3. The *cash surplus or deficit* section, which simply shows the difference between the cash receipts section and the cash disbursements section

4. The *financing* section, which provides a detailed account of the borrowings and repayments expected during the budgeting period

To illustrate, we will make the following assumptions:

- The company desires to maintain a $5,000 minimum cash balance at the end of each quarter.
- All borrowing and repayment must be in multiples of $500 at an interest rate of 10 percent per annum.
- Interest is computed and paid as the principal is repaid.
- Borrowing takes place at the beginning of each quarter and repayment at the end of each quarter.

The Budgeted Income Statement

The budgeted income statement summarizes the various component projections of revenue and expenses for the budgeting period. However, for control purposes the budget can be divided into quarters or even months depending on the need.

THE DELTA COMPANY

Cash Budget for the Year Ending December 31, 19XX

		Quarter				Total
		1	2	3	4	
Cash balance, beginning	Given	$10,000	$ 9,401	$ 5,461	$ 9,106	$ 10,000
Add: Receipts:						
Collection from customers		54,300	57,120	66,080	64,960	242,460
Total cash available		$64,300	$66,521	$71,541	$74,066	$252,460
Less: Disbursements:						
Direct materials		4,549	4,560	4,860	5,113	19,082
Direct labor		19,750	18,000	22,250	20,500	80,500
Factory overhead		10,650	9,950	11,650	10,950	43,200
Selling and admin.		15,950	12,750	14,750	13,150	56,600
Machinery purchase	Given	—	24,300	—	—	24,300
Income tax	Given	4,000	—	—	—	4,000
Total disbursements		54,899	69,560	53,510	49,713	227,682

268

Cash surplus (deficit)	9,401	(3,039)	18,031	24,353	24,778
Financing:					
Borrowing	—	8,500	—	—	8,500
Repayment	—	—	(8,500)	—	(8,500)
Interest	—	—	(425)	—	(425)
Total financing	—	8,500	(8,925)	—	(425)
Cash balance, ending	$ 9,401	$ 5,461	$ 9,106	$24,353	$ 24,353

THE DELTA COMPANY

Budgeted Income Statement[a]
For the Year Ending December 31, 19XX

Sales (3,200 units @ $80)		$256,000
Less: Variable expenses		
Variable cost of goods sold (3,200 units @ $41)	$131,200	
Variable selling & admin.	12,800	144,000
Contribution margin		112,000
Less: Fixed expenses		
Factory overhead	24,000	
Selling & admin.	43,800	67,800
Net operating income		44,200
Less: Interest expense		425
Net income before taxes		43,775
Less: Income taxes 20%		8,755
Net income		$ 35,020

[a] Data are derived from previous budgets.

The Budgeted Balance Sheet

The budgeted balance sheet is developed by beginning with the balance sheet for the year just ended and adjusting it, using all the activities that are expected to take place during the budgeting period. Some of the reasons why the budgeted balance sheet must be prepared are:

- It could disclose some unfavorable financial conditions that management might want to avoid.
- It serves as a final check on the mathematical accuracy of all the other schedules.
- It helps management perform a variety of ratio calculations.
- It highlights future resources and obligations.

To illustrate, we will use the balance sheet on pages 272–273 for the year 19XA.

SOME FINANCIAL CALCULATIONS _____

To see what kind of financial condition the Delta Company is expected to be in for the budgeting year, a sample of financial ratio calculations are in order (Assume 19XA after-tax net income was $15,000):

	19XA	**19XB**
Current ratio (Current assets/ Current liabilities)	$23,254/$6,200 = 3.75	$51,993/$11,219 = 4.63
Return on total assets (Net income after taxes/ Total assets)	$15,000/$113,254 = 13.24%	$35,020/$153,293 = 22.85%

Sample calculations indicate that the Delta Company is expected to have better liquidity as measured by the current ratio. Overall performance will be improved as measured by return on total assets. This could be an indication that the contemplated plan may work out well.

COMPUTER-BASED MODELS FOR BUDGETING _____

More and more companies are developing computer-based models for financial planning and budgeting, using powerful, yet easy-to-use, financial modeling languages such as Execum's *Interactive Financial Planning System* (to be discussed in the next chapter).

Other popular packages include:

1. *Venture,* Team Tech Systems (Red Bank, N.J.), (908) 530-1805, $395.

2. *Encore! Plus,* Ferox Microsystems (Alexandria, Virginia), (703) 684-1660, $895.

3. *MicroFCS,* Pilot Executive Software (Boston, Massachusetts), (617) 350-7035, Price varies by site license.

THE DELTA COMPANY
Balance Sheet
December 31, 19XA

ASSETS			LIABILITIES AND STOCKHOLDERS' EQUITY		
Current Assets:			Current Liabilities:		
Cash		$ 10,000	Accounts payable		$ 2,200
Accounts receivable		9,500	Income tax payable		4,000
Material inventory		474	Total current liabilities		$ 6,200
Finished goods inventory		3,280			
Total current assets		$ 23,254			
			Stockholders' Equity:		
Fixed Assets:			Common stock, no-par		$ 70,000
Land		$ 50,000	Retained earnings		37,054
Building and equipment		100,000	Total stockholders' equity		107,054
Accumulated depreciation		(60,000)			
Total fixed assets		90,000			
Total assets		$113,254	Total liabilities and stockholders' equity		$113,254

THE DELTA COMPANY
Budgeted Balance Sheet December 31, 19XB

ASSETS			LIABILITIES AND STOCKHOLDERS' EQUITY		
Current Assets:			Current Liabilities:		
Cash	$ 24,353[a]		Accounts payable		$ 2,464[h]
Accounts receivable	23,040[b]		Income tax payable		8,755[i]
Material inventory	500[c]		Total current liabilities		$ 11,219
Finished goods inventory	4,100[d]				
Total current assets		$ 51,993			
Fixed Assets:			Stockholders' Equity:		
Land	$ 50,000[e]		Common stock, no-par		$ 70,000[j]
Building and equipment	124,300[f]		Retained earnings		72,074[k]
Accumulated depreciation	(73,000)[g]		Total stockholders' equity		142,074
Total fixed assets		101,300			
Total Assets		$153,293	Total liabilities and stockholders' equity		$153,293

[a] From cash budget.
[b] $9,500 + $256,000 sales − $242,460 receipts = $23,040.
[c] and [d] From Ending Inventory Budget.
[e] No change.
[f] $100,000 + $24,300 = $124,300.
[g] $60,000 + $13,000 = $73,000.

[h] $2,200 + $19,346 − $19,082 = $2,464 (all accounts payable relate to material purchases), or 50% of 4th quarter purchase = 50% ($4,928) = $2,464.
[i] From budgeted income statement.
[j] No change.
[k] $37,054 + $35,020 net income = $72,074.

273

The models help not only build a budget for profit planning but answer a variety of "what-if" scenarios. The resultant calculations provide a basis for choice among alternatives under conditions of uncertainty. Financial modeling can also be accomplished using spreadsheet programs such as *Lotus 1-2-3*, Microsoft's *Excel*, and *Quattro-pro*.

Can you use an electronic spreadsheet to develop a budget plan?

Example 2 showed a detailed procedure for formulating a master budget. However, in practice a short-cut approach to budgeting is quite common using computer technology. For an illustration of a short-cut method, we will show how to develop a projected income statement using *Lotus 1-2-3:*

JKS Furniture Co., Inc. expects the following for the coming 12 months, 19XB:

1. Sales for 1st month = $60,000.
2. Cost of sales = 60% of sales.
3. Operating expenses = $10,000 plus 5% of sales.
4. Income taxes = 25% of net income.
5. Sales increase by 5% each month.

Based on this information, we will develop a spreadsheet for the pro forma income statement for the next 12 months and in total, which is given in Figure 12–2. Using a spreadsheet program such as *Lotus 1-2-3,* financial managers will be able to evaluate various "what-if" scenarios.

FIGURE 12-2 JKS FURNITURE CO., INC. PRO FORMA INCOME STATEMENT FOR THE PERIOD ENDING DECEMBER 31, 19XB

	1	2	3	4	5	6	7	8	9	10	11	12	Total	Percent
Sales	$60,000	$63,000	$66,150	$69,458	$72,930	$76,577	$80,406	$84,426	$88,647	$93,080	$97,734	$102,620	$955,028	100%
Cost of sales	$36,000	$37,800	$39,690	$41,675	$43,758	$45,946	$48,243	$50,656	$53,188	$55,848	$58,640	$61,572	$573,017	60%
Gross profit	$24,000	$25,200	$26,460	$27,783	$29,172	$30,631	$32,162	$33,770	$35,459	$37,232	$39,093	$41,048	$382,011	40%
Op. expenses	$13,000	$13,150	$13,308	$13,473	$13,647	$13,829	$14,020	$14,221	$14,432	$14,654	$14,887	$15,131	$167,751	18%
Net income	$11,000	$12,050	$13,153	$14,310	$15,526	$16,802	$18,142	$19,549	$21,027	$22,578	$24,207	$25,917	$214,260	22%
Tax	$ 2,750	$ 3,013	$ 3,288	$ 3,578	$ 3,881	$ 4,200	$ 4,536	$ 4,887	$ 5,257	$ 5,644	$ 6,052	$ 6,479	$ 53,565	6%
NI after tax	$ 8,250	$ 9,038	$ 9,864	$10,733	$11,644	$12,601	$13,607	$14,662	$15,770	$16,933	$18,155	$19,438	$160,695	17%

13

Budgeting Through Financial Modeling

What is a financial (budgeting) model?

As discussed in the previous chapter, most companies are increasingly using financial modeling to develop their budgets, with the aid of computer software. This chapter introduces financial modeling. A financial model, narrowly called a budgeting model, is a system of mathematical equations, logic, and data that describes the relationships among financial and operating variables. A financial model can be viewed as a subset of broadly defined corporate planning models or a stand-alone functional system that attempts to answer a certain financial planning problem.

A financial model is one in which:

1. One or more financial variables appear (expenses, revenues, investment, cash flow, taxes, earnings, etc.);

2. The model user can manipulate (set and alter) the value of one or more financial variables; and

3. The purpose of the model is to influence strategic decisions by revealing to the decision maker the implications of alternative values of these financial variables.

What are the types of financial models?

Financial models fall into two types: simulation better known as what-if models and optimization models. What-if models attempt to simulate the effects of alternative management policies and assumptions about the firm's external environment. They are a tool for management's laboratory. Optimization models maximize or minimize an objective such as present value of profit or cost. Multi-objective techniques such as goal programming are being explored.

Models can be deterministic or probabilistic. Deterministic models do not include any random or probabilistic variables whereas probabilistic models incorporate random numbers and/or one or more probability distributions for variables such as sales, costs, and so on. Financial models can be solved and manipulated computationally to derive from it the current and projected future implications and consequences. Due to technological advances in computers (such as spreadsheets, financial modeling languages, graphics, data base management systems, and networking), more companies are using modeling.

Why use a financial model?

Basically, a financial model is used to build a comprehensive budget (that is, projected financial statements such as the income statement, balance sheet, and cash flow statement). Such a model can be called a budgeting model, since we are essentially developing a master budget with such a model. Applications and uses of the model, however, go beyond developing a budget. They include:

- Financial forecasting and analysis.
- Capital expenditure analysis.
- Tax planning.
- Exchange rate analysis.
- Analysis for mergers and acquisitions.
- Labor contract negotiations.
- Capacity planning.
- Cost-volume-profit analysis.
- New venture analysis.
- Lease/purchase evaluation.
- Appraisal of performance by segments.
- Market analysis.
- New product analysis.
- Development of long-term strategy.
- Planning financial requirements.
- Risk analysis.
- Cash flow analysis.
- Cost and price projections.

How is modeling used in practice?

The use of financial modeling, especially a computer-based financial modeling system is rapidly growing. The reason is quite simple: The growing need for improved and quicker support for management decisions as a decision support system (DSS) and wide and easy availability of computer hardware and software.

Some of the functions currently served by financial models are:

• Projecting financial results under any given set of assumptions; to evaluate the financial impact of various assumptions and alternative strategies; and to prepare long-range financial forecasts.

• Computing income, cash flow, and ratios for five years by months; also revenue, power generation requirements, operating and manufacturing expenses, manual or automatic financing, and rate structure analysis.

• Providing answers to insights into financial what-if questions, and to produce financial scheduling information.

• Forecast of balance sheet and income statement with emphasis on alternatives for the investment securities portfolio.

• Projecting operating results and various financing needs, such as plant and property levels and financing requirements.

• Computing manufacturing profit, given sales forecasts, and any desired processing sequence through the manufacturing facilities; simulate effect on profits of inventory policies.

• Generating profitability reports of various cost centers.

• Projecting financial implications of capital investment programs.

• Showing the effect of various volume and activity levels on budget and cash flow.

• Forecasting corporate sales, costs, and income by division, by month.

• Providing: (1) sales revenue for budget; (2) a basis for evaluating actual sales department performance; and (3) other statistical comparisons.

- Determine pro forma cash flow for alternative development plans for real estate projects.
- Analyzing the impact of acquisition on company earnings.
- Determining economic attractiveness of new ventures, products, facilities, acquisitions, and so on.
- Evaluate alternatives of leasing or buying computer equipment.
- Determining corporate taxes as a function of changes in price.
- Evaluate investments in additional capacity at each major refinery.
- Generating income statements, cash flow, present value, and discounted rate of return for potential ventures, based on production and sales forecasts.

Supported by the expanded capabilities provided by models, many CFOs are increasingly successful in including long-term strategic considerations in their business plans, thus enabling them to investigate the possible impact of their current decisions on the long term welfare of the organization.

How do you develop financial models?

Development of financial models essentially involves two steps: (1) definition of variables and input parameters and (2) model specification. As far as model specification goes, we will concentrate only on the simulation-type model in this section. Generally speaking, the model consists of three important ingredients:

- Variables.
- Input parameter values.
- Definitional and/or functional relationships.

Examples of Financial Models

An example of a financial model is given below:

1. SALES = A − B · PRICE + C · ADV
2. REVENUE = SALES · PRICE

3. CGS = .70 · REVENUE
4. GM = SALES – CGS
5. OE = $10,000 + .2 · SALES
6. EBT = GM – OE
7. TAX = .46 · EBT
8. EAT = EBT – TAX

In this example, the selling price (PRICE) and advertising expenses (ADV) are given. A, B, and C are parameters to be estimated and

SALES = sales volume in units
REVENUE = sales revenue
CGS = cost of goods sold
GM = gross margin
OE = operating expenses
EBT = earnings before taxes
TAX = income taxes
EAT = earnings after taxes

Another example of a financial model is presented below:

1. INT = .10 · DEBT
2. EARN = REVENUE – CGS – OE – INT – TAX – DIV
3. DEBT = DEBT(–1) + BOW
4. CASH = CASH(–1) + CC + BOW + EARN – CD – LP
5. BOW = MBAL – CASH

Note that earnings (EARN) in equation (2) is defined as sales revenue minus CGS, OE, interest expense (INT), TAX, and dividend payment (DIV). But INT is a percentage interest rate on total debt in equation (1). Total debt in equation (3) is equal to the previous period's debt (DEBT (–1)) plus new borrowings (BOW). New debt is the difference between a minimum cash balance (MBAL) minus cash. Finally, the ending cash balance in equation (5) is defined as the sum of the beginning balance (CASH(–1)), cash collection, new borrowings and earnings minus cash disbursements and loan payments of the existing debt (LP). Figure 13–1 illustrates a more comprehensive financial (budgeting) model.

What types of computer models are available for financial modeling?

Financial models are used to generate pro forma financial statements and financial ratios. These are the basic tools for budgeting and profit planning. Also, the financial model is a technique for risk analysis and what-if experiments. The financial model is also needed for day-to-day operational and tactical decisions for immediate planning problems. For these purposes, the use of computers is essential.

In recent years, spreadsheet software and computer-based financial modeling software have been developed and utilized for budgeting and planning in an effort to speed up the budgeting process and allow CFOs to investigate the effects of changes in budget assumptions and scenarios.

In what follows, we will discuss one of the most popular modeling language—IFPS—with illustrations.

What is Interactive Financial Planning System (IFPS)?

IFPS is a multipurpose, interactive financial modeling system, often called a *decision support system (DSS)*, which supports and facilitates the building, solving, and asking of "what-if" questions of financial models. The output from an IFPS model is in the format of a spreadsheet, that is a matrix or table in which:

• The rows representing user-specified variables such as market share, sales, growth in sales, unit price, gross margin, variable cost, contribution margin, fixed cost, net income, net present value, internal rate of return, and earnings per share.

• The column designates a sequence of user-specified time periods such as month, quarter, year, total, percentages, or divisions.

FIGURE 13-1   A COMPREHENSIVE FINANCIAL MODEL

Balance Sheet Equations

$\text{Cash}_t = \text{Cash}_{t-1} + \text{Cash receipts}_t - \text{Cash disbursements}_t$

$\text{Accounts receivable}_t = (1-a)\,\text{Sales}_t + (1-b-a)\,\text{Sales}_{t-1}$
$$+ (1-c-b-a)\,\text{Sales}_{t-2}$$

$\text{Inventory}_t = \text{Inventory}_{t-1} + \text{Inventory purchase}_t$
$$- \text{Variable cost per unit}\left(\frac{\text{Sales}_t}{\text{Selling price per unit}}\right)$$

$\text{Plant} = \text{Initial value}$

$\text{Accounts payable}_t = (m)\,\text{Variable selling/administrative expenses}_{t-1}$
$$+ (n)\,\text{Variable selling/administrative expenses}_t$$
$$+ \text{Inventory purchase}_t + \text{Fixed expenses}_t$$

$\text{Bank loan}_t = \text{Bank loan}_{t-1} + \text{Loan}_t - \text{Loan repayment}_t$

$\text{Common stock} = \text{Initial value}$

$\text{Retained earnings}_t = \text{Retained earnings}_{t-1} + \text{Net income}_t$

Income Statement and Cash Flow Equations

$\text{Cash receipts}_t = (a)\,\text{Sales}_t + (b)\,\text{Sales}_{t-1} + (c)\,\text{Sales}_{t-2} + \text{Loan}_t$

$\text{Cash disbursements}_t = \text{Accounts payable}_{t-1} + \text{Interest}_t + \text{Loan repayments}_t$

$\text{Inventory purchase}_t\ [\geq 0] = \text{Variable cost per unit}$
$$\left(\frac{\text{Sales}_t + \text{Sales}_{t-1} + \text{Sales}_{t-2} + \text{Sales}_{t-3}}{\text{Selling price per unit}}\right) - \text{Inventory}_{t-1}$$

$\text{Interest}_t = (i)\,\text{Bank loan}_t$

$\text{Variable cost of sales}_t = \text{Sales}_t\left(\frac{\text{Variable cost per unit}}{\text{Selling price per unit}}\right)$

$\text{Variable selling/administrative expenses}_t = (x)\,\text{Sales}_t$

$\text{Net income before taxes}_t = \text{Sales}_t - \text{Interest}_t$
$$+ \text{Variable cost of sales}_t$$
$$+ \text{Variable selling/administrative expenses}_t$$
$$- \text{Fixed expenses}_t - \text{Depreciation}_t$$

$\text{Tax expense}_t\ (\geq 0) = (r)\,\text{Net income before taxes}_t$

$\text{Net income}_t = \text{Net income before taxes}_t - \text{Tax expense}_t$

Input Variables (Dollars)

Sales$_{t-1,\,t-2,\,t-3}$
Loan$_t$
Loan repayment$_t$
Fixed expense$_t$
Depreciation$_t$
Selling price per unit
Variable cost per unit

FIGURE 13-1 *(Continued)*

Input Parameters

Accounts receivable collection patterns
a—Percent received within current period
b—Percent received with one-period lag
c—Percent received with two-period lag
$a + b + c < 1$

Lag in accounts payable cash flow
m—Percent paid from previous period
n—Percent paid from current period
$m + n = 1$

r = Tax rate
i = Interest rate
x = Ratio of variable selling/administrative expense to sales

Initial Values (Dollars)

Plant
Common stock
$Cash_{t-1}$
$Sales_{t-1,\,t-2}$
$Inventory_{t-1}$
$Retained\ earnings_{t-1}$
$Bank\ loan_{t-1}$
$Variable\ selling/adminstrative\ expenses_{t-1}$
$Accounts\ payable_{t-1}$

• The entries in the body of the table display the values taken by the model variable over time or by segments of the firm such as divisions, product lines, sales territories, and departments.

IFPS offers the following key features:

• Like other special purpose modeling languages, IFPS provides an English-like modeling language. That means without an extensive knowledge of computer programming, the CFO can build financial models of his or her own, and use them for what-if scenarios and managerial decisions.

• IFPS has a collection of built-in financial functions that perform calculations such as net present value (NPV), internal rate of return (IRR), loan amortization schedules, and depreciation alternatives.

- IFPS also has a collection of built-in mathematical and statistical functions such as linear regression, linear interpolations, polynomial autocorrelation, and moving average functions.
- IFPS supports use of leading and/or lagged variables which are commonly used in financial modeling. For example, cash collections lag behind credit sales of prior periods.
- IFPS also supports deterministic and probabilistic modeling. It offers a variety of functions for sampling from probability distributions such as uniform, normal, bivariate normal, and user-described empirical distributions.
- IFPS is nonprocedural; this means that the relationships, logic, and data used to calculate the various values in the output do not have to be arranged in any particular top-to-bottom order in an IFPS model. IFPS automatically detects and solves a system of two or more linear or nonlinear equations.
- IFPS has extensive editing capabilities that include adding statements to and deleting statements from a model, making changes in existing statements, and making copies of parts or all of a model.
- IFPS supports sensitivity analysis by providing the following solution options:

- What-If: The IFPS lets you specify one or more changes in the relationships, logic, data, and/or parameter values, in the existing model and recalculates the model to show the impact of these changes on the performance measures.
- Goal-Seeking: In the goal seeking mode, IFPS can determine what change would have to take place in the value of a specified variable in a particular time period to achieve a specified value for another variable. For example, the CFO can ask the system to answer the question "What would the unit sales price have to be for the project to achieve a target return on investment of 20%?"
- Sensitivity: This particular command is employed to determine the effect of a specified variable on one or more other variables. The

sensitivity command is similar to the what-if command but it produces a convenient, model-produced tabular summary for each new alternative value of the specified variable.

- Analyze: The analyze command examines in detail those variables and their values that have contributed to the value of a specified variable.
- Impact: The impact command is used to determine the effect on a specified variable of a series of percentage changes in one or more variables.
- IFPS/optimum: The IFPS/optimum routine is employed to answer questions of "What is the best?" type rather than what-if.
- Other features of IFPS include: routine graphic output, interactive color graphics, data files that contain both data and relationships, a consolidation capability that lets the financial officer produce composite reports from two or more models, extraction of data from existing non-IFPS data files and placing them in IFPS-compatible data files, and operating on all major computer mainframes and microcomputers.

In the following section, we present, step by step, how to build a model using IFPS. (The example on page 287 was adapted from Execucom, *IFPS Fundamental Seminar Book,* 1987, pp. 6–20, with permission).

EXAMPLE 1

The MCL Corporation is considering diversifying and wishes to evaluate the profitability of the new venture over the next two years. A quarterly profit picture is desired. Marketing research has provided the following information: (1) The total market for the product will be 7000 units at the start of production and will grow at the rate of 1% per quarter; (2) MCL's initial share of the market is 11%, and this is expected to grow at the rate of one-half % per quarter if intense marketing efforts are maintained; (3) The selling price is expected to be $2.50 per unit the first year and

$2.65 the following year; (4) The standard cost system has produced the following estimates: (a) selling expenses, $0.233 per unit; (b) labor cost, $0.61 per unit; and (c) raw materials, $0.42 per unit; (5) General and administrative expenses are estimated to be $450 in the first quarter with a quarterly growth rate of 1%; and (6) set-up costs for the line are $3500.

First, "log in" to your computer and access IFPS.

1. To establish the model:

```
ENTER NAME OF FILE CONTAINING MODELS AND REPORTS
? PROFIT

FILE PROFIT NOT FOUND – NEW FILE WILL BE CREATED
READY FOR EXECUTIVE COMMAND
? MODEL EXAMPLE

BEGIN ENTERING NEW MODEL
? AUTO 10, 5

10? (Model is entered)
```

2. The model is entered as listed (on pages 288–289) (from 10 on down).

3. The model is displayed:

Once the model is complete, the solution can be displayed by using a sequence of commands like the ones below. A brief discussion of each command follows the illustration.

```
180? SOLVE

MODEL NEWPROD VERSION OF 12/20/91 16:38 --
11 COLUMNS 17 VARIABLES

ENTER SOLVE OPTIONS

?   COLUMNS 1992 5-8,1991, GROWTH

?   WIDTH 72, 16, 8

?   ALL
```

ALL instructs IFPS to print the values of all variables. (See page 287.)

4. What-if analysis:

Instead of merely solving a model as it is, the WHAT IF command can be used to determine

IFPS OUTPUT

Example of IFPS

	1992	5	6	7	8	1993	Growth
*Sales data and projections:							
Price		2.650	2.650	2.650	2.650		
Market share		.1300	.1350	.1400	.1450		
Total market		7284	7357	7431	7505		
Sales volume	3341	946.9	993.2	1040	1088	4069	21.76
*Previous calculations:							
Sales revenue	8354	2509	2632	2757	2884	10782	29.07
Net income	2306	845.1	904.6	965.2	1027	3742	62.25
*Costs:							
Unit selling cost	.6100	.2330	.2330	.2330	.2330		
Unit labor cost	.4200	.6100	.6100	.6100			
Unit material cost	1.263	.4200	.4200	.4200			
Unit cost	4220	1.263	1.263	1.263			
Variable cost	1827	1196	1254	1314	1374	5139	21.76
Admin. expenses	6047	468.3	473.0	477.7	482.5	1901	4.060
Total expenses		1664	1727	1792	1857	7040	16.41
Performance measures							
Initial investment	3500	0	0	0	0	0	−100
Discount rate		.1200	.1200	.1200	.1200		
Present value		−623.5	139.7	931.3	1750		
Rate of return			.1676	.3988	.5812		

```
10    COLUMNS 1-8,1992,1993,GROWTH
15    *EXAMPLE OF IFPS
20    *
25    **
30    PERIODS 4
35    * SALES DATA AND PROJECTIONS
40    PRICE=2.5 FOR 4, 2.65
45    MARKET SHARE = .11,PREVIOUS MARKET SHARE + .005
50    TOTAL MARKET = 7000, PREVIOUS TOTAL MARKET*1.01
55    SALES VOLUME = L45*L50
60    * PREVIOUS CALCULATIONS
65    SALES REVENUE = SALES VOLUME*PRICE
70    NET INCOME = SALES REVENUE - TOTAL EXPENSES
75    * COSTS
80    UNIT SELLING COST = .233
85    UNIT LABOR COST = .61
90    UNIT MATERIAL COST = .42
95    UNIT COST = SUM(UNIT SELLING COST THRU UNIT MATERIAL COST)
100
65    SALES REVENUE = SALES VOLUME*PRICE
70    NET INCOME = SALES REVENUE - TOTAL EXPENSES
```

```
75      * COSTS
80      UNIT SELLING COST = .233
85      UNIT LABOR COST = .61
90      UNIT MATERIAL COST = .42
95      UNIT COST = SUM(UNIT SELLING COST THRU UNIT MATERIAL COST)
100     VARIABLE COST = UNIT COST*SALES VOLUME
105     ADMIN EXPENSES=450,PREVIOUS ADMIN EXPENSES*1.01
110     TOTAL EXPENSES=VARIABLE COST+ADMIN EXPENSES
115     *PERFORMANCE MEASURES
120     INITIAL INVESTMENT= 3500,0
125     DISCOUNT RATE=.12
130     PRESENT VALUE=NPVC(NET INCOME,DISCOUNT RATE,INITIAL INVESTMENT)
140     RATE OF RETURN=IRR(NET INCOME,INITIAL INVESTMENT)
145     *
150     COLUMN 1992 FOR L55,L65,L70,L100,L105,L110,L120='
155             SUM(C1 THRU C4)
160     COLUMN 1993 FOR L55,L65,L70,L100,L105,L110,L120='
165             SUM (C5 THRU C8)
170     COLUMN GROWTH FOR L55,L65,L70,L100,L105,L110,L120='
175             100*(C10-C9)/C9
END OF MODEL
```

the effect of changes in the definitions of variables in the model. The examples that follow show how these questions can be answered:

Case	Question
1	What if the total market size starts out at 6000 units instead of 7000, but grows by 5 percent per quarter, instead of 1 percent?
2	What if the selling price is $2.70 in the second year instead of $2.65 (and total market follows the original assumptions)?
3	What if, in addition to price being $2.70 in 1992, unit material cost is three cents higher than expected in both years?

Note that Cases 1 and 2 are independent while Case 3 builds on the changes made in Case 2. To handle both kinds of situations, two different WHAT IF commands are available:

WHAT IF	Enables the user to modify temporarily as many individual model statements as desired to determine the effect on the solution. Each WHAT IF erases the assumptions made by the previous one.
WHAT IF CONTINUE	Since each WHAT IF normally starts from the base case, this command makes possible successive, cumulative, WHAT IF statements.

In the print-out on pages 292–293, the user has asked to see only selected variables. In Case 1, individual variable names, separated by commas, are used. In Case 2, model line numbers have been used instead. Case 3 illustrates the use of THRU to print an inclusive list of variables.

The solve options entered earlier to specify columns and page layout remain in effect through the modeling session.

Summary of "What-If" Analysis

Case 1 If the total market size starts out at 6,000 units and grows by 5 percent per quarter, then net income will go up by 111.5 percent.

Case 2   If the selling price is $2.70 in the second year, then the net income will go up by 71.07 percent.

Case 3   If, in addition to price being $2.70 in 1992, unit material cost is three cents higher than expected in both years, then the variable cost will go up by 21.76 percent.

5. Goal seeking analysis:

The goal seeking command allows the user to work backwards. That is, the user tells IFPS what assumption can be adjusted and what objective is to be sought. IFPS then solves the model repetitively until it finds the value that yields the desired objective. To illustrate the use of this command, consider the following two situations:

Case	*Question*
1	Market share estimates could be less than originally expected. How low could it be and still provide first quarter net income of $700 and 3 percent more in each subsequent quarter?
2	The required initial investment might be larger than originally expected. How much larger could it be and still permit a 25 percent return over the eight-quarter horizon?

The first question is really asking what market share would have to be in *each column* in order to achieve a certain net income in the same column. The second question asks what investment has to be in column 1 to produce a certain rate of return in column 8.

As shown in the example on pages 294–295, the second question is handled by enclosing the column number in parentheses after the variable name. The variable is then said to be "subscripted."

The command BASE MODEL is issued before GOAL SEEKING. Without this command, modifications made by the last WHAT IF command would still be in effect

? WHAT IF

WHAT IF CASE 1
ENTER STATEMENTS

? TOTAL MARKET = 6000, PREVIOUS TOTAL MARKET * 1.05
? SOLVE

ENTER SOLVE OPTIONS

? NET INCOME, PRESENT WORTH, RATE OF RETURN

***** WHAT IF CASE 1 *****
1 WHAT IF STATEMENT PROCESSED

	1992	5	6	7	8	1993	GROWTH
NET INCOME	1941	846.7	960.9	1084	1215	4107	111.5
PRESENT WORTH		-966.3	-155.6	733.1	1702		
RATE OF RETURN		.0703	.3240	.5318			

ENTER SOLVE OPTIONS

? WHAT IF

WHAT IF CASE 2
ENTER STATEMENTS

? PRICE = 2.5 FOR 4, 2.70
? SOLVE

ENTER SOLVE OPTIONS

? L70, L130, L140

```
***** WHAT IF CASE 2 *****
1 WHAT IF STATEMENT PROCESSED

                   1992       5        6       7       8      1993    GROWTH

NET INCOME         2306     892.5    1017    1081     3945    71.07
PRESENT WORTH             -582.4     1057    1919
RATE OF RETURN            .1952     .4333   .6198

ENTER SOLVE OPTIONS

? WHAT IF CONTINUE

WHAT IF CASE 3
ENTER STATEMENTS

? UNIT MATERIAL COST = UNIT MATERIAL COST + .03
? SOLVE

ENTER SOLVE OPTIONS

? UNIT MATERIAL COST THRU VARIABLE COST

***** WHAT IF CASE 3 *****
2 WHAT IF STATEMENTS PROCESSED

                   1992       5        6       7       8      1993    GROWTH

UNIT MATERIAL             .4500    .4500   .4500
UNIT COST                1.293    1.293   1.293
VARIABLE COST      4320   1224     1345    1407     5261    21.76
```

ENTER SOLVE OPTIONS

? BASE MODEL
? GOAL SEEKING

GOAL SEEKING CASE 1
ENTER NAME OF VARIABLE TO BE ADJUSTED TO ACHIEVE PERFORMANCE

? MARKET SHARE

ENTER COMPUTATIONAL STATEMENT FOR PERFORMANCE

? NET INCOME = 700, PREVIOUS NET INCOME * 1.03

***** GOAL SEEKING CASE 1 *****

	1992	5	6	7	8	1993	GROWTH
MARKET SHARE	.1243	.1259	.1274	.1291			

ENTER SOLVE OPTIONS

? NET INCOME, PRESENT WORTH, RATE OF RETURN

	1992	5	6	7	8	1993	GROWTH
NET INCOME	2929	787.9	811.5	835.8	806.9	3296	12.55
PRESENT WORTH	-89.41	595.2	1281	1967			
RATE OF RETURN		2446	5494	7072			

ENTER SOLVE OPTIONS

? GOAL SEEKING

GOAL SEEKING CASE 2
ENTER NAME OF VARIABLE TO BE ADJUSTED TO ACHIEVE PERFORMANCE

? INITIAL INVESTMENT(1)

ENTER COMPUTATIONAL STATEMENT FOR PERFORMANCE

? RATE OF RETURN(8) = 25%

***** GOAL SEEKING CASE 2 *****

	1992	5	6	7	8	1993	GROWTH
INITIAL INVESTMENT 4595	0	0	0	0	0	0	-100

ENTER SOLVE OPTIONS

? RATE OF RETURN

	1992	5	6	7	8	1993	GROWTH
RATE OF RETURN			.0835	.2500			

ENTER SOLVE OPTIONS
?

Summary of "Goal-Seeking" Analysis

Case 1   The market share could be as low as .1243 in the first quarter and still provide first quarter net income of $700 and 3 percent more in each subsequent quarter.

Case 2   The initial investment would have to be $4,595 in order to permit a 25 percent return over the eight-quarter horizon.

14

Capital Budgeting

What is capital budgeting?

Capital budgeting is the process of making long-term planning decisions for alternative investment opportunities. There are many investment decisions that the company may have to make in order to grow. Examples of capital budgeting applications are product line selection, keep or sell a business segment, lease or buy, and which asset to invest in.

What are the types of investment projects?

There are typically two types of long-term investment decisions:

1. *Selection decisions* in terms of obtaining new facilities or expanding existing ones: Examples include: (a) Investments in property, plant, and equipment as well as other types of assets; (b) Resource commitments in the form of new product development, market research, introduction of a computer, refunding of long-term debt, and so on; (c) Mergers and acquisitions in the form of buying another company to add a new product line.

2. *Replacement decisions* in terms of replacing existing facilities with new ones. Examples include replacing an old machine with a high-tech machine.

What are the features of investment projects?

Long-term investments have three important features:

1. They typically involve a large amount of initial cash outlays which tend to have a long-term impact on the firm's future profitability. Therefore, this initial cash outlay needs to be justified on a cost-benefit basis.

2. There are expected recurring cash inflows (for example, increased revenues, savings in cash

operating expenses, etc.) over the life of the investment project. This frequently requires considering the *time value of money*.

3. Income taxes could make a difference in the accept or reject decision. Therefore, income tax factors must be taken into account in every capital budgeting decision.

TIME VALUE FUNDAMENTALS _____

A dollar now is worth more than a dollar to be received later. This statement sums up an important principle: Money has a time value. This is not because inflation might make the dollar received at a later time worth less in buying power. The reason is that you could invest the dollar now and have more than a dollar at a specified later date.

Time value of money is a critical consideration in financial and investment decisions. For example, compound interest calculations are needed to determine future sums of money resulting from an investment. Discounting, or the calculation of present value, which is inversely related to compounding, is used to evaluate the future cash flow associated with capital budgeting projects. There are plenty of applications of time value of money in accounting and finance.

What is money worth in the future?

A dollar in hand today is worth more than a dollar to be received tomorrow because of the interest it could earn from putting it in a savings account or placing it in an investment account. Compounding interest means that interest earns interest. For the discussion of the concepts of compounding and time value, let us define:

F_n = future value: the amount of money at the end of year n

P   = principal

i   = annual interest rate

n   = number of years

Then,

F_1 = the amount of money at the end of year 1
= principal and interest = $P + iP = P(1 + i)$

F_2 = the amount of money at the end of year 2
= $F_1(1 + i) = P(1 + i)(1 + i) = P(1 + i)^2$

The future value of an investment compounded annually at rate i for n years is

$$F_n = P(1 + i)^n = P \cdot T1(i,n)$$

where $T1(i,n)$ is the compound amount of $1 and can be found in Table A–1 in the Appendix.

EXAMPLE 1

You place $1,000 in a savings account earning 8 percent interest compounded annually. How much money will you have in the account at the end of 4 years?

$F_n = P(1 + i)^n$
$F_4 = \$1,000 \ (1 + 0.08)^4 = \$1,000 \ T1(8\%,4 \text{ years})$

From Table A–1, the T1 for 4 years at 8 percent is 1.361. Therefore,

$$F_4 = \$1,000 \ (1.361) = \$1,361.$$

EXAMPLE 2

You invested a large sum of money in the stock of Delta Corporation. The company paid a $3 dividend per share. The dividend is expected to increase by 20 percent per year for the next 3 years. You wish to project the dividends for years 1 through 3.

$F_n = P(1 + i)^n$
$F_1 = \$3(1 + 0.2)^1 = \$3 \ T1(20\%,1) = \$3 \ (1.200) = \$3.60$
$F_2 = \$3(1 + 0.2)^2 = \$3 \ T1(20\%,2) = \$3 \ (1.440) = \$4.32$
$F_3 = \$3(1 + 0.2)^3 = \$3 \ T1(20\%,3) = \$3 \ (1.728) = \$5.18$

What is the future value of an annuity?

An annuity is defined as a series of payments (or receipts) of a fixed amount for a specified number of periods. Each payment is assumed to occur at the end of the period. The future value of an annuity is a compound annuity which involves depositing or investing an equal sum of money at the end of each year for a certain number of years and allowing it to grow.

Let S_n = the future value on an n-year annuity and A = the amount of an annuity. Then we can write

$$S_n = A(1+i)^{n-1} + A(1+i)^{n-2} + \ldots + A(1+i)^0$$
$$= A[(1+i)^{n-1} + (1+i)^{n-2} + \ldots + (1+i)^0]$$
$$= A \cdot \sum_{t=0}^{n-1} (1+i)^t = A \cdot \left[\frac{(1+i)^n - 1}{i} \right] = A \cdot T2(i,n)$$

where $T2(i,n)$ represents the future value of an annuity of \$1 for n years compounded at i percent and can be found in Table A–2 in the Appendix.

EXAMPLE 3

You wish to determine the sum of money you will have in a savings account at the end of 6 years by depositing \$1,000 at the end of each year for the next 6 years. The annual interest rate is 8 percent. The T2 (8%, 6 years) is given in Table A–2 as 7.336. Therefore,

$$S_6 = \$1,000 \ T2(8\%,6) = \$1,000 \ (7.336) = \$7,336$$

EXAMPLE 4

You deposit \$30,000 semiannually into a fund for ten years. The annual interest rate is 8 percent. The amount accumulated at the end of the tenth year is calculated as follows:

$$S_n = A \cdot T2(i,n)$$

where A = \$30,000, i = 8%/2 = 4%, n = 10 × 2 = 20.

Therefore,

$$S_{20} = \$30,000 \ T2(4\%,20)$$
$$= \$30,000 \ (29.778) = \$893,340$$

What is present value?

Present value is the present worth of future sums of money. The process of calculating present values, or discounting, is actually the opposite of finding the compounded future value. In connection with present value calculations, the interest rate i is called the *discount rate.* The discount rate we use is more commonly called the *cost of capital,* which is the minimum rate of return required by the investor.

Recall that $F_n = P(1 + i)^n$. Therefore,

$$P = \frac{F_n}{(1 + i)^n} = F_n\left[\frac{1}{(1 + i)^n}\right] = F_n \cdot T3(i,n)$$

where T3 (i,n) represents the present value of $1 and is given in Table A–3 in the Appendix.

EXAMPLE 5

You have been given an opportunity to receive $20,000 6 years from now. If you can earn 10 percent on your investments, what is the most you should pay for this opportunity? To answer this question, you must compute the present value of $20,000 to be received 6 years from now at a 10 percent rate of discount. F_6 is $20,000, i is 10 percent, and n is 6 years. T3(10%,6) from Table A–3 is 0.565.

$$P = \$20,000\left[\frac{1}{(1 + 0.1)^6}\right] = \$20,000 \ T3(10\%,6)$$
$$= \$20,000(0.564) = \$11,280$$

This means that you can earn 10 percent on your investment, and you would be indifferent to receiving $11,280 now or $20,000 6 years from today since the amounts are time equivalent. In other words, you could invest $11,300 today at 10 percent and have $20,000 in 6 years.

How do you compute mixed streams of cash flows?

The present value of a series of mixed payments (or receipts) is the sum of the present value of each individual payment. We know that the present value of each individual payment is the payment times the appropriate T3 value.

EXAMPLE 6

You are thinking of starting a new product line that initially costs $32,000. Your annual projected cash inflows are:

1	$10,000
2	$20,000
3	$5,000

If you must earn a minimum of 10 percent on your investment, should you undertake this new product line?

The present value of this series of mixed streams of cash inflows is calculated as follows:

Year	Cash Inflows	× T3 (10%, n)	Present Value
1	$10,000	0.909	$ 9,090
2	$20,000	0.826	$16,520
3	$ 5,000	0.751	$ 3,755
			$29,365

Since the present value of your projected cash inflows is less than the initial investment, you should not undertake this project.

What is the present value of an annuity?

Interest received from bonds, pension funds, and insurance obligations all involve annuities. To compare these financial instruments, we need to know the present value of each. The present value of an annuity (P_n) can be found by using the following equation:

$$P_n = A \cdot \frac{1}{(1+i)^1} + A \cdot \frac{1}{(1+i)^2} + \ldots + A \cdot \frac{1}{(1+i)^n}$$

$$= A \left[\frac{1}{(1+i)^1} + \frac{1}{(1+i)^2} + \ldots + \frac{1}{(1+i)^n} \right]$$

$$= A \cdot \sum_{t=1}^{n} \frac{1}{(1+i)^t} = A \cdot \frac{1}{i} \left[1 - \frac{1}{(1+i)} \right] = A \cdot T4(i,n)$$

where T4(i,n) represents the present value of an annuity of \$1 discounted at i percent for n years and is found in Table A–4 in the Appendix.

EXAMPLE 7

Assume that the cash inflows in Example 6 form an annuity of \$10,000 for 3 years. Then the present value is

$$P_n = A \cdot T4(i,n)$$
$$P_3 = \$10,000 \; T4(10\%, 3 \text{ years})$$
$$= \$10,000 \; (2.487) = \$24,870$$

Using financial calculators and spreadsheet programs

There are many financial calculators that contain preprogrammed formulas to perform many present value and future value applications. They include Radio Shack EC5500, Hewlett-Packard 10B, Sharpe EL733, and Texas Instruments BA35. Furthermore, spreadsheet software such as Lotus 1-2-3 has built-in financial functions to perform many such applications.

What are the popular evaluation techniques?

Several methods of evaluating investment projects are as follows:

1. Payback period.
2. Discounted payback period.
3. Accounting (simple) rate of return (ARR).
4. Net present value (NPV).
5. Internal rate of return (IRR) (or time adjusted rate of return).
6. Profitability index (or present value index).

The NPV method and the IRR method are called *discounted cash flow (DCF) methods.* Each of these methods is discussed below.

PAYBACK PERIOD ───────────────────

How do you determine the payback period?

The payback period measures the length of time required to recover the amount of initial investment. It is computed by dividing the initial investment by the cash inflows through increased revenues or cost savings.

EXAMPLE 8

Assume Cost of investment = $18,000 and Annual after-tax cash savings $3,000.

Then, the payback period is:

$$\text{Payback period} = \frac{\text{Initial investment}}{\text{Cost savings}} = \frac{\$18,000}{\$3,000} = 6 \text{ years}$$

Decision rule: Choose the project with the shorter payback period. The rationale behind this choice is: The shorter the payback period, the less risky the project, and the greater the liquidity.

EXAMPLE 9

Consider the two projects whose after-tax cash inflows are not even. Assume each project costs $1,000.

	Cash Inflow	
Year	A($)	B($)
1	100	500
2	200	400
3	300	300
4	400	100
5	500	
6	600	

When cash inflows are not even, the payback period has to be found by trial and error. The payback period of project A is ($1,000 = $100 + $200 + $300 + $400) 4 years. The payback period of project B is ($1,000 = $500 + $400 + $100):

$$2 \text{ years} + \frac{\$100}{\$300} = 2^{1/3} \text{ years}$$

Project B is the project of choice in this case, since it has the shorter payback period.

What are the pros and cons of the payback period method?

The advantages of using the payback period method of evaluating an investment project are that (1) it is simple to compute and easy to understand, and (2) it handles investment risk effectively.

The shortcomings of this method are that (1) it does not recognize the time value of money, and (2) it ignores the impact of cash inflows received after the payback period; essentially, cash flows after the payback period determine profitability of an investment.

Discounted Payback Period

You can take into account the time value of money by using the discounted payback period. The payback period will be longer using the discounted method since money is worth less over time.

How do you determine the discounted payback period?

Discounted payback is computed by adding the present value of each year's cash inflows until they equal the initial investment.

$$\frac{\text{Discounted}}{\text{payback}} = \frac{\text{Initial cash outlays}}{\text{Discounted annual cash inflows}}$$

EXAMPLE 10

You invest $40,000 and receive the following cash inflows. The discounted payback period is calculated as follows:

Year	Cash Inflows	T1 Factor	Present Value	Accumulated Present Value
1	$15,000	.9091	$13,637	$13,637
2	20,000	.8264	16,528	30,165
3	28,000	.7513	21,036	51,201

Thus,

$$\$30,165 + \frac{\$40,000 - 30,165}{\$21,036} = 2 \text{ years} + .47 = 2.47 \text{ years}$$

ACCOUNTING (SIMPLE) RATE OF RETURN

What is the accounting rate of return?

Accounting rate of return (ARR) measures profitability from the conventional accounting standpoint by relating the required investment—or sometimes the average investment—to the future annual net income.

Decision rule: Under the ARR method, choose the project with the higher rate of return.

EXAMPLE 11

Consider the following investment:

Initial investment	$6,500
Estimated life	20 years
Cash inflows per year	$1,000
Depreciation per year (using straight line)	$325

The accounting rate of return for this project is:

$$ARR = \frac{\text{Net income}}{\text{Investment}} = \frac{\$1,000 - \$325}{\$6,500} = 10.4\%$$

If average investment (usually assumed to be one-half of the original investment) is used, then:

$$\text{ARR} = \frac{\$1,000 - \$325}{\$3,250} = 20.8\%$$

What are the benefits and drawbacks of the ARR method?

The advantages of this method are that it is easily understood, simple to compute, and recognizes the profitability factor.

The shortcomings of this method are that it fails to recognize the time value of money, and it uses accounting data instead of cash flow data.

THE NET PRESENT VALUE METHOD —————

What is net present value?

Net present value (NPV) is the excess of the present value (PV) of cash inflows generated by the project over the amount of the initial investment (I):

$$\text{NPV} = \text{PV} - \text{I}$$

The present value of future cash flows is computed using the so-called cost of capital (or minimum required rate of return) as the discount rate. When cash inflows are uniform, the present value would be

$$\text{PV} = \text{A} \cdot \text{T4 (i,n)}$$

where A is the amount of the annuity. The value of T4 is found in Table A–4 of the Appendix.

Decision rule: If NPV is positive, accept the project. Otherwise reject it.

EXAMPLE 12

Consider the following investment:

Initial investment	$12,950
Estimated life	10 years
Annual cash inflows	$3,000

Cost of capital (minimum required rate
   of return)   12%

Present value of the cash inflows is:

   PV = A · T4(i,n)
      = $3,000 · T4(12%,10 years)
      = $3,000 (5.650) $16,950
   Initial investment (I)   12,950
   Net present value (NPV = PV − I) $ 4,000

Since the NPV of the investment is positive,
the investment should be accepted.

What are the pros and cons of the NPV method?

The advantages of the NPV method are that it
obviously recognizes the time value of money
and it is easy to compute whether the cash flows
form an annuity or vary from period to period.

INTERNAL RATE OF RETURN _____

What is internal rate of return?

Internal rate of return (IRR), also called time
adjusted rate of return, is defined as the rate of
interest that equates I with the PV of future cash
inflows.

In other words, at IRR, I = PV or NPV = 0.

Decision rule: Accept the project if the IRR
exceeds the cost of capital. Otherwise, reject it.

EXAMPLE 13

Assume the same data given in Example 12,
and set the following equality (I = PV):

$$\$12,950 = \$3,000 \times T4(i,10 \text{ years})$$

$$T4(i,10 \text{ years}) = \frac{\$12,950}{\$3,000} = 4.317$$

which stands somewhere between 18 percent and
20 percent in the 10-year line of Table A–4. The
interpolation follows:

	PV of an Annuity of $1 Factor T4(i,10 years)	
18%	4.494	4.494
IRR	4.317	
20%		4.192
Difference	0.177	0.302

Therefore,

$$IRR = 18\% + \frac{0.177}{0.302}(20\% - 18\%)$$

$$= 18\% + 0.586(2\%) = 18\% + 1.17\% = 19.17\%$$

Since the IRR of the investment is greater than the cost of capital (12 percent), accept the project.

What are the benefits and drawbacks of the IRR method?

The advantage of using the IRR method is that it does consider the time value of money and, therefore, is more exact and realistic than the ARR method.

The shortcomings of this method are that (1) it is time-consuming to compute, especially when the cash inflows are not even, although most financial calculators and PCs have a key to calculate IRR, and (2) it fails to recognize the varying sizes of investment in competing projects.

PROFITABILITY INDEX (OR PRESENT VALUE INDEX) ————————

What is the profitability index?

The profitability index is the ratio of the total PV of future cash inflows to the initial investment, that is, PV/I. This index is used as a means of ranking projects in descending order of attractiveness.

Decision rule: If the profitability index is greater than 1, then accept the project.

EXAMPLE 14

Using the data in Example 12, the profitability index is

$$\frac{PV}{I} = \frac{\$16,950}{\$12,950} = 1.31$$

Since this project generates $1.31 for each dollar invested (i.e., its profitability index is greater than 1), accept the project.

The profitability index has the advantage of putting all projects on the same relative basis regardless of size.

LIMITED FUNDS FOR CAPITAL SPENDING

How do you select the best mix of projects with a limited budget?

Many firms specify a limit on the overall budget for capital spending. Capital rationing is concerned with the problem of selecting the mix of acceptable projects that provides the highest overall NPV. The profitability index is used widely in ranking projects competing for limited funds.

EXAMPLE 15

The Westmont Company has a fixed budget of $250,000. It needs to select a mix of acceptable projects from the following:

Projects	I($) (000s)	PV($) (000s)	NPV($) (000s)	Profit- ability Index	Ranking
A	70	112	42	1.6	1
B	100	145	45	1.45	2
C	110	126.5	16.5	1.15	5
D	60	79	19	1.32	3
E	40	38	-2	0.95	6
F	80	95	15	1.19	4

The ranking resulting from the profitability index shows that the company should select projects A, B, and D.

	I	PV
A	$ 70,000	$112,000
B	100,000	145,000
D	60,000	79,000
	$230,000	$336,000

Therefore,

$$NPV = \$336,000 - \$230,000 = \$106,000$$

A more general approach to solving capital rationing problems is the use of zero-one integer programming. Here the objective is to select the mix of projects that maximizes the net present value (NPV) subject to a budget constraint.

Using the data given in Example 14, we can set up the problem as a zero-one programming problem such that

$$x_j = \begin{cases} 1 \text{ if project j is selected} \\ 0 \text{ if project j is not selected } (j = 1,2,3,4,5,6) \end{cases}$$

The problem then can be formulated as follows:

Maximize
$$NPV = \$42,000 \times x_1 + \$45,000 \times x_2 + \$16,500 \times x_3$$
$$+ \$19,000 \times x_4 - \$2,000 \times x_5 + \$15,000 \times x_6$$

subject to

$$\$70,000 \times x_1 + \$100,000 \times x_2 + \$110,000 \times x_3$$
$$+ \$60,000 \times x_4 + \$40,000 \times x_5 + \$80,000 \times x_6$$
$$\leq \$250,000$$
$$x_j = 0,1 \ (j = 1,2, \ldots , 6)$$

Using the zero-one programming solution routine, shown on pages 312–313, the solution to the problem is:

$$x1 = A = 1, x2 = B = 1, x4 = D = 1$$

LINDO'S ZERO-ONE PROGRAMMING OUTPUT

: max   42000x1+45000x2+16500x3+19000x4=2000x5+15000x6
? st
? 70000x1+100000x2+110000x3+60000x4+40000x5+80000x6<250000
? x1+x=1
? end

: : integer   6
: : integer   x1
: : integer   x2
: : integer   x3
: : integer   x4
: : integer   x5
: : integer   x6
: : Go

                    OBJECTIVE FUNCTION VALUE

1)   106000.000   = NPV

VARIABLE	VALUE	REDUCED COST	Note:
X1	1.000000	-21500.000000	)
X2	1.000000	-30000.000000	)
X3	.000000	.000000	) X1=1=A
X4	1.000000	-30000.000000	) X2=1=B
X5	.000000	8000.000000	) X4=1=D
X6	.000000	3000.000000	)

ROW	SLACK OR SURPLUS	DUAL PRICES
2)	.000000	.150000
3)	.000000	10000.000000

NO. ITERATIONS=   0 DETERM=   11.00E   4
BRANCHES=   0
BOND ON OPTIMUM;   102000.0
ENUMERATION COMPLETE. BRANCHES=   0   PIVOTS=   2

LAST INTEGER SOLUTION IS THE BEST FOUND
RE-INSTALLING BEST SOLUTION . . . .

313

and the NPV is $106,000. Thus, projects A, B and D should be selected.

How do you choose between mutually exclusive investments?

A project is said to be mutually exclusive if the acceptance of one project automatically excludes the acceptance of one or more other projects. In the case where one must choose between mutually exclusive investments, the NPV and IRR methods may result in contradictory indications. The conditions under which contradictory rankings can occur are:

1. Projects that have different life expectancies.

2. Projects that have different sizes of investment.

3. Projects whose cash flows differ over time. For example, the cash flows of one project increase over time, while those of another decrease.

The contradictions result from different assumptions with respect to the reinvestment rate on cash flows from the projects.

1. The NPV method discounts all cash flows at the cost of capital, thus implicitly assuming that these cash flows can be reinvested at this rate.

2. The IRR method implies a reinvestment rate at IRR. Thus, the implied reinvestment rate will differ from project to project.

The NPV method generally gives correct ranking, since the cost of capital is a more realistic reinvestment rate.

EXAMPLE 16

Assume the following:

			Cash Flows			
	0	1	2	3	4	5
A	(100)	120				
B	(100)					201.14

Computing IRR and NPV at 10 percent gives the following different rankings:

	IRR	NPV at 10%
A	20%	9.01
B	15%	24.90

The NPV's plotted against the appropriate discount rates form a graph called a NPV profile (Figure 14–1).

At a discount rate larger than 14 percent, A has a higher NPV than B. Therefore, A should be selected. At a discount rate less than 14 percent, B has the higher NPV than A, and thus should be selected. The correct decision is to select the project with the higher NPV, since the NPV method assumes a more realistic reinvestment rate, that is, the cost of capital.

EFFECT OF INCOME TAXES ON CAPITAL BUDGETING DECISIONS

How do income tax factors affect investment decisions?

Income taxes make a difference in many capital budgeting decisions. The project which is attractive on a before-tax basis may have to be rejected on an after-tax basis. Income taxes typically affect both the amount and the timing of cash flows. Since net income, not cash inflows,

FIGURE 14–1 NPV PROFILE

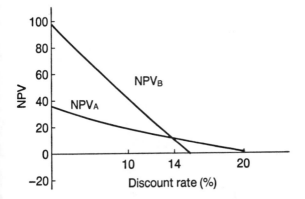

is subject to tax, after-tax cash inflows are not usually the same as after-tax net income.

Let us define:

$$S = \text{Sales}$$
$$E = \text{Cash operating expenses}$$
$$d = \text{Depreciation}$$
$$t = \text{Tax rate}$$

Then, before-tax cash inflows (or before-tax *cash savings*) = $S - E$ and net income = $S - E - d$.

By definition,

$$\begin{array}{c} \text{After-tax} \\ \text{cash inflows} \end{array} = \begin{array}{c} \text{Before-tax} \\ \text{cash inflows} \end{array} - \text{Taxes}$$

$$= (S - E) - (S - E - d)(t)$$

Rearranging gives the short-cut formula:

$$\text{After-tax cash inflows} = (S - E)(1 - t) + (d)(t)$$

or

$$= (S - E - d)(1 - t) + (d)$$

The deductibility of depreciation from sales in arriving at net income subject to taxes reduces income tax payments and thus serves as a tax shield.

$$\text{Tax shield} = \text{Tax savings on depreciation} = (d)(t)$$

EXAMPLE 17

Assume:

$$S = \$12,000$$
$$E = \$10,000$$
$$d = \$500 \text{ per year using the straight line method}$$
$$t = 30\%$$

Then,

$$\begin{array}{l} \text{After-tax} \\ \text{cash inflow} \end{array} = (\$12,000 - \$10,000)(1 - .3) + (\$500)(.3)$$

$$= (\$2,000)(.7) + (\$500)(.3)$$

$$= \$1,400 + \$150 = \$1,550$$

Note that a tax shield $=$ Tax savings on depreciation $= (d)(t)$

$$= (\$500)(.3) = \$150$$

Since the tax shield is dt, the higher the depreciation deduction, the higher the tax savings on depreciation. Therefore, an accelerated depreciation method (such as double-declining balance) produces higher tax savings than the straight-line method. Accelerated methods produce higher present values for the tax savings which may make a given investment more attractive.

EXAMPLE 18

The Shalimar Company estimates that it can save $2,500 a year in cash operating costs for the next ten years if it buys a special-purpose machine at a cost of $10,000. No salvage value is expected. Assume that the income tax rate is 30%, and the after-tax cost of capital (minimum required rate of return) is 10%. After-tax cash savings can be calculated as follows:

Note that depreciation by straight-line is $10,000/10 = $1,000$ per year. Here before-tax cash savings $= (S - E) = \$2,500$. Thus,

$$\text{After-tax cash savings} = (S - E)\,(1 - t) + (d)(t)$$
$$= \$2,500(1 - .3) + \$1,000(.3)$$
$$= \$1,750 + \$300 = \$2,050$$

To see if this machine should be purchased, the net present value can be calculated.

$$PV = \$2,050\ T4(10\%, 10\ \text{years}) = \$2,050\ (6.145)$$
$$= \$12,597.25$$

Thus, $NPV = PV - I = \$12,597.25 - \$10,000 = \$2,597.25$. Since NPV is positive, the machine should be bought.

What is the effect of ACRS on investment decisions?

Although the traditional depreciation methods still can be used for computing depreciation for book purposes, 1981 saw a new way of computing depreciation deductions for tax purposes. The new rule is called the *Accelerated Cost Recovery System* (ACRS) rule, as enacted by Congress in 1981 and then modified somewhat in 1986 under the Tax Reform Act of 1986. This rule is characterized as follows:

1. It abandons the concept of useful life and accelerates depreciation deductions by placing all depreciable assets into one of eight age property classes. It calculates deductions, based on an allowable percentage of the asset's original cost (see Tables 14–1 and 14–2 on the following pages).

With a shorter life than useful life, the company would be able to deduct depreciation more quickly and save more in income taxes in the earlier years, thereby making an investment more attractive. The rationale behind the system is that this way the government encourages the company to invest in facilities and increase its productive capacity and efficiency. (Remember that the higher d, the larger the tax shield (d)(t).)

2. Since the allowable percentages in Table 14–2 add up to 100%, there is no need to consider the salvage value of an asset in computing depreciation.

3. The company may elect the straight line method. The straight-line convention must follow what is called the *half-year convention.* This means that the company can deduct only half of the regular straight-line depreciation amount in the first year. The reason for electing to use the ACRS optional straight-line method is that some firms may prefer to stretch out depreciation deductions using the straight-line method rather than to accelerate them. Those firms are the ones that just start out or have little or no income and wish to show more income on their income statements.

EXAMPLE 19

Assume that a machine falls under a 3-year property class and costs $3,000 initially. The straight line option under ACRS differs from the traditional straight line method in that under

**TABLE 14-1   ACCELERATED COST RECOVERY SYSTEM
CLASSIFICATION OF ASSETS**

Year	Property Class					
	3-Yr. (%)	5-Yr. (%)	7-Yr. (%)	10-Yr. (%)	15-Yr. (%)	20-Yr. (%)
1	33.3	20.0	14.3	10.0	5.0	3.8
2	44.5	32.0	24.5	18.0	9.5	7.2
3	14.8[a]	19.2	17.5	14.4	8.6	6.7
4	7.4	11.5[a]	12.5	11.5	7.7	6.2
5		11.5	8.9[a]	9.2	6.9	5.7
6		5.8	8.9	7.4	6.2	5.3
7			8.9	6.6[a]	5.9[a]	4.9
8			4.5	6.6	5.9	4.5[a]
9				6.5	5.9	4.5
10				6.5	5.9	4.5
11				3.3	5.9	4.5
12					5.9	4.5
13					5.9	4.5
14					5.9	4.5
15					5.9	4.5
16					3.0	4.4
17						4.4
18						4.4
19						4.4
20						4.4
21						2.2
Total	100.0	100.0	100.0	100.0	100.0	100.0

[a]*Denotes the year of changeover to straight-line depreciation.*

TABLE 14-2 ACRS TABLES BY PROPERTY CLASS

ACRS Property Class and Depreciation Method	Useful Life (ADR Midpoint Life[a])	Examples of Assets
3-year property 200% declining balance	4 years or less	Most small tools are included; the law specifically *excludes* autos and light trucks from this property class.
5-year property 200% declining balance	More than 4 years to less than 10 years	Autos and light trucks, computers, typewriters, copiers, duplicating equipment, heavy general-purpose trucks, and research and experimentation equipment are included.
7-year property 200% declining balance	10 years or more to less than 16 years	Office furniture and fixtures and most items of machinery and equipment used in production are included.
10-year property 200% declining balance	16 years or more to less than 20 years	Various machinery and equipment, such as that used in petroleum distilling and refining and in the milling of grain, are included.
15-year property 150% declining balance	20 years or more to less than 25 years	Sewage treatment plants, telephone and electrical distribution facilities, and land improvements are included.
20-year property 150% declining balance	25 years or more	Service stations and other real property with an ADR midpoint life of less than 27.5 years are included.
27.5-year property Straight-line	Not applicable	All residential rental property is included.
31.5-year property Straight-line	Not applicable	All nonresidential real property is included.

ADR stands for *asset depreciation range*. Because the *useful life* of an asset in a business ranges, the appropriate ADR midpoint lives for assets are this method the company would deduct only $500 depreciation in the first year and the fourth year ($3,000/3 years = $1,000; $1,000/2 = $500). The table below compares the straight line with half-year convention with the ACRS.

Year	Straight Line (Half-Year) Depreciation	Cost	ACRS %	ACRS Deduction
1	$ 500	$3,000 ×	33.3%	$ 999
2	1,000	3,000 ×	44.5	1,335
3	1,000	3,000 ×	14.8	444
4	500	3,000 ×	7.4	222
	$3,000			$3,000

EXAMPLE 20

A machine costs $1,000. Annual cash inflows are expected to be $500. The machine will be depreciated using the ACRS rule and will fall under the 3-year property class. The cost of capital after taxes is 10%. The estimated life of the machine is 4 years. The tax rate is 30%. The formula for computation of after-tax cash inflows $(S - E)(1 - t) + (d)(t)$ needs to be computed separately. The NPV analysis can be performed as shown on the next page.

Therefore, NPV = PV − I = $1,359.08 − $1,000 = $359.08, which is positive, so that the machine should be bought.

$(S - E)(1 - t)$:

$500 (1 - .3) = \$350$ for 4 years

	Present Value Factor @ 10%	Present Value
	3.170[a]	\$1,109.5

(d) (t):

Year	Cost		ACRS %	d	(d) (t)	Present Value Factor @ 10%	Present Value
1	\$1,000	×	33.3%	\$333	\$ 99.9	.909[b]	90.81
2	\$1,000	×	44.5	445	133.5	.826[b]	110.27
3	\$1,000	×	14.8	148	44.4	.751[b]	33.34
4	\$1,000	×	7.4	74	22.2	.683[b]	15.16
							\$1,359.08

[a]T4 (10%, 4 years) = 3.170 (from Table 4).
[b]T3 values obtained from Table 3.

322

15

What and Why of Responsibility Accounting

What is responsibility accounting?

Responsibility accounting is the system for collecting and reporting revenue and cost information by areas of responsibility. It operates on the premise that managers should be held responsible for their performance, the performance of their subordinates, and all activities within their responsibility center.

What are the benefits of responsibility accounting?

Responsibility accounting, also called profitability accounting and activity accounting, has the following advantages:

1. It facilitates delegation of decision making.

2. It helps management promote the concept of management by objective. In management by objective, managers agree on a set of goals. The manager's performance is then evaluated based on his or her attainment of these goals.

3. It provides a guide to the evaluation of performance and helps to establish standards of performance which are then used for comparison purposes.

4. It permits effective use of the concept of management by exception, which means that the manager's attention is concentrated on the important deviations from standards and budgets.

What are the conditions for an effective responsibility accounting system?

For an effective responsibility accounting system, the following three basic conditions are necessary:

1. The organization structure must be well defined. Management responsibility and authority

must go hand in hand at all levels and must be clearly established and understood.

2. Standards of performance in revenues, costs, and investments must be properly determined and well-defined.

3. The responsibility accounting reports (or performance reports) should include only items that are controllable by the manager of the responsibility center. Also, they should highlight items calling for managerial attention.

What are the types of responsibility centers?

A well-designed responsibility accounting system establishes responsibility centers within the organization. A responsibility center is defined as a unit in the organization which has control over costs, revenues, and/or investment funds. Responsibility centers can be one of the following types:

• **Cost center.** A cost center is the unit within the organization which is responsible only for costs. Examples include production and maintenance departments of a manufacturing company. **Variance analysis** based on standard costs and flexible budgets would be a typical performance measure of a cost center.

• **Profit center.** A profit center is the unit which is held responsible for the revenues earned and costs incurred in that center. Examples might include a sales office of a publishing company, an appliance department in a retail store, and an auto repair center in a department store. The contribution approach to cost allocation is widely used to measure the performance of a profit center.

• **Investment center.** An investment center is the unit within the organization which is held responsible for the costs, revenues, and related investments made in that center. The corporate headquarters or division in a large decentralized organization would be an example of an investment center.

Figure 15–1 illustrates the manner in which responsibility accounting can be used within an organization and highlights profit and cost centers.

FIGURE 15-1 ORGANIZATION CHART COMPANY XYZ

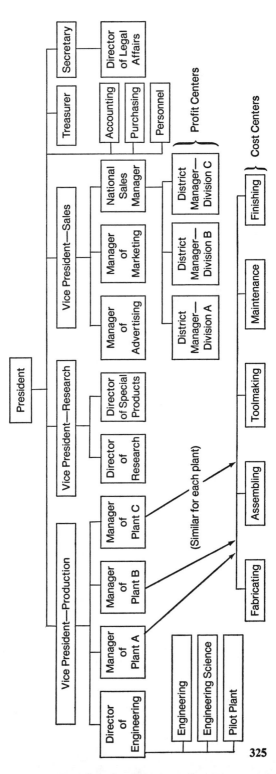

COST CENTER PERFORMANCE AND STANDARD COSTS _____

How do you measure the performance of a cost center?

One of the most important phases of responsibility accounting is establishing standard costs and evaluating performance by comparing actual costs with the standard costs. The difference between the actual costs and the standard costs, called the variance, is calculated for individual cost centers. Variance analysis is a key tool for measuring performance of a cost center.

Standard costs are costs that are established in advance to serve as targets to be met and after the fact, to determine how well those targets were actually met. The standard cost is based on physical and dollar measures: it is determined by multiplying the standard quantity of an input by its standard price.

Variance analysis based on standard costs and *flexible budgets* would be a typical tool for control of a *cost center* such as a production department.

General Model for Variance Analysis

Two general types of variances can be calculated for most cost items: a price variance and a quantity variance.

The price variance is calculated as follows:

$$\frac{\text{Price}}{\text{variance}} = \frac{\text{Actual}}{\text{quantity}} \cdot (\text{Actual price} - \text{Standard price})$$

$$= AQ \cdot (AP - SP)$$

$$= \underset{(1)}{(AQ \cdot AP)} - \underset{(2)}{(AQ \cdot SP)}$$

The quantity variance is calculated as follows:

$$\frac{\text{Quantity}}{\text{variance}} = \left(\frac{\text{Actual}}{\text{quantity}} - \frac{\text{Standard}}{\text{quantity}} \right) \cdot \frac{\text{Standard}}{\text{price}}$$

$$= (AQ - SQ) \cdot SP$$
$$= (AQ \cdot SP) - (SQ \cdot SP)$$
$$\quad\quad (2) \quad\quad\quad\quad (3)$$

Figure 15–2 shows a general model (3-column model) for variance analysis that incorporates items (1), (2), and (3) from the above equations. It is important to note four things:

1. A price variance and a quantity variance can be calculated for all three variable cost items—direct materials, direct labor, and the variable portion of factory overhead. The variance is not called by the same name, however. For example, a price variance is called a materials price variance in the case of direct materials, but a labor rate variance in the case of direct labor and a variable overhead spending variance in the case of variable factory overhead.

2. A cost variance is unfavorable (U) if the actual price AP or actual quantity AQ exceeds the standard price SP or standard quantity SQ; a variance is favorable (F) if the actual price or actual quantity is less than the standard price or standard quantity.

3. The standard quantity allowed for output—item (3)—is the key concept in variance analysis. This is the standard quantity that should have been used to produce actual output. It is computed by multiplying the actual output by the number of input units allowed.

4. Variances for fixed overhead are of questionable usefulness for control purposes, since these variances are usually beyond the control of the production department.

We will now illustrate the variance analysis for each of the variable manufacturing cost items.

How are material variances computed?

A materials purchase price variance is isolated at the time of purchase of the material. It is computed based on the actual quantity purchased. The purchasing department is responsible for any

FIGURE 15-2 A GENERAL MODEL FOR VARIANCE ANALYSIS OF VARIABLE MANUFACTURING COSTS

Actual Quantity of Inputs, at Actual Price (AQ · AP) (1)	Actual Quantity of Inputs, at Standard Price (AQ · SP) (2)	Standard Quantity Allowed for Output, at Standard Price (SQ · SP) (3)
	Price Variance (1) − (2)	Quantity Variance (2) − (3)
	Total (Flexible Budget) Variance (1) − (3)	
	• Materials purchase price variance	• Materials quantity (usage) variance
	• Labor rate variance	• Labor efficiency variance
	• Variable overhead spending variance	• Variable overhead efficiency variance

FIGURE 15-3 MATERIALS VARIANCES

Actual Quantity of Inputs, at Actual Price (AQ · AP) (1)	Actual Quantity of Inputs, at Standard Price (AQ · SP) (2)	Standard Quantity Allowed for Output, at Standard Price (SQ · SP) (3)
25,000 lb · $2.99 =$74,750	25,000 lb · $3.00 = $75,000	20,000 lb* · $3.00 = $60,000
	Price Variance = $250 (F)	
	20,750 lb · $3.00 = $62,250	Quantity Variance = $2,250 (U)

*10,000 units actually produced · 2 pounds allowed per unit = 20,000 pounds.

materials price variance that might occur. The materials quantity (usage) variance is computed based on the actual quantity used. The production department is responsible for any materials quantity variance.

Unfavorable price variances may be caused by: inaccurate standard prices, inflationary cost increases, scarcity in raw material supplies resulting in higher prices, and purchasing department inefficiencies. Unfavorable material quantity variances may be explained by poorly trained workers, by improperly adjusted machines, or by outright waste on the production line.

EXAMPLE 1

Dallas Ewing Corporation uses a standard cost system. The standard variable costs for product **J** are as follows:

Materials:	2 pounds at $3 per pound
Labor:	1 hour at $5 per hour
Variable overhead:	1 hour at $3 per hour

During March, 25,000 pounds of material were purchased for $74,750 and 20,750 pounds of material were used in producing 10,000 units of finished product. Direct labor costs incurred were $49,896 (10,080 direct labor hours) and variable overhead costs incurred were $34,776.

Using the general model (3-column model), the materials variances are shown in Figure 15–3.

It is important to note that the amount of materials purchased (25,000 pounds) differs from the amount of materials used in production (20,750 pounds). The materials purchase price variance was computed using 25,000 pounds purchased, whereas the materials quantity (usage) variance was computed using the 20,750 pounds used in production. A total variance cannot be computed because of the difference.

Alternatively, we can compute the materials variances as follows:

Materials purchase price variance = AQ (AP – SP)

$$= (AQ \cdot AP) - (AQ \cdot SP)$$
$$= (25{,}000 \text{ pounds}) (\$2.99 - \$3.00)$$
$$= \$74{,}750 - \$75{,}000$$
$$= \$250 \text{ (F)}$$

Materials quantity (usage) variance = (AQ – SQ) SP

$$= (20{,}750 \text{ pounds} - 20{,}000 \text{ pounds}) (\$3.00)$$
$$= \$62{,}250 - \$60{,}000$$
$$= \$2{,}250 \text{ (U)}$$

How are labor variances computed?

Labor variances are isolated when labor is used for production. They are computed in a manner similar to the materials variances, except that in the 3-column model the terms efficiency and rate are used in place of the terms quantity and price. The production department is responsible for both the prices paid for labor services and the quantity of labor services used. Therefore, the production department must explain why any labor variances occur.

Unfavorable rate variances may be explained by an increase in wages, or the use of labor commanding higher wage rates than contemplated. Unfavorable efficiency variances may be explained by poor supervision, poor quality workers, poor quality of materials requiring more labor time, or machine breakdowns.

EXAMPLE 2

Using the same data given in Example 1, the labor variances can be calculated as shown in Figure 15–4.

Alternatively, we can calculate the labor variances as follows:

$$\text{Labor rate variance} = AH (AR - SR)$$
$$= (AH \cdot AR) - (AH \cdot SR)$$
$$= (10{,}080 \text{ hours}) (\$4.95 - \$5.00)$$
$$= \$49{,}896 - \$50{,}400$$
$$= \$504 \text{ (F)}$$

FIGURE 15-4 LABOR VARIANCES

Actual Hours of Inputs, at Actual Rate (AH · AR) (1)	Actual Hours of Inputs, at Standard Rate (AH · SR) (2)	Standard Hours Allowed for Output, at Standard Rate (SH · SR) (3)
10,080 h · $4.95 = $49,896	10,080 h · $5.00 = $50,400	10,000 h~ · $5.00 = $50,000

Rate Variance (1) – (2) $504 (F)	Efficiency Variance (2) – (3) $400 (U)

Total Variance $104 (F)

~ 10,000 units actually produced · 1 hour (h) allowed per unit = 10,000 hours.

FIGURE 15-5 VARIABLE OVERHEAD VARIANCES

Actual Hours of Inputs, at Actual Rate (AH · AR) (1)	Actual Hours of Inputs, at Standard Rate (AH · SR) (2)	Standard Hours Allowed for Output, at Standard Rate (SH · SR) (3)
10,080 h · $3.45 = $34,776	10,080 h · $3.00 = $30,240	10,000 h# · $3.00 = $30,000

Spending Variance (1) – (2) $4,536 (U)	Efficiency Variance (2) – (3) $240 (U)

Total Variance $4,776 (U)

10,000 units actually produced · 1 hour (h) allowed per unit = 10,000 hours.

Note: The sumbols AQ, SQ, AP, and SP have been changed to AH, SH, AR, and SR to reflect the terms "hour" and "rate."

$$\text{Labor efficiency variance} = (AH - SH)\ SR$$

$$= \left(\frac{10,080}{\text{hours}} - \frac{10,000}{\text{hours}}\right) \cdot \$5.00$$

$$= \$50,400 - \$50,000$$

$$= \$400\ (U)$$

How are variable overhead variances computed?

The variable overhead variances are computed in a way very similar to the labor variances. The production department is usually responsible for any variable overhead variance.

Unfavorable variable overhead spending variances may be caused by a large number of factors: acquiring supplies for a price different from the standard, using more supplies than expected, waste, and theft of supplies. Unfavorable variable overhead efficiency variances might be caused by such factors as: poorly trained workers, poor-quality materials, faulty equipment, work interruptions, poor production scheduling, poor supervision, employee unrest, and so on.

When variable overhead is applied using direct labor hours, the efficiency variance will be caused by the same factors that cause the labor efficiency variance. However, when variable overhead is applied using machine hours, inefficiency in machinery will cause a variable overhead efficiency variance.

EXAMPLE 3

Using the same data given in Example 1, the variable overhead variances can be computed as shown in Figure 15–5.

Alternatively, we can compute the variable overhead variances as follows:

$$\text{Variable overhead spending variance} = AH\ (AR - SR)$$

$$= (AH \cdot AR) - (AH \cdot SR)$$

$$= (10,080\ \text{hours}) (\$3.45 - \$3.00)$$

$$= \$34,776 - \$30,240$$

$$= \$4,536 \text{ (U)}$$

Variable overhead efficiency variance $= (AH - SH) \text{ SR}$

$$= \left(\begin{matrix} 10,080 \\ \text{hours} \end{matrix} - \begin{matrix} 10,000 \\ \text{hours} \end{matrix} \right) \cdot \$3.00$$

$$= \$30,240 - \$30,000$$

$$= \$240 \text{ (U)}$$

FLEXIBLE BUDGETS AND PERFORMANCE REPORTS

How is a flexible budget used?

A flexible budget is useful in cost control. In contrast to a static budget, the flexible budget is characterized as follows:

1. It is geared toward a range of activity rather than a single level of activity.

2. It is dynamic in nature rather than static. By using the cost-volume formula (or flexible budget formula), a series of budgets can be easily developed for various levels of activity.

The static (fixed) budget is geared for only one level of activity and has problems in cost control. Flexible budgeting distinguishes between fixed and variable costs, thus allowing for a budget which can be automatically adjusted (via changes in variable cost totals) to the particular level of activity actually attained. Thus, variances between actual costs and budgeted costs are adjusted for volume ups and downs before differences due to price and quantity factors are computed.

The primary use of the flexible budget is to accurately measure performance by comparing actual costs for a given output with the budgeted costs for the same level of output.

EXAMPLE 4

To illustrate the difference between the static budget and the flexible budget, assume that the

Assembly Department of Jemco Industries, Inc. is budgeted to produce 6,000 units during June. Assume further that the company was able to produce only 5,800 units. The budget for direct labor and variable overhead costs is shown in Table 15–1.

If a static budget approach is used the performance report will appear as shown in Table 15–2. These cost variances are useless, in that they are comparing oranges with apples. The problem is that the budget costs are based on an activity level of 6,000 units, whereas the actual costs were incurred at an activity level below this (5,800 units). From a control standpoint, it makes no sense to try to compare costs at one activity level with costs at a different activity level. Such comparisons would make a production manager look good as long as the actual production is less than the budgeted production. Using the cost-volume formula and generating the budget based on the 5,800 actual units gives the performance report in Table 15–3. Notice that all cost variances are unfavorable (U), as compared to the favorable cost variances on the performance report based on the static budget approach.

How fixed overhead variances are computed?

By definition, fixed overhead does not change over a relevant range of activity; the amount of fixed overhead per unit varies inversely with the

TABLE 15-1   JEMCO INDUSTRIES, INC.
THE DIRECT LABOR AND VARIABLE OVERHEAD BUDGET
ASSEMBLY DEPARTMENT FOR THE MONTH OF JUNE

Budgeted production	6,000 units
Actual production	5,800 units
Direct labor	$39,000
Variable overhead costs:	
Indirect labor	6,000
Supplies	900
Repairs	300
	$46,200

TABLE 15-2 JEMCO INDUSTRIES, INC.
THE DIRECT LABOR AND VARIABLE OVERHEAD BUDGET
ASSEMBLY DEPARTMENT FOR THE MONTH OF JUNE

	Budget	Actual	Variance (U or F)*
Production in units	6,000	5,800	200U
Direct labor	$39,000	$38,500	$500F
Variable overhead costs:			
Indirect labor	6,000	5,950	50F
Supplies	900	870	30F
Repairs	300	295	5F
	$46,200	$45,615	$585F

*A variance represents the deviation of actual cost from the standard or budgeted cost. U and F stand for "unfavorable" and "favorable," respectively.

level of production. In order to calculate variances for fixed overhead, it is necessary to determine a standard fixed overhead rate, which requires the selection of a predetermined (denominator) level of activity. This activity should be measured on the basis of standard inputs allowed. The formula is:

$$\frac{\text{Standard fixed}}{\text{overhead rate}} = \frac{\text{Budgeted fixed overhead}}{\text{Budgeted level of activity}}$$

Total fixed overhead variance is simply under- or over-applied overhead. It is the difference between actual fixed overhead incurred and fixed overhead applied to production (generally, on the basis of standard direct labor hours allowed for actual production). Total fixed overhead variance combines fixed overhead spending (flexible-budget) variance and fixed overhead volume (capacity) variance.

1. Fixed overhead spending (flexible-budget) variance. It is the difference between actual fixed

TABLE 15-3 JEMCO INDUSTRIES, INC.
PERFORMANCE REPORT ASSEMBLY DEPARTMENT FOR THE MONTH OF JUNE

Budgeted production 6,000 units
Actual production   5,800 units

	Cost-Volume Formula	Budget 5,800 Units	Actual 5,800 Units	Variance (U or F)
Direct labor	$6.50 per unit	$37,700	$38,500	$800U
Variable overhead:				
Indirect labor	1.00	5,800	5,950	150U
Supplies	.15	870	870	0
Repairs	.05	290	295	5U
	$7.70	$44,660	$45,615	$955U

overhead incurred and budgeted fixed overhead. This variance is not affected by the level of production. Fixed overhead, by definition, does not change with the level of activity. The spending (flexible-budget) variance is caused solely by events such as unexpected changes in prices and unforeseen repairs.

2. Fixed overhead volume (capacity) variance. This variance results when the actual level of activity differs from the denominator activity used in determining the standard fixed overhead rate. Note that the denominator used in the formula is the expected annual activity level. Fixed overhead volume variance is a measure of the cost of failure to operate at the denominator (budgeted) activity level, and may be caused by such factors as failure to meet sales targets, idleness due to poor scheduling, and machine breakdowns. The volume variance is calculated as follows:

$$\begin{array}{l} \text{Fixed} \\ \text{overhead} \end{array} = \left(\begin{array}{l} \text{Budgeted} \\ \text{fixed overhead} \end{array} \right) - \left(\begin{array}{l} \text{Fixed} \\ \text{overhead applied} \end{array} \right)$$

or

$$= \left(\begin{array}{l} \text{Denominator} \\ \text{activity} \end{array} - \begin{array}{l} \text{Standard} \\ \text{hours allowed} \end{array} \right)$$

· Standard fixed overhead rate

When denominator activity exceeds standard hours allowed, the volume variance is unfavorable (U), because it is an index of less-than-denominator utilization of capacity.

It is important to note that there are no efficiency variances for fixed overhead. Fixed overhead does not change regardless of whether productive resources are used efficiently or not. For example, property taxes, insurance and factory rents are not affected by whether production is being carried on efficiently.

Figure 15–6 illustrates the relationship between the various elements of fixed overhead, and the possible variances.

EXAMPLE 5

The Geige Manufacturing Company has the following standard cost of factory overhead at a

FIGURE 15-6 FIXED OVERHEAD VARIANCES

	Incurred: Actual Hours × Actual Rate (1)	Flexible Budget Based on Actual Hours (2)	Flexible Budget Based on Standard Hours Allowed (3)	Applied (4)
3-way Analysis	Spending Variance (1) – (2)	Efficiency Variance (Not Applicable)	Volume Variance (3) – (4)	
2-way Analysis	Flexible Budget Variance (1) – (3)		Volume Variance (3) – (4)	
	(1) – (4) Under- or Over-Applied			

normal monthly production (denominator) volume of 1,300 direct labor hours:

> Variable overhead (1 hour @ $2)
> Fixed overhead (1 hour @ $5)

Fixed overhead budgeted is $6,500 per month. During the month of March, the following events occurred:

(a) Actual overhead costs incurred (for 1,350 units of output) were:

Variable	$2,053
Fixed	$6,725

(b) Standard hours allowed, 1,250 hours (1 hour × 1,250 units of output).

Note that:

(a) Flexible budget formula:

Variable overhead rate,	$2 per direct labor hour
Fixed overhead budgeted,	$6,500

(b) Standard overhead applied rates:

Variable,	$2 per direct labor hour
Fixed,	$5 per direct labor hour

Figure 15–7 shows all the variances for variable overhead as well as fixed overhead. Alternatively, fixed overhead volume variance can be calculated as follows:

$$\begin{array}{l} \text{Fixed overhead} \\ \text{volume variance} \end{array} = \left(\begin{array}{c} \text{Denominator} \\ \text{activity} \end{array} - \begin{array}{c} \text{Standard} \\ \text{hours allowed} \end{array} \right)$$

$$\cdot \text{ standard fixed overhead rate}$$

$$= (1,300 \text{ hours} - 1,250 \text{ hours}) \cdot \$5$$

$$= 50 \text{ hours} \cdot \$5 = \$250 \text{ U}$$

PRODUCTION MIX AND YIELD VARIANCES _____

What is the production mix variance?

The production mix variance is a cost variance that arises if the actual production mix

FIGURE 15-7 VARIANCE ANALYSIS FOR VARIABLE OVERHEAD AND FIXED OVERHEAD

	Incurred: Actual Hours × Actual Rate (1,350 hrs) (1)	Based on Actual Hours (1,350 hrs) (2)	Flexible Budget Based on Standard Hours Allowed (1,250 hrs) (3)	Applied (1,250 hrs) (4)
	V $2,853	$2,700 (1,350 × $2)	$2,500 (1,250 × $2)	$2,500
	F 6,725	6,500	6,500	6,250
	$9,578	$9,200	$9,000	$8,750

(3-way)

Spending Variance (1) − (2)
V $153 U
F 225 U
$378 U

Efficiency Variance (Not Applicable)
$200 U
Not Applicable
$200 U

Volume Variance (3) − (4)
Not Applicable
$250 U
$250 U

(2-way)

Flexible Budget Variance (1) − (3)
V $353 U + F $225 U = $578 U

Volume Variance (3) − (4)
Not Applicable
+ F $250 U = $250 U

Under- or Over-Applied (1) − (4)
V $353 U + F $475 U = $828 U

deviates from the standard or budgeted mix. In a multi-product, multi-input situation, the mix variances explain the portion of the quantity (usage, or efficiency) variance caused by using inputs (direct materials and direct labor) in ratios different from standard proportions, thus helping determine how efficiently mixing operations are performed.

The material mix variance indicates the impact on material costs of the deviation from the budgeted mix. The labor mix variance measures the impact of changes in the labor mix on labor costs.

$$\begin{matrix} \text{Material} \\ \text{mix} \\ \text{variance} \end{matrix} = \left(\begin{matrix} \text{Actual units} \\ \text{used at} \\ \text{standard mix} \end{matrix} - \begin{matrix} \text{Actual units} \\ \text{used at} \\ \text{actual mix} \end{matrix} \right) \cdot \begin{matrix} \text{Standard} \\ \text{unit price} \end{matrix}$$

$$\begin{matrix} \text{Labor} \\ \text{mix} \\ \text{variance} \end{matrix} = \left(\begin{matrix} \text{Actual hours} \\ \text{used at} \\ \text{standard mix} \end{matrix} - \begin{matrix} \text{Actual hours} \\ \text{used at} \\ \text{actual mix} \end{matrix} \right) \cdot \begin{matrix} \text{Standard} \\ \text{hourly rate} \end{matrix}$$

Probable causes of unfavorable production mix variances are as follows: (1) capacity restraints force substitution; (2) poor production scheduling; (3) lack of certain types of labor; and (4) certain materials are in short supply.

EXAMPLE 6

J Company produces a compound composed of Materials Alpha and Beta which is marketed in 20-lb. bags. Material Alpha can be substituted for Material Beta. Standard cost and mix data have been determined as follows:

Material	Unit Price	Standard Unit	Standard Mix Proportions
Alpha	$3	5 lb.	25%
Beta	4	15	75
		20 lb.	100%

Processing each 20 lbs. of material requires 10 hrs. of labor. The company employs two types of labor, "skilled" and "unskilled," working on two processes, assembly and finishing. The following standard labor cost has been set for a 20-lb. bag:

	Standard Hours	Standard Wage Rate	Total	Standard Mix Proportions
Unskilled	4 hr.	$2	$ 8	40%
Skilled	6	3	18	60
	10 hr.	$2.60	$26	100%

At standard cost, labor averages $2.60 per unit. During the month of December 100 20-lb. bags were completed with the following labor costs:

	Actual Hours	Actual Rate	Actual Wages
Unskilled	380 hr.	$2.50	$ 950
Skilled	600	3.25	1,950
	980 hr.	$2.96	$2,900

Material records show:

> Material Alpha actually used, 700 lb. @ $3.10
> Material Beta actually used, 1,400 lb. @ 3.90

Using the formulas above, the material mix variance and labor mix variance are computed as follows:

(a) Material Mix Variance:

Material	Actual Units Used at Standard Mix*	Actual Units at Actual Mix	Diff.	Standard Unit Price	Variance (U or F)
Alpha	525 lb.	700 lb.	175U	$3	$525U
Beta	1,575	1,400	175F	4	700F
	2,100	2,100			$175F

*This is the standard mix proportions of 25% and 75% applied to the actual material units used of 2,100 lbs.

(b) Labor Mix Variance:

	Actual Hrs. Used at Standard Mix*	Actual Hrs. at Actual Mix	Diff.	Standard Hourly Rate	Variance (U or F)
Unskilled	392 hr.	380 hr.	12F	$2	$24F
Skilled	588	600	12U	3	36U
	980	980			$12U

*This is the standard mix proportions of 40% and 60% applied to the actual total labor hours used of 980.

How do you compute the production yield variance?

The production yield variance is the difference between the actual yield and the standard yield. Yield is a measure of productivity. In other words, it is a measure of output from a given amount of input. For example, in the production of potato chips, we might expect a certain yield such as 40% yield or 40 pounds of chips for 100 pounds of potatoes.

If the actual yield is less than the expected or standard yield for a given level of input, the yield variance is unfavorable. A yield variance is computed for labor as well as materials. A labor yield variance is considered the result of the quantity and/or the quality of labor used. The yield variance explains the remaining portion of the quantity variance and is caused by a yield of finished product that does not correspond with the quantity that actual inputs should have produced. When there is no mix variance, the yield variance equals the quantity variance.

$$\begin{array}{c}\text{Material}\\ \text{yield}\\ \text{variance}\end{array} = \left(\begin{array}{cc}\text{Actual units} & \text{Actual output}\\ \text{used at} & - \text{ units used at}\\ \text{standard mix} & \text{standard mix}\end{array}\right) \cdot \begin{array}{c}\text{Standard}\\ \text{unit}\\ \text{price}\end{array}$$

$$\begin{array}{c}\text{Labor}\\ \text{yield}\\ \text{variance}\end{array} = \left(\begin{array}{cc}\text{Actual hours} & \text{Actual output}\\ \text{used at} & - \text{ hours used at}\\ \text{standard mix} & \text{standard mix}\end{array}\right) \cdot \begin{array}{c}\text{Standard}\\ \text{hourly}\\ \text{rate}\end{array}$$

The probable causes of unfavorable production yield variances are: (1) use of low quality materials and/or labor; (2) the existence of faulty equipment; (3) the use of improper production methods; and (4) an improper or costly mix of materials and/or labor.

EXAMPLE 7

A company uses a standard cost system for its production of a chemical product. This chemical is produced by mixing three major raw materials, A, B, and C. The company has the following standards:

36 lb. of Material A @ 1.00	= $ 36.00
48 lb. of Material B @ 2.00	= $ 96.00
36 lb. of Material C @ 1.75	= $ 63.00
120 lb. of standard mix @ 1.625	= $195.00

The company should produce 100 lb. of finished product at a standard cost of $1.625 per lb. ($195/120 lb.). To convert 120 lb. of materials into 100 lb. of finished chemical requires 400 direct labor hours at $3.50 per hour, or $14 per lb. During the month of December, the company completed 4,250 lb. of output with the following labor: direct labor 15,250 hours @ $3.50. Material records show:

Material A	1,160 lb. used
Material B	1,820
Material C	1,480

Material yield variance can be calculated as shown on the next page.

With a standard yield of 83⅓% (100/120), 4,250 lb. of completed output should have required 17,000 hours of direct labor (4,250 lb. × 400 direct labor hours/100). Comparing the hours allowed for the actual input, 14,866.67 hours with the hours allowed for actual output, 17,000 hours, we find a favorable labor yield variance of $7,466.66, as shown below:

Labor Yield Variance:

Actual hours at expected output	$52,033.34
Actual output (4,250 lb. × 400/100 = 17,000 hr. @ $3.50 or 4,250 lb. @ $14.00)	59,500.00
	$ 7,466.66F

Material	Actual Input Units at Standard Mix	Actual Output Units at Standard Mix*	Diff.	Standard Unit Price	Variance (U or F)
A	1,338 lb.	1,275 lb.	63U	$1.00	$ 63U
B	1,784	1,700	84F	2.00	168U
C	1,338	1,275	63U	1.75	110.25U
	4,460	4,250			$341.25U

*This is the standard mix proportions of 30%, 40%, and 30% applied to the actual output units used of 4,250 lb.

16

Control of Profit Centers

How do you evaluate profit centers?

Segmental reporting is the process of reporting activities of profit centers such as divisions, product lines, or sales territories. The *contribution approach* is valuable for segmented reporting because it emphasizes the cost behavior patterns and the controllability of costs that are generally useful for profitability analysis of various segments of an organization.

The contribution approach is based on the thesis that:

1. Fixed costs are much less controllable than variable costs.

2. Direct fixed costs and common fixed costs must be clearly distinguished. Direct fixed costs are those fixed costs which can be identified directly with a particular segment of an organization, whereas common fixed costs are those costs which cannot be identified directly with the segment.

3. Common fixed costs should be clearly identified as unallocated in the contribution income statement by segments. Any attempt to allocate these types of costs, on some arbitrary basis, to the segments of the organization can destroy the value of responsibility accounting. It would lead to unfair evaluation of performance and misleading managerial decisions.

The following concepts are highlighted in the contribution approach:

1. Contribution margin—Sales minus variable costs.

2. Segment margin—Contribution margin minus direct (tracable) fixed costs. Direct fixed costs include discretionary fixed costs such as certain advertising, research and development,

sales promotion, and engineering as well as tracable and commited fixed costs such as depreciation, property taxes, insurance and the segment managers' salaries.

3. Net income—Segment margin less unallocated common fixed costs. Segmental reporting can be made by division, product or product line, sales territory, service center, salesperson, store or branch office, or domestic or foreign operations.

Figure 16–1 illustrates two levels of segmental reporting: (1) By segments defined as divisions and (2) by segments defined as product lines of a division.

The segment margin is the best measure of the profitability of a segment. Unallocated fixed costs are common to the segments being evaluated and should be left unallocated in order not to distort the performance results of segments.

FIGURE 16-1 SEGMENTAL INCOME STATEMENT

(1) Segments Defined as Divisions

	Total Company	Segments Division 1	Segments Division 2
Sales	$150,000	$90,000	$60,000
Less: Variable costs			
Manufacturing	40,000	30,000	10,000
Selling and admin.	20,000	14,000	6,000
Total variable costs	$ 60,000	$44,000	$16,000
Contribution margin	$ 90,000	$46,000	$44,000
Less: Direct fixed costs	70,000	43,000	27,000
Divisional segment margin	$ 20,000	$ 3,000	$17,000
Less: Unallocated common fixed costs	10,000		
Net income	$ 10,000		

FIGURE 16-1 *(Continued)*

(2) Segments Defined as Product Lines of Division 2

	Division 2	Deluxe Model	Regular Model
		Segments	
Sales	$ 60,000	$20,000	$40,000
Less: Variable costs			
Manufacturing	10,000	5,000	5,000
Selling and administrative	6,000	2,000	4,000
Total variable costs	$ 16,000	$ 7,000	$ 9,000
Contribution margin	$ 44,000	$13,000	$31,000
Less: Direct fixed costs	26,500	9,500	17,000
Product line margin	$ 17,500	$ 3,500	$14,000
Less: Unallocated common fixed costs	500		
Divisional segment margin	$ 17,000		

PROFIT VARIANCE ANALYSIS

How does profit variance analysis work?

Profit variance analysis, often called gross profit analysis, deals with how to analyze the profit variance that constitutes the departure between actual profit and the previous year's income or the budgeted figure. The primary goal of profit variance analysis is to improve performance and profitability in the future.

Profit, whether it is gross profit or contribution margin, is affected by at least three basic items: sales price, sales volume, and costs. In addition, in a multi-product firm, if not all products are equally profitable, profit is affected by the mix of products sold.

The difference between budgeted and actual profits are due to one or more of the following:

1. Changes in unit sales price and cost, called sales price and cost price variances, respectively. The difference between sales price variance and cost price variance is often called a contribution-margin-per-unit variance or a gross-profit-per-unit variance, depending upon what type of costing system being referred to, that is absorption costing or direct costing. Contribution margin is considered, however, a better measure of product profitability because it deducts from sales revenue only the variable costs that are controllable in terms of fixing responsibility. Gross profit does not reflect cost-volume-profit relationships. Nor does it consider directly tracable marketing costs.

2. Changes in the volume of products sold summarized as the sales volume variance and the cost volume variance. The difference between the two is called the total volume variance.

3. Changes in the volume of the more profitable or less profitable items referred to as the sales mix variance.

Detailed analysis is critical to management when multi-products exist. The volume variances may be used to measure a change in volume (while holding the mix constant) and the mix may be employed to evaluate the effect of a change in sales mix (while holding the quantity constant). This type of variance analysis is useful when the products are substituted for each other, or when products which are not necessarily substitutes for each other are marketed through the same channel.

What are the types of standards in profit variance analysis?

To determine the various causes for a favorable variance (an increase) or an unfavorable variance (a decrease) in profit we need some kind of yardstick to compare against the actual results. The yardstick may be based on the prices and costs of the previous year, or any year selected as the base periods. Some companies summarize profit variance analysis data in their annual report by showing departures from the previous year's reported income. However, one can establish a more effective control and budgetary method rather than the previous year's data. Standard or budgeted mix can be determined using such sophisticated techniques as linear and goal programming.

How do you calculate profit variances for single product firms?

Profit variance analysis is simplest in a single product firm, for there is only one sales price, one set of costs (or cost price), and a unitary sales volume. An unfavorable profit variance can be broken down into four components: a sales price variance, a cost price variance, a sales volume variance, and a cost volume variance.

The sales price variance measures the impact on the firm's contribution margin (or gross profit) of changes in the unit selling price. It is computed as:

$$\text{Sales price variance} = (\text{Actual price} - \text{Budget price}) \times \text{Actual sales}$$

If the actual price is lower than the budgeted price, for example, this variance is unfavorable; it tends to reduce profit. The cost price variance, on the other hand, is simply the summary of price variances for materials, labor, and overhead. (This is the sum of material price, labor rate, and factory overhead spending variances.) It is computed as:

$$\text{Cost price variance} = (\text{Actual cost} - \text{Budget cost}) \times \text{Actual sales}$$

If the actual unit cost is lower than budgeted cost, for example, this variance is favorable; it tends to increase profit. We simplify the computation of price variances by taking the sales price variance less the cost price variance and call it the gross-profit-per-unit variance or contribution-margin-per-unit variance.

The sales volume variance indicates the impact on the firm's profit of changes in the unit sales volume. This is the amount by which sales would have varied from the budget if nothing but sales volume had changed. It is computed as:

$$\frac{\text{Sales volume}}{\text{variance}} = (\text{Actual sales} - \text{Budget sales}) \times \frac{\text{Budget}}{\text{price}}$$

If actual sales volume is greater than budgeted sales volume, this is favorable; it tends to increase profit. The cost volume variance has the same interpretation. It is:

$$(\text{Actual sales} - \text{Budget sales}) \times \text{Budget cost per unit}$$

The difference between the sales volume variance and the cost volume variance is called the total volume variance.

How do you calculate variances for multi-product firms?

When a firm produces more than one product, there is a fourth component of the profit variance. This is the sales mix variance, the effect on profit of selling a different proportionate mix of products than that which has been budgeted. This variance arises when different products have different contribution margins. In a multi-product firm, actual sales volume can differ from that budgeted in two ways. The total number of units sold could differ from the target aggregate sales. In addition, the mix of the products actually sold may not be proportionate to the target mix. Each of these two different types of changes in volume is reflected in a separate variance.

The total volume variance is divided into the two: the sales mix variance and the sales quantity variance. These two variances should be used to evaluate the marketing department of the firm. The sales mix variance shows how well the department has done in terms of selling the more profitable products while the sales quantity variance measures how well the firm has done in terms of its overall sales volume. They are computed as:

$$\begin{array}{l} \text{Sales mix} \\ \text{variance} \end{array} = \left(\begin{array}{c} \text{Actual sales at} \\ \text{budget mix} \end{array} - \begin{array}{c} \text{Budget sales} \\ \text{at budget mix} \end{array} \right)$$

$$\times \text{Budget CM (or gross profit)/unit}$$

$$\begin{array}{l} \text{Sales quantity} \\ \text{variance} \end{array} = \left(\begin{array}{c} \text{Actual sales at} \\ \text{budget mix} \end{array} - \begin{array}{c} \text{Actual sales} \\ \text{at budget mix} \end{array} \right)$$

$$\times \text{Budget CM (or gross profit)/unit}$$

$$\begin{array}{l} \text{Total volume} \\ \text{variance} \end{array} = \left(\begin{array}{c} \text{Actual sales at} \\ \text{actual mix} \end{array} - \begin{array}{c} \text{Budget sales} \\ \text{at budget mix} \end{array} \right)$$

$$\times \text{Budget CM (or gross profit)/unit}$$

EXAMPLE 1

The controller of the Royalla Publishing Company prepared the following comparative statement of operations for 19XA and 19XB.

	19XA	19XB
Sales in units	97,500	110,000
Selling price	$9.00	$8.80
Sales revenue	$877,500	$968,000
Cost of goods sold	$585,000	$704,000
Gross profit	$292,500	$264,000

The controller was very pleased with the performance of the company in 19XA. Analyze the decline in gross profit between 19XA and 19XB by calculating:

(a) Sales price variance.
(b) Cost price variance.
(c) Sales volume variance.
(d) Cost volume variance.
(e) Total volume variance (sales volume variance – cost volume variance) or (sales mix variance + sales quantity variance).
(f) Sales mix variance.
(g) Sales quantity variance.

19XA gross profit	$292,500
19XB gross profit	264,000
Decrease in gross profit to be accounted for	$ 28,500

(a) *Sales price variance:*

19XB actual sales revenue	$968,000
19XB actual sales revenue at 19XA price (110,000 at $9)	990,000
	$ 22,000U

(b) *Cost price variance:*

19XB actual	$704,000
19XB actual at 19XA cost per unit (110,000 at $6*)	660,000
	$ 44,000U

19XA cost per unit = $585,000/97,500 = $6

(c) *Sales volume variance:*

19XB actual volume at 19XA price	$990,000 (110,000 × $9)
19XA actual volume at 19XA price	877,500
(19XB actual – 19XA actual) × 19XA price	$112,500F

(d) *Cost volume variance:*

19XB actual volume at 19XA cost	$660,000 (110,000 × $6)
19XA actual volume at 19XA cost	585,000
(19XB actual – 19XA actual) × 19XA cost	$ 75,000U

(e) *Total volume variance* = sales volume variance − cost volume variance = $112,500F − $75,000U = $37,500F, which is broken down into the sales mix variance and the sales quantity variance as follows:

(f) *Sales mix variance* = 0 since we have only one product in this problem.

(g) *Sales quantity variance*

19XB Actual Volume	19XA Budgeted Volume	Diff.	19XA Gross Profit per Unit*	Variance ($)
110,000	97,500	12,500F	$3	$37,500F

*19XA gross profit per unit = 19XA selling price − 19XA cost of goods sold = $9 − $6 = $3

The decline in gross profit of $28,500 can be explained as follows:

	Gains	Losses
Gain due to favorable sales volume variance	$112,500F	
Losses due to:		
unfavorable sales price variance		$ 22,000U
unfavorable cost price variance		44,000U
unfavorable cost volume variance		75,000U
	$112,500F	$141,000U

The decrease in gross profit is thus accounted for:

$$141,000U − $112,500F = $28,500U$$

EXAMPLE 2

The Lake Tahoe Ski Store sells two ski models—Model X and Model Y. For the years 19X1 and 19X2, the store realized a gross profit of $246,640 and $211,650, respectively. The owner of the store was astounded since the total sales volume in dollars and in units was higher for 19X2 than for 19X1 yet the gross profit achieved actually declined. Given below are the store's unaudited operating results for 19X1 and 19X2. No fixed costs were included in the cost of goods sold per unit.

Year	Selling Price	Model X Cost of Goods Sold per Unit	Sales (in Units)	Sales Revenue
1	$150	$110	2,800	$420,000
2	160	125	2,650	424,000

Year	Selling Price	Model Y Cost of Goods Sold per Unit	Sales (in Units)	Sales Revenue
1	$172	$121	2,640	$454,080
2	176	135	2,900	510,400

Explain why the gross profit declined by $34,990. Include a detailed variance analysis of price changes and changes in volume both for sales and cost. Also subdivide the total volume variance into changes in price and changes in quantity.

Sales price and sales volume variances measure the impact on the firm's CM (or GP) of changes in the unit selling price and sales volume. In computing these variances, all costs are held constant in order to stress changes in price and volume. Cost price and cost volume variances are computed in the same manner, holding price and volume constant. All these variances for the Lake Tahoe Ski Store are computed below.

Sales Price Variance

Actual sales for 19X2:
  Model X 2,650 × $160 = $424,000
  Model Y 2,900 × 176 = 510,400 $934,400

Actual 19X2 sales at 19X1 prices:
  Model X $2,650 \times \$150 = \$397,500$
  Model Y $2,900 \times 172 = 498,800$ 896,300
                                                    $\overline{\underline{\$\ 38,100F}}$

Sales Volume Variance

Actual 19X2 sales at 19X1 prices: \$896,300
Actual 19X1 sales (at 19X1 prices):
  Model X $2,800 \times \$150 = \$420,000$
  Model Y $2,640 \times 172 = 454,080$ 874,080
                                                    $\overline{\underline{\$\ 22,220F}}$

Cost Price Variance

Actual cost of goods sold for 19X2:
  Model X $2,650 \times \$125 = \$331,250$
  Model Y $2,900 \times 135 = 391,500$ \$722,750
Actual 19X2 sales at 19X1 costs:
  Model X $2,650 \times \$110 = \$291,500$
  Model Y $2,900 \times 121 = 350,900$ 642,400
                                                    $\overline{\underline{\$\ 80,350U}}$

Cost Volume Variance

Actual 19X2 sales at 19X1 costs: \$642,400
Actual 19X1 sales (at 19X1 costs):
  Model X $2,800 \times \$110 = \$308,000$
  Model Y $2,640 \times 121 = 319,440$ 627,440
                                                    $\overline{\underline{\$\ 14,960U}}$

Total volume variance = sales volume variance
                      − cost volume variance
                      = \$22,220 F − \$14,960 U
                      = $\underline{\underline{\$\ 7,260}}$ F

The total volume variance is computed as the
sum of a sales mix variance and a sales quantity
variance as follows:

Sales Mix Variance

Model	19X2 Actual Sales at 19X1 Mix*	19X2 Actual Sales at 19X2 Mix	Diff.	19X1 Gross Profit per Unit	Variance ($)
X	2,857	2,650	207 U	$40	$ 8,280 U
Y	2,693	2,900	207 F	51	10,557 F
	5,550	5,550			$ 2,277 F

This is the 19X1 mix (used as standard or budget) proportions of 51.47% (or 2,800/5,440 = 51.47%) and 48.53% (or 2,640/5,440 = 48.53%) applied to the actual 19X2 sales figure of 5,550 units.

Sales Quantity Variance

Model	19X2 Actual Sales at 19X1 Mix*	19X1 Actual Sales at 19X1 Mix	Diff.	19X1 Gross Profit per Unit	Variance ($)
X	2,857	2,800	57 F	$40	$2,280 F
Y	2,693	2,640	53 F	51	2,703 F
	5,550	5,440			$4,983 F

This is the 19X1 mix (used as standard or budget) proportions of 51.47% (or 2,800/5,440 = 51.47%) and 48.53% (or 2,640/5,440 = 48.53%) applied to the actual 19X2 sales figure of 5,550 units.

A favorable total volume variance is due to a favorable shift in the sales mix (that is, from Model X to Model Y) and also to a favorable increase in sales volume (by 110 units) which is shown as follows.

Sales mix variance	$ 2,277F
Sales quantity variance	4,983F
	$ 7,260F

However, there remains the decrease in gross profit. The decrease in gross profit of $34,990 can be explained as follows.

	Gains	Losses
Gain due to increased sales price	$38,100F	
Loss due to increased cost		$80,350U
Gain due to increase in units sold	4,983F	
Gain due to shift in sales mix	2,277F	
	$45,360F	$80,350U

Hence, net decrease in gross profit = $80,350 − $45,360 = $34,990 U.

Despite the increase in sales price and volume and the favorable shift in sales mix, the Lake Tahoe Ski Store ended up losing $34,990 compared to 19X1. The major reason for this comparative loss was the tremendous increase in cost of goods sold, as indicated by an unfavorable cost price variance of $80,350. The costs for both Model X and Model Y went up significantly over 19X1. The Store has to take a close look at the cost picture. Even though only variable costs were included in cost of goods sold per unit, both variable and fixed costs should be analyzed in an effort to cut down on controllable costs. In doing that, it is essential that responsibility be clearly fixed to given individuals. In a retail business like the Lake Tahoe Ski Store, operating expenses such as advertising and payroll of store employees must also be closely scrutinized.

How do you improve sales mix?

Many product lines include a lower-margin price leader model, and often a high-margin deluxe model. For example, the automobile industry includes in its product line low-margin energy-efficient small cars and higher margin deluxe models. In an attempt to increase over-all profitability, management would wish to emphasize the higher margin expensive items, but salesmen might find it easier to sell low-margin cheaper models. Thus, a salesman might meet his unit sales quota with each item at its budgeted price, but because of mix shifts, he could be far short of contributing his share of budgeted profit.

CFOs should realize that (1) greater proportions of more profitable products mean higher profits and (2) higher proportions of lower margin sales reduce overall profit despite the increase in overall sales volume. That is, an unfavorable mix may easily offset a favorable increase in volume, and vice versa.

What should performance reports look like?

Profit variance analysis aids in fixing responsibility by separating the causes of the change in profit into price, volume, and mix factors. With responsibility resting in different places, the segregation of the total profit variance is essential. The performance reports based on the analysis of profit variances must be prepared for each responsibility center, indicating the following:

1. Is it controllable?

2. Is it favorable or unfavorable?

3. If it is unfavorable, is it significant enough for further investigation?

4. Who is responsible for what portion of the total profit variance?

5. What are the causes for an unfavorable variance?

6. What is the remedial action to take?

The performance report must address these types of questions. The report is useful in two ways: (1) in focusing attention on situations in need of management action and (2) in increasing the precision of planning and control of sales and costs. The report should be produced as part of the overall responsibility accounting system.

17

Performance Investment Centers and Transfer Pricing

Is the investment center healthy?

The ability to measure performance is essential in developing management incentives and controlling the operation toward the achievement of organizational goals. A typical decentralized subunit is an investment center that is responsible for an organization's invested capital (operating assets) and the related operating income. There are two widely used measurements of performance for the investment center: the rate of return on investment (ROI) and residual income (RI).

Why is transfer pricing important?

Goods and services are often exchanged between various divisions of a decentralized organization. The transfer price is the selling price credited to the selling division and the cost charged to the buying division for an internal transfer of a good or service. The choice of transfer prices not only affects divisional performance but is also important in decisions involving make or buy, whether to buy internally or outside, and choosing between production possibilities.

RATE OF RETURN ON INVESTMENT (ROI)

How do you calculate ROI?

ROI relates a division's operating income to operating assets:

$$\text{ROI} = \frac{\text{Operating income}}{\text{Operating assets}}$$

EXAMPLE 1

Consider the following financial data for a division:

> Operating assets $100,000
> Operating income $ 18,000
>
> $$ROI = \frac{\$18,000}{\$100,000} = 18\%$$

RESIDUAL INCOME (RI) ————————————

What is residual income?

Another approach to measuring performance in an investment center is residual income (RI). RI is the operating income which an investment center is able to earn above some minimum rate of return on its operating assets. RI, unlike ROI, is an absolute amount of income rather than a specific rate of return:

$$RI = \frac{\text{Operating}}{\text{income}} - \left(\frac{\text{Minimum required}}{\text{rate of return}} \times \frac{\text{Operating}}{\text{assets}}\right)$$

EXAMPLE 2

In Example 1, assume the minimum required rate of return is 13%. Then the residual income of the division is

$$\$18,000 - (13\% \times \$100,000) = \$18,000 - \$13,000$$
$$= \$5,000$$

What are the benefits of RI?

When RI is used to evaluate divisional performance, the objective is to maximize the total amount of residual income, not to maximize the overall ROI figure. RI is regarded as a better measure of performance than ROI because it encourages investment in projects that would be rejected under ROI. A major disadvantage of RI, however, is that it cannot be used to compare divisions of different sizes. RI tends to favor the larger divisions due to the larger amount of dollars involved.

INVESTMENT DECISIONS
UNDER ROI AND RI _____

How can you use ROI and RI?

The decision whether to use ROI or RI as a measure of divisional performance affects chief financial officers' investment decisions. Under the ROI method, division managers tend to accept only the investments whose returns exceed the division's ROI; otherwise, the division's overall ROI would decrease. Under the RI method, on the other hand, division managers would accept an investment as long as it earns a rate in excess of the minimum required rate of return. The addition of such an investment will increase the division's overall RI.

EXAMPLE 3

Consider the same data given in Examples 1 and 2:

Operating assets	$100,000
Operating income	$ 18,000
Minimum required rate of return	13%
ROI = 18% and RI = $5,000	

Assume that the division is presented with a project that would yield 15% on a $10,000 investment. The division manager would not accept this project under the ROI approach since the division is already earning 18%. Acquiring this project will bring down the present ROI to 17.73%, as shown below:

	Present	New Project	Overall
Operating assets (a)	$100,000	$10,000	$110,000
Operating income (b)	18,000	1,500*	19,500
ROI (b / a)	18%	15%	17.73%

$10,000 × 15% = $1,500

Under the RI approach, the manager would accept the new project since it provides a higher rate than the minimum required rate of return (15% vs. 13%). Accepting the new project will increase the overall residual income to $5,200, as shown below:

	Present	New Project	Overall
Operating assets (a)	$100,000	$10,000	$110,000
Operating income (b)	18,000	1,500	19,500
Minimum required income at 13% (c)	13,000	1,300*	14,300
RI (b − c)	$ 5,000	$ 200	$ 5,200

*$10,000 × 13% = $1,300

TRANSFER PRICING

How are transfer prices determined?

Goods and services are often exchanged between various divisions of a decentralized organization. A major goal of transfer pricing is to enable divisions that exchange goods or services to act as independent businesses.

The question then is: What monetary values should be assigned to these exchanges or transfers? Market price? Some kind of cost? Some version of either? Unfortunately, there is no single transfer price that will please everybody—that is, top management, the selling division, and the buying division—involved in the transfer. Various transfer pricing schemes are available, such as market price, cost-based price, or negotiated price.

The choice of a transfer pricing policy (i.e., which type of transfer price to use) is normally decided by top management. The decision will typically include consideration of the following:

• *Goal congruence.* Will the transfer price promote the goals of the company as a whole? Will it harmonize the divisional goals with organizational goals?

• *Performance evaluation.* Will the selling division receive enough credit for its transfer of goods and services to the buying division? Will the transfer price hurt the performance of the selling division?

• *Autonomy.* Will the transfer price preserve autonomy; the freedom of the selling and buying division managers to operate their divisions as decentralized entities?

• Other factors such as minimization of tariffs and income taxes and observance of legal restrictions.

What are alternative transfer pricing schemes?

Transfer prices can be based on:

• Market price
• Cost-based price—variable or full cost
• Negotiated price
• General formula, which is usually the sum of variable costs per unit and opportunity cost for the company as a whole (lost revenue per unit on outside sales)

How suitable is market price for transfers?

Market price is the best transfer price in the sense that it will maximize the profits of the company as a whole, if it meets the following two conditions:

1. There exists a competitive market price.
2. Divisions are independent of each other.

If either one of these conditions is violated, market price will not lead to an optimal economic decision for the company.

What are the pros and cons of cost-based prices?

Cost-based transfer price, another alternative transfer pricing scheme, is easy to understand and convenient to use. But there are some disadvantages, including:

• Inefficiencies of selling divisions are passed on to the buying divisions with little incentive to control costs. The use of standard costs is recommended in such a case.

• The cost-based method treats the divisions as cost centers rather than profit or investment centers. Therefore, measures such as ROI and RI cannot be used for evaluation purposes.

The variable-cost-based transfer price has an advantage over the full cost method because in the short run it may tend to ensure the best utilization of the overall company's resources. The reason is that, in the short run, fixed costs do not change. Any use of facilities, without incurrence of additional fixed costs, will increase the company's overall profits.

When is negotiated price used?

A negotiated price is generally used when there is no clear outside market. A negotiated price is a price agreed upon between the buying and selling divisions that reflects unusual or mitigating circumstances. This method is widely used when no intermediate market price exists for the product transferred and the selling division is assured of a normal profit.

EXAMPLE 4

Company X just purchased a small company that specializes in the manufacture of part no. 323. Company X is a decentralized organization, and will treat the newly acquired company as an autonomous division called Division B with full profit responsibility.

Division B's fixed costs total $30,000 per month, and variable costs per unit are $18. Division B's operating capacity is 5,000 units. The selling price per unit is $30. Division A of company X is currently purchasing 2,500 units of part no. 323 per month from an outside supplier at $29 per unit, which represents the normal $30 price less a quantity discount.

Top management wishes to decide what transfer price should be used. The following are alternative prices:

1. $30 market price.
2. $29, the price that Division A is currently paying to the outside supplier.

3. $23.50 negotiated price, which is $18 variable cost plus $1/2$ of the benefits of an internal transfer [($29 – $18) × 1/2].

4. $24 full cost, which is $18 variable cost plus $6 ($30,000/5,000 units) fixed cost per unit.

5. $18 variable cost.

We will discuss each of these prices:

1. $30 would not be an appropriate transfer price. Division B cannot charge a price more than the price Division A is paying now ($29).

2. $29 would be an appropriate transfer price if top management wishes to treat the divisions as autonomous investment centers. This price would cause all of the benefits of internal transfers to accrue to the selling division, with the buying division's position remaining unchanged.

3. $23.50 would be an appropriate transfer price if top management wishes to treat the divisions as investment centers, but wishes to share the benefits of an internal transfer equally between them, as follows.

Variable costs of Division B	$18.00
$1/2$ of the difference between the variable costs of Division B and the price Division A is paying ($29 – $18) × 1/2	5.50
Transfer price	$23.50

Note that $23.50 is just one example of a negotiated transfer price. The exact price depends on how the benefits are divided.

4. $24   [$24 = $18 + ($30,000/5,000   units)] would be an appropriate transfer price if top management treats divisions like cost centers with no profit responsibility. All benefits from both divisions will accrue to the buying division. This will maximize the profits of the company as a whole, but affect adversely the performance of the selling division. Another disadvantage of this cost-based approach is that inefficiencies (if any) of the selling division are being passed on to the buying division.

5. $18 would be an appropriate transfer price for guiding top management in deciding whether

transfers between the two divisions should take place. Since $18 is less than the outside purchase price of the buying division, and the selling division has excess capacity, the transfer should take place, because it will maximize the profits of the company as a whole. However, if $18 is used as a transfer price, then all of the benefits of the internal transfer accrue to the buying division and it will hurt the performance of the selling division.

When can you use a general formula for pricing transfers?

It is not easy to find a cure-all answer to the transfer pricing problem, since the three problems of goal congruence, performance evaluation, and autonomy must all be considered simultaneously. It is generally agreed, however, that some form of competitive market price is the best approach to the transfer pricing problem. The following formula would be helpful in this effort:

$$\text{Transfer price} = \text{Variable costs per unit} + \text{Opportunity costs per unit for the company as a whole}$$

Opportunity costs are defined as net revenue foregone by the company as a whole if the goods and services are transferred internally. The reasoning behind this formula is that the selling division should be allowed to recover its variable costs plus opportunity cost (i.e., revenue that it could have made by selling to an outsider) of the transfer. The selling department should not have to suffer lost income by selling within the company.

EXAMPLE 5

Company X has more than 50 divisions, including A, B, and K. Division A, the buying division, wants to buy a component for its final product and has an option to buy from Division B or from an outside supplier at the market price of $200. If Division A buys from the outside supplier, it will in turn buy selected raw materials from Division K for $40. This will increase its contribution to overall company profits by $30

($40 revenue minus $10 variable costs). Division B, on the other hand, can sell its component to Division A or to an outside buyer at the same price. Division B, working at full capacity, incurs variable costs of $150. Will the use of $200 as a transfer price lead to optimal decisions for the company as a whole? Figure 17–1 depicts the situation.

The optimal decision from the viewpoint of Company X as a whole can be looked at in terms of its net cash outflow, as follows:

	Division A's Action	
	Buy from B	**Buy from Outsider**
Outflow to the company as a whole	$(150)	$(200)
Cash inflows	—	to B:$50($200–$150) to K:$30($ 40–$ 10)
Net cash outflow to the company as a whole	$(150)	$(120)

To maximize the profits of Company X, Division A should buy from an outside supplier. The

FIGURE 17–1 TRANSFER PRICING SITUATION

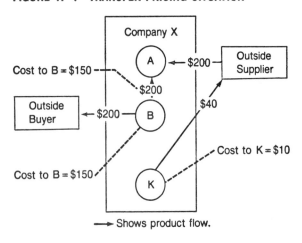

→ Shows product flow.

transfer price that would force Division A to buy outside should be the sum of variable costs and opportunity costs, that is,

$$\$150 + \$50 + \$30 = \$230 \text{ per unit}$$

In other words, if Division B charges $230 to Division A, Division A will definitely buy from the outside source for $200.

18

How to Analyze and Improve Corporate Profitability and Shareholder Value

How do you measure managerial performance and the return to stockholders?

The ability to measure performance is essential in developing incentives and controlling operations toward the achievement of organizational goals. Perhaps the most widely used single measure of profitability of an organization is the rate of return on investment (ROI). Related is the return to stockholders, known as the return on equity (ROE).

What is return on investment (ROI)?

ROI relates net income to invested capital (total assets). It provides a standard for evaluating how efficiently management employs the average dollar invested in a firm's assets, whether that dollar came from owners or creditors. Furthermore, a better ROI can also translate directly into a higher return on the stockholders' equity. ROI is calculated as:

$$\text{ROI} = \frac{\text{Net profit after taxes}}{\text{Total assets}}$$

EXAMPLE 1

Consider the following financial data:

Total assets	$100,000
Net profit after taxes	18,000

Then,

$$\text{ROI} = \frac{\text{Net profit after taxes}}{\text{Total assets}} = \frac{\$18,000}{\$100,000} = 18\%$$

The problem with this formula is that it only tells you about how a company did and how well it fared in the industry. Other than that, it has very little value from the standpoint of profit planning.

What is ROI made up of—DuPont formula?

In the past, managers have tended to focus only on the margin earned and have ignored the turnover of assets. It is important to realize that excessive funds tied up in assets can be just as much of a drag on profitability as excessive expenses. The DuPont Corporation was the first major company to recognize the importance of looking at both net profit margin and total asset turnover in assessing the performance of an organization. The ROI breakdown, known as the DuPont formula, is expressed as a product of these two factors, as shown below.

$$\text{ROI} = \frac{\text{Net profit after taxes}}{\text{Total assets}}$$

$$= \frac{\text{Net profit after taxes}}{\text{Sales}} \times \frac{\text{Sales}}{\text{Total assets}}$$

$$= \text{Net profit margin} \times \text{Total asset turnover}$$

The DuPont formula combines the income statement and balance sheet into this otherwise static measure of performance. Net profit margin is a measure of profitability or operating efficiency. It is the percentage of profit earned on sales. This percentage shows how many cents attach to each dollar of sales. On the other hand, total asset turnover measures how well a company manages its assets. It is the number of times by which the investment in assets turn over each year to generate sales.

The breakdown of ROI is based on the thesis that the profitability of a firm is directly related to management's ability to manage assets efficiently and to control expenses effectively.

EXAMPLE 2

Assume the same data as in Example 1. Also assume sales of $200,000. Then,

$$ROI = \frac{\text{Net profit after taxes}}{\text{Total assets}} = \frac{\$18,000}{\$200,000} = 18\%$$

Alternatively,

$$\text{Net profit margin} = \frac{\text{Net profit after taxes}}{\text{Sales}}$$

$$= \frac{\$18,000}{\$100,000} = 9\%$$

$$\frac{\text{Total asset}}{\text{turnover}} = \frac{\text{Sales}}{\text{Total assets}} = \frac{\$200,000}{\$100,000} = 2 \text{ Times}$$

Therefore,

$$ROI = \text{Net profit margin} \times \text{Total asset turnover}$$
$$= 9\% \times 2 \text{ Times} = 18\%$$

The breakdown provides a lot of insights to CFOs on how to improve profitability of the company and investment strategy. (Note that net profit margin and total asset turnover are called hereafter margin and turnover, respectively, for short.) Specifically, it has several advantages over the original formula (i.e., net profit after taxes/total assets) for profit planning. They are:

1. Focusing on the breakdown of ROI provides the basis for integrating many of the management concerns that influence a firm's overall performance. This will help managers gain an advantage in the competitive environment.

2. The importance of turnover as a key to overall return on investment is emphasized in the breakdown. In fact, turnover is just as important as profit margin in enhancing overall return.

3. The importance of sales is explicitly recognized, which is not there in the original formula.

4. The breakdown stresses the possibility of trading one off for the other in an attempt to improve the overall performance of a company. The margin and turnover complement each other. In other words, a low turnover can be made up for by a high margin; and vice versa.

EXAMPLE 3

The breakdown of ROI into its two components shows that a number of combinations of margin and turnover can yield the same rate of return, as shown below:

	Margin	×	Turnover	= ROI
(1)	9%	×	2 times	= 18%
(2)	6	×	3	= 18
(3)	3	×	6	= 18
(4)	2	×	9	= 18

The turnover-margin relationship and its resulting ROI is depicted in Figure 18–1.

Is there an optimal ROI?

Figure 18–1 can also be looked at as showing four companies that performed equally well (in terms of ROI), but with varying income statements and balance sheets. There is no ROI that is satisfactory for all companies. Manufacturing firms in various industries will have low rates of return. Structure and size of the firm influence the rate considerably. A company with a diversified product line might have only a fair return rate when all products are pooled in the analysis. In such cases, it seems advisable to establish

FIGURE 18-1   THE MARGIN-TURNOVER RELATIONSHIP

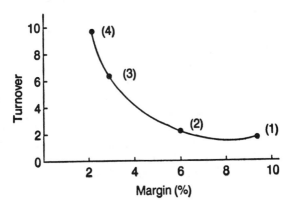

separate objectives for each line as well as for the total company.

Sound and successful operation must point toward the optimum combination of profits, sales, and capital employed. The combination will necessarily vary depending upon the nature of the business and the characteristics of the product. An industry with products tailor-made to customers' specifications will have different margins and turnover ratios, compared with industries that mass produce highly competitive consumer goods. For example, the combination (4) may describe a supermarket operation which inherently works with low margin and high turnover, while the combination (1) may be a jewelry store that typically has a low turnover and high margin.

How do you use ROI for profit planning?

The breakdown of ROI into margin and turnover gives management insight into planning for profit improvement by revealing where weaknesses exist: margin or turnover, or both. Various actions can be taken to enhance ROI. Generally, management can:

1. Improve margin.
2. Improve turnover.
3. Improve both.

Alternative 1 demonstrates a popular way of improving performance. Margins may be increased by reducing expenses, raising selling prices, or increasing sales faster than expenses. Some of the ways to reduce expenses are:

- Use less costly inputs of materials.
- Automate processes as much as possible to increase labor productivity.
- Bring the discretionary fixed costs under scrutiny, with various programs either curtailed or eliminated. Discretionary fixed costs arise from annual budgeting decisions by management. Examples include advertising, research and development, and management

development programs. The cost-benefit analysis is called for in order to justify the budgeted amount of each discretionary program.

A company with pricing power can raise selling prices and retain profitability without losing business. Pricing power is the ability to raise prices even in poor economic times when unit sales volume may be flat and capacity may not be fully utilized. It is also the ability to pass on cost increases to consumers without attracting domestic and import competition, political opposition, regulation, new entrants, or threats of product substitution. The company with pricing power must have a unique economic position. Companies that offer unique, high-quality goods and services (where the service is more important than the cost) have this economic position.

Alternative 2 may be achieved by increasing sales while holding the investment in assets relatively constant, or by reducing assets. Some of the strategies to reduce assets are:

- Dispose of obsolete and redundant inventory. The computer has been extremely helpful in this regard, making perpetual inventory methods more feasible for inventory control.
- Devise various methods of speeding up the collection of receivables and also evaluate credit terms and policies.
- See if there are unused fixed assets.
- Use the converted assets obtained from the use of the previous methods to repay outstanding debts or repurchase outstanding issues of stock. You may release them elsewhere to get more profit, which will improve margin as well as turnover.

Alternative 3 may be achieved by increasing sales or by any combinations of alternatives 1 and 2.

Figure 18–2 shows complete details of the relationship of ROI to the underlying ratios—margin and turnover—and their components. This will help identify more detailed strategies to improve margin, turnover, or both.

FIGURE 18-2 RELATIONSHIPS OF FACTORS INFLUENCING ROI

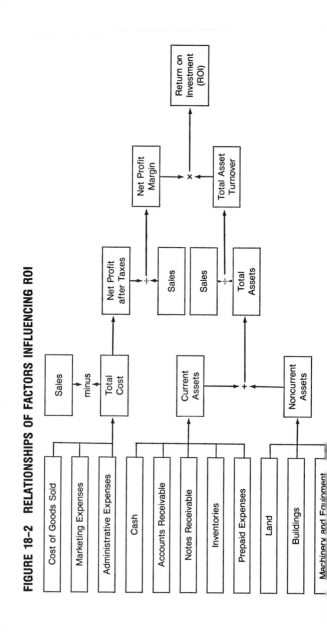

EXAMPLE 4

Assume that management sets a 20% ROI as a profit target. It is currently making an 18% return on its investment.

$$\text{ROI} = \frac{\text{Net profit after taxes}}{\text{Total assets}} = \frac{\text{Net profit after taxes}}{\text{Sales}}$$
$$\times \frac{\text{Sales}}{\text{Total assets}}$$

Present situation:

$$18\% = \frac{18,000}{200,000} \times \frac{200,000}{100,000}$$

The following are illustrative of the strategies which might be used (each strategy is independent of the other).

Alternative 1: Increase the margin while holding turnover constant. Pursuing this strategy would involve leaving selling prices as they are and making every effort to increase efficiency so as to reduce expenses. By doing so, expenses might be reduced by $2,000 without affecting sales and investment to yield a 20% target ROI, as follows:

$$20\% = \frac{20,000}{200,000} \times \frac{200,000}{100,000}$$

Alternative 2: Increase turnover by reducing investment in assets while holding net profit and sales constant. Working capital might be reduced or some land might be sold, reducing investment in assets by $10,000 without affecting sales and net income to yield the 20% target ROI as follows:

$$20\% = \frac{18,000}{200,000} \times \frac{200,000}{90,000}$$

Alternative 3: Increase both margin and turnover by disposing of obsolete and redundant inventories or through an active advertising campaign. For example, trimming down $5,000 worth of investment in inventories would also reduce the inventory holding charge by $1,000. This strategy would increase ROI to 20%.

$$20\% = \frac{19,000}{200,000} \times \frac{200,000}{95,000}$$

Excessive investment in assets is just as much of a drag on profitability as excessive expenses. In this case, cutting unnecessary inventories also helps cut down expenses of carrying those inventories, so that both margin and turnover are improved at the same time. In practice, alternative 3 is much more common than alternative 1 or 2.

What is the relationship between ROI and return on equity (ROE)?

Generally, a better management performance (i.e., a high or above-average ROI) produces a higher return to investors (equity holders). However, even a poorly managed company that suffers from a below-average performance can generate an above-average return on the stockholders' equity, simply called the return on equity (ROE). This is because borrowed funds can magnify the returns a company's profits represent to its stockholders.

Another version of the DuPont formula, called the modified DuPont formula reflects this effect. The formula ties together the ROI and the degree of financial leverage (use of borrowed funds). The financial leverage is measured by the equity multiplier, which is the ratio of a company's total asset base to its equity investment, or, stated another way, the ratio of how many dollars of assets held per dollar of stockholders' equity. It is calculated by dividing total assets by stockholders' equity. This measurement gives an indication of how much of a company's assets are financed by stockholders' equity and how much with borrowed funds.

The return on equity (ROE) is calculated as:

$$ROE = \frac{\text{Net profit after taxes}}{\text{Stockholders' equity}}$$

$$= \frac{\text{Net profit after taxes}}{\text{Total assets}} \times \frac{\text{Total assets}}{\text{Stockholders' equity}}$$

$$= \text{ROI} \times \text{Equity multiplier}$$

ROE measures the returns earned on the owners' (both preferred and common stockholders') investment. The use of the equity multiplier to convert the ROI to the ROE reflects the impact of the leverage (use of debt) on stockholders' return:

$$\text{The equity multiplier} = \frac{\text{Total assets}}{\text{Stockholders' equity}}$$

$$= \frac{1}{(1 - \text{Debt ratio})}$$

Figure 18–3 shows the relationship among ROI, ROE, and financial leverage.

EXAMPLE 5

In Example 1, assume stockholders' equity of $45,000. Then,

$$\text{Equity multiplier} = \frac{\text{Total assets}}{\text{Stockholders' equity}}$$

$$= \frac{\$100,000}{\$45,000} = 2.22$$

$$= \frac{1}{(1 - \text{Debt ratio})} = \frac{1}{(1 - .55)} = \frac{1}{.45} = 2.22$$

$$\text{ROE} = \frac{\text{Net profit after taxes}}{\text{Stockholders' equity}} = \frac{\$18,000}{\$45,000} = 40\%$$

$$\text{ROE} = \text{ROI} \times \text{Equity multiplier} = 18\% \times 2.22 = 40\%$$

If the company used only equity, the 18% ROI would equal ROE. However, 55% of the firm's capital is supplied by creditors ($45,000/$100,000 = 45% is the equity-to-asset ratio; $55,000/$100,000 = 55% is the debt ratio). Since the 18% ROI all goes to stockholders, who put up only 45% of the capital, the ROE is higher than 18%. This example indicates the company was using leverage (debt) favorably.

FIGURE 18-3 ROI, ROE, AND FINANCIAL LEVERAGE (MODIFIED DUPONT FORMULA)

Modified DuPont Formula

$$\text{Return on Equity (ROE)} = \frac{\text{Net profit after taxes}}{\text{Stockholders' equity}}$$

Measures the returns earned on the owners' (both preferred and common stockholders') investment

=

DuPont Formula

$$\text{Return on Investment (ROI)} = \frac{\text{Net profit after taxes}}{\text{Total assets}}$$

Measures overall effectiveness in generating profits with available assets

$$\text{Net profit margin} = \frac{\text{Net profits after taxes}}{\text{Sales}}$$

Measures profitability with respect to sales generated

×

$$\text{Total asset turnover} = \frac{\text{Sales}}{\text{Total assets}}$$

Measures efficiency in using assets to generate sales

$$\frac{1}{1 - \dfrac{\text{Debt Ratio} = \dfrac{\text{Total liabilities}}{\text{Total assets}}}{}}$$

Measures the proportion of total assets provided by the firm's creditors

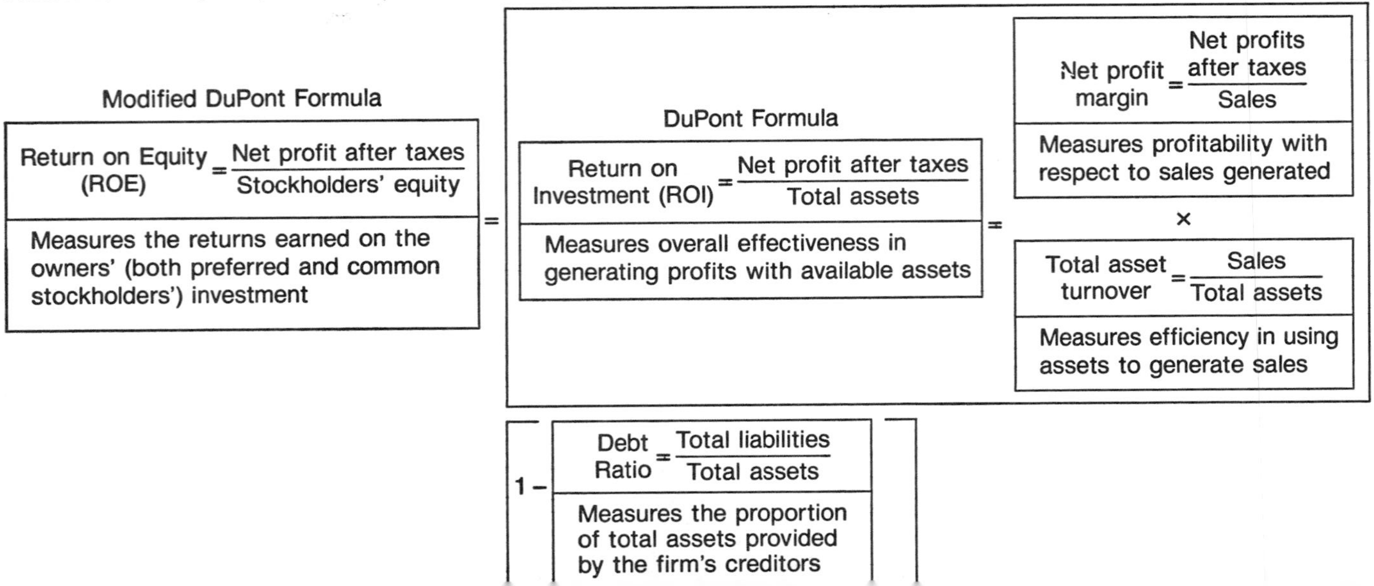

EXAMPLE 6

To further demonstrate the interrelationship between a firm's financial structure and the return it generates on the stockholders' investments, let us compare two firms that generate $300,000 in operating income. Both firms employ $800,000 in total assets, but they have different capital structures. One firm employs no debt, whereas the other uses $400,000 in borrowed funds. The comparative capital structures are shown as:

	A	B
Total assets	$800,000	$800,000
Total liabilities	—	400,000
Stockholders' equity (a)	800,000	400,000
Total liabilities and stockholders' equity	$800,000	$800,000

Firm B pays 10% interest for borrowed funds. The comparative income statements and ROEs for firms A and B would look as follows:

	A	B
Operating income	$300,000	$300,000
Interest expense	—	(40,000)
Profit before taxes	$300,000	$260,000
Taxes (30% assumed)	(90,000)	(78,000)
Net profit after taxes (b)	$210,000	$182,000
ROE [(b)/(a)]	26.25%	45.5%

The absence of debt allows firm A to register higher profits after taxes. Yet the owners in firm B enjoy a significantly higher return on their investments. This provides an important view of the positive contribution debt can make to a business, but within a certain limit. Too much debt can increase the firm's financial risk and thus the cost of financing.

If the assets in which the funds are invested are able to earn a return greater than the fixed rate of return required by the creditors, the leverage is positive and the common stockholders benefit. The advantage of this formula is that it enables the company to break its ROE into a profit margin portion (net profit margin), an efficiency-of-asset-utilization portion (total asset turnover), and a use-of-leverage portion (equity multiplier). It shows that the company can raise shareholder return by employing leverage—taking on larger amounts of debt to help finance growth.

Since financial leverage affects net profit margin through the added interest costs, management must look at the various pieces of this ROE equation, within the context of the whole, to earn the highest return for stockholders. CFOs have the task of determining just what combination of asset return and leverage will work best in its competitive environment. Most companies try to keep at least a level equal to what is considered to be "normal" within the industry.

19

Just-in-Time (JIT) Costing

How do you handle the inventory control problem?

The inventory control problem occurs in almost every type of organization. It exists whenever products are held to meet some expected future demand. In most industries, cost of inventory represents the largest liquid asset under the control of management. Therefore, it is very important to develop a production and inventory planning system that will minimize both purchasing and carrying costs.

Effective purchasing and management of materials is a high priority in most manufacturing firms. Material cost, as a proportion of total product cost, has continued to rise significantly during the last few years and hence is a primary concern of top management.

What is Just-in-Time (JIT)?

In recent years, the Japanese have demonstrated the ability to manage their production systems effectively. Much of their success has been attributed to what is known as the Just-in-Time (JIT) approach to production and inventory control, which has generated a great deal of interest among practitioners. The "Kanban" system—as they call it—has been a focal point of interest, with its dramatic impact on the inventory performance and productivity of the Japanese auto industry.

JIT is a demand-pull system. Demand for customer output (not plans for using input resources) triggers production. Production activities are "pulled," not "pushed," into action. JIT production, in its purest sense, is buying and producing in very small quantities just in time for use. The basic idea has its roots in Japan's densely populated industrial areas and its lack of resources, both of which have produced frugal personal habits among the Japanese people. The idea was developed into a formal management system by Toyota in order to meet the precise demands of customers for various vehicle models and colors with minimum delivery delays.

As a philosophy, JIT targets inventory as an evil presence that obscures problems that should be solved, and that by contributing significantly to costs, large inventories keep a company from being as competitive or profitable as it otherwise might be. Practically speaking, JIT has as its principal goal the elimination of waste, and the principal measure of success is how much or how little inventory there is. Virtually anything that achieves this end can be considered a JIT innovation.

Furthermore, the little inventory that exists in a JIT system must be of good quality. This requirement has led to JIT purchasing practices uniquely able to deliver high-quality materials.

JIT systems integrate five functions of the production process—sourcing, storage, transportation, operations, and quality control—into one controlled manufacturing process. In manufacturing, JIT means that a company produces only the quantity needed for delivery to dealers or customers. In purchasing, it means suppliers deliver subassemblies just in time to be assembled into finished goods. In delivery, it requires selecting a transportation mode that will deliver purchased components and materials in small-lot sizes at the loading dock of the manufacturing facilities just in time to support the manufacturing process.

How is JIT compared with traditional manufacturing?

JIT manufacturing is a demand-pull, rather than the traditional "push" approach. The philosophy underlying JIT manufacturing is to produce a product when it is needed and only in the quantities demanded by customers. Demand pulls products through the manufacturing process. Each operation produces only what is necessary to satisfy the demand of the succeeding operation. No production takes place until a signal from a succeeding process indicates a need to produce. Parts and materials arrive just in time to be used in production.

To illustrate the differences between pull and push systems of material control, the example of a fast food restaurant is used:

> At McDonald's, the customer orders a hamburger, the server gets one from the rack, the hamburger maker keeps an eye on the rack and makes new burgers when the number gets too low. The manager orders more ground beef when the maker's inventory gets too low. In effect, the customer's purchase triggers the pull of materials through the system. . . . . . In a push system, the caterer estimates how many steaks are likely to be ordered in any given week. He/she reckons how long it takes to broil a steak: he/she can figure out roughly how many meals are needed in a certain week. . . . (See Karmarkar, Uday, "Getting Control of Just-in-Time, *Harvard Business Review,* September-October 1989, pp. 122–131)

Reduced Inventories

The primary goal of JIT is to reduce inventories to insignificant or zero levels. In traditional manufacturing, inventories result whenever production exceeds demand. Inventories are needed as a buffer when production does not meet expected demand.

Manufacturing Cells and Multifunction Labor

In traditional manufacturing, products are moved from one group of identical machines to another. Typically, machines with identical functions are located together in an area referred to as a department or process. Workers who specialize in the operation of a specific machine are located in each department. JIT replaces this traditional pattern with a pattern of manufacturing cells or work centers. Robots supplement people to do many routine operations.

Manufacturing cells contain machines that are grouped in families, usually in a semicircle.

The machines are arranged so that they can be used to perform a variety of operations in sequence. Each cell is set up to produce a particular product or product family. Products move from one machine to another from start to finish. Workers are assigned to cells and are trained to operate all machines within the cell.

Thus, labor in a JIT environment is multifunction labor, not specialized labor. Each manufacturing cell is basically a minifactory or a factory within a factory. A comparison of the physical layout of JIT with the traditional system is shown in Figure 19–1.

Total Quality Control

JIT goes with it a stronger emphasis on quality control. A defective part brings production to a grinding halt. Poor quality simply cannot be tolerated in a stockless manufacturing environment. In other words, JIT cannot be implemented without a commitment to *total quality control (TQC)*. TQC is essentially an endless quest for perfect quality. This approach to quality is opposed to the traditional belief, called *acceptable quality level (AQL)*. AQL allows defects to occur provided they are within a predetermined level.

Decentralization of Services

JIT requires easy and quick access to support services, which means that centralized service departments must be scaled down and their personnel assigned to work directly to support production. For example, with respect to raw materials, JIT calls for multiple stock points, each one near where the material will be used. There is no need for a central warehouse location.

Suppliers as Outside Partners

The most important aspects of the JIT purchasing concept focus on (1) new ways of dealing with suppliers, and (2) a clear-cut recognition of the appropriate purchasing role in developing corporate strategy. Suppliers should be viewed as

FIGURE 19-1 PHYSICAL LAYOUT: TRADITIONAL VERSUS JIT MANUFACTURING

Traditional Manufacturing

Department A	Department B	Department C
X X	Y Y	Z Z
P1 >		
P2 >		
	> P1 >	> P1 >
	> P2 >	> P2 >

Each product passes through departments which specialize in one process. Departments process multiple products.

JIT Manufacturing

Product 1 (P1)
Manufacturing Cell 1
Y

P1 >   X   Z

Product 2 (P2)
Manufacturing Cell 2
Y

P2 >   X   Z

Notice that each product passes through its own cell. All machines necessary to process each product are placed within the cell. Each cell is dedicated to the production of one product or one subassembly.

Symbols: X = Machine A   P1 = Product 1
Y = Machine B   P2 = Product 2
Z = Machine C

387

"outside partners" who can contribute to the long-run welfare of the buying firm rather than as outside adversaries.

Better Cost Management

Cost management differs from cost accounting in that it refers to the management of cost, whether or not the cost has direct impact on inventory or the financial statements. The JIT philosophy simplifies the cost accounting procedure and helps managers manage and control their costs, which will be discussed in detail later in the chapter.

JIT recognizes that with simplification comes better management, better quality, better service, and better cost. Traditional cost accounting systems have a tendency to be very complex, with many transactions and reporting of data. Simplification of this process will transform a cost "accounting" system into a cost "management" system that can be used to support management's needs for better decisions about product design, pricing, marketing, and mix, and to encourage continual operating improvements.

The major differences between JIT manufacturing and traditional manufacturing are summarized in Table 19–1.

TABLE 19–1   COMPARISON OF JIT AND TRADITIONAL MANUFACTURING

JIT	Traditional
1. Pull system	1. Push system
2. Insignificant or zero inventories	2. Significant inventories
3. Manufacturing cells	3. "Process" structure
4. Multifunction labor	4. Specialized labor
5. Total quality control (TQC)	5. Acceptable quality level (AQL)
6. Decentralized services	6. Centralized services
7. Simple cost accounting	7. Complex cost accounting

What are the benefits of JIT?

The potential benefits of JIT are numerous. First, JIT practice reduces inventory levels, which means lower investments in inventories. Since the system requires only the smallest quantity of materials needed immediately, it reduces the overall inventory level substantially.

In many Japanese companies that use the JIT concept, inventory levels have been reduced to the point that makes the annual working capital turnover ratio much higher than that experienced by U.S. counterparts. For instance, Toyota reported inventory turnover ratios of 41 to 63, while comparable U.S. companies reported inventory turnover ratios of 5 to 8.

Second, since purchasing under JIT requires a significantly shorter delivery lead time, lead time reliability is greatly improved. Reduced lead time and increased reliability also contribute to a significant reduction in the safety stock requirements.

Third, reduced lead times and set-up times increase scheduling flexibility. The cumulative lead time, which includes both purchasing and production lead times, is reduced. Thus, the firm schedule within the production planning horizon is reduced. This results in a longer "look-ahead" time that can be used to meet shifts in market demand. The smaller lot size production made possible by reduced set-up time, also adds flexibility.

Fourth, improved quality levels have been reported by many companies. When the order quantity is small, sources of quality problems are quickly identifiable, and can be corrected immediately. In many cases, employee quality consciousness also tends to improve, producing an improvement in quality at the production source.

Fifth, the costs of purchased materials may be reduced through more extensive value analysis and cooperative supplier development activities.

Sixth, other financial benefits reported include:

1. Lower investments in factory space for inventories and production

2. Less obsolescence risk in inventories

3. Reduction in scrap and rework

4. Decline in paperwork

5. Reduction in direct material costs through quantity purchases.

What are the examples of JIT implementation in the United States?

The following are some of the many implementation experiences of JIT in the United States:

1. The Oldsmobile division of General Motors (GM) has implemented a JIT project which permits immediate electronic communication between Oldsmobile and 70 of its principal suppliers who provide 700 to 800 parts representing around 85% of the parts needed for the new GM-20 cars.

2. PTC Components, a supplier to GM, has assisted GM in its use of stockless production by sending one truck a week to deliver timing chains to several GM's engine plants rather than accumulate a truckload to ship to each plant.

3. Ford introduced JIT production at its heavy-duty truck plant in Kentucky, which forced Firestone to switch the tire searching point from Mansfield to Dayton, Ohio. By combining computerized ordering and halving inventory, Firestone has been able to reduce its own finished goods inventory. In addition, its production planning is no longer guesswork.

4. Each day a truck from Harley-Davidson Motor Co. transports 160 motorcycle seats and assorted accessories 800 miles overnight to Harley's assembly plant in York, Pa., as a part of their advanced Materials-as-Needed (MAN) program—its version of JIT.

5. The Hoover Company has used JIT techniques in its two plants at North Canton, Ohio, for a number of years for production scheduling and material flow control of 360 different models and 29,000 part numbers.

6. Some plants of DuPont used JIT and had an inventory savings of 30 cents on the dollar for the first year.

7. The Vancouver division of Hewlett-Packard reported the following benefits two years after the adoption of the JIT method:

Work-in-process inventory dollars	down 82%
Space used	down 40%
Scrap/rework	down 30%
Production time:	
Impact printers	down 7 days to 2 days
Thermal printers	down 7 days to 3 hours
Labor efficiency	up 50%
Shipments	up 20%

Note: The implementation experiences listed above do not suggest a quick or across-the-board adoption of this concept. In many companies (particularly U.S. firms), the JIT purchasing concept simply may not be practical or feasible. In others, it may not be applicable to all product lines. However, many progressive companies currently are either investigating or implementing some form of the system.

How does JIT simplify the costing system?

The cost accounting system of a company adopting JIT will be quite simple compared to job order or process costing. Under JIT, raw materials and work-in-process (WIP) accounts are typically combined into one account called "resources in process" (RIP) or "raw and in-process." Under JIT, the materials arrive at the receiving area and are whisked immediately to the factory area. Thus, the Stores Control account vanishes. The journal entries that accompany JIT costing are remarkably simple as follows:

Raw and in-process (RIT) inventory	45,000	
Accounts payable or cash		45,000
To record purchases		
Finished goods	40,000	
RIP inventory		40,000
To record raw materials in completed units.		

As can be seen, there is no Stores Control and WIP accounts under JIT.

In summary, JIT costing can be characterized as follows:

1. There are less inventory accounts.

2. There are no work orders. Thus, there is no need for detailed tracking of actual raw materials.

3. With JIT, activities can be eliminated on the premise that they do not add value. Prime target for elimination are storage areas for WIP inventory and material handling facilities.

4. Direct labor costs and factory overhead costs are not tracked to specific orders. Direct labor is now regarded as just another part of factory overhead. Furthermore, factory overhead is accounted for as follows. Virtually all of the factory overhead incurred each month, now including direct labor, flows through to cost of goods sold in the same month. Tracking overhead through WIP and finished goods inventory provides no useful information. Therefore, it makes sense to treat manufacturing overhead as an expense charged directly to cost of goods sold.

How does JIT enhance product costing accuracy and facilitate cost management?

The costs of many activities previously classified as indirect costs have been transferred to direct cost in the JIT environment. For example, under the JIT system workers on the production line will do plant maintenance and setups, while under traditional systems these activities were done by other workers classified as indirect labor. Table 19–2 compares the traceability of some manufacturing costs under the traditional system with their traceability in the JIT environment.

We can see that JIT manufacturing increases direct traceability in many manufacturing costs, thus enhancing the accuracy of product costing. *Note:* JIT does not convert all indirect costs into direct costs. Even with JIT installed, still some overhead activities remain common to the work centers. Nonetheless, JIT, coupled with activity-based accounting (ABC), gives rise to a

TABLE 19-2   TRACEABILITY OF PRODUCT COST TRADITIONAL VERSUS JIT MANUFACTURING

	Traditional	**JIT**
Direct labor	Direct	Direct
Direct materials	Direct	Direct
Material handling	Indirect	Direct
Repairs and maintenance	Indirect	Direct
Energy	Indirect	Direct
Operating supplies	Indirect	Direct
Supervision	Indirect	Direct
Insurance and taxes	Indirect	Indirect
Building depreciation	Indirect	Indirect
Equipment depreciation	Indirect	Direct
Building occupancy	Indirect	Indirect
Product support services	Indirect	Indirect

tremendous improvement in product costing accuracy over the traditional approach.

In traditional purchasing environments many firms place great emphasis on purchase price variances. Favorable purchasing price variances can sometimes be achieved by buying larger quantities to take advantage of price discounts or by buying lower quality materials. In JIT, the emphasis is on quality, availability, and the total cost of operations and not just the purchase price of materials.

In many traditional plants, much of the internal accounting effort is devoted to setting labor and overhead standards and in calculating and reporting variances from these standards. Firms using JIT report reduced emphasis on the use of labor and overhead variances. Even firms retaining variance analysis stress that a change in *focus* is appropriate in a JIT plant. The emphasis is on the analysis at the plant level with focus on *trends* that may be occurring in the manufacturing process rather than the absolute magnitude of individual variances.

Furthermore, traditional performance measures (such as labor efficiency and machine utilization) that are commonplace in many cost accounting systems are not appropriate within the JIT philosophy of cost management. They are all inappropriate for the following reasons:

1. They all promote building inventory beyond what is needed in the immediate time frame.

2. Emphasizing performance to standard gives priority to output, at the expense of quality.

3. Direct labor in the majority of manufacturers accounts for only 5 to 15% of total product cost.

4. Using machine utilization is inappropriate because it encourages results in building inventory ahead of needs.

Table 19-3 lists typical performance measures under the traditional and JIT systems.

TABLE 19-3   PERFORMANCE MEASURES TRADITIONAL VERSUS JIT

Traditional	JIT
Direct labor efficiency	Total head count productivity
Direct labor utilization	Return on assets
Direct labor productivity	Days of inventory
Machine utilization	Group incentives
	Lead time by product
	Response time to customer feedback
	Number of customer complaints
	Cost of quality
	Setup reduction

PART IV

MANAGEMENT OF ASSETS AND PAYABLES

20

Working Capital and Cash Management*

The ability to manage working capital will enhance the return and lower the risk of running short of cash. There are a number of ways to manage working capital and cash to result in optimal balances including quantitative techniques. The amount invested in any current asset may change daily and requires close monitoring. Current assets are being improperly managed when funds tied up in them can be used more productively elsewhere.

EVALUATING WORKING CAPITAL

How can working capital be managed to achieve the best results?

Working capital equals current assets less current liabilities. In optimally managing working capital, current assets and current liabilities have to be constantly regulated. A consideration must be given to how assets should be financed (e.g., short-term debt, long-term debt, or equity). There is a trade-off between return and risk that has to be taken into account. If funds move from fixed assets to current assets, there is a reduction in liquidity risk, greater ability to obtain short-term financing, and more flexibility, because the company can better adjust current assets to changes in sales volume. However, less of a return is typically earned on current assets than fixed assets. The advantage with using noncurrent debt relative to short-term debt is that it involves less liquidity risk. However, long-term debt usually has a higher cost than short-term debt arising from the uncertainty of the longer

*Chung J. Liew, Ph.D., consultant and associate professor of decision sciences at the University of Oklahoma and the University of Central Oklahoma, coauthored this chapter.

time period. The increased financing cost lowers profitability.

What to do: The hedging approach to finance should be used where assets are financed by liabilities of similar maturity. This results in sufficient funds to pay debt when due. For example, long-term assets should be financed with long-term debt rather than short-term borrowings.

Rule of thumb: The longer it takes to buy or manufacture goods, the more working capital needed. Working capital is also affected by the volume of purchases and the unit cost. For example, if the company can receive a raw material in three weeks, it needs to hold less inventory than if there was a one month lead time. *Tip:* Buy material early if lower prices are available and if the material's cost savings exceed inventory carrying costs.

CASH MANAGEMENT

Without monitoring your cash—how to measure it, invest it, borrow it and collect it—you can cheat yourself out of extra profits or even avoid trouble with creditors and bankruptcy.

What should be done about cash balances?

A centralized cash management system minimizes idle cash and maximizes available cash. The cash management system should integrate all the cash flows flowing into and out of the business including domestic and international divisions and subsidiaries. A centralized system "flags" situations where one subsidiary is borrowing at high interest rates while another subsidiary has idle cash. A coordination of cash processes should exist such as investment, disbursement, and collection.

Cash should be made available to cash-using divisions from cash-generating ones to keep borrowing at a minimum. For example, foreign currency payments should be netted among divisions to eliminate currency conversion and reduce float time between operations. There should be an integration of foreign currency requirements between the parent and subsidiaries. A multinational company must use a bank known for *quality* international services including networking, cash concentration, and clearing. The CFO should obtain competitive quotations before making a disbursement in a foreign country.

The objective of cash management is to invest excess cash for a return and at the same time have sufficient liquidity for future needs. The cash balance should neither be excessive nor deficient. For example, companies with many bank accounts may be accumulating excessive balances. Do you know how much cash you need, how much you have, where the cash is, what the sources of cash are, and where the cash will be used? This is especially crucial in recession. Cash forecasting determines (1) the best time to incur and pay back debt and (2) the amount to transfer daily between accounts. A daily computerized listing of cash balances and transaction reporting should be prepared so the CFO has up-to-date information in order to make decisions on how best to use funds. A listing of daily transactions identifies any problems so immediate rectification may be made.

Recommendation: The CFO should establish, control, and report bank accounts, services, and activities. Are banking services cost-effective? Analyze each bank account as to type, balance, and cost. What is the processing cost for checks, bank transfers, and direct debits? The adequacy of controls for intercompany transactions and transfers should be reviewed. When cash receipts and cash payments are synchronized and predictable, smaller cash balances may be maintained. If immediate liquidity is desired, invest in marketable securities.

General rule: Additional cash should be invested in income-producing securities with maturities structured to provide the necessary liquidity.

A financially strong company that is able to borrow at favorable interest rates even in difficult financial times may hold a lower cash balance than a highly leveraged company having a poor credit risk.

A high-tech company may need more cash on hand to withstand unexpected eventualities and financial problems. A mature, established company may hold minimal cash with short-term cash requirements met through short-term debt.

How much cash should be held?

The minimum cash to hold is the greater of (1) compensating balances (a deposit held by a bank to compensate it for providing services) or (2) precautionary balances (money held in cash for an emergency) plus transaction balances (money to cover uncleared checks). The company needs sufficient cash to satisfy daily requirements.

The longer the time period between cash payment to cash receipt, the higher the cash balance should be. A declining trend in cash may mean a looming "cash crisis." If collections are not received timely you may be unable to make payments to suppliers and for operating expenses. Major capital expenditures should be timed when cash is plentiful. Factors in determining the amount of cash to hold include:

- Overdraft protection.
- Instability in business activity.
- Length of the planning period.
- Overall financial strength and liquidity.
- Ability to borrow on favorable terms.
- Payment dates of debt.
- Expected future cash flows taking into account the probabilities of different cash flows under alternative circumstances. Since cash forecasting may result in errors, there should be excess cash on hand or short-term debt capacity to cover such eventuality.
- Overall business risks.
- Likelihood of unexpected problems (e.g., customer defaults).
- Rate of return.

There is less cash needed on hand when a company can borrow quickly from a bank, such as under a *line of credit agreement,* which allows a firm to borrow immediately up to a predetermined maximum amount. Check to see the commitment fee, if any, on the unused portion of the line.

Watch the amount of the compensating balance, since the portion of a loan that serves as collateral is restricted and unavailable for use. Are compensating balances too costly? Is cash unnecessarily tied up in other accounts (e.g., loans to employees, insurance deposits)? *Warning:* Liquid asset holdings are needed during a downturn in a company's cycle, when funds from operations decline.

The CFO should invest excess cash in marketable securities for a return. The marketable securities may then be sold when funds are needed. For example, a seasonal company may buy marketable securities when it has excess funds and then sell the securities when cash deficits occur. A firm may also invest in marketable securities when funds are held temporarily in anticipation of short-term capital expansion. In selecting an investment portfolio, consider return, marketability, default risk, and maturity date.

Coupon and security collection assures that any interest the company is entitled to is received and that securities maturing or sold are properly collected and deposited.

Recommendation: Do not fund peak seasonal cash requirements internally. Rather, borrow on a short-term basis to enable internal funds to be used more profitably throughout the year, such as by investing in plant and equipment.

The thrust of cash management is to accelerate cash receipts and delay cash payments.

Acceleration of Cash Inflow

You should appraise the reasons and take corrective steps to rectify any delays in receiving and depositing cash. WHAT TO DO: Ascertain how and where cash receipts come, how cash is transferred from outlying accounts to the main corporate account, banking policy on fund availability, and time lag between receiving a check and depositing it.

What is the float time?

The types of delays in processing checks are:

- Mail float: The time it takes for a check to move from customer to the company.

- Processing float: The time it takes for the company to record the payment in the books.
- Deposit collection float: The time for a check to clear.

Figure 20–1 depicts the total float of a check.

The CFO should evaluate the causes and take corrective measures for delays in having cash receipts deposited. Ascertain how and where the cash receipts come, how cash is transferred to your bank account, banking policy regarding availability of funds, and time lag between receiving a check and depositing it.

What does the amount of float depend upon?

The amount of float depends on both the time lag and the dollars involved. Float may be determined in dollar-days multiplying the lag in days by the dollar amount delayed. The cost of float is the interest lost because the money was not available for investment or the interest paid because money had to be borrowed during the lag period. The cost of float is computed by multiplying the average daily float by the cost of capital (opportunity cost) for the time period involved.

EXAMPLE 1

FLOAT MEASUREMENT

Item	Dollar Amount	×	Number of Days	=	Dollar Days
1	$20,000	×	3	=	$ 60,000
2	10,000		2		20,000
3	30,000		4		120,000
	$60,000				$200,000

$$\text{Average daily float} = \frac{\$200,000}{30} = \$6,667$$

$$\text{Average daily receipts} = \frac{\$60,000}{30} = \$2,000$$

Average daily float = $2,000 × 3.333 = $6,667

Average cost of float = $6,667 × .09 = $600

FIGURE 20-1 FLOAT DUE TO A CHECK ISSUED AND MAILED BY PAYER TO PAYEE

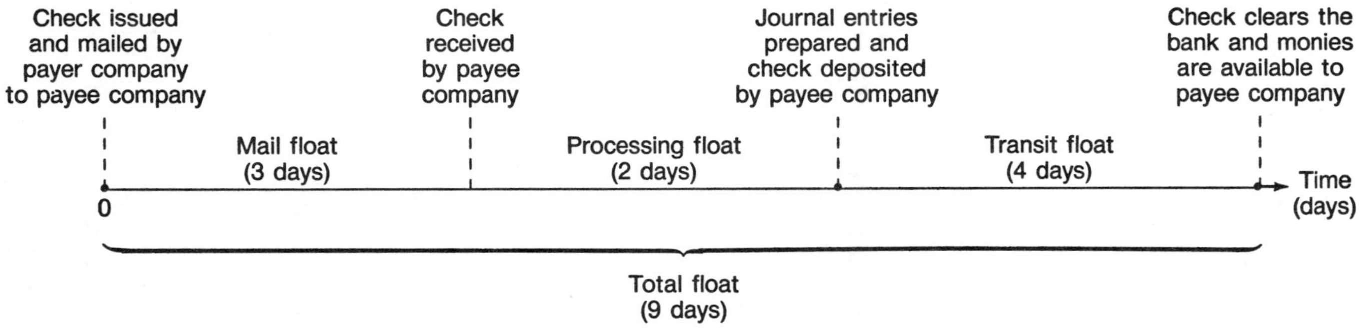

How may cash be received sooner?

There are many ways to accelerate cash receipts including:

• Lockbox arrangement where the collection points are situated closer to customers. Customer payments are mailed to strategic post office boxes to speed mailing and depositing time. Banks collect from these boxes several times a day and make deposits to the corporate account. Further, arrange for weekend deposits into the lockbox. There is a computer listing of payments received by account and a daily total.

Recommendation: Undertake a cost-benefit analysis to assure that the lockbox arrangement results in net savings. Determine the average face value of checks received, cost of operations eliminated, reducible processing overhead, and reduction in "mail float" days. Because per-item processing cost is usually significant, it is beneficial to use a lockbox with low-volume, high-dollar collections. However, lockboxes are becoming available to companies with high-volume, low-dollar receipts as technological advances (such as machine-readable documents) lower the per-item cost. *Tip:* Compare the return earned on freed cash to the cost of the lockbox. A *wholesale lockbox* is used for checks received from other *companies*. The average cash receipts is large and the number of cash receipts is small. The bank prepares an electronic list of payments received and transmits the information to the company. A wholesale lockbox strengthens internal control because there is a separation between billing and receivables processing. Many wholesale lockboxes only result in mail time reductions of no more than one business day, and check clearing time reductions of only a few tenths of one day. Wholesale lockboxes are cost-effective for companies having gross revenues of at least several million dollars. It is best when large checks are received from distant customers. A *retail lockbox* is used for a company dealing with the *public* (retail consumers as distinguished from companies). Retail lockboxes usually have numerous transactions of a nominal amount. The lockbox reduces float and transfers workload from the company to the bank. The "bottom line" should be more cash flow and less expenses.

• Identify and monitor changes in collection patterns. The reasons for delays should be ascertained, and the underlying problems should be corrected.

• On the return envelope for customer remission, use bar codes, nine-digit code numbers, and post office box numbers. *Note:* Accelerated Reply Mail (ARM) is the assignment of a unique "truncating" ZIP code to payments, such as lockbox receivables. The coded remittances are removed from the postal system and processed by banks or third parties.

• Send customers preaddressed, stamped envelopes. Include an "Attention" line on the return envelope to speed delivery within the company. Return envelopes reduce customers' errors in addressing and accelerating mail handling.

• Obtain permission from a customer to have a pre-authorized debit (PAD) charged to the customer's bank account automatically for recurring charges. An example is an insurance company that has PADs charged to its policyholders for insurance premiums. These debits take the form of paper pre-authorized checks (PACs) or paperless automatic clearing house entries. PADs result in cost savings because they avoid the process of billing a customer, receiving and processing a payment, and depositing a check. *Note:* Variable payments are not as efficient as fixed payments because the amount of the PAD must be changed each period and usually the customer must be notified by mail of the amount of the debit. PADs are suggested for constant, relatively nominal periodic (e.g., monthly, semi-weekly) payments.

• Transfer funds between banks by wire transfers or depository transfer checks (DTCs). *Wire transfers* may be used for intracompany transactions. Wire transfers may be made by computer terminal and telephone. A wire transfer allows for the same day transfer of funds. It should only be made for significant dollar amounts since per wire transfer fees are charged by both the originating bank and the receiving bank. Examples include making transfers to and from investments, placing funds in an account the day checks are expected to clear, and placing funds in any other account that requires immediate fund availability. Two types of wire transfers are preformatted (recurring) and free-form (nonrepetitive). In the case of preformatted wire transfers, extensive authorization is *not* required. This type is appropriate for usual transfers such as for investments and other company accounts. The company specifies an issuing bank and a receiving bank along with the account number. There is greater control for nonrecurring transfers. The control includes written confirmation rather than confirmation from telephone or computer terminal. Wire transfers may also be used to fund other types of checking accounts, such as payroll accounts. In order to control balances in the account, the account may be funded on a staggered basis. However, to guard against an overdraft, balances should be maintained in another account at the bank.

Paper or paperless depository transfer checks may be used to transfer funds between the company's bank accounts. Although no signature is required on depository transfer checks, the check is still payable to the bank for credit to the company's account. However, there must be controls in place so an employee does not use depository transfer checks to transfer money from an account on which he or she does not have signature authorization to an account in which he or she does. Depository transfer checks usually clear in one day. If *manual* depository transfer checks are used, pre-printed checks include all information except the amount and date. Manual preparation is suggested if there are only a few checks prepared daily. If there are *automated* depository transfer checks, they are printed as needed.

Tip: It is typically cheaper to use the bank's printer than the company buying its own. Automatic check preparation is suggested when there are many transfer checks to be prepared daily.

- Encourage customers to use a "purchase order with payment voucher attached" (POPVA). The payment voucher is a blank draft which the seller fills out, detaches, and then deposits. It is usually for amounts less than $1,000. Buyers will only deal with sellers they trust to make this arrangement.
- Accelerate billing. Send out bills to customers immediately when the order is shipped. Also, send out individual invoices rather than only a monthly statement. Correct invoice errors immediately.
- Require deposits on large or custom orders or progress billings as the work progresses.
- Promptly correct invoice errors. Customers should be encouraged to call an 800 telephone number if discrepancies exist.
- Charge interest on delinquent accounts receivable.
- Employ personal collection efforts.
- Offer discounts for early payment.
- Have postdated checks from customers.
- Provide cash-on-delivery terms.
- Deposit checks immediately.
- Make repeated collection calls and visits.

EXAMPLE 2

The CFO is considering whether to start a lockbox arrangement that will cost $150,000 annually. The daily average collections are $700,000. The system will reduce mailing and processing time by 2 days. The rate of return is 14%.

Return on freed cash ($14\% \times 2 \times \$700,000$)	$196,000
Annual cost	150,000
Net advantage of lockbox system	$ 46,000

EXAMPLE 3

You currently have a lockbox arrangement with Bank X in which it handles $5 million a day in return for an $800,000 compensating balance.

You are considering cancelling this arrangement and further dividing your western region by entering into contracts with two other banks. Bank Y will handle $3 million a day in collections with a compensating balance of $700,000, and Bank Z will handle $2 million a day with a compensating balance of $600,000. Collections will be half a day faster than at present. The rate of return is 12%.

Accelerated cash receipts	
($5 million per day × 0.5 day)	$2,500,000
Increased compensating balance	500,000
Improved cash flow	$2,000,000
Rate of return	× 0.12
Net annual savings	$ 240,000

How may cash payments be delayed to earn a greater return?

An evaluation should be made of who the payees are and to what degree time limits may be stretched.

Approaches to delay cash payments include:

• Centralize the payables operation so that debt may be paid at the most opportune time and so that the amount of disbursement float may be determined. Never pay vendors early.

• Establish zero balance accounts for all disbursing units. These accounts are in the same concentration bank. Checks are drawn against these accounts, with the balance in each account never exceeding $0. Divisional disbursing authority is maintained at the local management level. The benefits of zero balance accounts are enhanced control over cash payments, reduction in excess cash balances maintained in regional banks, and a possible increase in disbursing float. Under the zero balance account arrangement, the company only deposits funds into its payroll and payables checking accounts when it anticipates checks will clear. This strategy is aggressive. *Caution:* Be on guard against overdrafts and service charges. In a zero balance account (ZBA) arrangement, the bank *automatically* transfers money from a master (concentration) account as checks are presented against the payroll and payables accounts. Hence, payroll and payable accounts are retained at zero balances. Under ZBA, the CFO does not have to anticipate clearing times on each account.

• Use controlled disbursing in which checks are drawn against a bank that has the capability to inform the issuer early enough each day to allow funding in an exact amount the same day.

• Make partial payments and/or postdate checks.

• Request additional information about an invoice before paying it.

• Use payment drafts, where payment is *not* made on demand. Instead, the draft is presented for collection to the bank, which in turn goes to the issuer to accept it. A draft may be used to allow for inspection before payment. When approved, the company deposits the funds. *Net result:* There is less of a checking balance required. *Note:* The use of drafts involves bank charges (e.g., fixed monthly fee) and the inconveniences of always having to formerly approve the draft before paying it.

• Draw checks on remote banks (e.g., a New York Company using a Texas bank).

• Mail from post offices with limited service or where mail has to go through numerous handling points. *Tip:* If you use float properly you can maintain higher bank balances than the actual lower book balances. For example, if you write checks averaging $200,000 each day and three days are needed for them to clear, you will have a $600,000 checking balance less than the bank's records.

• Use remote mailing which is mailing checks from a location far removed from both the payee and drawee bank. A company having a centralized processing of accounts payable may install remote check printers in their plants and offices around the country. The central computer determines which banks to draw the check and which check printer to use to maximize delay time.

• Use probability analysis to determine the expected date for checks to clear. *Suggestion:* Have separate checking accounts (e.g., payroll, dividends) and monitor check clearing dates. Payroll checks are not all cashed on the payroll date, so funds can be deposited later to earn a return.

• Use a computer terminal to transfer funds between various bank accounts at opportune times.

• Use a charge account to lengthen the time between buying goods and paying for them.

• Stretch payments as long as there is no associated finance charge or impairment in credit. Prepare a priority list of who should get paid first and who should get paid last.

• Do not pay bills before they are due.

• Avoid making prepaid expenses. For example, if you are going to prepay insurance do it for one year not three years.

• Compensate others with noncash consideration such as stock or notes.

• Delay the frequency of payments to employees (e.g., expense account reimbursements, payrolls). Avoid giving employees cash advances such as for travel and entertainment or loans. Have a monthly payroll rather than a weekly payroll. In recession, the employer may eliminate or delay payroll payments to employees. Employees may be asked to take furloughs (e.g., two weeks off without pay) or give up current pay to be paid at a later date (e.g., postponing one week's pay to a later year or at retirement).

• Pay commissions on sales when the receivables are collected instead of when the sales are made.

• Mail payments late in the day or on Fridays.

• Engage in barter arrangements to avoid a cash payment. However, barter transactions are reportable for tax purposes based on the fair market value of what has been exchanged.

A cash management system is shown in Table 20–1.

EXAMPLE 4

Every 2 weeks the company issues checks that average $500,000 and take 3 days to clear. The CFO wants to find out how much money can be

TABLE 20-1 CASH MANAGEMENT SYSTEM

Acceleration of Cash Receipts	Delay of Cash Payments
Lock-box system	Pay by draft
Concentration banking	Requisition more frequently
Pre-authorized checks	Disbursing float
Pre-addressed stamp envelopes	Make partial payments
Obtain deposits on large orders	Use charge accounts
Charge interest on overdue receivables	Delay frequency of paying employees

saved annually if the transfer of funds is delayed from an interest-bearing account that pays 0.0384% per day (annual rate of 14%) for those 3 days:

$$\$500,000 \times (0.000384 \times 3) = \$576$$

The savings per year is $\$576 \times 26$ (yearly payrolls) = $\$14,976$

Cash Flow Software

Computer software allows for day-to-day cash management, determining cash balances, planning and analyzing cash flows, finding cash shortages, and investing cash surpluses. Spreadsheet software such as Lotus 1-2-3 can assist in developing cash projections and answering "what if" questions.

How do you use cash models to determine the optimal cash balance?

William Baumol developed a model (Figure 20–2) to determine the optimum amount of transaction cash under conditions of certainty. The objective is to minimize the sum of the fixed costs of

FIGURE 20-2

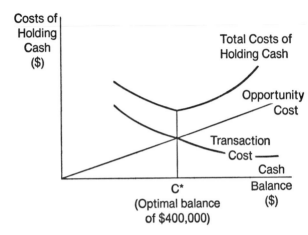

transactions *and* the opportunity cost of holding cash balances. These costs are expressed as:

$$F \times \frac{(T)}{C} + i \frac{(C)}{2}$$

where F = the fixed cost of a transaction, T = the total cash needed for the time period involved, i = the interest rate on marketable securities, and C = cash balance.

The optimal level of cash is determined using the following formula:

$$C^* = \sqrt{\frac{2FT}{i}}$$

EXAMPLE 5

You estimate a cash need for $4,000,000 over a one-month period where the cash account is expected to be disbursed at a constant rate. The opportunity interest rate is 6% per annum, or 0.5 percent for a one-month period. The transaction cost each time you borrow or withdraw is $100.

The optimal transaction size (the optimal borrowing or withdrawal lot size) and the number of transactions you should make during the month follow:

$$C^* = \sqrt{\frac{2FT}{i}} = \sqrt{\frac{2(100)(4,000,000)}{0.005}} = \$400,000$$

The optimal transaction size is $400,000. The average cash balance is:

$$\frac{C^*}{2} = \frac{\$400,000}{2} = \$200,000$$

The number of transactions required are:

$$\frac{\$4,000,000}{\$400,000} = 10 \text{ transactions during the month.}$$

You can use a stochastic model for cash management where uncertainty exists for cash payments. The Miller-Orr model places an upper and lower limit for cash balances. When the upper limit is reached a transfer of cash to marketable securities is made. When the lower limit is reached a transfer from securities to cash occurs. A transaction will not occur as long as the cash balance falls within the limits.

The Miller-Orr model takes into account the fixed costs of a securities transaction (F), assumed to be the same for buying as well as selling, the daily interest rate on marketable securities (i), and the variance of daily net cash flows (σ^2). The purpose is to satisfy cash requirements at the least cost. A major assumption is the randomness of cash flows. The two control limits in the Miller-Orr model may be specified as "d" dollars as an upper limit and zero dollars at the lower limit. When the cash balance reaches the upper level, d less z dollars of securities are bought and the new balance becomes z dollars. When the cash balance equals zero, z dollars of securities are sold and the new balance again reaches z. Of course, practically speaking you should note that the minimum cash balance is established at an amount greater than zero due to delays in transfer as well as to having a safety buffer.

The optimal cash balance z is computed as follows:

$$z = \sqrt[3]{\frac{3F\sigma^2}{4i}}$$

The optimal value for d is computed as 3z. The average cash balance will approximate $\frac{(z+d)}{3}$.

EXAMPLE 6

You wish to use the Miller-Orr model. The following information is supplied:

Fixed cost of a securities transaction	$10
Variance of daily net cash flows	$50
Daily interest rate on securities (10%/360)	0.0003

The optimal cash balance, the upper limit of cash needed, and the average cash balance follow:

$$z = \sqrt[3]{\frac{3(10)(50)}{4(0.0003)}} = \sqrt[3]{\frac{3(10)(50)}{.0012}} = \sqrt[3]{\frac{1,500}{0.0012}}$$

$$= \sqrt[3]{1,250,000} = \$102$$

The optimal cash balance is $102. The upper limit is $306 (3 × $102). The average cash balance is

$$\$136 \frac{(\$102 + \$306)}{3}$$

A brief elaboration on these findings is needed for clarification. When the upper limit of $306 is reached, $204 of securities ($306 – $102) will be purchased to bring you to the optimal cash balance of $102. When the lower limit of zero dollars is reached, $102 of securities will be sold to again bring you to the optimal cash balance of $102. See Figure 20–3.

BANKING RELATIONSHIPS _____

How should you deal with banks?

The company may want to restrict the maximum total deposit at a bank experiencing financial difficulties to no more than the amount

FIGURE 20-3

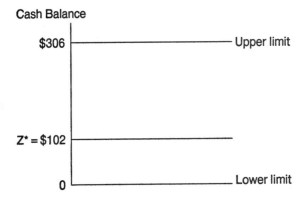

Cash Balance

federally insured. *Note:* With a checking account, the maximum deposit may be exceeded on the bank's records but not on the company's books because of the clearing time for checks and concentration entries.

A maximum deposit should be determined to keep at specific banks that exceeds the insurance limit. Deposits of unlimited amounts should be authorized at financial institutions.

Some banks offer better services than others in meeting company needs. In selecting a bank, consider:

- Location (affects lockboxes and disbursement points).
- Type and cost of services.
- Fund availability.

The financial strength of the bank should be determined. Reference may be made to ratings provided by services tracking banks.

Each bank account should be analyzed by comparing the value of the company balance kept at the bank to the service charges. While the bank will provide such analysis for you, it is biased and must be carefully evaluated.

A balance reporting system may be used where the lead bank gathers information for all other banks. The information may then be transferred to the company through telecommunications. The cost-effectiveness of the system should be periodically appraised.

Most checks clear in one business day. Clearing time of three or more business days is unusual. Ask the financial institution to give same-day credit on a deposit received before a specified cutoff time. However, if the deposit is made over-the-counter with a letter, immediate availability of those funds may not be received. If the deposit is made early enough, particularly through a lockbox, immediate fund availability may be achieved.

It is typically financially better to pay a higher deposited item charge in return for accelerated fund availability.

In performing an account reconciliation, the bank sorts checks into serial number order, lists all checks cleared, and matches issued checks provided by the company to paid checks so as to list outstanding checks and exception items. One objective is to reconcile the cash balances on deposit at various banks for control purposes. The services are only cost-effective when many checks are involved.

A bank reconciliation is prepared of each bank account to ensure the balance per books equals the balance per bank after adjusting for reconciling items. The bank reconciliation serves as an internal control measure.

INTERNATIONAL CASH MANAGEMENT _____

How should cash be managed when international dealings are involved?

International cash management minimizes the exposure of foreign located funds to exchange rate risks and minimizes governmental restrictions on the movement of funds among countries. Will the foreign country delay or block payments? For example, exchange control regulations may result in long delays in getting funds out of the country, or civil disturbances may interfere with payment. You must analyze the political and economic trends in the foreign country. For example, cash held in a socially depressed country is subject to risk.

Cash may be accelerated by having bank accounts in each country. In many countries, customers pay their bills by requesting their bank to deduct the amount owed from their account and to transfer the funds to another firm's account.

Multinational commercial banks, particularly those with branches or affiliates in many countries, can be helpful to multinational firms. Some of the larger U.S. multinational commercial banks have foreign departments whose only purpose is to assist multinational companies solve international cash management problems. An international bank can hasten funds flow and thus reduce the multinational company's exposure to foreign exchange rate risk. The bank can recommend the best route for the transfer of funds, and the national currency to be used. The time for foreign transactions can be as long as two weeks, and such delays can tie up significant funds. Multinational commercial banks aid in reducing this delay because they can transfer funds between countries on the same day provided there are affiliated branches in the two countries. We assume here that government restrictions on the remission of funds do *not* exist.

21

Management of Accounts Receivable

Accounts receivable management directly affects corporate profitability and cash flow. For example, too much money tied up in accounts receivable would be a "drag" on earnings. The CFO must consider discount policy, whether to grant credit to marginal customers, ways to hasten collections and reducing uncollectible accounts, and establishing credit terms.

How should accounts receivable be handled?

The order entry, billing, and accounts receivable activities should be evaluated to assure proper procedures and controls exist from the day an order is received until collection is made. What is the average time lag between completing the sales transaction and invoicing the customer? If it is excessive, why?

There are two kinds of float in accounts receivable management—invoicing and mail. *Invoicing float* is the days between the time goods are shipped to the customer and the time the invoice is rendered. Invoices should be timely processed. *Mail float* is the time between the preparation of an invoice and the time it is received by the customer. Mail float may be reduced by the following:

- Decentralizing invoicing and mailing.
- Coordinating outgoing mail with post office schedules.
- Using express mail services for large invoices.
- Enforcing due dates.
- Offering discounts.

In managing accounts receivable, the CFO should take into account the opportunity cost of holding receivables. The opportunity cost is tying up money in accounts receivable that could be invested elsewhere for a return. Therefore, ways to analyze and hasten collections should be undertaken.

An important consideration is the amount and credit terms given to customers since this will impact sales volume and collections. For example, a longer credit term will likely increase sales. The credit terms have a direct bearing on the costs and revenue derived from receivables. If credit terms are stringent, there will be less investment in accounts receivable and less bad debts. However, this will result in lower sales, reduced profits, and adverse customer reaction. If credit terms are lax, there will be higher sales and gross profit. However, this will result in greater bad debts and a higher opportunity cost of carrying the investment in accounts receivable because marginal customers take longer to pay. Receivable terms should be liberalized when you want to dispose of excessive inventory or obsolete items. Longer receivable terms are recommended for industries in which products are sold before retail seasons (e.g., swim suits). In the case of perishable goods, short receivable terms or even payment on delivery is advised.

In appraising a prospective customer's ability to pay, take into account the customer's honesty, financial strength, and pledged security. A customer's credit worthiness may be evaluated by using quantitative techniques such as regression analysis. These models are useful when there are many small customers. Bad debt losses can be accurately forecasted when a company sells to many customers and when its credit policies have remained static.

The CFO has to consider the costs of granting credit including administrative costs of the credit department, computer services, fees to rating agencies, and periodic field investigations.

What references may be made to credit reporting agencies?

Reference may be made to retail credit bureaus and credit reference services in evaluating a customer's ability to pay. One service is Dun and

Bradstreet (D&B), which rates companies. D&B reports contain information about a company's nature of business, financial status, prior payment history as reported by suppliers, amounts currently owed and past due, lawsuits, insurance coverage, audit opinion, leases, number of employees, terms of sale, banking relationships and account information (e.g., current bank loans), location of business, criminal proceedings, and seasonality characteristics.

What standards should be used in accounts receivable operations?

To monitor and improve accounts receivable activities, unit credit standards may be established. For invoice preparation, a cost per invoice, order, or item may be set. For credit investigation and approval, unit cost standards may include cost per account, sales order, or credit sales transaction. In examining credit correspondence records, cost per sales order, account sold, or letter may be used. In preparing customer statements, unit cost standards may be cost per statement or account sold. The standard for the computation of commissions on cash collections may be based on cost per remittance.

How may accounts receivable be effectively managed to maximize earnings?

There are many means to optimize profitability from accounts receivable and keep losses to a minimum. These include:

• Minimize "billing float" referring to the amount of time between the time of shipment, when a bill or invoice could have been rendered, to the time a bill or invoice is actually mailed. Billing may be accelerated through electronic data interchange (EDI) rather than using the mails.

• "Cycle bill" for uniformity in the billing process.

• Mail customer statements within 24 hours of the end of the accounting period.

• Mail an invoice to customers when the order is processed at the warehouse rather than when merchandise is shipped.

• Bill for services periodically when work is performed or charge a retainer. *Tip:* Bill large sales immediately.

• Use seasonal datings. *Recommendation:* When business is slow sell to customers with delayed payment terms to stimulate demand from those who cannot pay until later in the season. WHAT TO DO: Compare profitability on incremental sales plus the reduction in inventory carrying costs, which have to exceed the opportunity cost on the additional investment in average accounts receivable.

• Carefully evaluate customer financial statements before granting credit. Ratings should be obtained from financial advisory services.

• Avoid high-risk receivables (e.g., customers in a financially depressed industry or locality). Be careful of accounts in business less than one year (about 50% of businesses fail within the first two years).

• Note that customer receivables have greater default risk than corporate accounts.

• Adjust credit limits based on changes in customer's financial soundness.

• Accelerate collections from customers having financial difficulties. Also, withhold products or services until payment is received.

• Request collateral for questionable accounts. *Tip:* The collateral value should equal or exceed the account balance.

• Age accounts receivable to identify delinquent customers. Interest should be charged on such accounts. Aged receivables can be compared to previous years, industry standards, and competition. Bad Debt Loss Reports should be prepared showing cumulative bad debt losses detailed by customer, size of account, and terms of sale. These reports should be summarized by department, product line, and type of customer (e.g., industry). *Note:* Bad debt losses are usually higher for smaller companies than for larger ones. The company should charge back to the salesperson the commission already paid on an uncollectible account.

• Use outside collection agencies when net savings result.

• Factor accounts receivable when immediate funds are needed. However, confidential information may have to be disclosed.

• Have credit insurance to guard against unusual bad debt losses. *What to consider:* In deciding whether to obtain this insurance, consider expected average bad debt losses, financial soundness of your firm to withstand the losses, and the insurance cost.

• Consider marketing factors since a "tight" credit policy might mean less business.

• Monitor customer complaints about order item and invoice errors and orders not filled on time.

• Identify customers taking cash discounts who have not paid within the discount period.

• Look at the relationship of credit department costs to credit sales.

The collection period for accounts receivable partly depends on corporate policy and conditions. In granting trade credit, competition and economic conditions have to be considered. In recession, the CFO may liberalize the credit policy to obtain additional business. For example, the company may not rebill customers who take a cash discount even after the discount period expires. On the other hand, in times of short supply, credit policy may be tightened because the seller has the upper hand.

What are the attributes of a good credit system?

A credit system should be:

• Clear, fast, and consistent.
• Does not invade customer's privacy.

- Inexpensive (e.g., credit analysis and decision making is centralized).
- Based upon prior experience, taking into account characteristics of good, questionable, and bad accounts.

Tip: Determine the correlation between customer characteristics and future uncollectibility.

INVESTMENT IN ACCOUNTS RECEIVABLE ___

The CFO must determine the dollar investment tied up in accounts receivable. The accounts receivable balance depends on many factors including terms of sale, financial soundness of customers, product quality, interest rates, and economic conditions.

EXAMPLE 1

A company sells on terms of net/30. The accounts are on average 20 days past due. Annual credit sales are $600,000. The investment in accounts receivable is:

$$\frac{50}{360} \times \$600,000 = \$83,333.28$$

EXAMPLE 2

The cost of a product is 30 percent of selling price, and the cost of capital is 10 percent of selling price. On average, accounts are paid 4 months after sale. Average sales are $70,000 per month.

The investment in accounts receivable from this product is:

Accounts receivable (4 months × $70,000)	$280,000
Investment in accounts receivable [$280,000 × (0.30 + 0.10)]	112,000

EXAMPLE 3

You have accounts receivable of $700,000. The average manufacturing cost is 40% of the sales price. The before-tax profit margin is 10%. The carrying cost of inventory is 3% of selling price. The sales commission is 8% of sales. The investment in accounts receivable is:

$$\$700,000\ (0.40 + 0.03 + 0.08) = \$700,000\ (0.51)$$
$$= \$357,000$$

Should customers be offered a discount for the early payment of account balances?

The CFO has to compare the return on freed cash resulting from customers paying earlier to the cost of the discount.

EXAMPLE 4

The following data are provided:

Current annual credit sales	$14,000,000
Collection period	3 months
Terms	net/30
Minimum rate of return	15%

The company is considering offering a 3/10, net/30 discount. We expect 25 percent of the customers to take advantage of it. The collection period will decline to two months.

The discount should be offered, as indicated in the following calculations:

Advantage
Increased profitability:
  Average accounts receivable balance
  before a change in policy

$$\frac{\text{Credit sales}}{\text{Accounts receivable turnover}} \quad \frac{\$14,000,000}{4} \qquad \$3,500,000$$

  Average accounts receivable balance
  after change in policy

$$\frac{\text{Credit sales}}{\text{Average receivable turnover}} \quad \frac{\$14,000,000}{6} \qquad \underline{2,333,333}$$

Reduction in average accounts receivable balance	$1,116,667
Rate of return	×.15
Return	$ 175,000

Disadvantage

Cost of the discount 0.30 × 0.25 × $14,000,000	$ 105,000
Net advantage of discount	$ 70,000

Should the company give credit to marginal customers?

In granting credit to marginal customers, compare the profit on sales to the added cost of the receivables. NOTE: If idle capacity exists, the additional profit is the contribution margin on the sales because fixed costs are constant. The additional cost on the additional receivables results from the increased number of bad debts and the opportunity cost of tying up funds in receivables for more days.

EXAMPLE 5

Sales price per unit	$120
Variable cost per unit	$80
Fixed cost per unit	$15
Annual credit sales	$600,000
Collection period	1 month
Minimum return	16%

If you relax the credit policy, you estimate that

- Sales will increase by 40%.
- The collection period on total accounts will be two months.
- Bad debts on the increased sales will be 5%.

Preliminary calculations:

Current units ($600,000/$120)	5,000
Additional units (5,000 × 0.4)	2,000

The new average unit cost is now calculated:

	Units	×	Unit cost	=	Total cost
Current units	5,000	×	$95		$475,000
Additional units	2,000	×	$80		160,000
Total	7,000				$635,000

$$\text{New average unit cost} = \frac{\text{Total cost}}{\text{Units}}$$

$$= \frac{\$635,000}{7,000} = \$90.71$$

Since at idle capacity fixed cost remains constant, the incremental cost is only the variable cost of $80 per unit. This will result in a decline in the new average unit cost.

Advantage
Additional profitability:

Incremental sales volume units	2,000
× Contribution margin per unit (Selling price – variable cost) $120 – $80	× $40
Incremental profitability	$ 80,000

Disadvantage
Incremental bad debts:

Incremental units × Selling price 2,000 × $120	$240,000
Bad debt percentage	× 0.05
Additional bad debts	$ 12,000

Opportunity cost of funds tied up in accounts receivable:

Average investment in accounts receivable after change in policy:

$$\frac{\text{Credit sales}}{\text{Accounts receivable turnover}} \times \frac{\text{Unit cost}}{\text{Selling price}}$$

$$\frac{\$840,000 @}{6} \times \frac{\$90.71}{\$120} \qquad \$105,828$$

@ 7,000 units × $120 = $840,000.

Current average investment in accounts receivable:

$\dfrac{\$600,000}{12} \times \dfrac{\$95}{\$120}$	39,583
Additional investment in accounts receivable	$ 66,245
Minimum return	×0.16
Opportunity cost of funds tied up	$ 10,599

Net advantage of relaxation in credit standards:

Additional earnings		$ 80,000
Less:		
Additional bad debt losses	$12,000	
Opportunity cost	10,599	22,599
Net savings		$ 57,401

The company may have to decide whether to extend full credit to presently limited credit customers or no-credit customers. Full credit should be given only if net profitability occurs.

EXAMPLE 6

Category	Bad Debt Percentage	Collection Period	Credit Policy	Increase in Annual Sales if Credit Restrictions Are Relaxed
X	2%	30 days	Unlimited	$ 80,000
Y	5%	40 days	Restricted	600,000
Z	30%	80 days	No Credit	850,000

Gross profit is 25% of sales. The minimum return on investment is 12%.

EXAMPLE 7

You are considering liberalizing the credit policy to encourage more customers to purchase

	Category Y	Category Z
Gross profit		
$600,000 × .25	$150,000	
$850,000 × .25		$ 212,500
Less bad debts		
$600,000 × .05	−30,000	
$850,000 × .30		−255,000
Incremental average investment in accounts receivable		
40/360 × (0.75 × $600,000)	$50,000	
80/360 × (0.75 × $850,000)		$141,667
Opportunity cost of incremental investment in accounts receivable	× 0.12	× 0.12
	−6,000	−17,000
Net earnings	$114,000	$(−59,500)

Credit should be extended to category Y.

on credit. Currently, 80% of sales are on credit and there is a gross margin of 30%. Other relevant data are:

	Currently	Proposal
Sales	$300,000	$450,000
Credit sales	240,000	360,000
Collection expenses	4% of credit sales	5% of credit sales
Accounts receivable turnover	4.5	3

An analysis of the proposal yields the following results:

Average accounts receivable balance (credit sales/accounts receivable turnover)	
Expected average accounts receivable $360,000/3	$120,000
Current average accounts receivable $240,000/4.5	53,333
Increase	$ 65,667
Gross profit:	
Expected increase in credit sales ($360,000 – $240,000)	$120,000
Gross profit rate	× 0.30
Increase	$ 36,000
Collection expenses:	
Expected collection expenses 0.05 × $360,000	$ 18,000
Current collection expenses 0.04 × $240,000	9,600
Increase	$ 8,400

A more liberal credit policy should be instituted.

EXAMPLE 8

The company is planning a sales campaign in which it will offer credit terms of 3/10, net/45. We expect the collection period to increase from

	Without Sales Campaign		With Sales Campaign	
Gross margin (0.3 × $8,000,000)		$2,400,000	0.3 × $10,000,000	$3,000,000
Sales subject to discount				
0.65 × $8,000,000	$5,200,000			
0.85 × $10,000,000			$8,500,000	
Sales discount	× 0.03	−156,000	× 0.03	−255,000
Investment in average accounts receivable				
60/360 × $8,000,000 × 0.7	$933,333			
80/360 × $10,000,000 × 0.7			$1,555,555	
Return rate	× 0.14	−130,667	× 0.14	−217,778
Net profit		$2,113,333		$2,527,222

430

60 days to 80 days. Relevant data for the contemplated campaign follow:

	Percent of Sales Before Campaign	Percent of Sales During Campaign
Cash sales	40	30
Payment from		
1–10	25	55
11–100	35	15

The proposed sales strategy will probably increase sales from $8 million to $10 million. There is a gross margin rate of 30%. The rate of return is 14%. Sales discounts are given on cash sales.

The company should undertake the sales campaign, because earnings will increase by $413,889 ($2,527,222 – $2,113,333).

How are your receivable records excluding those for customers?

Some receivable transactions other than regular sales may result in losses. Examples include insurance and freight claims. The CFO should formulate a plan to handle these transactions. Unfortunately, some companies lack the needed recordkeeping. In fact, some firms only retain pieces of correspondence.

22

Inventory Management*

The objective of inventory management is to formulate policies that will result in an optimal inventory investment. The optimal inventory level varies among industries and among companies in a given industry. The successful management of inventory minimizes inventory at all manufacturing stages while retaining cost-efficient production volume. This improves corporate earnings and cash flow. By operating with minimum inventory and with short production lead times, the company increases its flexibility. This flexibility immediately responds to changing market conditions.

What inventory records should be kept?

Inventory files should contain balance on hand, quantity committed, and inventory location. The inventory balance must be adequate to maintain production schedules, properly utilize machines, and meet customer orders. Some inventory must be kept at the different manufacturing stages as hedges against the variabilities of supply and demand as well as hedging in the case problems arise in the manufacturing process. A sales forecast is the beginning step for effective inventory management since expected sales determines how much inventory is required.

Inventory records should provide information to meet the needs of the financial, production, sales, and purchasing managers. Inventory information may include the following by major type: unit cost, quantity on order, historical usage, minimum-maximum quantities, quantities in transit, scheduling dates, delivery times, and quantities set aside for specific customers,

---

*Dr. Anthony Akel, managerial consultant and director of the business program at C.W. Post College, coauthored this chapter.

production orders, and contracts. With regard to minimum-maximum quantities, such a procedure is practical when *stability* exists in the rate of sale or use of the product and where the order time is short. The minimum is a "cushion" in case of an emergency. The maximum is the "ceiling" desired inventory. The reorder point is between the minimum and maximum.

A master item file should exist containing identification, description, and specifications of the item's raw material, component parts, and assembly relationship. An item specification should include current information about the part, the uses of the item, possible substitutions, the production process, demand information, overall supply, and competitive factors. Information may also be provided about suppliers, and the availability and price of the item.

What inventory balance should be kept?

The inventory balance depends on many variables including sales, production cycle, cyclicality, perishability and obsolescence, inventory financing, liquidity, and markdowns in the industry. The objective is to maximize sales with minimum inventory. Therefore, inventory levels should be closely correlated to the selling cycle. A poor inventory management system may be indicated by the failure to achieve production plans, manufacturing bottlenecks, downtime, slow-moving or obsolete merchandise, expediting of parts, "rush" jobs, poor customer service, poor forecasts and inadequate performance reporting, and internal conflicts between members of the organization such as production and marketing.

An advantage of a "bloated" inventory is the reduction in manufacturing costs from larger production runs. It also provides a safety buffer if there is a nondelivery of raw materials or the previous department's manufacturing process breaks down.

Accurate sales forecasting is essential because a high sales estimate can result in high inventory levels, obsolescence, markdowns, and inventory write-offs. A low sales estimate can result in low inventory and lost sales.

Suppliers should be appraised in terms of fair pricing, meeting delivery dates, quality of goods shipped (e.g., consistent with product specifications), and ability to meet "rush" orders.

What inventory management policies should be practiced?

There are many benefits to sound inventory management including:

• Reduces waste and cost from excess storage, handling, and obsolescence.

• Reduces manufacturing delays because sufficient raw material balances are maintained. This results in lower production costs and longer runs.

• Reduces the chance of inventory theft.

• Improves customer service because materials are available.

Inventory Management Policies

• Evaluate the adequacy of raw materials, which depends on expected production, condition of equipment, supplier reliability, and seasonality. Raw material requirements may be projected using such techniques as statistical analysis of historical trends and cycles, econometric models, and Delphi methods. *Recommendation:* Use material management guidelines to specify what and how much should be stored. The manufacturing process requires an appropriate balance of parts to produce an end item. *What to watch for:* A situation in which you have two of three components because this results in having two excess inventories when there is a stockout of the third.

• Forecast future movements in raw material prices, so that if prices are expected to increase, additional materials are purchased at lower prices.

• Discard slow-moving merchandise to reduce inventory carrying costs and improve cash flow.

• Stock higher profit margin items.

• Guard against inventory buildup because of carrying and opportunity costs.

• Minimize inventory when there are liquidity and/or inventory financing difficulties.

• Plan for a stock balance that will guard against and cushion the possible loss of business from a shortage in materials. The timing of an order also depends on seasonality factors.

• Ensure that inventory is received when needed for smooth production. *What to do:* Compare vendor and production receipts to promised delivery dates.

• A long sales order entry process requires the stocking of additional merchandise.

• Try to convince customers to retain higher stock levels to reduce the company's inventory of finished goods.

• Examine the quality of merchandise received. The ratio of purchase returns to purchases should be examined. A sharp increase in the ratio indicates that a new supplier may be needed. A performance measurement and evaluation system should exist to appraise vendor quality and reliability. If the vendor is unreliable, problems will occur in production scheduling, imbalances in work-in-process, and "rush" purchase orders.

• Keep a careful record of back orders. A high back-order level indicates that less inventory is required because back orders may be used as an indicator of the production required, resulting in improved manufacturing planning and procurement. The trend in the ratio of the dollar amount of back orders to the average per-day sales is enlightening.

• Evaluate the purchase and inventory control functions. Any problems must be identified and solved. If controls are deficient, inventory balances should be minimized.

• Accuracy is needed for the bills of materials to indicate the parts and quantities received to produce an end product. *What to do:* Conduct audits on the production floor when the parts are assembled.

• Have accurate inventory records and assign inventory responsibilities to managers. For example, assign to the engineering manager responsibility for the bills of material. Do you have the necessary inventory measurement tools (e.g., scales)?

• Closely supervise warehouse and materials handling staff to guard against theft and to maximize efficiency.

• Frequently review stock lines for poor earnings.

• Minimize the lead time in the acquisition, manufacturing, and distribution functions. The lead time is how long it takes to receive merchandise from suppliers after an order is placed. Depending upon lead times, an increase in inventory stocking may be required or the purchasing pattern may have to be altered. *What to do:* Calculate the ratio of the value of outstanding orders to average daily purchases to indicate the lead time for receiving orders from suppliers. The ratio indicates whether the inventory balance should be increased or buying patterns changed. Are vendors keeping their promises?

• Examine the time between raw material input and the completion of production to determine if production and engineering techniques can be instituted to speed the production process.

• Appraise the degree of and reasons for spoilage and take corrective measures.

• Prepare an inventory analysis report presenting the number of months of insurance coverage. The report should highlight items with excess inventory coverage resulting from such causes as changes in customer demand or poor inventory practices.

• Maintain adequate inventory control such as by applying computer techniques. For example, a point-of-sale computerized electronic register may be used by a retail business. The register updates inventory for sales and purchases facilitating the computation of reorder points and quantity per order.

• Examine the trend in unit cost. The causes for variations should be studied to determine if they arise from factors within or beyond management control (i.e., increase in oil prices, financial management deficiencies).

• Have economies in production run size to reduce setup costs and idle time.

• Have vendors consign inventory to you and invoice as used.

• Use computer techniques and operations research to control inventory. For example, statistical forecasting techniques may be used to compute inventory levels related to a predetermined acceptability level.

How can the purchasing department help?

The purchasing department can aid in inventory management as follows:

• Determine a price for raw materials that will protect the business in unstable markets.

• Gradually increase the purchase order as you get to know the supplier better.

• Have blanket orders for operating supplies.

• Utilize stringent control over subcontracted operations.

• Schedule delivery of raw materials using statistical and just-in-time techniques.

What are the signs of inventory problems?

The symptoms of inventory management problems are:

• Inventory writedowns.

• Differing rates of turnover among inventory items within the same inventory class.

• Material shortages.

• Uneven production and downtime.

• Order cancellations.

• Periodic extension of back orders.

• Lack of storage facilities.

• Frequent layoffs and rehirings.

What inventory control measures can be taken?

Internal controls over inventory guard against theft and other irregularities. A periodic surprise count will confirm agreement between the book inventory and physical inventory. There should be controlled audit groups of work-in-process moving through the manufacturing stages to assure that work-in-process is properly documented.

Shortages may occur and go unnoticed for a long time if controls are deficient. Controls are required in the acquisition and handling phases. There should be segregation in the purchasing, receiving, storing and shipping of inventories.

An inventory control system should achieve the following objectives: (1) proper record keeping, (2) aiding in forecasting usage and needs, (3) reporting exceptions, (4) maintaining safeguards against misuse, and (5) implementing inventory decision models.

How can you appraise and evaluate inventory?

Inventory analysis considers the following:

• Inventory months' supply on hand by period for each major product.

• Customer order backlog relative to the inventory balance.

• Customer order backlog in weeks as a percent of the production process cycle (lead time).

• Safety stock and slow-moving (obsolete) goods as a percent of cost of sales and of the inventory balance.

• Inventory carrying cost by month, quarter, and year.

Work-in-process should be completed in a timely manner to realize sales and cash flow.

The marketing department should be held responsible for obsolete and slow-moving merchandise that they originally recommended. Before a product design is altered at the suggestion of marketing, it should be carefully studied.

Inventory items vary in profitability and the amount of space occupied. Inventory management involves a trade-off between the costs of keeping inventory compared to the benefits of holding it. Higher inventory balances result in increased costs from storage, spoilage, theft and casualty insurance, higher property taxes for larger facilities, increased manpower requirements, and interest on borrowed funds to finance inventory purchase. However, an increase in inventory lowers the possibility of lost sales from stockouts and the incidence of production slowdowns. Further, large volume purchases will result in greater purchase discounts. Inventory levels are also affected by short-term interest rates. For example, as short-term interest rates increase, the optimum level of holding inventory decreases.

How may handling costs be reduced?

To reduce costs of handling inventory, do the following:

- Minimize seasonal stocking.
- Decrease the time between filling an order and replacing the stock sold.
- Consolidate the number of inventory storage locations and/or warehouses.
- Avoid shutting down the plant, such as by having varying vacations.
- Simplify and standardize the product.
- Stop supplying "old" service parts but rather give customers the blueprint so they may internally produce them.
- Speed routing reproduction by using standardized forms.
- Keep materials at subassemblies, not final assemblies.
- Use several assembly lines and move crews to the next line which has already been setup.

What influences inventory balances?

The inventory balance depends upon:

- Reliability in estimating customer needs. Consideration should be given to the forecasting error.
- Accuracy of manufacturing documents (e.g., bill of materials, route sheets).
- Vertical integration of the product line as indicated by manufactured vs. purchased parts.

The inventory of raw materials depends upon the anticipated level and seasonality of production, and the reliability of supply sources.

Work-in-progress usually varies the most and depends upon the timing of the production run, stages in the manufacturing cycle, quality problems, lead time, and lot-sizing.

Work-in-progress is a "liability" to inventory managers because it takes away production capacity and cash while increasing the obsolescence and shrinkage risk. While machine utilization is good, a buildup of work-in-progress is bad.

The CFO may have to decide whether it is more profitable to sell inventory as is, or sell it after further processing. Assume inventory can be sold as is for $600,000, or sold for $800,000 if it is put into further processing costing $30,000. The latter should be chosen because further processing results in $770,000 profit compared to $600,000 for the current sale.

There should be periodic counts of inventory to check it on an ongoing basis as well as to reconcile the book and physical amounts. *Recommendation:* Standardized labeling and quantity markings will reduce counting time, and result in orderly warehouse stocking. *Tip:* The count should be during nonworking hours. Alternatively, warehouse pickers could carefully enter daily movement when the cycle count occurs. The advantages to cyclic counting are:

• Does not require a plant shutdown, as does a year-end count.

• Enables the timely detection and correction of the causes of inventory error.

• Allows the efficient use of a few full-time experienced counters throughout the year.

• Facilitates the modification of computer inventory programs.

WHAT ARE THE INVENTORY COSTS? _____

What are the costs associated with inventory?

Inventory carrying costs include handling, warehousing, insurance, and property taxes. Further, there is an opportunity cost of holding inventory. A provisional cost for spoilage and obsolescence should also be included. Carrying cost increases as the size of the inventory increases. Carrying cost equals:

$$\text{Carrying cost} = \frac{Q}{2} \times C$$

where Q/2 represents average quantity and C is the carrying cost per unit.

Inventory ordering costs are the costs of placing an order and receiving the goods. They include freight and the clerical costs to place the order. The ordering costs can be reduced by placing less orders. In the case of manufactured items, ordering cost includes the scheduling cost. Ordering cost equals:

$$\text{Ordering cost} = \frac{S}{Q} \times P$$

where S = total usage, Q = quantity per order, and P = cost of placing an order.

The total inventory cost is therefore:

$$\frac{QC}{2} + \frac{SP}{C}$$

There is a tradeoff between ordering and carrying costs. A greater order quantity will increase carrying costs but lower ordering costs.

WHAT IS THE ECONOMIC ORDER QUANTITY (EOQ)?

The economic order quantity (EOQ) is the optimum amount of goods to order each time so that total inventory costs are minimized. The EOQ should be determined for each major product:

$$EOQ = \sqrt{\frac{2SP}{C}}$$

Assumptions underlying the EOQ model are:

- Demand is constant and known.
- No discount is given for quantity purchases.

• Depletion of stock is linear and constant.

• *Lead time,* which is the time between placing an order and receiving delivery, is a constant, i.e., stockout is not possible.

The number of orders for a period is the usage (S) divided by the EOQ.

EXAMPLE 1

You want to know how often to place orders. The following information exists:

$$S = 500 \text{ units per month}$$
$$P = \$40 \text{ per order}$$
$$C = \$4 \text{ per unit}$$

$$EOQ = \sqrt{\frac{2SP}{C}} = \sqrt{\frac{2(500)(40)}{4}} = \sqrt{10,000} = 100 \text{ units}$$

The number of orders each month is:

$$S/EOQ = 500/100 = 5$$

Therefore, an order should be placed about every 6 days (31/5).

EXAMPLE 2

You want to determine how often to place an order for product X. The purchase price is \$15. The annual carrying cost is \$200. The ordering cost is \$10. You expect to sell 50 units per month. The desired average inventory is 40 units.

$$S = 50 \times 12 = 600$$
$$P = \$10$$
$$C = \frac{\text{Purchase price} \times \text{Carrying cost}}{\text{Average investment}}$$
$$= \frac{\$15 \times \$200}{40 \times \$15} = \$5$$
$$EOQ = \sqrt{\frac{2SP}{C}} = \sqrt{\frac{2(600)(10)}{5}} = \sqrt{\frac{12,000}{5}}$$
$$= \sqrt{2,400} = 49 \text{ (rounded)}$$

The number of orders per year is:

$$\frac{S}{EOQ} = \frac{600}{49} = 12 \text{ orders (rounded)}$$

You should place an order approximately every 30 days (365/12).

WHAT IS THE REORDER POINT? _____

The reorder point (ROP) is the inventory level at which to place an order. However, the reorder point requires a knowledge of the lead time from placing to receiving an order. The reorder point may be affected by the months of supply or total dollar ceilings on inventory to be held or to be ordered.

Reorder point equals:

ROP = Lead time × Average usage per unit of time

This reveals the inventory level at which a new order should be placed. If a safety stock is needed, then add this amount to the ROP.

The more the *vendor's* backlog, the greater will be the work-in-process. This results in a longer and more inaccurate lead time. If a product is made to a customer's order, the lead time is the run time, queue time, move time, setup time, and procurement time for raw material.

EXAMPLE 3

A company needs 6,400 units evenly throughout the year. There is a lead time of one week. There are 50 working weeks in the year. The reorder point is:

$$1 \text{ week} \times \frac{6,400}{50 \text{ weeks}} = 1 \times 128 = 128 \text{ units}$$

When the inventory level drops to 128 units, a new order should be placed.

An optimal inventory level can be based on comparing the incremental profitability resulting from having more merchandise to the opportunity cost of carrying the higher inventory balances.

EXAMPLE 4

The current inventory turnover is 12 times. Variable costs are 60% of sales. An increase in inventory balances is expected to prevent stockouts, thus increasing sales. Minimum rate of return is 18%. Relevant data follow.

Sales	Turnover
$800,000	12
890,000	10
940,000	8
980,000	7

(1)	(2)	(3) [(1)/(2)] Average Inventory Balance
Sales	Turnover	
$800,000	12	$66,667
890,000	10	89,000
940,000	8	117,500
980,000	7	140,000

(4) Opportunity Cost of Carrying Incremental Inventory[a]	(5) Increased Profitability[b]	(6) [(5)–(4)] Net Savings
—	—	—
$4,020	$36,000	$31,980
5,130	20,000	14,870
4,050	16,000	11,950

[a] Increased inventory × 0.18.
[b] Increased sales × 0.40.

The optimal inventory level is $89,000, because it results in the highest net savings.

How are stockouts avoided?

The stockout of raw materials or work-in-process can cause a production slowdown. A safety stock should be held to avoid a stockout situation. Safety stock is the minimum inventory for an item based on anticipated usage (demand) and delivery (lead) time of materials. A safety stock guards against unusual product demand or unexpected delivery problems. The variability in demand of the item can be measured by the standard deviation or mean absolute deviation. The standard deviation measures the degree to which the actual level at the end of the cycle differs from the normal level. The trend period in computing standard deviations should consider market characteristics, product maturity, and demand volatility. A large standard deviation indicates significant inventory variation. Therefore, the probability of being out of stock at various times during the year is high if there is no safety stock. Safety stock prevents the potential damage to customer relations and to future sales that can occur when there is a lack of inventory to fill an order. A safety stock increases the inventory balance. In effect, safety stock requires a balancing of expected costs of stockouts against the costs of carrying the additional inventory. *Rule of thumb:* A typical inventory management system uses a 5% stockout factor.

EXAMPLE 5

An order is placed when the inventory level reaches 210 units rather than 180 units. The safety stock is thus 30 units. In other words, you expect to be stocked with 30 units when the new order is received.

The optimum safety stock is the point where the increased carrying cost equals the opportunity cost of a potential stockout. The increased carrying cost equals the carrying cost per unit multiplied by the safety stock.

$$\frac{\text{Stockout}}{\text{cost}} = \frac{\text{Number}}{\text{of orders}} \left(\frac{\text{Usage}}{\text{Order quantity}} \right)$$

$$\times \frac{\text{Stockout}}{\text{units}} \times \frac{\text{Unit stockout}}{\text{cost}}$$

$$\times \text{Probability of a stockout}$$

EXAMPLE 6

A company uses 100,000 units annually. Each order is for 10,000 units. Stockout is 1,000 units; this amount is the difference between the maximum daily usage during the lead time less the reorder point, ignoring a safety stock factor. The acceptable stockout probability is 30%. The per unit stockout cost is $2.30. The carrying cost per unit is $5.

The stockout cost is:

$$\frac{100,000}{10,000} \times 1,000 \times \$2.30 \times .3 = \$6,900$$

The amount of safety stock is computed below:

$$\text{Let } X = \text{Safety stock}$$
$$\text{Stockout cost} = \text{Carrying cost of safety stock}$$
$$\$6,900 = \$5X$$
$$1,380 \text{ units} = X$$

EXAMPLE 7

A company uses 250,000 units per year. Each order is for 25,000 units. Stockout is 4,000 units. The tolerable stockout probability is 25%. The per unit stockout cost is $4. The carrying cost per unit is $8.

$$\text{Stockout cost} = \frac{250,000}{25,000} \times 4,000 \times \$4 \times 0.25 = \$40,000$$

$$\text{Amount of safety stock needed} = \frac{\text{Stockout cost}}{\text{Carrying cost per unit}}$$

$$= \frac{\$40,000}{\$8} = 5,000 \text{ units}$$

HOW TO FIND THE OPTIMAL STOCK SIZE

Service level can be defined as the probability that demand will not exceed supply during lead time. Thus, a service level of 80% implies a

TABLE 22-1 VALUES OF z_p FOR SPECIFIED PROBABILITIES P

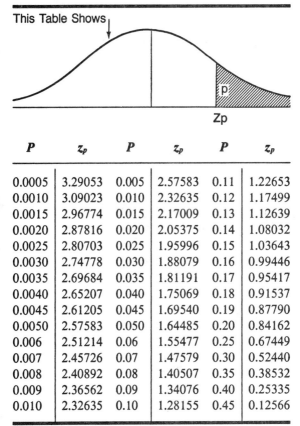

This Table Shows

P	z_p	P	z_p	P	z_p
0.0005	3.29053	0.005	2.57583	0.11	1.22653
0.0010	3.09023	0.010	2.32635	0.12	1.17499
0.0015	2.96774	0.015	2.17009	0.13	1.12639
0.0020	2.87816	0.020	2.05375	0.14	1.08032
0.0025	2.80703	0.025	1.95996	0.15	1.03643
0.0030	2.74778	0.030	1.88079	0.16	0.99446
0.0035	2.69684	0.035	1.81191	0.17	0.95417
0.0040	2.65207	0.040	1.75069	0.18	0.91537
0.0045	2.61205	0.045	1.69540	0.19	0.87790
0.0050	2.57583	0.050	1.64485	0.20	0.84162
0.006	2.51214	0.06	1.55477	0.25	0.67449
0.007	2.45726	0.07	1.47579	0.30	0.52440
0.008	2.40892	0.08	1.40507	0.35	0.38532
0.009	2.36562	0.09	1.34076	0.40	0.25335
0.010	2.32635	0.10	1.28155	0.45	0.12566

z_p *is the value of the standardized normal (mean = 0, standard deviation = 1) random variable z such that the probability of obtaining a sample z value at least as large as z_p is P. The value of P must be doubled if two sided statements are made using the same z_p value.*

Source: *Croxton/Cowden/Bolch*, Practical Business Statistics, *4th Ed., © 1969, p. 393. Reprinted by permission of Prentice-Hall, Inc., Englewood Cliffs, N.J.*

probability of 80% that demand will not exceed supply. To determine the optimal level of safety stock size, ascertain the costs of not having enough inventory (stockout costs). Here are three cases for computing the safety stock. The first two do not recognize stockout costs; the third case does.

Case 1: Variable usage rate, constant lead time

$$\text{ROP} = \text{Expected usage during lead time}$$
$$+ \text{safety stock}$$
$$= \overline{\mu}\text{LT} + Z\ \text{LOT}\ (\sigma\mu)$$

where $\overline{\mu}$ = average usage rate, LT = lead time, σ_μ = standard deviation of usage rate, Z = standard normal variable as defined in Table 22–1.

For a normal distribution, a given service level amounts to the shaded area under the curve to the left of ROP in Figure 22–1.

EXAMPLE 8

A company uses large cases of a product at an average rate of 50 units per day. Usage can be approximated by a normal distribution with a standard deviation of five units per day. Lead time is four days. Thus:

$$\overline{\mu} = 50 \text{ units per day}$$
$$\sigma_\mu = 5 \text{ units}$$
$$\text{LT} = 4 \text{ days}$$

FIGURE 22–1   SERVICE LEVEL

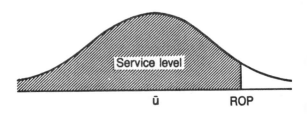

FIGURE 22-2 SERVICE LEVEL = 99%

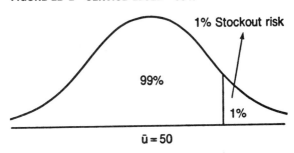

For a service level of 99% (see Figure 22-2), $Z = 2.33$ (from Table 22-1) Thus:

$$\text{Safety stock} = 2.33 \sqrt{4}\ (5) = 23.3 \text{ cans}$$
$$\text{ROP} = 50(4) + 23.3 = 223.3 \text{ cans}$$

Case 2: Constant usage rate, variable lead time

For constant usage with variable lead time, the reorder point is computed as follows:

$$\text{ROP} = \text{Expected usage during lead time}$$
$$+ \text{Safety stock}$$
$$= \overline{\mu}\text{LT} + Z\mu\sigma_{LT}$$

where μ = constant usage rate, $\overline{LT}$ = average lead time, and σ_{LT} = standard deviation of lead time.

EXAMPLE 9

A company uses 10 gallons of product X per day. Lead time is normally distributed with a mean of six days and a standard deviation of two days. Thus,

$$\mu = 10 \text{ gallons per day}$$
$$\overline{LT} = 6 \text{ days}$$
$$\sigma_{LT} = 2 \text{ days}$$

$$\text{Safety stock} = 2.33\ (10)(2) = 46.6 \text{ gallons}$$
$$\text{ROP} = 10(6) + 46.6 = 106.6 \text{ gallons}$$

Figure 22–3 shows the changes in level of inventory over time.

The product generating the highest contribution margin per square foot should usually have the most priority in allocating space.

EXAMPLE 10

The following information pertains to product X:

Sales price	$ 15
Variable cost per unit	5
Contribution margin per unit	$ 10
Contribution margin per dozen	$120
Storage space per dozen	2 cubic feet
Contribution margin per cubic foot	$ 60
Number of units sold per period	4
Expected contribution margin per cubic foot	$240

ABC INVENTORY CONTROL _____

ABC analysis concentrates on the most important items considering gross profitability, sensitive

FIGURE 22–3　CHANGES IN LEVEL OF INVENTORY OVER TIME

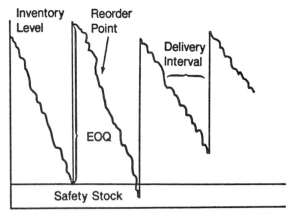

Time

price or demand patterns, and supply excesses or shortages. The ABC method involves the classification of inventory into one of four categories A, B, C, or D. The grouping is based on the potential savings associated with a proper level of control.

Perpetual inventory records should be kept for A items because of the required accuracy and frequent attention, often daily. A items usually refer to one out of every ten items in inventory typically representing 70% of the dollar value of inventory. Group B items are less expensive but are still important and require intermediate control. The group B items usually account for both 20% of the number of inventory items and 20% of the dollar value. Group C items constitute most of the inventory. Since they are usually less expensive and less used, there is less attention paid to them. There is typically a high safety stock level for C items. There should be blanket purchase orders for A items and only "spot buys" for Bs and Cs. Group D items are the *losers*. There has been no usage of D items for an extended time period (e.g., six months). D items should not be reordered without special authorization. Items may be reclassified as needed. For example, a "fragile" item or one being stolen can be reclassified from C to A.

The higher the value of the inventory items, the more control required. For example, in looking at A items, carefully examine records, bills of material, customer orders, open purchase orders, and open manufacturing orders.

The steps in ABC are:

1. Segregate inventory into components.

2. Compute annual dollar usage by inventory type.

3. Rank inventory according to dollar usage ranging from high to low (e.g., As in top 30%, Bs in next 50%, and Cs in last 20%).

4. Tag inventory with the appropriate classification so proper attention may be given to them.

5. Record classifications in the inventory records.

SERVICE BUSINESS ─────────────

How should a service business handle inventory?

In a service business, inventories are less tangible than durable goods and they are perishable by nature. Examples of inventory in a service business are an empty seat in an airplane, empty hotel room, and empty table in a restaurant. In these instances, inventory is lost as time passes and the "empty" condition continues. Inventory also includes service parts.

Inventory in a service business consists of the following levels:

1. *Primary Level.* This level represents the capacity of the facility or equipment to provide the service.

2. *Secondary Level.* This level is the variable capacity used at different time periods to deliver the service.

Marginal pricing may be used to obtain income from otherwise lost opportunities. Examples are hotels offering "week-end specials" and airlines with "off-peak" fares. The aim is to divert minimal income from the normal service customer by attracting lower margin business. The profit of the service business is influenced by the perishability of the service inventory.

The labor force should be such that labor costs are matched with the ability to sell the product.

23

Management of Payables

The CFO must assure that there is a well-managed accounts payable system. Any warning signs of problems with payables must be identified and solved.

ACCOUNTS PAYABLE SYSTEM

The control of the cash that leaves the company is as important as controlling the cash that comes in. To achieve control, payables must be aggressively managed in accordance with the company's financial position and goals. Payment of bills must not be simply made but *planned*. Above all, payables must be viewed as a flexible system that the CFO can manipulate in response to other factors such as sales decreases or slowdowns in collections.

A well-managed accounts payable system should:

• *Evaluate cash flow.* Every accounts payable strategy should be rooted in the realities of the company's cash flow status. For example, if it takes 90 days to collect from customers, it is financially self-destructive to pay bills within 45 days.

How long does it take dollars spent to be replaced? The CFO should monitor the cash-to-cash cycle representing the length of time elapsing from the expenditure of dollars on inventory to the receipt of cash from sales. Take for instance a retailer who buys a product on January 1 and pays for it on January 30; it takes the retailer 60 days from that point to sell that product (which brings the retailer to March 31) and 45 days after that to collect the cash (May 15). The cash-to-cash cycle adds up to 105 days, which is the length of time the retailer is behind after expending the cash.

• *Set goals.* Once cash flow has been appraised, establish written payment goals so there

454 MANAGEMENT OF ASSETS AND PAYABLES

can be no confusion among bill payers. Avoid a situation in which staff make the decisions about which bills are to be paid and when—usually, suppliers who complain the most are paid first, regardless of overall benefit to the business.

The payment of bills should be timed to coordinate exactly with formal disbursement goals. This means checks should be dated no earlier than the dates upon which payments are due (and suppliers should receive checks no more than a day or two earlier than the due date). The goal should be to hold cash in interest-bearing accounts until the last possible minute in which payments must be made and still maintain good relations with suppliers.

• *Establish payment priorities.* It is advisable to establish a two-tiered list of payment priorities, which then becomes part of the formal payment strategy. Tier one, the group that should be paid at all costs and at whatever terms have been agreed upon, should include major vendors and service suppliers, bankers, and the state and federal tax authorities. Tier two, which offers more room for short-term maneuvering during cash-flow crunches, should consist of minor suppliers whose goodwill is less vital to the overall well-being of the company. Payment priorities should be in writing.

• *Aggressively negotiate payment.* Granted, there is not much room for negotiation with bankers or tax collectors, but once they are taken care of, everything else on the payables front is open for discussion. The CFO has leverage to negotiate better-than-usual terms from major suppliers, especially during recessionary times, when vendors are afraid of losing business. Determine the optimal payment terms (using the cash-to-cash or other cash flow information as a guide; then when orders are placed, not when bills become due or overdue, negotiate to achieve those terms.

• *Forecast cash needs.* The CFO should predict how much cash is needed—and when—to fulfill the payables obligations. That forecast becomes an important tool in averting cash flow problems. Will funds be available at the right time from bank accounts or bank credit lines? If funds will not be available, take precautionary measures such as stepping up customer collection efforts.

• *Keep good payables records.* Payable records include weekly updates about the aging of every outstanding bill; documentation that matches each bill paid with its original sales order, delivery records, and payment invoice; and total cost records, including interest penalties paid on each bill. The last is important because it may not be evident how much it adds to the cost of doing business when the company winds up having to pay interest charges to finance late payables.

• *Review payables records regularly.* Payables reports are as important as other cash flow documents and must be evaluated. Review payables—aging schedules—weekly; cost records can be appraised monthly.

• *Recognize warning signs.* Since cash flow cycles vary, there may be periods when payables get stretched without any long-term risk. But it is essential to spot indications of more serious problems. One approach is to draw up a "payables problems" checklist, which breaks down average bill age, promptness of tax payments, any interest charges and other warning factors.

• *Paying the right amount.* Payments should be made in accordance with purchase order terms and discounts taken where allowed. Payments should only be made against the original invoice to prevent a duplicate payment against a photocopy or summary statement. Match all vendor invoices against receiving reports and purchase orders.

In managing payables, what must be considered?

Sound management of accounts payable takes into account the following:

• *Prioritize.* Financial obligations fall into three categories: the bills to be paid as soon as they are due (wages and salaries, bank loans, and taxes), bills to be paid within 15 days (to important contractors for services already performed), and bills you try to pay within 30 days (all others). As your business begins to feel the recessionary pinch, try to stretch that third category out longer. In looking at cash flow, accounts payable are something that the CFO has some control over-and suppliers can be "played with" if needed.

• *Negotiate.* Negotiate longer payment terms in advance, although the process can be time consuming. Contact major vendors to ask when they absolutely have to have their money. This information should then get recorded in each vendors' accounts payable file. It sets the guidelines for payment of all major outstanding obligations. With smaller suppliers, however, there may not be much potential payoff from stretching out payments.

• *Monitor payables closely.* Each week analyze an accounts payable aging schedule along with other cash flow documents. As a last resort, the company should use its credit line to make payments if cash collections from customers are behind schedule.

• *Demonstrate good faith.* When money does not come in, the company is in a jam. One possible solution: Pay only *absolute essentials* such as salaries, rent, taxes, and loans. These expenditures cannot be delayed. Suppliers are more tolerant and flexible since they need the business. However, try to pay more to the demanding vendors and less to those more likely to wait. A partial payment shows vendors that the company is trying to pay them. Don't just send the money— get on the phone and explain what is happening and why and set up an informal payment schedule. Let the vendors know when they can expect to receive the balance due. A follow-up letter should confirm the telephone conversation.

Is your business heading for accounts payable problems?

Some typical symptoms of accounts payable problems are:

• *Aged payables.* Chances are that the company is heading for trouble when bills start becoming, on average, 45 to 60 days past due. (The only exception: bills whose issuers have approved late payment terms without interest penalties, at the time of order).

• *Interest penalties.* Do not box yourself in by paying interest charges on overdue bills—unless there are clear financial benefits from using funds elsewhere. Once the company is paying penalties to even a few vendors on a regular monthly basis, it is in trouble. Instead, approach creditors with a workout plan that will reduce or perhaps eliminate interest charges.

• *Hassles from creditors.* Make it a habit to communicate informally with creditors whenever there is a developing cash crunch. Creditors are typically understanding if the company has good intentions and is honest.

What information should you obtain from vendors?

Money may be saved by getting to know the policies of vendors and suppliers. Probe them for the best prices and terms. Ask open-ended questions such as "What else can you do for me?" Ask vendors to complete an information sheet that forces them to write down the terms and conditions of their sales plans. With this form, their verbal promises become written ones. The following is a list of useful information:

• Vendor's name, address, and phone number (Will the vendor accept collect calls? Is there an 800 number?).

• Sales representative's name, phone number, and qualifications.

• Amount of minimum purchase.

• Quantity discounts available.

• Advertising/promotion allowances.

• Availability of extended payment terms.

• Financing charge on overdue accounts.

• Delivery terms.

• Service policies.

• Return privileges for damaged goods (who pays the freight?).

• Credit terms (how flexible is it?).

PART V

FINANCING THE BUSINESS

24

Short-Term and Intermediate-Term Financing

This chapter provides information about short-term and intermediate-term financing sources. Short-term financing is typically used to meet seasonal and temporary fluctuations in funds position. For example, short-term financing may provide working capital, finance current assets (such as receivables and inventory), or furnish interim financing for a long-term project or capital asset until long-term financing may be issued. Long-term financing may not be currently suitable because of long-term credit risk or unusually high cost. Intermediate-term financing is primarily obtained from banks and lessors.

SHORT-TERM FINANCING

Before deciding on how much short-term financing is needed, the CFO should consider the company's cash flow on a monthly and even weekly basis taking into account economic conditions, timing of receipts and payments, and seasonality.

When compared to long-term financing, how does short-term financing stack up?

Short-term financing has several beneficial aspects including being easier to arrange, being less costly, and having greater flexibility. The drawbacks of short-term financing are that interest rates fluctuate more often, refinancing is usually needed, and the risk of inability to pay along with its associated consequences (e.g., credit rating).

What sources of short-term financing may be tapped?

The CFO may decide to use trade credit, bank loans, bankers' acceptances, finance company loans, commercial paper, receivable financing, and inventory financing. A particular source may be more appropriate in a specific situation. Some sources are more beneficial than others depending upon interest rates and collateral requirements.

What variables have to be taken into account when deciding which short-term financing source to use?

The factors influencing the selection of a particular financing source include:

• *Cost* including interest rate and front-end fees (e.g., legal fees, points).
• *Prepayment penalties.*
• *Impact on financial ratios.*
• *Effect on credit rating.* Some sources of short-term financing may negatively impact the company's credit rating, such as factoring accounts receivable.
• *Risk.* Consider the reliability of the source of funds for future borrowing. If the company is significantly affected by external factors, it will need more stability and reliability in financing.
• *Restrictions.* Certain creditors may impose limitations, such as requiring a minimum working capital.
• *Flexibility.* Certain lenders are more willing to accommodate the company, for example, to periodically adjust the amount of funds needed.
• *Anticipated money market conditions* (e.g., future interest rates) and availability of future financing.
• *Inflation rate.*
• *Profitability and liquidity positions.*
• *Stability and maturity of operations.*
• *Tax rate.*

If the firm will be short of cash during certain periods, the CFO should arrange for financing (such as a line of credit) in advance rather than waiting for a crisis.

How may trade credit best be used?

Trade credit is a spontaneous (recurring) financing source since it comes from normal operations. It is the least costly way to finance inventory. The benefits of trade credit are: it is readily available from suppliers; no collateral requirement; interest is usually nonexistent; it is convenient; and trade creditors are generally tolerant if the company gets into financial straits. If the business has liquidity problems, it may be able to stretch accounts payable; however, among the disadvantages of doing so are the giving up of any cash discount offered and the probability of lowering the company's credit rating. The CFO may prepare a report evaluating accounts payable in terms of lost discounts, aged unpaid invoices, and days to pay.

Should creditors be paid earlier to obtain a cash discount?

It is usually best to take advantage of a cash discount on the early payment of accounts payable because the failure to do so results in a high opportunity cost. The cost of not taking a discount equals:

$$\left(\frac{\text{Discount lost}}{\begin{array}{c}\text{Dollar proceeds you}\\\text{have use of by not}\\\text{taking the discount}\end{array}} \right) \times \left(\frac{360}{\begin{array}{c}\text{Number of days you have}\\\text{use of the money by not}\\\text{taking the discount}\end{array}} \right)$$

EXAMPLE 1

The company buys $100,000 in raw materials on terms of 2/10, net/30. The company fails to take the discount and pays the bill on the 30th day. The cost of the discount is:

$$\frac{\$20,000}{\$980,000} \times \frac{360}{20} = 36.7\%$$

The company is advised to take the discount because the opportunity cost is 36.7%, even if it had to borrow the funds from the bank. The interest rate on a bank loan would be much less than 36.7%.

When are bank loans advisable?

Banks give the business the ability to operate with minimal cash and still be confident of planning activities even in light of uncertainty.

Bank loans are not spontaneous financing as is trade credit. One example is a self-liquidating (seasonal) loan used to pay for a temporary increase in accounts receivable or inventory. As soon as the assets realize cash, the loan is repaid.

Bank financing may take the following forms: unsecured loans, secured loans, lines of credit, and installment loans.

How do unsecured loans work?

Most short-term unsecured (no collateral) loans are self-liquidating. This kind of loan is suggested if the company has an excellent credit rating. It is typically used to finance projects having fast cash flows. It is advisable when the company has immediate cash and can either repay the loan in the near term or quickly obtain longer-term financing. Seasonal cash shortfalls and desired inventory buildups are reasons to use an unsecured loan. The disadvantages of such a loan are that, because it is made for the short term, it has a higher interest rate than a secured loan and payment in a lump sum is required.

When is a collateralized loan necessary?

If the company's credit rating is poor, the bank may require security. Collateral may be in the form of inventory, marketable securities, or fixed assets. *Tip:* Even though the company can obtain an unsecured loan, it may still give security to get a lower interest rate.

How much line of credit can the company get?

Under a line of credit, the bank contracts to lend money on a recurring basis up to a given amount. Credit lines are usually for one year and are renewable. The CFO should determine whether the line of credit is sufficient for current and future needs.

The advantages of a line of credit are the easy and quick availability of funds during credit crunches and the ability to borrow only as much as needed and repay when adequate cash is available. *Recommendation:* Use a line of credit if the company is working on large long-term projects when receipts are minimal or nonexistent until job completion. The disadvantages of a credit line are the collateral requirements and the additional financial disclosure that must be furnished to the bank. Further, the bank may place restrictions upon the company, such as a ceiling on fixed asset acquisitions or the maintenance of a minimum working capital. The bank often imposes a commitment fee on the amount of the unused credit line.

A line of credit agreement may require the company to maintain a compensating balance with the bank. The compensating balance is stated as a percentage of the loan and increases the effective interest rate.

EXAMPLE 2

The company borrows $200,000 and must keep a 12% compensating balance. It also has an unused credit line of $100,000, for which there is a 10% compensating balance. The minimum balance to maintain is:

$$(\$200,000 \times .12) + (\$100,000 \times .10)$$
$$= \$24,000 + \$10,000 = \$34,000$$

The bank may test the company's financial soundness by requiring it to repay the loan for a brief time during the year (e.g., for 1 month). If the company is unable to do so, it should probably finance long-term. The payment shows the bank that the loan is actually seasonal instead of permanent.

Why would a letter of credit be used?

A letter of credit is a conditional bank commitment on behalf of the firm to pay a third party based on specified terms. A payment is made on presentation of proof of shipment or other performance. The advantages of a letter of credit are that the company does not have to pay cash before shipment and funds could be used elsewhere for a return. Banks impose a fee and a rate for bankers' acceptances arising after shipment which approximates the prime interest rate.

What is the benefit of a revolving credit agreement?

A revolving credit arrangement involves short-term notes (usually 90 days). The loan may be renewed or additional funds borrowed up to a maximum amount. The advantages of revolving credit are readily available and fewer restrictions compared to the line-of-credit arrangement.

Is an installment loan advisable?

In an installment loan, there are monthly payments. When the principal on the loan decreases sufficiently, refinancing can occur at a lower interest rate. This loan may be tailored to meet the company's seasonal financing needs.

What is the real cost of borrowing?

Interest on a loan may be paid either at maturity (ordinary interest) or in advance (discounting the loan). When interest is paid in advance, the loan proceeds are reduced and the effective (true) interest cost is increased.

EXAMPLE 3

The company borrows $300,000 at 16% interest per annum on a discount basis. The loan is repaid one year later. The effective interest rate is:

Interest	$= \$300,000 \times .16$	$= \$48,000$
Proceeds	$= \$300,000 - \$48,000$	$= \$252,000$

$$\frac{\text{Effective}}{\text{interest rate}} = \frac{\text{Interest}}{\text{Proceeds}} = \frac{\$48,000}{\$252,000} = 19\%$$

A compensating balance increases the effective interest rate.

EXAMPLE 4

The effective interest rate for a 1-year, $600,000 loan that has a nominal interest rate of 19%, with interest due at maturity and requiring a 15% compensating balance follows.

Effective interest rate (with compensating balance) equals:

$$\frac{\text{Interest rate} \times \text{Principal}}{\text{Proceeds (\%)} \times \text{Principal}} = \frac{.19 \times \$600,000}{(1.00 - .15) \times \$600,000}$$

$$= \frac{\$114,000}{\$510,000} = 22.4\%$$

EXAMPLE 5

Assume the same facts as in the previous example, except that the loan is discounted. The effective interest rate is:

Effective interest rate (with discount) equals:

$$\frac{\text{Interest rate} \times \text{Principal}}{(\text{Proceeds (\%)} \times \text{Principal}) - \text{Interest}}$$

$$\frac{0.19 \times \$600,000}{(0.85 \times \$600,000) - \$114,000} = \frac{\$114,000}{\$396,000} = 28.8\%$$

EXAMPLE 6

The company has a credit line of $400,000 but must keep a compensating balance of 13% on outstanding loans and a compensating balance of 10% on the unused credit. The interest rate on the loan is 18%. The company borrows $275,000. The effective interest rate is computed as follows. The compensating balance is:

$$
\begin{array}{lr}
.13 \times \$275,000 & \$35,750 \\
.10 \times \ \ 125,000 & \underline{12,500} \\
& \overline{\$48,250}
\end{array}
$$

Effective interest rate (with line of credit) equals:

$$\frac{\text{Interest rate (on loan)} \times \text{Principal}}{\text{Principal} - \text{Compensating balance}}$$

$$\frac{0.18 \times \$275,000}{\$275,000 - \$48,250} = \frac{\$49,500}{\$226,750} = 21.8\%$$

The effective interest rate associated with an installment loan is illustrated below. Assume a 1-year loan due in equal monthly installments. The effective rate will be based on the average amount outstanding for the year. The interest is computed on the face amount of the loan.

EXAMPLE 7

The company borrows $400,000 at an interest rate of 10% to be paid in 12 monthly installments. The average loan balance is $400,000/ 2 = $200,000. The effective interest rate is $40,000/$200,000 ≈ 20%.

EXAMPLE 8

Assume the same information as in Example 7 except that the loan is discounted. The interest of $40,000 is deducted in advance so the proceeds received are $400,000 − $40,000 ≈ $360,000. The average loan balance is $360,000/2 ≈ $180,000. The effective interest rate is $40,000/$180,000 ≈ 22.2%.

The effective interest cost computation may be more complicated when there are differing installment payments. The true interest cost of an installment loan is the internal rate of return of the applicable cash flows converted on an annual basis (if desired).

EXAMPLE 9

The company borrows $100,000 and will repay it in 3 monthly installments of $25,000, $25,000, and $50,000. The interest rate is 12%. Amount of borrowing equals:

Installment loan	$100,000
Less: Interest on first installment	
($100,000 × .25 × .12)	3,000
Balance	$ 97,000

Effective interest cost of installment loan equals:

$$0 = -\$97,000 + \$25,000/(1 + \text{Cost})$$
$$+ \$25,000/(1 + \text{Cost})2 + \$50,000/(1 + \text{Cost})3$$

$$= 1.37\% \text{ on monthly basis}$$

$$= 1.37\% \times 12 = 16.44\% \text{ on annual basis}$$

Interest rate hedging may be accomplished with swaps, caps, and collars. These products protect the company from rising interest rates. In a swap, the borrower substitutes a variable interest rate loan for a fixed rate loan. In a cap, the borrower for an upfront fee puts a limit of how high a floating interest rate may go. A collar puts a cap or rising interest rates and a floor on decreasing interest rates. The collar has a lower upfront charge than a cap because of the advantage of falling interest rates to the borrower. The benefits of interest rate hedging are: (1) the company locks in a maximum financing cost; (2) there is more flexibility; and (3) interest rates are known in advance reducing the speculative risk of changing interest rates. These strategies are especially appealing to seasonal borrowers.

What is a banker's acceptance?

A banker's acceptance is a short-term non-interest bearing draft (up to 6 months), drawn by the company and accepted by a bank, that orders payment to a third party at a future date. It is usually issued up to $1 million on a discount basis. The creditworthiness of the draft is of good quality because it has the backing of the bank, not the drawer. It is, in effect, a debt instrument arising from a self-liquidating transaction. Bankers' acceptances are often used to finance the shipment and handling of both domestic and foreign goods. Acceptances typically have maturities of less than 180 days.

Is the company forced to take out a commercial finance loan?

When bank credit is not available, the company may need to contact a commercial finance company. The finance company loan has a higher interest rate than a bank loan, and is typically secured. The amount of collateral will generally be more than the balance of the loan. Commercial finance companies also finance the installment purchases of industrial equipment.

Is the company financially strong enough to issue commercial paper?

Commercial paper can be issued only if the company has a strong credit rating. Therefore, the interest rate is below that of a bank loan, usually ½% less than the prime interest rate. Commercial paper is unsecured and sold at a discount (below face value). The maturity date is typically less than 270 days, otherwise Securities and Exchange Commission (SEC) registration is required. Since the note is issued at a discount, the interest is immediately deducted from the face of the note by the creditor, but the company will pay the full face value. Commercial paper may be issued through a dealer or directly placed to an institutional investor.

The advantages of commercial paper are the absence of collateral, and a lower interest rate. The disadvantage is that commercial paper can be issued only by large, financially secure companies.

EXAMPLE 10

A company's balance sheet appears below:

ASSETS	
Current assets	$ 540,000
Fixed assets	800,000
Total assets	$1,340,000

LIABILITIES AND STOCKHOLDERS' EQUITY	
Current liabilities:	
Notes payable to banks	$ 100,000
Commercial paper	650,000
Total current liabilities	$ 750,000
Long-term liabilities	260,000
Total liabilities	$1,010,000
Stockholders' equity	330,000
Total liabilities and stockholders equity	$1,340,000

The company has issued a high percentage of commercial paper relative to both its current liabilities, 86.7% ($650,000/$750,000), and its total liabilities, 64.4% ($650,000/$1,010,000). The company should probably do more bank borrowing because in a money market squeeze it is advantageous to have a working relationship with a bank.

EXAMPLE 11

The company needs $300,000 for the month of November. Its options are:

1. A one-year line of credit for $300,000 with a bank. The commitment fee is 0.5%, and the interest charge on the used funds is 12%.

2. Issue two-month commercial paper at 10% interest. Because the funds are only needed for one month, the excess funds ($300,000) can be invested in 8% marketable securities for December. The total transaction fee for the marketable securities is 0.3%.

The line of credit costs:

Commitment fee for unused period (0.005)(300,000)(11/12)	$1,375
Interest for one month (0.12)(300,000) (1/12)	3,000
Total cost	$4,375

The commercial paper costs:

Interest charge (0.10)(300,000)(2/12)	$5,000
Transaction fee (0.003)(300,000)	900
Less interest earned on marketable securities (0.08)(300,000)(1/12)	(2,000)
Total cost	$3,900

The commercial paper arrangement is less costly.

Should receivables be used for financing?

In accounts receivable financing, the accounts receivable are the collateral for the loan as well as the source of repayment.

Receivable financing avoids the need for long-term financing and generates recurring cash flow. However, there are high administrative costs when many small accounts exist.

Accounts receivable may be financed under either a factoring or assignment (pledging) arrangement. *Factoring* is the sale of accounts receivable to a finance company *without recourse.* The purchaser assumes all credit and collection risks. The amount received equals the face value of the receivables less the commission charge, which is usually 2 to 4% higher than the prime interest rate. The cost of factoring is the factor's commission for credit investigation, interest on the unpaid balance of advanced funds, and a discount from the face value of the receivables where high credit risk exists. Customer payments are made directly to the factor.

The advantages of factoring are immediate availability of money, reduction in overhead since the credit examination activity is no longer needed, obtaining financial advice, receipt of seasonal advances, and strengthening of the balance sheet position.

The disadvantages of factoring are the high cost and the customer's negative impression because of the change in ownership of the receivables. Further, factors may antagonize customers by their demanding collection methods of delinquent accounts.

In an *assignment* (pledging), there is no transfer of the ownership of the accounts receivable. Receivables are given to a finance company *with recourse.* The finance company typically advances between 50 and 85% of the face value of the receivables in cash. The company incurs a service charge, interest on the advance, and bad debt losses. Customer remissions continue to be made directly to the company.

The assignment of accounts receivable has the advantages of immediate availability of cash, cash advances available on a seasonal basis, and avoidance of negative customer reaction. The disadvantages include the high cost, the continuance of clerical work on the accounts receivable, and the bearing of all credit risk.

The CFO has to recognize the impact of a change in accounts receivable policy on the cost of financing receivables. The cost of financing may rise or fall under different conditions. For example, (1) when credit standards are eased, costs rise; (2) when recourse for defaults is given to the finance company, costs decrease; and (3) when the minimum invoice amount of a credit sale is increased, costs decline.

EXAMPLE 12

A factor will purchase the company's $120,000 per month accounts receivable. The factor will advance up to 80% of the receivables for an annual charge of 14%, and a 1.5% fee on receivables purchased. The cost of this factoring arrangement is:

Factor fee [0.015 × ($120,000 × 12)]	$21,600
Cost of borrowing [0.14 × ($120,000 × 0.8)]	13,440
Total cost	$35,040

EXAMPLE 13

A factor charges a 3% fee per month. The factor lends the company up to 75% of receivables purchased for an additional 1% per month. Credit sales are $400,000 per month. As a result of the factoring arrangement, the company saves $6,500 per month in credit costs and a bad debt expense of 2% of credit sales.

XYZ Bank has offered an arrangement to lend the company up to 75% of the receivables. The bank will charge 2% per month interest plus a 4% processing charge on receivable lending.

The collection period is 30 days. If the company borrows the maximum per month, should it stay with the factor or switch to XYZ Bank?

Cost of factor:

Purchased receivables (0.03 × $400,000)	$12,000
Lending fee (0.01 × $300,000)	3,000
Total cost	$15,000

474

Cost of bank financing:	
Interest (0.02 × $300,000)	$6,000
Processing charge (0.04 × $300,000)	12,000
Additional cost of not using the factor:	
Credit costs	6,500
Bad debts (0.02 × $400,000)	8,000
Total cost	$32,500

The company should stay with the factor.

EXAMPLE 14

A company needs $250,000 and is considering the alternatives of arranging a bank loan or going to a factor. The bank loan terms are 18% interest, discounted, with a compensating balance of 20%. The factor will charge a 4% commission on invoices purchased monthly, and the interest rate on the purchased invoices is 12%, deducted in advance. By using a factor, the company will save $1,000 monthly credit department costs, and uncollectible accounts estimated at 3% of the factored accounts receivable will not occur. Which is the better option?

The bank loan which will net the company its desired $250,000 in proceeds is:

$$\frac{\text{Proceeds}}{(100\% - \text{Proceeds deducted})} = \frac{\$250,000}{100\% - (18\% + 20\%)}$$

$$\frac{\$250,000}{1.0 - 0.38} = \frac{\$250,000}{0.62} = \$403,226$$

The effective interest rate of the bank loan is:

$$\text{Effective interest rate} = \frac{\text{Interest rate}}{\text{Proceeds (\%)}} = \frac{.18}{.62} = 29.0\%$$

The amount of accounts receivable that should be factored to net the firm $250,000 is:

$$\frac{\$250,000}{1.0 - 0.16} = \frac{\$250,000}{0.84} = \$297,619$$

The total annual cost of the bank arrangement is:

Interest ($250,000 × 0.29)	$72,500
Additional cost of not using a factor:	
Credit costs ($1,000 × 12)	12,000
Uncollectible accounts ($297,619 × 0.03)	8,929
Total cost	$93,429

The effective interest rate associated with factoring accounts receivable is:

$$\text{Effective interest rate} = \frac{\text{Interest rate}}{\text{Proceeds (\%)}}$$

$$= \frac{12\%}{100\% - (12\% + 4\%)}$$

$$= \frac{0.12}{0.84} = 14.3\%$$

The total annual cost of the factoring alternative is:

Interest ($250,000 × 0.143)	$35,750
Factoring ($297,619 × 0.04)	11,905
Total cost	$47,655

The factoring arrangement should be selected because it costs almost half as much as the bank loan.

EXAMPLE 15

A company is examining a factoring arrangement. The company's sales are $2,700,000, accounts receivable turnover is 9 times, and a 17% reserve on accounts receivable is required. The factor's commission charge on average accounts receivable payable at the point of receivable purchase is 2.0%. The factor's interest charge is 16% of receivables after subtracting the commission charge and reserve. The interest charge reduces the advance. The annual effective cost under the factoring arrangement is computed next.

$$\frac{\text{Average accounts}}{\text{receivable}} = \frac{\text{Credit sales}}{\text{Turnover}}$$

$$= \frac{\$2,700,000}{9} = \$300,000$$

The company will receive the following amount by factoring its accounts receivable:

Average accounts receivable	$300,000
Less: Reserve ($300,000 × 0.17)	−51,000
Commission ($300,000 × 0.02)	−6,000
Net prior to interest	$243,000
Less: Interest ($243,000 × (16%/9)	4,320
Proceeds received	$238,680

The annual cost of the factoring arrangement is:

Commission ($300,000 × 0.02)	$ 6,000
Interest ($243,000 × (16%/9)	4,320
Cost each 40 days (360/9)	$10,320
Turnover	× 9
Total annual cost	$92,880

The annual effective cost under the factoring arrangement based on the amount received is:

$$\frac{\text{Annual cost}}{\text{Average amount received}} = \frac{\$92,880}{\$238,680} = 38.9\%$$

Should inventories be used for financing?

Inventory may be financed when the company has fully exhausted its borrowing capacity on receivables. Inventory financing requires marketable, nonperishable, and standardized merchandise with a fast turnover. The goods should not be susceptible to rapid obsolescence. Inventory is of better collateral if it can be marketed apart from the company's marketing organization. Inventory financing should take into account the price stability of the product and its selling costs.

The advance is high when marketable inventory exists. In general, the financing of raw materials and finished goods is about 75% of their value. The interest rate approximates 3 to 5 points over the prime interest rate.

The drawbacks to inventory financing include the high interest rate and the inventory restrictions.

The types of inventory financing include a floating (blanket) lien, warehouse receipt, and trust receipt. A *floating lien* has the creditor's security in the aggregate inventory rather than in its components. Even though the company sells and restocks, the lender's security interest continues. A *warehouse receipt* has the lender obtain an interest in the inventory stored at a public warehouse; however, the fixed costs of this arrangement are high. In a field warehouse arrangement, the warehouser provides a secured area at the company's location. The company has access to the goods but must account for them. A *trust receipt* loan is when the creditor has title to the goods but releases them to the company to sell on the creditor's behalf. As merchandise are sold, the company remits the funds to the lender. An example of trust receipt use is automobile dealer financing. The drawback of the trust receipt arrangement is that it only applies to specific items.

A collateral certificate may be issued by a third party to the lender guaranteeing the existence of pledged inventory. The advantage of a collateral certificate is flexibility because merchandise does not have to be segregated or possessed by the lender.

EXAMPLE 16

The company wants to finance $500,000 of inventory. Funds are required for 3 months. A warehouse receipt loan may be taken at 16% with a 90% advance against the inventory's value. The warehousing cost is $4,000 for the 3-month period. The cost of financing the inventory is:

Interest [$0.16 \times 0.90 \times \$500,000 \times (3/12)$]	$18,000
Warehousing cost	4,000
Total cost	$22,000

EXAMPLE 17

The company experiences growth in operations but is having liquidity problems. Six large
financially strong companies are customers, being responsible for 75% of sales. On the basis of
the below financial information for 19X1,
should the company borrow on receivables or inventory? (See Figure 24–1.)

Selected income statement information follows:

Sales	$1,800,000
Net income	130,000

FIGURE 24–1 BALANCE SHEET

ASSETS		
Current assets		
Cash	$ 27,000	
Receivables	380,000	
Inventory (consisting of 55% of work-in-process)	320,000	
Total current assets		$727,000
Fixed assets		250,000
Total assets		$977,000

LIABILITIES AND STOCKHOLDERS' EQUITY		
Current liabilities		
Accounts payable	$260,000	
Loans payable	200,000	
Accrued expenses	35,000	
Total current liabilities		$495,000
Noncurrent liabilities		
Bonds payable		110,000
Total liabilities		$605,000
Stockholders' equity		
Common stock	$250,000	
Retained earnings	122,000	
Total stockholders' equity		372,000
Total liabilities and stockholders' equity		$977,000

Receivable financing should be used since a high percentage of sales are made to only six large financially strong companies. Receivables appear collectible. It is easier to control a few large customer accounts.

Inventory financing is not likely because of the high percentage of partially completed items. Lenders are reluctant to finance inventory when there is a large work-in-process balance because the goods will be difficult to process and sell by lenders.

What other assets may be used for financing?

Assets other than inventory and receivables may be used as collateral for short-term bank loans such as real estate, plant and equipment, cash surrender value of life insurance, and securities. Lenders are usually receptive to advance a high percentage of the market value of bonds. Further, loans may be made based on a guaranty of a third party. Major features of short-term financing sources are presented in Table 24–1.

How is short-term financing different from long-term financing?

Short-term financing is easier to obtain, has lower cost, and is more flexible than long-term financing. However, short-term financing makes the borrower susceptible to interest rate fluctuations, requires earlier refinancing, and is more difficult to repay. *Recommendation:* Use short-term financing as additional working capital, finance short-lived assets, or as interim financing on long-term projects. Long-term financing is suitable to finance long-term assets or construction projects.

INTERMEDIATE-TERM FINANCING ⎯⎯⎯⎯

Should you take out an intermediate-term bank loan?

Intermediate-term loans mature in more than one year. They are suitable when short-term unsecured loans are not, such as when a business is bought, capital assets are purchased, and

TABLE 24-1 SUMMARY OF MAJOR SHORT-TERM FINANCING SOURCES

Type of Financing	Source	Cost or Terms	Features
A. Spontaneous Sources			
Accounts payable	Suppliers	No explicit cost but there is an opportunity cost if a cash discount for early payment is not taken. Companies should take advantage of the discount offered.	The main source of short-term financing typically on terms of 0 to 120 days.
Accrued expenses	Employees and tax agencies	None	Expenses incurred but not yet paid (e.g., accrued wages payable, accrued taxes payable).
B. Unsecured Sources			
Bank loans			
Single-payment note	Commercial banks	Prime interest rate plus risk premium. The interest rate may be fixed or variable. Unsecured loans are less costly than secured loans.	A single-payment loan to satisfy a funds shortage to last a short time period.
Lines of credit	Commercial banks	Prime interest rate plus risk premium. The interest rate may be fixed or variable. A compensating balance is typically required. The line of credit must be "cleaned up" periodically.	An agreed-upon borrowing limit for funds to satisfy seasonal needs.
Commercial paper	Commercial banks, insurance companies, other financial institutions, and other companies	A little less than the prime interest rate.	Unsecured, short-term note of financially strong companies.

C. Secured Sources

Accounts receivable as collateral

	Source	Cost	Description
Pledging	Commercial banks and finance companies	2% to 5% above prime plus fees (usually 2%–3%). Low administrative costs. Advances typically ranging from 60% to 85%.	Qualified accounts receivable accounts serve as collateral. Upon collection of the account, the borrower remits to the lender. Customers are not notified of the arrangement. With recourse meaning that the risk of nonpayment is borne by the company.
Factoring	Factors, commercial banks, and commercial finance companies	Typically a 2%–3% discount from the face value of factored receivables. Interest on advances of almost 3% over prime. Interest on surplus balances held by factor of about 1/2% per month. Costs with factoring are higher than with pledging.	Certain accounts receivable are sold on a discount basis without recourse. Customers are notified of the arrangement. The factor provides more services than is the case with pledging.

Inventory collateral

	Source	Cost	Description
Floating liens	Commercial banks and commercial finance companies	About 4% above prime. Advance is about 40% of collateral value.	Collateral is all the inventory. There should be a stable inventory with many inexpensive items.
Trust receipts (floor planning)	Commercial banks and commercial finance companies	About 3% above prime. Advances ranging from 80% to 100% of collateral value.	Collateral is specific inventory that is typically expensive. Borrower retains collateral. Borrower remits proceeds to lender upon sale of the inventory.
Warehouse receipts	Commercial banks and commercial finance companies	About 4% above prime plus about a 2% warehouse fee. Advance of about 80% of collateral value.	Collateralized inventory is controlled by lender. A warehousing company issues a warehouse receipt hold by the lender. The warehousing company acts as the lender's agent.

long-term debt is retired. If a company wants to issue long-term debt or equity securities but market conditions are unfavorable, it may take an intermediate loan to bridge the gap until long-term financing can be arranged on favorable terms. A firm may employ extendable debt when there is a continuing financing need. This reduces the time and cost of many debt issuances.

The interest rate on an intermediate-term loan is usually more than on a short-term loan because of the longer maturity. The interest rate may be either fixed or variable (e.g., based on changes in the prime interest rate). The cost of an intermediate-term loan depends on the amount of the loan and the company's financial standing.

Ordinary intermediate-term loans are due in periodic equal installments except for the last payment, which may be higher (referred to as a balloon payment). The schedule of loan payments should be based on the company's cash flow status. The periodic payment equals:

$$\text{Periodic payment} = \frac{\text{Amount of loan}}{\text{Present value factor}}$$

EXAMPLE 18

The company contracts to repay a term loan in five equal year-end installments. The amount of the loan is $150,000 and the interest rate is 10%. The payment each year is:

$$\frac{\$150,000}{3.7908^*} = \$39,569.48$$

*Present value of annuity for 5 years at 10%.

The total interest on the loan is:

Total payments (5 × $39,569.48)	$197,847.40
Principal	150,000.00
Interest	$ 47,847.40

EXAMPLE 19

The company takes out a term loan in 20 year-end annual installments of $2,000 each. The interest rate is 12%. The amount of the loan is:

$$\$2,000 = \frac{\text{Amount of loan}}{7.4694*}$$

Amount of loan = $\$2,000 \times 7.4694 = \$14,939.80$

Present value of annuity for 20 years at 12%.

The amortization schedule for the first 2 years is:

Year	Payment	Interest*	Principal	Balance
0				$14,938.80
1	$2,000	$1,792.66	$207.34	14,731.46
2	2,000	1,767.78	232.22	14,499.24

12% times the balance of the loan at the beginning of the year.

What restrictions does the company face?

Restrictive provisions that the lender may insist upon in an intermediate-term loan are:

• General provisions used in most agreements which vary based upon the company's financial position. Examples are current ratio and debt-equity ratio.

• Routine (uniform) provisions that are used universally in most agreements. Examples are the payment of taxes and the maintenance of insurance to assure maximum lender protection.

• Specific provisions tailored to a particular situation. Examples are the placing of limits on future loans and the carrying of adequate life insurance for executives.

What are the advantages and disadvantages of intermediate-term loans?

The advantages of intermediate-term loans are:

• Flexibility in that the terms may be changed as the company's financing requirements change.

• Financial information is kept confidential because there is no public issuance.

• The loan may be arranged quickly compared to a public offering.

- Avoids the possible nonrenewal of a short-term loan.
- There are no public flotation costs.

The disadvantages of intermediate-term loans are:

- Collateral and possible restrictive covenants are required, as opposed to none for commercial paper and unsecured short-term bank loans.
- Budgets and financial statements may have to be routinely submitted to the lender.
- "Sweeteners" such as stock warrants or a share of the profits are sometimes asked for by the bank.

What is a revolving credit agreement?

Revolving credit, typically used for seasonal financing, may have a 3-year maturity, but the notes are short-term, usually 90 days. The advantages of revolving credit are flexibility and ready availability. The company may renew a loan or enter into additional financing up to a maximum amount. A revolving credit agreement usually has less restrictions than a line of credit but there is a slightly higher interest rate.

How may an insurance company term loan be used?

Insurance companies and other institutional lenders may extend intermediate-term loans. Insurance companies usually accept loan maturity dates exceeding 10 years, but their rate of interest is often higher than that of bank loans. Insurance companies do not require compensating balances, but usually there is a prepayment penalty, which is often not the case with a bank loan. A company may take out an insurance company loan when it wants a longer maturity period.

How does equipment financing work?

Equipment may serve as security for a loan. An advance is made against the market value of the equipment. The more marketable the equipment is, the higher the advance will be. The cost of selling the equipment is also relevant. The repayment schedule is structured so that the market value of the equipment at any time exceeds the unpaid loan principal.

Equipment financing may be obtained from banks, finance companies, and equipment manufacturers. Equipment loans may be collateralized by a chattel mortgage or a conditional sales contract. A chattel mortgage is a lien on property except for real estate. A *conditional sales contract* is when the seller of the equipment keeps title to it until the buyer has met the terms; otherwise the seller repossesses the equipment. The buyer makes periodic payments over a given time period. A conditional sales contract is usually used by a small company with a poor credit standing.

Equipment trust certificates may be issued to finance the acquisition of readily salable equipment. Preferably, the equipment should be general purpose and movable. A trust is formed to buy the equipment and lease it to the user. The trust issues the certificates to finance about 80% of the purchase price and holds title to the equipment until *all* the certificates have been repaid at which time the title passes to the lessee.

Are you better-off leasing?

The lessee uses property in exchange for making rental payments. The advantages of leasing are:

• Immediate cash payment is not required.

• Provides for *temporary* equipment need and flexibility in operations.

• A purchase option may exist allowing the company to obtain the property at a bargain price at the termination date of the lease. This provides the flexibility to make the purchase decision based on the value of the property at the expiration date.

• Lessor's service capability is used.

• There are usually less financing restrictions (e.g., limitations on dividends) by the lessor compared to a lender.

- Obligation for future rental payment does not have to be reported as a liability on the balance sheet for an *operating lease.*
- Leasing permits the company, in effect, to depreciate land, which is not allowed if land is bought.
- In bankruptcy or reorganization, the maximum claim of lessors is 3 years of rental payments. With debt, creditors have a claim for the entire balance.
- Eliminates equipment disposal.

Leasing may be better than buying when a company cannot use all of the tax deductions and tax credits associated with the assets in a timely fashion.

The drawbacks to leasing are:

- Higher cost than if the asset is bought. The lessee is not building equity.
- Interest cost of leasing is usually higher than the interest cost on debt.
- If the property reverts to the lessor at the end of the lease, the lessee must either sign a new lease or buy the property at higher current prices. Further, the salvage value of the property is realized by the lessor.
- May have to keep property no longer desired (i.e., obsolete equipment).
- Unable to make improvements to the leased property without the lessor's consent.

EXAMPLE 20

The company enters into a lease for a $100,000 machine. It is to make 10 equal annual payments at year-end. The interest rate on the lease is 14%. The periodic payment equals:

$$\frac{\$100,000}{5.2161^*} = \$19,171$$

*The present value of an ordinary annuity factor for $n = 10$, $i = 14\%$ is 5.2161.

EXAMPLE 21

Assume the same facts as in Example 19, except that now the annual payments are to be made at the beginning of each year. The periodic payment equals:

Year	Factor
0	1.0
1–9	4.9464
	5.9464

$$\frac{\$100,000}{5.9464} = \$16,817$$

The interest rate on a lease can be computed. Divide the value of the leased property by the annual payment to obtain the factor, which is then used to find the interest rate with the aid of an annuity table.

EXAMPLE 22

The company leased $300,000 of property and is to make equal annual payments at year-end of $40,000 for 11 years. The interest rate on the lease agreement is:

$$\frac{\$300,000}{\$40,000} = 7.5$$

Going to the present value of annuity table and looking across 11 years to a factor nearest to 7.5, we find 7.4987 at a 7% interest rate. Thus, the interest rate in the lease agreement is 7%.

The capitalized value of a lease can be found by dividing the annual lease payment by an appropriate present value of annuity factor.

EXAMPLE 23

Property is to be leased for 8 years at an annual rental payment of $140,000 payable at the beginning of each year. The capitalization rate is 12%. The capitalized value of the lease is:

$$\frac{\text{Annual lease payment}}{\text{Present value factor}} = \frac{\$140,000}{1 + 4.5638} = \$25,163$$

Is it cheaper to buy or lease an asset?

A decision may have to be made whether it is cheaper to buy an asset or lease it. Present value analysis may be used for this purpose (see Chapter 14).

25

Long-Term Financing

Long-term financing is for more than five years. The CFO should be familiar with the what, why, and how of equity and long-term debt financing. Equity financing consists of issuing preferred stock and common stock while long-term debt financing consists primarily of issuing bonds. Long-term financing is often used to finance long-lived assets (e.g., plant) or construction projects. A capital intensive business will have a greater reliance on long-term debt and equity. A comparison of public versus private placement of securities is given. The advantages and disadvantages of issuing long-term debt, preferred stock, and common stock are presented. The financing strategy most appropriate under a set of circumstances is discussed. The financing policies should be in response to the overall strategic direction of the company.

A company's mix of long-term funds is referred to as the *capital structure.* The ideal capital structure maximizes the total value of the company and minimizes the overall cost of capital. The formulation of an appropriate capital structure takes into account the nature of the business and industry, corporate business plan, current and historical capital structure, and planned growth rate.

Should securities be publicly or privately placed?

Equity and debt securities may be issued either publicly or privately. A consideration in determining whether to issue securities to the public or privately is the type and amount of required financing.

In a public issuance, the shares are bought by the general public. In a private placement, the company issues securities directly to either one or a few large institutional investors.

Private placement has the following advantages relative to a public issuance:

• The flotation cost is less. It is the expense of registering and selling the stock issue. The flotation cost for common stock exceeds that for preferred stock. The flotation cost expressed as a percentage of gross proceeds is higher for smaller issues than for larger ones.

• It avoids SEC filing requirements.

• It avoids the disclosure of information to the public.

• There is less time involved in obtaining funds.

• There is greater flexibility.

Private placement has the following drawbacks relative to a public issuance:

• There is a higher interest rate due to less liquidity of a debt issue relative to public issuance.

• There is typically a shorter maturity period than for a public issue.

• It is more difficult to obtain significant amounts of money privately than publicly.

• Large investors typically use stringent credit standards requiring the company to be in strong financial condition. In addition, there are more restrictive terms.

• Large institutional investors may watch more closely the company's activities than smaller investors in a public issue.

• Large institutional investors are more capable of obtaining voting control of the company.

TYPES OF LONG-TERM DEBT AND WHEN EACH SHOULD BE USED _____

We now discuss the characteristics, advantages, and disadvantages of long-term debt financing. In addition to the various types of debt instruments, the circumstances in which a particular type of debt is most appropriate are mentioned. Sources of long-term debt include mortgages and bonds. The amount of debt a company may have depends largely on its available collateral. Bond refunding is also discussed.

What should you know about mortgages?

Mortgages are notes payable that have as collateral real assets and require periodic payments. Mortgages can be undertaken to finance the purchase of assets, construction of plant, and modernization of facilities. The bank will require that the value of the property exceed the mortgage on that property. Most mortgage loans are for between 70% and 90% of the value of the collateral. Mortgages may be obtained from a financial institution, typically a bank. It is easier to obtain mortgage loans for multiple-use real assets than for single-use ones.

There are two types of mortgages: a *senior* mortgage, which has first claim on assets and earnings, and a *junior* mortgage, which has a subordinate lien.

A mortgage may have a closed-end provision that prevents the company from issuing additional debt of the same priority against the specific property. If the mortgage is open-ended, the company can issue additional first-mortgage bonds against the property.

Mortgages have a number of advantages, including favorable interest rates, less financing restrictions, extended maturity date, and availability. A drawback is the collateral requirement.

When should bonds be issued?

The *indenture* describes the features of the bond issue. It may provide for certain restrictions on the company such as a limitation on dividends and minimum working capital requirements. If a provision of the indenture is violated, the bonds are in default. The indenture may have a negative pledge clause, which precludes the issuance of new debt taking priority over existing debt. The clause can apply to currently-held and future assets.

The price of a bond depends on several factors such as maturity date, interest rate, and collateral. In selecting a maturity date, consider the debt repayment schedule which should not be overloaded at one time. Further, if the company's credit rating is expected to improve in the near term, short-term debt should be issued because the company will be able to refinance at a lower interest rate.

Bond prices and market interest rates are inversely related. For example, as market interest rates increase, the price of the existing bond falls because investors can invest in new bonds paying higher interest rates.

What types of bonds may be issued?

The various types of bonds are:

• *Debentures:* Because debentures are unsecured (no collateral) debt, they can be issued only by large, financially strong companies with excellent credit ratings.

• *Subordinated Debentures:* The claims of the holders of these bonds are subordinated to those of senior creditors. Debt having a prior claim over the subordinated debentures is set forth in the bond indenture. Typically, in liquidation, subordinated debentures come after short-term debt.

• *Mortgage Bonds:* These are bonds secured by real assets. The first-mortgage claim must be met before a distribution is made to a second-mortgage claim. There may be several mortgages for the same property (e.g., building).

• *Collateral Trust Bonds:* The collateral for these bonds is the company's security investments in other companies (bonds or stocks), which are given to a trustee for safekeeping.

• *Convertible Bonds:* These may be converted to stock at a later date based on a specified conversion ratio. The *conversion ratio* equals the par value of the convertible security divided by the conversion price. Convertible bonds are typically issued in the form of subordinated debentures. Convertible bonds are more marketable and are typically issued at a lower interest rate than are regular bonds because they offer the *conversion right* to common stock. Of course, if bonds are converted to stock, debt repayment is not involved. A convertible bond is a quasi-equity security because its market value is tied to its value if converted rather than as a bond.

- *Income Bonds:* These bonds pay interest only if there is a profit. The interest may be cumulative or noncumulative. If cumulative, the interest accumulates regardless of earnings, and if bypassed, must be paid in a later year when adequate earnings exist. Income bonds are appropriate for companies with large fixed capital investments and large fluctuations in earnings, or for emerging companies with the expectation of low earnings in the early years.

- *Guaranteed Bonds:* These are debt issued by one party with payment guaranteed by another.

- *Serial Bonds:* A portion of these bonds comes due each year. At the time serial bonds are issued, a schedule shows the yields, interest rates, and prices for each maturity. The interest rate on the shorter maturities is lower than the interest rate on the longer maturities because less uncertainty exists regarding the future.

- *Deep Discount Bonds:* These bonds have very low interest rates and thus are issued at substantial discounts from face value. The return to the holder comes primarily from appreciation in price rather than from interest payments. The bonds are volatile in price. Since these bonds are typically callable at par, this reduces the refunding flexibility of the issuer.

- *Zero Coupon Bonds:* These bonds do not provide for interest. The return to the holder is in the form of appreciation in price. *Note:* Lower interest rates may be available for zero coupon bonds (and deep discount bonds) because of the lack of callability and possible foreign tax laws.

- *Variable Rate Bonds:* The interest rates on the bonds are adjusted periodically to changes in money market conditions (e.g., prime interest rate). These bonds are popular when there is uncertainty of future interest rates and inflation.

- *Deferred Interest Bonds:* Bonds in which the periodic interest payments are fully or partially deferred in the first few years (usually 3–7 years). In another version, the bond payments lower coupons during the deferred years and higher (stepped-up) coupons in later years. They may be used in a buyout or financial restructuring arrangement. The deferred period allows the issuer to improve operations, sell-off assets, and refinance. The bonds are typically subordinated, have a call feature, and provide a conversion option. In deciding whether this type of bond is suitable, the issuer should consider anticipated future interest rates, current debt position, and expected future cash flows.

• *Eurobonds:* Bonds issued outside the country in whose currency the bonds are denominated. Eurobonds cannot be issued to U.S. investors but only to foreign investors because they are not registered with the Securities and Exchange Commission. The bonds are typically in bearer form. *Tip:* Check to see if at the present time the Eurodollar market will give the company a lower cost option than the U.S. market. These bonds usually can only be issued by high quality borrowers.

A summary of the characteristics and priority claims of bonds appears in Table 25–1.

If the company is small and emerging with an unproven track record, it may have to issue "junk bonds" (high-yielding risky bonds).

What are the advantages and disadvantages to debt financing?

The advantages of issuing long-term debt include:

• Interest is tax-deductible but dividends are not.

• Bondholders do not share in superior earnings of the company.

• The repayment of debt is in cheaper dollars during inflation.

• There is no dilution of company control.

• Financing flexibility can be accomplished by including a call provision in the bond indenture which allows the company to retire the debt before maturity.

TABLE 25-1 SUMMARY OF CHARACTERISTICS AND PRIORITY CLAIMS OF BONDS

Bond Type	Characteristics	Priority of Lender's Claim
Debentures	Available only to financially strong companies. Convertible bonds are typically debentures	General creditor
Subordinated Debentures	Comes after senior debt holders	General creditor
Mortgage Bonds	Collateral is real property or buildings	Paid from the proceeds from the sale of the mortgaged assets. If any deficiency exists, general creditor status applies
Collateral Trust Bonds	Secured by stock and(or) bonds owned by the issuer. Collateral value is usually 30% more than bond value	Paid from the proceeds of stock and(or) bond that is collateralized. If there is a deficiency, general creditor status applies.
Income Bonds	Interest is only paid if there is net income. Often issued when a company is in reorganization because of financial problems	General creditor
Deep Discount (and Zero Coupon) Bonds	Issued at very low or no (zero) coupon rates. Issued at prices significantly below face value. Usually callable at par value.	Unsecured or secured status may apply depending on the features of the issue
Variable Rate Bonds	Coupon rate changes within limits based on changes in money or capital market rates. Appropriate when uncertainty exists regarding inflation and future interest rates. Because of the automatic adjustment to changing market conditions, the bonds sell near face value	Unsecured or secured status may apply depending on the features of the issue

• It may safeguard the company's financial stability, for example, in tight money markets when short-term loans are not available.

The disadvantages of issuing long-term debt include:

- Interest must be paid even if profits are low or there are losses.
- Debt must be repaid at maturity.
- Higher debt indicates financial risk which may increase the interest cost.
- Indenture provisions may place stringent restrictions on the company.
- Overcommitments may arise because of forecasting errors.

How does issuing debt compare with issuing equity securities?

The advantages of issuing debt instead of equity are that interest is tax deductible whereas dividends are not, during inflation the payback will be in cheaper dollars, there is no dilution of voting control, and flexibility in financing is possible by including a call provision in the bond indenture. The disadvantages of issuing debt rather than equity are that interest and principal must be paid regardless of the company's cash flow, and indenture restrictions often exist.

The mixture of long-term debt to equity depends on company policy, credit availability, and after-tax cost of financing. When debt is high, the company should minimize other corporate risks (e.g., product risk). The amount of leverage in the capital structure depends upon the company's inclination toward risk and the debt levels at competing companies.

When should long-term debt be issued?

Debt financing is appropriate when:

• The interest rate on debt is below the rate of return earned on the money borrowed. By using other people's money (OPM), corporate after-tax profit will increase.

• There is stability in revenue and earnings so that the company will be able to pay interest and principal in both good and bad years. However, cyclicality should not prevent a company from having any debt. The important thing is to accumulate no more interest and principal obligations than you can handle in bad times.

• The profit margin is satisfactory so that earnings are sufficient to meet debt obligations.

• The company's cash flow and liquidity are adequate.

• The debt/equity ratio is low so the company can absorb additional obligations.

• There is a low risk level.

• Stock prices are depressed so that it is not advisable to issue common stock at the current time.

• There is a concern that if common stock was issued greater control might fall in the wrong hands.

• The company is mature.

• Inflation is expected so that debt can be paid back in cheaper dollars.

• A lack of competition exists such as barriers of entry into the industry.

• The company is growing.

• There is a high tax rate making the deductibility of interest attractive.

• Bond indenture restrictions are not excessive.

• The money market trends are favorable to obtain financing.

What if there are financing problems?

If your company may want to refinance short-term debt on a long-term basis (such as by extending the maturity dates of loans) to alleviate current liquidity and cash flow problems.

As the default risk of your company becomes higher, so will the interest rate to compensate for the greater risk.

The threat of financial distress or even bankruptcy is the ultimate limitation on leverage. Beyond a debt limit, the tax savings on interest expense will be offset by an increased interest rate demanded by creditors for the greater risk. Excessive debt may lower the market price of stock because of the greater risk associated with it.

Should bonds be refunded?

Bonds may be refunded prior to maturity by either issuing a serial bond or exercising a call privilege on a straight bond. The issuance of serial bonds permits the company to refund the debt over the life of the issue. A call feature allows the company to retire a bond before the expiration date.

If future interest rates are expected to decrease, a call provision is advisable since the company can buy back the higher-interest bond and issue a lower-interest one. The timing for the refunding depends on expected future interest rates. A call price is usually established above the face value of the bond. The resulting call *premium* equals the difference between the call price and the maturity value. The company pays the premium to the bondholder in order to acquire the outstanding bonds before the maturity date. The call premium is typically equal to one year's interest if the bond is called in the first year, and it declines at a constant rate each subsequent year.

A callable bond usually has a lower offering price, and will be issued at an interest rate higher than one without the call provision.

EXAMPLE 1

Your company has a $20 million, 10% bond issue outstanding that has 10 years to maturity. The call premium is 7% of face value. The company can issue 10-year bonds in the amount of $20 million at an 8% interest rate. The flotation costs of the new issue are $600,000.

There should be refunding of the original bond issue as shown next:

Old interest payments
($20,000,000 × 0.10) $2,000,000

New interest payments		
($20,000,000 × 0.08)		1,600,000
Annual savings		$ 400,000
Call premium ($20,000,000 × 0.07)		$1,400,000
Flotation cost		600,000
Total cost		$2,000,000

Year	Calculation	Present Value
0	−$2,000,000 × 1	−$2,000,000
1–10	$ 400,000 × 6.71*	2,684,000
Net present value		$ 684,000

Present value of annuity factor for i = 8%, n = 10.

EXAMPLE 2

Your company is considering calling a $10 million, 20-year bond that was issued 5 years ago at a nominal interest rate of 10%. The call price on the bonds is 105. The bonds were initially sold at 90. The discount on bonds payable at the time of sale was, therefore, $1 million and the net proceeds received were $9 million. The initial flotation cost was $100,000. The firm is considering issuing $10 million, 8 percent, 15-year bonds and using the net proceeds to retire the old bonds. The new bonds will be issued at face value. The flotation cost for the new issue is $150,000. The company's tax rate is 46 percent. The after-tax cost of new debt ignoring flotation costs, is 4.32% (8% × 54%). With the flotation cost, the after-tax cost of new debt is estimated at 5%. There is an overlap period of 3 months in which interest must be paid on the old and new bonds.

The initial cash outlay is:

Cost to call old bonds	
($10,000,000 × 105%)	$10,500,000
Cost to issue new bond	150,000
Interest on old bonds for overlap	
period ($10,000,000 × 10% × 3/12)	250,000
Initial cash outlay	$10,900,000

The initial cash inflow is:

Proceeds from selling new bond		$10,000,000
Tax-deductible items		
Call premium	$500,000	
Unamortized discount ($1,000,000 × 15/20)	750,000	
Overlap in interest ($10,000,000 × 10% ×3/12)	250,000	
Unamortized issue cost of old bond ($100,000 × 15/20)	75,000	
Total tax-deductible items	$1,575,000	
Tax rate	× 0.46	
Tax savings		724,500
Initial cash inflow		$10,724,500

The *net* initial cash outlay is therefore:

Initial cash outlay	$10,900,000
Initial cash inflow	10,724,500
Net initial cash outlay	$ 175,500

The annual cash flow for the old bond is:

Interest (10% × $10,000,000)		$1,000,000
Less: Tax-deductible items		
Interest	$1,000,000	
Amortization of discount ($1,000,000/20 years)	50,000	
Amortization of issue cost ($100,000/20 years)	5,000	
Total tax-deductible items	$1,055,000	
Tax rate	× 0.46	
Tax savings		485,300
Annual cash outflow with old bond		$ 514,700

The annual cash flow for the new bond is:

Interest		$800,000
Less: Tax-deductible items		
Interest	$800,000	

Amortization of issue cost		
($150,000/15 years)	10,000	
Total tax-deductible items	$810,000	
Tax rate	× 0.46	
Tax savings		372,600
Annual cash outflow with new bond		$427,400

The net annual cash savings with the new bond compared to the old bond is:

Annual cash outflow with old bond	$514,700
Annual cash outflow with new bond	427,400
Net annual cash savings	$ 87,300

The net present value associated with the refunding is:

	Calculation	Present Value
Year 0	−$175,500 × 1	−$175,500
Years 1–15	$87,300 × 10.38*	+906,174
Net present value		$730,674

Present value of annuity factor for i = 5%, n = 15.

Since a positive net present value exists, the refunding of the old bond should be made.

What are variable notes?

Variable coupon renewable notes are long-term financing instruments with the potential of significant cost savings. They are usually for 50 years and contain a put feature allowing note holders to accept a reduced coupon spread for the last three payments. The coupon is changed weekly based on a spread over the rates for three-month treasury bills. Interest is paid quarterly. The issuer may use this as a long-term financing source while paying short-term interest rates.

THE ISSUANCE OF EQUITY SECURITIES _____

The sources of equity financing consist of preferred stock and common stock. The advantages and disadvantages of issuing preferred and common are addressed, along with the various circumstances in which either financing source is most suited. Stock rights are also described.

When should preferred stock be issued?

Preferred stock is a hybrid between bonds and common stock. Preferred stock comes after debt but before common stock in liquidation and in the distribution of earnings. Preferred stock may be issued when the cost of common stock is high. The best time to issue preferred stock is when the company has excessive debt and an issue of common stock might cause control problems. Preferred stock is a more expensive way to raise funds than a bond issue because the dividend payment is not tax-deductible.

Preferred stock may be cumulative or noncumulative. *Cumulative* preferred stock means that if any prior year's dividend payments have been missed, they must be paid before dividends can be paid to common stockholders. If preferred dividends are in arrears for a long time, the company may find it difficult to resume its dividend payments to common stockholders. With *noncumulative* preferred stock, the company need not pay missed preferred dividends. Preferred stock dividends are limited to the rate specified, which is based on the total par value of the outstanding shares. Most preferred stock is cumulative.

Participating preferred stock means that if declared dividends exceed the amount typically given to preferred stockholders and common stockholders, the preferred and common stockholders will participate in the excess dividends. Unless stated otherwise, the distribution of the excess dividends will be based on the relative total par values. Nonparticipating preferred stock does *not* participate with common stock in excess dividends. Most preferred stock is nonparticipating.

Preferred stock may be callable. The call provision is beneficial when interest rates decline because the company has the option of discontinuing payment of dividends at a rate that has become excessive by buying back preferred stock that was issued when bond interest rates were high. Unlike bonds, preferred stock *rarely* has a maturity date. However, if preferred stock has a sinking fund provision, this establishes a maturity date for repayment.

There are different types of preferred stock. Limited life preferred stock has a maturity date or can be redeemed at the holder's option. Perpetual preferred stock automatically converts to common stock at a specified date. There are also preferred stock with "floating rate" dividends so as to keep the preferred stock at par by changing the dividend rate.

The cost of preferred stock is typically tied to changes in interest rates. The cost of preferred stock will most likely be low when interest rates are low. When the cost of common stock is high, preferred stock issuance may be at a lower cost.

What are the advantages and disadvantages of issuing preferred stock?

A preferred stock issue has the following advantages:

• Preferred dividends do not have to be paid (important in times of financial problems), whereas interest on debt must be paid.

• Preferred stockholders cannot force the company into bankruptcy.

• Preferred shareholders do not share in unusually high earnings because the common stockholders are the real owners of the business.

• A growth company can earn better profits for its original owners by issuing preferred stock having a fixed dividend rate than by issuing common stock.

• Preferred stock issuance does not dilute the ownership interest of common stockholders in terms of earnings participation and voting rights.

• The company does not have to use assets as security as might be the case with issuing debt.

• There is an improvement in the debt to equity ratio.

A preferred stock issue has the following disadvantages:

- Preferred stock requires a higher yield than bonds because of increased risk.
- Preferred dividends are not deductible on the tax return.
- There are higher flotation costs than with bonds.

How does preferred stock compare to bonds and common stock?

The advantages of preferred stock relative to bonds is that the company can omit a dividend readily, no maturity date exists, and no sinking fund is required. Preferred stock has a number of advantages over common stock. It avoids both dilution of control and the equal participation in profits that are afforded to common stockholders. Disadvantages of preferred stock issuance compared to bonds are that it requires a higher yield than debt because it is more risky to the holder and dividends are not tax deductible.

When is the issuance of common stock advised?

Common stock is the residual equity ownership in the business. Common stockholders have voting power but come after preferred stockholders in receiving dividends and in liquidation. Common stock does not involve fixed charges, maturity dates, or sinking fund requirements.

In timing a public issuance of common stock, the following should be considered:

- Do not offer shares near the expiration date for options on the company's stock since the option related transaction may impact share price.
- Offer higher yielding common stock just prior to the ex-dividend date to attract investors.
- Issue common stock when there is little competition of share issuance by other companies in the industry.
- Issue shares in bull markets and refrain from issuing them in bear markets.

How is market price of stock estimated?

The estimated market price per share for a company can be determined as follows:

$$\frac{\text{Expected dividend}}{\text{Cost of capital} - \text{Growth rate in dividends}}$$

EXAMPLE 3

Your company expected the dividend for the year to be $10 a share. The cost of capital is 13%. The growth rate in dividends is expected to be constant at 8%. The price per share is:

$$\frac{\text{Price}}{\text{per share}} = \frac{\text{Expected dividend}}{\text{Cost of capital} - \text{Growth rate in dividends}}$$

$$= \frac{\$10}{0.13 - 0.08 = 0.05} = \$200$$

The price/earnings (P/E) ratio is another way to price the share of stock of a company.

EXAMPLE 4

Your company's earnings per share is $7. It is expected that the company's stock should sell at eight times its earnings. The market price per share is therefore:

$$\text{P/E} = \frac{\text{Market price per share}}{\text{Earnings per share}}$$

$$\frac{\text{Market price}}{\text{per share}} = \text{P/E multiple} \times \text{Earnings per share}$$

$$= 8 \times \$7 = \$56$$

You may want to determine the market value of your company's stock. There are a number of ways to do this.

EXAMPLE 5

Assuming an indefinite stream of future dividends of $300,000 and a required return rate of 14%, the market value of the stock equals:

$$\text{Market value} = \frac{\text{Expected dividends}}{\text{Rate of return}}$$

$$= \frac{\$300,000}{0.14} = \$2,142,857$$

If there are 200,000 shares, the market price per share is:

$$\text{Market value} = \frac{\$2,142,857}{200,000} = \$10.71$$

EXAMPLE 6

Your company is considering a public issue of its securities. The average price/earnings multiple in the industry is 15. The company's earnings is $400,000. There will be 100,000 shares outstanding after the issuance of the stock. The expected price per share is:

$$\begin{array}{c}\text{Total market} \\ \text{value}\end{array} = \begin{array}{c}\text{Net} \\ \text{income}\end{array} \times \begin{array}{c}\text{Price/earnings} \\ \text{multiple}\end{array}$$

$$= \$400,000 \times 15 = \$6,000,000$$

$$\begin{array}{c}\text{Price} \\ \text{per share}\end{array} = \frac{\text{Market value}}{\text{Shares}}$$

$$= \frac{\$6,000,000}{100,000} = \$60$$

EXAMPLE 7

Your company issues 400,000 new shares of common stock to current stockholders at a $25 price per share. The price per share before the new issue was $29. Currently, there are 500,000 outstanding shares. The expected price per share after the new issue is:

Value of outstanding shares (500,000 × $29)	$14,500,000
Value of newly issued shares (400,000 × $25)	10,000,000
Value of entire issue	$24,500,000

$$\text{Value per share} = \frac{\text{Value of entire shares}}{\text{Total number of shares}}$$

$$= \frac{\$24,500,000}{900,000} = \$27.22$$

EXAMPLE 8

Your company is considering constructing a new plant. The firm has usually distributed all its earnings in dividends. Capital expansion has been financed through the issue of common stock. The firm has no preferred stock or debt. The following expectations exist:

Net income	$23,000,000
Shares outstanding	5,000,000
Construction cost of new plant	$16,000,000

Incremental annual earnings expected because of the new plant is $2 million. The rate of return expected by stockholders is 12 percent per annum. The total market value of the firm if the plant is financed through the issuance of common stock is:

$$\frac{\text{Total net income}}{\text{Rate of return}} = \frac{\$25,000,000}{0.12} = \$208,330,000$$

The CFO may want to compute the company's price-earnings ratio and required rate of return.

EXAMPLE 9

Your company has experienced an 8 percent growth rate in earnings and dividends. Next year, it anticipates earnings per share of $4 and dividends per share of $2.50. The company will be having its first public issue of common stock. The stock will be issued at $50 per share.
The price-earnings ratio is:

$$\frac{\text{Market price per share}}{\text{Earnings per share}} = \frac{\$50}{\$4} = 12.5 \text{ times}$$

The required rate of return on the stock is:

$$\frac{\text{Dividends per share}}{\text{Market price per share}} + \text{Growth rate in dividends}$$

$$\frac{\$2.50}{\$50.00} + 0.08 = 0.13$$

If your company has *significant* debt, it would be better off financing with an equity issue to lower overall financial risk.

What are the advantages and disadvantages of issuing common stock?

The issuance of common stock has the following advantages:

- There is no requirement to pay fixed charges such as interest or dividends.
- There is no repayment date or sinking fund stipulation.
- A common stock issue improves the company's credit rating compared to the issuance of debt. For example, the debt-equity ratio is improved.

The issuance of common stock has the following disadvantages:

- Dividends are not tax-deductible.
- Ownership interest is diluted. The additional voting rights could vote to take control away from the current ownership group.
- Earnings and dividends are spread over more shares outstanding.
- The flotation costs of a common stock issue are higher than with preferred stock and debt financing.

It is less costly to finance operations from internally generated funds because financing out of retained earnings involves no flotation costs. Retained earnings may be used as equity funding if the company believes its stock price is lower than the real value of its assets. Retained earnings is also preferred if transaction costs are high for external financing.

The company may use dividend reinvestment plans and employee stock option plans to raise financing and thus avoid issuance costs and the market effect of a public offering.

A summary comparison of bonds and common stocks is presented in Table 25–2.

What are stock rights?

Stock rights are options to buy securities at a given price at a future date. They are a good source of common stock financing. The *preemptive right* means existing stockholders have the first option to buy additional shares to maintain their ownership percentage.

The CFO may participate in deciding on the life of the right (typically about two months), its price (usually below the current market price), and the number of shares required to buy a share.

TABLE 25–2 SUMMARY COMPARISON OF BONDS AND COMMON STOCK

Bonds	Common Stock
Bondholders are creditors.	Stockholders are owners.
No voting rights exist.	Voting rights exist.
There is a maturity date.	There is no maturity date.
Bondholders have prior claims on profits and assets in bankruptcy.	Stockholders have residual claims on profits and assets in bankruptcy.
Interest payments represent fixed charges.	Dividend payments do not constitute fixed charges.
Interest payments are deductible on the tax return.	There is no tax deductibility for dividend payments.
The rate of return required by bondholders is typically lower than that by stockholders.	The required rate of return by stockholders is typically greater than that by bondholders.

EXAMPLE 10

Your company has 500,000 shares of common stock outstanding and is planning to issue another 100,000 shares through stock rights. Each current stockholder will receive one right per share. Each right permits the stockholder to buy $1/5$ of a share of new common stock (100,000 shares/500,000 shares). Hence, 5 rights are needed to buy one share of stock. Hence, a shareholder holding 10,000 shares would be able to buy 2,000 new shares $(10,000 \times 1/5)$. By exercising his or her right, the stockholder would now have a total of 12,000 shares, representing a 2% interest (12,000/600,000) in the total shares outstanding. This is the same 2% ownership (10,000/500,000) the stockholder held prior to the rights offering.

How many rights are needed to buy one share?

Once the subscription price has been decided upon, the number of rights needed to purchase a share of stock may be determined as follows:

$$\text{Shares to be sold} = \frac{\text{Amount of funds to be obtained}}{\text{Subscription price}}$$

The number of rights needed to acquire one share equals:

$$\text{Rights per share} = \frac{\text{Total shares outstanding}}{\text{Shares to be sold}}$$

EXAMPLE 11

Your company wants to obtain $800,000 by a rights offering. There are presently 100,000 shares outstanding. The subscription price is $40 a share. The shares to be sold equal:

$$\text{Shares to be sold} = \frac{\text{Amount of funds to be obtained}}{\text{Subscription price}}$$

$$= \frac{\$800,000}{\$40} = 20,000 \text{ shares}$$

The number of rights needed to acquire one share equals:

$$\text{Rights per share} = \frac{\text{Total shares outstanding}}{\text{Shares to be sold}}$$

$$= \frac{100,000}{20,000} = 5$$

Thus, 5 rights will be required to buy each new share at \$40. Each right enables the holder to buy ⅕ of a share of stock.

How do you determine what a right is worth?

The value of a right should, theoretically, be the same whether the stock is selling with rights on or with ex rights.

When stock is selling with rights on, the value of a right equals:

$$\frac{\text{Market value of stock with rights on} - \text{Subscription price}}{\text{Number of rights needed to buy one share} + 1}$$

EXAMPLE 12

Your company's common stock sells for \$55 a share with rights on. Each stockholder is given the right to buy one new share at \$35 for every four shares held. The value of each right is:

$$\frac{\$55 - \$35}{4 + 1} = \frac{\$20}{5} = \$4$$

When stock is traded ex rights, the market price is expected to decline by the value of the right. The market value of stock trading ex rights should theoretically equal:

Market value of stock with rights on – Value of a right when stock is selling rights on.

The value of a right when stock is selling ex rights equals:

$$\frac{\text{Market value of stock trading ex rights} - \text{Subscription price}}{\text{Number of rights needed to buy one new share}}$$

EXAMPLE 13

Assuming the same information as in Example 12, the value of the company's stock trading ex rights should equal:
Market value of stock with rights on – value of a right when stock is selling rights on:

$$\$55 - \$4 = \$51$$

The value of a right when stock is selling ex rights is therefore:

$$\frac{\text{Market value of stock trading ex rights} - \text{Subscription price}}{\text{Number of rights needed to buy one new share}}$$

$$\frac{\$51 - \$35}{4} = \frac{\$16}{4} = \$4$$

Note: The theoretical value of the right is identical when the stock is selling rights on or ex rights.

FINANCING STRATEGY

Some companies obtain most of their funds from issuing stock and from earnings retained in the business. Other companies borrow to the limit and obtain additional money from stockholders only when they can no longer borrow. Most companies are somewhere in between.

The CFO must select the best source of financing based on the situation. He or she has to consider the various circumstances to determine the best mix of financing.

In formulating a financing strategy in terms of source and amount, the CFO should take into account the following:

• The cost and risk of alternative financing sources.

• The trend in market conditions and how they will effect the future availability of funds and interest rates. For example, if interest rates are expected to increase, the company would be advised to finance with long-term debt at the currently lower interest rates. If stock prices are high, equity issuance may be preferred over debt.

- The current debt to equity ratio. An excessive ratio, for example, reflects financial risk indicating that further financing should be from equity sources.

- The maturity dates of debt. For example, the company should refrain from having all debt expire at one time because in an economic crisis the company may not have sufficient cash to make payment.

- The restrictions in loan agreements. For example, a restriction may place a limit on the debt-equity ratio.

- The type and amount of security demanded by long-term creditors.

- The ability to modify financing strategy to meet the changing economic climate. For example, a company susceptible to cyclical variations should have less debt so as to meet principal and interest at the trough of the cycle. If profits are unstable and/or there is strong competition, greater reliance should be on equity financing.

- The amount, nature, and stability of internally generated funds. If there is adequacy and stability in earnings, the company can tolerate more debt.

- The adequacy of credit lines to meet present and future needs.

- The inflation rate since paying debt will be in cheaper dollars.

- The corporate earning power and liquidity. For example, a liquid business is able to repay debt.

- The type and riskiness of assets. Poor quality assets lack cash realizability to meet debt payments.

- The nature of the product line. A company that has technological obsolescence risk in its product line (e.g., computers) should use less debt.

- The uncertainty of large expenditures. If major cash outlays may be needed (e.g., lawsuit), there should be unused debt capacity available.

• The tax rate. A higher tax rate makes debt more attractive because of the tax deductibility of interest.

• Foreign operations. If operations are in high risk foreign areas and foreign competition is keen, or the exchange rate vacillates widely, a conservative debt posture is warranted.

What financing situations does the company face and what is it doing about it?

Let us select the best possible source of financing based on the facts of each situation below.

EXAMPLE 14

Your company is considering issuing either debt or preferred stock to finance the purchase of a plant costing $1.3 million. The interest rate on the debt is 15%. The dividend rate on the preferred stock is 10%. The tax rate is 34%.

The annual interest payment on the debt is:

$$15\% \times \$1,300,000 = \$195,000$$

The annual dividend on the preferred stock is:

$$10\% \times \$1,300,000 = \$130,000$$

The required earnings before interest and taxes to meet the dividend payment is:

$$\frac{\$130,000}{(1 - 0.34)} = \$196,970$$

If your company anticipates earning $196,970 without a problem, it should issue the preferred stock.

EXAMPLE 15

Your company has sales of $30 million a year. It needs $6 million in financing for capital expansion. The debt/equity ratio is 68%. Your company is in a risky industry, and net income is not stable. The common stock is selling at a high P/E ratio compared to competition. Under consideration is either the issuance of common stock or debt.

Because your company is in a high-risk industry and has a high debt/equity ratio and unstable earnings, issuing debt would be costly, restrictive, and potentially dangerous to future financial health. The issuance of common stock is recommended.

EXAMPLE 16

Your company is a mature one in its industry. There is limited ownership. The company has vacillating sales and earnings. Your firm's debt/equity ratio is 70% relative to the industry standard of 55%. The after-tax rate of return is 16%. Since your company is a seasonal business, there are certain times during the year when its liquidity position is inadequate. Your company is unsure on the best way to finance.

Preferred stock is one possible means of financing. Debt financing is not recommended due to the already high debt/equity ratio, the fluctuation in profit, seasonal nature of the business, and the deficient liquidity posture. Because of the limited ownership, common stock financing may not be appropriate because this would dilute the ownership.

EXAMPLE 17

A new company is established and it plans to raise $15 million in funds. The company expects that it will obtain contracts that will provide $1,200,000 a year in before-tax profits. The firm is considering whether to issue bonds only or an equal amount of bonds and preferred stock. The interest rate on AA corporate bonds is 12 percent. The tax rate is 50 percent.

The company will probably have difficulty issuing $15 million of AA bonds because the interest cost of $1,800,000 (12% × $15,000,000) associated with these bonds is greater than the estimated earnings before interest and taxes.

The issuance of debt by a new company is a risky alternative.

Financing with $7.5 million in debt and $7.5 million in preferred stock is also not recommended. While some debt may be issued, it is not practical to finance the balance with preferred stock. In the case that $7.5 million of AA bonds were issued at the 12 percent rate, the company would be required to pay $900,000 in interest. In this event, a forecasted income statement would look as follows:

Earnings before interest and taxes	$1,200,000
Interest	900,000
Taxable income	$ 300,000
Taxes	150,000
Net income	$ 150,000

The amount available for the payment of preferred dividends is only $150,000. Hence, the maximum rate of return that could be paid on $7.5 million of preferred stock is .02 ($150,000/$7,500,000).

Stockholders would not invest in preferred stock that offers only a 2% rate of return.

The company should consider financing with common stock.

EXAMPLE 18

Your company wants to construct a plant that will take about 1½ years to construct. The plant will be used to produce a new product line, for which your company expects a high demand. The new plant will materially increase corporate size. The following costs are expected:

The cost to build the plant	$800,000
Funds needed for contingencies	$100,000
Annual operating costs	$175,000

The asset, debt, and equity positions of your company are similar to industry standards. The market price of the company's stock is less than it should be, taking into account the future earning power of the new product line. What would be an appropriate means to finance the construction?

Since the market price of stock is less than it should be and considering the potential of the product line, convertible bonds and installment bank loans might be appropriate means of financing, since interest expense is tax-deductible. Additionally, the issuance of convertible bonds might not require repayment, since the bonds are likely to be converted to common stock because of the company's profitability. Installment bank loans can be gradually paid off as the new product generates cash inflow. Funds needed for contingencies can be in the form of open bank lines of credit.

If the market price of the stock was not at a depressed level, financing through equity would be an alternative financing strategy.

EXAMPLE 19

Your company wants to acquire another business but has not determined an optimal means to finance the acquisition. The current debt/equity position is within the industry guideline. In prior years, financing has been achieved through the issuance of short-term debt.

Profit has shown vacillation and as a result the market price of the stock has fluctuated. Currently, however, the market price of stock is strong. Your company's tax bracket is low.

The purchase should be financed through the issuance of equity securities for the following reasons:

• The market price of stock is currently at a high level.

• The issuance of long-term debt will cause greater instability in earnings because of the high fixed interest charges. In consequence, there will be more instability in stock price.

• The issuance of debt will result in a higher debt/equity ratio relative to the industry norm. This will negatively impact the company's cost of capital and availability of financing.

• Because it will take a long time to derive the funds needed for the purchase price, short-term debt should not be issued. If short-term debt is issued, the debt would have to be paid before the receipt of the return from the acquired business.

EXAMPLE 20

Breakstone Corporation wants to undertake a capital expansion program and must, therefore, obtain $7 million in financing. The company has a good credit rating. The current market price of its common stock is $60. The interest rate for long-term debt is 18%. The dividend rate associated with preferred stock is 16%, and Breakstone's tax rate is 46%.

Relevant ratios for the industry and the company are:

	Industry	Breakstone
Net income to total assets	13%	22%
Long-term debt to total assets	31%	29%
Total liabilities to total assets	47%	45%
Preferred stock to total assets	3%	0
Current ratio	2.6	3.2
Net income plus interest to interest	8	17

Dividends per share is $8, the dividend growth rate is 7%, no sinking fund provisions exist, the trend in earnings shows stability, and the present ownership group wishes to retain control. The cost of common stock is:

$$\frac{\text{Dividends per share}}{\text{Market price per share}} + \text{Dividend growth rate}$$

$$\frac{\$8}{\$60} + 0.07 = 20.3\%$$

The after-tax cost of long-term debt is 9.7% (18% × 54%). The cost of preferred stock is 16%. How should Breakstone finance its expansion?

The issuance of long-term debt is more appropriate for the following reasons:

1. Its after-tax cost is the lowest.

2. The company's ratios of long-term debt to total assets and total liabilities to total assets are less than the industry average, pointing to the company's ability to issue additional debt.

3. Corporate liquidity is satisfactory based on the favorable current ratio relative to the industry standard.

4. Fixed interest charges can be met, taking into account the stability in earnings, the earning power of the firm, and the very favorable times-interest-earned ratio. Additional interest charges should be met without difficulty.

5. The firm's credit rating is satisfactory.

6. There are no required sinking fund provisions.

7. The leveraging effect can take place to further improve earnings.

In the case that the firm does not want to finance through further debt, preferred stock would be the next best financing alternative, since its cost is lower than that associated with common stock and no dilution in the ownership interest will take place.

EXAMPLE 21

Harris Corporation has experienced growth in sales and net income but is in a weak liquidity position. The inflation rate is high. At the end of 19X5, the company needs $600,000 for the following reasons:

New equipment	$175,000
Research and development	95,000
Paying overdue accounts payable	215,000
Paying accrued liabilities	60,000
Desired increase in cash balance	55,000
	$600,000

Exhibit 25–1 is the financial statement for 19X5.

EXHIBIT 25–1   HARRIS CORPORATION
BALANCE SHEET
DEC. 31 19X5

ASSETS
Current assets
Cash	$ 12,000	
Accounts receivable	140,000	
Notes receivable	25,000	
Inventory	165,000	
Office supplies	20,000	
Total current assets		$362,000
Fixed assets		468,000
Total assets		$830,000

LIABILITIES AND
STOCKHOLDERS' EQUITY
Current liabilities
Loans payable	$ 74,000	
Accounts payable	360,000	
Accrued liabilities	55,000	
Total current liabilities		$489,000
Long-term debt		61,000
Total liabilites		$550,000
Stockholders' equity		
Common stock	$200,000	
Retained earnings	80,000	
Total stockholders' equity		280,000
Total liabilities and stockholders' equity		$830,000

HARRIS CORPORATION
INCOME STATEMENT
FOR THE YEAR ENDED DEC. 31, 19X5

Sales	$1,400,000
Cost of sales	750,000
Gross margin	$ 650,000
Operating expenses	480,000
Income before tax	$ 170,000
Tax	68,000
Net income	$ 102,000

It is anticipated that sales will increase on a yearly basis by 22% and that net income will increase by 17%. What time of financing is best suited for Harris Corporation?

The most suitable source of financing is long-term. A company in a growth stage needs a large investment in equipment, and research and development expenditure. With regard to 19X5, $270,000 of the $600,000 is required for this purpose. A growth company also needs funds to satisfy working capital requirements. Here, 45.8% of financing is necessary to pay overdue accounts payable and accrued liabilities. The firm also needs sufficient cash to capitalize on lucrative opportunities. The present cash balance to total assets is at a low 1.4%.

Long-term debt financing is recommended for the following reasons:

1. The ratio of long-term debt to stockholders' equity is a low 21.8%. The additional issuance of long-term debt will not impair the overall capital structure.

2. The company has been profitable and there is an expectation of future growth in earnings. Internally generated funds should therefore ensue, enabling the payment of fixed interest charges.

3. During inflation, the issuance of long-term debt generates purchasing power gains because the firm will be repaying creditors in cheaper dollars.

4. Interest expense is tax-deductible.

EXAMPLE 22

On average over the past 10 years, Tektronix's return on equity has not been sufficient to finance growth of the business, thus an infusion of new capital from outside sources has been required. Most of the additional capital has been in the form of long-term debt, which represented 13% of total capital in fiscal 1977 and 21% of total capital in fiscal 1981.

With expansion of the business expected to accelerate in the next few years after the current lull, but, with return on equity likely to remain somewhat depressed because of competitive factors and costs associated with "preparing for the 1980s," a need for additional capital is developing. Also, of the $146 million of long-term debt outstanding at the fiscal 1981 year-end, nearly $65 million matures in the fiscal 1982 to fiscal 1984 period. Thus, it is possible that as much as $100 million of capital may have to be raised to meet all requirements.

In anticipation of capital needs, Tektronix in fiscal 1981 borrowed funds in the commercial paper market, and the company intends to replace these commercial paper borrowings at some future time with long-term financing.

Given the foregoing circumstances, and also given that Tektronix common stock currently is quoted on the New York Stock Exchange at 160% of book value and that the current interest rate on newly issued triple-A industrial bonds of long maturity is 14%, evaluate on an immediate and longer term basis each of the following options. Include economic and capital market assumptions. (*a*) Tektronix is selling 2 million shares of common stock at $50 per share, (*b*) Tektronix is selling a $100 million straight debenture issue maturing in 20 years, and (*c*) Tektronix is selling a $100 million bond issue convertible into common stock and maturing in 20 years. (CFA, adapted.)

SOLUTION

1. From the timing viewpoint, selling equity is attractive considering price-to-book rates (160%) and comparatively modest dilution (2 million shares represents 11 percent of currently outstanding shares, less impact of after-tax cost of borrowing to be retired). However, price soon could move higher given a better economic environment, earnings recovery, and resultant stronger general stock market. Long-term, selling equity is expensive, as continuing dividend service is with after-tax dollars. Also, immediate return on equity capital will diminish with reduced leverage as debt matures.

2. Increasing debt, net of maturities, to a larger part of total capital is tolerable by most standards. According to the data provided, debt of about $146 million would increase to around $181 million ($146 + $100 − $65), and by 1984 this sum presumably would not represent much more than the current 21 percent subject to earnings retention during the interim. However, this would be an appealing option only if interest rate assumptions indicate other than a rather meaningful decline over the next year or two, and if pro forma interest charge coverage and/or the current lull in the business do not seriously impact the rating and issue price of the bonds. The after-tax cost of debt service will be comparatively low, and so would be the net cost of capital. Another consideration will be sinking fund requirements and call restrictions and price.

3. A convertible bond issue has certain disadvantages but it also had advantages; (1) it can be sold at a lower interest cost than a straight debt, and (2) the potential dilution is less than an issue of common reflecting the premium over the common market.

26

Warrants and Convertibles

Warrants and convertibles are unique compared to other types of securities because they may be converted into common stock. The CFO needs to have a good understanding of warrants and convertibles along with their valuation, their advantages and disadvantages, and when their issuance is recommended.

WARRANTS

A *warrant* is the option given holders to buy a predetermined number of shares of stock at a given price. Warrants may be detachable or nondetachable. A *detachable* warrant may be sold separately from the bond it is associated with. Thus, the holder may exercise the warrant but not redeem the bond. Your company may issue bonds with detachable warrants to purchase additional bonds so as to hedge the risk of adverse future interest rate movements since the warrant is convertible into a bond at a fixed interest rate. If interest rates increase, the warrant will be worthless, and the issue price of the warrant will partially offset the higher interest cost of the future debt issue. A *nondetachable* warrant is sold with its bond to be exercised by the bond owner simultaneously with the convertible bond.

Your company may sell warrants separately (e.g., American Express) or in combination with other securities (e.g., MGM/UA).

To obtain common stock the warrant must be given up along with the payment of cash called the *exercise price*. Although warrants usually mature on a specified date, some are perpetual. A holder of a warrant may exercise it by purchasing the stock, sell it on the market to other investors, or continue to hold it. The company cannot force the exercise of a warrant.

If desired, the company may have the exercise price of the warrant change over time (e.g., increase each year).

If a stock split or stock dividend is issued before the warrant is exercised, the option price of the warrant will be adjusted for it.

Warrants may be issued to obtain additional funds. When a bond is issued with a warrant, the warrant price is usually established between 10% and 20% above the stock's market price. If the company's stock price increases above the option price, the warrants will be exercised at the option price. The closer the warrants are to their maturity date, the greater is the likelihood that they will be exercised.

What is a warrant worth?

The theoretical value of a warrant is computed by a formula. The formula value is typically less than the market price of the warrant because the speculative appeal of a warrant allows the investor to obtain personal leverage:

$$\begin{matrix}\text{Value of a} \\ \text{Warrant}\end{matrix} = \left(\begin{matrix}\text{Market price} \\ \text{per share}\end{matrix} - \begin{matrix}\text{Exercise} \\ \text{price}\end{matrix}\right)$$

$$\times \begin{matrix}\text{Number of shares} \\ \text{that may be bought}\end{matrix}$$

EXAMPLE 1

A warrant for XYZ Company's stock gives the owner the right to buy one share of common stock at $25 a share. The market price of the common stock is $53. The formula price of the warrant is $28 (($53 – $25) × 1).

If the owner had the right to buy three shares of common stock with one warrant, the theoretical value of the warrant would be $84 ($53 – $25) × 3).

If the stock is selling for an amount below the option price, there will be a negative value. Since this is illogical, a zero value is assigned.

EXAMPLE 2

Assume the same facts as in Example 1, except that the stock is selling at $21 a share. The formula amount is – $4 (($21—$25) × 1). However, zero will be assigned.

Warrants do not have an investment value because there is *no* interest, dividends, or voting rights. Therefore, the market value of a warrant is only attributable to its convertibility feature into common stock. However, the market price of a warrant is typically more than its theoretical value, which is referred to as the *premium* on the warrant. The lowest amount that a warrant will sell for is its theoretical value.

The value of a warrant depends on the remaining life of the option, dividend payments on the common stock, the fluctuation in price of the common stock, whether the warrant is listed on the exchange, and the investor's opportunity. There is a higher price for a warrant when its life is long, the dividend payment on common stock is small, the stock price is volatile, it is listed on the exchange, and the value of funds to the investor is great (because the warrant requires a lesser investment).

EXAMPLE 3

ABC stock has a market value of $50. The exercise price of the warrant is also $50. Thus, the theoretical value of the warrant is $0. However, the warrant will sell at a premium (positive price) if there is the possibility that the market price of the common stock will exceed $50 prior to the expiration date of the warrant. The more distant the expiration date, the greater will be the premium, since there is a longer period for possible price appreciation. The lower the market price relative to the exercise price, the less the premium will be.

EXAMPLE 4

Assume the same facts as in Example 3, except that the current market price of the stock is $35. In this case, the warrant's premium will be much lower since it would take longer for the stock's price to increase above $50 a share. If investors expect that the stock price would not increase above $50 at a later date, the value of the warrant would be $0.

If the market price of ABC stock rises above $50, the market price of the warrant will increase and the premium will decrease. In other words, when the stock price exceeds the exercise price, the market price of the warrant approximately equals the theoretical value so the premium disappears. The reduction in the premium arises because of the lessening of the advantage of owning the warrant compared to exercising it.

Should you issue a warrant?

The advantages of issuing warrants are:

• They serve a "sweetener" for an issue of debt or preferred stock.

• They permit the issuance of debt at a low interest rate.

• They allow for balanced financing between debt and equity.

• Funds are received when the warrants are exercised.

The disadvantages of issuing warrants are:

• When exercised they will result in a dilution of common stock which in turn lowers the market price of stock.

• They may be exercised when the business has no need for additional capital.

CONVERTIBLE SECURITIES ────────

What is a convertible security and when should it be issued?

A *convertible security* may be exchanged for common stock by the holder, and in some cases the issuer, according to specified terms. Examples are convertible bonds and convertible preferred stock. Common shares are issued when the convertible security is exchanged. The *conversion ratio* equals:

$$\text{Conversion ratio} = \frac{\text{Par value of convertible security}}{\text{Conversion price}}$$

The *conversion price* is the price the holder pays for the common stock when the conversion is made. The conversion price and the conversion ratio are established at the date the convertible security is issued. The conversion price should be tied to the growth prospects of the company. The greater the potential, the greater the conversion price.

A convertible bond is a quasi-equity security because its market value is keyed to its value if converted instead of as a bond. The convertible bond may be deemed a delayed issue of common stock at a price above the current level.

EXAMPLE 5

A $1,000 bond is convertible into 30 shares of stock. The conversion price is $33.33 ($1,000/30 shares).

EXAMPLE 6

A share of convertible preferred stock with a par value of $50 is convertible into four shares of common stock. The conversion price is $12.50 ($50/4).

EXAMPLE 7

A $1,000 convertible bond is issued that allows the holder to convert the bond into 10 shares of common stock. Thus, the conversion ratio is 10 shares for 1 bond. Since the face value of the bond is $1,000 the holder is tendering this amount upon conversion. The conversion price equals $100 per share ($1,000/10 shares).

EXAMPLE 8

Y Company issued a $1,000 convertible bond at par. The conversion price is $40. The conversion ratio is:

$$\text{Conversion ratio} = \frac{\text{Par value of convertible security}}{\text{Conversion price}}$$

$$= \frac{\$1,000}{\$40} = 25$$

The conversion value of a security is computed as follows:

$$\text{Conversion value} = \text{Common stock price} \times \text{Conversion ratio}$$

When a convertible security is issued, it is priced higher than its conversion value. The difference is the conversion premium. The percentage conversion premium is computed as follows:

$$\text{Percentage conversion premium} = \frac{\text{Market value} - \text{Conversion value}}{\text{Conversion value}}$$

EXAMPLE 9

LA Corporation issued a $1,000 convertible bond at par. The market price of the common stock at the date of issue was $48. The conversion price is $55.

$$\text{Conversion ratio} = \frac{\text{Par value of convertible security}}{\text{Conversion price}} = \frac{\$1,000}{\$55} = 18.18$$

Conversion value of the bond equals:

$$\text{Common stock price} \times \text{Conversion ratio} = \$48 \times 18.18 = \$872$$

The difference between the conversion value of $872 and the issue price of $1,000 is the conversion premium of $128. The conversion premium may also be expressed as a percentage of the conversion value. The percent in this case is:

Percentage conversion premium equals:

$$\frac{\text{Market value} - \text{Conversion value}}{\text{Conversion value}} = \frac{\$1,000 - \$872}{\$872} = \frac{\$128}{\$872} = 14.7\%$$

The conversion terms may increase in steps over specified time periods. As time elapses, fewer common shares are exchanged for the

bond. In some cases, after a specified time period the conversion option may expire.

A convertible security usually includes a clause
that protects it from dilution caused by stock dividends, stock splits, and stock rights. The clause
typically prevents the issuance of common stock
at a price lower than the conversion price. The
conversion price is adjusted for a stock split or
stock dividend enabling the common shareholder
to retain his or her percentage interest.

EXAMPLE 10

A 3-for-1 stock split requires a tripling of the
conversion ratio. A 20% stock dividend necessi-
tates a 20% increase in the conversion ratio.

The voluntary conversion of a security by the
holder depends on the relationship of the interest
on the bond compared to the dividend on the
stock, the risk preference of the holder (stock has
a greater risk than a bond), and the current and
expected market price of the stock.

What is the value of a convertible security?

A convertible security is a hybrid security, because it has attributes similar to common stock
and bonds. It is expected that the holder will
eventually receive both interest yield and capital
gain. Interest yield is the coupon interest relative
to the amount invested. The capital gain yield
applies to the difference between the conversion
price and the stock price at the issuance date and
the expected growth rate in stock price.

The investment value of a convertible security
is the value of the security, assuming it was not
convertible but had all other attributes. For a
convertible bond, its investment value equals the
present value of future interest payments plus
the present value of the maturity amount. For
preferred stock the investment value equals the
present value of future dividend payments plus
the present value of expected selling price.

Conversion value is the value of the stock received upon converting the bond. As the price of
the stock increases so will its conversion value.

EXAMPLE 11

A $1,000 bond is convertible into 18 shares of common stock with a market value of $52 per share. The conversion value of the bond equals:

$$\$52 \times 18 \text{ shares} = \$936$$

EXAMPLE 12

At the date a $100,000 convertible bond is issued, the market price of the stock is $18 a share. Each $1,000 bond is convertible into 50 shares of stock. The conversion ratio is thus 50. The number of shares the bond is convertible into is:

$$\frac{100 \text{ bonds}}{(\$100,000/\$1,000)} \times 50 \text{ shares} = 5,000 \text{ shares}$$

The conversion value is $90,000 ($18 × 5,000 shares).

If the stock price is anticipated to grow at 6% per year, the conversion value at the end of the first year is:

Shares	5,000
Stock price ($18 × 1.06)	$19.08
Conversion value	$95,400

A convertible security will not sell at less than its value as straight debt (nonconvertible security). This is because the conversion privilege has to have some value in terms of its potential convertibility to common stock and in terms of reducing the holder's risk exposure to a declining bond price (convertible bonds fall off less in price than straight debt issues). Market value will equal investment value only when the conversion privilege is worthless because of a low market price of the common stock relative to the conversion price.

When convertible bonds are issued, the business expects that the value of common stock will appreciate and that the bonds will eventually be converted. If conversion does occur, the company could then issue another convertible bond referred to as "leapfrog financing."

If the market price of common sock decreases instead of increasing, the holder will not convert the debt into equity. In this case, the convertible security remains as debt and is termed a "hung" convertible.

A convertible security holder may prefer to hold the security rather than converting it even though the conversion value exceeds the investment cost. First, as the price of the common stock increases so will the price of the convertible security. Second, the holder receives regular interest payments or preferred dividends. To force conversion, companies issuing convertibles often have a call price. The call price is above the face value of the bond (about 10 percent to 20 percent higher). This forces the conversion of stock provided the stock price exceeds the conversion price. The holder would prefer a higher-value common stock than a lower call price for the bond.

The issuing company may force conversion of its convertible bond to common stock when financially advantageous such as when the market price of the stock has declined, or when the interest rate on the convertible debt is currently higher than the "going" market interest rates. An example of a company that has in the past had a conversion of its convertible bond when the market price of its stock was low was United Technologies.

EXAMPLE 13

The conversion price on a $1,000 debenture is $40 and the call price is $1,100. In order for the conversion value of the bond to equal the call price, the market price of the stock would have to be $44 ($1,100/25). If the conversion value of the bond is 15 percent higher than the call price, the approximate market price of common stock would be $51 (1.15 × $44). At a $51 price, conversion is assured because if the investor did not convert he or she would experience an opportunity loss.

EXAMPLE 14

ABC Company's convertible bond has a conversion price of $80. The conversion ratio is 10. The market price of the stock is $140. The call price is $1,100. The bondholder would prefer to convert to common stock with a market value of $1,400 ($140 × 10) than have his or her convertible bond redeemed at $1,100. In this situation, the call provision forces the conversion when the bondholder might be inclined to wait longer.

Does it pay to issue a convertible security?

The advantages of issuing convertible securities are:

• It is a "sweetener" in a debt offering by giving the investor an opportunity to share in the price appreciation of common stock.

• The issuance of convertible debt allows for a lower interest rate on the financing compared to issuing straight debt.

• There are fewer financing restrictions with a convertible security.

• Convertibles provide a means of issuing equity at prices higher than current market prices.

• A convertible security may be issued in a tight money market, when it is difficult for a creditworthy company to issue a straight bond or preferred stock.

• The call provision enables the company to force conversion whenever the market price of the stock exceeds the conversion price.

• If the company issued straight debt now and common stock later to meet the debt, they would incur flotation costs twice, whereas with convertible debt, flotation costs would occur only once, with the initial issuance of the convertible bonds.

The disadvantages of issuing convertible securities are:

• If the company's stock price appreciably increases, it would have been better off financing through a regular issuance of common stock by waiting to issue it at the higher price rather than allowing conversion at the lower price.

• The company has to pay the convertible debt if the stock prices does not appreciate.

What should be the financing policy?

When a company's stock price is depressed, convertible debt rather than common stock issuance may be advisable if the price of stock is expected to increase. A conversion price above the current market price of stock will involve the issuance of less shares when the bonds are converted relative to selling the shares at a current lower price. Further, there is less share dilution. The conversion will take place only if the price of the stock rises above the conversion price. The drawback is that if the stock price does not increase and conversion does not occur, an additional debt burden is placed upon the firm.

The issuance of convertible debt is recommended when the company wants to leverage itself in the short-term but desires not to pay interest and principal on the convertible debt in the long-term (due to its conversion).

A convertible issue is a good financing instrument for a growth company with a low dividend yield on stock. The higher the growth rate, the earlier the conversion. For example, a convertible bond may be a temporary source of funds in a construction period. It is a relatively inexpensive source for financing growth. A convertible issuance is not recommended for a company with a modest growth rate since it would take a long time to force conversion. During such a time the company will not be able to easily issue additional financing. A long conversion period may imply to investors that the stock has not done as well as expected. The growth rate of the firm is an important factor in determining whether convertibles should be issued.

Your company may also issue bonds exchangeable for the common stock of other companies. Your company may do this if it owns a sizable stake in another company's stock and it wants to raise cash. There is an intention to sell shares at a later date because of an expectation of share price appreciation.

In conclusion, a convertible bond is a delayed common equity financing. The issuer expects stock price to rise in the future (e.g., 2–4 years) to stimulate conversion. Convertible bonds may be appropriate for smaller, rapidly growing companies.

Note: If your company has an uncertain future tax position, it may issue convertible preferred stock exchangeable at the option of the company (i.e., when it becomes a taxpayer) into convertible debt of the company.

How do convertibles compare with warrants?

The differences between convertibles and warrants are:

• Exercising convertibles does not usually generate additional funds to the company, while the exercise of warrants does.

• When conversion takes place the debt ratio is reduced. However, the exercise of warrants adds to the equity position with debt still remaining.

• Due to the call feature, the company has more control over the timing of the capital structure with convertibles than with warrants.

27

Cost of Capital and Capital Structure Decisions

The cost of capital is defined as the rate of return that is necessary to maintain the market value of the firm (or price of the firm's stock). CFOs must know the cost of capital (the minimum required rate of return) in (1) making capital budgeting decisions, (2) helping to establish the optimal capital structure, and (3) making decisions such as leasing, bond refunding, and working capital management. The cost of capital is used either as a discount rate under the NPV method or as a hurdle rate under the IRR method. The cost of capital is computed as a weighted average of the various capital components, which are items on the right-hand side of the balance sheet such as debt, preferred stock, common stock, and retained earnings.

How do you compute individual costs of capital?

Each element of capital has a component cost that is identified by the following:

k_i = before-tax cost of debt

$k_d = k_i (1 - t)$ = after-tax cost of debt, where t = tax rate

k_p = cost of preferred stock

k_s = cost of retained earnings (or internal equity)

k_e = cost of external equity, or cost of issuing new common stock

k_o = firm's overall cost of capital, or a weighted average cost of capital

COST OF DEBT

The before-tax cost of debt can be found by determining the internal rate of return (or yield to maturity) on the bond cash flows.

However, the following short-cut formula may be used for approximating the yield to maturity on a bond:

$$k_i = \frac{I + (M - V)/n}{(M + V)/2}$$

where I = annual interest payments in dollars, M = par or face value, usually $1,000 per bond, V = market value or net proceeds from the sale of a bond, and n = term of the bond n years.

Since the interest payments are tax-deductible, the cost of debt must be stated on an after-tax basis. The after-tax cost of debt is:

$$k_d = k_i (1 - t)$$

where t is the tax rate.

EXAMPLE 1

Assume that the Carter Company issues a $1,000, 8%, 20-year bond whose net proceeds are $940. The tax rate is 40%. Then, the before-tax cost of debt, k_i, is:

$$k_i = \frac{I + (M - V)/n}{(M + V)/2}$$

$$= \frac{\$80 + (\$1,000 - \$940)/20}{(\$1,000 + \$940)/2} = \frac{\$83}{\$970} = 8.56\%$$

Therefore, the after-tax cost of debt is:

$$k_d = k_i (1 - t) = 8.56\% (1 - 0.4) = 5.14\%$$

COST OF PREFERRED STOCK _____

The cost of preferred stock, k_p, is found by dividing the annual preferred stock dividend, d_p, by the net proceeds from the sale of the preferred stock, p, as follows:

$$k_p = \frac{d_p}{p}$$

Since preferred stock dividends are not a tax-deductible expense, these dividends are paid after taxes. Consequently, no tax adjustment is required.

EXAMPLE 2

Suppose that the Carter Company has preferred stock that pays a $13 dividend per share and sells for $100 per share in the market. The flotation (or underwriting) cost is 3%, or $3 per share. Then the cost of preferred stock is:

$$k_p = \frac{d_p}{P} = \frac{\$13}{\$97} = 13.4\%$$

COST OF EQUITY CAPITAL _____

The cost of common stock, k_e, is generally viewed as the rate of return investors require on a firm's common stock. Two techniques for measuring the cost of common stock equity capital are widely used: (1) the Gordon's growth model and (2) the *capital asset pricing model* (CAPM) approach.

The Gordon's growth model is:

$$P_0 = \frac{D_1}{r - g}$$

where P_0 = value (or market price) of common stock, D_1 = dividend to be received in 1 year, r = investor's required rate of return, and g = rate of growth (assumed to be constant over time).

Solving the model for r results in the formula for the cost of common stock:

$$r = \frac{D_1}{P_0} + g \text{ or } k_e = \frac{D_1}{P_0} + g$$

Note that the symbol r is changed to k_e to show that it is used for the computation of cost of capital.

EXAMPLE 3

Assume that the market price of the Carter Company's stock is $40. The dividend to be paid at the end of the coming year is $4 per share and is expected to grow at a constant annual rate of 6%. Then the cost of this common stock is:

$$k_e = \frac{D_1}{P_0} + g = \frac{\$4}{\$40} + 6\% = 16\%$$

The cost of new common stock, or external equity capital, is higher than the cost of existing common stock because of the *flotation costs* involved in selling the new common stock. Flotation costs, sometimes called *issuance costs,* are the total costs of issuing and selling a security that include printing and engraving, legal fees, and accounting fees.

If f is flotation cost in percent, the formula for the cost of new common stock is:

$$k_e = \frac{D_1}{P_0\,(1-f)} + g$$

EXAMPLE 4

Assume the same data as in Example 3, except the firm is trying to sell new issues of stock A and its flotation cost is 10%. Then:

$$k_e = \frac{D_1}{P_0\,(1-f)} + g = \frac{\$4}{\$40(1-0.1)} + 6\% = \frac{\$4}{\$36} + 6\%$$

$$= 11.11\% + 6\% = 17.11\%$$

The Capital Asset Pricing Model (CAPM) Approach. An alternative approach to measuring the cost of common stock is to use the CAPM, which involves the following steps:

1. Estimate the risk-free rate, r_f, generally taken to be the United States Treasury bill rate.

2. Estimate the stock's beta coefficient, b, which is an index of systematic (or nondiversifiable market) risk.

3. Estimate the rate of return on the market portfolio, r_m, such as the Standard & Poor's 500 Stock Composite Index or Dow Jones 30 Industrials.

4. Estimate the required rate of return on the firm's stock, using the CAPM equation:

$$k_e = r_f + b(r_m - r_f)$$

Again, note that the symbol r_j is changed to k_e.

EXAMPLE 5

Assuming that r_f is 7%, b is 1.5, and r_m is 13 percent, then:

$$k_e = r_f + b(r_m - r_f) = 7\% + 1.5 \ (13\% - 7\%) = 16\%$$

This 16% cost of common stock can be viewed as consisting of a 7% risk-free rate plus a 9% risk premium, which reflects that the firm's stock price is 1.5 times more volatile than the market portfolio to the factors affecting nondiversifiable, or systematic, risk.

COST OF RETAINED EARNINGS _____

The cost of retained earnings, k_s, is closely related to the cost of existing common stock, since the cost of equity obtained by retained earnings is the same as the rate of return investors require on the firm's common stock. Therefore,

$$k_e = k_s$$

How the overall cost of capital is determined?

The firm's overall cost of capital is the weighted average of the individual capital costs, with the weights being the proportions of each type of capital used. Let k_o be the overall cost of capital.

$k_o = \Sigma$ (percentage of the total capital structure supplied by each source of capital × cost of capital for each source)

$= \Sigma w_d \, k_d + w_p \, k_p + w_e \, k_e + w_s \, k_s$

where w_d = % of total capital supplied by debts, w_p = % of total capital supplied by preferred stock, w_e = % of total capital supplied by external equity, and w_s = % of total capital supplied by retained earnings (or internal equity).

The weights can be *historical, target,* or *marginal.*

HISTORICAL WEIGHTS

Historical weights are based on a firm's existing capital structure. The use of these weights is based on the assumption that the firm's existing capital structure is optimal and therefore should be maintained in the future. Two types of historical weights can be used—book value weights and market value weights.

Book Value Weights

The use of book value weights in calculating the firm's weighted cost of capital assumes that new financing will be raised using the same method the firm used for its present capital structure. The weights are determined by dividing the book value of each capital component by the sum of the book values of all the long-term capital sources. The computation of overall cost of capital is illustrated in the following example.

EXAMPLE 6

Assume the following capital structure and cost of each source of financing for the Carter Company:

Source		Cost
Mortgage bonds ($1,000 par)	$20,000,000	5.14% (Example 1)
Preferred stock ($100 par)	5,000,000	13.40% (Example 2)
Common stock ($40 par)	20,000,000	17.11% (Example 4)
Retained earnings	5,000,000	16.00% (Example 3)
Total	$50,000,000	

The book value weights and the overall cost of capital are computed as follows:

Source	Book Value	Weights	Cost	Weighted Cost
Debt	$20,000,000	40%[a]	5.14%	2.06%[b]
Preferred stock	5,000,000	10	13.40%	1.34
Common stock	20,000,000	40	17.11%	6.84
Retained earnings	5,000,000	10	16.00%	1.60
	$50,000,000	100%		11.84

Overall cost of capital = k_o = 11.84%

[a] $20,000,000/$50,000,000 = .40 = 40%
[b] 5.14% × 40% = 2.06%

Market Value Weights

Market value weights are determined by dividing the market value of each source by the sum of the market values of all sources. The use of market value weights for computing a firm's weighted average cost of capital is theoretically more appealing than the use of book value weights because the market values of the securities closely approximate the actual dollars to be received from their sale.

EXAMPLE 7

In addition to the data from Example 6, assume that the security market prices are as follows:

Mortgage bonds = $1,100 per bond
Preferred stock = $90 per share
Common stock = $80 per share

The firm's number of securities in each category is:

$$\text{Mortgage bonds} = \frac{\$20,000,000}{\$1,000} = 20,000$$

$$\text{Preferred stock} = \frac{\$5,000,000}{\$100} = 50,000$$

$$\text{Common stock} = \frac{\$20,000,000}{\$40} = 500,000$$

Therefore, the market value weights are:

Source	Number of Securities	Price	Market Value
Debt	20,000	$1,100	$22,000,000
Preferred stock	50,000	$ 90	4,500,000
Common stock	500,000	$ 80	40,000,000
			$66,500,000

The $40 million common stock value must be split in the ratio of 4 to 1 (the $20 million common stock versus the $5 million retained earnings in the original capital structure), since the market value of the retained earnings has been impounded into the common stock.

The firm's cost of capital is as follows:

Source	Market Value	Weights	Cost	Weighted Average
Debt	$22,000,000	33.08%	5.14%	1.70%
Preferred stock	4,500,000	6.77	13.40%	0.91
Common stock	32,000,000	48.12	17.11%	8.23
Retained earnings	8,000,000	12.03	16.00%	1.92
	$66,500,000	100.00%		12.76%

Overall cost of capital = k_o = 12.76%

TARGET WEIGHTS

If the firm has a target capital structure (desired debt-equity mix), which is maintained over the long term, then the use of that capital structure and associated weights can be used in calculating the firm's weighted cost of capital.

MARGINAL WEIGHTS _____

Marginal weights involves the use of *actual* financial mix used in financing the proposed investments. In using target weights, the firm is concerned with what it believes to be the optimal capital structure or target percentage. In using marginal weights, the firm is concerned with the actual dollar amounts of each type of financing to be needed for a given investment project. This approach, while attractive, presents a problem. The cost of capital for the individual sources depend on the firm's financial risk, which is affected by the firm's financial mix. If the company alters its present capital structure, the individual costs will change, which makes it more difficult to compute the weighted cost of capital. The important assumption needed is that the firm's financial mix is relatively stable and that these weights will closely approximate future financing practice.

EXAMPLE 8

The Carter Company is considering raising $8 million for plant expansion. The CFO estimates using the following mix for financing this project:

Debt	$4,000,000	50%
Common stock	2,000,000	25%
Retained earnings	2,000,000	25%
	$8,000,000	100%

The company's cost of capital is computed as:

Source	Marginal Weights	Cost	Weighted Cost
Debt	50%	5.14%	2.57%
Common stock	25	17.11%	4.28
Retained earnings	25	16.00%	4.00
	100%		10.85%

Overall cost of capital = k_o = 10.85%

How do you determine the firm's optimal capital structure?

The concepts to be covered in this chapter relate closely to the cost of capital, and also extend to the crucial problem of determining the firm's optimal capital structure. We will cover three methods that show how to build an appropriate financing mix.

EBIT-EPS APPROACH TO CAPITAL STRUCTURE DECISIONS

This analysis is a practical tool that enables the CFO to evaluate alternative financing plans by investigating their effect on EPS over a range of EBIT levels. Its primary objective is to determine the EBIT break-even, or indifference, points between the various alternative financing plans. The indifference point identifies the EBIT level at which the EPS will be the same regardless of the financing plan chosen by the CFO.

This indifference point has major implications for capital structure decisions. At EBIT amounts in excess of the EBIT indifference level, the more heavily levered financing plan will generate a higher EPS. At EBIT amounts below the EBIT indifference level, the financing plan involving less leverage will generate a higher EPS. Therefore, it is of critical importance for the CFO to know the EBIT indifference level. The indifference points between any two methods of financing can be determined by solving for EBIT in the following equality:

$$\frac{(\text{EBIT} - I)(1 - t) - \text{PD}}{S_1} = \frac{(\text{EBIT} - I)(1 - t) - \text{PD}}{S_2}$$

where t = tax rate, PD = preferred stock dividends, S_1 and S_2 = number of shares of common stock outstanding after financing for plan 1 and plan 2, respectively.

EXAMPLE 9

Assume that ABC Company, with long-term capitalization consisting entirely of $5 million in stock, wants to raise $2 million for the acquisition of special equipment by (1) selling 40,000 shares of common stock at $50 each, (2) selling bonds at 10% interest, or (3) issuing preferred stock with an 8% dividend. The present EBIT is $800,000, the income tax rate is 50% and 100,000 shares of common stock are now outstanding. To compute the indifference points, we begin by calculating EPS at a projected EBIT level of $1 million.

	All Common	All Debt	All Preferred
EBIT	$1,000,000	$1,000,000	$1,000,000
Interest		200,000	
Earnings before taxes (EBT)	$1,000,000	$ 800,000	$1,000,000
Taxes	500,000	400,000	500,000
Earnings after taxes (EAT)	$ 500,000	$ 400,000	$ 500,000
Preferred stock dividend			160,000
Earnings available to common stockholders	$ 500,000	$ 400,000	$ 340,000
Number of shares	140,000	100,000	100,000
EPS	$3.57	$4.00	$3.40

Now connect the EPSs at the level of EBIT of $1 million with the EBITs for each financing alternative on the horizontal axis to obtain the EPS-EBIT graphs. We plot the EBIT necessary to cover all fixed financial costs for each financing alternative on the horizontal axis. For the common stock plan, there are no fixed costs, so the intercept on the horizontal axis is zero. For the debt plan, there must be an EBIT of $200,000 to cover interest charges. For the preferred stock plan, there must be an EBIT of $320,000 [$160,000/1 − 0.5)] to cover $160,000 in preferred stock dividends at a 50% income tax rate; so $320,000 becomes the horizontal axis intercept. (See Figure 27–1.) In this example, the

FIGURE 27-1 EPS-EBIT GRAPH

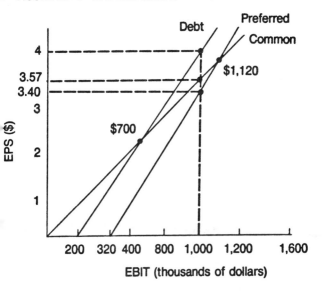

indifference point between all common and all debt is:

$$\frac{(EBIT - I)(1 - t) - PD}{S_1} = \frac{(EBIT - I)(1 - t) - PD}{S_2}$$

$$\frac{(EBIT - 0)(1 - 0.5) - 0}{140,000} = \frac{(EBIT - 200,000)(1 - 0.5) - 0}{100,000}$$

Rearranging yields:

$$0.5(EBIT)(100,000) = 0.5(EBIT)(140,000)$$
$$- 0.5(200,000)(140,000)$$
$$20,000 \ EBIT = 14,000,000,000$$
$$EBIT = \$700,000$$

Similarly, the indifference point between all common and all preferred would be:

$$\frac{(EBIT - I)(1 - t) - PD}{S_1} = \frac{(EBIT - I)(1 - t) - PD}{S_2}$$

$$\frac{(EBIT - 0)(1 - 0.5) - 0}{140,000} = \frac{(EBIT - 0)(1 - 0.5) - 160,000}{100,000}$$

Rearranging yields:

$$0.5(\text{EBIT})(100,000) = 0.5(\text{EBIT})(140,000)$$
$$- 160,000(140,000)$$
$$20,000 \; \text{EBIT} = 22,400,000,000$$
$$\text{EBIT} = \$1,120,000$$

Based on the above computations and observing Figure 27–1, we can draw the following conclusions:

1. At any level of EBIT, debt is better than preferred stock, since it gives a higher EPS.

2. At a level of EBIT above $700,000, debt is better than common stock. If EBIT is below $700,000, the reverse is true.

3. At a level of EBIT above $1,120,000, preferred stock is better than common. At or below that point, the reverse is true.

A Word of Caution

It is important to realize that financial leverage is a two-edge sword. It can magnify profits but it can also increase losses. The EBIT-EPS approach helps the CFO examine the impact of financial leverage as a financing method. Investment performance is crucial to the successful application of any leveraging strategy.

ANALYSIS OF CORPORATE CASH FLOWS

A second tool of capital structure management involves the *analysis of cash flows*. When considering the appropriate capital structure, among other things, it is important to analyze the cash-flow ability of the firm to service fixed charges. The greater the dollar amount of debt and/or preferred stock the firm issues and the shorter their maturity, the greater the fixed charges of the firm. These charges include principal and interest payments on debt, lease payments, and preferred stock dividends. Before assuming additional fixed charges, the firm should analyze its expected future cash flows, for fixed charges must be met with cash. The inability to meet these charges, with the exception of preferred stock dividends, may result in insolvency. The greater and more stable the expected future cash flows of the firm, the greater the debt capacity of the company.

COVERAGE RATIOS

A third tool is the calculation of *comparative coverage ratios.* Among the ways we can gain insight into the debt capacity of a firm is through the use of coverage ratios. In the computation of these ratios, a CFO typically uses EBIT as a rough measure of the cash flow available to cover debt-servicing obligations. Perhaps the most widely used coverage ratio is *times interest earned,* which is simply:

$$\text{Times interest earned} = \frac{\text{EBIT}}{\text{Interest on debt}}$$

Assume that the most recent annual EBIT for a company was $4 million, and that interest payments on all debt obligations were $1 million. Therefore, times interest earned would be four times. This tells us that EBIT can drop by as much as 75% and the firm still will be able to cover its interest payments out of earnings.

However, a coverage ratio of only 1.0 indicates that earnings are just sufficient to satisfy the interest burden. While it is difficult to generalize as to what is an appropriate interest coverage ratio, a CFO usually is concerned when the ratio gets much below 3:1. However, it all depends. In a highly stable industry, a relatively low times-interest-earned ratio may be appropriate, whereas it is not appropriate in a highly cyclical one.

Unfortunately, the times-interest-earned ratio tells us nothing about the ability of the firm to meet principal payments on its debt. The inability to meet a principal payment constitutes the same legal default as failure to meet an interest payment. Therefore, it is useful to compute the coverage ratio for the full debt-service burden. This ratio is:

$$\text{Debt-service coverage} = \frac{\text{EBIT}}{\text{Interest} + \dfrac{\text{Principal payments}}{1 - \text{Tax rate}}}$$

Here principal payments are adjusted upward for the tax effect. The reason is that EBIT represents earnings before taxes. Because principal payments are not tax deductible, they must be paid out of after-tax earnings. Therefore, we must adjust principal payments so that they are consistent with EBIT. If principal payments in our previous example were $1.5 million per annum and the tax rate were 34%, the debt-service coverage ratio would be:

$$\text{Debt-service coverage} = \frac{\$4 \text{ million}}{\$1 \text{ million} + \dfrac{\$1.5 \text{ million}}{1 - .34}} = 1.22$$

A coverage ratio of 1.22 means that EBIT can fall by only 22% before earnings coverage is insufficient to service the debt. The closer the ratio is to 1.0, the worse things are, all other things being equal. However, even with a coverage ratio of less than 1.0, a company may still meet its obligations if it can renew some of its debt when it comes due.

The financial risk associated with leverage should be analyzed on the basis of the firm's ability to service total fixed charges. While lease financing is not debt per se, its impact on cash flows is exactly the same as the payment of interest and principal on a debt obligation. Therefore, annual lease payments should be added to the denominator of the formula in order to properly reflect the total cash-flow burden associated with financing.

Two types of comparison should be undertaken with a coverage ratio. First, it should be compared with past and expected future ratios of the same company. The idea behind *trend analysis* is to determine if there has been an improvement or a deterioration in coverage over time. Another method of analyzing the appropriate capital structure for a company is to evaluate the capital structure of other companies having similar business risk. Companies used in this comparison may be those in the same industry. If the firm is contemplating a capital structure significantly out of line with that of similar companies, it is conspicuous to the marketplace. This is not to say, however, that the firm is wrong; other companies in the industry may be too conservative with respect to the use of debt. The optimal capital structure for all companies in the industry might call for a higher proportion of debt to equity than the industry average. As a result, the firm may well be able to justify more debt than the industry average. Because investment analysts and creditors tend to evaluate companies by industry, however, the firm should be able to justify its position if its capital structure is noticeably out of line in either direction.

Ultimately, a CFO wants to make generalizations about the appropriate amount of debt (and leases) for a firm to have in its capital structure. It is clear that over the long run the source to service debt for a going concern is earnings. Therefore, coverage ratios are an important analytical tool. However, coverage ratios are but only one tool by which a CFO is able to reach conclusions with respect to the company's best capital structure. Coverage ratios are subject to certain limitations and, consequently, cannot be used as a sole means for determining the capital structure. For one thing, the fact that EBIT falls below the debt-service burden does not spell immediate doom for the company. Often alternative sources of funds, including renewal of a loan, are available, and these sources must be considered.

CAPITAL STRUCTURE DECISIONS ⎯⎯⎯⎯⎯⎯

How are capital structure decisions made in practice?

How do companies decide in practice which route to go in raising capital? It is a complex decision, related to a company's balance sheet, market conditions, outstanding obligations and a host of other factors.

Many CFOs believe that the following factors influence capital structure:

1. Growth rate and stability of future sales.

2. Competitive structure in the industry.

3. Asset makeup of the individual firm.

4. The business risk to which the firm is exposed.

5. Control status of owners and management.

6. Lenders' attitudes toward the industry and the company.

Surveys indicate that the majority of CFOs of large firms believe in the concept of an optimal capital structure. The optimal capital structure is approximated by the identification of target debt ratios. The most frequently mentioned factor that affects the level of the target debt ratio was the company's ability to service fixed financing costs. Other factors identified as affecting the target were (1) maintaining a desired bond rating, (2) providing an adequate borrowing reserve, and (3) exploiting the advantages of financial leverage.

28

Dividend Policy

Your company's dividend policy is important for the following reasons:

- It impacts the financing program and capital budget.
- It affects cash flow. A company experiencing liquidity problems may be forced to restrict its dividend payments.
- It influences investor attitudes. For example, stockholders do not like dividends cut because they associate it with corporate financial problems. Further, in formulating a dividend policy, the CFO must determine and fulfill the owners' objectives. Otherwise, the stockholders may sell their shares, which in turn may lower the market price of the stock. Stockholder dissatisfaction raises the possibility that control of the company may be acquired by an outside group.
- It lowers stockholders' equity since dividends reduce retained earnings, and so results in a higher debt to equity ratio.

If your company's cash flows and investment requirements are unstable, the CFO should not recommend a high regular dividend. It would be better to establish a low regular dividend that can be met even in bad years.

What dividend policy is best for your company?

The company's dividend policy should maximize owner wealth while providing adequate financing for the business. When the company's profitability increases, the CFO does *not* automatically raise the dividend. Generally, there is a time lag between increased earnings and the payment of a higher dividend. The CFO should be optimistic that the increased earnings will be sustained before he or she increases the dividend. If dividends are increased, they should continue to be paid at the higher rate. There are different

types of dividend policies the CFO may choose
from including:

1. *Stable dividend-per-share policy.* Many
companies use a stable dividend-per-share policy
because it is looked upon favorably by investors.
A stable dividend implies a low-risk company.
The dividend should be maintained even in loss
years because the shareholders are more apt to
consider the losses as temporary. Further, some
stockholders rely on the receipt of stable dividends for income. A stable dividend policy is also
necessary for a company to be placed on a list of
securities in which financial institutions (pension funds, insurance companies) invest. The inclusion on the list provides greater marketability
for corporate shares.

2. *Constant dividend-payout ratio (dividends
per share/earnings per share).* A constant percentage of earnings is paid out in dividends. Because net income fluctuates, dividends paid will
also vary using this policy. A problem arises if
the company's earnings fall drastically or there is
a loss because the dividends paid will be significantly reduced or nonexistent. This policy will
not maximize market price per share since most
stockholders do not want variability in their dividend receipts.

3. *A compromise policy.* A compromise between the policies of a stable dollar amount and a
percentage amount of dividends is for a company
to pay a lower dollar amount per share plus a
percentage increment in good years. While this
policy provides flexibility, it also results in uncertainty in the minds of investors as to the
amount of dividends they are likely to receive.
Stockholders typically do not like such uncertainty. However, this policy may be suitable
when earnings vary considerably over the years.
The percentage, or extra, portion of the dividend
should not be paid regularly; otherwise it becomes meaningless.

4. *Residual-dividend policy.* When a company's investment opportunities are not stable,
the CFO may wish to consider a vacillating dividend policy. The amount of earnings retained

depends upon the availability of investment opportunities. Dividends represent the *residual* amount from earnings after the company's investment needs are satisfied.

EXAMPLE 1

Company A and company B are identical except for their dividend policies. Company A pays out a constant percentage of its net income (40% dividends), while company B pays out a constant dollar dividend. Company B's market price per share is higher than that of company A because the stock market looks favorably upon stable dollar dividends which imply less uncertainty.

EXAMPLE 2

Hayes Manufacturing Company had a net income of $800,000 in 19X1. Earnings have grown at an 8% annual rate. Dividends in 19X1 were $300,000. In 19X2, the net income was $1,100,000. This was much higher than the typical 8% annual growth rate. It is anticipated that profits will be back to the 8% rate in future years. The investment in 19X2 was $700,000.

Assuming a stable dividend payout ratio of 25%, the dividends to be paid in 19X2 will be $275,000 ($1,100,000 × 25%).

If a stable dollar dividend policy is maintained, the 19X2 dividend payment will be $324,000 ($300,000 × 1.08).

Assuming a residual dividend policy is maintained and 40 percent of the 19X2 investment is financed with debt, the 19X2 dividend will be:

Equity needed = $700,000 × 60% = $420,000

Since net income exceeds the equity needed, all of the $420,000 of equity investment will be derived from net income.

Dividend = $1,100,000 − $420,000 = $680,000

If the investment for 19X2 is to be financed with 80% debt and 20% retained earnings, and any net income not invested is paid out in dividends, then the dividends will be:

$$\text{Earnings retained} = \$700,000 \times 20\% = \$140,000$$

Dividend = Net income – Earnings retained

$960,000 = \$1,100,000 - \$140,000$

In theory, how much should be paid in dividends?

Theoretically, the company should retain earnings rather than distribute them when the corporate return exceeds the return investors can obtain on their money elsewhere. Further, if the company obtains a return on its profits that exceeds the cost of capital, the market price of its stock will be maximized. On the other hand, the company should not, theoretically, keep funds for investment if it earns less of a return than what the investors can earn elsewhere. If the owners have better investment opportunities outside the company, the firm should pay a high dividend.

Although theoretical considerations from a financial perspective should be taken into account when establishing dividend policy, the *practicality* of the situation is that investors expect to be paid dividends. Psychological factors come into play which may adversely impact the market price of the stock of a company that does not pay dividends.

What are the important variables in establishing dividend policy?

A company's dividend policy depends on many variables, some of which have already been mentioned. Other factors to be considered are:

• *Profitability.* Dividend distribution is tied to earnings.

• *Earnings stability.* A company with stable earnings is better able to distribute a higher percentage of its profit than one with unstable earnings.

• *Tax penalties.* The tax penalties for excess accumulation of retained earnings may result in high dividend payouts.

• *Financial leverage.* A company with a high debt-to-equity ratio is more likely to retain profits so that it will have the funds to pay interest and principal on debt when due.

• *Restrictive covenants.* There may be a restriction in a loan agreement limiting the dividend payments.

• *Growth rate.* A rapidly growing company, even if profitable, may have to cut back on dividends to keep funds within the business for growth.

• *Uncertainty.* The payment of dividends reduces the uncertainty in stockholders' minds about the firm's financial condition.

• *Ability to finance externally.* A company that is able to obtain outside financing can afford to have a higher dividend payout ratio. When external sources of funds are limited, more earnings will be retained for planned financial needs.

• *Age and size.* An older, established, large company is usually better able to maintain dividend payments.

• *Maintenance of control.* Management that is reluctant to issue additional common stock because it does not want to dilute control of the firm will retain a higher percentage of its earnings. Internal financing enables control to be kept within.

How does stock repurchase benefit or hinder the company?

The purchase of treasury stock is an alternative to paying dividends. Since outstanding shares will be fewer after stock has been repurchased, earnings per share will increase (assuming net income is held constant). The increase in earnings per share may result in a higher market price per share.

EXAMPLE 3

A company earned $2.5 million in 19X1. Of this amount, it decided that 20% would be used to buy treasury stock. Currently, there are 400,000 shares outstanding. Market price per share is $18.

The company can use $500,000 (20% × $2.5 million) to buy back 25,000 shares through a tender offer of $20 per share. The offer price of $20 is higher than the current market price of $18 because the company feels its buy back will drive up the price of existing shares due to the demand/supply relationship.

Current earnings per share is:

$$\text{EPS} = \frac{\text{Net income}}{\text{Outstanding shares}} = \frac{\$2,500,000}{400,000} = \$6.25$$

The current P/E multiple is:

$$\frac{\text{Market price per share}}{\text{Earnings per share}} = \frac{\$18}{\$6.25} = 2.88 \text{ times}$$

Earnings per share after treasury stock is acquired becomes:

$$\frac{\$2,500,000}{400,000 - 25,000} = \frac{\$2,500,000}{375,000} = \$6.67$$

The expected market price, assuming the P/E ratio (multiple) remains the same, is:

$$\text{P/E multiple} \times \frac{\text{New earnings}}{\text{per share}} = \frac{\text{Expected}}{\text{market price}}$$

$$2.88 \quad \times \quad \$6.67 \quad = \quad \$19.21$$

The benefits from a stock repurchase include the following:

• Treasury stock can be resold if additional funds are needed. If the treasury stock was acquired for a price less than the current market price, the excess increases paid-in-capital.

• If there is temporary excess cash, the CFO may prefer to repurchase stock than to pay a higher dividend that he or she believes cannot be maintained.

• Treasury stock can be used for stock options or future acquisitions.

• If management is holding stock, they would favor a stock repurchase rather than a dividend because of the favorable tax treatment.

The disadvantages of treasury stock acquisition include:

• If investors believe that the company is engaging in a repurchase plan because there are no alternative good investment prospects, a decline in the market price of stock may occur. However, there are instances when this has not happened, such as when General Electric announced in 1989 its plan of periodic reacquisition of stock because of a lack of more attractive investment opportunities.

• If the reacquisition of stock appears to be manipulation, the Securities and Exchange Commission (SEC) may investigate. Further, if the Internal Revenue Service (IRS) concludes that the repurchase is designed to avoid the payment of tax on dividends, tax penalties may be imposed because of the improper accumulation of earnings.

29

Financial Management of Multinational Corporations

Many companies are multinational corporations (MNCs) that have significant foreign operations deriving a high percentage of their sales overseas. CFOs of MNCs require an understanding of the complexities of international finance to make sound financial and investment decisions. International finance involves consideration of managing working capital, financing the business, control of foreign exchange and political risks, and foreign direct investments. Most importantly, the CFO has to consider the value of the U.S. dollar relative to the value of the currency of the foreign country in which business activities are being conducted. Currency exchange rates may materially affect receivables and payables, and imports and exports of the U.S. company in its multinational operations. The effect is more pronounced with increasing activities abroad.

What is unique about the financial management of a multinational corporation (MNC)?

• *Multiple-currency problem.* Sales revenues may be collected in one currency, assets denominated in another, and profits measured in a third.

• *Various legal, institutional, and economic constraints.* There are variations in such things as tax laws, labor practices, balance of payment policies, and government controls with respect to the types and sizes of investments, types and amount of capital raised, and repatriation of profits.

• *Internal control problem.* When the parent office of a MNC and its affiliates are widely located, internal organizational difficulties arise.

What are popular financial goals of MNCs?

A survey made on CFOs of MNCs lists the financial goals of MNCs in the following order of importance:

1. Maximize growth in corporate earnings, whether total earnings, earnings before interest and taxes (EBIT), or earnings per share (EPS).

2. Maximize return on equity.

3. Guarantee that funds are always available when needed.

What types of foreign operations are right for you?

When strong competition exists in the United States, a company may look to enter or expand its foreign base. However, if a company is unsuccessful in the domestic market, it is likely to have problems overseas as well. Further, the CFO must be cognizant of local customs and risks in the international markets.

A large, well-established company with much international experience may eventually have wholly-owned subsidiaries. However, a small company with limited foreign experience operating in "risky areas" may be restricted to export and import activity.

If the company's sales force has minimal experience in export sales, it is advisable to use foreign brokers when specialized knowledge of foreign markets is needed. When sufficient volume exists, the company may establish a foreign branch sales office including sales people and technical service staff. As the operation matures, production facilities may be located in the foreign market. However, some foreign countries require licensing before foreign sales and production can take place. In this case, a foreign licensee sells and produces the product. A problem with this is that confidential information and knowledge are passed on to the licensees who can then become a competitor at the expiration of the agreement.

A joint venture with a foreign company is another way to proceed internationally and share the risk. Some foreign governments require this to be the path to follow to operate in their countries. The foreign company may have local goodwill to assure success. A drawback is less control over activities and a conflict of interest.

In evaluating the impact that foreign operations have on the entity's financial health, the CFO should consider the extent of intercountry transactions, foreign restrictions and laws, tax structure of the foreign country, and the economic and political stability of the country. If a subsidiary is operating in a high-tax country with a double-tax agreement, dividend payments are not subject to further U.S. taxes. One way to transfer income from high tax areas to low tax areas is to levy royalties or management fees on the subsidiaries.

What is the foreign exchange market?

Except in a few European centers, there is no central marketplace for the foreign exchange market. Rather, business is carried out over telephone or telex. The major dealers are large banks. A company that wants to buy or sell currency typically uses a commercial bank. International transactions and investments involve more than one currency. For example, when a U.S. company sells merchandise to a Japanese firm, the former wants to be paid in dollars but the Japanese company typically expects to receive yen. Due to the foreign exchange market, the buyer may pay in one currency while the seller can receive payment in another currency.

What are spot and forward foreign exchange rates?

An exchange rate is the ratio of one unit of currency to another. An exchange rate is established between the different currencies. The conversion rate between currencies depends on the demand/supply relationship. Because of the change in exchange rates, companies are susceptible to exchange rate fluctuation risks because of a net asset or net liability position in a foreign currency. (See Figure 29–1.)

FIGURE 29-1   FOREIGN EXCHANGE RATES (FRIDAY, OCTOBER 4, 1991)

Country	Contract	U.S. Dollar Equivalent	Currency per U.S. $
Britain	Spot	1.7350	.5764
(Pound)	30-day future	1.7272	.5790
	90-day future	1.7142	.5834
	180-day future	1.6963	.5895
Germany	Spot	.5952	1.6800
(Mark)	30-day future	.5933	1.6856
	90-day future	.5894	1.6965
	180-day future	.5839	1.7126
Japan	Spot	.007681	130.20
(Yen)	30-day future	.007670	130.37
	90-day future	.007670	130.55
	180-day future	.007650	130.72

Exchange rates may be in terms of dollars per foreign currency unit (called a *direct quote*) or units of foreign currency per dollar (called an *indirect quote*). Therefore, an indirect quote is the reciprocal of a direct quote and vice versa:

$$\text{An indirect quote} = 1/\text{direct quote}$$
$$\text{Pound/\$} = 1/(\text{\$/pound})$$

EXAMPLE 1

A rate of 1.735/British pound means each pound costs the U.S. company $1.735. In other words, the U.S. company gets $1/1.735 = .5764$ pounds for each dollar.

The spot rate is the exchange rate for immediate delivery of currencies exchanged, while the forward rate is the exchange rate for later delivery of currencies exchanged. For example, there may be a 90-day exchange rate. The forward exchange rate of a currency will be slightly different from the spot rate at the current date because of future expectations and uncertainties.

Forward rates may be greater than the current spot rate (premium) or less than the current spot rate (discount).

What are cross rates?

A cross rate is the indirect calculation of the exchange rate of one currency from the exchange rates of two other currencies.

EXAMPLE 2

The dollar per pound and the yen per dollar rates are given in Figure 29–1. From this information, you could determine the yen per pound (or pound per yen) exchanges rates. For example, you see that:

$$(\$/\text{pound}) \times (\text{yen}/\$) = (\text{yen}/\text{pound})$$
$$1.7350 \times 130.20 = 225.897 \text{ yen/pound}$$

Thus, the pound per yen exchange rate is

$$1/225.897 = .004427 \text{ pound per yen}$$

Note: The Wall Street Journal routinely publishes key currency cross rates, as shown in Figure 29–2.

EXAMPLE 3

On February 1, 19X5, forward rates on the British pound were at a premium in relation to the spot rate, while the forward rates for the Japanese yen were at a discount from the spot rate. This means that participants in the foreign exchange market anticipated that the British pound would appreciate relative to the U.S. dollar in the future but the Japanese yen would depreciate against the dollar.

The percentage discount or premium is computed as follows. Forward premium (or discount) equals:

$$\frac{\text{Forward rate} - \text{spot rate}}{\text{Spot rate}} \times \frac{12}{\substack{\text{Length of forward} \\ \text{contract in months}}} \times 100$$

where if the forward rate > the spot rate, the result is the annualized premium in percent; otherwise, it is the annualized discount in percent.

FIGURE 29-2 KEY CURRENCY CROSS RATES
LATE NEW YORK TRADING OCT. 31, 1991

	Dollar	Pound	SFranc	Guilder	Yen	Lira	D-Mark	FFranc	CdnDlr
Canada	1.1228	1.9525	.76480	.59612	.00858	.00090	.67153	.19648	
France	5.7145	9.938	3.8924	3.0340	.04367	.00456	3.4178		5.0895
Germany	1.6720	2.9076	1.1389	.88771	.01278	.00133		.29259	1.4891
Italy	1253.0	2179.0	853.48	665.25	9.576		749.40	219.27	1116.0
Japan	130.85	227.55	89.129	69.472		.10443	78.260	22.898	116.54
Netherlands	1.8835	3.2754	1.2830		.01439	.00150	1.1265	.32960	1.6775
Switzerland	1.4681	2.5530		.77945	.01122	.00117	.87805	.25691	1.3075
U.K.	.57504		.39169	.30531	.00439	.00046	.34393	.10063	.51215
U.S.		1.7390	.68115	.53093	.00764	.00080	.59809	.17499	.89063

Source: Telerate

EXAMPLE 4

On October 4, 1991, a 30-day forward contract in British pounds was selling at a 5.39% discount:

$$\frac{1.7350 - 1.7272}{1.7350} \times \frac{12 \text{ months}}{1 \text{ month}} \times 100 = 5.39\%$$

How do you control foreign exchange risk?

Foreign exchange rate risk exists when the contract is written in terms of the foreign currency or denominated in foreign currency. The exchange rate fluctuations increase the riskiness of the investment and incur cash losses. The CFOs must not only seek the highest return on temporary investments but must also be concerned about changing values of the currencies invested. You do not necessarily eliminate foreign exchange risk. You may only try to contain it.

FINANCIAL STRATEGIES ⸻

In countries where currency values are likely to drop, CFOs of the subsidiaries should:

• Avoid paying advances on purchase orders unless the seller pays interest on the advances sufficient to cover the loss of purchasing power.

• Not have excess idle cash. Excess cash can be used to buy inventory or other real assets.

• Buy materials and supplies on credit in the country in which the foreign subsidiary is operating, extending the final payment date as long as possible.

• Avoid giving excessive trade credit. If accounts receivable balances are outstanding for an extended time period, interest should be charged to absorb the loss in purchasing power.

• Borrow local currency funds when the interest rate charged does not exceed U.S. rates after taking into account expected devaluation in the foreign country.

What are three different types of foreign exchange exposure?

MNCs' CFOs are faced with the dilemma of three different types of foreign exchange risk. They are:

- *Translation exposure,* often called *accounting exposure,* measures the impact of an exchange rate change on the firm's financial statements. An example would be the impact of a French Franc devaluation on a U.S. firm's reported income statement and balance sheet.

- *Transaction exposure* measures potential gains or losses on the future settlement of outstanding obligations that are denominated in a foreign currency. An example would be a U.S. dollar loss after the Franc devalues, on payment received for an export invoiced in Francs before that devaluation.

- *Operating exposure,* often called *economic exposure,* is the potential for the change in the present value of future cash flows due to an unexpected change in the exchange rate.

TRANSLATION EXPOSURE _____

A major purpose of translation is to provide data of expected impacts of rate changes on cash flow and equity. In the translation of the foreign subsidiaries' financial statements into the U.S. parent's financial statements, the following steps are involved:

1. The foreign financial statements are put into U.S. generally accepted accounting principles.

2. The foreign currency is translated into U.S. dollars. Balance sheet accounts are translated using the current exchange rate at the balance sheet date. If a current exchange rate is not available at the balance sheet date, use the first exchange rate available after that date. Income statement accounts are translated using the weighted-average exchange rate for the period.

Current (1986) FASB rules require translation by the *current rate* method. Under the current rate method:

• All balance sheet assets and liabilities are translated at the current rate of exchange in effect on the balance sheet date.

• Income statement items are usually translated at an average exchange rate for the reporting period.

• All equity accounts are translated at the historical exchange rates that were in effect at the time the accounts first entered the balance sheet.

• Translation gains and losses are reported as a separate item in the stockholders' equity section of the balance sheet. Translation gains and losses are only included in net income when there is a sale or liquidation of the entire investment in a foreign entity.

TRANSACTION EXPOSURE _____

Foreign currency transactions may result in receivables or payables fixed in terms of the amount of foreign currency to be received or paid. Transaction gains and losses are reported in the income statement.

Foreign currency transactions are those transactions whose terms are denominated in a currency other than the entity's functional currency. Foreign currency transactions take place when a business:

• Buys or sells on credit goods or services the prices of which are denominated in foreign currencies.

• Borrows or lends funds, and the amounts payable or receivable are denominated in a foreign currency.

• Is a party to an unperformed forward exchange contract.

• Acquires or disposes of assets, or incurs or settles liabilities denominated in foreign currencies.

Note: Transaction losses differ from translation losses, which do not influence taxable income.

What is long versus short position?

When there is a devaluation of the dollar, foreign assets and income in strong currency countries are worth more dollars as long as foreign liabilities do not offset this beneficial effect.

Foreign exchange risk may be analyzed by examining expected receipts or obligations in foreign currency units. A company expecting receipts in foreign currency units ("long" position in the foreign currency units) has the risk that the value of the foreign currency units will drop. This results in devaluing the foreign currency relative to the dollar. If a company is expecting to have obligations in foreign currency units ("short" position in the foreign currency units), there is risk that the value of the foreign currency will rise and it will need to buy the currency at a higher price.

If net claims are greater than liabilities in a foreign currency, the company has a "long" position since it will benefit if the value of the foreign currency rises. If net liabilities exceed claims with respect to foreign currencies, the company is in a "short" position because it will gain if the foreign currency drops in value.

What is your monetary position?

Monetary balance is avoiding either a net receivable or a net payable position. Monetary assets and liabilities do not change in value with devaluation or revaluation in foreign currencies.

A company with a long position in a foreign currency will be receiving more funds in the foreign currency. It will have a net monetary asset position (monetary assets exceed monetary liabilities) in that currency.

A company with net receipts is a net monetary creditor. Its foreign exchange rate risk exposure has a net receipts position in a foreign currency that is susceptible to a drop in value.

A company with a future net obligation in foreign currency has a net monetary debtor position. It faces a foreign exchange risk of the possibility of an increase in the value of the foreign currency.

What are some ways to neutralize foreign exchange risk?

Foreign exchange risk can be neutralized or hedged by a change in the asset and liability position in the foreign currency. Here are some ways to control exchange risk.

• Entering a money-market hedge. Here the exposed position in a foreign currency is offset by borrowing or lending in the money market.

EXAMPLE 5

XYZ, an American importer enters into a contract with a British supplier to buy merchandise for 4,000 pounds. The amount is payable on the delivery of the good, 30 days from today. The company knows the exact amount of its pound liability in 30 days. However, it does not know the payable in dollars. Assume that the 30-day money-market rates for both lending and borrowing in the United States and United Kingdom are 0.5% and 1%, respectively. Assume further that today's foreign exchange rate is $1.50 per pound.

In a money-market hedge, XYZ can take the following steps:

Step 1. Buy a one-month U.K. money market security, worth $4,000/(1 + .005) = 3,980$ pounds. This investment will compound to exactly 4,000 pounds in one month.

Step 2. Exchange dollars on today's spot (cash) market to obtain the 3,980 pounds. The dollar amount needed today is 3,980 pounds × $1.7350 per pound = $6,905.30.

Step 3. If XYZ does not have this amount, it can borrow it from the U.S. money market at the going rate of 1%. In 30 days, XYZ will need to repay $6,905.30 \times (1 + .1) = \$7,595.83$.

Note: XYZ need not wait for the future exchange rate to be available. On today's date, the future dollar amount of the contract is known with certainty. The British supplier will receive 4,000 pounds, and the cost of XYZ to make the payment is $7,595.83.

• Hedging by purchasing forward (or futures) exchange contracts. Forward exchange contracts is a commitment to buy or sell, at a specified future date, one currency for a specified amount of another currency (at a specified exchange rate). This can be a hedge against changes in exchange rates during a period of contract or exposure to risk from such changes. More specifically, you do the following: (1) Buy foreign exchange forward contracts to cover payables denominated in a foreign currency and (2) sell foreign exchange forward contracts to cover receivables denominated in a foreign currency. This way, any gain or loss on the foreign receivables or payables due to changes in exchange rates is offset by the gain or loss on the forward exchange contract.

EXAMPLE 6

In the previous example, assume that the 30-day forward exchange rate is $1.7272. XYZ may take the following steps to cover its payable.

Step 1. Buy a forward contract today to purchase 4,000 pounds in 30 days.

Step 2. On the 30th day pay the foreign exchange dealer 4,000 pounds × $1.7272 per pound = $6,908.80 and collect 4,000 pounds. Pay this amount to the British supplier.

Note: Using the forward contract XYZ knows the exact worth of the future payment in dollars ($6,908.80).

Note: The basic difference between futures contracts and forward contracts is that futures contracts are for specified amounts and maturities, whereas forward contracts are for any size and maturity desired.

• Hedging by foreign currency options. Foreign currency options can be purchased or sold in three different types of markets: (a) Options on the physical currency, purchased on the over-the-counter (interbank) market, (b) options on the physical currency, on organized exchanges such as the Philadelphia Stock Exchange and the Chicago Mercantile Exchange, and (c) options on futures contracts, purchased on the International

Monetary Market (IMM) of the Chicago Mercantile Exchange. *Note:* The difference between using a futures contract and using an option on a futures contract is that with a futures contract, the company must deliver one currency against another, or reverse the contract on the exchange, while with an option the company may abandon the option and use the spot (cash) market if that is more advantageous.

• Repositioning cash by *leading* and *lagging* the time at which an MNC makes operational or financial payments. Often, money- and forward-market hedges are not available to eliminate exchange risk. Under such circumstances, leading (accelerating) and lagging (decelerating) may be used to *reduce* risk. *Note:* A net asset position (i.e., assets minus liabilities) is not desirable in a weak or potentially depreciating currency. In this case, you should expedite the disposal of the asset. By the same token, you should lag or delay the collection against a net asset position in a strong currency.

• Maintaining balance between receivables and payables denominated in a foreign currency. MNCs typically set up "multilateral netting centers" as a special department to settle the outstanding balances of affiliates of a MNC with each other on a net basis. It is the development of a clearing house for payments by the firm's affiliates. If there are amounts due among affiliates they are offset insofar as possible. The net amount would be paid in the currency of the transaction. The total amounts owed need not be paid in the currency of the transaction; thus, a much lower quantity of the currency must be acquired. *Note:* The major advantage of the system is a reduction of the costs associated with a large number of separate foreign exchange transactions.

• Positioning of funds through *transfer pricing*. A transfer price is the price at which an MNC sells goods and services to its foreign affiliates or, alternatively, the price at which an affiliate sells to the parent. For example, a parent that wishes to transfer funds from an affiliate in a depreciating-currency country may charge a higher price on the goods and services sold to this affiliate by the parent or by affiliates from strong-currency countries. Transfer pricing affects not only transfer of funds from one entity to another but also the income taxes paid by both entities.

OPERATING EXPOSURE ⎯⎯⎯⎯⎯⎯⎯

Operating (economic) exposure is the possibility that an unexpected change in exchange rates will cause a change in the future cash flows of a firm and its market value. It differs from translation and transaction exposures in that it is subjective and thus not easily quantified. *Note:* The best strategy to control operation exposure is to diversify operations and financing internationally.

What are some key questions to ask that help to identify foreign exchange risk?

A systematic approach to identifying an MNC's exposure to foreign exchange risk is to ask a series of questions regarding the net effects on profits of changes in foreign currency revenues and costs. The questions are:

• Where is the MNC selling? (Domestic vs. foreign sales share)
• Who are the firm's major competitors? (Domestic vs. foreign)
• Where is the firm producing? (Domestic vs. foreign)
• Where are the firm's inputs coming from? (Domestic vs. foreign)
• How sensitive is quantity demanded to price? (Elastic vs. inelastic)
• How are the firm's inputs or outputs priced? (Priced in a domestic market or a global market; the currency of denomination)

Can you forecast foreign exchange rates?

The forecasting of foreign exchange rates is a formidable task. Most MNCs rely primarily on bank and bank services for assistance and information in preparing exchange rate projections. The following economic indicators are considered to be the most important for the forecasting process:

- Recent rate movements.
- Relative inflation rates.
- Balance of payments and trade.
- Money supply growth.
- Interest rate differentials.

INTEREST RATES

Interest rates have an important influence on exchange rates. In fact, there is an important economic relationship between any two nations' spot rates, forward rates, and interest rates. This relationship is called the *interest rate parity theorem* (IRPT). The IRPT states that the ratio of the forward and spot rates is directly related to the two interest rates:

$$\frac{F}{S} = \frac{1 + i_\$}{1 + i_F}$$

where F = forward exchange rate (\$/foreign currency), S = spot exchange rate (\$/foreign currency), $i_\$$ = U.S. interest rate, and i_F = foreign interest rate.

EXAMPLE 7

Assume the following data concerning U.S. and French currency.

$$F = \$0.210/FR$$
$$S = \$0.200/FR$$
$$i_F = 10\%$$

Then

$$\frac{0.210}{0.200} = \frac{1 + i_\$}{1.10}$$

So

$$i_\$ = 0.155 = 15.5\%$$

Note that the forward franc is selling at a premium and U.S. interest rates are higher than French interest rates.

INFLATION

Inflation, which is a change in price levels, also affect future exchange rates. The mathematical relationship that links changes in exchange rates and changes in price level is called the *purchasing power parity theorem* (PPPT). The PPPT states that the ratio of the forward and spot rates is directly related to the two inflation rates:

$$\frac{F}{S} = \frac{1 + I_\$}{1 + I_F}$$

where F = forward exchange rate (\$/foreign currency), S = spot exchange rate (\$/foreign currency), $I_\$$ = U.S. inflation rate, and I_F = foreign inflation rate.

EXAMPLE 8

Assume the following data:

Expected U.S. inflation rate   = 5%
Expected French inflation rate = 10%
$$S = \$0.220/FR$$

Then,

$$\frac{F}{0.220} = \frac{1.05}{1.10}$$

So

$$F = \$0.210/FR$$

Note: If France has the higher inflation rate, then the purchasing power of the franc is declining faster than that of the dollar. This will lead to a forward discount on the franc relative to the dollar.

APPRAISING FOREIGN INVESTMENTS ――――

How do you analyze foreign investments?

Foreign investment decisions are basically capital budgeting decisions at the international level. The decision requires three major components:

• *The estimation of the relevant future cash flows.* Cash flows are the dividends and possible future sales price of the investment. The estimation depends on the sales forecast, the effects on exchange rate changes, the risk in cash flows, and the actions of foreign governments.

• *The choice of the proper discount rate (cost of capital).* The cost of capital in foreign investment projects is higher due to the increased risks of:

- Currency risk (or foreign exchange risk)—changes in exchange rates. This risk may adversely affect sales by making competing imported goods cheaper.

- Political risk (or sovereignty risk)—possibility of nationalization or other restrictions with net losses to the parent company.

EXAMPLES OF POLITICAL RISKS ――――――

• Expropriation of plants and equipment without compensation or with minimal compensation that is below actual market value.

• Nonconvertibility of the affiliate's foreign earnings into the parent's currency—the problem of "blocked funds."

• Substantial changes in the laws governing taxation.

• Government controls in the host country regarding wages, compensation to the personnel, hiring of personnel, the sales price of the product, making of transfer payments to the parent, and local borrowing.

How do you measure political risk?

Many MNCs and banks have attempted to measure political risks in their businesses. They even hire or maintain a group of political risk analysts. Several independent services provide political risk and country risk ratings.

• *Euromoney* magazine's annual *Country Risk Rating,* which is based on a measure of different countries' access to international credit, trade finance, political risk and a country's payment record. The rankings are generally confirmed by political risk insurers and top syndicate managers in the Euromarkets.

• Rating by *Economist Intelligence Unit,* a New York-based subsidiary of the *Economist Group,* London, which is based on such factors as external debt and trends in the current account, the consistency of the government policy, foreign-exchange reserves, and the quality of economic management.

• *International Country Risk Guide,* put out by a U.S. division of *International Business Communications, Ltd.,* London, which offers a composite risk rating, as well as individual ratings for political, financial and economic risk (see Figure 29–3 for a 1991 global rating). The political variable—which makes up half of the composite index—includes factors such as government corruption and how economic expectations diverge from reality. The financial rating looks at such things as the likelihood of losses from exchange controls and loan defaults. Finally, economic ratings consider such factors as inflation and debt-service costs.

What are the methods for dealing with political risk?

To the extent that forecasting political risks is a formidable task, what can a MNC do to cope with them? There are several methods suggested. They are:

• *Avoidance* Try to avoid political risk by minimizing activities in or with activities with countries that are considered to be of high risk and by using a higher discount rate for projects in riskier countries.

FIGURE 29-3   A 1991 GLOBAL RANKING

COUNTRY	POLITICAL RISK	FINANCIAL RISK	ECONOMIC RISK	COMPOSITE RISK
1 Switzerland	93.0	50.0	39.5	91.5
2 Luxembourg	93.0	49.0	36.0	89.0
3 Norway	87.0	47.0	42.0	88.0
4 Austria	88.0	47.0	39.5	87.5
5 Germany	83.0	50.0	38.5	86.0
5 Netherlands	85.0	46.0	40.5	86.0
7 Brunei	81.0	48.0	41.5	85.5
8 Japan	80.0	50.0	39.0	84.5
9 Singapore	79.0	48.0	39.5	83.5
9 U.S.	78.0	49.0	39.5	83.5
11 Canada	81.0	48.0	37.0	83.0
12 Belgium	82.0	45.0	36.5	82.0
12 Denmark	86.0	41.0	37.0	82.0
14 Sweden	81.0	47.0	35.0	81.5
14 Taiwan	71.0	49.0	43.0	81.5
16 United Kingdom	76.0	50.0	36.0	81.0
17 Finland	85.0	44.0	32.0	80.5
18 France	79.0	46.0	34.5	80.0
18 Ireland	80.0	42.0	37.5	80.0
20 New Zealand	78.0	46.0	35.0	79.5
21 Australia	76.0	45.0	37.0	79.0
21 Iceland	82.0	42.0	33.5	79.0
23 Malaysia	71.0	45.0	38.5	77.5
24 Italy	72.0	47.0	35.0	77.0
25 Venezuela	75.0	40.0	36.0	75.5
26 Portugal	69.0	42.0	38.5	75.0
27 South Korea	63.0	47.0	36.5	73.5
28 Botswana	70.0	34.0	42.0	73.0

Source: International Country Risk Guide

FIGURE 29-3 (cont.)

COUNTRY	POLITICAL RISK	FINANCIAL RISK	ECONOMIC RISK	COMPOSITE RISK
28 Cyprus	69.0	39.0	38.0	73.0
30 Bahamas	66.0	39.0	36.5	71.0
30 Spain	65.0	42.0	35.0	71.0
32 Malta	64.0	34.0	43.0	70.5
32 Mexico	71.0	41.0	28.5	70.5
32 Oman	65.0	34.0	42.0	70.5
35 Chile	67.0	42.0	30.5	70.0
36 Czechoslovakia	73.0	36.0	30.0	69.5
37 Costa Rica	71.0	35.0	32.0	69.0
38 Indonesia	57.0	44.0	35.5	68.5
38 Uruguay	66.0	39.0	32.0	68.5
40 Thailand	57.0	42.0	37.0	68.0
41 Colombia	60.0	41.0	34.0	67.5
41 Hong Kong	58.0 .	42.0	35.0	67.5
43 Paraguay	59.0	39.0	34.5	66.5
44 Qatar	56.0	33.0	42.0	65.5
45 Gabon	57.0	33.0	39.0	64.5
45 Mongolia	65.0	36.0	28.0	64.5
47 Greece	65.0	33.0	29.5	64.0
48 Jamaica	66.0	37.0	24.0	63.5
49 Saudi Arabia	60.0	31.0	35.5	63.5
50 Israel	58.0	33.0	34.5	63.0
50 Trinidad/Tobago	59.0	35.0	31.5	63.0
50 U.A.E.	53.0	33.0	39.5	63.0
53 Bahrain	54.0	30.0	40.5	62.5
54 Brazil	67.0	34.0	23.0	62.0
54 Hungary	68.0	32.0	24.0	62.0
56 Gambia	53.0	33.0	35.5	61.0
56 Poland	62.0	29.0	31.0	61.0

FIGURE 29-3 (*cont.*)

COUNTRY	POLITICAL RISK	FINANCIAL RISK	ECONOMIC RISK	COMPOSITE RISK
58 China	58.0	24.0	38.0	60.0
59 South Africa	56.0	30.0	32.5	59.5
60 Bolivia	52.0	34.0	32.0	59.0
60 Cote d'Ivoire	66.0	29.0	23.0	59.0
62 Algeria	54.0	30.0	32.5	58.5
63 Argentina	63.0	30.0	23.0	58.0
63 Senegal	53.0	29.0	33.5	58.0
65 Bulgaria	61.0	28.0	25.5	57.5
66 Ecuador	58.0	29.0	26.0	56.5
66 Egypt	54.0	30.0	29.0	56.5
66 Libya	52.0	27.0	34.0	56.5
66 Nigeria	49.0	29.0	35.0	56.5
70 Syria	53.0	23.0	36.0	56.0
71 Iran	56.0	28.0	26.5	55.5
71 Morocco	52.0	28.0	30.5	55.5
71 U.S.S.R.	53.0	36.0	21.5	55.5
74 Ghana	53.0	30.0	27.0	55.0
75 Namibia	47.0	24.0	38.0	54.5
75 Panama	47.0	28.0	34.0	54.5
75 Tunisia	54.0	23.0	32.0	54.5
78 Cameroon	47.0	27.0	34.0	54.0
78 Papua	54.0	26.0	28.0	54.0
80 Dominican Rep.	53.0	23.0	30.5	53.5
81 Congo	52.0	20.0	33.5	53.0
81 Tanzania	56.0	27.0	23.0	53.0
83 Angola	45.0	19.0	41.0	52.5
83 Honduras	49.0	28.0	28.0	52.5
85 Albania	55.0	33.0	16.0	52.0
85 Malawi	51.0	28.0	25.0	52.0

FIGURE 29-3 (cont.)

	COUNTRY	POLITICAL RISK	FINANCIAL RISK	ECONOMIC RISK	COMPOSITE RISK
87	Madagascar	57.0	20.0	26.0	51.5
88	Togo	41.0	26.0	35.0	51.0
89	Guyana	51.0	29.0	20.5	50.5
90	Burkina Faso	41.0	23.0	36.0	50.0
90	Kenya	48.0	26.0	26.0	50.0
90	Zimbabwe	51.0	25.0	23.5	50.0
93	Romania	55.0	29.0	15.0	49.5
93	Turkey	52.0	19.0	27.5	49.5
95	Niger	45.0	24.0	29.0	49.0
96	Guinea	48.0	21.0	28.0	48.5
97	Guatemala	41.0	24.0	30.5	48.0
97	Jordan	45.0	20.0	30.5	48.0
99	Peru	45.0	28.0	21.5	47.5
99	Sri Lanka	36.0	26.0	32.5	47.5
99	Suriname	44.0	23.0	28.0	47.5
102	Philippines	41.0	22.0	29.5	46.5
102	Yugoslavia	45.0	24.0	23.5	46.5
104	Kuwait	38.0	24.0	29.5	46.0
104	New Caledonia	44.0	13.0	34.5	46.0
106	North Korea	59.0	15.0	16.0	45.0
106	Mali	40.0	19.0	30.5	45.0
106	Zambia	45.0	19.0	25.5	45.0
109	Nicaragua	44.0	27.0	17.0	44.0
109	Pakistan	34.0	22.0	32.0	44.0
109	Vietnam	50.0	18.0	20.0	44.0
112	El Salvador	37.0	18.0	32.0	43.5
113	India	34.0	25.0	27.0	43.0
113	Mozambique	44.0	26.0	15.5	43.0
115	Yemen	49.0	23.0	12.0	42.0

FIGURE 29-3 (*cont.*)

COUNTRY	POLITICAL RISK	FINANCIAL RISK	ECONOMIC RISK	COMPOSITE RISK
116 Cuba	54.0	16.0	12.0	41.0
117 Bangladesh	33.0	18.0	29.0	40.0
118 Lebanon	32.0	11.0	35.0	39.0
118 Sierra Leone	37.0	20.0	20.5	39.0
120 Guinea-Bissau	46.0	19.0	12.0	38.5
121 Zaire	30.0	18.0	20.0	34.0
122 Haiti	28.0	12.0	26.5	33.5
123 Ethiopia	22.0	16.0	25.0	31.5
124 Uganda	36.0	21.0	5.0	31.0
125 Burma	27.0	9.0	22.5	28.5
126 Iraq	19.0	4.0	25.5	24.5
127 Sudan	15.0	10.0	22.5	24.0
128 Somalia	22.0	12.0	5.0	19.5
129 Liberia	10.0	8.0	12.0	15.0

• *Adaptation* Try to reduce such risk by adapting the activities (for example, by using hedging techniques discussed previously).
• *Diversification* Diversity across national borders, so that problems in one country do not risk the company.
• *Risk transfer* Buy insurance policies for political risks.

EXAMPLE 9

Most developed nations offer insurance for political risk to their exporters. Examples are:

• In the United States, the *Eximbank* offers policies to exporters that cover such political risks as war, currency inconvertibility, and civil unrest. Furthermore, the *Overseas Private Investment Corporation (OPIC)* offers policies to U.S. foreign investors to cover such risks as currency inconvertibility, civil or foreign war damages, or expropriation.

• In the United Kingdom, similar policies are offered by the *Export Credit Guarantee Department (ECGD);* in Canada, by the *Export Development Council (EDC);* and in Germany, by an agency called *Hermes.*

FINANCING

What are international sources of financing?

A company may finance its activities abroad, especially in countries it is operating in. A successful company in domestic markets is more likely to be able to attract financing for international expansion.

The most important international sources of funds are the Eurocurrency market and the Eurobond market. Also, MNCs often have access to national capital markets in which their subsidiaries are located. (See Figure 29–4.)

The Eurocurrency market is a largely short-term (usually less than one year of maturity) market for bank deposits and loans denominated in any currency except the currency of the country where the market is located. For example, in London, the Eurocurrency market is a market for bank deposits and loans denominated in dollars, yen, franc, marks, and any other currency except British pounds. The main instruments used in this market are CDs and time deposits, and bank loans. *Note:* The term "market" in this context is not a physical market place, but a set of bank deposits and loans.

The Eurobond market is a long-term market for bonds denominated in any currency except the currency of the country where the market is located. Eurobonds may be of different types such as straight, convertible, and with warrants. While most Eurobonds are fixed rate, variable rate bonds also exist. Maturities vary but 10 to 12 years is typical.

Although Eurobonds are issued in many currencies, you wish to select a stable, fully convertible, and actively traded currency. In

FIGURE 29–4 INTERNATIONAL FINANCIAL MARKETS

Market	Instruments	Participants	Regulator
International monetary system	Special drawing rights; gold; foreign exchange	Central banks; International Monetary Fund	International Monetary Fund
Foreign exchange markets	Bank deposits; currency; futures and forward contracts	Commercial and central banks; firms; individuals	Central bank in each country
National money markets (short term)	Bank deposits and loans; short-term government securities; commercial paper	Banks; firms; individuals; government agencies	Central bank; other government agencies
National capital markets (long term)	Bonds; long-term bank deposits and loans; stocks; long-term government securities	Banks; firms; individuals; government agencies	Central bank; other government agencies
Eurocurrency market	Bank deposits; bank loans; eurocommercial paper	Commercial banks; firms; government agencies	Substantially unregulated
Eurobond market	Bonds	Banks; firms; individuals; government agencies	Substantially unregulated

some cases, if a Eurobond is denominated in a weak currency the holder has the option of requesting payment in another currency.

Sometimes, large MNCs establish wholly owned offshore finance subsidiaries. These subsidiaries issue Eurobond debt and the proceeds are given to the parent or to overseas operating subsidiaries. Debt service goes back to bondholders through the finance subsidiaries.

If the Eurobond was issued by the parent directly, the U.S. would require a withholding tax on interest. There may also be an estate tax when the bondholder dies. These tax problems do not arise when a bond is issued by a finance subsidiary incorporated in a tax haven. Hence, the subsidiary may borrow at less cost than the parent.

In summary, the Euromarkets offers borrowers and investors in one country the opportunity to deal with borrowers and investors from many other countries, buying and selling bank deposits, bonds, and loans denominated in many currencies.

Figure 29–5 provides a list of funding sources available to a foreign affiliate of an MNC (debt and equity).

EXAMPLE 10

In what follows, we will illustrate a case of multinational capital budgeting. We will analyze a hypothetical foreign investment project by a U.S. manufacturing firm in Korea. The analysis is based on the following Am-tel data gathered by a project team:

• *Product.* The company (to be called "Ko-tel" hereafter) is expected to be a wholly owned Korean manufacturer of customized integrated circuits (ICs) for use in computers, automobiles, and robots. Ko-tel's products would be sold primarily in Korea, and all sales would be denominated in Korean won.

• *Sales.* Sales in the first year are forecasted to be Won 26,000 million. Sales are expected to grow at 10% per annum for the foreseeable future.

FIGURE 29-5 INTERNATIONAL SOURCES OF CREDIT

Borrowing	Domestic Inside the Firm	Domestic Market	Foreign Inside the Firm	Foreign Market	Euromarket
Direct, short-term	Intrafirm loans, transfer pricing, royalties, fees, service charges	Commercial paper	International intrafirm loans, international transfer pricing, dividends, royalties, fees		Eurocommercial paper
Intermediated short-term		Short-term bank loans, discounted receivables	International back-to-back loans	Short-term bank loans, discounted receivables	Euro short-term loans
Direct, long-term	Intrafirm loans, invested in affiliates	Stock issue Bond issue	International intrafirm long-term loans, FDI	Stock issue Bond issue	Eurobonds
Intermediated, long-term		Long-term bank loans	International back-to-back loans	Long-term bank loans	Euro long-term loans

- *Working capital.* Ko-tel needs gross working capital (that is, cash, receivables, and inventory) equal to 25% of sales. Half of gross working capital can be financed by local payables, but the other half must be financed by Ko-tel or Am-tel.

- *Parent-supplied components.* Components sold to Ko-tel by Am-tel have a direct cost to Am-tel equal to 95% of their sales price. The margin is therefore 5%.

- *Depreciation.* Plant and equipment will be depreciated on a straight-line basis for both accounting and tax purposes over an expected life of 10 years. No salvage value is anticipated.

- *License fees.* Ko-tel will pay a license fee of 2.5% of sales revenue to Am-tel. This fee is tax-deductible in Korea but provides taxable income to Am-tel.

- *Taxes.* The Korean corporate income tax rate is 35%, and the U.S. rate is 38%. Korea has no withholding tax on dividends, interest, or fees paid to foreign residents.

- *Cost of capital.* The cost of capital (or minimum required return) used in Korea by companies of comparable risk is 22%. Am-tel also uses 22% as a discount rate for its investments.

- *Inflation.* Prices are expected to increase as follows:

Korean general price level:	+9% per annum
Ko-tel average sales price:	+9% per annum
Korean raw material costs:	+3% per annum
Korean labor costs:	+12% per annum
U.S. general price level:	+5% per annum

- *Exchange rates.* In the year in which the initial investment takes place, the exchange rate is Won 750 to the dollar. Am-tel forecasts the won to depreciate relative to the dollar at 4% per annum.

- *Dividend policy.* Ko-tel will pay 70% of accounting net income to Am-tel as an annual cash dividend. Ko-tel and Am-tel estimate that over a five-year period the other 30% of net income must be reinvested to finance working capital growth.

• *Financing.* Ko-tel will be financed by Am-tel with a $11,000,000 purchase of Won 8,250,000,000 common stock, all to be owned by Am-tel.

In order to develop the normal cash flow projections, Am-tel has made the following assumptions.

1. Sales revenue in the first year of operations is expected to be Won 26,000 million. Won sales revenue will increase annually at 10% because of physical growth and at an additional 9% because of price increases. Consequently, sales revenue will grow at $(1.1)(1.09) = 1.20$, or 20% per annum.

2. Korean raw material costs in the first year are budgeted at Won 4,000 million. Korean raw material costs are expected to increase at 10% per annum because of physical growth and at an additional 3% because of price increases. Consequently, raw material cost will grow at $(1.1)(1.03) = 1.13$, or 13% per annum.

3. Parent-supplied component costs in the first year are budgeted at Won 9,000 million. Parent-supplied component costs are expected to increase annually at 10% because of physical growth, plus an additional 5% because of U.S. inflation, plus another 4% in won terms because of the expected deterioration of the won relative to the dollar. Consequently, the won cost of parent-supplied imports will increase at $(1.1)(1.05)(1.04) = 1.20$ or 20% per annum.

4. Direct labor costs and overhead in the first year are budgeted at Won 5,000 million. Korean direct labor costs and overhead are expected to increase at 10% per annum because of physical growth, and at an additional 12% because of increase in Korean wage rates. Consequently, Korean direct labor and overhead will increase at $(1.1)(1.12) = 1.1222$, or 12.2% per annum.

5. Marketing and general and administrative expenses are budgeted at Won 4,000 million, fixed plus 4% of sales.

6. Liquidation value. At the end of five years, the project (including working capital) is expected

to be sold on a going-concern basis to Korean investors for Won 9,000 million, equal to $9,863,014 at the expected exchange rate of won 912.50/$. This sales price is free of all Korean and U.S. taxes, and will be used as a terminal value.

Given the facts and stated assumptions, the beginning balance sheet is presented in Example 11; Example 12 shows revenue and cost projections for Ko-tel over the expected five-year life of the project.

EXAMPLE 11

BEGINNING BALANCE SHEET, KO-TEL

	Millions of Won	Thousands of Dollars
Assets		
1 Cash balance	650	867
2 Accounts receivable	0	0
3 Inventory	1050	1400
4 Net plant and equipment	7000	9333
5 Total	8700	11600
Liabilities and Net Worth		
6 Accounts payable	700	933
7 Common stock equity	8000	10667
8 Total	8700	11600

Example 13 shows how the annual increase in working capital investment is calculated. According to the facts, half of gross working capital must be financed by Ko-tel or Am-tel. Therefore, half of any annual increase in working capital would represent an additional required capital investment.

Example 14 forecasts project cash flows from the viewpoint of Ko-tel. Thanks to healthy liquidation value, the project has a positive NPV and an IRR greater than the 22% local (Korean) cost of capital for projects of similar risk. Therefore,

EXAMPLE 12—SALES AND COST DATA

Item	Year 1	2	3	4	5
1 Total sales revenue	26000	31174	37378	44816	53734
2 Korean raw material	4000	4532	5135	5818	6591
3 Components purchases from Am-tel	9000	10811	12986	15599	18737
4 Korean labor and overhead	5000	6160	7589	9350	11519
5 Depreciation	700	700	700	700	700
6 Cost of sales [(2) + (3) + (4) + (5)]	18700	22203	26410	31466	37548
7 Gross margin [(1) − (6)]	7300	8971	10968	13350	16187
8 License fee [2.5% of (1)]	650	779	934	1120	1343
9 Marketing and general & administrative	5040	5247	5495	5793	6149
10 EBIT [(7) − (8) − (9)]	1610	2945	4538	6437	8694
11 Korean income taxes (35%)	564	1031	1588	2253	3043
12 Net income after Korean taxes [(10) − (11)]	1047	1914	2950	4184	5651
13 Cash dividend [70% of (12)]	733	1340	2065	2929	3956

EXAMPLE 13—WORKING CAPITAL CALCULATION

Item	Year				
	1	2	3	4	5
1 Total revenue	26000	31174	37378	44816	53734
2 Net working capital needs at year-end [25% of (1)]	6500	7794	9344	11204	13434
3 Less year-beginning working capital	1700	6500	7794	9344	11204
4 Required addition to working capital	4800	1294	1551	1860	2230
5 Less working capital financed in Korean by payables	2400	647	775	930	1115
6 Net new investment in working capital	2400	647	775	930	1115

EXAMPLE 14—CASH FLOW PROJECTION—NPV AND IRR FOR KO-TEL

Item	0	1	2	3	4	5
1 EBIT [Ex. 12, (10)]		1610	2945	4538	6437	8694
2 Korean income taxes (35%)		564	1031	1588	2253	3043
3 Net income, all equity basis		1047	1914	2950	4184	5651
4 Depreciation		700	700	700	700	700
5 Liquidation value						9000
6 Half of addition to working capital		2400	647	775	930	1115
7 Cost of project	−8000					
8 Net cash flow	−8000	−654	1967	2874	3954	14236
9 PV factor (22%)	1.000	0.820	0.672	0.551	0.451	0.370
10 PV each year	−8000	−536	1322	1584	1783	5267
11 Cumulative NPV	−8000	−8536	−7214	−5630	−3847	1421
12 IRR = 26.77%	0.267657					

Year

592

EXAMPLE 15—AFTER-TAX DIVIDEND RECEIVED BY AM-TEL

Item	Year					
	0	1	2	3	4	5
In Millions of Won						
1 Cash dividend paid [Ex. 12, (13)]		733	1340	2065	2929	3956
2 A 70% of Korean income tax [Ex. 12, (11)]		394	721	1112	1577	2130
3 Grossed-up dividend [(1) + (2)]		1127	2061	3177	4506	6086
4 Exchange-rate (won/$)	750.00	780.00	811.20	843.65	877.39	912.49
In Thousands of Dollars						
5 Grossed-up dividend [(3)/(4) × 1000]		1444.9	2541.2	3765.5	5135.2	6669.3
6 U.S. tax (38%)		549.1	965.7	1430.9	1951.4	2534.3
7 Credit for Korea taxes [(2)/(4) × 1000]		505.7	889.4	1317.9	1797.3	2334.3
8 Additional U.S. Tax due [(6) − (7), if (6) is larger]		43.3	76.2	113.0	154.1	200.1
9 Excess U.S. tax credit [(7) − (6), if (7) is larger]		0.0	0.0	0.0	0.0	0.0
10 Dividend received by Am-tel after all taxes [(1)/(4) × 1000 − (8)]		895.8	1575.5	2334.6	3183.8	4135.0

593

EXAMPLE 16—NPV AND IRR FOR AM-TEL

Item	Year					
	0	1	2	3	4	5
In Million of Won						
1 License fee from Ko-tel (2.5%) [Ex. 12, (7)]		650	779	934	1120	1343
2 Margin on exports to Ko-tel [5% of (3) in Ex. 12]		450	541	649	780	937
3 Total receipts		1100	1320	1584	1900	2280
4 Exchange rate (won/$)	750.00	780.00	811.20	843.65	877.39	912.49
In thousands of Dollars						
5 Pre-tax receipts [(3)/(4) × 1000]	1410.3	1627.1	1877.2	2165.9	2498.9	2949.6
6 U.S. taxes (38%)		535.9	618.3	713.4	823.0	949.6
7 License fees and export profits, after tax		874.4	1008.8	1163.9	1342.8	1549.3
8 After-tax dividend [Ex. 15, (10)]		895.8	1575.5	2334.6	3183.8	4135.0
9 Project cost		−11000.0				
10 Liquidation value						9863.0
11 Net cash flow	−11000.0	1770.2	2584.3	3498.5	4526.7	15547.3
12 PV factor (22%)	1.000	0.820	0.672	0.551	0.451	0.370
13 PV each year	−11000.0	1451.5	1736.7	1927.7	2041.5	5752.5
14 Cumulative NPV	−11000.0	−9548.5	−7811.8	−5884.1	−3842.6	1909.9
15 IRR = 27.48%	0.274782					

Ko-tel passes the first of the two tests of required rate of return.

Does Ko-tel also pass the second test? That is, does it show at least a 22% required rate of return from the viewpoint of Am-tel?

Example 15 shows the calculation for expected after-tax dividends from Ko-tel to be received by Am-tel. For purposes of this example, note that Am-tel must pay regular U.S. corporate income taxes (38% rate) on dividends received from Ko-tel. However, the U.S. tax law allows Am-tel to claim a tax credit for income taxes paid to Korea on the Korean income that generated the dividend. The process of calculating the regional income in Korea is called "grossing up" and is illustrated in Example 15, line (1), (2), and (3).

This imputed Korean won income is converted from won to dollars in lines (4) and (5). Then the U.S. income tax is calculated at 38% in line (6). A tax credit is given for the Korean income taxes paid, as calculated in line (7). Line (8) then shows the net additional U.S. tax due, and line (10) shows the net dividend received by Am-tel after the additional U.S. tax is paid.

Finally, Example 16 calculates the rate of return on cash flows from Ko-tel from the viewpoint of Am-tel. Again, Ko-tel passes the test because it has a positive NPV and an IRR, higher than the 22% rate of return required by Am-tel.

What-If Analysis

So far the project investigation team has used a set of "most likely" assumptions to forecast rates of return. It is now time to subject the most likely outcome to sensitivity analyses. The many probabilistic techniques are available to test the sensitivity of results to political and foreign exchange risks as are used to test sensitivity to business and financial risk. But it is more common to test sensitivity to political and foreign exchange risk by simulating what would happen to net present value and earnings under a variety of "what if" scenarios. Spreadsheet programs such as Lotus 1-2-3 can be utilized to test various scenarios.

PART VI

FINANCIAL ANALYSIS

30

Financial Statement Analysis

Financial statement analysis examines a company's historical financial performance and its future prospects. It appraises the health and operating performance of the business. This chapter covers analytical techniques in appraising the balance sheet, analyzing the income statement, and evaluating the financial structure. CFOs analyze the financial statements to see how the company looks to the financial community and what corrective actions can be taken to minimize and solve financial problems. Areas of risk are identified. Means to efficiently utilize assets and earn greater returns are emphasized. Financial statement analysis aids in determining the appropriateness of mergers and acquisitions.

A company's financial condition influences its price-earnings ratio, bond rating, cost of financing, and availability of financing.

What kind of financial comparisons should CFOs make?

To obtain worthwhile conclusions from financial ratios, the CFO has to make two comparisons.

• *Industry comparison.* The CFO should compare the company's ratios to those of competing companies in the industry or with industry standards. Industry norms can be obtained from such services as Standard and Poor's and Moody's.

In analyzing the company, the CFO should appraise the trends in the industry. What is the pattern of growth or decline? The profit dollar is worth more if earned in a healthy, expanding industry than in a declining one.

The CFO should make certain that the financial data of competitors are comparable to his or her company. For example, the CFO will have difficulty comparing the profitability of his or her company if it uses FIFO with a competitor that uses LIFO for inventory valuation. In this case, the CFO should restate the earnings of both companies on a comparative basis.

• *Trend analysis.* A company's ratio may be compared over several years to identify direction of financial position and operating performance. An attempt should be made to uncover the reasons for the change.

What are some tips when doing financial analysis?

The optimum value for any ratio varies across industry lines, through time, and within different companies in the same industry. In other words, a ratio deemed optimum for one company may be inadequate for another. A ratio is typically deemed optimum within a given range of values. An increase or decrease beyond this range points to something unusual requiring investigation. *Example:* While a low current ratio may indicate deficient liquidity, a very high current ratio may reflect inefficient utilization of assets (e.g., excessive inventory) or inability to use short-term credit to the firm's advantage.

For a seasonal business, the CFO may find that year-end financial data are not representative. Thus, quarterly or monthly averages may be used to level out seasonality effects.

When computing ratios for *analytical* purposes, the CFO may also want to use the realistic values for balance sheet accounts instead of historical amounts. For example, investments in securities are recorded at the lower of cost or market value applied on a total portfolio basis. Thus, if cost is $4,000,000 and market value is $4,800,000, the portfolio would be shown at $4,000,000. However, the securities are actually worth $4,800,000.

A distorted trend indicates a problem mandating management attention. However, a lack of change does not always infer normalcy. For example, manpower growth may have increased but production/sales may be constant or decreasing. Thus, manpower costs may be disproportionate to operational activity.

What is the difference between horizontal and vertical analysis?

Horizontal analysis looks at the trend in accounts over years and assists in spotting areas of wide divergence requiring additional attention. Horizontal analysis may also be presented by showing trends relative to a base year.

In *vertical analysis,* a significant item on a financial statement is used as a base value, and all other items on the financial statement are compared to it. In performing vertical analysis for the balance sheet, total assets is assigned 100%. Each asset is expressed as a percentage of total assets. Total liabilities and stockholders' equity is also assigned 100%. Each liability and stockholders' equity account is then expressed as a percentage of total liabilities and stockholders' equity. In the income statement, net sales is given the value of 100% and all other accounts are appraised in comparison to net sales. The resulting figures are then given in a common size statement.

Vertical analysis is helpful in disclosing the internal structure of the business and potential problem areas. It reveals the relationship between each income statement account and revenue. It indicates the mix of assets that generate income and the mix of the sources of financing, whether by current or noncurrent liabilities or by equity. Besides making internal evaluation possible, vertical analysis may be used to appraise the company's relative position in the industry. Horizontal and vertical analysis point to possible problem areas to be evaluated by the CFO.

BALANCE SHEET ANALYSIS _____

A CFO may analyze asset and liability accounts, evaluate liquidity, appraise solvency, and look to signs of possible business failure. The CFO is concerned with the realizability of assets, turnover, and earning potential. Besides analyzing financial health, the CFO will want to make recommendations for improvement so that financial problems are rectified. Also, the CFO should identify strengths which may further be taken advantage of.

Are assets of high or low quality?

Asset quality relates to the certainty of the amount and timing of the realization of the assets in cash. Therefore, assets should be categorized by risk category. *What to Do:* Calculate the following ratios: (1) high-risk assets to total assets and (2) high-risk assets to sales. If high risk exists in assets, future write-offs may occur. For example, the realization of goodwill is more doubtful than equipment. The risk of each major asset category should also be appraised. For example, receivables from an economically unstable government (e.g., Brazil) has greater risk than a receivable from General Electric. *Note:* Single-purpose assets have greater risk than multi-purpose ones.

What to Watch For: Assets with no separable value that cannot be sold easily, such as intangibles and work-in-process. On the other hand, marketable securities are readily salable.

In evaluating realization risk, the impact of changing government policies on the entity has to be considered. Risk may exist with chemicals and other products deemed hazardous to health. Huge inventory losses may arise.

We will now analyze each of the major assets.

What should be considered in evaluating the cash account?

The CFO should determine how much of the cash balance is unavailable or restricted. Examples are a compensating balance and cash held in a foreign country when remission restrictions exist. *Note:* Foreign currency holdings are generally stated at year-end exchange rates but may change rapidly.

The CFO should determine the ratio of sales to cash. A high turnover rate may indicate a deficient cash position leading to financial problems if additional financing is not available at reasonable interest rates. A low turnover ratio may indicate excessive cash being retained.

EXAMPLE 1

	19X1	19X2
Cash	$ 500,000	$ 400,000
Sales	8,000,000	9,000,000
Industry norm for cash turnover rate	15.8 times	16.2 times

The turnover of cash is 16 ($8,000/$500,000) in 19X1 and 22.5 ($9,000/$400,000) in 19X2. The company has a cash deficiency in 19X2, which implies a possible liquidity problem.

The CFO should distinguish between two types of cash: that needed for operating purposes and that required for capital expenditures. While the former must be paid, the latter is postponable.

How is an analysis of accounts receivable useful?

Realization risk in receivables can be appraised by studying the nature of the receivable balance. Examples of high risk receivables include amounts from economically unstable foreign countries, receivables subject to offset provisions, and receivables due from a company experiencing severe financial problems. Further, companies dependent on a few customers have greater risk than those with a large number of important accounts. Receivables due from industry are typically safer than receivables arising from consumers. Fair trade laws are more protective of consumers.

Accounts receivable ratios include the accounts receivable turnover and the average collection period. The *accounts receivable turnover ratio* indicates the number of times accounts receivable is collected during the period. It equals net sales divided by average accounts receivable. A higher turnover rate reveals faster collections. On the other hand, an excessively high ratio may point to a tight credit policy, with the company not tapping the potential for profit through sales to customers in higher risk categories. However, in changing its credit policy, the company must consider the profit potential against the risk in selling to more marginal customers.

The *average collection period* (days sales in receivables) is the number of days it takes to collect receivables. It equals 365 days divided by the accounts receivable turnover.

Collection periods may be calculated by type of customer, product line, and market territory.

An increase in collection days may indicate customer balances becoming uncollectible. One reason for an increase may be that the company is now selling to highly marginal customers. An *aging schedule* is helpful.

The quality of receivables may also be appraised by referring to customer ratings issued by credit agencies.

The CFO should look for a buildup in the ratios of (1) accounts receivable to total assets and (2) accounts receivable to sales as indicative of a collection problem. Receivables outstanding in excess of the expected payment date and relative to industry norm implies a higher probability of uncollectibility.

The trend in sales returns and allowances is a reflection of the quality of merchandise sold.

What are important concerns when analyzing inventories?

An inventory buildup may mean realization problems. The buildup may be at the plant, wholesaler, or retailer. A sign of a buildup is when inventory increases at a much faster rate than the increase in sales. *What to Watch For:* A decline in raw materials coupled with a rise in work-in-process and finished goods pointing to a future production slowdown.

If the company is holding excess inventory, there is an opportunity cost of tying up money in inventory. Further, there is a high carrying cost for storing merchandise. Why aren't certain types of merchandise selling well? Calculate turnover rates for each inventory category and by department. Possible reasons for a low turnover rate are overstocking, obsolescence, product line deficiencies, or poor marketing efforts. There are cases where a low inventory rate is appropriate. *Examples:* A higher inventory level may arise because of expected future increases in price or when a new product has been introduced for which the advertising efforts have not been felt yet.

Note: The turnover rate may be unrepresentatively high when the business uses a "natural year-end" because at that time the inventory balance will be exceptionally low. *What to Do:* Compute the number of days inventory is held and compare it to the industry norm and previous years.

$$\text{Inventory turnover} = \frac{\text{Cost of goods sold}}{\text{Average inventory}}$$

$$\text{Age of inventory} = \frac{365}{\text{Turnover}}$$

Also look at the trend in inventory to sales. A high turnover rate may point to inadequate inventory, possibly leading to a loss in business.

What to Watch For: Merchandise that is susceptible to price variability, "fad," specialized, perishable, technological, and luxurious goods. On the contrary, low realization risk is with standardized, staple, and necessity items.

Note: Raw material inventory is safer than finished goods or work-in-process since raw material has more universal and varied uses.

Questions to be asked:

• Is inventory collateralized against a loan? If so, creditors can retain it in the event of nonpayment of the obligation.

• Is there adequate insurance? There is a particular problem when insurance cannot be obtained for the item because of high risk (e.g., geographic location of inventory is in a high crime area or there is susceptibility to floods).

• Is it subject to political risk (e.g., big cars and an oil crisis)?

Look for inventory that is overstated due to mistakes in quantities, costing, pricing, and valuation.

Warning: The more technical a product and the more dependent the valuation on internally developed cost records, the more susceptible are cost estimates to error.

In gauging manufacturing efficiency, you should look at the relationship between indirect labor and direct labor since a constant level of both are needed to efficiently run the organization.

EXAMPLE 2

A company presents the following makeup of inventory:

	19X1	19X2
Raw materials	$89,000	$ 78,000
Work-in-process	67,000	120,000
Finished goods	16,000	31,000

The CFO's analysis of inventory shows there was a material divergence in the inventory components between 19X1 and 19X2. There was a reduction in raw material by 12.4% ($11,000/$89,000), while work-in-process rose by 79.1% ($53,000/$67,000) and finished goods rose by 93.8% ($15,000/$16,000). The lack of consistency in the trend between raw materials relative to work-in-process and finished goods may imply a forthcoming cutback in production. An obsolescence problem may also exist applicable to work-in-process and finished goods due to the sizable buildup.

The company's operating cycle should be determined which equals the average collection period plus the average age of inventory. A short operating cycle is desired so that cash flow is expedited.

What are the key areas when looking at the investment portfolio?

An indication of the fair value of investments may be the revenue (dividend income, interest income) obtained from them. Have decreases in portfolio market values been recognized in the accounts? Higher realization risk exists where there is a declining trend in the percentage of earnings derived from investments to their carrying value. Also check for unrealized losses in the portfolio occurring after year-end.

EXAMPLE 3

Company X presents the following information:

	19X1	19X2
Investments	$50,000	$60,000
Investment income	$ 7,000	$ 5,000

The percent of investment income to total investments decreased from 14% in 19X1 to 8.3% in 19X2, pointing to higher realization risk in the portfolio.

If a company is buying securities in other companies for diversification purposes, this will reduce overall risk. Risk in an investment portfolio can be ascertained by computing the standard deviation of its rate of return.

When an investment portfolio has a market value above cost, it constitutes an undervalued asset.

An investment portfolio of securities fluctuating widely in price is of higher realization risk than a portfolio that is diversified by industry and economic sector. But the former portfolio will show greater profitability in a bull market. *Recommendations:* Appraise the extent of diversification and stability of the investment portfolio. There is less risk when securities are negatively correlated (price goes in opposite directions) or not correlated compared to a portfolio of positively correlated securities (price goes in same direction). Is the portfolio of poor quality securities, such as "junk" bonds?

Note cases in which debt securities have a cost in excess of market value.

In evaluating fixed assets, what should be considered?

Is there sufficient maintenance of productive assets to ensure current and future earning power? Lessened operational efficiency and breakdowns occur when obsolete assets have not been replaced and/or required repairs made. *What to Do:* Determine the age and condition of each major asset category, as well as the cost to replace old assets. Determine output levels, downtime, and temporary discontinuances. Inactive and unproductive assets are a drain on the firm. Are the fixed assets specialized or risky, making them susceptible to obsolescence?

Note: Pollution-causing equipment may require replacement or modification to satisfy governmental ecology standards.

Ratio trends to be calculated are:

• Fixed asset acquisitions to total assets. The trend is particularly revealing for a technological company that has to keep up-to-date. A decrease in the trend points to the failure to replace older assets on a timely basis.

• Repairs and maintenance to fixed assets.

• Repairs and maintenance to sales.

• Sales to fixed assets.

• Net income to fixed assets.

The fixed asset turnover ratio (net sales to average fixed assets) aids in appraising a company's ability to use its asset base efficiently to obtain revenue. A low ratio may mean that investment in fixed assets is excessive relative to the output generated.

A high ratio of sales to floor space indicates the efficient utilization of space.

A company having specialized or risky fixed assets has greater vulnerability to asset obsolescence. Examples include machinery used to manufacture specialized products and "fad" items.

When a company's rate of return on assets (e.g., net income to fixed assets) is poor, the firm may be justified in not maintaining fixed assets. If the industry is declining, fixed asset replacement and repairs may have been restricted.

It is better for a company when assets are mobile and/or can easily be modified since it affords the firm greater flexibility. If the assets are easily accessible, it will also be easier to repair them. The location of the assets is also important since that may affect their condition and security. The location will also affect property taxes, so a company may be able to save on taxes by having the plant located in a low tax area.

What to Watch For: A material decline in sales coupled with a significant increase in capital expenditures may be inconsistent. It may point to overexpansion.

EXAMPLE 4

Company T presents the following information regarding its fixed assets:

	19X1	19X2
Fixed assets	$120,000	$105,000
Repairs and maintenance	6,000	4,500
Replacement cost	205,000	250,000

The company has inadequately maintained its assets as indicated by:

• The reduction in the ratio of repairs and maintenance to fixed assets from 5% in 19X1 to 4.3% in 19X2.

• The material variation between replacement cost and historical cost.

• The reduction in fixed assets over the year.

How should property, plant and equipment be managed and controlled?

Fixed assets should meet the operational needs of the business with maximum productivity at minimum cost. These long-term expenditures are significant in amount, and can result in great loss to the company if fixed assets are improperly managed. Capital investments result in a higher break-even point due to the resulting costs associated with them including depreciation, insurance, and property taxes.

A new company requires greater capital expansion for growth. There is less of a need for additional capital facilities by an established, mature company with strong market share.

For control purposes, unique control numbers should be securely affixed to fixed assets. There should be periodic appraisals of the adequacy of insurance coverage.

The company should not buy elaborate manufacturing facilities for a new product until it has shown success. In the beginning stages, production may be subcontracted. With an established product, productivity is achieved through internal capital expansion. In appraising production facilities, scrap, rejects, cost per unit, and malfunctioning time should be considered.

The CFO is concerned with the following in managing fixed assets:

• Purchasing the "right" equipment for the company's needs.

• Proper timing of capital expenditures.

• Keeping capital expenditures within the financial capabilities of the business.

• Physical care and security of property.

What are some concerns when appraising intangibles?

Realization risk is indicated when there is a high ratio of intangible assets to total assets. The amounts recorded for intangibles may be overstated relative to their market value or to their future income-generating capacity.

What to Do: Calculate trends in the following ratios:

• Intangible assets to total assets

• Intangible assets to stockholders' equity

• Intangible assets to sales

• Intangible assets to net income

• Dubious intangible assets (e.g., goodwill) to total assets

What to Watch For: Leasehold improvements because they have no cash realizability.

Note: In some cases, intangibles may be undervalued, such as a successful patented product. However, can the patented product be infringed upon by minor alteration? What is the financial strength of the company to defend itself against those infringing upon its patented product? What are the expiration dates of patents, and are new products being developed?

A company's goodwill account should be appraised to ascertain whether the firm acquired has superior earning potential to justify the excess of cost over fair market value of net assets paid for it. If the acquired company does not have superior profit potential, the goodwill has no value because excess earnings do not exist relative to other companies in the industry. However, internally developed goodwill is expensed and not capitalized. It represents an undervalued asset, such as the good reputation of McDonald's.

Are the company's assets being properly utilized?

Asset utilization may be measured by the total asset turnover (net sales/average total assets). The ratio is useful in appraising an entity's ability to use its asset base efficiently to generate revenue. A low ratio may be caused from numerous factors, and it is essential to identify the causes. For example, it must be determined if the investment in assets is excessive relative to production. If so, the business may wish to consolidate its present operation, perhaps by selling some of its assets and investing the funds for a higher return or using them to expand into a more profitable area.

The operating assets ratio (total operating assets to total assets) concentrates on those assets *actively employed in current operations.* Such assets exclude (1) past-oriented assets and (2) future-oriented assets. Past-oriented assets arise from prior errors, inefficiencies, or losses because of competitive factors or changes in business plans. These assets have not yet been formerly recognized in the accounts. Examples are obsolete goods, idle plants, receivables under litigation, delinquent receivables, and nonperforming loans (no interest being recognized). Future-oriented assets are acquired for corporate growth or generating future sales. Examples are land held for speculation and factories under construction. Nonoperating assets reduce profits and return on investment because no benefit to current operations occurs. They neither generate sales nor reduce costs. Rather, they are a "drain" on the company and may require financing.

What is the nature of the assets?

Are any of the current assets used to secure long-term debt or contingent liabilities as pledges or guarantees?

Even though current assets are about the same or slightly above current liabilities, the company may still experience liquidity difficulties if the maturity schedule of the liabilities is ahead of the expected cash realization of the assets. For example, the payment schedule of the debts may be concentrated towards the beginning of the year but the cash realization of the assets may be evenly disbursed throughout the year. If this occurs, the company may be forced to discount its receivables or quickly liquidate inventory at lower prices. Although this will generate immediate cash, it dilutes the realizable value of the current assets. In effect, the actual value of the assets becomes less than the fair value of the liabilities.

Assets that are interdependent create a financial disadvantage. For example, the sale of equipment on the assembly line may adversely affect the remaining equipment. On the other hand, one marketable security may be sold without affecting the others.

Wide variability in the price of assets is a negative sign because the company may be forced to sell an asset at a time of financial need at significant loss (i.e., market value is materially below book value).

There is more liquidity risk with noncurrent assets than with current assets because of the greater disposition difficulty.

The CFO should determine whether off-balance-sheet assets exist. Examples are a tax loss carryforward benefit, expected rebates, and a purchase commitment to acquire an item at a price lower than the prevailing one. The CFO should also identify assets reflected on the balance sheet at an amount substantially less than their real value. Examples are patents recorded at cost, even though the present value of future benefits substantially exceeds it, and land that does not reflect its appreciated value.

FASB 87 on pension plans does not allow the recognition of a minimum asset for the excess of the fair value of pension plan assets less the accumulated benefit obligation. For analytical purposes, such minimum asset should be considered as an unrecorded asset for the excess of fair value of plan assets over the projected benefit obligation.

Recommendation: Note the existence of unrecorded assets representing resources of the business or items expected to have future economic benefit.

What should be taken into account when evaluating liabilities?

The CFO should calculate the trends in the ratios of:

- Current liabilities to total liabilities
- Current liabilities to stockholders' equity
- Current liabilities to sales

Increasing trends point to liquidity difficulty. *Caution:* Stretching short-term payables is not a good sign.

The CFO should determine the trend in "patient" (e.g., supplier) to "pressing" (e.g., bank, IRS) liabilities. When liquidity problems exist, the company is better-off with patient creditors who will work with it. Thus, a high ratio of pressing liabilities to total liabilities is unfavorable.

EXAMPLE 5

A company presents the following information:

	19X1	19X2
Current Liabilities		
Trade payables	$ 33,000	$ 28,000
Bank loans	51,000	78,000
Commercial paper	35,000	62,000
Taxes payable	8,000	12,000
Total current liabilities	$ 127,000	$ 180,000
Total noncurrent liabilities	$ 310,000	$ 315,000
Total liabilities	$ 437,000	$ 495,000
Total revenue	$1,100,000	$1,150,000

Relevant ratios are

Current liabilities to total revenue	11.5%	15.7%
Current liabilities to total liabilities	29.1%	36.4%
Pressing current liabilities to patient current liabilities	2.85	5.43

There is more liquidity risk in 19X2, as reflected by the higher ratios. In fact, the number of pressing liabilities has significantly risen in terms of percentage.

Certain liabilities should not be considered obligations for analytical purposes because they may not require future payment. Examples are:

• The deferred tax credit account if it applies to a temporary difference that will keep recurring (e.g., depreciation as long as capital expansion occurs).

• Unearned revenue related to passive income sources, such as rents.

• Convertible bonds with an attractive conversion feature.

Corporate obligations that are not recorded in the balance sheet must be considered when evaluating the entity's going-concern potential. Examples are lawsuits, dispute under a government contract, operating leases, commitments for future loans to a troubled company, guarantees of future performance, and bonus payment obligations.

The minimum liability for the pension plan equals the accumulated benefit obligation less the fair value of pension plan assets. However, the projected benefit obligation (based on anticipated future salaries) is a better measure of the plan's obligation than the accumulated benefit obligation (based on current salaries). Therefore, the CFO should consider as an unrecorded liability the excess of the projected benefit obligation over the accumulated benefit obligation.

EXAMPLE 6

Accumulated benefit obligation	$50,000,000
Less: Fair value of plan assets	40,000,000
Minimum (booked) liability	$10,000,000

If the projected benefit obligation is $58 million, the unrecorded liability is $8 million ($58 million less $50 million).

An equity account may be in essence a liability, such as preferred stock with a maturity date or subject to sinking fund requirements.

How easily can the company obtain financing?

The company's ability to obtain financing at reasonable rates is affected by external considerations (e.g., Federal Reserve policy) and internal considerations (e.g., degree of existing debt).

The extent of loan restrictions on the company should be examined. How close is the company to violating a given restriction, which may in turn call the loan?

Can the company issue commercial paper and short-term bank debt? If there is a loan, has the collateral value of the loan diminished relative to the balance of the loan? If so, additional security may be required. Also examine the trend in the effective interest rate and compensating balance requirement relative to competition. Does the weighted-average debt significantly exceed the year-end debt balance?

How should liabilities be managed and controlled?

In managing liabilities, a major concern is whether the business has adequate resources to meet maturing debt. Otherwise, the company will be in financial difficulty. The debt structure affects both the short-term and long-term financial status of the enterprise.

The CFO must be assured that all financial obligations are presented and disclosed in the financial statements. Further, the liability position and related ratios must be in compliance with any restrictions in loan agreements. The company must borrow money when needed in a timely fashion and at a reasonable interest rate.

Liability management involves the proper planning of all types of obligations. The CFO must know current balances of say accounts payable and accrued expenses, and how far they may be stretched. Are liabilities within acceptable industry norms? Can the company withstand periods of adversity? How does the overall economic picture look, and what effect does it have on the business?

The CFO should prepare a number of reports to analyze the actual status of liabilities and to properly plan the debt structure. Some useful reports include:

• Periodic reports (e.g., quarterly, monthly) on the status of material liabilities, such as pensions, leases, and health care.

• Periodic reports comparing actual liabilities to allowable amounts in credit agreements.

• Comparisons of budgeted liabilities to actual liabilities.

• Listing and status of contingent liabilities and their amounts.

• Aging of accounts payable.

How is an analysis of stockholders' equity useful?

If management reduces or omits its dividends, it may imply that the company has financial difficulties. Management is better-off varying its dividends rather than paying constant dividends so it can more easily reduce dividends in troubled times. If stockholders are used to receiving constant dividends, it will be more difficult for management to lower its dividends without upsetting stockholders.

If a loan agreement places restrictions on the company, such as its ability to pay dividends, this inhibits management's freedom of action and is a negative sign.

If treasury stock is acquired, the market price of the company's stock will rise because less shares will be on the market. If a company had previously purchased treasury stock at a cost which is significantly below the current market price, it is "sitting on" a significant potential increase in cash flow and paid-in-capital.

If a company issues preferred stock for the first time or if it substantially issues preferred stock in the current year, it may mean the company had problems with issuing its common stock. This is a negative sign since the investing public may be viewing its common stock as risky.

If convertible bonds or convertible preferred stock are converted to common stock that means that bondholders or preferred stockholders are optimistic about the company. However, this will result in a drop in the market price of common stock as more shares are issued. On the plus side, the company will be able to omit the interest payment on bonds and the dividend payment on preferred stock.

A high ratio of retained earnings to stockholders' equity is a good sign because it indicates that capital financing is being achieved internally.

Stockholders are interested in dividends and prefer high ratios for dividend yield (dividends per share/market price per share) and dividend payout (dividends per share/earnings per share). A decline in these ratios may cause concern among stockholders.

Is the company liquid?

Liquidity is the company's ability to convert noncash assets into cash or to obtain cash to pay current debt. The CFO has to examine the stock and flow of liquid resources. The timing of the cash inflows and outflows also has to be considered.

Liquidity is crucial in carrying out business activity, particularly in times of adversity, such as when a business is shut down by a strike or when operating losses result from a recession or a significant rise in raw material prices. If liquidity is inadequate to cushion such losses, serious financial difficulties may result.

Liquidity is affected by the company's ability to obtain financing (e.g., lines of credit) and to postpone cash payments. The mixture of current assets and current liabilities is also relevant. How "near to cash" are assets and liabilities? A deficient liquidity position may render a company unable to make timely interest and principal payments on debt.

Liquidity ratios are static at year-end. Thus, it is important for the CFO to analyze expected *future* cash flows. If future cash outflows are much more than cash inflows, there will be a deteriorating liquidity position.

What to Watch For: If your a seasonal business, year-end financial data are not representative. In this case, use averages based on quarterly or monthly data to level out seasonal effects.

A seasonal business that is a net borrower should use long-term financing as a precautionary measure. Further, a company with financial difficulties should have debts mature during the peak rather than the trough of the season.

Can you modify unexpected difficulties by changing the amount and timing of future cash flows? This involves consideration of the closeness of assets to cash, ability to obtain financing, amount of nonoperating assets that can be sold, ability to alter operating and investing activities, and payback periods on projects.

What ratios may be used to appraise liquidity?

Some important funds flow ratios are:

$$\text{Current ratio} = \frac{\text{Current assets}}{\text{Current liabilities}}$$

Seasonal variability effects this ratio. The current ratio appraises the company's ability to pay current debt out of current assets. A high ratio is needed if the company has a problem borrowing quickly, and if there are troubling business conditions, among other reasons. A limitation of this ratio is that it may increase just before financial distress because of a company's attempt to improve its cash position by selling fixed assets. Such dispositions have a negative impact upon productive capacity. Another limitation of the ratio is that it will be higher when inventory is carried on a LIFO basis. *Note:* Current assets that are pledged to secure long-term liabilities are not available to pay current debt. If these current assets are included in the calculation, a distorted ratio arises.

$$\text{Quick ratio} = \frac{\text{Cash} + \text{Marketable securities} + \text{Accounts receivable}}{\text{Current liabilities}}$$

This is a more stringent test of liquidity than the current ratio because it excludes inventories and prepaid expenses.

$$\text{Working capital} = \text{Current assets} - \text{Current liabilities}$$

A high working capital helps when the company has difficulty borrowing on short notice. However, an excess working capital may be bad because funds could be invested in noncurrent assets for a greater return. Compare working capital to other financial statement items such as sales and total assets. For example, working capital to sales indicates if the company is optimally using its liquid resources. To identify changes in the composition of working capital, the CFO should determine the trend in the percentage of each current asset to total current assets. A movement from cash to inventory, for example, indicates less liquidity.

• *Working Capital/Long-Term Debt:* This ratio indicates if there is adequate working capital to pay long-term debt.

• *Working Capital/Current Liabilities:* A low ratio reveals deficient liquidity since liquid funds are inadequate to meet current debt.

• *A Specific Current Asset/Total Current Assets:* For example, a shift of cash to inventory means less liquidity.

• *Sales/Current Assets:* A high ratio indicates inadequate working capital. Current liabilities may be due before inventories and receivables turn over to cash.

• *Working Capital Provided from Operations/ Net Income:* A high ratio is desirable because it indicates earnings are backed up by liquid funds.

• *Working Capital Provided from Operations/ Total Liabilities:* This ratio reveals how much internally generated working capital can meet obligations.

• *Cash + Marketable Securities/Current Liabilities:* This ratio reveals the cash available to pay short-term debt.

• *Cost of Sales, Operating Expenses, and Taxes/ Average Total Current Assets:* This ratio indicates the adequacy of current assets in meeting ongoing expenses.

• *Quick Assets/Year's Cash Expenses:* This tells how many days of expenses the highly liquid assets could support.

• *Sales/Short-Term Trade Liabilities:* This ratio indicates if the business could partly finance operations with cost-free funds. If the company can easily obtain trade credit, this is a positive sign. A decline in trade credit means creditors have less faith in the financial soundness of the business.

• *Net Income/Sales:* This ratio indicates the profitability generated from revenue and is an important measure of operating performance. It also provides clues to a company's pricing, cost structure, and manufacturing efficiency. If the ratio declines, loan repayment problems may exist because a lack in earnings spells financial distress.

• *Fixed Assets/Short-Term Debt:* If you finance long-term assets with current debt, there may be a problem in paying the debt because the return and proceeds from the fixed asset will not be realized before the maturity dates of the current debt.

• *Short-Term Debt/Long-Term Debt:* A high ratio means greater liquidity risk. The company is susceptible in a money-market squeeze.

• *Accounts Payable/Average Daily Purchases:* This ratio is the number of days needed for the company to pay creditors. Is the company meeting its payables commitment? Accounts payable payment period (in days) equal to: *365/Accounts Payable Turnover.* (The accounts payable turnover equals purchases divided by accounts payable).

A decline in the payment period may indicate the company is taking advantage of prompt payment discounts, or has used the shorter purchase terms as leverage in negotiating with suppliers so as to lower the purchase price. However, an extension in payment terms infers the company is having financial difficulties. Perhaps that is why the company is stretching its payables. Alternatively, the lengthening of the payment terms may mean the business is properly managing its payables. In delaying payments to creditors, the company is taking advantage of interest-free financing.

• *Current Liabilities/Total Liabilities:* A high ratio means less liquidity because there is a greater proportion of current debt.

• *(Accounts Receivable + Inventory) – (Accounts Payable + Accrued Expenses Payable):* Some banks look at this figure as an indication of a company's liquid position because it concentrates on the major current accounts.

• *Liquidity Index.* This is the number of days current assets are removed from cash. A shorter period is preferred.

EXAMPLE 7

	Amount		Days Removed from Cash	Total
Cash	$ 10,000	×	—	—
Accounts receivable	40,000	×	25	$1,000,000
Inventory	60,000	×	40	2,400,000
	$110,000			$3,400,000

$$\text{Index} = \frac{\$3,400,000}{\$\ 110,000} = 30.9 \text{ days}$$

EXAMPLE 8

Company B provides the following financial information:

Current assets	$ 400,000
Fixed assets	800,000
Current liabilities	500,000
Noncurrent liabilities	600,000
Sales	5,000,000
Working capital provided from operations	100,000
Industry norms are:	
Fixed assets to current liabilities	4.0 times
Current liabilities to noncurrent liabilities	45.0%
Sales to current assets	8.3 times
Working capital provided from operations to total liabilities	30.5%
Company B's ratios are:	
Fixed assets to current liabilities	1.6 times
Current liabilities to noncurrent liabilities	83.3%

Sales to current assets	12.5 times
Working capital provided from operations to total liabilities	9.1%

Company B's liquidity ratios are all unfavorable relative to industry standards. There is high short-term debt and deficient current assets. Further, there is inadequacy in working capital provided from operations to meet total debt.

What is the trade-off between liquidity risk and return?

Liquidity risk is reduced by holding greater current assets than noncurrent assets. However, the return rate will decrease because the return on current assets (e.g., marketable securities) is typically less than the rate earned on productive fixed assets. Further, excessively high liquidity may mean that management has not aggressively sought out desirable capital investment opportunities. A proper balance between liquidity and return is crucial to the overall financial standing of the business.

Is the company solvent?

Solvency is a company's ability to pay long-term debt payments (principal and interest). The CFO should consider the long-term financial and operating structure of the business. An evaluation is made of the magnitude of noncurrent debt and the realization risk in noncurrent assets. A high ratio of long-term assets to long-term liabilities is desirable. Solvency depends on earning power because a company will not be able to pay obligations unless it is profitable.

When practical the CFO should use the market value of assets rather than book value in ratio computations because the former are more representative.

What ratios may be used to evaluate solvency?

A stable earnings and cash flow from operations enhances confidence in the company's ability to pay debt. Long-term debt ratios to be computed are:

• *Total Liabilities to Total Assets.* This ratio indicates the percentage of total funds obtained from creditors. If the company owes too much, it may have difficulty in repaying the debt. At the optimum debt/assets ratio, the weighted-average cost of capital is less than at any other debt to asset level.

• *Long-Term Debt to Stockholders' Equity.* High leverage indicates risk because it may be difficult for the company to meet interest and principal payments as well as obtain reasonable financing. The problem is acute when there are cash problems. Excessive debt means less financial flexibility because the company will have a problem in obtaining funds during a tight money market. A desirable debt/equity ratio depends on many factors including the rates of other firms in the industry, the access to debt financing, and stability in earnings.

• *Cash Flow from Operations to Long-Term Debt.* This ratio shows whether internally generated funds are sufficient to meet noncurrent liabilities.

• *Interest Coverage (Net Income + Interest + Taxes/Interest).* A high ratio indicates that earnings are adequate to meet interest charges. It is a safety margin indicator showing how much of a decline in profit the company can tolerate.

• *Cash Flow Generated from Operations Plus Interest to Interest.* This ratio indicates available cash to meet interest charges. Cash rather than profit pays interest. A higher ratio is needed for a cyclical business.

• *Net Income Before Taxes and Fixed Charges to Fixed Charges.* This ratio helps evaluate the company's ability to meet fixed costs. A low ratio points to risk because when corporate activity falls, the company is unable to pay fixed charges.

• *Cash Flow from Operations Plus Fixed Charges to Fixed Charges.* A high ratio indicates the company's ability to meet fixed charges. Further, a company with stable operations is more apt to handle fixed costs.

• *Noncurrent Assets to Noncurrent Liabilities.* Long-term debt is eventually paid from long-term assets. A high ratio affords more protection for long-term creditors.

• *Retained Earnings to Total Assets.* The trend in this ratio reflects the company's profitability over the years.

• *Total Liabilities to Sales.* This ratio indicates the amount of sales financed by creditors.

• *Stockholders' Equity to Sales.* This ratio indicates the proportion of sales financed by stockholders' equity. It is generally safer for sales to be financed by equity than debt. A review of the ratio reveals if the owners are investing too much or too little relative to the sales volume. Is owners' equity being employed effectively?

EXAMPLE 9

The following partial balance sheet and income statement data are provided for Company D:

Long-term assets	$700,000
Long-term liabilities	500,000
Stockholders' equity	300,000
Net income before tax	80,000
Cash flow provided from operations	100,000
Interest expense	20,000
Average norms taken from competitors:	
Long-term assets to long-term liabilities	2.0
Long-term debt to stockholders' equity	.8
Cash flow to long-term liabilities	.3
Net income before tax plus interest to interest	7.0
Company D's ratios are:	
Long-term assets to long-term liabilities	1.4
Long-term debt to stockholders' equity	1.67
Cash flow to long-term liabilities	.2
Net income before tax plus interest to interest	5.0

After comparing the company's ratios with the industry averages, it appears that the company's solvency is worse than its competition as evidenced by the greater long-term liabilities in the capital structure and lower interest coverage.

POTENTIAL FOR BUSINESS FAILURE _____

Bankruptcy occurs when the company cannot pay maturing financial obligations. We are particularly interested in predicting cash flow. Financial problems affect the P/E ratio, bond rating, and cost of capital.

A quantitative indicator in predicting failure is *Altman's Z-score*. The Z-score is about 90% accurate in predicting failure one year in advance and about 80% reliable in forecasting it two years in advance. For a detailed discussion of Z-score, see Edward I. Altman, "Financial Ratios, Discriminant Analysis, and the Prediction of Corporate Bankruptcy," *Journal of Finance*, September 1968.

The Z-score equals:

$$\frac{\text{Working capital}}{\text{Total assets}} \times 1.2 + \frac{\text{Retained earnings}}{\text{Total assets}} \times 1.4$$

$$\frac{\text{Operating income}}{\text{Total assets}} \times 3.3 + \frac{\substack{\text{Market value of} \\ \text{common and preferred}}}{\text{Total liabilities}}$$

$$\times 0.6 + \frac{\text{Sales}}{\text{Total assets}} \times 0.999$$

The scores and the probability of short-term illiquidity follow:

Score	Probability of Illiquidity
1.80 or less	Very high
1.81–2.99	Not sure
3.0 or greater	Not likely

EXAMPLE 10

A company presents the following information:

Working capital	$280,000
Total assets	875,000
Total liabilities	320,000
Retained earnings	215,000
Sales	950,000
Operating income	130,000

Common stock	
Book value	220,000
Market value	310,000
Preferred stock	
Book value	115,000
Market value	170,000

The Z-score equals:

$$\frac{\$280,000}{\$875,000} \times 1.2 + \frac{\$215,000}{\$875,000} \times 1.4 + \frac{\$130,000}{\$875,000} \times 3.3$$

$$+ \frac{\$480,000}{\$320,000} \times 0.6 + \frac{\$950,000}{\$875,000} \times 0.999$$

$$= 0.384 + 0.344 + 0.490 + 0.9 + 1.0857 = \underline{\underline{3.2037}}$$

The probability of failure is not likely.

There are updated versions of Altman's model. You may refer to Altman's *Corporate Financial Distress* (New York: John Wiley, 1983). An excellent step by step discussion on how to develop a spreadsheet and graphing for the Z-score model can be found in Charles W. Kyd, "Forecasting Bankruptcy with Z-Scores," *Lotus,* September 1985, pp. 43–47. For more on this and other prediction models, see Chapter 38.

The liquidation value of a company may be estimated by using J. Wilcox's gambler's ruin prediction formula:

Cash + (Marketable securities at market value)
+ (70% of inventory, accounts receivable, and prepaid expenses)
+ (50% of other assets)
– (Current liabilities
+ Long-term liabilities)

What warning signs exist as to future corporate failure?

The CFO should note the following quantitative factors in predicting corporate failure:

• Low cash flow to total liabilities.
• High debt-to-equity and high debt to total assets.

- Low return on investment.
- Low profit margin.
- Low retained earnings to total assets.
- Low working capital to total assets and low working capital to sales.
- Low fixed assets to noncurrent liabilities.
- Inadequate interest-coverage.
- Instability in earnings.
- Small-size company in terms of sales and/or total assets.
- Sharp decline in price of stock, bond price, and earnings.
- A significant increase in Beta. Beta is the fluctuation in the price of the company's stock compared to a market index.
- Market price per share is materially below book value per share.
- Cut back in dividends.
- A significant increase in the weighted-average cost of capital.
- High fixed cost to total cost structure (high operating leverage).
- Failure to maintain capital assets. An example is a decline in the ratio of repairs to fixed assets.

The CFO should note the following qualitative factors in predicting failure:

- Inability to control costs.
- New company.
- Declining industry.
- High degree of competition.
- Inability to obtain suitable financing, and when obtained there are significant loan restrictions.
- Inability to meet past-due obligations.
- Moving into new areas in which expertise is lacking.
- Failure to keep up-to-date such as a technologically oriented business.
- High business risk (e.g., positive correlation in the product line; vulnerability to strikes).

- Inadequate insurance.
- Cyclicality in business operations.
- Inability to adjust production to meet consumption needs.
- Susceptibility to stringent governmental regulation (e.g., companies in the real estate industry).
- Susceptibility to unreliable suppliers and energy shortages.
- Renegotiation of debt and/or lease agreements.

What can be done to avoid business failure?

If the CFO can predict with reasonable accuracy that the company is developing financial distress, he or she can recommend corrective actions.

The CFO may use the following financial/quantitative factors to minimize the potential for failure:

- Avoid heavy debt. If liabilities are excessive, finance with equity.
- Dispose of unprofitable divisions and product lines.
- Manage assets for maximum return at the least practical risk.
- Stagger and extend the maturity dates of debt.
- Use quantitative techniques such as multiple regression analysis to compute the correlation between variables and the possibility of business failure.
- Assure that a "safety buffer" exists between actual status and compliance requirements (e.g., working capital) in loan agreements.
- Have a negative correlation between products and investments.
- Lower dividend payouts.

The CFO may employ the following nonfinancial factors that minimize the potential for failure:

- Vertically and horizontally diversify the product line and operations.
- Diversify geographically.
- Finance assets with liabilities of similar maturity (hedging).

- Have adequate insurance.
- Enhance marketing efforts (e.g., advertise in the right place).
- Implement cost reduction programs.
- Improve productivity.
- Minimize the adverse impact of inflation and recession on the business (e.g., price on a next-in, first-out basis).
- Invest in multi-purpose, rather than single-purpose, assets, because of their lower risks.
- Reconsider entering industries with a high rate of failure.
- Have many projects, rather than only a few, that significantly affect operations.
- Consider introducing product lines that are the least affected by the business cycle and have stable demand.
- Avoid going from a labor-intensive to a capital-intensive business, because the latter has a high degree of operating leverage.
- Avoid long-term fixed-fee contracts to customers. Incorporate inflation adjustment and energy-cost indices in contracts.
- Avoid entering markets on the downturn or that are highly competitive.
- Adjust to changes in technology.

INCOME STATEMENT ANALYSIS _____

What should be considered in analyzing the income statement?

The analysis of the income statement indicates a company's earning power, earnings quality, and operating performance. The CFO should be familiar with the important factors in appraising the income statement. Net income backed-up by cash is essential for corporate liquidity. The accounting policies should be realistic in reflecting the substance of the transactions. Accounting changes should only be made for legitimate reasons. Further, a high degree of estimation in the income measurement process results in uncertainty in reported figures. Earnings stability enhances the predictability of future results based on currently reported profits.

In analyzing the income statement, the CFO should look at quantitative (e.g., ratio analysis) and qualitative factors (e.g., pending litigation).

Earnings potential and earnings quality affect the price-earnings ratio, bond rating, effective interest rate, compensating balance requirement, availability of financing, and desirability of the firm as either an acquirer or acquiree.

Why are discretionary costs important to look at?

Discretionary costs can be changed at will. They may be decreased when a company is having problems. *What to Do:* Examine current discretionary costs relative to previous years and to future requirements. An index number may be used to compare the current year discretionary cost to the base amount. A reduction in discretionary costs (e.g., advertising, research, repairs) is undesirable if their absence will have a negative effect on the future. *Recommendation:* Analyze the trend in the following ratios: (1) discretionary costs to sales and (2) discretionary costs to assets. If a cost reduction program produces substantial cuts in discretionary costs, future profitability will suffer. However, cost control is justified when (1) in previous years discretionary expenditures were excessive because of deficient and ill-conceived corporate strategy or (2) competition has decreased. A material increase in discretionary costs may have a significant positive impact on corporate earning power and future growth.

EXAMPLE 11

The following data are supplied:

	19X1	19X2	19X3
Sales	$95,000	$125,000	$84,000
Research	9,000	14,000	3,000

The most representative year (base year) is 19X1. After 19X4, the CFO believes that research is essential for the company's success because of the technological nature of the industry.

	19X1	19X2	19X3
Research to sales	9.5%	11.2%	3.6%

Looking in base dollars, 19X1 represents 100. 19X2 is 156 ($14,000/$9,000). 19X3 has an index of 33 ($3,000/$9,000).

A red flag is posted for 19X3. Research is lower than in previous years. There should have been a boost in research considering the technological updating needed for 19X4.

EXAMPLE 12

The following information on plant assets applies for a company:

	19X1	19X2
Equipment	$4,500	$4,800
Less: Accumulated depreciation	3,000	3,200
Book value	$1,500	$1,600
Repairs	400	320
Replacement cost of equipment	6,800	7,700
CPI value of equipment	7,400	8,500
Revenue	48,000	53,000
Working capital	2,900	2,600
Cash	1,100	970
Debt-to-equity ratio	42%	71%
Downtime of equipment	2%	5%

Finance company loans have increased relative to bank loans over the year.

The CFO wants to analyze equipment and repairs.

Repairs to gross equipment decreased from 8.9% in 19X1 ($400/$4,500) to 6.7% in 19X2 ($320/$4,800). In a similar vein, repairs to revenue went from 0.83% in 19X1 ($400/$48,000) to 0.6% in 19X2 ($320/$53,000).

Over the year there was a greater variation between replacement cost and book value and CPI value and book value, indicating equipment is aging.

The increased downtime means there is more equipment malfunctioning.

Equipment purchased over the year was minimal, 6.7% ($300/$4,500).

The company's capital maintenance is inadequate. Repairs to fixed assets and repairs to revenue are down, and there are insufficient replacements. Perhaps these are the reasons for the increased downtime.

The company may have a problem purchasing fixed assets when needed because of a deteriorating liquidity position. Financial leverage has significantly increased over the year. It is difficult for the company to obtain adequate financing at reasonable interest rates, as evidenced by the need to borrow from finance companies.

How much of the earnings are supported by cash?

Cash flow from operations equals net income plus noncash expenses less noncash revenue. The CFO should examine the trend in the ratio of cash flow from operations to net income. A high ratio is warranted because it means that earnings are backed-up by cash.

In evaluating cash adequacy, compute the following:

• Cash flow generated from operations before interest expense.

• Cash flow generated from operations less cash payments to meet debt principal, dividends, and capital expenditures.

What tax factors have to be considered in appraising earnings?

Earnings are not really available if there is a high percentage of foreign profits that will not be repatriated back to the U.S. for an extended time period.

It is better if the company's earnings and growth do not rely on a lowered tax rate that is susceptible to a future change in the tax law or that places restrictions on the firm.

Of what value is residual income?

Residual income is an economic income considering the opportunity cost of placing funds in the business. An increasing trend in residual income to net income indicates strong corporate profitability because the company is earning enough to meet its imputed cost of capital.

Residual income equals:

Net income
Less: Minimum return (cost of capital)
   × Total assets
Residual income

EXAMPLE 13

A company's net income is $800,000, total assets are $4,600,000, and cost of capital is 13.40%.

Residual income equals:

Net income	$800,000
Less: Minimum return × Total assets	
13.40% × $4,600,000	616,400
Residual income	$183,600

The ratio of residual income to net income is 23% ($183,600/$800,000).

(Residual income is discussed in more detail in Chapter 17.)

Are accounting policies realistic?

The accounting policies should be realistic in reflecting the economic substance of the company's transactions. The underlying business and financial realities of the company and industry have to be considered. For example, the depreciation method should most approximately measure the decline in service potential of the asset. Examples of realistic accounting policies are cited in AICPA Industry Audit Guides.

How certain are the earnings?

The more subjective the accounting estimates in the income measurement process, the greater is the uncertainty associated with net income. *What to Do:* Examine the difference between actual experience and the estimates used. A wide difference implies uncertain earnings.

Examine the trend in the following ratios:

- High estimation assets (e.g., fixed assets) to total assets.
- Cash expenses to revenue.
- Estimated expenses to revenue.
- Cash revenue to revenue.
- Estimated revenue to revenue.
- Estimated expenses to net income.
- Estimated revenue to net income.

EXAMPLE 14

The following information applies to a company:

	19X1	19X2
Cash and near-cash revenue	$ 98,000	$107,000
Noncash revenue items	143,000	195,000
Total revenue	$241,000	$302,000
Cash and near-cash expenses	$ 37,000	$ 58,000
Noncash expenses	67,000	112,000
Total expenses	$104,000	$170,000
Net income	$137,000	$132,000

Estimation-related ratios can now be calculated:

	19X1	19X2
Estimated revenue to total revenue	59%	65%
Estimated revenue to net income	104%	148%
Estimated expenses to total expenses	64%	66%
Estimated expenses to total revenue	28%	37%
Estimated expenses to net income	49%	85%

In each case, there was greater estimation in the income measurement process in 19X2 compared to 19X1. A high degree of estimation results in uncertain profits.

What is the significance of discontinued operations?

Income from discontinued operations is typically of a one-time nature and should be ignored when predicting future earnings. Further, a discontinued operation implies the company is in a state of decline or that a poor management decision is the reason for the firm's entering the discontinued line of business initially.

What are some useful profitability ratios?

A sign of good financial health and how effectively the company is managed is its ability to generate earnings and return on investment. Absolute dollar profit is of minimal significance unless it is compared to the assets generating it.

A company's profit margin (net income to sales) indicates how well it is managed and provides clues to a company's pricing, cost structure, and manufacturing efficiency. A high gross profit percent (gross profit to sales) is favorable because it indicates the company can control its production costs.

Return on investment is how much profit is achieved from the investment. Two key ratios of return on investment are *return on total assets* and *return on owners' equity.*

The *return on total assets* (net income/average total assets) indicates the efficiency with which management has used its resources to obtain revenue. Further, a decline in the ratio may stem from a productivity problem.

The *return on common equity* (earnings available to common stock/average stockholders' equity) measures the rate of return on the common stockholders' investment.

(Return on investment is fully discussed in Chapter 17.)

An increase in the gross profit margin (gross profit to sales) may mean the company was able to increase its sales volume or selling price, or to reduce its cost of sales. Manufacturers typically have higher gross profit rates than merchandisers.

The net operating profit ratio (net operating profit to sales) may be used to evaluate operating managers. The analysis is before considering interest expense since financing is usually arranged by the finance managers.

A high ratio of sales to working capital indicates efficient utilization of liquid funds. The sales backlog should be used to monitor sales status and planning. Compute the days of sales in backlog equal to:

$$\frac{\text{Backlog balance}}{\text{Sales volume divided by days in period}}$$

Is the backlog for long-range delivery (e.g., 5 years from now) or on a recurring basis to maintain continuing stability?

Some other ratios reflective of operations are:

• Revenue to number of employees as well as revenue to employee salaries. Higher ratios are reflective of better employee productivity.

• Average yearly wage per employee and average hourly wage rate. These ratios examine the ability to control labor costs.

• Average fixed assets per employee. This shows the productivity of using fixed assets by employees.

• Indirect labor to direct labor. A low ratio is reflective of controlling the labor component of overhead.

• Purchase discounts to purchases. A high ratio indicates effective management of purchases.

• General and administrative expenses to selling expense. This ratio indicates control of G&A expenses. G&A expenses relative to selling expenses should decline with increased sales volume. If the ratio increases, inadequate controls over administrative activities exist.

How is the growth rate computed?

A company's growth rate should be compared to that of competitors and industry averages. Measures of growth rate include:

$$\frac{\text{Change in retained earnings}}{\text{Stockholders' equity at beginning of year}}$$

$$\frac{\text{EPS (end of year)} - \text{EPS (beginning of year)}}{\text{EPS (beginning of year)}}$$

The growth rate in sales, dividends, total assets, and the like may be computed in a similar fashion.

MARKET VALUE RATIOS

What are some important market value ratios?

The market value ratios apply to a comparison of the company's stock price relative to its earnings (or book value) per share. The dividend-related ratios are also considered. The ratios include:

• Earnings per share (net income divided by outstanding shares).

• Price-earnings ratio (market price per share divided by earnings per share).

• Book value per share. This equals:

$$\frac{\begin{array}{c}\text{Total stockholders' equity} - \\ \text{(Liquidation value of preferred stock} + \\ \text{Preferred dividends in arrears)}\end{array}}{\text{Common stock outstanding}}$$

A comparison of book value per share to market price per share indicates how investors feel about the company.

• Dividend yield (dividends per share divided by market price per share).

• Dividend payout (dividends per share divided by earnings per share).

Investors look unfavorably upon lower dividends since dividend payout is a sign of the financial health of the business.

ANALYZING THE FINANCIAL STRUCTURE OF THE FIRM _____

Quantitative measures can be used to evaluate the company's stability. Comparisons should be made to prior years of the firm, competing companies, and industry norms.

Types of stability measurements include:

• *Trend in average reported earnings.* Average earnings over a long time period (such as five years) will level out abnormal and erratic income statement components as well as cyclical factors.

• *Average pessimistic earnings.* This represents the average earnings based on the *worst* possible scenario for the company's operational activities. The average minimum earnings is useful in appraising a company having high risk operations.

• *Standard Deviation*

$$S.D. = \sqrt{\frac{\Sigma(y - \overline{y})^2}{n}}$$

where $\overline{y}$ = net income for period t, $\overline{y}$ = average net income, and n = number of periods. The higher the standard deviation, the greater is the instability.

• *Coefficient of Variation*

$$C.V. = \frac{S.D.}{\overline{y}}$$

The coefficient of variation is a relative measure of instability to facilitate a comparison between competing companies. The higher the coefficient, the greater the risk.

• *Instability Index of Earnings*

$$I = \sqrt{\frac{\Sigma(y - y^T)^2}{n}}$$

where y^T = trend earnings for period t, and is determined as follows:

$$y^T = a + bt$$

where a = dollar intercept, b = slope of trend line, and t = time period.

Trend income is computed using a simple trend equation solved by computer. The index reflects the deviation between actual income and trend income. A higher index indicates greater stability.

• *Beta.* Beta is computed by a computer run based on the following equation:

$$r_{jt} = a_j + B_j r_{Mt} + E_{jt}$$

where r_{jt} = return of security j for period t, a_j = constant, B_j = Beta for security j, r_{Mt} = return on a market index such as the New York Stock Exchange Index, and E_{jt} = error term.

Beta measures the systematic risk of a stock. A Beta greater than 1 indicates the company's market price of stock fluctuates more than the change in the market index, indicating a risky security. A fluctuation in stock price infers greater business risk and instability. For example, a Beta of 1.4 means the company's stock price rises or falls 40 percent faster than the market. A Beta of 1 means the company's stock price moves the same as the market index. A Beta of less than 1 indicates the company's stock price fluctuates less than the stock market index, indicating lower corporate risk. Of course, a company's Beta may change over time. The Betas for individual companies may be obtained from various sources such as Standard and Poors.

EXAMPLE 15

A company shows the following trend in reported earnings:

19X0	$100,000
19X1	110,000
19X2	80,000
19X3	120,000
19X4	140,000

$$\text{Standard Deviation} = \sqrt{\frac{\Sigma(y - y)^2}{n}}$$

$$\bar{y} = \Sigma \frac{y}{n} = \frac{\begin{array}{c}100,000 + 110,000 + 80,000 \\ + 120,000 + 140,000\end{array}}{5}$$

$$= \frac{550,000}{5} = 110,000$$

Year	$(y - \bar{y})$	$(y - \bar{y})^2$
19X0	−10,000	100,000,000
19X1	0	0
19X2	−30,000	900,000,000
19X3	+10,000	100,000,000
19X4	+30,000	900,000,000
		2,000,000,000

$$\text{Standard Deviation} = \sqrt{\frac{2,000,000,000}{5}}$$

$$= \sqrt{400,000,000} = 20,000$$

$$\text{Coefficient of Variation} = \frac{\text{Standard Deviation}}{\bar{y}}$$

$$= \frac{20,000}{110,000}$$

$$= 18.2\%$$

To what extent are costs highly leveraged?

Operating leverage is the degree to which fixed charges exist in a company's cost structure. Measures of operating leverage are:

- Fixed costs to total costs.
- Percentage change in operating income to the percentage change in sales volume.
- Net income to fixed costs.

Note: An increase in (1) and (2) or decrease in (3) indicates greater earnings instability because of the high fixed costs.

A high percentage of variable costs to total costs indicates greater earnings stability. Variable costs can be adjusted more readily than fixed costs to meet declining product demand.

A high break-even company is vulnerable to economic declines.

What is the nature of the product line?

A company's product line affects its overall stability and profitability. Where possible, product risk should be minimized, such as by moving toward negative correlation among products.

Product Line Measures

- The degree of correlation between products is evident from a correlation matrix determined by a computer run.
- Product demand elasticity is determined as follows:

$$\frac{\text{Percentage change in quantity}}{\text{Percentage change in price}}$$

If > 1 Elastic demand
If = 1 Unitary demand
If < 1 Inelastic demand

- *Red Flag.* Products that are positively correlated and have elastic demands are of high risk. On the other hand, companies with product lines having negative correlations and inelastic demand (e.g., health-care products) are stable. Further, products with different seasonal peaks should be added to stabilize production and marketing operations.

EXAMPLE 16

The correlation matrix of a product line follows:

Product	A	B	C	D	E	F
A	1.0	.13	−.02	−.01	−.07	.22
B	.13	1.0	−.02	−.07	.00	.00
C	−.02	−.02	1.0	.01	.48	.13
D	−.01	−.07	.01	1.0	.01	−.02
E	−.07	.00	.48	.01	1.0	.45
F	.22	.00	.13	−.02	.45	1.0

Perfect correlation exists with the same product. For instance, the correlation between product F and product F is 1.0.

High positive correlation exists between products E and C (.48) and products E and F (.45). Because these products are tightly interwoven, risk exists.

Low negative correlation exists between products A and D (−.01) and products A and C (−.02).

No correlation is present between products B and E (.00) and products B and F (.00).

It would be better if some products had significant negative correlations (e.g., −.7) but such is not the case.

EXAMPLE 17

Data for products X and Y follow:

	X	Y
Selling price	$10	$8
Unit sales	10,000	13,000

If the selling price of product X is increased to $11, it is predicted that sales volume will decrease by 500 units. If the selling price of product Y is raised to $9.50, sales volume is anticipated to fall by 4,000 units.

Product demand elasticity equals:

$$\frac{\text{Percentage change in quantity}}{\text{Percentage change in price}}$$

Inelastic demand exists with product X:

$$\frac{\dfrac{500}{10,000}}{\dfrac{\$1}{\$10}} = \frac{.05}{.10} = .5$$

Elastic demand occurs with product Y:

$$\frac{\dfrac{4,000}{13,000}}{\dfrac{\$1.50}{\$8.00}} = \frac{.307}{.188} = 1.63$$

What are some financial measures of marketing effectiveness?

The CFO may evaluate marketing effectiveness as follows:

• Appraise product warranty complaints and their dispositions.

• Calculate revenue, cost, and profit by product line, customer, industry segment, geographic area, distribution channel, type of marketing effort, and average order size.

• Evaluate new products in terms of risk and profitability.

• Appraise strengths and weaknesses of competition as well as their reactions to the company's promotion efforts.

• Determine revenue, marketing costs, and profits before, during, and after promotion programs.

• Appraise sales generated by different types of selling efforts (e.g., direct mail, television, newspaper).

• Analyze sales force effectiveness by determining the profit generated by salespeople, call frequency, sales incentives, sales personnel costs (e.g., auto), and dollar value of orders obtained per hour spent.

• Determine sales and/or net income per employee.

• Examine the trend in the ratio of marketing costs to sales.

How may risk be appraised?

In appraising risk, the CFO should compare the company's risk exposure to the competition and to past trends of the firm. Uncertainty makes it difficult to predict future performance. The major risks faced by the company are:

• Corporate risk, such as the underinsurance of assets (e.g., declining trend in insurance expense to fixed assets, unusual casualty losses). A way to reduce corporate risk is diversification.

• Industry risk, such as an industry under public and governmental scrutiny (e.g., real estate industry). An approach to diminish industry risk is to move toward a variable-cost-oriented business.

• Economic risk, such as the effect of a recession on product demand. This risk may be curtailed by having a low-priced product substitute for a high-priced item (e.g., cereal for meat).

• Political risk, such as the need for lobbying efforts. Avoid operations in highly regulated areas.

• Social risk, such as a company experiencing customer boycotts or bias suits. A way to reduce this risk is community involvement.

• Environmental risk, such as a product line or service exposed to the weather. A way to lower this risk is to have counterseasonal products.

What is the nature of your industry?

Labor-intensive businesses typically have greater stability than capital-intensive ones since the former have a higher percentage of variable costs whereas the latter have a higher percentage of fixed costs. Capital-intensive industries are susceptible to cyclicality. Companies in a staple industry have greater stability because of inelastic product demand.

A company may have variability because of an industry cycle. An example is the steel industry, which has a five- to ten-year cycle because of the refurbishing of steel furnaces.

Industry Characteristics Indicative of Greater Risk

• Competition. What is the ease of entry, price wars, and cheaper imports?

• Technological (e.g., computers) causing obsolescence risk and difficulty in keeping up-to-date.

• Governmental regulation such as by a utility regulatory commission.

• Susceptibility to cyclical effects.

• High-risk product line without adequate insurance coverage.

If you have difficulty obtaining insurance in your industry, try to pool risks by setting up mutual insurance companies.

Are you vulnerable to political uncertainties?

Political risk refers to foreign operations and governmental regulation. Multinational companies with foreign exposure have uncertainties in repatriation of funds, currency fluctuations, and local customs and regulations. Operations in politically and economically unstable foreign regions means instability.

Ratios to Be Examined

- Questionable foreign revenue to total revenue
- Questionable foreign earnings to net income
- Total export revenue to total revenue
- Total export earnings to net income
- Total assets in "questionable" foreign countries to total assets
- Total assets in foreign countries to total assets

Considerations in Foreign Operations

- Foreign exchange rates. *Red Flag:* Vacillating foreign exchange rates, which can be measured by the percentage change over time and/or its standard deviation. The trend in foreign translation gains and losses (reported in the stockholders' equity section) should be examined. When foreign assets are balanced against foreign liabilities, you are better insulated from changes in exchange rates. Evaluate your exposed position for each major foreign country. When the dollar is devalued, net foreign assets and income in countries with strong currencies are worth more dollars. Forward exchange contracts should be viewed positively because the company is minimizing its foreign currency exposure by hedging against exchange risk from foreign currency transactions.
- Foreign country's tax rate and duties.

Companies dependent on government contracts have more instability because government spending is vulnerable to political whims of legislators and war-threatening situations. *Suggestion:* Determine the percentage of earnings from government contract work, and the extent to which such work is recurring.

Look at government regulation over the company because it influences the bottom line (e.g., utility rate increases are less than that which has been asked for). *Recommendation:* Examine present and future effects of governmental interference on the company by studying current and proposed governmental laws and regulations. The sources of such information include legislative hearings, trade journals, and newspapers. Stringent environmental and safety regulations "eat into" profits.

Analyze the effect of present and proposed tax legislation. What are the areas of IRS scrutiny?

31

Analysis, Evaluation, and Control of Revenue and Costs

A company can improve its bottom-line and overall operations by analyzing, planning, monitoring, and controlling revenue and costs. Control reports help in this process. This chapter provides some benchmarks in this evaluation and control process.

CONTROL REPORTS

Control reports are issued to highlight poor performance so that timely corrective action may be taken. The reports should be frequent, detailed, and look at each important operational level.

Summary reports should present performance over a long time period (e.g., monthly) and provide an overview of performance.

The form and content of the control report varies depending upon the functions and responsibilities of the executives receiving it. The reports may be narrative, tabular, or graphic. A lower level manager is more concerned with details. A higher level manager is more interested with summaries, trends, and relationships. The reports may be in both financial and nonfinancial terms.

How may revenue be controlled?

Important questions needing answering in sales analysis are: What was sold? Where was it sold? Who sold it? What was the profit?

Sales and profitability analysis involves the following:

• *Customer.* Industry or retail, corporate or governmental, domestic or foreign.

• *Product.* Type of commodity, size, price, quality, size, and color.

- *Distribution channel.* Wholesaler, retailer, agent, broker.
- *Sales effort.* Personal visit, direct mail, coupon, ad (e.g., newspaper, magazine), media (television, radio).
- *Territory.* Country, state, city, suburb.
- *Order size.* Individual purchase.
- *Organization.* Department, branch.
- *Salesperson.* Group, individual.
- *Terms of sale.* Cash purchase, cash on delivery, charge account, installment purchase.

Profitability may be determined by territory, product, customer, channel of distribution, salesmen, method of sale, organization, and operating division. In deciding upon a product line, economies of production have to be considered.

The CFO should watch out for significant changes in sales trends in terms of profit margin and distribution channels. How do actual sales conform to sales goals and budgets? In analyzing the trend in sales, the CFO may see the need to redirect sales effort and/or change the product. The types and sizes of desirable accounts and orders should be determined. Volume selling price breaks may be given for different order sizes.

In appraising sales volume and prices, the CFO should not ignore the possibility that unfavorable variances have arisen from salespeople having excessive authority in establishing selling prices.

Pricing should be periodically reviewed after considering relevant factors such as increasing costs. All types of cost must be considered including total cost, marginal cost, and out-of-pocket costs.

The CFO should compare the profit margins on alternative products in deciding which ones to emphasize. He or she should also consider the probable effect of volume on the profit margin. Consideration should also be given to the importance of changes in composition, manufacturing processes, and quality on the costs to produce and distribute the product.

The CFO should determine the following:

- The least cost geographic location for warehouses.
- The minimum acceptable order.
- How best to serve particular accounts, such as by mail order, telephone, jobber etc.

The CFO may find that most sales are concentrated in a few products. In fact, a few customers may represent a significant portion of company sales. This involves a small amount of the sales effort. The CFO may be able to reduce selling costs by concentrating sales effort on the major customers and products. Perhaps salesperson assignments should be modified, such as concentrating on only a few territories. Perhaps a simplification of the product line is needed.

The CFO should provide the alternative costs for the varying methods of sale. For example, how should samples be distributed to result in the best effect on sales at minimum cost.

In evaluating sales effort, we should consider the success of business development expense (e.g., promotion and entertainment) by customer, territory, or salesperson.

How may customers be analyzed?

Customer analysis should indicate the number of accounts and dollar sales by customer volume bracket and average order size. A small order size may result in unprofitable sales because of such factors as high distribution costs and high order costs. In this case, the CFO should analyze distribution costs by size of order in order to bring the problem under control and take appropriate corrective action.

It may cost more to sell to certain types of customers than others among different classes as well as within a particular class. For example, a particular customer may require greater services than typical, such as delivery and warehousing. A particular customer may demand a different price, such as for volume purchases. Profitability analysis by customer should be made so as to see where to place salespeople time, what selling price to establish, where to control distribution costs, and what customer classes to discontinue. A determination should also be made as to which customers have increasing or decreasing sales volume. Sales effort may be curtailed on: (1) large volume accounts that only buy low profit margin items and (2) low volume accounts that are at best marginally profitable.

It may not pay to carry all varieties, sizes, and colors from a sales and profitability perspective. The company should emphasize the profitable products which may *not* be the *odd* items (e.g., unusual colors, odd sizes).

What analysis may be made of sales?

Sales which have not been realized should be listed and analyzed, particularly with regard to any problems that may have been experienced. Such analysis involves the following:

- Orders received.
- Unfilled orders.
- Lost sales.
- Cancellations. Why?

Note: The analysis of orders is particularly crucial when goods are made to order.

Sales deductions should be analyzed to indicate problems possibly leading to deficient profits. Problems may be indicated when excessive discounts, allowances, and freight costs exist. What is the extent and reasons for returns, price adjustments, freight allowances, etc. A determination should be made of whom is responsible. A defective product is the responsibility of manufacturing. An excessive freight cost or wrong delay is the responsibility of traffic.

Sales should be analyzed in terms of both price and volume to identify unfavorable trends, weaknesses, and positive directions.

CONTROL OF COSTS ──────────

Cost control must be exercised over manufacturing and nonmanufacturing costs. Costs should only be incurred for necessary business expenditures that will provide revenue benefit to the firm.

How may manufacturing costs be controlled?

The purpose of cost control is to obtain an optimum product consistent with quality standards from the various input factors including material, labor, and facilities. The input-output relationship is crucial. In other words, the best result should be forthcoming at the least cost. The office should be shut down when the factory is not in operation. Since most costs are controllable by someone within the organization, responsibility should be assigned.

Changes in standard prices for material, labor, and overhead should be noted along with their effects upon the unit standard cost of the product. Perhaps there is a need for material substitutions or modifications in specifications or processes.

Labor control should be jointly developed between staff and management. Line supervisors have prime responsibility to control labor costs. Actual performance of labor should be compared against a realistic yardstick. Unfavorable discrepancies should be followed up.

The CFO may assist in controlling labor costs in the following ways:

• Prepare an analysis of overtime hours and cost. Make sure overtime is approved in advance.

• Prepare a report on labor turnover, training cost, and years of service.

• Determine the standard man-hours for the production program.

• Establish procedures to limit the number of employees placed on the payroll to that called for by the production plan.

• Make sure that an employee is performing services per his/her job description. Are high-paid employees doing menial work?

• Consider overtime hours and cost, turnover rate, output per worker, and relationship between indirect labor and direct labor.

- Working conditions should be improved to enhance productivity.
- Analyze machinery to assure they are up-to-date.

Because most overhead items are small in amount, proper control may be neglected. Of course, in the aggregate overhead may be substantial. Areas to look at include the personal use of supplies and xeroxing, and use of customized forms when standardized ones would suffice.

In order to control overhead, standards must be established and compared against actual performance. Periodic reports of budget and actual overhead costs should be prepared to identify problem areas. Preplanning of overhead costs may be done such as planning indirect labor staff (e.g., maintenance) to avoid excessive hours. The preplanning approach may be beneficial when significant dollar cost is involved, such as in the purchase of repair material and supplies. A record of purchases by responsibility unit may be helpful. Purchase requirements should be properly approved.

The cost of idle equipment should be determined to gauge whether facilities are being utilized properly. What is the degree of plant utilization relative to what is normal?

What can be done to minimize manufacturing costs?

The control of distribution costs is a much more difficult problem than the control of manufacturing costs. In distribution, we have to consider the varying nature of the personality of seller and buyer. Competitive factors must be taken into account. On the contrary, in production the worker is the only human element. In marketing, there is more methods and greater flexibility relative to production. Several distribution channels may be used. Because of the greater possibility for variability, distribution processes are more difficult to standardize than production activities. If distribution costs are excessive, who and where does the responsibility lie? Is it a problem territory? Is the salesperson doing a poor job?

Distribution costs and effort must be planned, controlled, and monitored. Distribution costs may be analyzed by functional operation, nature of expense, and application of distribution effort.

In functional operation, distribution costs are analyzed in terms of individual responsibility. This is a particularly useful approach in large companies. Functional operations requiring measurement are identified. Examples of such operations might be circular mailing, warehouse shipments, and salespeople calls on customers.

In looking at the nature of the expense, costs are segregated by month and trends in distribution costs are examined. The ratio of distribution costs to sales over time should be enlightening. A comparison to industry norms is recommended.

In looking at the manner of application, distribution costs must be segregated into direct costs, indirect costs, and semidirect costs.

Direct costs are specifically identifiable to a particular segment. Examples of direct costs assignable to a salesperson are salary, commission, and travel and entertainment expense. But these same costs may be indirect or semidirect if attributable to product analysis. An expense that is direct in one application may not be in another.

Indirect costs are general corporate costs and must be allocated to segments (e.g., territory, product) on a rational basis. Examples are corporate advertising and salaries of general sales executives. Advertising may be allocated based on sales. General sales executives' salaries may be allocated based on time spent by territory or product. Here, a time log may be kept.

Semidirect costs are related in some measurable way to particular segments. Such costs may be distributed in accordance with the services required. For example, the variable factor for warehousing may be weight handled. Order handling costs may be in terms of the number of orders. The allocation base is considerably less arbitrary than with indirect costs.

A comparison should be made between actual and budgeted figures for salesperson salaries, bonuses, and expenses. The salary structure in the industry may serve as a good reference point.

An examination should be made as to the effect of advertising on sales. Perhaps a change in media is needed.

Telephone expense may be controlled in the following ways:

- Prior approval for long-distance calls.
- Controls to restrict personal use of the telephone, such as a key lock.
- Discarding or returning unnecessary equipment.

The trend in warehouse expense to sales should be analyzed. Increasing trends may have to be investigated.

To control dues and subscription expenses, a control is necessary such as having a card record of each publication by subscribed to, by whom, and why. If another employee must use that publication, he or she knows where to go.

There should be centralized control over contributions such as in the hands of a committee of senior management. A general policy must be established as to amount and for what purposes.

32

Insurance and Legal Considerations

The CFO should be familiar with insurance and law. Insurance coverage protects against fire and theft losses, product liability, and contract repudiation. Federal and state laws deal with the relationship between the employer and employee.

What kind of insurance protection do you need?

In a large company, a risk manager should exist to handle insurance issues. He or she should report directly to the CFO. In a smaller company, the CFO may be responsible for insurance matters himself or herself.

Insurance protection minimizes the risk of loss. Insurance may be mandated by law such as worker's compensation. Insurance coverage may be required by contract such as fire insurance in order to adhere to the provisions of a loan agreement. The CFO must understand insurance requirements and procedures, and must monitor and control insurance costs while maintaining sufficient insurance coverage. The CFO has to consider the limits for risk assumption or retention, self-insurance and uninsurable risks. Further, suitable documentation of insurance procedures is needed.

What are your duties in the insurance area?

The CFO has many responsibilities in insurance protection including identifying and appraising risks, monitoring changes in the corporate environment as it affects insurance, estimating the probability of loss, maintaining insurance records, keeping abreast of new developments in insurance, and assuring compliance with federal and local regulatory laws.

The CFO in evaluating insurable hazards should examine in detail properties along with related contractual obligations (e.g., leases, mortgages). Each structure should be listed along with its condition, safety, location, and replacement cost.

In insignificant risk areas, deductibles should be established to satisfy company needs and result in premium savings. *Tip:* A new business should have higher deductibles until experience is gained of loss incidences and their financial effect.

Insurance policies should be periodically reviewed to avoid uninsured losses. As the company changes in size, products, geographic areas, etc., it may have to alter the type and amount of insurance. There may have to be a revision in policy limits and deductibles based on the company's current situation. If the deductible is increased, the premium will be decreased. When reviewing insurance, the CFO has to consider new risks, trends in litigation, changes in inventory policy, sale or purchase of fixed assets, switch in distribution channels, and fair market value of property.

Note: Insurance is not needed for everything. In some nonessential areas, self insurance may be enough. In deciding whether to insure against a risk, the CFO must weigh the probable loss against the insurance premium. If the difference is negligible, it may not pay to insure the item. GENERAL RULE: Insure potential catastrophes that would significantly impair ongoing operations.

What insurance records are needed?

There are many insurance records that should be maintained including:

• Records of premiums, losses, and settlements. The ratio of premiums to losses should be computed.

• Expense distribution records including information about payments, refunds, accruals, write-offs, and allocation amounts and bases to segments.

• Claim records including the names of claim representatives, claim procedures, documentation, claim information (e.g., date), and status of the claim.

- Records of the values of insured items.
- Binder records of *pending* insurance.
- Location records of insured items.
- Transportation logs for corporate vehicles including delivery trucks and automobiles. Information includes miles driven and to be driven, condition, and location.
- Other files including due dates for premiums, notice of hearings, and inspections.

An insurance manual should be kept detailing the procedures to be followed on all aspects of insurance coverage by type including obtaining insurance, filing claims, financial reporting and presentation, allocation bases to allocate premiums to reporting units, and settlement issues.

All insurable losses must be immediately reported and documented. The CFO must know what types of losses have occurred, where, and magnitude. The damaged items must be segregated until the adjuster has made a review. The CFO should determine the reason for the loss and recommend remedial steps.

At year-end, an insurance report should be prepared containing a description of the types of insurance and coverage, premiums paid, self-insured items, and the adequacy of established reserves.

The insurance record (Table 32–1) lists the insurance policies, policy dates, annual premium, and coverage.

The CFO should keep records of the use and sale of property. Insurance claim information should be maintained for such items as cash, securities, inventory, and fixed assets. The CFO should check the track record, support, and documentation for all claims.

How do you know what insurance broker to use?

In choosing an insurance broker, the following should be considered:

- Insurer's financial condition.
- Types of coverage, insurance products available, and rates.

TABLE 32-1 INSURANCE RECORD

Insurance Company	Broker	Identifying Number of Policy	Amount of Policy	Term	Expiration Date	Annual Premium	Coverage	Exclusions

- Timely and full resolution of insurance claims.
- Services provided and expertise of staff.

TYPES OF INSURANCE

The types of business insurance include product liability, commercial property, umbrella excess policy, marine, contingent business interruption, automobile, and aircraft.

To what extent are you affected by product liability?

Insurance coverage is needed for losses arising from damages suffered by other parties because of defects in the company's products, services, operations, or employee actions. An evaluation should be conducted of contracts, leases, and sales orders. What federal and state product liability statutes apply? What is the probability of loss, the degree, and the frequency?

What is covered under commercial property insurance?

The commercial property policy is a comprehensive one insuring inventory on the premises, warehouses, and in-transit. It also covers property damage, personal injuries, product liability, advertising liability, fire damage on rental premises, flood and earthquake losses, and loss of valuable records. The coverage *excludes* certain items such as cash and securities, property sold under installments, precious metals, aircraft, and imports or exports. These are covered under other types of policies.

The commercial property policy is the prime "all-risk" policy of the company. Losses exceeding policy limits are recoverable under the umbrella policy.

How do you determine the insurance reimbursement?

Casualty insurance covers such items as fire loss and water damage. The premiums are typically paid in advance and debited to Pre-paid Insurance which is then amortized over the policy period. Casualty insurance reimburses the holder for the fair market value of lost property. Insurance companies usually have a coinsurance provision so that the insured bears a portion of the loss. The insurance reimbursement formula follows (assumes an 80% coinsurance clause):

$$\frac{\text{Face of policy}}{.8 \times \text{Fair market value of insured property}} \times \frac{\text{Fair market value of loss}}{} = \frac{\text{Possible reimbursement}}{}$$

Insurance reimbursement is based on the lower of the face of the policy, fair market value of loss, or possible reimbursement.

EXAMPLE 1

Case	Face of Policy	Fair Market Value of Property	Fair Market Value of Loss
A	$ 4,000	$10,000	$ 6,000
B	6,000	10,000	10,000
C	10,000	10,000	4,000

Insurance reimbursement follows:

Case A:
$$\frac{\$4,000}{.8 \times \$10,000} \times \$6,000 = \$3,000$$

Case B:
$$\frac{\$6,000}{.8 \times \$10,000} \times \$10,000 = \$7,500$$

Case C:
$$\frac{\$10,000}{.8 \times \$10,000} \times \$4,000 = \$5,000$$

A blanket policy covers several items of property. The face of the policy is allocated based upon the fair market values of the insured assets.

EXAMPLE 2

A blanket policy of $15,000 applies to equipment I and equipment II. The fair values of equipment I and II are $30,000 and $15,000, respectively. Equipment II is partially destroyed resulting in a fire loss of $3,000.

The policy allocation to equipment II is computed below:

	Fair Market Value	Policy
Equipment I	$30,000	$10,000
Equipment II	15,000	5,000
	$45,000	$15,000

The insurance reimbursement is:

$$\frac{\$5,000}{.8 \times \$15,000} \times \$3,000 = \$1,500$$

When there is a fire loss, the destroyed asset must be removed from the books. Fire loss is charged for the book value of the property. The insurance reimbursement reduces the fire loss. The fire loss is an extraordinary item shown net of tax.

EXAMPLE 3

Merchandise costing $5,000 is fully destroyed. There is no insurance for it. Furniture costing $10,000 with accumulated depreciation of $1,000 and having a fair market value of $7,000 is fully destroyed. The policy is for $10,000. Building costing $30,000 with accumulated depreciation of $3,000 and having a fair market value of $20,000 is 50% destroyed. The face of the policy is $15,000. The journal entries to record the fire loss on the books follow:

Fire loss	5,000	
Inventory		5,000
Fire loss	9,000	

Accumulated Depreciation	1,000	
Furniture		10,000
Fire loss	13,500	
Accumulated depreciation	1,500	
Building		15,000

Insurance reimbursement totals $16,375 computed as follows:

Furniture:
$$\frac{\$10,000}{.8 \times \$7,000} \times \$7,000 = \$12,500$$

Building:
$$\frac{\$15,000}{.8 \times \$20,000} \times \$10,000 = \$9,375$$

The journal entry for the insurance reimbursement is:

Cash	16,375	
Fire loss		16,375

The net fire loss is $11,125 ($27,500 − $16,375).

What is boiler explosion insurance?

This insurance covers losses of property arising from an explosion.

What is an umbrella policy?

The umbrella policy insures against all risks not covered under another policy. For example, if the commercial property policy covers up to $15 million, the umbrella policy would provide coverage in excess of $15 million but not to exceed $40 million. It is an "excess coverage" policy taking effect after another policy has paid its limit. The umbrella policy is essential in a comprehensive insurance program.

How does marine insurance work?

Marine insurance applies to the importing of merchandise on terms of FOB shipping point.

The policy covers goods in transit. Insurance coverage is required because the company obtains title when the goods are shipped. Each shipment is covered separately and the premium is based on the value of that shipment. The marine coverage should be to the receiving warehouse dock. Once at the warehouse, the commercial property policy is in effect. *Note:* A General Term Bond for Entry of Merchandise should also be taken out covering landed merchandise while it passes through customs and brokers' hands.

What if there is an interruption in your business?

This insurance applies when operations are disturbed or ceased because of an unforeseen or infrequent event, such as fire, flood, tornado, earthquake, and vandalism. This policy covers the loss in profit during the shutdown, continuing fixed costs, incremental costs to replace equipment, overtime, or the cost of having the product produced elsewhere. There may also be coverage for losses arising from a supplier's inability to deliver goods due to an unexpected occurrence.

What does insurance on vehicles involve?

This insurance applies to a company's owned vehicles. The insurance for corporate planes includes normal property damage and liability insurance to insured parties.

How are insurance bonds helpful?

There are several kinds of insurance bonds including comprehensive, miscellaneous, and performance. A comprehensive bond is fidelity coverage for employees due to theft of cash or property. If your company sells to a municipality, it may be required to have miscellaneous bid and performance bonds. The bid bond is usually in place of a certified check which has to accompany government bonds. The performance bond insures against the company's failure to perform under the government contract.

Medical and Catastrophe Coverage

Many employers provide medical and catastrophe insurance for present and retired employees.

What is workmen's compensation?

This policy reimburses the employer for liability arising from occupational health hazards falling under state law. It usually covers the employer's liability for employee lawsuits alleging personal injuries. The premium is based on the total dollar payroll.

Does the state require disability insurance?

Some states require that the employee be covered for accidents and disabilities occurring off the job. The premium is dictated by state law and paid for by the employee. The employer may opt to pay the entire premium as a fringe benefit. If a state does not have a disability law, private insurance may be carried.

How does life insurance work?

The lives of "key" executives may be insured. The insurance may provide cash to buy the deceased's common stock. *Note:* If the company is the beneficiary, the premiums are *not* tax deductible. However, they are expensed for financial reporting purposes. The proceeds received upon death is *not* taxable income.

The cash surrender value of life insurance is the sum payable upon cancellation of the policy by the insured; the insured will of course receive less than the premium paid. Cash surrender value is classified under long-term investments. It applies to ordinary life and limited payment policies. It is *not* typically applicable to term insurance. The insurance premium consists of two elements—expense and cash surrender value.

EXAMPLE 4

A premium of $6,000 is paid that increases the cash surrender value by $2,000. The appropriate entry is:

Life insurance expense	4,000	
Cash surrender value of life insurance	2,000	
Cash		6,000

The gain on a life insurance policy is *not* typically considered an extraordinary item since it is in the ordinary course of business.

Liability Insurance Coverage for CFOs

In today's litigious environment, CFOs need coverage for their activities resulting in losses to investors and creditors. Liability exposure exists for corporate financial problems due to the default of junk bonds, failure of an initial public offering (IPO), governmental action (e.g., SEC), and so on.

BUSINESS LAW

A brief discussion of business law follows. The CFO should consult with legal counsel about all legal issues.

Laws involving the employer-employee relationship include:

• *Federal Insurance Contribution Act (FICA),* commonly referred to as social security, requires a FICA tax to be withheld from the employee's salary with an equal matching by the employer.

• *Fair Labor Standards Act (FLSA)* deals with wages and hours. A minimum wage is specified, and employees must receive equal pay for equal work. Thus, wage discrimination is prohibited due to race, sex, age, etc. Certain employees must receive time and one-half for overtime. An employer cannot hire a child below a certain age, typically 16.

• *Occupational Safety and Health Act (OSHA)* mandates that the employer provide a safe and healthy working environment.

• *Employee Retirement Income Security Act (ERISA)* requires pension plans to be in conformity with specified requirements including vesting, funding, participation, and disclosure.

- *Workmens' Compensation* applies to on the job injuries. The employer pays a specified amount into an insurance fund.

- *Employment Discrimination* prohibits employer discrimination on the basis of sex, national origin, race, color, or religion. Employees between the ages of 40 and 65 may not be discriminated against unless a legitimate reason exists because of the type of position.

Antitrust laws exist regarding restraints of trade and monopoly.

The following agreements are illegal:

- Price-fixing.
- Division of markets.
- Requiring the customer to buy a second product if he or she orders a first one.
- Sale of product to retailer only if the retailer contracts not to resell the product below a certain price.
- Group boycott of a customer.

The CFO who files a registration statement for a public offering of equity and debt securities must have some flexibility with security laws and regulations.

The legal ramifications of a manufacturer's potential liability causes the CFO to assume responsibility for "risk assessment" in contracts. A major consideration is controlling payments and receipts when contracts are canceled and in estimating liquidated or consequential damages for product failure.

Environmental laws must be conformed to otherwise substantial fines may be assessed. Environmental obligations may include clean-up costs, civil and/or criminal litigation over injury and damage claims, constraints on future operations, and uninsurable accidents. Reference should be made to the regulations of the Environmental Protection Agency (EPA) and proper insurance carried. The CFO may have to prepare annual reports under the Superfund Amendments and Reauthorization Act (SARA). The CFO continually must appraise the company's internal procedures to monitor and conform with federal, state, and local dictates. Besides complying with existing regulations why not plan ways to comply with proposed regulations. *Tip:* Undertake an environmental audit to measure the company's environmental performance against internal company policies and procedures and external environmental requirements. Such an audit is also of assistance in valuing a potential targeted company.

33

Basics of Economics

The CFO should have an understanding of economics and its effect on the company. The CFO should know how to read and interpret various economic indices and statistics which are vital to the success of the business in a dynamic, ever changing economic environment. This knowledge will enable better financial and investment decisions.

How can you keep track of the economy with economic and monetary indicators?

To sort out the confusing mix of statistics that flow almost daily from the government and to help you keep track of what is going on in the economy, we examine various economic and monetary indicators.

Economic and monetary indicators reflect where the economy seems to be headed and where it's been. Each month government agencies, including the Federal Reserve Board, and several economic institutions publish various indicators. These may be broken down into six broad categories:

1. Measures of Overall Economic Performance

These measures include gross national and domestic products, industrial production, personal income, housing starts, unemployment rate, and retail sales.

• *Gross National Product (GNP).* GNP measures the value of all goods and services produced in the economy and is the nation's broadest gauge of economic health. GNP is normally stated in annual terms, though data are compiled and released quarterly. GNP is often a measure of the state of the economy. For example, many economists speak of recession when there has been a decline in GNP for two consecutive quarters. *Warning:* Unfortunately, there is no way of measuring whether we are in a recession or prosperity based on the GNP measure. Only after the quarter is over can it be determined if there was growth or decline. In addition, an increasing number of economists believe the GNP criteria for a recession are no longer valid. Experts look upon other measures as recession indicators such as unemployment rate, industrial production, durable orders, corporate profits, retail sales, and housing starts.

The following diagram shows how GNP typically impacts companies, charting a series of events leading from a declining GNP to lower security prices.

GNP down → Corporate profits down →
            Dividends down → Security prices down

• *Gross Domestic Product (GDP).* Unlike GNP, GDP only includes the values of goods and services earned by a nation *within* its boundaries. Thus, it includes only the income derived from factories within the country (and *not* without). For example, when General Motor's British unit repatriates dividends, profits, or interest on loans, the money is counted as part of GNP, whereas British GM profits is not included in GDP. *Note:* As of December 1991, the Department of Commerce began focusing on GDP instead of GNP when reporting the nation's economic condition.

• *Industrial Production.* This index shows changes in the output of U.S. plants, mines, and utilities. Detailed breakdowns of the index provide a reading on how individual industries are faring. The index is issued monthly by the Federal Reserve Board.

• *Personal Income.* This shows the before-tax income received by individuals and unincorporated businesses such as wages and salaries, rents, and interest and dividends, and other payments such as unemployment and Social Security. They represent consumers' spending power. When personal income rises, it usually means that consumers will increase their purchases, which will in turn affect favorably the economic climate. *Note:* Consumer spending makes a major contribution (67%) to the nation's GNP. Personal income data are released monthly by the Commerce Department.

• *Housing Starts.* Housing starts is an important economic indicator that offers an estimate of the number of dwelling units on which construction has begun. The figures are issued monthly by the Bureau of Census. When an economy is going to take a downturn, the housing sector (and companies within it) is the first to decline. This indicates the future strength of the housing sector of the economy. At the same time, it is closely related to interest rates and other basic economic factors.

• *Unemployment Rate.* No one economic indicator is able to point to the direction to which an economy is heading. It is common that many indicators give mixed signals regarding, for example the possibility of a recession. When the various leading indicators are mixed, many economists look to the unemployment rate as being the most important.

• *Retail Sales.* Retail sales is the estimate of total sales at the retail level. It includes everything from groceries to durable goods. It is used as a measure of future economic conditions: A long slowdown in sales could spell cuts in production. Retail sales are a major concern because they represent about half of overall consumer spending. *Note:* Consumer spending accounts for about two-thirds of the nation's GNP. The amount of retail sales depends heavily on consumer confidence. The data are issued monthly by the Commerce Department.

2. Price Indices

Price indices are designed to measure the rate of inflation. Various price indices are used to measure living costs, price level changes, and inflation. They are:

• *Consumer Price Index (CPI).* The Consumer Price Index (CPI) is the most well-known inflation gauge. The CPI measures the cost of buying a fixed bundle of goods (some 400 consumer goods and services), representative of the purchase of the typical working-class urban family. The fixed basket is divided into the following categories: food and beverages, housing, apparel, transportation, medical care, entertainment, and other. Generally referred to as a "cost-of-living index," it is published by the Bureau of Labor Statistics of the U.S. Department of Labor. The CPI is widely used for escalation clauses. The base year for the CPI index was 1982–84 at which time it was assigned 100. The following diagram charts a chain of events leading from lower rates of inflation to increased consumer spending and possibly the up security market.

CPI down → Real personal income up →
Consumer confidence up → Consumer spending
up (Retail sales up + Housing starts up +
Auto sales up) → Security market up.

• *Producer Price Index (PPI).* Like the CPI, the PPI is a measure of the cost of a given basket of goods priced in wholesale markets, including raw materials, semifinished goods, and finished goods at the early stage of the distribution system.

The PPI is published monthly by the Bureau of Labor Statistics of the Department of Commerce. The PPI signals changes in the general price level, or the CPI, some time before they actually materialize. (Since the PPI does not include services, caution should be exercised when the principal cause of inflation is service prices). For this reason, the PPI and especially some of its subindexes, such as the index of sensitive materials, serve as one of the leading indicators that are closely watched by policy makers. It is the one that signals changes in the general price level, or the CPI, some time before they actually materialize.

• *GNP Deflator (Implicit Price Index).* The GNP implicit deflator is the third index of inflation that is used to separate price changes in GNP calculations from real changes in economic activity. The GNP Deflator is a weighted average of the price indexes used to deflate the components of GNP. Thus, it reflects price changes for goods and services bought by consumers, businesses, and governments. The GNP deflator is found by dividing current GNP in a given year by constant (real) GNP. Because it covers a broader group of goods and services, than the CPI and PPI, the GNP Deflator is a very widely used price index that is frequently used to measure inflation. The GNP deflator, unlike the CPI and PPI, is available only quarterly—not monthly. It is published by the U.S. Department of Commerce.

3. Indices of Labor Market Conditions

Indicators covering labor market conditions are unemployment rate, average work week of production workers, applications for unemployment compensation, and hourly wage rates.

4. Money and Credit Market Indicators

Most widely reported in the media are money supply, consumer credit, the Dow Jones Industrial Average (DJIA), and the Treasury bill rate.

5. Index of Leading Indicators

This most widely publicized signal caller is made up of 11 data series. They are money supply, stock prices, vendor performance, average workweek, new orders, contracts, building permits, inventory change, consumer confidence, change in sensitive prices, and change in total liquid assets. They monitor certain business activities that can signal a change in the economy. A more detailed discussion will follow shortly.

6. Measures for Major Product Markets

These measures are designed to be indicators for segments of the economy such as housing, retail sales, steel, and automobile. Examples are 10-day auto sales, advance retail sales, housing starts and construction permits.

Note: Indicators are only signals, telling the CFO something about the economic conditions in the country, a particular area, and industry and, over time, the trends that seem to be shaping up.

INDICES OF LEADING, COINCIDENT, AND LAGGING ECONOMIC INDICATORS _____

The Index of Leading Economic Indicators is the economic series of indicators that tend to predict future changes in economic activity; officially called *Composite Index of 11 Leading Indicators.* This index reveals the direction of the economy in the next six to nine months.

Note: If the index is rising, even only slightly, the economy is chugging along and a setback is unlikely. If the indicator drops for three or more consecutive months, look for an economic slowdown and possibly a recession in the next year or so.

This series is the government's main barometer for forecasting business trends. Each of the series has shown a tendency to change before the economy makes a major turn—hence, the term "leading indicators." The index is designed to forecast economic activity six to nine months ahead (1982 = 100). The series is published monthly by the U.S. Department of Commerce, consisting of:

• *Average work week of production workers in manufacturing.* Employers find it a lot easier to increase the number of hours worked in a week than to hire more employees.

• *Initial claims for unemployment insurance.* The number of people who sign up for unemployment benefits signals changes in present and future economic activity.

• *Change in consumer confidence.* It is based on the University of Michigan's survey of consumer expectations. The index measures consumers' optimism regarding the present and future state of the economy and is based on an index of 100 in 1966. *Note:* Consumer spending buys two-thirds of GNP (all goods and services produced in the economy), so any sharp change could be an important factor in an overall turnaround.

• *Percent change in prices of sensitive crude materials.* Rises in prices of such critical materials as steel usually mean factory demands are going up, which means factories plan to step up production.

• *Contracts and orders for plant and equipment.* Heavier contracting and ordering usually lead economic upswings.

• *Vendor performance.* Vendor performance represents the percentage of companies reporting slower deliveries. As the economy grows, firms have more trouble filling orders.

• *Stock index prices.* A rise in the common stock indicates expected profits and lower interest rates. Stock market advances usually precede business upturns by three to eight months.

• *Money supply.* A rising money supply means easy money that sparks brisk economic activity. This usually leads recoveries by as much as fourteen months.

• *New orders for manufacturers of consumer goods and materials.* New orders mean more workers hired, more materials and supplies purchased and increased output. Gains in this series usually lead recoveries by as much as four months.

• *Residential building permits for private housing.* Gains in building permits signal business upturns.

• *Factory backlogs of unfilled durable goods orders.* Backlogs signify business upswings.

Note: These 11 components of the index are adjusted for inflation. Rarely do these components of the index all go in the same direction at once. Each factor is weighted. The composite figure is designed to tell only in which direction business will go. It is not intended to forecast the magnitude of future ups and downs.

What are coincident indicators?

Coincident indicators are the types of economic indicator series that tend to move up and down in line with the aggregate economy and therefore are measures of current economic activity. They are intended to gauge current economic conditions. Examples are Gross National Product (GNP), employment, retail sales, and industrial production.

What are lagging indicators?

Lagging indicators are the ones that follow or trail behind aggregate economic activity. There are currently six lagging indicators published by the government, including unemployment rate, labor cost per unit, loans outstanding, average prime rate charged by banks, ratio of consumer installment credit outstanding to personal income, and ratio of manufacturing and trade inventories to sales.

OTHER IMPORTANT ECONOMIC INDICES

There are other important indices with which the CFO should be familiar. Some widely watched indices are given below.

What is the Forbes Index?

Forbes publishes *The Forbes Index.* This index (1976 = 100) is a measure of U.S. economic activity composed of 8 equally weighted elements: total industrial production, new claims for unemployment, cost of services relative to all consumer prices, housing starts, retail sales, the level of new orders for durable goods compared with manufactures' inventories, personal income, and total consumer installment credit.

What is the Purchasing Index?

The *National Association of Purchasing Management* releases its monthly *Purchasing Index* which tells about buying intentions of corporate purchasing agents.

What is the Dodge Index?

The *Dodge Index* prepared by the F.W. Dodge Division of McGraw-Hill is a monthly market index that assesses the building industry in terms of the value of new construction projects.

What is the Help-Wanted Index?

The Conference Board of New York, an industry-sponsored, non-profit economic research institute, publishes two indices: The Help-Wanted Advertising Index and Consumer Confidence Index (to be discussed later). The *Help-Wanted Index* measures the amount of help-wanted advertising in 51 newspapers and tells about the change in labor market conditions.

What are two major consumer confidence indices?

The *Consumer Confidence Index* measures consumer optimism and pessimism about general business conditions, jobs, and total family income.

The University of Michigan Survey Research Center is another research organization that compiles its own index called the *Index of Consumer Sentiment.* It measures consumers' personal financial circumstances and their outlook for the future. The survey is compiled through a telephone survey of 500 households. The index is used by the Commerce Department in its monthly *Index of Leading Economic Indicators* and regularly charted in the Department's *Business Conditions Digest.*

What is the Optimism Index?

The National Federation of Independent Business, a Washington-based advocacy group, publishes the *Optimism Index* which is based on small-business owners' expectations for the economy. The benchmark year is 1978.

MONETARY INDICATORS AND HOW THEY IMPACT THE ECONOMY

What are monetary indices?

Monetary indicators apply to Federal Reserve actions and the demand for credit. These are of particular importance to CFOs because they greatly impact the firms in terms of the costs of debt and equity financing and security prices. They involve consideration of long-term interest rates, which are important since bond yields compete with stock yields. Monetary and credit indicators are often the first signs of market direction. If monetary indicators move favorable, this is an indication that a decline in stock prices may be over. A stock market top may be ready for a contraction if the Federal Reserve tightens credit, making consumer buying and corporate expansion more costly and difficult.

Monetary indicators that are regularly watched are:

- Dow Jones twenty-bond index.
- Dow Jones utility average.
- NYSE utility average.
- T-Bill yield.
- 30-year T-Bond yield.

Bonds and utilities are yield instruments and therefore money-sensitive. They are impacted by changing interest rates. If the above monetary indicators are active and pointing higher, it is a sign the stock market will start to take off. In other words, an upward movement in these indicators take place in advance of a stock market increase.

A brief description of monetary and economic variables that should be carefully watched by CFOs follows.

What is the money supply?

This is the level of funds available at a given time for conducting transactions in an economy, as reported by the Federal Reserve Board. The Federal Reserve System can influence money supply through its monetary policy measures. There are several definitions of the money supply: M1 (which is currency in circulation, demand deposits, traveler's checks, and those in interest-bearing NOW accounts), M2 (the most widely followed measure, it equals M1 plus savings deposits, money market deposit accounts, and money market funds), and M3 (which is M2 plus large CDs). Moderate growth is thought to have a positive impact on the economy. A rapid growth is viewed as inflationary; in contrast, a sharp drop in the money supply is considered recessionary.

What are interest rates?

Interest rates represent the costs to borrow money and come in many forms. There are long-term and short-term interest rates, depending on the length of the loan; there are interest rates on super-safe securities (such as U.S. T-bills) and there are interest rates on "junk bonds" of financially troubled companies; there are nominal (coupon) interest rates, real (inflation-adjusted) or risk adjusted interest rates, and effective interest rates (or yields). Interest rates depend upon the maturity of the security. The longer the period, the higher will be the interest rate because of the greater uncertainty.

Some of the more important interest rates are briefly explained below.

• *Prime rate.* The rate banks charge their best customers for short-term loans. This is a bellwether rate in that it is construed as a sign of rising or falling loan demand and economic activity. When the prime rate is climbing, it means companies are borrowing heavily and the economy is still on an upward swing.

• *Federal funds rate.* The rate on short-term loans among commercial banks for overnight use. The Fed influences this rate by open market operations and by changing the bank's required reserve.

• *Discount rate.* The charge on loans to depository institutions by the Federal Reserve Board. A change in the discount rate is considered a major economic event and is expected to have an impact on security prices, especially bonds. A change in the prime rate usually follows the change in the discount rate.

• *90-Day Treasury bills.* This yield represents the direction of short-term rates, a closely watched indicator. When yields on 90-day bills rise sharply, this may signal a resurgence of inflation. Subsequently, the economy could slow down.

• *5-Year and 10-year Treasury notes.* The yields on these notes give an idea of the prevailing interest rates for intermediate-term fixed-income securities.

• *30-Year Treasury bonds.* This yield, also called the long bond yield, is a closely watched bellwether indicator of long-term interest rates since the entire bond market (and sometimes the stock market as well) often moves in line with this rate.

Interest rates are controlled by the Fed's monetary policy. The Fed's monetary policy tools involve: (1) changes in the required reserve ratio; (2) changes in the discount rate; and (3) open market operations—that is, purchase and sale of government securities. Cuts in the discount rate are aimed at stimulating the economy—a positive development for stocks. A summary of the effect of cutting the discount rate on the economy follows.

The Effects of Lowering the Discount Rate

• *The players:* The Federal Reserve Board is the nation's central bank. It regulates the flow of money through the economy.

• *The action:* Discount rate is what the Federal Reserve charges on short-term loans to member banks. When the Fed cuts the discount rate, it means banks can get cash cheaper and thus charge less on loans.

• *The first effect:* Within a few days, banks are likely to start passing on the discounts by cutting their prime rate, which is what banks charge on loans to their best corporate customers.

• *Impact:* Businesses are more likely to borrow. Second, adjustable consumer loans are tied to the prime, such as credit card rates. These become cheaper, stimulating spending.

• *The second effect:* Within a few weeks, rates on mortgage, auto and construction loans drop.

• *The third effect:* The lower rates go, the more investors move their cash to stocks, creating new wealth.

• *The goal:* To kick start the economy. If lower interest rates cause businesses to start growing again, laid-off workers get jobs, retailers start selling, and the economy starts to roll again.

The following diagram summarizes the impact of open market operations on the money supply, level of interest rates, and loan demand.

Easy Money Policy:
> Fed buys securities → Bank reserve up →
> Bank lending up → Money supply up →
> Interest rates down → Loan demand up

Tight Money Policy:
> Fed sells securities → Bank reserve down →
> Bank lending down → Money supply down →
> Interest rates up → Loan demand down

What is inflation?

Inflation is the general rise in prices of consumer goods and services. The federal government measures inflation by comparing prices today—measured in terms of the CPI, PPI, and/or GNP Deflator—to a two-year period, 1982–84. As prices increase, lenders and investors will demand greater returns to compensate for the decline in purchasing power. Companies may reduce borrowing because of higher interest rates. This leads to less capital expenditures for property, plant and equipment. As a result, output may decrease resulting in employee layoffs. During inflation, selling prices may increase to keep pace with rising price levels but the company's sales in real dollars remain the same. You still lose out since your company's tax liability will increase.

Most likely, the Federal Reserve will tighten the money supply and raise interest rates (such as discount rate or federal fund rate). It would be too expensive to borrow money. Therefore, there is less demand for products, which in turn pushes

prices down. The following diagram shows how
inflation affects the prices of products:

Inflation → Fed raises discount rate →
Interest rates up → Demand for money down →
Demand for products down → Prices down

Interest rates are no more than a reflection of
what expectations are for inflation. Inflation
therefore means higher interest rates and thus
higher borrowing cost to the company.

Productivity and Unit Labor Costs

The data on productivity and unit labor costs is
released by the Labor Department. Increased
productivity, or getting more worker output per
hour on the job, is considered vital to increasing
the nation's standard of living without **inflation**.
Meanwhile, unit labor costs is a key gauge of
future price inflation along with the CPI, PPI,
and GNP Deflator.

What is recession?

Recession means a sinking economy. Unfortunately, there is no consensus definition and
measure of recession. Three or more straight
monthly drops of the Index of Leading Economic
Indicators are generally considered a sign of recession. Or, two consecutive quarterly drops of
GNP signals recession. Or, consecutive monthly
drops of durable goods orders which most likely
results in less production and increasing layoffs
in the factory sector. Recession tends to dampen
the spirits of consumers and thus depress prices
of products and services.

To kick start the economy the Fed will loosen
the money supply and lower interest rates such as
the discount rate. When the Fed cuts the discount rate, it means banks can get cash cheaper
and thus charge less on loans.

Note that the size of the cut is a critical consideration. For example, a half-point discount rate
cut itself is not strong enough to get the economy
moving fast. External political conditions (such

as a crisis in the Middle East), the federal deficit and problems in the bank and S&L industry would make companies hesitant to start expanding again and also make consumers nervous for a longer time that the Fed would anticipate.

What is the federal deficit?

The national debt is the sum of all money the government has borrowed to finance budget deficits. The only way for a government to reduce its debt is to run a budget surplus, to obtain more money than it spends. The surplus must then be used to pay off maturing debt (bonds, notes, etc.) rather than replacing them (rolling them over) with more debt. This federal deficit affects the economy as a whole.

Economists generally believe that larger federal deficits result in higher interest rates for two reasons. First, increased budget deficits raise the demand for the loanable funds resulting in higher interest rates. Second, larger deficits are apt to lead to higher inflation. This may be true either because the sources of the increased deficits—larger government spending and/or lower taxes—result in greater pressure for loan demand and hence inflation, or because the deficit will induce the Fed to expand the money supply to help finance the deficit, thus causing inflation. In any case, if the increased deficit elevate the public's expectation of inflation, it will tend to raise the level of interest rates. Furthermore, the financing of the deficit by issuance of government debt securities will compete for funds to be raised by companies and will deter economic expansion. It also forces companies to borrow at higher interest rates. This is called the "crowding-out effect."

What is the balance of payments?

A balance of payments is a systematic record of a country's receipts from, or payments to, other countries. The "balance of trade" usually refers to goods within the goods and services category. It is also known as merchandise or "visible" trade because it consists of tangibles like foodstuffs, manufactured goods, and raw materials. "Services," the other part of the category, is known as "invisible" trade and consists of intangibles such as interest or dividends, technology transfers, services (like insurance, transportation, financial), and so forth.

When the net result of both the current account and the capital account yields more credits than debits, the country is said to have a surplus in its balance of payments. When there are more debits than credits, the country has a deficit in the balance of payments. *Note:* When deficits persist, this generally depresses the value of the dollar and can boost inflation. The reason is a weak dollar makes foreign goods relatively expensive, often allowing U.S. makers of similar products to raise prices as well. It is necessary for a CFO to know the condition of a country's balance of payments, since its resulting inflation and value of the dollar will affect the company's product demand.

What is better, a strong dollar (appreciation in foreign exchange rate) or a weak dollar (depreciation in foreign exchange rate)?

The answer is, unfortunately, it depends. *Note:* This is a matter of concern particularly to the CFOs of multinational corporations. A strong dollar makes Americans' cash go further overseas and reduces import prices—generally good for U.S. consumers and for foreign manufacturers. If the dollar is overvalued, U.S. products are harder to sell abroad and at home, where they compete with low-cost imports.

A weak dollar can restore competitiveness to American products by making foreign goods comparatively more expensive. But too weak a dollar can spawn inflation, first through higher import prices and then through spiraling prices for all goods. Even worse, a falling dollar can drive foreign investors away from U.S. securities, which lose value along with the dollar. A strong dollar can be induced by interest rates. Relatively higher domestic interest rates than abroad will attract money dollar-denominated

FIGURE 33-1   THE IMPACTS OF CHANGES IN
FOREIGN EXCHANGE RATES

	Strong Dollar (Appreciation)	Weak Dollar (Depreciation)
Imports	Cheaper	More expensive
Exports	More expensive	Cheaper
Payables	Cheaper	More expensive
Receivables	More expensive	Cheaper

investments which will raise the value of the
dollar. Figure 33–1 summarizes the impacts of
changes in foreign exchange rates on the company's products and services.

PART VII

INVESTMENTS

34

Corporate Investments in Securities

This chapter covers how to manage a company's surplus liquidity funds. A firm's surplus funds or idle cash are usually considered only of a temporary nature. The funds should be made available to cover a shortfall in cash flow or working capital or to serve as a reservoir for capital spending and acquisition. Most CFOs are conservative (not speculative) when considering investing idle cash in financial securities since the money should be on hand without loss in value of the funds when needed.

How is this surplus cash used?

Generally, there are three choices:

1. Investing in marketable securities
2. Reducing outstanding debt
3. Increasing compensating balances at banks.

According to a survey, only 14 out of 61 firms responded that they normally apply surplus funds toward paying off debt or building up compensating balances at their banks; the majority (47) prefer to invest excess funds in securities.

What are the investment practices?

Here are some new insights on the investment tendencies of corporate investment officers, based on the Fortune 1000 list of large industrial firms. Respondents were asked to describe their own approach to cash management—aggressive, moderate, and passive. We focus on two types—aggressive and moderate. They were asked to identify the percentage of their short-term portfolios invested in the typical marketable securities. The five most popular vehicles and the respective percentages are presented on the next page.

Type of Security	Aggressive Manager	Moderate Manager
Treasury securities	5.55%	8.82%
Commercial paper	18.16	17.53
Domestic certificates of deposits (CDs)	11.45	6.87
Eurodollar CDs	36.77	24.28
Repurchase agreements (Repos)	11.27	18.99

Source: Frankle, A. W., and J. M. Collins, "Investment Practices of the Domestic Cash Managers," Journal of Cash Management, (May/June 1987), pp. 50–53.

The survey indicates that Eurodollar CDs are preferred by aggressive cash managers with commercial paper being ranked second and domestic CDs ranked third. The moderate cash managers also preferred Eurodollar CDs, with repos ranked second and commercial paper ranked third.

As for the question on which investment attributes shaped their ultimate investment decisions, the aggressive cash managers ranked *yield* first, *risk of default* second, and *maturity* third, while the moderate managers ranked *risk of default* first, *yield* second, and *maturity* third.

What are the types of securities?

Securities cover a broad range of investment instruments, including common stocks, preferred stocks, bonds, and options. There are two broad categories of securities available to corporate investors: equity securities, which represent ownership of a company, and debt (or fixed income) securities, which represent a loan from the investor to a company or government. Fixed income securities generally stress current fixed income and offer little or no opportunity for appreciation in value. They are usually liquid and bear less market risk than other types of investments. This type of investment performs well during stable economic conditions and lower inflation. Examples of fixed income securities include: corporate bonds, government securities, mortgage-backed securities, preferred stocks, and short-term debt securities.

Each type of security has not only distinct characteristics, but also advantages and disadvantages which vary by a corporate investor. This chapter focuses on investing in fixed income (debt) securities—with especially short- and intermediate-term maturity—normally utilized by corporate investors.

What are the factors to be considered in investment decisions?

Consideration should be given to safety of principal, yield and risk, stability of income, and marketability and liquidity.

• *Security of principal.* It is the degree of risk involved in a particular investment. The company will not want to lose part or all of the initial investment.

• *Yield and risk.* The primary purpose of investing is to earn a return on invested money in the form of: interest, dividends, rental income, and capital appreciation. However, increasing total returns would entail greater investment risks. Thus, yield and degree of risk are directly related. Greater risk also means sacrificing security of principal. A CFO has to choose the priority that fits the corporation's financial circumstances and objectives.

• *Stability of income.* When steady income is the most important consideration, bond interest or preferred stock dividends should be emphasized. This might be the situation if the company needs to supplement its earned income on a regular basis with income from its outside investment.

• *Marketability and liquidity.* It is the ability to find a ready market to dispose of the investment at the right price.

• *Tax Factors.* Corporate investors in high tax brackets will have different investment objectives than those in lower brackets. If the company is in a high tax bracket, it may prefer municipal bonds (interest is not taxable) or investments that provide tax credits or tax shelters, such as those in oil and gas.

In addition, there are many other factors to be considered, including:

- Current and future income needs.
- Hedging against inflation.
- Ability to withstand financial losses.
- Ease of management.
- Amount of investment.
- Diversification.
- Long-term versus short-term potential.

What are the questions to be asked?

In developing the corporation's investment strategy, it will be advisable to ask the following questions:

- What proportions of funds does the company want safe and liquid?
- Is the company willing to invest for higher return but greater risk?
- How long of a maturity period is the company willing to take on its investment?
- What should be the mix of its investments for diversification?
- Does the company need to invest in tax-free securities?

What are the types of fixed income investment instruments?

There are many fixed income securities a CFO can choose from. They can be categorized into short-term and long-term investments, as follows:

Short-Term Vehicles
   U.S. Treasury bills
   Certificates of deposit (CDs)
   Banker's acceptances (BAs)
   Commercial paper
   Repurchase agreements (Repos)
   Money market funds
   Eurodollar time deposits

Long-Term Vehicles
    U.S. Treasury notes and bonds
    Corporate bonds
    Mortgage-backed securities
    Municipal bonds
    Preferred stock, fixed or adjustable
    Bond funds
    Unit investment trusts

What are the advantages and disadvantages of owning bonds?

A bond is a certificate or security showing the corporate investor loaned funds to an issuing company or to a government in return for fixed future interest and repayment of principal. Bonds have the following advantages:

- There is fixed interest income each year.
- Bonds are safer than equity securities such as common stock. This is because bondholders come before common stockholders in the event of corporate bankruptcy.

Bonds suffer from the following disadvantages:

- They do not participate in incremental profitability.
- There are no voting rights.

TERMS AND FEATURES OF BONDS _____

There are certain terms and features of bonds a corporate investment officer should be familiar with, including:

- *Par value.* The par value of a bond is the face value, usually $1,000.
- *Coupon rate.* The coupon rate is the nominal interest rate that determines the actual interest to be received on a bond. It is an annual interest per par value. For example, if a corporate investor owns a $1,000,000 bond having a coupon rate of 10%, the annual interest to be received will be $100,000.

• *Maturity date.* It is the final date on which repayment of the bond principal is due.

• *Indenture.* The bond indenture is the lengthy, legal agreement detailing the issuer's obligations pertaining to a bond issue. It contains the terms and conditions of the bond issue as well as any restrictive provisions placed on the firm, known as restrictive covenants. The indenture is administered by an independent trustee. A restrictive covenant includes maintenance of (a) required levels of working capital, (b) a particular current ratio, and (c) a specified debt ratio.

• *Trustee.* The trustee is the third party with whom the indenture is made. The trustee's job is to see that the terms of the indenture are actually carried out.

• *Yield.* The yield is different than the coupon interest rate. It is the effective interest rate the corporate investor earns on the bond investment. If a bond is bought below its face value (i.e., purchased at a discount), the yield is higher than the coupon rate. If a bond is acquired above its face value (i.e., bought at a premium), the yield is below the coupon rate.

• *Call provision.* A call provision entitles the issuing corporation to repurchase, or "call" the bond from their holders at stated prices over specified periods.

• *Sinking fund.* In a sinking fund bond, money is put aside by the issuing company periodically for the repayment of debt, thus reducing the total amount of debt outstanding. This particular provision may be included in the bond indenture to protect investors.

What are the types of bonds?

There are many types of bonds according to different criteria including:

• *Mortgage bonds.* Mortgage bonds are secured by physical property. In case of default, the bondholders may foreclose on the secured property and sell it to satisfy their claims.

• *Debentures.* Debentures are unsecured bonds. They are protected by the general credit of the issuing corporation. Credit ratings are very important for this type of bond. Federal, state, and municipal government issues are debentures. Subordinated debentures are junior issues ranking after other unsecured debt as a result of explicit provisions in the indenture. Finance companies have made extensive use of these types of bonds.

• *Convertible bonds.* These bonds are subordinated debentures which may be converted, at the investor's option, into a specified amount of other securities (usually common stock) at a fixed price. They are hybrid securities having characteristics of both bonds and common stock in that they provide fixed interest income and potential appreciation through participation in future price increases of the underlying common stock.

• *Income bonds.* In income bonds, interest is paid only if earned. They are often called reorganization bonds.

• *Tax-exempt bonds.* Tax-exempt bonds are usually municipal bonds where interest income is not subject to federal tax, although the Tax Reform Act (TRA) of 1986 imposed restrictions on the issuance of tax-exempt municipal bonds. Municipal bonds may carry a lower interest rate than taxable bonds of similar quality and safety. However, after-tax yield from these bonds are usually more than a bond with a higher rate of taxable interest. Note that municipal bonds are subject to two principal risks—interest rate and default.

• *U.S. government and agency securities.* They include Treasury bills, notes, bonds, and mortgage-backed securities such as "Ginnie Maes." Treasury bills represent short-term government financing and mature in twelve months or less. U.S. Treasury notes have a maturity of one to ten years whereas U.S. Treasury bonds have a maturity of ten to twenty five years and can be purchased in denominations as low as $1,000. All these types of U.S. government securities are subject to federal income taxes, but not subject to state and local income taxes. "Ginnie Maes" represent pools of 25- to 30-year Federal Housing

Administration (FHA) or Veterans Administration (VA) mortgages guaranteed by the Government National Mortgage Association.

• *Zero coupon bonds.* With zero coupon bonds, the interest instead of being paid out directly is added to the principal semiannually and both the principal and accumulated interest are paid at maturity. *Tip:* This compounding factor results in the investor receiving higher returns on the original investment at maturity. Zero coupon bonds are not fixed income securities in the historical sense, because they provide no periodic income. The interest on the bond is paid at maturity. However, accrued interest, though not received, is taxable yearly as ordinary income. Zero coupon bonds have two basic advantages over regular coupon-bearing bonds: (1) A relatively small investment is required to buy these bonds; and (2) The investor is assured of a specific yield throughout the term of the investment.

• *Junk bonds.* Junk bonds, or high-yield bonds, are bonds with a speculative credit rating of Baa or lower by *Moody's* and BBB or lower by *Standard & Poor's* rating systems. Coupon rates on junk bonds are considerably higher than those of better quality issues. Note that junk bonds are issued by companies without track records of sales and earnings and therefore are subject to high default risk. Today, many non-mortgage-backed bonds issued by corporations are junk. Very recently, a large number of junk bonds have been issued as part of corporate mergers or takeovers. Junk bonds are known for their high yields and high risk. Many risk-oriented corporate investors including banks specialize in trading them. However, the bonds may be defaulted on. During the periods of recession and high interest rates where servicing debts is very difficult, junk bonds can pose a *serious default risk* to corporate investors.

How do you select a bond?

When selecting a bond, corporate investors should take into consideration basically four factors:

1. Investment quality— Rating of bonds
2. Length of maturity—Short-term
$\qquad$ (0–5 years)
$\qquad$ Medium
$\qquad$ (6–15 years)
$\qquad$ Long-term
$\qquad$ (over 15 years)
3. Features of bonds—call or conversion features
4. Tax status
5. Yield to maturity

• *Bond ratings.* The investment quality of a bond is measured by its bond rating which reflects the probability that a bond issue will go into default. The rating should influence the investor's perception of risk and therefore have an impact on the interest rate the investor is willing to accept, the price the investor is willing to pay, and the maturity period of the bond the investor is willing to accept.

Bond investors tend to place more emphasis on independent analysis of quality than do common stock investors. Bond analysis and ratings are done, among others, by Standard & Poor's and Moody's. Table 34–1 is an actual listing of the designations used by these well-known independent agencies. Descriptions on ratings are summarized. For original versions of descriptions, see Moody's *Bond Record* and Standard & Poor's *Bond Guide.*

Corporate investors should pay careful attention to ratings since they can affect not only potential market behavior but relative yields as well. Specifically, the higher the rating, the lower the yield of a bond, other things being equal. It should be noted that the ratings do change over time and the rating agencies have "credit watch lists" of various types. Corporate investment policy should specify this point: for example, the company is allowed to invest in only those bonds rated Baa or above by Moody's or BBB or above by Standard & Poor's, even though doing so means giving up about $3/4$ of a percentage point in yield.

TABLE 34-1   DESCRIPTION OF BOND RATINGS

Moody's	Standard & Poor's	Quality Indication
Aaa	AAA	Highest quality
Aa	AA	High quality
A	A	Upper medium grade
Baa	BBB	Medium grade
Ba	BB	Contains speculative elements
B	B	Outright speculative
Caa	CCC & CC	Default definitely possible
Ca	C	Default, only partial recovery likely
C	D	Default, little recovery likely

Ratings may also have + or − signs to show relative standings in each class.

• *Maturity.* In addition to the ratings, an investment officer can control the risk element through maturities. The maturity indicates how much the company stands to lose if interest rates rise. The longer a bond's maturity, the more volatile its price. There is a trade-off: Shorter maturities usually mean lower yields. A conservative corporate investor, which is typical, may select bonds with shorter maturities.

• *Features.* Check to see whether a bond has a call provision, which allows the issuing company to redeem its bonds after a certain date if it chooses to, rather than at maturity. The investor is generally paid a small premium over par if an issue is called but not as much as the investor would have received if the bond was held until maturity. That is because bonds are usually called only if their interest rates are higher than the going market rate. Try to avoid bonds of companies that have a call provision and may be involved in "event risk" (mergers and acquisitions, leveraged buyouts, etc.).

Also check to see if a bond has a convertible feature. Convertible bonds can be converted into common stock at a later date. They provide fixed income in the form of interest. The corporate investor also can benefit from the appreciation value of common stock.

• *Tax status.* If the investing company is in a high tax bracket, it may want to consider tax-exempt bonds. Most municipal bonds are rated A or above, making them a good grade risk. They can also be bought in mutual funds.

• *Yield to maturity.* Yield has a lot to do with the rating of a bond. How to calculate various yield measures is taken up later.

How do you calculate yield (effective rate of return) on a bond?

Bonds are evaluated on many different types of returns including current yield, yield to maturity, yield to call, and realized yield.

• *Current yield.* The current yield is the annual interest payment divided by the current price of the bond. This is reported in *The Wall Street Journal,* among others.

The current yield is:

$$\frac{\text{Annual interest payment}}{\text{Current price}}$$

EXAMPLE 1

Assume a 12% coupon rate $1,000 par value bond selling for $960. The current yield = $120/$960 = 12.5%

The problem with this measure of return is that it does not take into account the maturity date of the bond. A bond with 1 year to run and another with 15 years to run would have the same current yield quote if interest payments were $120 and the price were $960. Clearly, the one year bond would be preferable under this circumstance because you would not only get $120 in interest, but also a gain of $40 ($1000 − $960) with a one-year time period, and this amount could be reinvested.

• *Yield to maturity (YTM).* The yield to maturity takes into account the maturity date of the bond. It is the real return the investor would receive from interest income plus capital gain assuming the bond is held to maturity. The exact way of calculating this measure is a little complicated and not presented here. But the approximate method is:

$$\text{Yield} = \frac{I + (\$1,000 - V)/n}{(\$1,000 + V)/2}$$

where V = the market value of the bond, I = dollars of interest paid per year, and n = number of years to maturity.

EXAMPLE 2

An investor bought a 10-year, 8% coupon, $1,000 par value bond at a price of $877.60. The rate of return (yield) on the bond if held to maturity is:

$$\text{Yield} = \frac{\$80 + (\$1,000 - \$877.60)/10}{(\$1,000 + \$877.60)/2} = \frac{\$80 + \$12.24}{\$938.80}$$

$$= \frac{\$92.24}{\$938.80} = 9.8\%$$

As can be seen, since the bond was bought at a discount, the yield (9.8%) came out greater than the coupon rate of 8%.

• *Yield to call.* Not all bonds are held to maturity. If the bond may be called prior to maturity, the yield to maturity formula will have the call price in place of the par value of $1,000.

EXAMPLE 3

Assume a 20-year bond was initially bought at a 13.5% coupon rate, and after two years, rates have dropped. Assume further that the bond is currently selling for $1,180, the yield to maturity on the bond is 11.15%, and the bond can be called in five years after issue at $1,090. Thus if the investor buys the bond two years after issue, the bond may be called back after three more years at $1,090. The yield to call can be calculated as follows:

$$\frac{\$135 + (\$1,090 - \$1,180)/3}{(\$1,090 + \$1,180)/2} = \frac{\$135 + (-\$90/3)}{\$1,135}$$

$$= \frac{\$105}{\$1,135} = 9.25\%$$

Note: The yield to call figure of 9.25% is 190 basis points less than the yield to maturity of 11.15%. Clearly, you need to be aware of the differential because a lower return is earned.

• *Realized yield.* The investor may trade in and out of a bond long before it matures. The investor obviously needs a measure of return to evaluate the investment appeal of any bonds that are intended to be bought and quickly sold. Realized yield is used for this purpose. This measure is simply a variation of yield to maturity, as only two variables are changed in the yield to maturity formula. Future price is used in place of par value ($1,000), and the length of the holding period is substituted for the number of years to maturity.

EXAMPLE 4

In Example 2, assume that the investor anticipates holding the bond only three years and that the investor has estimated interest rates will change in the future so that the price of the bond will move to about $925 from its present level of $877.70. Thus, the investor will buy the bond today at a market price of $877.70 and sell the issue three years later at a price of $925. Given these assumptions, the realized yield of this bond would be:

$$\frac{\text{Realized}}{\text{yield}} = \frac{\$80 + (\$925 - \$877.70)/3}{(\$925 + \$877.70)/2} = \frac{\$80 + \$15.77}{\$901.35}$$

$$= \frac{\$95.77}{\$901.35} = 10.63\%$$

Note: Use a bond table to find the value for various yield measures. A source is *Thorndike Encyclopedia of Banking and Financial Tables* by Warren, Gorham & Lamont (Boston).

• *Equivalent before-tax yield.* Yield on a municipal bond needs to be looked at on an equivalent before-tax yield basis, because the interest received is not subject to federal income taxes. The formula used to equate interest on municipals to other investments is:

Tax equivalent yield = Tax-exempt yield/(1 − tax rate)

EXAMPLE 5

If a company has a marginal tax rate of 34% and is evaluating a municipal bond paying 10% interest, the equivalent before-tax yield on a taxable investment would be:

$$10\%/(1 - .34) = 15.15\%$$

Thus, the company could choose between a taxable investment paying 15.15% and a tax-exempt bond paying 10% and be indifferent between the two.

How is interest-rate risk determined?

Interest-rate risk can be determined in two ways. One way is to look at the term structure of a debt security by measuring its average term to maturity—a duration. The other way is to measure the sensitivity of changes in a debt security's price associated with changes in its yield to maturity. We will discuss two measurement approaches: Macaulay's duration coefficient and the interest rate elasticity.

• *Macaulay's duration coefficient.* Macaulay's duration (D) is an attempt to measure risk in a bond. It is defined as the weighted average number of years required to recover principal and all interest payments. A simple example below illustrates the duration calculations.

EXAMPLE 6

A bond pays a 7% coupon rate annually on its $1,000 face value that has 3 years until its maturity and has a YTM of 6%. The computation of Macaulay's duration coefficient involves the following three steps:

Step 1. Calculate the present value of the bond for each year.

Step 2. Express present values as proportions of the price of the bond.

Step 3. Multiply proportions by years' digits to obtain the weighted average time.

(1)	(2)	(3)	(Step 1) (4)	(Step 2) (5)	(Step 3) (6)
Year	Cash Flow	PV Factor @ 6%	PV of Cash Flow	PV as Proportion of Price of Bond	Column (1) × Column (5)
1	$ 70	.9434	$ 66.04	.0643	.0643
2	70	.8900	62.30	.0607	.1214
3	1,070	.8369	898.39	.8750	2.6250
			$1,026.73	1.0000	2.8107

This 3-year bond's duration is a little over 2.8 years. In all cases, a bond's duration is less than or equal to its term to maturity. Only a pure discount bond—that is, one with no coupon or sinking-fund payments—has duration equal to the maturity.

The higher the D value, the greater the interest rate risk, since it implies a longer recovery period.

• *Interest rate elasticity.* A bond's interest rate elasticity (E) is defined as

$$E = \frac{\text{Percentage change in bond price}}{\text{Percentage change in YTM}}$$

Since bond prices and YTMs always move inversely, the elasticity will always be a negative number. Any bond's elasticity can be determined directly with the above formula. Knowing the duration coefficient (D), we can calculate the E using the following simple formula:

$$(-1)\, E = D \frac{\text{YTM}}{(1 + \text{YTM})}$$

EXAMPLE 7

Using the same data in Example 6, the elasticity is calculated as follows:

$$(-1)\, E = 2.8107\ [0.6/(1.06)] = .1586$$

How do you invest in a bond fund?

It is possible that a corporate investor may decide to invest in a bond fund. There are the following three key facts about the bonds in any portfolio.

• *Quality.* Check the credit rating of the typical bond in the fund. Ratings by Standard & Poor's and Moody's show the relative danger that an issuer will default on interest or principal payments. AAA is the best grade. A rating of BB or lower signifies a junk bond.

• *Maturity.* The average maturity of your fund's bonds indicates how much a corporate investor stands to lose if interest rates rise. The longer the term of the bonds, the more volatile is the price. For example, a 20-year bond may fluctuate in price four times as much as a four-year issue.

• *Premium or discount.* Some funds with high current yields hold bonds that trade for more than their face value, or at a premium. Such funds are less vulnerable to losses if rates go up. Funds that hold bonds trading at a discount to face value can lose most.

Corporate investors must keep in mind the following guidelines:

• Rising interest rates drive down the value of all bond funds. For this reason, rather than focusing only on current yield, the investor should look primarily at total return (yield plus capital gains from falling interest rates or minus capital losses if rates climb).

• All bond funds do not benefit equally from tumbling interest rates. If a corporate investment officer thinks interest rates will decline and he/she wants to increase total return, he/she should buy funds that invest in U.S. Treasuries or top-rated corporate bonds. The investment officer should consider high-yield corporate bonds (junk bonds) if he/she believes interest rates are stabilizing and is willing to take risk.

• Unlike bonds, bond funds do not allow the corporate investor to lock in a yield. A mutual fund with a constantly changing portfolio is not like an individual bond, which can be kept to maturity. If the investor wants steady, secure income over several years or more, he/she should consider, as alternatives to funds, buying individual top-quality bonds or investing in a municipal bond *unit trust,* which maintains a fixed portfolio.

Should you consider unit investment trusts?

Like a mutual fund, a unit investment trust offers to investors the advantages of a large, professionally selected and diversified portfolio. Unlike a mutual fund, however, its portfolio is fixed; once structured, it is not actively managed. Unit investment trusts are available of tax-exempt bonds, money market securities, corporate bonds of different grades; mortgage-backed securities; preferred stocks; utility common stocks; and other investments. Unit trusts are most suitable for corporate investors who need a fixed income and a guaranteed return of capital. They disband and pay off investors after the majority of their investments have been redeemed.

MORGAGES _____

How about mortgage-backed securities?

A mortgage-backed security is a share in an organized pool of residential mortgages. Some are pass-through securities where the principal and interest payments on them are passed through to shareholders, usually monthly. There are several kinds of mortgage-backed securities. They include:

• *Government National Mortgage Association (GNMA—Ginnie Mae)* securities. GNMA primarily issues pass-through securities. These securities pass through all payments of interest and principal received on a pool of federally insured mortgage loans. GNMA guarantees that all payments of principal and interest will be made on the mortgages on a timely basis. Since many mortgages are repaid before maturity, corporate investors in GNMA pools usually recover most of their principal investment well ahead of schedule. Ginnie Mae is considered an excellent investment. The higher yields, coupled with the U.S. government guarantee, provide a competitive edge over other intermediate-term to long-term securities issued by the U.S. government and other agencies.

• *Federal Home Loan Mortgage Corporation (FHLMC—Freddie Mac)* securities. Freddie Mac was established to provide a secondary market for conventional mortgages. It can purchase conventional mortgages for its own portfolio. Freddie Mac also issues pass-through securities—called participation certificates (PCs)—and guaranteed mortgage certificates (GMCs) that resemble bonds. Freddie Mac securities do not carry direct government guarantees and are subject to state and federal income tax.

• *Federal National Mortgage Association (FNMA—Fannie Mae)* securities. The FNMA is a publicly held corporation whose goal is to provide a secondary market for government-guaranteed mortgages. It does so by financing its purchase by selling debentures with maturities of several years and short-term discount notes from 30 to 360 days to private investors. The FNMA securities are not government guaranteed and are an unsecured obligation of the issuer. For this reason, they often provide considerably higher yields than Treasury securities.

• *Collaterized mortgage obligations (CMOs)*. CMOs are mortgage-backed securities that separates mortgage pools into short-, medium-, and long-term portions. Corporate investors can choose between short-term pools (such as 5-year pools) and long-term pools (such as 20-year pools).

Mortgage-backed securities enjoy liquidity and a high degree of safety since they are either government-sponsored or otherwise insured.

OTHER FIXED INCOME INVESTMENTS

Other short-term fixed income securities?

Besides bonds and mortgage-backed securities, there are other significant forms of debt instruments from which corporate investors may choose, and they are primarily short-term in nature.

• *Certificates of deposit (CDs).* These safe instruments are issued by commercial banks and thrift institutions and have traditionally been in amounts of $10,000 or $100,000 (jumbo CDs). CDs have a fixed maturity period varying from several months to many years. However, there is a penalty for cashing in the certificate prior to the maturity date.

• *Repurchase agreements (repos).* Repurchase agreements is a form of loan in which the borrower sells securities (such as government securities and other marketable securities) to the lender, but simultaneously contracts to repurchase the same securities either on call or on a specified date at a price that will produce an agreed yield. For example, a corporate investment officer agrees to buy a 90-day Treasury bill from a bank at a price to yield 7% with a contract to buy the bills back one day later. Repos are attractive to corporate investors because, unlike demand deposits, repos pay explicit interest and it may be difficult to locate a one-day-maturity government security. Although repos can be a sound investment, it will cost to buy them (such as bank safekeeping fees, legal fees, and paperwork).

• *Banker's acceptances (BAs).* A banker's acceptance is a draft drawn on a bank by a corporation to pay for merchandise. The draft promises payment of a certain sum of money to its holder at some future date. What makes BAs unique is that by prearrangement a bank accepts them, thereby guaranteeing their payment at the stated time. Most BAs arise in foreign trade transactions. The most common maturity for BAs is three months, although they can have maturities of up to 270 days. Their typical denominations are $500,000 and $1 million. BAs offer the following advantages as a corporate investment vehicle:

- Safety.
- Negotiability.
- Liquidity since an active secondary market for instruments of $1 million or more exists.
- BAs offer several basis points higher yield spread than those of T-bills.
- Smaller investment amount producing a yield similar to that of a CD with a comparable face value.
- *Commercial paper.* Commercial paper is issued by large corporations to the public. It usually comes in minimum denominations of $25,000. It represents an unsecured promissory note. It usually carries a higher yield than small CDs. The maturity is usually 30, 60, and 90 days. The degree of risk depends on the company's credit rating.
- *Treasury bills.* Treasury bills have a maximum maturity of one year and common maturities of 91 and 182 days. They trade in minimum units of $10,000. They do not pay interest in the traditional sense; they are sold at a discount, and redeemed when the maturity date comes around, at face value. T-bills are extremely liquid in that there is an active secondary or resale market for these securities. T-bills have an extremely low risk because they are backed by the U.S. government.

Yields on discount securities such as T-bills are calculated using the formula:

$$\frac{P_1 - P_0}{P_0} \times \frac{52}{n}$$

where P_1 = redemption price, P_0 = purchase price, and n = maturity in weeks.

EXAMPLE 8

Assume that P_1 = $10,000, P_0 = $9,800, and n = 13 weeks. Then the T-bill yield is:

$$\frac{\$10,000 - \$9,800}{\$9,800} \times \frac{52}{13} = \frac{\$200}{\$9,800} \times 4 = .0816 = 8.16\%$$

• *Eurodollar time deposits and CDs.* Eurodollar time deposits are essentially nonnegotiable, full liability, U.S. dollar-denominated time deposits in an offshore branch of a U.S. or foreign bank. Hence, these time deposits are not liquid or marketable. Eurodollar CDs, on the other hand, are negotiable and typically offer a higher return than domestic CDs because of its exposure to sovereign risk.

• *Student Loan Marketing Association (Sallie Mae) Securities.* Sallie Mae purchases loans made by financial institutions under a variety of federal and state loan programs. Sallie Mae securities are not guaranteed, but generally insured by the federal government and its agencies. These securities include floating rate and fixed rate obligations with maturities of five years or more as well as discount notes with maturities from a few days to 360 days.

How do you choose money market funds?

Money market funds is a special form of mutual funds. The investor can own a portfolio of high-yielding CDs, T-bills, and other similar securities of short-term nature, with a small amount to invest. There is a great deal of liquidity and flexibility in withdrawing funds through check-writing privileges. Money market funds are considered very conservative, because most of the securities purchased by the funds are quite safe.

Money market mutual funds invest in short-term government securities, commercial paper, and certificates of deposits. They provide more safety of principal than other mutual funds since net asset value never fluctuates. Each share has a net asset value of $1. The yield, however, fluctuates daily. The advantages are:

- Money market funds are no-load.
- There may be a low deposit in these funds.
- The fund is a form of checking account, allowing a firm to write checks against its balance in the account.

Disadvantage: The deposit in these funds is not insured as it is in a money market account or other federally insured deposit in banks.

Table 34–2 ranks various short-term investment vehicles in terms of their default risk.

Is investing in preferred stock desirable?

Preferred stock carries a fixed dividend that is paid quarterly. The dividend is stated in dollar terms per share, or as a percentage of par (stated) value of the stock. Preferred stock is considered a hybrid security because it possesses features of both common stock and a corporate bond. It is like common stock in that:

- It represents equity ownership and is issued without stated maturity dates;
- It pays dividends.

TABLE 34–2 DEFAULT RISK AMONG SHORT-TERM INVESTMENT VEHICLES

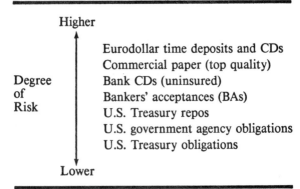

	Higher
Degree of Risk	Eurodollar time deposits and CDs Commercial paper (top quality) Bank CDs (uninsured) Bankers' acceptances (BAs) U.S. Treasury repos U.S. government agency obligations U.S. Treasury obligations
	Lower

Preferred stock is also like a corporate bond in that:

• It provides for prior claims on earnings and assets.

• Its dividend is fixed for the life of the issue.

• It can carry call and convertible features and sinking fund provisions.

Since preferred stocks are traded on the basis of the yield offered to investors, they are in effect viewed as fixed income securities and, as a result, are in competition with bonds in the marketplace. *Note:* Corporate bonds, however, occupy a position senior to preferred stocks.

Advantages of owning preferred stocks include:

• Their high current income, which is highly predictable.

• Safety.

• Lower unit cost ($10 to $25 per share).

Disadvantages are:

• Their susceptibility to inflation and high interest rates.

• They lack substantial capital gains potential.

Preferred Stock Ratings

Like bond ratings, Standard & Poor's and Moody's have long rated the investment quality of preferred stocks. S&P uses basically the same rating system as they do with bonds, except that triple A ratings are not given to preferred stocks. Moody's uses a slightly different system, which is given below. These ratings are intended to provide an indication of the quality of the issue and are based largely on an assessment of the firm's ability to pay preferred dividends in a prompt and timely fashion. *Note:* Preferred stock ratings should not be compared with bond ratings as they are not equivalent; preferred stocks occupy a position junior to bonds.

MOODY'S PREFERRED STOCK RATING SYSTEM

Rating Symbol	Definition
aaa	Top quality
aa	High grade
a	Upper medium grade
baa	Lower medium grade
ba	Speculative type
b	Little assurance of future dividends
caa	Likely to be already in arrears

How do you calculate expected return from preferred stock?

The expected return from preferred stock is calculated in a manner similar to the expected return on bonds. The calculations depend upon whether the preferred stock is issued in perpetuity or if it has a call that is likely to be exercised.

• *A Perpetuity.* Since preferred stock usually has no maturity date when the company must redeem it, you cannot calculate a yield to maturity. You can calculate a current yield as follows:

$$\text{Current yield} = D/P$$

where D = annual dividend, and P = the market price of the preferred stock.

EXAMPLE 9

A preferred stock paying $4.00 a year in dividends and having a market price of $25 would have a current yield of 16% ($4/$25).

• *Yield to Call.* If a call is likely, a more appropriate return measure is yield to call (YTC). Theoretically, YTC is the rate that equates the present value of the future dividends and the call price with the current market price of the preferred stock. Two examples are given on the following page.

EXAMPLE 10

Consider the following two preferreds:

Preferreds	Market Price	Call Price	Dividends	Term to Call	YTC
A	$ 8/share	$9	$1/year	3 years	16.06%
B	10	9	$1	3	6.89

• *Comparison to Bond Yields.* The example shows that yields on straight preferreds are closely correlated to bond yields, since both are fixed income securities. However, yields on preferreds are often below bond yields, which seems unusual because preferreds have a position junior to bonds. The reason is that corporate investors favor preferreds over bonds because of a dividend exclusion allowed in determining corporate taxable income, which will be explained next.

Should you consider adjustable rate preferred stock (ARPS)?

CFOs with excess funds can make short-term investments in long-term securities such as long-term bonds and common and preferred stocks. They may be naturally adverse to the price volatility of long-term bonds, especially when they put money aside for a specific payment such as income taxes. Perhaps for a similar reason, common and preferred stocks would be equally unattractive for short-term investments. But this is not quite true, since these securities provide an interesting tax advantage for corporations. For example, if the company invests its surplus funds in a short- or long-term debt, it must pay tax on the interest received. Thus, for $1 of interest, a corporation in a 46 percent marginal tax bracket ends up with only $0.54. However, companies pay tax on only 20 percent of dividends received from investments in stocks. (Under current tax laws, corporations are allowed to exclude 80 percent of the dividends they receive from a stock (either common or preferred) from their taxable income. Thus, for $1 of dividends received, the firm winds up with $1 - (.20 \times .46) = 0.91. The effective tax rate is only 9.1%.

The problem with preferred stocks is that since preferred dividends are fixed, the prices of preferred shares change when long-term interest rates change. Many corporate money managers are reluctant to buy straight preferred because of its interest risk. To encourage corporate investments in preferred shares, a new type of preferred stock was introduced in May 1982 by Chemical New York Corporation. These securities—the so-called *adjustable rate (floating rate) preferreds*—pay dividends that go up and down with the general level of interest rates. The prices of these securities are therefore less volatile than fixed-dividend preferreds, and they are a safer haven for the corporation's excess cash. Yields obtained from preferreds may be lower than the debt issue. The corporations buying the preferreds would still be happy with the lower yield because 80% of the dividends they receive escape tax.

Money Market Preferred Stock: A Newest Investment Form

The money market preferred stock (MMPS), also known as auction-rate preferred stock, is the newest and most popular member of the preferred stock group attractive to corporate investors since it offers the following advantages:

- Low market risk in the event of price decline.
- Competitive yield.
- Liquidity.

MMPS pays dividends and adjusts rates up or down, depending on the current market, every seven weeks. Unlike other adjustable preferreds, the market, not the issuer, sets the rate at the auction. If no bids are placed for a stock, MMPS' dividend rate is automatically set at the 60-day AA commercial paper rate quoted by the Federal Reserve Bank. There is a possibility, however, of a failed auction if no buyers show up at the auction. Corporate investors must take into account the credit quality of a money market preferred stock. Money market preferreds include:

- Short-Term Auction Rate Stock (STARS).
- Dutch-Auction Rate Transferable Securities (DARTS).
- Market-Auction Preferred Stock (MAPS).
- Auction-Market Preferred Stock (AMPS).
- Cumulative Auction-Market Preferred Stock (CAMPS).

PART VIII

TAXATION

35

Tax Factors in Financial Decision Making*

There are many taxing agencies, including federal, state, and local, to which your company pays tax. If your company is operating internationally, it has the additional problem of applying tax laws of foreign countries. Taxes may be levied on income, sales, and property. The federal corporate income tax (filed on Form 1120) is the most important because it often represents the largest tax liability. Thus, it can have a major effect on your financial decisions.

What should you know about taxes?

To make sound financial and investment decisions, you must have an understanding of the basic concepts underlying the U.S. tax structure and how they affect your decisions. This section discusses first the general structure of the corporate income tax, such as taxable income, capital gains and losses, deductible expenses, operating loss carrybacks and carryforwards, tax rates, and tax prepayments and credits. Then, it reviews various tax planning strategies to minimize your company's income tax liability in the current year and postpone the payment of taxes to later years. The advantages of electing S corporation status will also be discussed.

The general tax formula for corporations is shown on the following page.

---

*This chapter was written by Loc T. Nguyen, LL.M., CPA, a tax consultant to industry and Professor of Taxation at California State University, Long Beach, CA.

Gross income
Less: Deductions
= Taxable income
     × Tax rates
= Gross tax
Less: Tax credits and prepayments
= Tax due (or Refund)

A brief review of the various elements of this tax formula will give us a general understanding needed for effective tax planning.

What does gross income consist of?

Corporate gross income is of two types:

• Ordinary income, which includes income from normal business operations as well as miscellaneous incomes such as rents, interest, and dividends. Ordinary income is fully taxable, however the corporation has a special exclusion for dividends received from taxable domestic corporations. Generally, 70% of the dividends received may be excluded from the corporation's gross income. For example, if a $100 dividend is received by the corporation, $70 can be excluded and only $30 of the dividend is included in taxable income. This 70% exclusion can be increased to 80% if the corporation receiving the dividend owns at least 20% but less than 80% of the dividend paying corporation's stock. And for ownership exceeding 80% of the dividend paying corporation, the dividend received deduction will be 100%.

• Capital gains or losses, resulting from the sale of capital assets. In general, assets bought and sold in the ordinary course of a company's business, such as inventory, receivables, and depreciable assets, generate ordinary income. The sale or exchange of all other assets, such as stocks, bonds, real estate investments, generate capital gains or losses.

Capital gains and losses are netted together and any net capital gain is taxed at either the applicable corporate rate or an alternative rate of 28%. However, unlike the case with individuals, corporations cannot deduct a net capital loss from ordinary income in the year of the loss, i.e., there is no capital loss deduction against ordinary income. Thus, a corporation's capital losses can only be used to offset the current year capital gains. However, any unused capital loss may be carried back to the three years preceding the year of loss to offset capital gains and, if not completely absorbed, may be then carried forward for up to five years subsequent to the loss year. For example, any unused capital loss in the current year may be carried back to the third prior tax year to offset any capital gain reported by the corporation in that year. Any remaining unused capital loss is then carried to the second prior year and, if necessary, to the last taxable year. After carrying back the current year capital loss to the three prior years, the corporation can continue to carry forward any remaining capital loss to offset against capital gains realized in the next five years. Any loss not utilized by the end of the fifth subsequent year will expire without tax benefit.

Capital gains and losses are classified as long term or short term. A long-term capital gain is a gain from the sale of assets held for more than one year. The highest tax rate on capital gains is 28%.

What are the allowable tax deductions?

All of a regular corporation's activities are considered to be connected with the conduct of a trade or business. Therefore, all the ordinary and necessary expenses paid or incurred during the year by your business are tax deductible.

Business meals and entertainment expenses are 80% deductible. The meal must have a direct relationship to carrying out your business activities. Business must be discussed before, during, and after the meal. The meal or beverage cannot be "lavish or extravagant." Transportation to and from the restaurant is 100% deductible. However, parking at a sports arena is only 80% deductible.

EXAMPLE 1

You took a customer out to dinner and drinks, and it costs $125. The business meal is limited in terms of tax deductibility to $125 × 80% = $100. In addition, the taxi fare to the restaurant was $20. This is fully deductible.

Generally, food- and entertainment-related employee benefits are fully deductible. Examples are departmental and office parties.

Promotional items for public distribution are fully deductible (e.g., samples). Deductions for business gifts are limited to $25 per individual customer, client, or other business contact. Items clearly of an advertising nature that cost $4 or less and are imprinted with the company's name (e.g., pens, calendars, etc. . . .) do not have to be included in the $25 limitation.

EXAMPLE 2

You gave business gifts to 17 customers. These gifts, which were not of an advertising nature, had the following fair market value: 4 @ $10, 4 @ $25, 4 @ $50, and 5 @ $100. These gifts are deductible as business expenses for $365 computed as follows:

4 @ $10	$40
13 @ $25	325
Total	$365

All bad debts incurred by the corporation are business-related and can be used to offset the corporation's ordinary income. The corporation can no longer use the reserve method which allows deductions for estimated bad debts. Instead, it must use the direct write-off method which allows a bad debt deduction only at the time the debt actually becomes partially or totally worthless.

A charitable contribution made in cash or property is deductible. For contributions of inventory used to care for the ill, the needy, or infants and contributions of scientific property to an educational institution to be used for research, the amount of deduction is the cost of the property plus one half of the potential profit (but not exceeding two times the cost). The deduction is generally limited to 10% of taxable income computed by excluding the charitable contribution itself, the dividends-received exclusion, and the net operating loss and capital loss carrybacks. Any charitable contribution in excess of the limitation may be carried forward and deducted in any of the 5 succeeding years.

With life insurance premiums, there are some circumstances in which a corporation may claim a deduction. These include premiums paid for "key man" life insurance (i.e., life insurance for any officer, employee who may have a financial interest in the company) and for group-term life insurance when the company is not the beneficiary. "Key man" life insurance premiums are deductible only if (1) the premium payments are an ordinary business expense as additional compensation to the "key" employee, and (2) the total amount of all compensation paid to that employee is not unreasonable. As for group-term insurance, the premiums paid for coverage of up to $50,000 per employee are a deductible expense for the corporation and are not taxable income to the employee. For coverage above $50,000, the employee must include in income an amount equivalent to the cost of the additional protection. The group-term insurance policy must be nondiscriminatory, i.e., it must provide coverage for all employees with only few permitted exceptions such as those who work part-time, who are under age 21, or who have not been employed for at least 6 months.

Other deductible expenses include interest, professional fees (e.g., independent accountants, outside attorneys), casualty and theft losses, and bad debts when a specific amount is deemed uncollectible. Nondeductible expenses include fines, penalties, and illegal payments.

How much of depreciation is tax-deductible?

Your company has the choice of depreciating tangible assets under the straight line method or the modified accelerated cost recovery (MACRS) method. The basis for determining depreciation is the cost of the assets and improvements. If land and building are purchased together, the purchase price must be apportioned between the land and the building because only the building cost is depreciable. The portion allocated to the land cannot be depreciated since land is considered to have unlimited useful life.

ACRS depreciation lowers taxes in the early years of an asset's life, thus improving corporate cash flow and making funds available for investment. The faster the cash flow, the greater the rate of return earned on the investment.

Your company may elect to deduct immediately part or all of the cost of a depreciable asset in the year of purchase rather than depreciating it over its useful life. This provision relates to personal property qualifying under ACRS and acquired for trade or business use. However, the maximum amount that may be expensed is $10,000 per year.

Business automobiles are subject to a special set of depreciation rules. Starting from 1987, automobiles must be depreciated over five years. In addition, the maximum amount of annual depreciation in 1991 is subject to the following ceilings:

1st year	$2,660
2nd year	4,300
3rd year	2,550
4th year and thereafter	1,575

The effect of these rules is to limit the annual depreciation for a car costing more than $13,300 in 1991. For these more expensive cars, depreciation can be continued after the fifth year, subject to the maximum annual limitation. In addition, if the car is used less than 100 percent for business, the maximum amount of annual depreciation allowed must be reduced proportionately.

Amortization

Some types of intangible assets may be amortized (i.e., written off systematically over their estimated useful lives) for tax purposes. For instance, a new company's organization costs may be amortized over a period of not less than 60 months.

What do you do about losses in the current year?

If a company has a net operating loss, the loss may be applied against income in other years. The loss can be carried back 3 years and then forward 15 years (capital loss can be carried back for 3 years and forward for 5 years only). Note that the taxpayer must first apply the loss against the taxable income in the 3 prior years. If the loss is not completely absorbed by the profits in these 3 years, it may be carried forward to each of the following 15 years. The taxpayer has the option of foregoing the carryback and can elect to carry the loss forward only. After the 15 years, any loss remaining may no longer be used as a tax deduction. To illustrate, a 19X5 net operating loss may be used to recover, in whole or in part, the taxes paid during 19X2, 19X3, and 19X4. Thus, the net operating loss can be carried back first to 19X2 and treated as a newly discovered deduction to be subtracted from the gross income reported in 19X2. If the corporation had taxable income and paid a tax in 19X2. If the corporation had taxable income and paid a tax in 19X2, the corporation can get a refund of part or all of the taxes paid for that year. If there is still a remaining unabsorbed loss, the corporation can carry it to the second prior year (19X3), and then to the first prior year (19X4). Finally, if any part of the loss remains after the carryback to the three prior years, this unabsorbed loss may be used to reduce taxable income, if any, during the 15-year period from 19X6 through 20X0.

What tax rates apply?

The federal income tax rate is graduated, meaning that as additional profits are earned, the tax rate on the incremental earnings increases.

The federal corporate tax rates are as follows:

Taxable Income	Tax Rates
$0–$50,000	15%
$50,001–$75,000	25%
Over $75,000	34%

There is an additional 5% surtax on taxable income between $100,000 and $335,000.

The highest tax rate used in computing your company's total tax obligation is referred to as the marginal tax rate, which is the tax rate applicable to the next dollar of income. In addition to the marginal tax rate, the average (effective) tax rate is the one applicable to all taxable income. It is computed as follows:

$$\text{Effective tax rate} = \frac{\text{Total tax liability}}{\text{Taxable income}}$$

The maximum federal tax rate for corporations is 34%. In addition, companies have state and local income taxes that are typically based on federal taxable income. As a result, the effective tax rate a company pays is generally higher than 34%.

EXAMPLE 3

Your company's taxable income is $160,000. The tax obligation is:

$50,000 × 15%	$7,500
$25,000 × 25%	6,250
$85,000 × 34%	28,900
$60,000 × 5%	3,000
	$45,650

The average (effective) tax rate is $45,650/$160,000 = 28.5%.

Because you are concerned with the tax obligation on the additional profit, the marginal tax rate must be considered when making financial decisions.

Were your tax prepayments adequate?

Under the principle of pay-as-you-go of our tax system, the corporation must prepay (1) 90% of its tax liability, or (2) 100% of the tax for the preceding year. The quarterly estimated payments are to be made on April 15, June 15, September 15, and December 15 for calendar year taxpayers.

Are you entitled to a tax credit?

A tax credit reduces dollar for dollar the amount of tax otherwise payable. A foreign tax credit is allowed for income taxes paid to a foreign country. However, the foreign tax credit cannot be used to reduce the U.S. tax liability on income from U.S. sources. The allowable credit is calculated as follows:

$$\frac{\text{Foreign}}{\text{tax credit}} = \frac{\text{Foreign source income}}{\text{Worldwide income}} \times \frac{\text{U.S. tax}}{\text{liability}}$$

EXAMPLE 4

In 19X8, your company had worldwide taxable income of $675,000 and tentative U.S. income tax of $270,000. The company's taxable income from business operations in Country X was $300,000, and foreign income taxes charged were $135,000 stated in U.S. dollars. The credit for foreign income taxes that can be claimed on the U.S. tax return for 19X8 is:

$$\frac{\text{Foreign}}{\text{tax credit}} = \frac{\$300,000}{\$675,000} \times \$270,000 = \$120,000$$

How may tax planning reduce your taxes?

You have to analyze the tax consequences of alternative approaches in financial decision making. Ignoring the effect of income taxes will cause an overstatement in estimated income. An otherwise positive cash flow from an investment may become negative when the tax is taken into consideration. As a result, an investment alternative may be chosen that does not sufficiently generate the needed return for the risk exposure taken.

Tax planning includes the minimization of tax payments by attempting to eliminate the tax entirely or providing for taxation at lower tax rates. But reducing the tax ultimately payable is often not possible. As an alternative, much tax planning is concerned with deferring tax payments from the current year to a future tax year. Tax deferrals can contribute a great deal to the efficient use of resources available to the company. The deferral is equivalent to an interest-free loan from the taxing authority. In addition, the business earns a return for another year on the funds that would have had to be paid to the federal and local taxing authorities; future tax payments will be made with "cheaper" dollars; and there may eventually be no tax payment (e.g. new tax laws). Thus, corporate taxes should be deferred when there will be a lower tax bracket in a future year, or when the firm lacks the funds to meet the present tax obligation.

In tax planning, income and expenses should be shifted into tax years that will result in the least tax liability. In general, income should be deferred to future years and expenses should be accelerated into the current year.

How may income be deferred for tax purposes?

A good tax strategy is to defer income into a year in which it will be taxed at a lower rate. For example, if you expect tax rates to drop next year, you can reduce the tax obligation by deferring income into the next year. Thus, instead of selling an asset outright, the corporation can exchange that asset for a like-kind asset, and the gain on the exchange will be tax-deferred. For example, a tangible asset such as equipment, machinery, autos, etc. . . . held for productive use in business or for investment can be exchanged tax-free for another tangible asset. Similarly, realty such as land, building, warehouse, etc. . . . can be exchanged tax-free for another piece of real property. Another method to defer income is to report the gain from an asset sale under the installment method. This method can be used when the sale price is collected over more than one year. The company must determine a gross profit ratio for an installment sale and then apply this ratio to the cash collections each year to determine the amount of gain that is taxable in that year.

Can you obtain tax-exempt income?

The company should try to convert income to less taxed or even tax-exempt sources. For example, a change from investing in corporate bonds into investing in state and local obligations can convert taxable interest income into tax-exempt income. Interest earned on municipal bonds is not subject to federal taxes and is exempt from tax of the state in which the bond is issued. Of course, the market value of the bond changes with changes in the "going" interest rate.

Tax-free income is worth much more than taxable income. That is why tax-free bonds almost always have lower pre-tax yields. You can determine the equivalent taxable return as follows:

$$\text{Equivalent taxable return} = \frac{\text{Tax-free return}}{1 - \text{Marginal tax rate}}$$

EXAMPLE 5

A municipal bond pays interest at the rate of 6%. The company's marginal tax rate is 34%. The equivalent rate on a taxable instrument is:

$$\frac{.06}{1 - .34} = \frac{.06}{.66} = 9.1\%$$

When should you accelerate expenses?

Pay tax-deductible expenses in a year in which you will receive the most benefit. Accelerate expenses which will no longer be deductible or will be restricted in the future. Also, accelerate deductions into the current year if you anticipate lower tax rates in the next period. For example, if your company is a cash-basis taxpayer, prepay your future tax obligations, such as property taxes and estimated income taxes, to bring the deductible expenses into the current year. Also, selling a loss asset prior to year-end can accelerate a tax loss into the current year.

The company may donate property instead of cash. By donating appreciated property to a charity, the business can deduct the full market value and avoid paying tax on the gain.

Is a small business better-off filing as an S Corporation?

A small business corporation having 35 or less stockholders and only one class of stock may elect to be taxed as a Subchapter S corporation (more commonly known as an S corporation). An S corporation is taxed like a partnership. There is no tax at the corporate level and all corporate income and losses are passed through to the stockholders. Income is allocated and taxed directly to the stockholders regardless of whether it is actually received by them. An S corporation files an information tax return on Form 1120S, and attaches a Schedule K-1 for each stockholder, showing his/her portion of taxable income or loss for the year. The corporate income is taxed only once to the stockholders at their individual tax rates.

The election to be taxed as an S corporation may be made by a qualified corporation at any time during the preceding taxable year or in the first 75 days of the year during which it applies. For the election to be valid, all stockholders must consent to the election in a signed statement.

An S corporation is advantageous because there is no tax at the corporate level and because the maximum tax rate to individuals is lower (generally 31%) than that of the corporation (generally 34%). Thus, stockholders still obtain the benefits of a corporation such as limited liability while escaping the double taxation typically associated with the distribution of corporate profits.

However, certain tax advantages that companies obtain do not go to S corporations. For example, fringe benefits paid to shareholders owning more than 2 percent of the stock are treated as distributions to the shareholders and are not deductible by the corporation. In addition, items that would be subject to special limitations on the shareholders' individual returns, such as interest, dividends, capital gains and losses, charitable contributions, etc. . . , cannot be netted against the S corporation's income; instead they must be allocated to the shareholders' directly.

PART **IX**

MERGERS, DIVESTITURES, FAILURE, AND REORGANIZATION

36

Mergers and Acquisitions*

In a merger, we have to value the targeted company. As a starting point in valuation, the key financial data must be accumulated and analyzed including historical financial statements, forecasted financial statements, and tax returns. The assumptions of the valuation must be clearly spelled out.

How do you value a targeted company?

The valuation approaches may be profit- or asset-oriented. Adjusted earnings may be capitalized at an appropriate multiple. Future adjusted cash earnings may be discounted by the rate of return that may be earned. Assets may be valued at fair market value, e.g., through appraisal. Comparative values of similar companies may serve as benchmarks. Commercial software programs are available to do merger analysis.

How do you do a comparison with industry averages?

Valid comparisons can be made between the entity being valued and others in the same industry. Industry norms should be noted. General sources of comparative industry data found in financial advisory services include Standard and Poor's, Moody's, Value Line, Dun and Bradstreet, and Robert Morris Associates. Trade publications may also be consulted. Reference may be made to the *Almanac of Business and Industrial Financial Ratios* (based on corporate tax returns to the Internal Revenue Service) written by Leo Troy (Englewood Cliffs, NJ: Prentice-Hall). If a small company is being acquired, reference may be made to *Financial Studies of Small Businesses* published annually by Financial Research

*This chapter was coauthored by Stan Chu, MS, CPA, consultant and professor at the City University of New York.

Associates (Washington, DC: Financial Research Associates, 1984).

Publicly available information on the targeted company includes the annual report, SEC Forms 10-K, 10-Q, and 8-K, interim shareholder reports, proxy statements, press releases, and offering prospectuses.

We will look at the various approaches to business valuation including capitalization of earnings, capitalization of excess earnings, capitalization of cash flow, present value (discounted) of future cash flows, book value of net assets, tangible net worth, economic net worth, fair market value of net assets, gross revenue multiplier, profit margin/capitalization rate, price-earnings factor, comparative value of similar going concerns, and recent sales of stock. A combination of approaches may be used to obtain a representative value.

CAPITALIZATION OF EARNINGS ⎯⎯⎯⎯⎯

How does capitalization of earnings influence value?

Primary consideration should be given to earnings when valuing a company. Historical earnings is typically the beginning point in applying a capitalization method to most business valuations. In general, historical earnings are a reliable predictor of future earnings. According to IRS Revenue Ruling 59-60, 1959-1, C.B. 237, the greatest emphasis should be placed on profitability when looking at a "going concern."

The value of the business may be based on its adjusted earnings times a multiplier for what the business sells for in the industry.

How is net income adjusted?

Net income should be adjusted for unusual and nonrecurring revenue and expense items. In adjusting net income of the business, we should add back the portion of the following items if personal rather than business-related: auto expense, travel expense, and promotion and entertainment expense. Interest expense should also be added back to net income because it is the cost to borrow funds to buy assets or obtain working capital, and as such is not relevant in determining the operating profit of the business. In the event lease payments arise from a low-cost lease, earnings should be adjusted to arrive at a fair rental charge. Extraordinary items (e.g., gain on the sale of land) should be removed from earnings to obtain typical earnings. If business assets are being depreciated at an accelerated rate, you should adjust net income upward. Therefore, the difference between the straight-line method and an accelerated depreciation method should be added back.

We should add back expenses for a closely held business solely for fringe benefits, health plan, pension plan, and life insurance. In addition, we should add back excessive salary representing the difference between the owner's salary and what a reasonable salary would be if we hired someone to do the job. All compensation should be considered including perks. Thus, if the owner gets a salary of $300,000 and a competent worker would get $80,000, the add back to net income is $220,000.

A tax provision (if none exists) should be made in arriving at the adjusted net income. The tax provision should be based on the current rates for each of the years.

If the company has a significant amount of investment income (e.g., dividend income, interest income, rental income from nonoperating property), net income may be reduced for the investment income with taxes being adjusted accordingly. We are primarily concerned with the income from operations.

What multiplier of earnings should be used?

The adjusted (restated) earnings results in a quality of earnings figure. The restated earnings is then multiplied by a multiplier to determine the value of a business. The multiplier should be higher for a low risk business but generally not more than 10. The multiplier should be lower for a high risk business, often only 1 or 2. An average multiplier is used when average risk exists, such as 5. The P/E ratio for a comparable company would be a good benchmark.

Some investment bankers use in valuation a multiple of the latest year's earnings, or the annual rate of earnings of a current interim period (if representative). An example follows based on a multiplier of one-year profits.

EXAMPLE 1

Adjusted net income for the current year	$400,000
× Multiplier	× 4
Valuation	$1,600,000

The adjusted net income is computed below:

Reported net income	$325,000
Adjustments:	
Personal expenses (e.g., promotion and entertainment)	50,000
Extraordinary or nonrecurring gain	(60,000)
Owner's fringe benefits (e.g., pension plan)	40,000
Excessive owner's salary relative to a reasonable salary	30,000
Interest expense	20,000
Dividend revenue	(10,000)
Low cost rental payments relative to a fair rental charge	(5,000)
Excess depreciation from using an accelerated method	10,000
Restated net income	$400,000

Typically, a five-year average adjusted historical earnings figure is used. The five years' earnings up to the valuation date demonstrates past earning power. Note that for SEC registration and reporting purposes a five-year period is used. Assuming a simple average is used, the computation follows:

Simple average adjusted earnings over 5 years × Multiplier (Capitalization factor, P/E Ratio) of 5 (based on industry standard) = Value of business

EXAMPLE 2

Assume the following net incomes:

19X9	$120,000
19X8	$100,000
19X7	$110,000
19X6	$ 90,000
19X5	$115,000

The multiplier is 4.

$$\text{Simple average earnings} = \frac{\$120,000 + \$100,000 + \$110,000 + \$90,000 + \$115,000}{5}$$

$$= \frac{\$535,000}{5} = \$107,000$$

Simple average adjusted earnings over 5 years	$107,000
× Multiplier	× 4
Value of business	$428,000

Instead of a simple average, a weighted-average adjusted historical earnings figure is recommended. This gives more weight to the most recent years which reflects higher current prices and recent business performance. If a five-year weighted-average is used, the current year is given a weight of 5 while the first year is assigned a weight of 1. The multiplier is then applied to the weighted-average five-year adjusted earnings to get the value of the business.

EXAMPLE 3

Year	Net Income (000s)	×	Weight	=	Total (000s)
19X9	$120	×	5	=	$ 600
19X8	100	×	4	=	400
19X7	110	×	3	=	330
19X6	90	×	2	=	180
19X5	115	×	1	=	115
			15		$1,625

Weighted-average 5-year earnings:

$$\$1,625,000/15 = \$108,333$$

Weighted-average 5-year earnings	$108,333
× Capitalization factor	× 4
Capitalization-of-earnings valuation	$433,332

The capitalization factor should be based on such factors as risk, stability of earnings, expected future earnings, liquidity, etc.

Has the owner of a closely held company failed to record cash sales to hide income? One way of determining this is to take purchases and add a typical profit markup in the industry. To verify reported profit, you can multiply the sales by the profit margin in the industry. If reported earnings is significantly below what the earnings should be based on the industry standard, there may be some hidden income.

CAPITALIZATION OF EXCESS EARNINGS _____

How do we treat excess earnings?

The best method is to capitalize excess earnings. The normal rate of return on the weighted-average net tangible assets is subtracted from the weighted-average adjusted earnings to determine excess earnings. It is suggested that the weighting be based on a five year period. The excess earnings are then capitalized to determine the value of the intangibles (primarily goodwill). The addition of the value of the intangibles and the fair market value of the net tangible assets equals the total valuation. As per IRS Revenue Ruling 68-609, 1968-2 C.B. 327, the IRS recommends this method to value a business for tax purposes. The Revenue Ruling states that the return on average net tangible assets should be the percentage prevailing in the industry. If an industry percentage is not available, an 8% to 10% rate may be used. An 8% return rate is used for a business with a small risk factor and stable earnings while a 10% rate of return is used for a business having a high risk factor and unstable earnings. The capitalization rate for excess earnings should be 15% (multiple of 6.67) for a business with a small risk factor and stable earnings and a 20% capitalization rate (multiple of 5) should be used for a business having a high risk factor and unstable earnings. Thus, the suggested return rate range is between 8% to 10%. The range for the capitalization rate may be between 15% to 20%.

EXAMPLE 4

Weighted average net tangible assets is computed below:

Year	Amount (000s)	×	Weight	=	Total (000s)
19X1	$ 950	×	1		$ 950
19X2	1,000	×	2		2,000
19X3	1,200	×	3		3,600
19X4	1,400	×	4		5,600
19X5	1,500	×	5		7,500
			15		$19,650

Weighted-average net tangible assets:

$$\$19,650,000/15 = \$1,310,000$$

Weighted-average adjusted net income (5 years) – assumed	$ 600,000
Reasonable rate of return on weighted-average tangible net assets ($1,310,000 × 10%)	131,000
Excess earnings	$ 469,000
Capitalization rate (20%)	x 5
Value of intangibles	$2,345,000
Fair market value of net tangible assets	3,000,000
Capitalization-of-excess-earnings valuation	$5,345,000

CAPITALIZATION OF CASH FLOW

The adjusted cash earnings may be capitalized in arriving at a value for the firm. This method may be suitable for a service business.

EXAMPLE 5

Adjusted cash earnings	$100,000
× Capitalization factor (25%)	× 4
Capitalization of cash flow	$400,000
Less liabilities assumed	50,000
Capitalization-of-cash-flow earnings	$350,000

PRESENT VALUE OF FUTURE CASH FLOWS

What steps are involved in discounting?

A business is worth the discounted value of future cash earnings plus the discounted value of the expected selling price. Cash flow may be a more valid criterion of value than book profits because cash flow can be used for reinvestment. The growth rate in earnings may be based on past growth, future expectations, and the inflation rate. This approach is suggested in a third-party sale situation. We also have more confidence in it when the company is strong in the industry and has solid earnings growth. The problem with the method is the many estimates required of future events. It probably should not be used when there has been an inconsistent trend in earnings.

Step 1: Present Value of Cash Earnings. The earnings should be estimated over future years using an estimated growth rate. A common time frame for a cash flow valuation is ten years. Once the future earnings are determined, they should be discounted. Future earnings may be based on the prior years' earnings and the current profit margin applied to sales. Cash earnings equals net income plus noncash expense adjustments such as depreciation.

Step 2: Present Value of Sales Price. The present value of the expected selling price of the business at the date of sale should be determined. This residual value may be based on a multiple of earnings or cash flow, expected market value, etc.

You may use as the discount rate the minimum acceptable return to the buyer for investing in the target company. The discount rate may take into account the usual return rate for money, inflation rate, a risk premium (based on such factors as local market conditions, earnings instability, and level of debt), and maybe a premium for the illiquidity of the investment. If the risk-free interest rate is 7% (on government bonds), the risk premium is 8%, and the illiquidity premium is 7%, the capitalization (discount) rate will be 22%. The risk premium may range from 5% to 10% while the illiquidity premium may range from 5% to 15%. Some evaluators simply use as the discount rate the market interest rate of a low risk asset investment.

Assuming you expect to hold the business for 14 years, and anticipate a 12% rate of return, and a constant earnings each year, the value of the business is based on:

For cash earnings. Present value of an ordinary annuity for n = 14, i = 12%.

For selling price. Present value of $1 for n = 14, i = 12%.

If earnings grow at an 8% rate, Table A-3 (Appendix) would be used to discount the annual earnings that would change each year.

EXAMPLE 6

In 19X1, the net income is $200,000. Earnings are expected to grow at 8% per year. The discount rate is 10%. You estimate that the business is worth the discounted value of future earnings. The valuation equals:

Year	Net Income (Based on an 8% Growth Rate)	PV of $1 Factor (at 10% Interest)	Present Value
19X1	$200,000	× .909	$181,800
19X2	208,000	× .826	171,808
19X3	224,600	× .751	168,675
19X4	242,568	× .683	165,674
19X5	261,973	× .621	162,685
Present Value of Future Earnings			$850,642

If the expected selling price at the end of year 19X5 is $600,000, the valuation of the business equals:

Present value of earnings	$ 850,642
Selling price in 19X5 $600,000 × .621	372,600
Valuation	$1,223,242

OPERATING CASH FLOW

Some businesses may be valued at a multiple of operating cash flow. For example, radio and TV stations often sell for between 8 to 12 times operating cash flow.

BOOK VALUE

How do asset approaches work?

The business may be valued based on the book value of the net assets (assets less liabilities) at the most recent balance sheet date. This method is unrealistic because it does not take into account current values. It may only be appropriate when it is impossible to determine fair value of net assets and/or goodwill. However, book value may be adjusted for obvious understatements such as excess depreciation, LIFO reserve, favorable leases, and for low debt (e.g., low rental payments or unfunded pension and postretirement benefits). Unfortunately, it may be difficult for a buying company to have access to information regarding these adjustments.

TANGIBLE NET WORTH

The valuation of the company is its tangible net worth for the current year equal to:

Stockholders' equity
Less: Intangible assets
Tangible net worth
Economic net worth (adjusted book value)

Economic net worth equals:

> Fair market value of net assets
> Plus: Goodwill (as per agreement)
> Economic net worth

FAIR MARKET VALUE OF NET ASSETS _____

The fair market value of the net tangible assets of the business may be determined through independent appraisal. To it, we add the value of the goodwill (if any). Note that goodwill applies to such aspects as reputation of the company, customer base, and high quality merchandise. IRS Appeals and Review Memorandums (ARM) 34 and 38 present formula methods to value goodwill. In case of a small business, a business broker may be retained to do the appraisal of property, plant and equipment. A business broker is experienced because he or she puts together the purchase of small businesses. According to Equitable Business Brokers, about 25% of businesses changing hands are sold through business brokers. Typically, the fair value of the net tangible assets (assets less liabilities) is higher than book value.

The general practice is to value inventory at a maximum value of cost. IRS Revenue Procedure 77-12 provides acceptable ways to allocate a lump-sum purchase price to inventories.

Unrecognized and unrecorded liabilities should be considered when determining the fair market value of net assets. For example, one company had both an unrecorded liability for liquidated damages for non-union contracts of $3,100,000 and an unrecorded liability for $4,900,000 related to the estimated employer final withdrawal liability. As a result of unrecorded liabilities the value of a business will be reduced further.

A tax liability may also exist that has not been recognized in the accounts. For example, the company's tax position may be adjusted by the IRS which is currently auditing the tax return. This contingent liability should be considered in valuing the business.

Similarly, unrecorded and undervalued assets should be considered because they increase the value of the business such as customer lists, patents, and licensing agreements.

Note: IRS Revenue Ruling 65-193 approves only those approaches where valuations can be determined separately for tangible and intangible assets.

LIQUIDATION VALUE

Liquidation value is a conservative figure of value because it does not take into account the earning power of the business. Liquidation value is a "floor" price in negotiations. Liquidation value is the estimated value of the company's assets and assuming their conversion into cash in a short time period. All liabilities and the costs of liquidating the business (e.g., appraisal fees, real estate fees, legal and accounting fees, recapture taxes) are subtracted from the total cash to obtain net liquidation value.

Liquidation value may be computed based on an orderly liquidation or a forced (rapid) liquidation. In the case of the latter, there will obviously be a lower value.

REPLACEMENT VALUE

What is replacement cost?

Replacement cost ("new") is the cost of duplicating from scratch the business's assets on an "as-if-new" basis. It will typically result in a higher figure than book value or fair market value of existing assets. Replacement cost provides a meaningful basis of comparison with other methods but should not be used as the acquisition value. A more accurate indicator of value is when replacement cost is adjusted for relevant depreciation and obsolescence.

SECURED LOAN VALUE

What is the secured-loan value?

The secured loan-value reflects the borrowing power of the seller's assets. Typically, banks will lend up to 90% of accounts receivable and 10 to 60% of the value of inventory depending on how much represents finished goods, work-in-process, and raw materials. The least percentage amount will be work-in-process because of its greater realization risk and difficulty of sale. Also considered are turnover rates.

CAPITALIZATION OF REVENUE _____

How is revenue capitalized?

The value of the business may be determined by multiplying the revenue by the gross revenue multiplier common in the industry. The industry standard gross revenue multiplier is based on the average ratio of market price to sales prevalent in the industry. This approach may be used when earnings are questionable.

EXAMPLE 7

If revenue is $14,000,000 and the multiplier is .2, the valuation is: $14,000,000 × .2 = $2,800,000.

Similarly, insurance agencies often sell for about 150% of annual commissions.

PROFIT MARGIN/CAPITALIZATION RATE _____

The profit margin divided by the capitalization rate provides a multiplier which is then applied to revenue. A multiplier of revenue that a company would sell at is the company's profit margin. The profit margin may be based on the industry average. The formula is:

$$\frac{\text{Profit margin}}{\text{Capitalization rate}} = \frac{\text{Net income/sales}}{\text{Capitalization rate}} = \text{Multiplier}$$

The capitalization rate in earnings is the return demanded by investors. In arriving at a capitalization rate, the prime interest rate may be taken into account. The multiplier is what the buyer is willing to pay.

EXAMPLE 8

Assume sales of $14,000,000, a profit margin of 5%, and a capitalization rate of 20%. The multiplier is 25% (5%/20%). The valuation is:

$$\text{Sales} \times 25\%$$
$$\$14,000,000 \times 25\% = \$3,500,000$$

The IRS and the courts have considered recent sales as an important factor.

PRICE-EARNINGS RATIO ⎯⎯⎯⎯⎯⎯⎯⎯

Can we use the price-earnings multiplier?

The value of a business may be based on the price-earnings factor applied to current (or expected) earnings per share (EPS). For publicly traded companies, the PE ratio is known. Valuation for a privately held company is more difficult. Historical earnings must be adjusted for a closely held company to be consistent with the reported earnings of a public company. After suitable adjustments have been made, the average P/E ratio for the industry or for several comparable public companies is used to arrive at a value. Typically, a premium is added to the value estimate to incorporate uncertainty and additional risk and lack of marketability associated with private companies. A variation of the P/E method may also be used. Assuming an expected earnings growth rate of the seller and a desired ROI, the acquirer determines an earnings multiple he would pay to achieve the ROI goal. Under this approach, the buyer determines the price he would be willing to pay instead of using a stock-market related price.

EXAMPLE 9

Net income	$800,000
Outstanding shares	/100,000
EPS	$ 8
PE Ratio	× 10
Market price per share	$ 80

| × Number of shares outstanding | × 100,000 |
| Price-earnings valuation | $8,000,000 |

SIMILAR BUSINESSES

What are other businesses worth?

What would someone pay for this business? Reference may be made to the market price of similar publicly traded companies. Under this approach, you obtain the market prices of companies in the industry similar in nature to the one being examined. Recent sale prices of similar businesses may be used, and an average taken. Upward or downward adjustments to this average will be made depending on the particular circumstances of the company being valued. There are two ways of arriving at an adjusted averaged value for a company based on comparable transactions. Under the equivalency adjustment method, you make an adjustment to each transaction before averaging based on such factors as size, profitability, earnings stability, and transactions structure. Transactions are adjusted downward if you deem a higher price was paid than would be appropriate for the target company, and vice versa. The average of the adjusted comparables approximates the estimated value of the target company. With the simple averaging method, you determine a simple average of the comparable transactions, after excluding noncomparable cases, and adjust the target company's price in so far as it differs from the average features of the companies purchased in comparable transactions. The former approach is suggested where extensive data is available on the comparable transactions, and where they differ substantially in their features. The latter approach is preferable where the comparable transactions are broadly similar, or where many comparable transactions have occurred.

While a perfect match is not possible, the companies should be reasonably similar (e.g., size, product, structure, geographic locations, diversity). The comparable transactions value will often be higher than the market value of the target's stock price. Several sources of industry information are Standard & Poor's, Dow Jones-Irwin, on-line information services (e.g., Compustat, Media General), and trade association reports. Extensive databases exist to assist in the analysis of merger-market history.

EXAMPLE 10

A competing company has just been sold for $6,000,000. We believe the company is worth 90 percent of the competing business. Therefore, the valuation is $5,400,000.

SALES OF STOCK ————————————

Can value be based on sales of stock?

The value of the business may be based on the outstanding shares times the market price of the stock. For an actively traded stock, the stock price provides an important benchmark. For a thinly traded stock, the stock price may not reflect an informed market consensus. Typically, the market price of the stock should be based on a discounted amount from the current market price since if all the shares are being sold the market price per share may drop somewhat based on the demand/supply relationship. Further, market value of stock is of use only in planning the actual strategy of acquiring a target company since the stock may be overvalued or undervalued relative to the worth of the target company to the acquirer.

COMBINATION OF METHODS ——————

The value of the business may be approximated by determining the average value of two or more methods.

EXAMPLE 11

Assume that the fair market value of net assets approach gives a value of $2,100,000 while the capitalization of excess earnings method provides a value of $2,500,000. The value of the business would then be the average of these two methods, or $2,300,000 ($2,100,000 + $2,500,000/2).

Some courts have found a combination of methods supportable as long as greater weight is given to the earnings methods. The most weight should be placed on the earnings approaches and less on the asset approaches.

EXAMPLE 12

Using the same information as the prior example, if a 2 weight was assigned to the earnings approach and a 1 weight was assigned to the fair market value of net assets method, the valuation would be:

Method	Amount	× Weight =	Total
Fair market value of net assets	$2,100,000 ×	1	$2,100,000
Capitalization-of-excess earnings	2,500,000 ×	2	5,000,000
		3	$7,100,000
			/3
Valuation			$2,366,667

ACCOUNTING ADJUSTMENTS _____

Material accounting adjustments should be made to the acquired company's figures to place them on a comparable basis to those of the acquirer. Adjustments should be made, where practical, for savings in administrative, technical, sales, plant, and clerical personnel costs resulting from the combination. These savings arise from the elimination of duplicate personnel, plant, office, and warehouse facilities. Savings in freight may result from the combination by shifting production to plants closer to markets.

37 _____

Divestiture

The divestiture of business segments by corporations has become an accepted strategy for growth rather than diversification. Divestiture involves the partial or complete conversion, disposition and reallocation of people, money, inventories, plants, equipment and products. It is the process of eliminating a portion of the enterprise for subsequent use of the freed resources for some other purpose. A divestment may involve a manufacturing, marketing, research or other business function.

Why divest?

A business segment may be subject to divestiture if they:

1. Do not produce an acceptable return on invested capital.

2. Do not generate sufficient cash flow.

3. Fit in with the overall corporate strategy.

4. The worth of the pieces is greater than that of the whole.

Resource allocation becomes an important consideration in a diversified business. These resources are not only capital but also include management talent. If management finds itself spending an excessive amount of time and energy on one segment of the corporation, that segment may be a candidate for divestiture. Then those resources can be redirected to the growing segments of the business. However, this operation also requires the attention of management.

What are the objectives and types of divestitures?

The usual objectives behind divestiture are to reposition the company in a market, raise cash, and to reduce losses. The other alternatives to divestiture are liquidation and bankruptcy, however, in this time of acquisitions and buyouts usually a buyer can be found for the other guy's dog. There are four primary types of divestitures:

1. Sale of an operating unit to another firm.
2. Sale of the managers of the unit being divested.
3. Setting up the business to be divested as a separate corporation and then giving (or spinning off) its stock to the divesting firm's stockholders on a pro rata basis.
4. Outright liquidation of assets.

When the divestiture is in the form of a sale to another firm, it usually involves an entire division or unit and is generally for cash but sometimes for stock of the acquiring firm. In a managerial buyout, the division managers themselves purchase the division, often through a leverage buyout (LBO), and reorganize it as a closely held firm. In a spin-off, the firm's existing stockholders are given new stock representing separate ownership in the company that was divested. The new company establishes its own board of directors and officers and operates as a separate entity. In a liquidation, the assets of the divested unit are sold off separately instead of as a whole.

What are the reasons for divestiture?

Prior to formulating a divestiture strategy and determining which segments should be divested, the reasons for divestiture need to be listed. Table 37–1 summarizes the reasons given by management for divesting segments of their business.

How do you determine what areas/units should be sold?

When trying to determine which areas or units of the company to sell, there are some simple guidelines that CFOs should follow:

• The sum of a division's parts may be greater in value than the whole division.
• Simple components of a division may be sold more easily than the whole division itself.

TABLE 37-1   REASONS CITED FOR DIVESTING

	Frequency Cited
Poor performance	26%
Changes in plans	23%
Excessive resource needs	19%
Constraints in operation	15%
Source of funds	10%
Anti-trust	7%
	100%

Source: *L. Vignola, Jr.* Strategic Divestment *(New York: Amacon, 1974), p. 52.*

• The disposal of a corporate division is a major marketing operation.

• Planning should include an evaluation from the viewpoint of the potential buyer.

• A spin-off should be considered if the division is large enough and may be potentially publicly traded.

In addition, the CFO must review existing operations and identify those divisions that don't relate to the primary focus of the company or don't meet internal financial and performance standards. Special strength of each division must also be considered. Does a division provide a unique service, have a special marketing, distribution system or production facilities that may be of more value to another company? Also, the financial aspects must be considered. The historical and projected return on investment need to be calculated and tabulated for each division.

Using these guidelines and the information determined above, the CFO can focus on three topics. First, the attractiveness and value to others versus the arguments for keeping the division. Second, what corrective action would be needed to be taken to make the division a keeper. Third, the current value of the division to the company. Only after considering all of these factors can a divestiture decision be made for a division.

How do you value and appraise divestiture?

Valuation of a division is not an exact science, and in the final analysis the value of a division is in the eye of the purchaser. Valuation methods will be broken down into asset valuation methods, those based on sales and income, and those based on market comparisons. Although these methods vary in their applicability and depend on certain facts and circumstances they can be used to determine a range of values for a division.

Methods of valuation or appraisal include: (1) asset valuation methods, (2) sales and income methods, (3) market comparison methods, and (4) discounted cash flow methods.

ASSET VALUATION METHODS ⸻

Asset valuation methods are based on the asset value of a business segment. Four popular methods are described next.

• *Adjusted Net Book Value.* One of the most conservative methods of valuation is the adjusted net book value, because it determines the value based on historical (book) value and not on market value. This can be adjusted to compensate for this shortage by adding in such items as favorable lease arrangements, and other intangible items such as customer lists, patents, and goodwill.

• *Replacement Cost.* Another method is the replacement cost technique. It asks "what would it cost to purchase the division's assets new?" This method will give a higher division value than the adjusted net book value method and is therefore good for adjusting the book value to account for new costs. This figure can also be used as a basis for determining the liquidation value of the division's assets. The most reasonable value comes from adjusting the replacement value for depreciation and obsolescence of equipment.

• *Liquidation Value.* The liquidation value is also a conservative estimate of a division's value since it does not consider the division's ongoing earning power. The liquidation value does provide the seller with a bottom line figure as to how low the price can be. The liquidation value is determined by estimating the cash value of assets assuming that they are to be sold in a short period of time. All the liabilities, real and estimated, are then deducted from the cash that was raised to determine the net liquidation value. Liquidation value can be determined based on fire sale prices or on a longer term sales price. The fire sale value would be lower.

• *Secured Loan Value.* The secured loan value technique is based on the borrowing power of the division's assets. Banks will usually lend up to 90% of the value of accounts receivable and anywhere from 10 to 60% on the value of inventory depending on the quantity of the inventory in the conversion process.

PROFITABILITY METHODS ─────────────

How are sales and income factors used?

Using sales and/or income figures as the basis for valuation can be made in two different ways.

• *Price-Earnings (P/E) Ratios.* The P/E ratio for publicly held companies is known and therefore valuation is made easy. The division's value can be determined by multiplying the P/E ratio by the expected earnings for the division. This will give a derived price that all suitors can readily understand. The earnings can be estimated from quarterly or annual reports published by the company.

For privately held companies, however, it is difficult to determine a P/E ratio as the stock of the company is not traded and the earnings are rarely disclosed. However, the earnings can be estimated and an industry average P/E ratio can be used in the calculation to estimate the private company's sales value.

• *Sales or Earnings Multiples.* There are many rules of thumb that can be used when estimating a division's value based on a multiple of sales or earnings. For example, insurance agencies sell for 200% of annual commissions or liquor stores sell for 10 times monthly sales. Another example would be radio stations selling for 8 times earnings or cash flow. These rules are fast and dirty and may result in a completely erroneous estimate of a division's value. Most business brokers will know these rule of thumb values to assist the CFO in estimating the value of a division.

MARKET-BASED COMPARISONS _____

Every day that a public company is traded on the stock market a new value is assigned to it by the traders. Thus, the stock price can be compared to equivalent companies, in terms of products, size of operations, and average P/E ratios. From these P/E ratios, an estimated sales price can be estimated as described earlier.

In the case of private companies, it is difficult for the buyer to determine the earnings of the company. However, they can compare the company to other companies that are publicly traded. Comparison to publicly traded companies is necessary as the sales price is typically disclosed in the sale or acquisition announcement.

DISCOUNTED CASH FLOW ANALYSIS _____

Another method of determining value of a business segment is to use discounted cash flow (DCF) analysis. This bases the value of the segment on the current value of its projected cash flow. In theory, this method should result in a division's value being equal to that determined by one of the P/E ratio calculations, since both reflect the current worth of the company's earnings. In actuality, discounted cash flow is basing the value of the company on actual forecasted cash flows whereas the stock market is basing the stock price on other things including the markets perception of the company and its potential cash flow.

The DCF method requires information on

- Forecasted actual cash flows.
- Assumed terminal (residual) value of the division at the end of the forecast period (book value, zero, or a multiple of earnings are frequently used).
- Discount rate.

Choosing the right discount rate is the key to the successful use of the DCF technique. It must take into account the following factors:

- Purchaser's expected return on investment (ROI).
- Purchaser's assessment of risk.
- Cost of capital.
- Projected inflation rates.
- Current interest rates.

Whichever method of evaluation is chosen it is wise to check that resulting value with at least one other method to see if it is a reasonable figure. We have to be careful of excessively high or low figures. It is also a good idea to determine the liquidation value of the company or division as this will set a *floor* for negotiations.

AN ILLUSTRATION: DISCOUNTED CASH FLOW ANALYSIS

The CFO will choose to divest a segment of the business if he or she perceives that the action will increase the wealth of the stockholders, as reflected in the price of the firm's stock. It can be further said that the price of the firm's stock will react favorably to a divestiture if the new present value of the transaction is perceived by the market to be positive.

Should a profitable business segment be retained and not divested, it would generate annual cash inflows for a particular or infinite number of years. Discounted cash flow analysis involves a comparison of initial incoming cash flows resulting from the sale of a business unit with the present value of the foregone future cash inflows given up by the firm. Foregone future cash flows refer to the cash flows that the business unit is anticipated to generate and will do so for the acquiring firm. The divesting firm gives up these cash inflows in exchange for the selling price of the business segment. For divestiture analysis to be of any value, the foregone future cash flow must be accurately estimated. The present value of these future inflows are found by discounting them at the firm's weighted average cost of capital, k.

EXAMPLE 1

Table 37-2 shows estimated cash inflows and outflows for a fictitious divestment candidate (FDC) over the next five years. The cash flows represent the best estimates by the CFO of FDC's parent company and he or she further believes that FDC will be able to be sold at its residual value of $58.7 million in five years. The firm's cost of capital is assumed to be known and is 15%.

The net present value of the future cash inflows of FDC is $47.3 million. If FDC were to be divested, the CFO of its parent company should only consider selling prices greater than this amount. This logic also assumes that the $47.3 million can be reinvested at a 15% rate of return.

Another way of looking at this valuing task makes use of the following equation for divestiture net present value (DNPV):

$$DNPV = P - \Sigma \frac{NCFt}{(1 + k)^t}$$

where P = the selling price of the business unit and NCFt = net cash flow in period t. If a $50 million offer was made by a firm for FDC, the DNPV will equal $2.7 million:

$$DNPV = 50 - \frac{9.8}{1.15} + \frac{.4}{(1.15)^2} + \frac{2.4}{(1.15)^3}$$
$$+ \frac{5.8}{(1.15)^4} + \frac{62.9}{(1.15)^5}$$
$$= 50 - 47.3 = \$2.7 \text{ million}$$

From a financial point of view, this divestment is acceptable. If the divestment candidate has an unlimited life, such as a division in a healthy industry, then cash flows must be forecasted to infinity. This task is made simple by treating the cash flows similarly to a constant growth stock and value accordingly. If the cash inflows are expected to remain constant (zero growth) to

TABLE 37-2 FDC'S CASH FLOW PROJECTIONS (IN MILLIONS)

	1	2	3	4	5
Cash Inflows					
Net operating profit	$ 3.1	$ 3.6	$ 4.0	$ 5.1	$ 6.0
Depreciation	2.1	2.4	1.8	2.3	2.1
Residual value					58.7
Total	$ 5.2	$ 6.0	$ 5.8	$ 7.4	$ 66.8
Cash Outflows					
Capital expenditure	$ 1.7	$ 1.3	$ 0.8	$ 2.1	$ 1.7
Increase (decrease) in working capital	(6.3)	1.3	2.6	(0.5)	2.2
Total	$ (4.6)	$ 2.6	$ 3.4	$ 1.6	$ 3.9
Net cash inflow (NCF)	$ 9.8	$ 3.4	$ 2.4	$ 5.8	$ 62.9
PVIF (T3)*	0.8696	0.7561	0.6575	0.5718	0.4972
Net present value (NPV)	$ 8.5	$ 2.6	$ 1.6	$ 3.3	$ 31.3
Total NPV	$ 47.3				

*PVIF = Present value interest factor for the cost of capital of 15%. From Table A-3.

infinity, then the present value of the NCF can be determined in the same manner as for a preferred stock, or perpetuity. In this case, the DNPV will be:

$$DNPV = P - \frac{NCF}{k}$$

For future cash flows that are expected to grow at an after tax rate of g, the present value of those flows can be found using the constant growth valuation model. In this case, the DNPV will be:

$$DNPV = P - \frac{NCF_1}{k - g}$$

where $NCF_1 =$ the expected NCF in the next period.

A final situation encountered often when evaluating divestiture candidates is the case where the NCFs are expected to be uneven for a number of years followed by even growth. In this case, the DNPV can be found as:

$$DNPV = R - \frac{NCF_1}{(1 + k)} + \frac{NCF_2}{(1 + k)^2} + \cdots$$
$$+ \frac{NCF_{c-1}}{(k - g)} \cdot \frac{1}{(1 + k)}$$

where NCF_1 and NCF_2 represent foregone cash flows in periods 1 and 2 and c = the first year in which constant growth applies.

Firms should only divest of assets with positive DNPVs. To do so will increase the value of the firm and subsequently, the price of its stock. If two different candidates are mutually exclusive, the one with the highest DNPV should be chosen since this will increase the value of the firm the most. If divestiture is forced by the government, for example, and the firm finds it has a choice of candidates, all with negative DNPVs, it should divest the one whose DNPV is closest to zero, since this will reduce the value of the firm the least.

DIVESTITURE WITH UNCERTAINTY _____

Due to the difficulty in predicting the NCFs and also in knowing what kinds of prices will be offered for the divestment candidate, the divestment's net present value is normally uncertain.

For situations involving an unknown selling price (due to a lack of offers) the parent firm can either elect not to divest of the candidate or set its asking price such that the DNPV will equal zero. This should be the minimum they are willing to accept. They can also look for other divestment candidates that offer promising DNPVs.

Adjusting for uncertain NCFs is much more difficult and while there is no generally accepted method for accounting for this risk, there are a number of useful techniques that are borrowed from capital budgeting and can be used here.

Risk Adjusted Discount Rate

Employing a risk adjusted discount rate is one technique that can be used to account for the uncertainty of the expected NCFs. In the previous examples, the firm's weighted average cost of capital was used to discount the NCFs to their present value. This is an appropriate choice when the divestiture candidate is as risky as the firm itself. When it is more risky, the use of a higher discount rate can be used for adjustment. This will reduce the present values of the cash flows and increase the DNPV. This is logical since a relatively risky divestment candidate with uncertain cash flows will be of less value to the firm, in present dollars. The added benefit of divesting such a candidate will be reflected in the increased DNPV. On the other hand, when the NCFs are more certain than those of the rest of the firm, the discount rate should be lowered. This lowers the DNPV and makes the divestiture less attractive. The first equation can be rewritten as:

$$DNPV = P - E\frac{NCF_t}{(1 + k')^t}$$

where all terms are the same except for k' which now is the adjusted rate to be used for discounting the cash flows. Using data from Table 37–2 and assuming that the divestment candidate is less risky than the firm as a whole (lowering k from .15 to .14) shows:

$$DNPV = 50 - \frac{9.8}{1.14} + \frac{3.4}{(1.14)^2} + \frac{2.4}{(1.14)^3}$$

$$+ \frac{5.8}{(1.14)^4} + \frac{62.9}{(1.14)^5}$$

$$= 50 - 48.9 = \$1.1 \text{ million}$$

Using a lower discount rate lessened the DNPV by \$1.6 million (\$2.7 million – \$1.1 million). This is reasonable in that the attractiveness of a divestment candidate at a certain selling price will be lessened as the candidate is found to be less risky.

Sensitivity Analysis

Sensitivity analysis is another technique that can be used in making divestiture decisions. In sensitivity analysis, the parent company evaluates the effect that certain factors have on the NCFs. For example, a divestment candidate's NCFs might be largely influenced by the price of copper, the U.S. Navy Defense budget, and upcoming union contract talks. For these three influencing factors, a number of different scenarios or forecasts, can be projected, each with their expected NCFs. For instance, the expected NCFs would be highest in the scenario where all three influencing factors are favorable. Having evaluated the NCFs and DNPVs for different scenarios, the parent firm has a better understanding of the range that the NCFs might fall in and also what factors influence them the most. Further, if the probability of the scenarios can be forecasted, statistical techniques can be used to give the probability of realizing a negative DNPV, the expected DNPV and the standard deviation, and coefficient of variation of DNPVs. This information would be very useful in making divestment decisions. It should be noted that the NCFs using sensitivity analysis are discounted at the firm's weighted average cost of capital.

Simulation

Simulation is a third technique used to account for the uncertainty of future cash flows. It is similar to but more sophisticated than the sensitivity analysis previously discussed. In simulation, the parent firm's CFO first identifies key factors which he or she believes are likely to influence the NCFs of a divestment candidate. Next the CFO creates a probability distribution describing the future outcome of each key factor. The CFO finally specifies the impact of each key variable on the NCFs and ultimately the DNPVs. The firm's cost of capital is again used to discount the NCFs. Computer programs are available to assist CFOs in the simulation analysis. After the data has been input and the program run, the computer will estimate NCFs and corresponding DNPVs over the whole range of probabilities. From this distribution, the CFO can determine the expected DNPV and the probability that the actual DNPV will be above or below some critical value. The uncertainty associated with the DNPV can also be determined, as measured by the dispersion of possible DNPV values. It is important to note that this technique is only as good as the input it receives from CFOs, and even then, it cannot make a firm's divestment decision. It does, however, provide a comprehensive evaluation of the divestiture proposal.

38

Forecasting Corporate Financial Distress*

There have been an increasing number of bank-ruptcies. Will your company be one? Will your major customers or suppliers go bankrupt? What warning signs exist and what can be done to avoid corporate failure?

Bankruptcy is the final declaration of the inability of a company to sustain current operations given the current debt obligations. The majority of firms require loans and therefore increase their liabilities during their operations in order to expand, improve or even just survive. The degree to which a firm has current debt in excess of assets is the most common factor in bankruptcy.

If you can predict with reasonable accuracy ahead of time that your company is developing financial distress, you can better protect yourself and your company. The CFO can reap significant rewards and benefits from a *predictive* model for his or her own purposes. For example,

1. *Merger analysis.* The predictive model can help identify potential problems with a merger candidate.

2. *Legal analysis.* Those investing or giving credit to your company may sue for losses incurred. The model can help in your company's defense.

CFOs have to try to build early warning systems to detect the likelihood of bankruptcy. While financial ratio analysis is useful in predicting failure, it is limited because the methodology is basically *univariate*. Each ratio is examined in

*This chapter is adapted from Shim, Jae K., "Predicting Corporate Bankruptcy," Journal of Business Forecasting, Spring, 1992. The author is indebted to Gregory Fong and Thomas McKnight for their computer assistance during this project.

isolation and it is up to the CFO to use professional judgement to determine whether a set of financial ratios are developing into a meaningful analysis.

In order to overcome the shortcomings of financial ratio analysis, it is necessary to combine mutually exclusive ratios into groups to develop a meaningful predictive model. *Regression analysis* and *multiple discriminant analysis (MDA)* are two statistical techniques that have been used to predict the financial strength of a company.

How can you use three different models?

Three predictive bankruptcy models will be illustrated, with the aid of a spreadsheet program. They are the Z-score model, the degree of relative liquidity model, and the Lambda index model.

The *Z-score model* evaluates a combination of several financial ratios to predict the likelihood of future bankruptcy. The model, developed by Edward Altman, uses multiple discriminant analysis to give a relative prediction of whether a firm will go bankrupt within five years. The *degree of relative liquidity model,* on the other hand, evaluates a firm's ability to meet its short-term obligations. This model also uses discriminant analysis by combining several ratios to derive a percentage figure that indicates the firm's ability to meet short-term obligations. Third, the *Lambda index model* evaluates a firm's ability to generate or obtain cash on a short-term basis to meet current obligations and therefore predict solvency.

Lotus 1-2-3 models have been developed to calculate the prediction of bankruptcy using data extracted from *Moody's* and *Standard & Poor's.* Two companies—Navistar International (formerly International Harvester), that continues to struggle in the heavy and medium truck industry, and Best Products, Inc., that has recently declared bankruptcy as of January 1991—have been selected for our study. Financial data has been collected for the period 1979 thru 1990 for both companies.

What is Z-score analysis?

Using a blend of the traditional financial ratios and multiple discriminant analysis, Altman developed a bankruptcy prediction model that produces a Z score as follows:

$$Z = 1.2 \cdot X1 + 1.4 \cdot X2 + 3.3 \cdot X3 + 0.6 \cdot X4 + 0.999 \cdot X5$$

where $X1$ = Working capital/Total assets, $X2$ = Retained earnings/Total assets, $X3$ = Earnings before interest and taxes (EBIT)/Total assets, $X4$ = Market value of equity/Book value of debt, and $X5$ = Sales/Total assets.

Altman established the following guideline for classifying firms:

Z Score	Probability of Short-Term Illiquidity
1.8 or less	Very high
1.81 – 2.99	Not sure
3.0 or higher	Unlikely

The Z score is about 90% accurate in forecasting business failure one year in the future and about 80% accurate in forecasting it two years in the future. With the many important changes in reporting standards since the late 1960s, the Z-Score model is somewhat out of date. A second-generation model known as *zeta analysis* adjusts for these changes, primarily the capitalization of financial leases. The resulting zeta discriminant model is extremely accurate for up to 5 years before failure. This analysis is proprietary, so the exact weights for the model's seven variables cannot be specified here. The new study resulted in the following variables explaining corporate failure.

$X1$ = Return on Assets. Earnings before interest and taxes to total assets.

$X2$ = Stability of earnings. Measure by the "normalized measure of the standard error of estimate around a 10-year trend in $X1$."

X3 = Debt service. Earnings before interest and taxes to total interest payments.

X4 = Cumulative profitability. Retained earnings to total assets.

X5 = Liquidity. Current assets to current liabilities.

X6 = Capitalization. Equity to total capital.

X7 = Size measured by the firm's total assets.

Figure 38–1 shows a Lotus 1-2-3 spreadsheet of the 12-year (1979 to 1990) financial history and the Z scores of Navistar International. Figure 38–2 displays a Z-score chart for the company. The graph shows that Navistar International performed at the edge of the ignorance zone (unsure area), for the year 1979. Since 1980, the company started signalling a sign of failure. However, by selling stock and assets, the firm managed to survive. Since 1983, the company showed an improvement in its Z scores, although the firm continually scored in the danger zone.

The 1990 Z score of 1.60 is in the high probability range of <1.81, and yet it is above the firm's norm or average over the past decade. Based on this assumption, it seems unlikely that Navistar will go bankrupt by 1992. If their financial position erodes below the firm's norm, the prediction for beyond 1992 might change. If the 1991 Z score increases over 1989 and 1990, it may be indicating that Navistar is improving its financial position and becoming a more viable company. Because Navistar is a struggling company, its securities might be undervalued. If they are undervalued and an improvement in the Z score indicates a turning point, this may be a positive signal.

Best Products, Inc. has had a Z score in the 2.44 to 2.98 range from 1984 to 1988. The strong decline in 1989 may have correctly indicated the pending bankruptcy of Best in January 1991. (See Figures 38–3 and 38–4.)

How does the degree of relative liquidity (DRL) model work?

The DRL has been proposed as an alternative method for measuring the liquidity of a small

FIGURE 38-1 NAVISTAR INTERNATIONAL (NYSE-NAV) FORMERLY, INTERNATIONAL HARVESTOR Z SCORE DATA

			Balance Sheet				
Year	Cur Asts	Total Asts	Current Liab	Total Liab	Retained Erngs	Net Worth	Wrkng Captl
	Graph CA	TA	CL	TL	RE	NW	WC
1979	3266	5247	1873	3048	1505	2199	1393
1980	3427	5843	2433	3947	1024	1896	994
1981	2672	5346	1808	3864	600	1482	864
1982	1656	3699	1135	3665	-1078	34	521
1983	1388	3362	1367	3119	-1487	243	21
1984	1412	3249	1257	2947	-1537	302	155
1985	1101	2406	988	2364	-1894	42	113
1986	698	1925	797	1809	-1889	53	-100
1987	785	1902	836	1259	-1743	643	-51
1988	1280	4037	1126	1580	150	866	154
1989	986	3609	761	1257	175	914	225
1990	2663	3795	1579	2980	81	815	1084

FIGURE 38-1 (cont.)

Income S	Stk Data		Calculations						Misc Graph Values		Year
		Market Val	WC/ TA	RE/ TA	EBIT/ TA	MKT/ TL	SALES/ TA	Z Score	TOP GRAY	BOTTOM GRAY	
SALES	EBIT	MKT						A	B	C	X
SALES	EBIT										
8426	719	1122	0.2655	0.2868	0.1370	0.3681	1.6059	3.00	2.99	1.81	1979
6000	-402	1147	0.1701	0.1753	-0.0688	0.2906	1.0269	1.42	2.99	1.81	1980
7018	-16	376	0.1616	0.1122	-0.0030	0.0973	1.3128	1.71	2.99	1.81	1981
4322	-1274	151	0.1408	-0.2914	-0.3444	0.0412	1.1684	-0.18	2.99	1.81	1982
3600	-231	835	0.0062	-0.4423	-0.0687	0.2677	1.0708	0.39	2.99	1.81	1983
4861	120	575	0.0477	-0.4731	0.0369	0.1951	1.4962	1.13	2.99	1.81	1984
3508	247.1	570	0.0470	-0.7872	0.1027	0.2411	1.4580	0.89	2.99	1.81	1985
3357	163	441	-0.0517	-0.9813	0.0846	0.2436	1.7436	0.73	2.99	1.81	1986
3530	219	1011	-0.0267	-0.9162	0.1153	0.8026	1.8558	1.40	2.99	1.81	1987
4082	451	1016	0.0381	0.0372	0.1117	0.6430	1.0111	1.86	2.99	1.81	1988
4241	303	1269	0.0623	0.0485	0.0840	1.0095	1.1751	2.20	2.99	1.81	1989
3854	111	563	0.2856	0.0213	0.0292	0.1888	1.0155	1.60	2.99	1.81	1990

FIGURE 38-2 ALTMAN'S Z SCORE

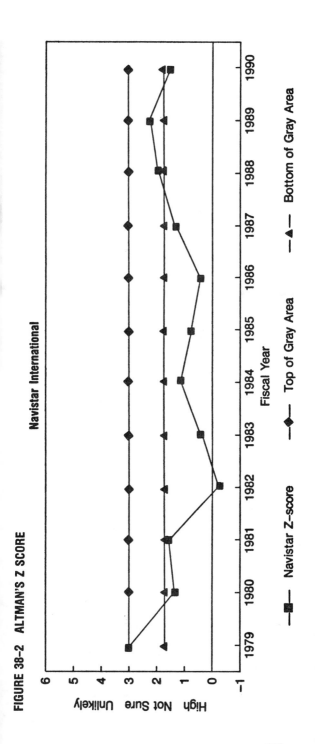

Navistar International

—■— Navistar Z-score   —◆— Top of Gray Area   —▲— Bottom of Gray Area

FIGURE 38-3 BEST PRODUCTS, INC. Z SCORE DATA

				Balance Sheet				
Year	Cur Asts	Total Asts	Current Liab	Total Liab	Retained Erngs	Net Worth	Wrkng Captl
	Graph CA	TA	CL	TL	RE	NW	WC
1984	745228	1202138	468590	787135	186486	415003	276638
1985	723684	1178424	443752	759278	193568	419146	279932
1986	840686	1331975	529690	916579	189306	415396	310996
1987	816853	1265637	400403	878479	160455	387158	416450
1988	811314	1239860	426065	836956	190960	402904	385249
1989	877937	1735595	738837	1646302	39293	89293	139100
1990	583773	1438208	412732	1366974	−14516	71234	171041

FIGURE 38-3 (cont.)

Income St		Stk Data	Calculations					Z Score	Misc Graph Values		Year
		Market Val	WC/TA	RE/TA	EBIT/TA	MKT/TL	SALES/TA		TOP GRAY	BOTTOM GRAY	
SALES	EBIT	MKT						A	B	C	X
2081328	106952	319048	0.2301	0.1551	0.0890	0.4053	1.7314	2.76	2.99	1.81	1984
2252656	66705	407604	0.2375	0.1643	0.0566	0.5368	1.9116	2.93	2.99	1.81	1985
2234768	47271	253041	0.2335	0.1421	0.0355	0.2761	1.6778	2.44	2.99	1.81	1986
2142118	25372	202988	0.3290	0.1268	0.0200	0.2311	1.6925	2.47	2.99	1.81	1987
2066589	93226	672300	0.3107	0.1540	0.0752	0.8033	1.6668	2.98	2.99	1.81	1988
809457	96440	672300	0.0801	0.0226	0.0556	0.4084	0.4664	1.02	2.99	1.81	1989
2094570	73512	672300	0.1189	−0.0101	0.0511	0.4918	1.4564	2.05	2.99	1.81	1990

FIGURE 38-4   Z SCORE

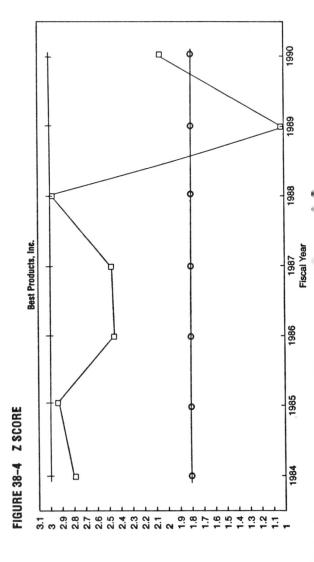

Best Products, Inc.

Fiscal Year

firm and can have significant applications for larger companies. It has been compared to the two common liquidity ratios, the *current* and *acid-test* (or *quick*) *ratios,* which are often used to evaluate the liquidity of a firm. However, under certain circumstances, these two ratios sometimes provide incomplete and often misleading indications of a firm's ability to meet its short-term obligations and may be opposite to the trend at hand. A logical approach to evaluating several liquidity measures simultaneously is to consider how appropriately each measure responds to changes relative to direction and degree of sensitivity. Examples where the current or acid-test ratio may give misleading indications are:

• *Current.* An obsolete or slow-moving inventory and uncollectible accounts receivable may distort this ratio.

• *Acid-test.* Uncollectible receivables and the exclusion of inventories can provide an incomplete picture.

The DRL represents the percentage of a firm's cash expenditure requirements which could be secured from beginning working capital and from cash generated through the normal operating process. An emphasis is placed upon the availability of cash sources relative to cash needs, omitting sources and uses of cash such as:

• Capital expenditures and sale of fixed assets.

• Sale and extinguishment of capital stock.

• Receipt and repayment of long-term borrowings.

• Investments and liquidations in marketable securities and bonds.

The DRL is calculated by dividing the total cash potential by the expected cash expenditures. In equation form:

$$\text{DRL} = \frac{\text{TCP}}{\text{E}} \quad \text{or} \quad \frac{\text{WC} + (\text{OT} \times \text{SVI})}{\text{NSV} - [(\text{NI} + \text{NON}) + \text{WCC}]}$$

where TCP = Total cash potential, E = Cash expenditures for normal operations, WC = Beginning working capital (Beginning current assets − Beginning current liabilities), OT = Operating turnover, or Sales/(Accounts receivable + Inventory × Sales/cost of sales), SVI = Sales value of inventory (Inventory at cost × Sales/cost of sales), NSV = Net sales values, NI = Net income, NON = Noncash expenditures (such as depreciation and amortization), and WCC = Change in working capital.

If the DRL ratio is greater than 1.00 (or 100%), the firm can meet its current obligations for the period and have *some* net working capital available at the end of the period. If the DRL is less than 1.00, the firm should seek outside working capital financing before the end of the period.

The DRL may be derived by dividing the total cash potential (TCP) by expected cash expenditures (E) in the operating period. The TCP is the sum of initial cash potential and the cash potential from normal operations. The initial cash potential is reflected in the beginning working capital (WC) assuming reported values can be realized in cash. The cash potential from operations can be determined by multiplying the operating turnover rate (OT) by the sales of value of existing finished goods inventory (SVI). The operating turnover rate (OT) reflects the number of times the sales value of finished goods inventory (at retail) and accounts receivables (net of uncollectibles) is converted into cash in an operating period. The sales value of finished goods inventory (SVI) is the adjustment of inventory at cost to retail value.

The expected cash expenditures (E) are derived by subtracting cash flow from operations from net sales (NSV). Cash flow from operations can be derived by accrual net income (NI) plus noncash expenses (NON) plus the change in working capital (WCC).

Application

The DRL is calculated for the prior 12 years for Navistar International (see Figures 38–5 and 38–6). The results show a rather bleak liquidity

FIGURE 38-5 NAVISTAR INTERNATIONAL (NYSE-NAV) FORMERLY, INTERNATIONAL HARVESTOR DRL DATA

	Balance Sheet						Income Statement			
	ACCTS. REC.	INVENTORY	CURRENT ASSETS	CURRENT LIAB.	ENDING W.C.	BEGINNING W.C.	N.S.V.	COST OF SALES	NET INCOME	NON-CASH EXPENSES
YEAR	AR	INV	CA	CL	E-WC	B-WC	NSV	COS	NI	NON
1979	806	2343	3266	1873	1393	1210	8392	6904	370	127
1980	769	2332	3427	2480	947	1393	6312	5700	-397	130
1981	555	1634	2672	1846	826	947	6298	5750	-351	144
1982	306	759	1768	1135	633	826	4292	4150	-1738	149
1983	255	619	1388	1366	22	633	3601	3325	-485	131
1984	226	693	1412	1257	155	22	3382	2934	-55	100
1985	133	334	1101	988	113	155	3508	3084	-364	41
1986	111	293	680	797	-117	113	3357	3009	2	40
1987	114	266	785	836	-51	-117	3530	3054	33	41
1988	376	316	1280	1126	154	-51	4080	3574	244	49
1989	1629	336	2965	1731	1234	154	4023	3637	87	60
1990	1627	343	2663	1579	1084	1234	3854	3376	-11	66

FIGURE 38-5 (cont.)

Calculations | | | | | | | Graph Values

OPER. TURNOVER OT =	SALES VALUE OF INVENT. SVI =	OPERATIONS CASH POTENTIAL OCP =	CHANGE WORKING CAPITAL WCC =	TOTAL CASH POTENTIAL TCP =	EXPENDITURES E =	DEGREE OF RELATIVE LIQUIDITY DRL =	BASE
2.3	2848	6541	183	7751	7712	1.005	1.000
1.9	2582	4864	-446	6257	7025	0.891	1.000
2.7	1790	4807	-121	5754	6626	0.868	1.000
3.9	785	3088	-193	3914	6074	0.644	1.000
3.9	670	2609	-611	3242	4566	0.710	1.000
3.3	799	2636	133	2658	3204	0.830	1.000
6.8	380	2598	-42	2753	3873	0.711	1.000
7.7	327	2506	-230	2619	3545	0.739	1.000
8.4	307	2575	66	2458	3390	0.725	1.000
5.5	361	1998	205	1947	3582	0.543	1.000
2.0	372	747	1080	901	2796	0.322	1.000
1.9	392	748	-150	1982	3949	0.502	1.000

CALCULATIONS:

$OT = NSV/(AR + INV \cdot NSV/COS)$ $WCC = E-WC - B-WC$ $E = NSV - (NI + NON) - WCC$

$SVI = INV \cdot NSV/COS$ $TCP = B-WC + (OT \cdot SVI)$ $DRL = TCP/E$

$OCP = OT \cdot SVI$

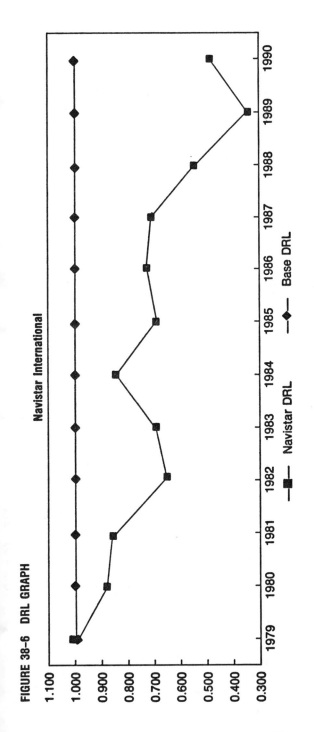

FIGURE 38-6 DRL GRAPH

Navistar International

Navistar DRL   Base DRL

position with all figures under the 1.00 zone except 1979. This indicates that Navistar has not been able to generate the working capital internally through operations, rather they have had to continually seek outside working capital sources since 1979.

Best Products, Inc., has had a DRL which has remained above 1.000 since 1985, peaking at 1.194 in 1987. (See Figures 38–7 and 38–8.) However, its DRL has been dropping since 1987 and took a significant plunge in 1990 down to 1.039. Although the DRL is above 1.000, the significant drop may have indicated a worsening situation for Best and predicted their bankruptcy in January 1991.

Based on just two companies, the DRL appears to have shown that the change in relative liquidity than the absolute measure is more relevant in predicting corporate bankruptcy.

What is the Lambda index?

The *Lambda index* is a ratio which focuses on two relevant components of liquidity—short-term cash balances and available credit to gauge the probability that a firm will become insolvent. The index measures the probability of a company going bankrupt and it includes the key aspect of uncertainty in cash-flow measurement by utilizing a sample standard deviation. In consequence, it can be used like a *z* value from the standard normal distribution table.

For a given period, Lambda is the sum of a company's initial liquid reserve and net flow of funds divided by the uncertainty associated with the flows:

$$\frac{\text{Initial liquid reserve} + \text{Total anticipated}}{\text{net cash flow during the analysis horizon}}$$
$$\text{Uncertainty about net cash flow}$$
$$\text{during the analysis horizon}$$

Net cash flow is the balance of cash receipts less cash outlays. Unused lines of credit, short-term investments, and cash balances make up the initial liquid reserve. The uncertainty is based on

FIGURE 38-7 BEST PRODUCTS, INC. DRL DATA

| | | Balance Sheet | | | | | | | Income Statement | | |
| | ACCTS. REC. | INVENTORY | CURRENT ASSETS | CURRENT LIAB. | ENDING W.C. | BEGINNING W.C. | N.S.V. | COST OF SALES | NET INCOME | NON-CASH EXPENSES |
YEAR	AR	INV	CA	CL	E-WC	B-WC	NSV	COS	NI	NON
1985	46746	658880	723684	443752	279932	276638	2252656	1692568	13609	65764
1986	45050	757051	840686	529690	310996	279932	2234768	1685198	2223	67341
1987	29670	649162	816853	400403	416450	310996	2142118	1592984	−25593	66647
1988	28571	670236	811314	426065	385249	416450	2066589	1499641	30527	38544
1989	32614	579651	877937	738837	139100	385249	809457	575467	39297	13216
1990	32213	509617	583773	412732	171041	139100	2094570	1529598	−53809	56008

FIGURE 38-7 (cont.)

Calculations

OPER. TURNOVER	SALES VALUE OF INVENT.	OPERATIONS CASH POTENTIAL	CHANGE WORKING CAPITAL	TOTAL CASH POTENTIAL	EXPENDITURES	DEGREE OF RELATIVE LIQUIDITY	BASE
OT =	SVI =	OCP =	WCC =	TCP =	E =	DRL =	
2.4	876910	2138650	3294	2415288	2169989	1.113	1.000
2.1	1003937	2138793	31064	2418725	2134140	1.133	1.000
2.4	872941	2071704	105454	2382700	1995610	1.194	1.000
2.2	923623	2004580	-31201	2421030	2028719	1.193	1.000
1.0	815342	778324	-246149	1163573	1003093	1.160	1.000
2.9	697849	2002150	31941	2141250	2060430	1.039	1.000

Graph Values

CALCULATIONS: OT = NSV / (AR + INV · NSV/COS)
SVI = INV · NSV/COS
OCP = OT · SVI
WCC = E - WC - B - WC
TCP = B - WC + (OT · SVI)
E = NSV - (NI + NON) - WCC
DRL = TCP / E
NON-CASH EXPENSES INCLUDE DEPRECIATION ONLY.

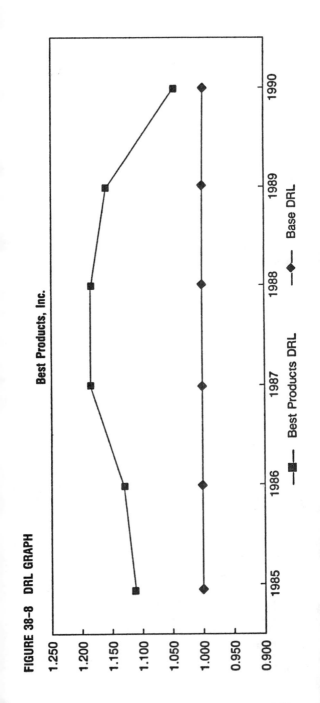

FIGURE 38-8   DRL GRAPH

Best Products, Inc.

— ■ — Best Products DRL   — ◆ — Base DRL

the standard deviation of net cash flow. In order to calculate and utilize the Lambda index, a cash forecast should be used.

A worksheet can be prepared to contain twelve line items in the following order from top to bottom: short-term line of credit, beginning liquid assets, adjustments, initial liquid reserve, total sources of funds, total uses of funds, ending liquid assets, ending liquid reserve, standard deviation, the Lambda index, and finally, additional cash required to maintain a Lambda of three.

A firm's short-term line of credit may not change during the course of the forecast (i.e., 1 year), which simplifies calculations. Liquid assets, by definition, include marketable securities and cash at the start of the forecast summary. By having an adjustments line item one can see the result of decreasing or increasing the cash level. The initial liquid reserve is the total short-term line of credit with any adjustments. The total sources and uses of funds are forecasts by company management, resulting in a positive or negative net cash flow. The Lambda value should rise if a firm's short-term line of credit doesn't change and it has a positive net cash flow. Ending liquid assets is the sum of three values: beginning liquid assets, adjustments, and net cash flow. Ending liquid reserve is the sum of two values: short-term line of credit and ending liquid assets. The standard deviation is drawn from the net cash flows from period to period. Next, the Lambda index is calculated by dividing the ending liquid reserve by the standard deviation.

And finally, the last line item is additional cash needed to hold a Lambda of three. A negative number here indicates a Lambda value of greater than three and hence, a safer firm financially. A high negative value here, assuming that management is confident of its forecasts, may point out that those funds could be better utilized somewhere else.

Once an index value has been determined using the equation, the pertinent odds can be found by referencing a standard normal distribution table (see Table 38–1). For example, a Lambda of

TABLE 38-1 STANDARD NORMAL DISTRIBUTION TABLE

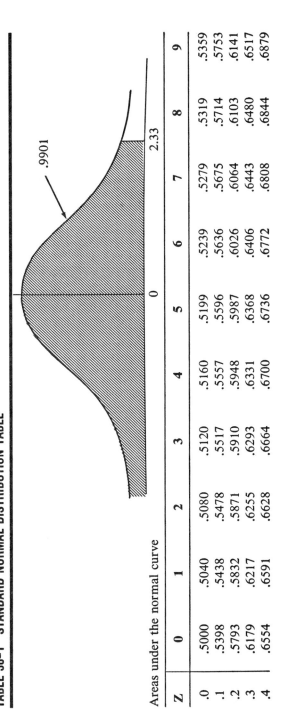

Areas under the normal curve

Z	0	1	2	3	4	5	6	7	8	9
.0	.5000	.5040	.5080	.5120	.5160	.5199	.5239	.5279	.5319	.5359
.1	.5398	.5438	.5478	.5517	.5557	.5596	.5636	.5675	.5714	.5753
.2	.5793	.5832	.5871	.5910	.5948	.5987	.6026	.6064	.6103	.6141
.3	.6179	.6217	.6255	.6293	.6331	.6368	.6406	.6443	.6480	.6517
.4	.6554	.6591	.6628	.6664	.6700	.6736	.6772	.6808	.6844	.6879

TABLE 38–1 (*cont.*)

Z	0	1	2	3	4	5	6	7	8	9
.5	.6915	.6950	.6985	.7019	.7054	.7088	.7123	.7157	.7190	.7224
.6	.7257	.7291	.7324	.7357	.7389	.7422	.7454	.7486	.7517	.7549
.7	.7580	.7611	.7642	.7673	.7703	.7734	.7764	.7794	.7823	.7852
.8	.7881	.7910	.7939	.7967	.7995	.8023	.8051	.8078	.8106	.8133
.9	.8159	.8186	.8212	.8238	.8264	.8289	.8315	.8340	.8365	.8389
1.0	.8413	.8438	.8461	.8485	.8508	.8531	.8554	.8577	.8599	.8621
1.1	.8643	.8665	.8686	.8708	.8729	.8749	.8770	.8790	.8810	.8830
1.2	.8849	.8869	.8888	.8907	.8925	.8944	.8962	.8980	.8997	.9015
1.3	.9032	.9049	.9066	.9082	.9099	.9115	.9131	.9147	.9162	.9177
1.4	.9192	.9207	.9222	.9236	.9251	.9265	.9278	.9292	.9306	.9319
1.5	.9332	.9345	.9357	.9370	.9382	.9394	.9406	.9418	.9430	.9441
1.6	.9452	.9463	.9474	.9484	.9495	.9505	.9515	.9525	.9535	.9545
1.7	.9554	.9564	.9573	.9582	.9591	.9599	.9608	.9616	.9625	.9633
1.8	.9641	.9648	.9656	.9664	.9671	.9678	.9686	.9693	.9700	.9706

TABLE 38-1 (cont.)

Z	0	1	2	3	4	5	6	7	8	9
1.9	.9713	.9719	.9726	.9732	.9738	.9744	.9750	.9756	.9762	.9767
2.0	.9772	.9778	.9783	.9788	.9793	.9798	.9803	.9808	.9812	.9817
2.1	.9821	.9826	.9830	.9834	.9838	.9842	.9846	.9850	.9854	.9857
2.2	.9861	.9864	.9868	.9871	.9874	.9878	.9881	.9884	.9887	.9890
2.3	.9893	.9896	.9898	.9901	.9904	.9906	.9909	.9911	.9913	.9916
2.4	.9918	.9920	.9922	.9925	.9927	.9929	.9931	.9932	.9934	.9936
2.5	.9938	.9940	.9941	.9943	.9945	.9946	.9948	.9949	.9951	.9952
2.6	.9953	.9955	.9956	.9957	.9959	.9960	.9961	.9962	.9963	.9964
2.7	.9965	.9966	.9967	.9968	.9969	.9970	.9971	.9972	.9973	.9974
2.8	.9974	.9975	.9976	.9977	.9977	.9978	.9979	.9979	.9980	.9981
2.9	.9981	.9982	.9982	.9983	.9984	.9984	.9985	.9985	.9986	.9986
3.	.9987	.9990	.9993	.9995	.9997	.9998	.9998	.9999	.9999	1.0000

2.33 has a value of .9901 from the table, which says that there is a 99% chance that problems won't occur and a 1% chance that they will.

Generally, a firm with a Lambda value of 9 or higher is financially healthy. And firms with a Lambda of 15 or more are considered very safe. A Lambda value of 3 translates to one chance in a thousand that necessary cash outlays will exceed available cash on hand. A Lambda value of 3.9 puts the probability at one in twenty thousand. A low Lambda of 1.64 is equivalent to a one in twenty chance of required disbursements exceeding available cash on hand. A work sheet that keeps a running tally of Lambda shows how changes in the financial picture affect future cash balances.

There are a number of positive aspects to using the Lambda index. The Lambda index focuses on the key factors of liquidity, available unused credit and cash flows, which by contrast are ignored by standard cash forecasts. Further, by including the standard deviation of cash flows, Lambda penalizes irregular cash flows. The result of higher changes in cash flows would be a lower Lambda.

A drawback to Lambda, however, is the fact that it's significantly tied to revenue forecasts, which at times can be suspect depending on the time horizon and the industry involved. A strong Lambda doesn't carry much weight if a firm isn't confident about its forecast.

Application

Figures 38–9 and 38–10 show that Navistar's Lambda index has remained very low since 1979, with a low point of 2.16 in 1982 to a high of 5.98 in 1989. Its Lambda value had increased from 1986 through 1989, however it dropped again in 1990. Using a Lambda value of 9 as a bench mark for what is considered a healthy firm, Navistar has been in trouble for some time.

Best Product's Lambda index was far lower than that of Navistar, with a low of 2.39 in 1986 and a high of 4.52 in 1989. Its Lambda index also

Year	1979	1980	1981	1982	1983	1984	1985	1986	1987	1988	1989	1990
Short-term line of credit	100000	100000	100000	100000	100000	100000	100000	100000	100000	100000	100000	100000
Beginning liquid assets	27256	25205	137103	393879	259452	391619	412970	323220	217745	383900	562400	674000
Adjustments												
Initial liquid reserve	127256	125205	237103	493879	359452	491619	512970	423220	317745	483900	662400	774000
Total sources of funds	-2051	111898	256776	-134427	132167	21351	-89750	-105475	166155	178500	111600	-86000
Total uses of funds												
Net cash flow	-2051	111898	256776	-134427	132167	21351	-89750	-105475	166155	178500	111600	-86000
Ending liquid assets, short-term debt, and adjustments (net)	25205	137103	393879	259452	391619	412970	323220	217745	383900	562400	674000	588000
Ending liquid reserve (net)	125205	237103	493879	359452	491619	512970	423220	317745	483900	662400	774000	688000
Standard deviation	NA	80574	129721	166384	147856	133909	135398	135804	135604	135181	129435	130297
Calculated Lambda index	NA	2.94	3.81	2.16	3.32	3.83	3.13	2.34	3.57	4.90	5.98	5.28
Additional cash required (remaining) to maintain Lambda of 3.0	NA	4619	-104716	139701	-48050	-111243	-17027	89666	-77087	-256856	-385696	-297108
Very Safe		15.00	15.00	15.00	15.00	15.00	15.00	15.00	15.00	15.00	15.00	15.00
Healthy		9.00	9.00	9.00	9.00	9.00	9.00	9.00	9.00	9.00	9.00	9.00
Slight - 1 in 20000		3.90	3.90	3.90	3.90	3.90	3.90	3.90	3.90	3.90	3.90	3.90
Low - 1 in 20		1.64	1.64	1.64	1.64	1.64	1.64	1.64	1.64	1.64	1.64	1.64

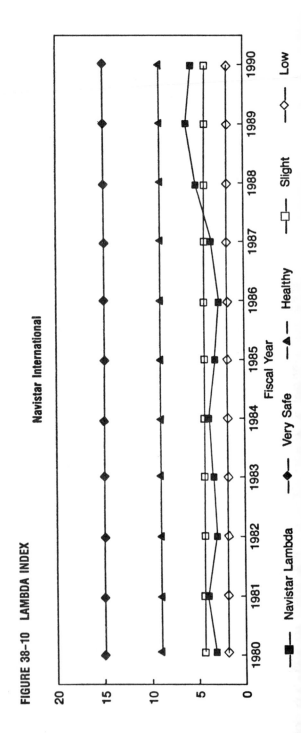

FIGURE 38-10 LAMBDA INDEX

Navistar International

Fiscal Year

— Navistar Lambda — Very Safe — Healthy — Slight — Low

dropped in 1990, reaching a level of .80. This is not surprising, since in January of 1991, Best filed for bankruptcy protection. (See Figures 38–11 and 38–12.)

Table 38–2 summarizes guidelines for classifying firms under the three models.

A word of Caution: The Z score may be used by different people for varying uses. The Z score offers an excellent measure of the probability of a firm's insolvency, but like any tool, one must use it with care and skill. The Z score should be evaluated over a number of years and should not be the sole basis of evaluation.

The Z score may also be used to compare the stability of different firms. Care should also be exercised when the Z-score is used for this purpose. The firms must be in the same market offering the same, if not very similar products. In addition, the measure must be taken across the same period of years. These similarities are requirements in order to eliminate external environmental factors which would be reflected in the score.

The DRL is a more comprehensive measure of liquidity than the current ratio or the acid-test ratio. However, like the current and the acid-test ratios, the DRL is a relative measure and should be used only in relation to either the firm's own historical DRL or to those of other businesses. Since the DRL does not incorporate the timing and variances in cash flows (assumed to be uniform and continuous), comparing the DRL of two dissimilar firms is hazardous. It is important to note that the DRL does correctly identify an improved or deteriorated liquidity position, however, it does not suggest explicit causes of change. On the other hand, the DRL does provide a basis from which to pursue an analysis and interpretation of those causes of change because the derivation of the DRL requires input for all the factors which are relevant to liquidity position.

As with DRL, the Lambda index is a method for gauging a firm's liquidity, but one should consider a firm's historical background and

FIGURE 38-11 BEST PRODUCTS, INC. LAMBDA INDEX

Year	1985	1986	1987	1988	1989	1990
Short-term line of credit	100000	100000	100000	100000	100000	100000
Beginning liquid assets	62933	4915	15126	103197	110243	253278
Adjustments						
Initial liquid reserve	162933	104915	115126	203197	210243	353278
Total sources of funds	-58018	10211	88071	7046	143035	-244843
Total uses of funds						
Net cash flow	-58018	10211	88071	7046	143035	-244843
Ending liquid assets, short-term debt, and adjustments (net)	4915	15126	103197	110243	253278	8435
Ending liquid reserve	104915	115126	203197	210243	353278	108435
Standard deviation	NA	48245	73097	59769	78245	135047
Calculated Lambda index	NA	2.39	2.78	3.52	4.52	0.80
Additional cash required (remaining) to maintain Lambda of 3.0	NA	29610	16095	-30936	-118542	296706
Very Safe		15.00	15.00	15.00	15.00	15.00
Healthy		9.00	9.00	9.00	9.00	9.00
Slight - 1 in 20000		3.90	3.90	3.90	3.90	3.90
Low - 1 in 20		1.64	1.64	1.64	1.64	1.64

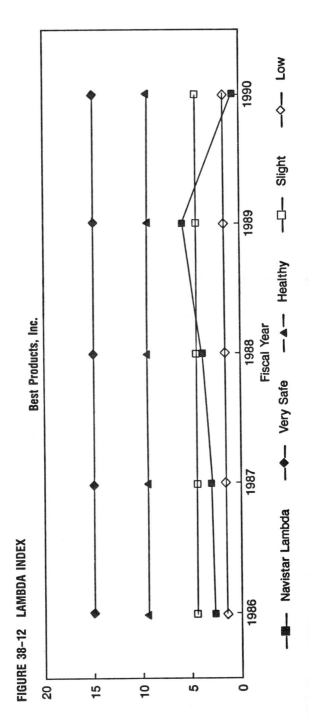

FIGURE 38-12 LAMBDA INDEX

Best Products, Inc.

TABLE 38–2   CLASSIFYING GUIDELINES UNDER THE THREE MODELS

Model	Guidelines
(1) Z-Score Model	
Z Score	*Probability of Short-Term Illiquidity*
1.8 or less	Very high
1.81–2.99	Not sure
3.0 or higher	Unlikely
(2) Degree of Relative Liquidity (DRL) Model	
DRL Score	*Probability of Short-Term Illiquidity*
Less than 1.00	Very high
Higher than 1.00	Unlikely
(3) Lambda Index	
Lambda Score	*Probability of Short-Term Illiquidity*
1.64	1 in 20
3.90	1 in 20,000
9.00 or higher	Unlikely

always use common sense in evaluating any calculated value. A weak point of this model is that in order to calculate the index, forecasted figures must be used, making the final Lambda value somewhat suspect in some cases.

39

Failure and Reorganization

When a company fails, it can either be reorganized or dissolved. There are a number of ways for business failure to occur including a poor rate of return, technical insolvency, or bankruptcy.

According to law, failure of a company can either be technical insolvency or bankruptcy. Creditors have recourse against the company's assets. Some reasons for business failure include poor management, lawsuit, overexpansion, an economic downturn affecting the company and/or industry, and catastrophe.

• *Deficient Rate of Return.* A company may fail if its rate of return is negative or very low. If operating losses exist, the company may not be able to pay its debt. A negative return will cause a decline in the market price of stock. If a company's return is less than its cost of capital, it is losing money. However, a poor return, in and of itself, does not constitute legal evidence of failure.

• *Technical Insolvency.* Technical insolvency means that the company cannot satisfy current obligations when due even if total assets exceed total liabilities.

• *Bankruptcy.* In bankruptcy, liabilities exceed the fair market value of assets. There is a negative real net worth.

How does a voluntary settlement work?

By voluntarily settling out of court with creditors, the company saves the costs associated with bankruptcy. The settlement allows the company to either continue or be liquidated and is initiated to enable the debtor firm to recover some of its investment.

A creditor committee may opt to allow the business to operate if it is expected that the company will recover. Creditors may also keep doing business with the firm. In sustaining the company's existence, there may be:

- An extension.
- A composition.
- Creditor control.
- Integration of each of the above.

What is an extension?

In an *extension,* creditors will receive the amounts owed to them but over an extended time period. Purchases are made with cash. Creditors may agree not only to extend the payment date but also to subordinate their claims to current debt for suppliers giving credit in the extension period. The creditors are hopeful that the debtor will be able to resolve some of its problems.

The creditor committee may insist upon certain controls such as legal control over the company's assets or common stock, obtaining collateral, and approving all cash payments.

If certain creditors dissent to the agreement, they may be paid off to prevent them from declaring the firm bankrupt.

How does a composition come about?

In a *composition,* a voluntary reduction of the balance the debtor owes the creditor is made. The creditor receives a percent of the obligation in *full* satisfaction of the debt. The arrangement allows the debtor to remain in business. The creditor may work with the debtor in resolving the company's financial problems, since a stable customer may ensue. The advantages of a composition are the elimination of court costs and the stigma of a bankrupt company.

If there are dissenting stockholders, they may be paid in full or they may be permitted to recover a higher percentage so that they do not force the business to close.

An extension or composition is feasible if the creditors expect that the debtor will recover.

What is creditor control?

A committee of creditors may take control of the company if they are not satisfied with management. They will operate the business until they are paid. Once paid, the creditors may recommend new management replace the old before further credit is granted.

How does integration work?

In an *integration,* the company and its creditors negotiate a plan involving a combination of extension, composition, and creditor control. For example, the agreement may stipulate a 20% cash payment of the balance owed plus five future payments of 10% each, typically in notes. Therefore, the total payment is 70%.

The advantages of a negotiated settlement are:

• They are easier to implement and less formal than bankruptcy proceedings.

• They cost less, especially in attorney fees.

The disadvantages of a negotiated settlement are:

• If the troubled debtor continues to control its affairs, there may be a further decline in asset values. However, creditor controls can provide some protection.

• Unrealistic small creditors may drain the negotiating process.

What is involved in a reorganization?

If a voluntary settlement does not occur, the company may be placed into bankruptcy by its creditors. The bankruptcy proceeding may either reorganize or liquidate the business.

Bankruptcy occurs when the company is unable to pay its bills or when liabilities exceed the fair market value of its assets. Here, legal bankruptcy may be declared. A company may file for reorganization under which it will formulate a plan for continued existence.

Chapter 7 of the Bankruptcy Reform Act of 1978 outlines the procedures in liquidation. This chapter applies when reorganization is not feasible. Chapter 11 provides the steps of reorganizing a failed business.

The two types of reorganization petitions are:

1. *Voluntary.* The company requests its own reorganization. It does not have to be insolvent to file for it.

2. *Involuntary.* Creditors file for an involuntary reorganization of the company. An involuntary petition must set forth either that the debtor firm is not paying debts when due or that a creditor or another party has taken custody or other control over the debtor's assets. In general, most of the creditors or claims must support the petition.

There are the following five steps in a reorganization:

1. A reorganization petition is filed under Chapter 11 in court.

2. A judge approves the petition and either appoints a trustee or permits the creditors to elect one to handle the sale of the assets.

3. The trustee specifies a fair plan of reorganization to the court.

4. The plan is given to the creditors and stockholders to approve.

5. The debtor pays the expenses associated with the reorganization proceedings.

The trustee in a reorganization values the business, recapitalizes the company, and exchanges outstanding debts for new securities.

What is involved in valuing the company?

In valuing the business, the trustee estimates its liquidation value and compares it to its value as a going concern. Liquidation is suggested when the liquidation value exceeds the continuity value. If the company is more valuable when operating, reorganization is justified. The value of the reorganized business must take into account expected future earnings. The going concern value represents the discounted value of future earnings.

EXAMPLE 1

A company's petition for reorganization was filed under Chapter 11. The trustee computed the firm's liquidation value net of expenses as $4.5 million. The trustee estimated that the reorganized business will throw off $530,000 in annual earnings. The cost of capital is 10%. Assuming the earnings continue indefinitely, the value of the business as a going concern is:

$$\$530,000/.10 = \$5,300,000$$

Since the company's value as a going concern ($5.3 million) exceeds its liquidation value ($4.5 million), reorganization is recommended.

What is recapitalization about?

If the trustee recommends reorganization, a plan must be drawn up. The obligations may be extended or equity securities may be issued in substitution of the debt. Income bonds may be given for the debentures. Income bonds pay interest only if the company has a profit. Recapitalization is the process of exchanging liabilities for other types of liabilities or equity securities. The purpose of recapitalization is to have a mixture of debt and equity that will permit the company to pay its debts and provide a reasonable profit for the owners.

EXAMPLE 2

The current capital structure of Y Corporation is:

Debentures	$1,500,000
Collateral bonds	3,000,000
Preferred stock	800,000
Common stock	2,500,000
Total	$7,800,000

There exists high financial leverage:

$$\frac{\text{Debt}}{\text{Equity}} = \frac{\$4,500,000}{\$3,300,000} = 1.36$$

Assuming the company is deemed to be worth $5 million as a going concern, the trustee can develop a less leveraged capital structure having a total capital of $5 million as:

Debentures	$1,000,000
Collateral bonds	1,000,000

Income bonds	1,500,000
Preferred stock	500,000
Common stock	1,000,000
Total	$5,000,000

The income bond of $1.5 million is similar to equity in appraising financial leverage, since interest is not paid unless there is income. The new debt/equity ratio is safer:

$$\frac{\text{Debt} + \text{Collateral bonds}}{\text{Income bonds} + \text{Preferred stock} + \text{Common stock}} = \frac{\$2,000,000}{\$3,000,000} = 0.67$$

What is the procedure in exchanging obligations?

In exchanging obligations to derive an optimal capital structure, priorities are followed. Senior claims come before junior ones. Senior debt holders receive a claim on new capital equal to their previous claims. The last priority goes to common stockholders in receiving new securities. A debt holder usually receives a combination of different securities. Preferred and common stockholders may receive nothing. Typically, they retain some small ownership. After the exchange, the debt holders may become the company's new owners.

What is liquidation due to bankruptcy?

When a company becomes bankrupt, it may be liquidated under Chapter 7 of the Bankruptcy Reform Act of 1978. The major elements of liquidation are legal considerations, claim priority, and dissolution.

What legal aspects exist in bankruptcy?

When a company is declared bankrupt, creditors have to meet between 10 and 30 days after that declaration. A judge or referee presides over the meeting, and creditors show evidence of their claims. A trustee is appointed by the creditors. The trustee handles the property, liquidates the business, makes payments, keeps records, evaluates the creditors' claims, and provides information of the liquidation process.

Who gets paid first in bankruptcy?

Some claims come before others in bankruptcy. The following ranking order exists:

1. *Secured claims.* Secured creditors receive the value of the pledged assets. If the value of the secured assets does not fully satisfy the claims, the balance reverts to general creditor status.

2. *Bankruptcy administrative costs.* The costs of handling bankruptcy including legal and trustee expenses.

3. *Unsecured salaries and commissions.* These claims are limited to a maximum specified amount per individual and must have been incurred within 90 days of the bankruptcy petition.

4. *Unsecured customer deposit claims.* These claims are limited to a nominal amount.

5. *Taxes.* Unpaid taxes owed to federal, state, and local governments.

6. *General creditor claims.* General creditors do not have specific collateral to support their claims. For example, debentures and accounts payable are unsecured.

7. *Preferred stockholders.*

8. *Common stockholders.*

How is the business dissolved?

After claims have been paid and an accounting of the proceedings made, an application may be filed to *discharge* the bankrupt business. In a *discharge,* the court releases the company from legitimate debts in bankruptcy, with the exception of debts that are immune to discharge. As long as a debtor has not been discharged within the previous 6 years and was not bankrupt because of fraud, the debtor may start a new business.

EXAMPLE 3

The balance sheet of Ace Corporation for the year ended December 31, 19X4, follows:

Balance Sheet

ASSETS	
Current assets	$400,000
Fixed assets	410,000
Total assets	$810,000
LIABILITIES	
Current liabilities	$475,000
Long-term liabilities	250,000
Common stock	175,000
Retained earnings	(90,000)
Total liabilities and stockholders' equity	$810,000

The company's liquidation value is $625,000. Rather than liquidate, there could be a reorganization with an investment of an additional $320,000. The reorganization is expected to generate earnings of $115,000 per year. A multiplier of 7.5 is appropriate. If the $320,000 is obtained, long-term debt holders will receive 40 percent of the common stock in the reorganized business in substitution for their current claims.

If $320,000 of further investment is made, the firm's going-concern value is $862,500 ($7.5 \times $115,000$). The liquidation value is given at $625,000. Since the reorganization value exceeds the liquidation value, reorganization is called for.

EXAMPLE 4

Fixed assets with a book value of $1.5 million were sold for $1.3 million. There are mortgage bonds on the fixed assets amounting to $1.8 million. The proceeds from the collateral sale are insufficient to pay the secured claim. The unsatisfied portion of $500,000 ($1,800,000 − $1,300,000) becomes a general creditor claim.

EXAMPLE 5

Land having a book value of $1.2 million was sold for $800,000. Mortgage bonds on the land are $600,000. The excess of $200,000 will be returned to the trustee to pay other creditors.

EXAMPLE 6

Charles Company is bankrupt. The book and liquidation values follow:

	Book Value	Liquidation Value
Cash	$ 600,000	$ 600,000
Accounts receivable	1,900,000	1,500,000
Inventory	3,700,000	2,100,000
Land	5,000,000	3,200,000
Building	7,800,000	5,300,000
Equipment	6,700,000	2,800,000
Total assets	$25,700,000	$15,500,000

The liabilities and stockholders' equity at the date of liquidation are:

Current liabilities		
Accounts payable	$1,800,000	
Notes payable	900,000	
Accrued taxes	650,000	
Accrued salaries*	450,000	
Total current liabilities		$ 3,800,000
Long-term liabilities		
Mortgage on land	$3,200,000	
First mortgage—building	2,800,000	
Second mortgage— building	2,500,000	
Subordinated debentures	4,800,000	
Total long-term liabilities		13,300,000
Total liabilities		$17,100,000
Stockholders' equity		
Preferred stock	$4,700,000	
Common stock	6,800,000	
Retained earnings	(2,900,000)	
Total stockholders' equity		8,600,000
Total liabilities and stockholders' equity		$25,700,000

*The salary owed each worker is below the specified amount and was incurred within 90 days of the bankruptcy petition.

Expenses of the liquidation including legal costs were 15 percent of the proceeds. The debentures are subordinated only with regard to the two first-mortgage bonds.

The distribution of the proceeds follows:

Proceeds		$15,500,000
Mortgage on land	$3,200,000	
First mortgage—building	2,800,000	
Second mortgage—building	2,500,000	
Liquidation expenses		
(15% × $15,500,000)	2,325,000	
Accrued salaries	450,000	
Accrued taxes	650,000	
Total		11,925,000
Balance		$ 3,575,000

The percent to be paid to general creditors is:

$$\frac{\text{Proceeds balance}}{\text{Total owed}} = \frac{\$3,575,000}{\$7,500,000} = 47.66667\%$$

The balance due general creditors follows:

General Creditors	Owed	Paid
Accounts payable	$1,800,000	$ 858,000
Notes payable	900,000	429,000
Subordinated debentures	4,800,000	2,288,000
Total	$7,500,000	$3,575,000

EXAMPLE 7

The balance sheet of the Oakhurst Company is presented below.

ASSETS
Current assets

Cash	$ 9,000	
Marketable securities	6,000	
Receivables	1,100,000	
Inventory	3,000,000	
Prepaid expenses	4,000	
Total current assets		$4,119,000

Noncurrent assets		
Land	$1,800,000	
Fixed assets	2,000,000	
Total noncurrent assets		3,800,000
Total assets		$7,919,000

LIABILITIES AND STOCKHOLDERS' EQUITY

Current liabilities		
Accounts payable	$ 180,000	
Bank loan payable	900,000	
Accrued salaries	300,000[a]	
Employee benefits payable	70,000[b]	
Customer claims— unsecured	80,000[c]	
Taxes payable	350,000	
Total current liabilities		$1,880,000
Noncurrent liabilities		
First mortgage payable	$1,600,000	
Second mortgage payable	1,100,000	
Subordinated debentures	700,000	
Total noncurrent liabilities		3,400,000
Total liabilities		$5,280,000
Stockholders' equity		
Preferred stock (3,500 shares)	$ 350,000	
Common stock (8,000 shares)	480,000	
Paid-in capital	1,600,000	
Retained earnings	209,000	
Total stockholders' equity		2,639,000
Total liabilities and stockholders' equity		$7,919,000

[a]The salary owed to each worker is below the specified amount and was incurred within 90 days of the bankruptcy petition.
[b]Employee benefits payable have the same limitations as unsecured wages and satisfy for eligibility in bankruptcy distribution.
[c]No customer claim is greater than the nominal amount.

Additional data are as follows:

1. The mortgages apply to the company's total noncurrent assets.

2. The subordinated debentures are subordinated to the bank loan payable. Therefore, they come after the bank loan payable in liquidation.

3. The trustee has sold the company's current assets for $2.1 million and the noncurrent assets for $1.9 million. Therefore, a total of $4 million was received.

4. The business is bankrupt, since the total liabilities of $5.28 million are greater than the $4 million of the fair value of the assets.

Assume that the administration expense for handling the bankrupt company is $900,000. This liability is not reflected in the above balance sheet.

The allocation of the $4 million to the creditors follows.

Proceeds		$4,000,000
Available to secured creditors		
First mortgage—payable from $1,900,000 proceeds of noncurrent assets	$1,600,000	
Second mortgage—payable from balance of proceeds of noncurrent assets	300,000	1,900,000
Balance after secured creditors		$2,100,000
Next priority		
Administrative expenses	$ 900,000	
Accrued salaries	300,000	
Employed benefits payable	70,000	
Customer claims —unsecured	80,000	
Taxes payable	350,000	1,700,000
Proceeds available to general creditors		$ 400,000

Now that the claims on the proceeds from liquidation have been met, general creditors receive the balance on a pro rata basis. The distribution of the $400,000 follows:

General Creditor	Amount	Pro Rata Allocation for Balance to Be Paid
Second-mortgage balance ($1,100,000–$300,000)	$ 800,000	$124,031
Accounts payable	180,000	27,907
Bank loan payable	900,000	248,062*
Subordinated debentures	700,000	0
Total	$2,580,000	$400,000

Since the debentures are subordinated, the bank loan payable must be satisfied in full before any amount can go to the subordinated debentures. The subordinated debenture holders therefore receive nothing.

EXAMPLE 8

Nolan Company is having severe financial problems. Jefferson Bank holds a first mortgage on the plant and has an $800,000 unsecured loan that is already delinquent. The Alto Insurance Company holds $4.7 million of the company's subordinated debentures to the notes payable. Nolan is deciding whether to reorganize the business or declare bankruptcy.

Another company is considering acquiring Nolan Company by offering to take over the mortgage of $7.5 million, pay the past due taxes, and pay $4.38 million for the firm.

Nolan's balance sheet follows:

ASSETS
Current assets	$ 2,800,000
Plant assets	11,700,000
Other assets	3,000,000
Total assets	$17,500,000

LIABILITIES AND STOCKHOLDERS' EQUITY

Current liabilities		
Accounts payable	$ 1,800,000	
Taxes payable	170,000	
Bank note payable	260,000	
Other current liabilities	1,400,000	
Total current liabilities		$ 3,630,000
Noncurrent liabilities		
Mortgage payable	$ 7,500,000	
Subordinated debentures	5,300,000	
Total noncurrent liabilities		12,800,000
Total liabilities		$16,430,000
Stockholders' equity		
Common stock	$ 1,000,000	
Premium on common stock	2,300,000	
Retained earnings	(2,230,000)	
Total stockholders' equity		1,070,000
Total liabilities and stockholders' equity		$17,500,000

The impact of the proposed reorganization on creditor claims is indicated below.

Outstanding obligations		$16,430,000
Claims met through the reorganization		
Mortgage payable	$7,500,000	
Taxes payable	170,000	
Total		7,670,000
Balance of claims		$ 8,760,000

The cash arising from reorganization is given as $4.38 million, which is 50% ($4,380,000/$8,760,000) of the unsatisfied claims.

The distribution to general creditors follows:

General Creditor	Liability Due	50%	Adjusted for Subordination
Bank note payable	$ 260,000	$ 130,000	$ 260,000*
Subordinated debenture	5,300,000	2,650,000	2,520,000
Other creditors (accounts payable + other current liabilities)	3,200,000	1,600,000	1,600,000
Total	$8,760,000	$4,380,000	$4,380,000

*The bank note payable is paid in full before the subordinated debenture.

APPENDIX

TABLE A-1 THE FUTURE VALUE OF $1.00 (COMPOUNDED AMOUNT OF $1.00) $(1 + i)^n = T_1(i,n)$

Periods	4%	6%	8%	10%	12%	14%	20%
1	1.040	1.060	1.080	1.100	1.120	1.140	1.200
2	1.082	1.124	1.166	1.210	1.254	1.300	1.440
3	1.125	1.191	1.260	1.331	1.405	1.482	1.728
4	1.170	1.263	1.361	1.464	1.574	1.689	2.074
5	1.217	1.338	1.469	1.611	1.762	1.925	2.488
6	1.265	1.419	1.587	1.772	1.974	2.195	2.986
7	1.316	1.504	1.714	1.949	2.211	2.502	3.583
8	1.369	1.594	1.851	2.144	2.476	2.853	4.300
9	1.423	1.690	1.999	2.359	2.773	3.252	5.160
10	1.480	1.791	2.159	2.594	3.106	3.707	6.192
11	1.540	1.898	2.332	2.853	3.479	4.226	7.430
12	1.601	2.012	2.518	3.139	3.896	4.818	8.916
13	1.665	2.133	2.720	3.452	4.364	5.492	10.699
14	1.732	2.261	2.937	3.798	4.887	6.261	12.839
15	1.801	2.397	3.172	4.177	5.474	7.138	15.407

TABLE A-1 *(cont.)*

Periods	4%	6%	8%	10%	12%	14%	20%
16	1.873	2.540	3.426	4.595	6.130	8.137	18.488
17	1.948	2.693	3.700	5.055	6.866	9.277	22.186
18	2.026	2.854	3.996	5.560	7.690	10.575	26.623
19	2.107	3.026	4.316	6.116	8.613	12.056	31.948
20	2.191	3.207	4.661	6.728	9.646	13.743	38.338
30	3.243	5.744	10.063	17.450	29.960	50.950	237.380
40	4.801	10.286	21.725	45.260	93.051	188.880	1469.800

TABLE A-2 THE FUTURE VALUE OF AN ANNUITY OF $1.00* (COMPOUNDED AMOUNT OF AN ANNUITY OF $1.00) $\dfrac{(1+i)^n - 1}{i} = T_2(i, n)$

Periods	4%	6%	8%	10%	12%	14%	20%
1	1.000	1.000	1.000	1.000	1.000	1.000	1.000
2	2.040	2.060	2.080	2.100	2.120	2.140	2.200
3	3.122	3.184	3.246	3.310	3.374	3.440	3.640
4	4.247	4.375	4.506	4.641	4.779	4.921	5.368
5	5.416	5.637	5.867	6.105	6.353	6.610	7.442
6	6.633	6.975	7.336	7.716	8.115	8.536	9.930
7	7.898	8.394	8.923	9.487	10.089	10.730	12.916
8	9.214	9.898	10.637	11.436	12.300	13.233	16.499
9	10.583	11.491	12.488	13.580	14.776	16.085	20.799
10	12.006	13.181	14.487	15.938	17.549	19.337	25.959
11	13.486	14.972	16.646	18.531	20.655	23.045	32.150
12	15.026	16.870	18.977	21.385	24.133	27.271	39.580
13	16.627	18.882	21.495	24.523	28.029	32.089	48.497

TABLE A-2 (cont.)

Periods	4%	6%	8%	10%	12%	14%	20%
14	18.292	21.015	24.215	27.976	32.393	37.581	59.196
15	20.024	23.276	27.152	31.773	37.280	43.842	72.035
16	21.825	25.673	30.324	35.950	42.753	50.980	87.442
17	23.698	28.213	33.750	40.546	48.884	59.118	105.930
18	25.645	30.906	37.450	45.600	55.750	68.394	128.120
19	27.671	33.760	41.446	51.160	63.440	78.969	154.740
20	29.778	36.778	45.762	57.276	75.052	91.025	186.690
30	56.085	79.058	113.283	164.496	241.330	356.790	1181.900
40	95.026	154.762	259.057	442.597	767.090	1342.000	7343.900

Payments (or receipts) at the end of each period.

TABLE A-3 PRESENT VALUE OF $1.00 $\frac{1}{(1+i)^n} = T_3(i, n)$

Periods	4%	6%	8%	10%	12%	14%	16%	18%	20%	22%	24%	26%	28%	30%	40%
1	.962	.943	.926	.909	.893	.877	.862	.847	.833	.820	.806	.794	.781	.769	.714
2	.925	.890	.857	.826	.797	.769	.743	.718	.694	.672	.650	.630	.610	.592	.510
3	.889	.840	.794	.751	.712	.675	.641	.609	.579	.551	.524	.500	.477	.455	.364
4	.855	.792	.735	.683	.636	.592	.552	.516	.482	.451	.423	.397	.373	.350	.260
5	.822	.747	.681	.621	.567	.519	.476	.437	.402	.370	.341	.315	.291	.269	.186
6	.790	.705	.630	.564	.507	.456	.410	.370	.335	.303	.275	.250	.227	.207	.133
7	.760	.665	.583	.513	.452	.400	.354	.314	.279	.249	.222	.198	.178	.159	.095
8	.731	.627	.540	.467	.404	.351	.305	.266	.233	.204	.179	.157	.139	.123	.068
9	.703	.592	.500	.424	.361	.308	.263	.225	.194	.167	.144	.125	.108	.094	.048
10	.676	.558	.463	.386	.322	.270	.227	.191	.162	.137	.116	.099	.085	.073	.035
11	.650	.527	.429	.350	.287	.237	.195	.162	.135	.112	.094	.079	.066	.056	.025
12	.625	.497	.397	.319	.257	.208	.168	.137	.112	.092	.076	.062	.052	.043	.018
13	.601	.469	.368	.290	.229	.182	.145	.116	.093	.075	.061	.050	.040	.033	.013
14	.577	.442	.340	.263	.205	.160	.125	.099	.078	.062	.049	.039	.032	.025	.009
15	.555	.417	.315	.239	.183	.140	.108	.084	.065	.051	.040	.031	.025	.020	.006

TABLE A-3 (*cont.*)

Periods	4%	6%	8%	10%	12%	14%	16%	18%	20%	22%	24%	26%	28%	30%	40%
16	.534	.394	.292	.218	.163	.123	.093	.071	.054	.042	.032	.025	.019	.015	.005
17	.513	.371	.270	.198	.146	.108	.080	.060	.045	.034	.026	.020	.015	.012	.003
18	.494	.350	.250	.180	.130	.095	.069	.051	.038	.028	.021	.016	.012	.009	.002
19	.475	.331	.232	.164	.116	.083	.060	.043	.031	.023	.017	.012	.009	.007	.002
20	.456	.312	.215	.149	.104	.073	.051	.037	.026	.019	.014	.010	.007	.005	.001
21	.439	.294	.199	.135	.093	.064	.044	.031	.022	.015	.011	.008	.006	.004	.001
22	.422	.278	.184	.123	.083	.056	.038	.026	.018	.013	.009	.006	.004	.003	.001
23	.406	.262	.170	.112	.074	.049	.033	.022	.015	.010	.007	.005	.003	.002	
24	.390	.247	.158	.102	.066	.043	.028	.019	.013	.008	.006	.004	.003	.002	
25	.375	.233	.146	.092	.059	.038	.024	.016	.010	.007	.005	.003	.002	.001	
26	.361	.220	.135	.084	.053	.033	.021	.014	.009	.006	.004	.002	.002	.001	
27	.347	.209	.125	.076	.047	.029	.018	.011	.007	.005	.003	.002	.001	.001	
28	.333	.196	.116	.069	.042	.026	.016	.010	.006	.004	.002	.002	.001	.001	
29	.321	.185	.107	.063	.037	.022	.014	.008	.005	.003	.002	.001	.001	.001	
30	.308	.174	.099	.057	.033	.020	.012	.007	.004	.003	.002	.001	.001	.001	
40	.208	.097	.046	.022	.011	.005	.003	.001	.001						

TABLE A-4 PRESENT VALUE OF AN ANNUITY OF \$1.00* $\dfrac{1}{i}\left[1-\dfrac{1}{(1+i)^n}\right] = T_4(i,n)$

Periods	4%	6%	8%	10%	12%	14%	16%	18%	20%	22%	24%	25%	26%	28%	30%	40%
1	0.962	0.943	0.926	0.909	0.893	0.877	0.862	0.847	0.833	0.820	0.806	0.800	0.794	0.781	0.769	0.714
2	1.886	1.833	1.783	1.736	1.690	1.647	1.605	1.566	1.528	1.492	1.457	1.440	1.424	1.392	1.361	1.224
3	2.775	2.673	2.577	2.487	2.402	2.322	2.246	2.174	2.106	2.042	1.981	1.952	1.923	1.868	1.816	1.589
4	3.630	3.465	3.312	3.170	3.037	2.914	2.798	2.690	2.589	2.494	2.404	2.362	2.320	2.241	2.166	1.849
5	4.452	4.212	3.993	3.791	3.605	3.433	3.274	3.127	2.991	2.864	2.745	2.689	2.635	2.532	2.436	2.035
6	5.242	4.917	4.623	4.355	4.111	3.889	3.685	3.498	3.326	3.167	3.020	2.951	2.885	2.759	2.643	2.168
7	6.002	5.582	5.206	4.868	4.564	4.288	4.039	3.812	3.605	3.416	3.242	3.161	3.083	2.937	2.802	2.263
8	6.733	6.210	5.747	5.335	4.968	4.639	4.344	4.078	3.837	3.619	3.421	3.329	3.241	3.076	2.925	2.331
9	7.435	6.802	6.247	5.759	5.328	4.946	4.607	4.303	4.031	3.786	3.566	3.463	3.366	3.184	3.019	2.379
10	8.111	7.360	6.710	6.145	5.650	5.216	4.833	4.494	4.192	3.923	3.682	3.571	3.465	3.269	3.092	2.414
11	8.760	7.887	7.139	6.495	5.938	5.453	5.029	4.656	4.327	4.035	3.776	3.656	3.544	3.335	3.147	2.438
12	9.385	8.384	7.536	6.814	6.194	5.660	5.197	4.793	4.439	4.127	3.851	3.725	3.606	3.387	3.190	2.456
13	9.986	8.853	7.904	7.103	6.424	5.842	5.342	4.910	4.533	4.203	3.912	3.780	3.656	3.427	3.223	2.468
14	10.563	9.295	8.244	7.367	6.628	6.002	5.468	5.008	4.611	4.265	3.962	3.824	3.695	3.459	3.249	2.477
15	11.118	9.712	8.559	7.606	6.811	6.142	5.575	5.092	4.675	4.315	4.001	3.859	3.726	3.483	3.268	2.484

TABLE A-4 (cont.)

Periods	4%	6%	8%	10%	12%	14%	16%	18%	20%	22%	24%	25%	26%	28%	30%	40%
16	11.652	10.106	8.851	7.824	6.974	6.265	5.669	5.162	4.730	4.357	4.033	3.887	3.751	3.503	3.283	2.489
17	12.166	10.477	9.122	8.022	7.120	6.373	5.749	5.222	4.775	4.391	4.059	3.910	3.771	3.518	3.295	2.492
18	12.659	10.828	9.372	8.201	7.250	6.467	5.818	5.273	4.812	4.419	4.080	3.928	3.786	3.529	3.304	2.494
19	13.134	11.158	9.604	8.365	7.366	6.550	5.877	5.316	4.844	4.442	4.097	3.942	3.799	3.539	3.311	2.496
20	13.590	11.470	9.818	8.514	7.469	6.623	5.929	5.353	4.870	4.460	4.110	3.954	3.808	3.546	3.316	2.497
21	14.029	11.764	10.017	8.649	7.562	6.687	5.973	5.384	4.891	4.476	4.121	3.963	3.816	3.551	3.320	2.498
22	14.451	12.042	10.201	8.772	7.645	6.743	6.011	5.410	4.909	4.488	4.130	3.970	3.822	3.556	3.323	2.498
23	14.857	12.303	10.371	8.883	7.718	6.792	6.044	5.432	4.925	4.499	4.137	3.976	3.827	3.559	3.325	2.499
24	15.247	12.550	10.529	8.985	7.784	6.835	6.073	5.451	4.937	4.507	4.143	3.981	3.831	3.562	3.327	2.499
25	15.622	12.783	10.675	9.077	7.843	6.873	6.097	5.467	4.948	4.514	4.147	3.985	3.834	3.564	3.329	2.499
26	15.983	13.003	10.810	9.161	7.896	6.906	6.118	5.480	4.956	4.520	4.151	3.988	3.837	3.566	3.330	2.500
27	16.330	13.211	10.935	9.237	7.943	6.935	6.136	5.492	4.964	4.524	4.154	3.990	3.839	3.567	3.331	2.500
28	16.663	13.406	11.051	9.307	7.984	6.961	6.152	5.502	4.970	4.528	4.157	3.992	3.840	3.568	3.331	2.500
29	16.984	13.591	11.158	9.370	8.022	6.983	6.166	5.510	4.975	4.531	4.159	3.994	3.841	3.569	3.332	2.500
30	17.292	13.765	11.258	9.427	8.055	7.003	6.177	5.517	4.979	4.534	4.160	3.995	3.842	3.569	3.332	2.500
40	19.793	15.046	11.925	9.779	8.244	7.105	6.234	5.548	4.997	4.544	4.166	3.999	3.846	3.571	3.333	2.500

*Payments (or receipts) at the end of each period.

INDEX